W9-DBT-488

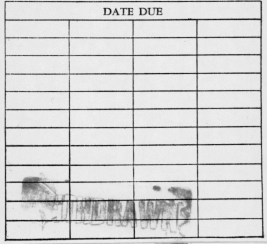

EVERYMAN, I will go with thee,

and be thy guide,

In thy most need to go by thy side

RICHARD HOOKER

Born in 1554 at Exeter. Educated at the grammar school there and at Corpus Christi College, Oxford. Becoming a fellow of his college in 1577, he was appointed Master of the Temple in 1585. He was presented to the living of Bishopsbourne, Kent, in 1595, and died there in 1600.

RICHARD HOOKER

Of the Laws of
Ecclesiastical
Polity

IN TWO VOLUMES · VOLUME ONE
(BOOKS I—IV)

INTRODUCTION BY
CHRISTOPHER MORRIS, M.A.
Fellow of King's College, Cambridge

DENT: LONDON
EVERYMAN'S LIBRARY
DUTTON: NEW YORK

NO. 201

INTRODUCTION

'HOOKER,' it might almost be said, is the name of a book rather than the name of a man; for there are few great writers since the Middle Ages of whom we know less. The story of Richard Hooker's life is soon told. He was born in 1554 in Exeter of burgess stock, his grandfather having been mayor. His uncle John Hooker had been an editor of Holinshed's *Chronicles*. The family was Protestant and also poor; but Richard showed promise at the local grammar-school and his uncle secured for him the patronage of John Jewel, Bishop of Salisbury, who got the boy into Corpus Christi College, Oxford, at the age of fourteen, first as a chorister and later as a clerk. At nineteen he became a scholar and at twenty-three a fellow of the college. His academic career was not outstanding but he acquired enough fame to become deputy Professor of Hebrew for a few days, and to be asked to preach at Paul's Cross in London in 1581, just after he had taken orders. In 1588 he married Joan Churchman, daughter of a future Master of the Merchant Taylors Company. Modern research has disposed of Izaak Walton's story that the Churchman family was in low financial water; but there may be truth in Walton's statement that Hooker was a henpecked husband—it would not be inconsistent with his known humility of character.

Before his marriage Hooker became Rector of Drayton Beauchamp, Buckinghamshire, in 1584 and, a year later, Master of the Temple. He was appointed over the head of the well-known Puritan Walter Travers, who, however, stayed on as a lecturer. The Master and the Lecturer were soon engaged in a public theological controversy for, in spite of a Puritanical background in his home and in his college, Hooker had already formed strongly Anglican views. The controversy, although it gave him personal pain, brought him into the limelight and attracted the interest both of Archbishop Whitgift and of Burghley. They soon saw in Hooker the champion for whom the Established Church was looking. In 1591 he ceased to be Master of the Temple and became Rector of Boscombe, Wiltshire, although almost certainly he continued to live in London.

The first four Books of the *Ecclesiastical Polity* appeared in
1593, Book V in 1597. Hooker died in 1600 at the age of
forty-six and was survived by his widow and four daughters.
He had been since 1595 Vicar of Bishopsbourne, Kent, where
he died and where the adjective 'judicious' appears on his
monument. The remaining three Books of the *Ecclesiastical
Polity* were completed, though not revised, before his death.
The manuscripts fell into careless or unscrupulous hands and
were not published until long afterwards (1648 to 1662), and
then only in mutilated form.

For Hooker's personal characteristics we have little
evidence apart from the *Life* by Walton, who was an unreliable gossip and generally moulded his subjects to fit a
ready-made pattern. But Hooker may well have been just
as bashful and retiring as Walton says and just as myopic and
'full of heat-pimples begot by his sedentary life.' We may
guess, however, from many shrewd observations in Hooker's
pages, that he knew rather more of men and of affairs than
Walton would suggest. There is certainly internal evidence
that Hooker had a sense of humour and that he could engage
in controversy without malice or uncharitableness. He
found the conflict with Travers all the more painful, he wrote
to Whitgift, 'because I believe him to be a good man.'
Hooker claimed, in the same letter, that he had no wish 'to
provoke any' but that he wrote only 'to satisfy all tender
consciences.' For the completion of his task he requested a
refuge where he might have 'peace and privacy and behold
God's blessing spring out of my Mother Earth and eat my
own bread without oppositions.'

The Elizabethan Church needed a champion of Hooker's
calibre. It had come into existence to save a political
situation and had sacrificed many things for the sake of
giving the Queen and the country a politically quiet life. A
vaguely Protestant theology had been adopted to placate the
Protestant intellectuals, who had to be given high office in the
Church, since the Catholic leaders were politically unreliable
and were also discredited by the Marian persecution. Yet in
ritual, vestments and liturgy many 'rags of Popery' had been
retained in order to hoodwink the Catholic powers abroad, or
else in order not to offend the conservative tastes and senti-
ments of the majority of the population. Episcopacy had of
course been kept, largely to secure royal control over the
clergy. Many abuses of lay patronage had been tolerated

for fear of alienating powerful magnates. Schemes to increase the number of educated clergy had been discountenanced for fear of causing 'disputaciousness'; and Hooker had to defend a system which did not aim at providing parishes with more than three or four sermons a year. He had also to defend the keeping of domestic chaplains in noble households on the grounds that, if the rich went to church with the poor, it would be 'repugnant to the majesty and greatness of English nobility.'

Anglican propaganda had been largely ineffectual because it had been largely negative. It had concentrated on saying what Anglicans did *not* believe. Anglicanism appeared to lack positive intellectual content and, significantly, many of the bright young men from the universities had been listening with more attention to voices from Rome or from Geneva. Both seemed to offer something more logical and consistent or more heroic and inspiring. Both kinds of extremist could very plausibly accuse the government of having sacrificed religious truth to 'reason of state.'

The war with Spain had largely killed the Catholic danger at home as well as abroad, by making Catholicism seem anti-English. But the war had increased the Puritans' prestige, since they had been the 'forward' anti-Spanish party. The Puritans, moreover, were persecuted by methods that could be likened to those of the Spanish Inquisition. Hooker's task in defending such persecution was not easy; and he could only do it by proving that the Puritans cut at the roots of all political obligation. To do this satisfactorily he had to examine the whole nature of law and of government, of society and indeed of man. It is this which caused him to create a masterpiece of systematic philosophy out of what might have been a mere political pamphlet.

Hooker's book is long and complex and his effects are cumulative. The natural unit of his prose, moreover, is the paragraph rather than the sentence. As Fuller put it, 'his style was long and pithy, driving on a whole flock of several clauses before he came to the close of a sentence.' Brief quotation, therefore, can do him little justice either as writer or as thinker. Yet he did as much perhaps for English prose as he did for the Anglican religion and for political philosophy. He never lost control of his sentences any more than of his argument; he had an exquisite ear for cadence; and the emphatic word falls inevitably into the emphatic place.

One of his opponents paid Hooker unwitting tribute in complaining that he had been 'by the sweet sound of your melodious style, almost cast into a dreaming sleep.' Hooker contrived also to be immensely learned without seeming pedantic and to be urbane without losing a certain trenchant, almost rustic pithiness. At times, too, he was master of a delicate and whimsical irony.

Among Hooker's merits was an intellectual honesty which allowed him to admit much of the Puritan case. He granted that the Anglican Church continued many practices not to be found in Scripture and shared many practices with Rome. He even admitted that 'Presbyter' was a word more consistent than 'Priest' 'with the drift of the whole Gospel of Jesus Christ,' and that episcopacy itself was only a 'custom' which might be abolished if it were found not to work. But all such things, he argued, were 'things indifferent,' that is to say, not the essentials of Christianity and not things affecting the salvation of souls. In all 'things indifferent' it was permissible and indeed desirable to follow tradition, authority, and, above all, reason, which the Puritans distrusted.

This is the crux of Hooker's argument. We need not and should not rely on scriptural authority alone, for we have other sources of knowledge and other means of discovering God's laws and will. We may trust and use such sources whenever they do not conflict with reason, which is an instrument given to men by God Himself for the express purpose of supplementing revelation. There was no need 'for men to be tied and led by authority, as it were with a kind of captivity of judgement, and though there be reason to the contrary not to listen to it, but to follow like beasts the first in the herd they know not nor care not whither, this were brutish.' It might, however, be presumed that practices and institutions which men had accepted for many centuries had been accepted just because they did conform to reason.

'The general and perpetual voice of men is as the sentence of God Himself. For that which all men have at all times learned, Nature herself must needs have taught; and God being the Author of Nature, her voice is but His instrument. . . . By force of the light of Reason, wherewith God illuminateth everyone which cometh into the world, men being enabled to know truth from falsehood and good from evil, do thereby learn in many things what the will of God is.' The function of reason was to discover law, particularly the

Natural Law, moral and physical, by which God regulates the universe.

In Book I of the *Ecclesiastical Polity* Hooker delineates the great hierarchy of the laws, ascending from the 'positive laws' made by individual earthly rulers to 'the Law which Angels in heaven obey.' It must be remembered that most Protestant philosophers had conceived the universe as being virtually lawless. For them there was only one law, the Law of God; and, since men are incapable of understanding this, God's operations must seem purely arbitrary or capricious acts of will. But Hooker's universe has laws appropriate to every sphere; and each is thought of as aspiring to the more perfect law of the sphere above it, God's law alone being perfect and complete, since the natural must fall short of the divine. It follows that all human or natural laws may, whenever necessary, be changed or improved. Hooker had a strong sense of historical development but this gave him more than mere reverence for the past. It enabled him to allow for improvement or reform. All 'things indifferent' were changeable things and therefore the outward forms of worship or of church government might be altered if circumstances required it. We should not 'lightly esteem . . . the judgment of antiquity' but 'all things cannot be of ancient continuance,' and a government or a church may on occasion 'ordain that which never was.' Hooker in fact was something much more than a conservative.

Law, for Hooker, rested upon instinct as well as upon reason, since he held that men naturally seek the social life and therefore seek to evolve law. Society is rooted in human nature and grows organically but it has also to satisfy reason and to embody agreement or consent. 'Laws they are not, therefore, which public approbation hath not made so.' Yet we are bound by the consent given by our ancestors, since 'corporations are immortal,' so that membership of a society commits men to obey its laws, which are 'the deed of the whole body politic whereof if ye judge yourselves to be any part, then is the law even your deed also.' Besides, 'the public power of all societies is above every soul contained in the same societies' and must be obeyed 'unless . . . the Law of Reason or of God doth enjoin the contrary. Because, except our own private and but probable resolutions be by the law of public determinations over-ruled, we take away all possibility of sociable life in the world.' In other words, the

Puritan who disobeys ecclesiastical law undermines the whole
of society; and neither reason nor conscience can bid him
disobey, since it is only in externals, in 'things indifferent,'
that he is asked to conform.   This of course begs the question,
for the Puritans would not have agreed with Hooker over
what were or were not 'things indifferent.'

Although the original contract which set up government,
once it is made, cannot be unmade, Hooker granted that the
people was originally free to set up any form of government
it chose.   There was, he thought, a slight presumption that
monarchy is the most satisfactory form; but Hooker did not
hold the full doctrine of the divine right of kings, for he
admitted that God had not commanded that 'the Christian
world should be ordered by kingly regiment.'   On the other
hand, 'unto kings by human right honour by very divine
right is due,' that is to say, God gives all legal government
the moral right to be obeyed.   Hooker was aware that some
kings might be tyrants but he provided no remedy beyond the
pious hope that rulers would normally find that it paid them
to keep the rules.   We must remember that Queen Elizabeth's government was opposed only by small minorities and
supported by the great majority of her subjects.   It was
therefore tacitly assumed by nearly all Elizabethans that a
serious clash between ruler and subject was an academic
hypothesis rather than a practical question.

Hooker saw, more clearly than most of his contemporaries,
that there must be a sovereign and that jurisdiction 'must
have necessarily a fountain that deriveth it to all others and
receiveth it not from any; because otherwise the course of
justice should go infinitely in a circle every superior having
his superior without end, which cannot be.'   Without this
sovereignty there was no safeguard against anarchy and no
power to enforce what was to the general interest against
particular interests or wills.   Yet Hooker clung to the idea
of constitutional monarchy: sovereignty was somehow to be
combined with the Rule of Law.   'What power the king
hath, he hath it by law; the bounds and limits of it are
known.'   What the bounds and limits are Hooker does not
clearly define; but had any man of his time been able to
define them clearly, England might have avoided her great
Civil War.

Perhaps Hooker looked, in this as in other matters, for a
compromise that was workable in practice rather than

precise in theory. He disliked logical extremes and over-simple generalizations. Nothing, he wrote, appealed more to men of 'gross' understanding than 'unlimited generalities, because of their plainness at first sight; nothing less with men of exact judgement.' He resented the Puritans' contempt for compromise and their refusal to accept the second best. Much, he thought, that was not demonstrably perfect, was nevertheless demonstrably good. Much might be good 'in gross' even if it fell short 'in some particular points.'

Queen Elizabeth's 'ecclesiastical polity' or system of church government, Hooker argued, might not be ideal and might not conform in all minutiae to a scriptural model; but there was nothing in it that was inconsistent either with the laws of God or with the laws of Nature and of Reason. And there was much in it that conformed to tradition and to common sense. The Puritans, however, saw in their own Presbyterian form of church government 'the only sovereign remedy of all evils.' This, Hooker thought, gave them an undeserved reputation for great acumen, since it was 'the nature . . . of the people . . . to imagine that anything, the virtue whereof they hear commended, would help them; but that most which they least have tried.'

The Puritan concept of the Church, however scriptural, was a narrow one since it implied 'a gathered church' consisting of the Elect alone. This in effect separated Church and State into two separate kingdoms. Besides, as Hooker observed, it was exclusive. 'They labour to appropriate the saving power of the Holy Ghost, they separate from all apparent hope of life and salvation thousands whom the goodness of Almighty God doth not exclude.'

Anglicanism, as Hooker conceived it, made every English-man a churchman, not excluding those whose ultimate salvation might be gravely doubted. For Hooker member-ship of Church and of Commonwealth was identical; Church and State were two complementary aspects of the same society. 'There is not any man of the Church of England but the same is a member of the Commonwealth, nor any man a member of the Commonwealth which is not also of the Church of England.' This involved the giving of religious responsibilities to the civil ruler. 'A gross error it is to think that regal power ought to serve for the good of the body and not of the soul, for men's temporal peace and not for their eternal safety: as if God had ordained kings for no other end

and purpose but only to fat up men like hogs and to see that
they have their mast.' King and Parliament therefore are
representative of the Church in England just as much as they
are of the State; they have both the right and the duty to
make laws concerning the externals of religious life.

There are weaknesses in this frankly Erastian position.
It suggests that the Church is more a national than an inter-
national community. It gives no reliable guarantee that
Caesar will not interfere in the things that are God's. It
almost admits that error is preferable to contention and
disunity; and it refuses to face the possibility that error or
serious disagreement might arise over things that are not
'indifferent.' Hooker indeed assumed too much when he
asserted that 'the law doth not make that to be truth which
before was not.' He might think it unlikely that the government would contravene any of the 'essentials' of Christianity,
but he had in effect made the government the judge of
what was 'essential' and of what was true.

His limitations are those of his time and situation; and it
is the more remarkable how often Hooker's argument tran-
scends the purely ephemeral purposes of his own day. Much
that he wrote was written in a sense 'for all time' and has
seemed valid and impressive to men of other generations.
Locke was to use Hooker's backing for his belief in the necessity of consent, while Burke was to find in Hooker confirmation of his belief that constitutions grow organically and
are rooted in a nation's history. Hobbes may have owed
something to Hooker's theory of a social compact that cannot
be unmade; and Rousseau could have found in Hooker the
germs of a theory of the General Will. But Hooker's achieve-
ment and influence extended more widely still; for it was he
more than any other man who contrived to reconcile Protestant theology with the long tradition of Natural Law which
can be traced through Catholic scholasticism right back to
the Stoics. He made it possible for men to accept the
Reformation and yet to retain the Renaissance belief in
man and in reason, a belief which Protestantism had nearly
destroyed. Yet he had found it possible to believe in reason
without going on to insist, as so many rationalists have done,
that what at first sight seems irrational must therefore be
abolished. He could argue that tradition and authority are
likely to be reasonable and that it is unreasonable to dig up
established institutions by the roots. He could be liberal

without becoming radical and conservative without resisting progress. He had found a way to harmonize the variability of human institutions with the universality of law. He recognised man's need for government but also man's right to be governed only by his free consent.

Above all, Hooker showed men how to philosophise without becoming doctrinaire, how to remain relatively tolerant and strikingly moderate in a fanatical world. Perhaps only Montaigne, of all Hooker's contemporaries, spoke in the same tone of voice. Hooker had kept his own temper and he had asked, firmly but courteously, that his opponents should keep theirs. 'Think ye are men, deem it not impossible for you to err.'

CHRISTOPHER MORRIS.

The present edition is a reprint of Books I to V of Richard Hooker's *Of the Laws of Ecclesiastical Polity*.

BIBLIOGRAPHICAL NOTE

The first four Books of Hooker's *Lawes of Ecclesiastical Politie* were published in 1593; Book V in 1597; Books VI and VIII in 1648 and 1651. Book VII first appeared in Bishop Gauden's edition of Hooker's *Works*, 1662.

The best edition of Hooker's *Works* is John Keble's (3 vols.), 1836, revised by R. W. Church and F. Paget, 1888. Book I was admirably edited by R. W. Church, 1876; Book V by F. Paget, 1899; and Book VIII by R. A. Houk, 1931. Each has an important introduction.

Izaak Walton's *Life* of Hooker, first published in 1665, has often been reprinted and is included in Keble's edition of the *Works*.

Reference may also be made to L. S. Thornton: *Richard Hooker: a Study of his Theology*, 1924; C. J. Sisson: *The Judicious Marriage of Mr Hooker and the Birth of the Laws of Ecclesiastical Polity*, 1940; E. T. Davies: *The Political Ideas of Richard Hooker*, 1946; P. Munz: *The Place of Hooker in the History of Thought*, 1952.

See also J. W. Allen: *A History of Political Thought in the Sixteenth Century*, 1928; A. P. d'Entrèves: *The Medieval Contribution to Political Thought*, 1939; C. Morris: *Political Thought in England: Tyndale to Hooker*, 1953.

CONTENTS OF VOL. I

A
LEARNED AND COMFORTABLE
SERMON

OF

THE CERTAINTY AND PERPETUITY OF FAITH
IN THE ELECT:

ESPECIALLY OF THE PROPHET HABAKKUK'S FAITH [1]

HABAK I. 4.

["Therefore the law is slacked, and judgment doth never go forth."]
Whether the Prophet Habakkuk, by admitting this cogitation into his
mind, "The law doth fail," did thereby shew himself an unbeliever.

WE have seen in the opening of this clause which concerneth the weakness of the prophet's faith, first what things
they are whereunto the faith of sound believers doth assent:
secondly wherefore all men assent not thereunto: and
thirdly why they that do, do it many times with small
assurance. Now because nothing can be so truly spoken,
but through misunderstanding it may be depraved; therefore to prevent, if it be possible, all misconstruction in this
cause, where a small error cannot rise but with great
danger, it is perhaps needful, ere we come to the fourth
point, that something be added to that which hath been
already spoken concerning the third.

[1] [This and the Discourse of Justification, are now placed first among
Hooker's Opuscula, as having probably been earliest written. See
Travers's Supplication to the Council, in Dobson's Hooker, ii. p. 464.
"Upon . . . occasion of this doctrine of his, that the assurance of that
we believe by the word is not so certain as of that we perceive by sense,
I . . . taught the doctrine otherwise.—According to which course of
late, when as he had taught, 'that the church of Rome is a true church,'
&c." Compare Hooker's Answer, § 9, 10, 11. It should seem as if
these two, and the Sermons on Pride, were portions of a series on the
Prophecy of Habakkuk preached in the Temple Church, 1585-6 ; and
the present arrangement sets them in the order of their texts.]

That mere natural men do neither know nor acknowledge the things of God, we do not marvel, because they are spiritually to be discerned; but they in whose hearts the light of grace doth shine, they that are taught of God, why are they so weak in faith? why is their assenting to the law so scrupulous? so much mingled with fear and wavering? It seemeth strange that ever they should imagine the law to fail. It cannot seem strange if we weigh the reason. If the things which we believe be considered in themselves, it may truly be said that faith is more certain than any science. That which we know either by sense, or by infallible demonstration, is not so certain as the principles, articles, and conclusions of Christian faith. Concerning which we must note, that there is a Certainty of Evidence, and a Certainty of Adherence. Certainty of Evidence we call that, when the mind doth assent unto this or that, not because it is true in itself, but because the truth is clear, because it is manifest unto us. Of things in themselves most certain, except they be also most evident, our persuasion is not so assured as it is of things more evident, although in themselves they be less certain. It is as sure, if not surer, that there be spirits, as that there be men; but we be more assured of these than of them, because these are more evident. The truth of some things is so evident, that no man which heareth them can doubt of them: as when we hear that "a part of any thing is less than the whole," the mind is constrained to say, this is true. If it were so in matters of faith, then, as all men have equal certainty of this, so no believer should be more scrupulous and doubtful than another. But we find the contrary. The angels and spirits of the righteous in heaven have certainty most evident of things spiritual: but this they have by the light of glory. That which we see by the light of grace, though it be indeed more certain; yet is it not to us so evidently certain, as that which sense or the light of nature will not suffer a man to doubt of. Proofs are vain and frivolous except they be more certain than is the thing proved: and do we not see how the Spirit every where in the Scripture proveth matters of faith, laboureth to confirm us in the things which we believe, by things whereof we have sensible knowledge? I conclude therefore that we have less certainty of evidence concerning things believed, than concerning sensible or naturally perceived. Of these who doth doubt at any time? Of them at some time who doubteth not? I will not here allege the sundry confessions of the perfectest that have lived upon earth concerning their great imperfections this way; which if I did, I should dwell too long upon a matter sufficiently known by every faithful man that doth know himself.

The other, which we call the Certainty of Adherence, is when the heart doth cleave and stick unto that which it doth believe. This certainty is greater in us than the other. The reason is this: the faith of a Christian doth apprehend the words of the law, the promises of God, not only as true, but also as good; and therefore even then when the evidence which he hath of the truth is so small that it grieveth him to feel his weakness in assenting thereto, yet is there in him such a sure adherence unto that which he doth but faintly and fearfully believe, that his spirit having once truly tasted the heavenly sweetness thereof, all the world is not able quite and clean to remove him from it; but he striveth with himself to hope against all reason of believing, being settled with Job upon this unmoveable resolution, " Though God kill me, I will not give over trusting in him." [1] For why? this lesson remaineth for ever imprinted in him, " It is good for me to cleave unto God." [2]

Now the minds of all men being so darkened as they are with the foggy damp of original corruption, it cannot be that any man's heart living should be either so enlightened in the knowledge, or so established in the love of that wherein his salvation standeth, as to be perfect, neither doubting nor shrinking at all. If any such were, what doth let why that man should not be justified by his own inherent righteousness? For righteousness inherent being perfect will justify. And perfect faith is a part of perfect righteousness inherent; yea a principal part, the root and the mother of all the rest: so that if the fruit of every tree be such as the root is, faith being perfect, as it is if it be not at all mingled with distrust and fear, what is there to exclude other Christian virtues from the like perfections? And then what need we the righteousness of Christ? His garment is superfluous: we may be honourably clothed with our own robes, if it be thus. But let them beware who challenge to themselves a strength which they have not, lest they lose the comfortable support of that weakness which indeed they have.

[1] [Job xiii. 15.]　　　[2] Psalm lxxiii. 28.

Some shew, although no soundness of ground, there is, which may be alleged for defence of this supposed perfection in certainty touching matters of our faith ; as first that Abraham did believe and doubted not : secondly, that the Spirit which God hath given us to no other end, but only to assure us that we are the sons of God, to embolden us to call upon him as our Father, to open our eyes, and to make the truth of things believed evident unto our minds, is much mightier in operation than the common light of nature, whereby we discern sensible things : wherefore we must needs be more sure of that we believe, than of that we see ; we must needs be more certain of the mercies of God in Christ Jesus, than we are of the light of the sun when it shineth upon our faces.

To that of Abraham, " He did not doubt ; " [1] I answer, that this negation doth not exclude all fear, all doubting, but only that which cannot stand with true faith. It freeth Abraham from doubting through Infidelity, not from doubting through Infirmity ; from the doubting of Unbelievers, not of weak Believers ; from such a doubting as that whereof the prince of Samaria is attainted, who hearing the promise of sudden plenty in the midst of extreme dearth, answered, " Though the Lord would make windows in heaven, were it possible so to come to pass ? " [2] But that Abraham was not void of all doubtings, what need we any other proof than the plain evidence of his own words ? [3]

The reason which is taken from the power of the Spirit were effectual, if God did work like a natural agent, as the fire doth inflame, and the sun enlighten, according to the uttermost ability which they have to bring forth their effects. But the incomprehensible wisdom of God doth limit the effects of his power to such a measure as seemeth best unto himself. Wherefore he worketh that certainty in all, which sufficeth abundantly to their salvation in the life to come ; but in none so great as attaineth in this life unto perfection. Even so, O Lord, it hath pleased thee ; even so it is best and fittest for us, that feeling still our own infirmities, we may no longer breathe than pray, " Adjuva, Domine ; " " Help, Lord, our incredulity." [4] Of the third question, this I hope will suffice, being added unto that which hath

---

[1] [Rom. iv. 20, οὐ διεκρίθη τῇ ἀπιστίᾳ.]   [2] [2 Kings vii. 2.]
[3] Gen. xvii. 17.   [4] [S. Mark ix. 24.]

been thereof already spoken. The fourth question resteth, and so an end of this point.

That which cometh last of all in this first branch to be considered concerning the weakness of the Prophet's faith, "Whether he did by this very thought, *The law doth fail*, quench the Spirit, fall from faith, and shew himself an unbeliever, or no?" The question is of moment; the repose and tranquillity of infinite souls doth depend upon it. The Prophet's case is the case of many; which way soever we cast for him, the same way it passeth for all others. If in him this cogitation did extinguish grace, why the like thoughts in us should not take the like effects, there is no cause. Forasmuch therefore as the matter is weighty, dear, and precious, which we have in hand, it behoveth us with so much the greater chariness to wade through it, taking special heed both what we build, and whereon we build, that if our building be pearl, our foundation be not stubble; if the doctrine we teach be full of comfort and consolation, the ground whereupon we gather it be sure: otherwise we shall not save but deceive both ourselves and others. In this we know we are not deceived, neither can we deceive you, when we teach that the faith whereby ye are sanctified cannot fail; it did not in the Prophet, it shall not in you. If it be so, let the difference be shewed between the condition of unbelievers and his, in this or in the like imbecility and weakness. There was in Habakkuk that which St. John doth call "the seed of God,"[1] meaning thereby the First Grace which God poureth into the hearts of them that are incorporated into Christ; which having received, if because it is an adversary to sin, we do therefore think we sin not both otherwise, and also by distrustful and doubtful apprehending of that which we ought steadfastly to believe, surely we do but deceive ourselves. Yet they which are of God do not sin either in this, or in any thing, any such sin as doth quite extinguish grace, clean cut them off from Christ Jesus; because the "seed of God" abideth in them, and doth shield them from receiving any irremediable wound. Their faith, when it is at the strongest, is but weak; yet even then when it is at the weakest, so strong, that utterly it never faileth, it never perisheth altogether, no not in them who think it extinguished in themselves. There are for whose sakes I dare

[1] [1 John iii. 9.]

not deal slightly in this cause, sparing that labour which must be bestowed to make it plain.   Men in like agonies unto this of the Prophet Habakkuk's are through the extremity of grief many times in judgment so confounded, that they find not themselves in themselves.   For that which dwelleth in their hearts they seek, they make diligent search and inquiry.   It abideth, it worketh in them, yet still they ask where ; still they lament as for a thing which is past finding : they mourn as Rachel, and refuse to be comforted, as if that were not which indeed is, and as if that which is not were ; as if they did not believe when they do, and as if they did despair when they do not. Which in some I grant is but a melancholy passion, proceeding only from that dejection of mind, the cause whereof is the body, and by bodily means can be taken away.   But where there is no such bodily cause, the mind is not lightly in this mood, but by some of these three occasions : one, that judging by comparison either with other men, or with themselves at some other time more strong, they think imperfection to be a plain deprivation, weakness to be utter want of faith.

Another cause is, they often mistake one thing for another. St. Paul wishing well to the Church of Rome prayeth for them after this sort : "The God of hope fill you with all joy of believing." [1]   Hence an error groweth, when men in heaviness of spirit suppose they lack faith, because they find not the sugared joy and delight which indeed doth accompany faith, but so as a separable accident, as a thing that may be removed from it ; yea there is a cause why it should be removed.   The light would never be so acceptable, were it not for that usual intercourse of darkness.   Too much honey doth turn to gall ; and too much joy even spiritually would make us wantons.   Happier a great deal is that man's case, whose soul by inward desolation is humbled, than he whose heart is through abundance of spiritual delight lifted up and exalted above measure.   Better it is sometimes to go down into the pit with him, who, beholding darkness, and bewailing the loss of inward joy and consolation, crieth from the bottom of the lowest hell, " My God, my God, why hast thou forsaken me ? " [2] than continually to walk arm in arm with angels, to sit as it were in Abraham's bosom, and to have no thought, no cogitation,

[1] [Rom. xv. 13.]   [2] [Psal. xxii. 1.]

but "I thank my God it is not with me as it is with other men." [1] No, God will have them that shall walk in light to feel now and then what it is to sit in the shadow of death. A grieved spirit therefore is no argument of a faithless mind

A third occasion of men's misjudging themselves, as if they were faithless when they are not, is, they fasten their cogitations upon the distrustful suggestions of the flesh, whereof finding great abundance in themselves, they gather thereby, Surely unbelief hath full dominion, it hath taken plenary possession of me; if I were faithful, it could not be thus: not marking the motions of the Spirit and of faith, because they lie buried and overwhelmed with the contrary: when notwithstanding as the blessed Apostle doth acknowledge, [2] that "the Spirit groaneth," and that God heareth when we do not; so there is no doubt, but that our faith may have and hath her privy operations secret to us, in whom, yet known to him by whom they are.

Tell this to a man that hath a mind deceived by too hard an opinion of himself, and it doth but augment his grief: he hath his answer ready, Will you make me think otherwise than I find, than I feel in myself? I have thoroughly considered and exquisitely sifted all the corners of my heart, and I see what there is; never seek to persuade me against my knowledge; "I do not, I know I do not believe."

Well, to favour them a little in their weakness; let that be granted which they do imagine; be it that they are faithless and without belief. But are they not grieved for their unbelief? They are. Do they not wish it might, and also strive that it may, be otherwise? We know they do. Whence cometh this, but from a secret love and liking which they have of those things that are believed? No man can love things which in his own opinion are not. And if they think those things to be, which they shew that they love when they desire to believe them; then must it needs be, that by desiring to believe they prove themselves true believers. For without faith, no man thinketh that things believed are. Which argument all the subtilty of infernal powers will never be able to dissolve.

The faith therefore of true believers, though it have many and grievous downfalls, yet doth it still continue invincible; it conquereth and recovereth itself in the end. The

[1] [Luke xviii. 11.]   [2] [Rom. viii. 26, 27.]

dangerous conflicts whereunto it is subject are not able to prevail against it. The Prophet Habakkuk remained faithful in weakness, though weak in faith.

It is true, such is our weak and wavering nature, we have no sooner received grace, but we are ready to fall from it: we have no sooner given our assent to the law, that it cannot fail, but the next conceit which we are ready to embrace is, that it may, and that it doth fail. Though we find in ourselves a most willing heart to cleave unseparably unto God, even so far as to think unfeignedly with Peter, "Lord, I am ready to go with thee into prison and to death;"[1] yet how soon and how easily, upon how small occasions are we changed, if we be but a while let alone and left unto ourselves? The Galatians to-day, for their sakes which teach them the truth of Christ, content, if need were, to pluck out their own eyes,[2] and the next day ready to pluck out theirs which taught them. The love of the Angel of the Church of Ephesus, how greatly inflamed, and how quickly slacked.[3]

The higher we flow, the nearer we are unto an ebb, if men be respected as mere men, according to the wonted course of their alterable inclination, without the heavenly support of the Spirit.

Again, the desire of our ghostly enemy is so uncredible, and his means so forcible to overthrow our faith, that whom the blessed Apostle knew betrothed and made hand-fast unto Christ, to them he could not write but with great trembling: "I am jealous over you with a godly jealousy, for I have prepared you to one husband to present you a pure virgin unto Christ: but I fear, lest as the serpent beguiled Eve through his subtilty, so your minds should be corrupted from the simplicity which is in Christ."[4] The simplicity of faith which is in Christ taketh the naked promise of God, his bare word, and on that it resteth. This simplicity the serpent laboureth continually to pervert, corrupting the mind with many imaginations of repugnancy and contrariety between the promise of God and those things which sense or experience or some other foreconceived persuasion hath imprinted.

The word of the promise of God unto his people is, "I will not leave thee nor forsake thee:"[5] upon this the

---

[1] [Luke xxii. 33.]   [2] [Gal. iv. 5.]   [3] [Apoc. ii. 2, 4.]
[4] 2 Cor. xi. 2, 3.   [5] Jos. i. 5; Heb. xiii. 5.

simplicity of faith resteth, and it is not afraid of famine. But mark how the subtilty of Satan did corrupt the minds of that rebellious generation, whose spirits were not faithful unto God. They beheld the desolate state of the desert in which they were, and by the wisdom of their sense concluded the promise of God to be but folly: "Can God prepare a table in the wilderness?"[1]

The word of the promise to Sarah was, "Thou shalt bear a son." Faith is simple, and doubteth not of it: but Satan, to corrupt the simplicity of faith, entangleth the mind of the woman with an argument drawn from common experience to the contrary: "A woman that is old! Sarah now to be acquainted again with forgotten passions of youth!"[2]

The word of the promise of God by Moses and the prophets made the Saviour of the world so apparent unto Philip, that his simplicity could conceive no other Messias, than Jesus of Nazareth the son of Joseph. But to stay Nathanael, lest being invited to come and see, he should also believe, and so be saved, the subtilty of Satan casteth a mist before his eyes, putteth in his head against this the common-conceived persuasion of all men concerning Nazareth: "Is it possible that a good thing should come from thence?"[3]

This stratagem he doth use with so great dexterity, the minds of all men are so strangely bewitched with it, that it bereaveth them for the time of all perceivance of that which should relieve them and be their comfort; yea it taketh all remembrance from them, even of things wherewith they are most familiarly acquainted. The people of Israel could not be ignorant, that he which led them through the sea was able to feed them in the desert: but this was obliterated and put out by the sense of their present want. Feeling the hand of God against them in their food, they remember not his hand in the day that he delivered them from the hand of the oppressor. Sarah was not then to learn, that "with God all things were possible."[4] Had Nathanael never noted how "God doth choose the base things of this world to disgrace them that are most honourably esteemed"?[5]

The Prophet Habakkuk knew that the promises of grace, protection, and favour, which God in the law doth make

[1] Psal. lxxviii. 19.　　　[2] Gen. xviii. 12.　　　[3] John i. 46.
[4] Matt. xix. 26.　　　[5] 1 Cor. i. 27, 28.

unto his people, do not grant them any such immunity as can free and exempt them from all chastisements: he knew that as God said, "I will continue my mercy for ever towards them;" so he likewise said, "Their transgressions I will punish with a rod:"[1] he knew that it cannot stand with any reason we should set the measure of our own punishments, and prescribe unto God how great or how long our sufferings shall be: he knew that we were blind, and altogether ignorant what is best for us; that we sue for many things very unwisely against ourselves, thinking we ask fish when indeed we crave a serpent: he knew that when the thing we ask is good, and yet God seemeth slow to grant it, he d th not deny but defer our petitions, to the end we might learn to desire great things greatly: all this he knew. But, beholding the land which God had severed for his own people, and seeing it abandoned unto heathen nations; viewing how reproachfully they did tread it down, and wholly make havock of it at their pleasure; beholding the Lord's own royal seat made a heap of stones, his temple defiled, the carcasses of his servants cast out for the fowls of the air to devour, and the flesh of his meek ones for the beasts of the field to feed upon; being conscious to himself how long and how earnestly he had cried, "Succour us, O God of our welfare, for the glory of thine own name;"[2] and feeling that their sore was still increased: the conceit of repugnancy between this which was object to his eyes, and that which faith upon promise of the law did look for, made so deep an impression and so strong, that he disputeth not the matter; but without any further inquiry or search inferreth, as we see, "The law doth fail."

Of us who is here which cannot very soberly advise his brother? Sir, you must learn to strengthen your faith by that experience which heretofore you have had of God's great goodness towards you: "Per ea quæ agnoscas præstita, discas sperare promissa;" "By those things which you have known performed, learn to hope for those things which are promised." Do you acknowledge to have received much? Let that make you certain to receive more: "Habenti dabitur;" "To him that hath more shall be given." When you doubt what you shall have, search what you have had at God's hands. Make this reckoning, that the benefits, which he hath bestowed, are bills obligatory and sufficient

[1] [Ps. lxxxix. 28, 32.]   [2] [Ps. lxxix. 9.]

sureties that he will bestow further. His present mercy is still a warrant of his future love, because, "whom he loveth, he loveth unto the end."[1] Is it not thus?

Yet if we could reckon up as many evident, clear, un-doubted signs of God's reconciled love towards us as there are years, yea days, yea hours, past over our heads ; all these set together have not such force to confirm our faith, as the loss, and sometimes the only fear of losing a little transitory goods, credit, honour, or favour of men,—a small calamity, a matter of nothing,—to breed a conceit, and such a conceit as is not easily again removed, that we are clean crost out of God's book, that he regards us not, that he looketh upon others, but passeth by us like a stranger to whom we are not known. Then we think, looking upon others, and com-paring them with ourselves, Their tables are furnished day by day ; earth and ashes are our bread : they sing to the lute, and they see their children dance before them ; our hearts are heavy in our bodies as lead, our sighs beat as thick as a swift pulse, our tears do wash the beds wherein we lie : the sun shineth fair upon their foreheads ; we are hanged up like bottles in the smoke, cast into corners like the sherds of a broken pot : tell not us of the promises of God's favour, tell such as do reap the fruit of them ; they belong not to us, they are made to others. The Lord be merciful to our weakness, but thus it is.

Well, let the frailty of our nature, the subtilty of Satan, the force of our deceivable imaginations be, as we cannot deny but they are, things that threaten every moment the utter subversion of our faith ; faith notwithstanding is not hazarded by these things. That which one sometimes told the senators of Rome,[2] "Ego sic existimabam, P. C. uti patrem sæpe meum prædicantem audiveram, qui vestram amicitiam diligenter colerent, eos multum laborem suscipere, cæterum ex omnibus maxime tutos esse ;" "As I have often heard my father acknowledge, so I myself did ever think, that the friends and favourers of this state charged them-selves with great labour, but no man's condition so safe as theirs ;" the same we may say a great deal more justly in this case : our Fathers and Prophets, our Lord and Master, hath full often spoken, by long experience we have found it true, as many as have entered their names in the mystical Book of Life, "Eos maximum laborem suscipere," they

[1] John xiii. 1.   [2] Sallust. Jugurth. c. 14.

have taken upon them a laboursome, a toilsome, a painful profession, "sed omnium maxime tutos esse," but no man's security like to theirs. "[1] Simon, Simon, Satan hath desired to winnow thee as wheat;" here is our toil: "but I have prayed for thee, that thy faith fail not;" this is our safety. No man's condition so sure as ours: the prayer of Christ is more than sufficient both to strengthen us, be we never so weak; and to overthrow all adversary power, be it never so strong and potent. His prayer must not exclude our labour: their thoughts are vain who think that their watching can preserve the city which God himself is not willing to keep: and are not theirs as vain, who think that God will keep the city, for which they themselves are not careful to watch? The husbandman may not therefore burn his plough, nor the merchant forsake his trade, because God hath promised "I will not forsake thee." And do the promises of God concerning our stability, think you, make it a matter indifferent for us to use or not to use the means whereby, to attend or not to attend to reading? to pray or not to pray that we "fall not into temptations?" Surely if we look to stand in the faith of the sons of God, we must hourly, continually, be providing and setting ourselves to strive. It was not the meaning of our Lord and Saviour in saying,[2] "Father, keep them in thy name," that we should be careless to keep ourselves. To our own safety, our own sedulity is required. And then blessed for ever and ever be that mother's child whose faith hath made him the child of God. The earth may shake, the pillars of the world may tremble under us, the countenance of the heaven may be appalled, the sun may lose his light, the moon her beauty, the stars their glory; but concerning the man that trusteth in God, if the fire have proclaimed itself unable as much as to singe a hair of his head, if lions, beasts ravenous by nature and keen with hunger, being set to devour, have as it were religiously adored the very flesh of the faithful man; what is there in the world that shall change his heart, overthrow his faith, alter his affection towards God, or the affection of God to him? If I be of this note, who shall make a separation between me and my God? "Shall tribulation, or anguish, or persecution, or famine, or nakedness, or peril, or sword?"[3] No; "I am persuaded that neither tribulation, nor anguish,

---

[1] Luke xxii. 31, 32.   [2] [John xvii. 11.]
[3] [Rom. viii. 35, 38, 39.]

nor persecution, nor famine, nor nakedness, nor peril, nor sword, nor death, nor life, nor angels, nor principalities, nor powers, nor things present, nor things to come, nor height, nor depth, nor any other creature," shall ever prevail so far over me. "I know in whom I have believed;" I am not ignorant whose precious blood hath been shed for me; I have a Shepherd full of kindness, full of care, and full of power: unto him I commit myself; his own finger hath engraven this sentence in the tables of my heart, "Satan hath desired to winnow thee as wheat, but I have prayed that thy faith fail not." therefore the assurance of my hope I will labour to keep as a jewel unto the end; and by labour, through the gracious mediation of his prayer, I shall keep it.

A

LEARNED DISCOURSE

OF

JUSTIFICATION, WORKS, AND HOW THE FOUNDATION OF FAITH IS OVERTHROWN [1]

HABAK. I. 4.

The wicked doth compass about the righteous : therefore perverse
judgment doth proceed.

FOR better [a] manifestation of the prophet's meaning in
this place, we are, first, to consider "the wicked," of whom
he saith, "that they compass about "the righteous :" secondly,
"the righteous" that are compassed about by them : and
thirdly, that which is inferred ; "therefore [b] perverse judgment proceedeth." Touching the first, there are two kinds
of wicked men, of whom in the fifth of the former to the
Corinthians,[c] the blessed Apostle speaketh thus : [2] "Do ye

[a] the better E.   [b] Ergo D.   [c] Corinthes D.

[1] [From a passage in Hooker's answer to Travers's Supplication, §
5. we know that this sermon was preached in the first year of Hooker's
mastership of the Temple. For he says, "I am able to prove that
myself have now *for a full yeer together* borne the continuance of such
dealings," &c. And it appears from Strype's Collections, inserted in
Walton's Life of Hooker, that the sermon was preached the 28th March,
and that Travers's notes of exception to it were "set down and shewed"
March 30, 1585 : but a MS. in the Harleian Collection, quoted above,
vol. i. 59, gives March 1, 1585, as the date of the sermon ; erroneously,
since the sermon was preached on a Sunday, (see Travers, Supplication,
p. 561, 562, *infra*) and the 1st March did not fall on a Sunday in
either of those years. The 28th did, in 1586. And this agrees with
what Travers in his Supplication states, "that Hooker according to his
course had *of late* taught that the church of Rome is a true church of
Christ." He had been made Master of the Temple March 17, 1584-5.
The sermon was collated by Archdeacon Cotton for the edition of 1836,
with a MS. (A. 5, 6.) in Trin. Coll. Dublin, here designated by D. :
the results of which collation, revised by Dr. Todd and Mr. Gibbings,
are given in the margin below.]

[2] 1 Cor. v. 12, 13.[*]

[*] *Om.* D.

14

not judge them that are within? but God judgeth them that are without." There are wicked, therefore, whom the Church may judge, and there are wicked whom God only judgeth; wicked within, and wicked without, the walls of the Church. If within the Church particular persons, being apparently such, cannot [d] otherwise be reformed, the rule of apostolical [e] judgment is this,[1] "Separate them from among [f] you:" if whole assemblies, this, "Separate yourselves from among [f] them: for what society hath light with darkness?" But the wicked, whom the prophet meaneth, were Babylonians, and therefore without. For which cause we have heard at large heretofore in what sort he urgeth God to judge them.

2. Now concerning the righteous, there neither is, nor ever [g] was, any mere natural man absolutely righteous in himself: that is to say, void of all unrighteousness, of all sin. We dare not except, no not the blessed Virgin herself; of whom although we say with St. Augustine,[2] for the honour's [h] sake which we owe to our Lord and Saviour Christ, we are not willing, in this cause, to move any question of [i] his mother; yet forasmuch as the schools of Rome have made it a question, we must [k] answer with Eusebius Emissenus,[3] who speaketh of her to [l] this effect: "Thou didst by special prerogative nine months together entertain within the closet of thy flesh the hope of all the ends of the earth, the honour of the world, the common joy of men. He, from whom all things had their beginning,

[d] be apparently such as cannot E.   [e] of the apostolical E.   [f] amongst D.
[g] never D.   [h] honour D.   [i] about D.   [k] may E.   [l] in E.

[1] 2 Cor. vi. 14–17.*

[2] [De Nat. et Grat. contra Pelag. § 42. x. 144. G. " Commemorat eos, qui non modo non peccasse, verum etiam juste vixisse referantur, Abel, Enoch, Melchisedech, &c. Adjungit etiam fœminas, . . . ipsam etiam Domini ac Salvatoris nostri matrem, quam dicit sine peccato confiteri necesse esse pietati. Excepta itaque sancta virgine Maria, de qua propter honorem Domini nullam prorsus, cum de peccatis agitur, haberi volo quæstionem, (unde enim scimus, quid ei plus gratiæ collatum fuerit ad vincendum omni ex parte peccatum, quæ concipere ac parere meruit, quem constat nullum habuisse peccatum?) hac ergo virgine excepta, si omnes illos sanctos et sanctas, cum hic viverent, congregare possemus, et interrogare utrum essent sine peccato; quid fuisse responsuros putamus; utrum hoc quod iste dicit, sive quod Joannes Apostolus?"]

[3] Or whosoever it be, that was the author of those Homilies, that go under his name.†

* *Om.* D   † Note *om.* D.

hath [m] had his own [n] beginning from thee; of thy body he took the blood which was to be shed for the life of the world; of thee he took that which even for thee he paid. '*A peccati enim veteris nexu, per se non est immunis nec ipsa genitrix Redemptoris:*'[1] The mother of the Redeemer herself, otherwise than by redemption, is not loosed from the band [o] of that ancient sin."[p][2] If Christ have paid a ransom for all, even for her, it followeth, that all without exception were captives. If one have died for all, all [q] were dead, dead in sin;[r] all sinful, therefore none absolutely righteous in themselves; but we are absolutely righteous in Christ. The world then must shew a Christian [s] man, otherwise it is not able to shew a man that is perfectly righteous: "Christ is made unto us wisdom, justice, sanctification, and redemption:"[3] wisdom, because he hath revealed his Father's will; justice, because he hath offered himself [t] a sacrifice for sin; sanctification, because he hath given us of [u] his Spirit; redemption, because he hath appointed a day to vindicate his children out of the bands of corruption into liberty which is glorious.[4] How Christ is made wisdom, and how redemption, it may be declared when occasion serveth; but how Christ is made the righteousness of men, we are now to declare.

3. There is a glorifying righteousness of men in the world to come: and [x] there is a justifying and a sanctifying righteousness here. The righteousness, wherewith we shall be clothed in the world to come, is both perfect and inherent. That whereby here we are justified is perfect, but not inherent. That whereby we are sanctified, in-

---

[m] hath *om.* E.   [n] own *om.* E.   [o] bond E.   [p] is not otherwise loosed from the bond of ancient sin, than by redemption E.   [q] then all E.   [r] were dead in sin E.   [s] righteous E.   [t] offered up himself E.   [u] of *om.* E.   [x] as E.

[1] Knowing how the schoolmen hold this question, some critical wits may perhaps half suspect that these two words, *per se*, are inmates. But, if the place which they have be their own, their sense can be none other than that which I have given them by a paraphrastical interpretation.[*]

[2] Hom. 2. de Nativ. Dom.[*] [t. v. pars ii. p. 545. Biblioth. Patr. Colon. "Spem terrarum, decus sæculorum, commune omnium gaudium, peculiari munere novem mensibus sola possides: initiator omnium rerum abs te initiatur, et profundendum pro mundi vita sanguinem de corpore tuo accepit, ac de te sumpsit, quod etiam pro te solvat. A peccati enim," &c.]

[3] [1 Cor. i. 30.]   [4] [Rom. viii. 21.]

[*] Both notes *om.* D.

herent,[y] but not perfect. This openeth a way to the plain[z] understanding of that grand question, which hangeth yet in controversy between us and the Church of Rome, about the matter of justifying righteousness.

4. First, although they imagine that the mother of our Lord and Saviour Jesus Christ were, for his honour, and by his special protection, preserved clean from all sin, yet touching the rest, they teach as we do, that all have sinned;[a] that infants which did never[b] actually offend, have their natures defiled, destitute of justice, and averted from God. They teach as we do, that God doth justify the soul of man alone, without any other coefficient cause of justice;[c] that in making man righteous, none do work efficiently[d] with God, but God.[1] They teach as we do, that unto justice no man ever attained, but by the merits of Jesus Christ. They teach as we do, that although Christ as God be the efficient, as man the meritorious cause of our justice; yet in us also there is something[e] required. God is the cause of our natural life; in him we live: but he quickeneth not the body without the soul in the body. Christ hath merited to make us just: but as a medicine which is made for health, doth not heal by being made, but by being applied; so, by the merits of Christ there can be no justification, without the application of his merits. Thus far we join hands with the Church of Rome.

5. Wherein then do we disagree? We disagree about the nature of the very essence[f] of the medicine whereby Christ cureth our disease; about the manner of applying it; about the number and the power of means, which God requireth in us for the effectual applying thereof to our soul's comfort. When they are required to shew, what the

---

[y] is inherent E.   [z] plain om. E.   [a] that all have sinned om. E.
[b] never did E.   [c] This clause in marg. E. which also reads coeffective for coefficient.   [d] work efficiently E.   [e] there is also somewhat D.
[f] nature and essence E.

[1] * "Deus sine medio coeffectivo animam justificat." Casal. de quadripart. Just. lib. vi. [pars I. lib. i. cap. 8, p. 24, G. ed. Venet. 1599.] Idem, lib. iii. c. 9. ["Salvator noster est nostra justificatio, quia nos justificat effective secundum naturam divinam ; estque nostra justificatio, quia nos justificat meritorie secundum naturam humanam," p. 304. Casal was bishop of Leiria in Portugal, and was distinguished at the council of Trent. See in Fra Paolo, vi. 53, his arguments for conceding the eucharistical cup to the laity ; and vii. 32, his assertion of the divine right of episcopacy.]

* Note om. D.

righteousness is whereby a Christian man is justified, they answer,[1] that it is a divine spiritual quality; which quality received into the soul, doth first make it to be one of them who are born of God : and, secondly, endue it with power to bring forth such works, as they do that are born of him ; even as the soul of man being joined unto [g] his body, doth first make him to be in [h] the number of reasonable creatures, and secondly enable [i] him to perform the natural functions which are proper to his kind; that it maketh the soul gracious and amiable [k] in the sight of God, in regard whereof it is termed Grace ; that it purgeth, purifieth, washeth out,[l] all the stains and pollutions of sin ;[m] that by it, through the merit of Christ we are delivered as from sin, so from eternal death and condemnation, the reward of sin   This grace they will have to be applied by infusion ; to the end, that as the body is warm by the heat which is in the body, so the soul might be righteous by inherent grace : which grace they make capable of increase ; as the body may be more and more warm, so the soul more and more justified,[2] according as grace shall be augmented; the aug-

[g] to E.   [h] of E.   [i] inhable D.   [k] amiable and gracious E.   [l] and washeth out E.   [m] sins E.

[1] * Tho. Aquin. Summ. Theol. ii. pars i. quæst. 100.   "Gratia gratum faciens, id est, justificans, est in anima quiddam reale et positivum ; qualitas quædam (art. ii. concl.) supernaturalis, non eadem cum virtute infusa, ut Magister, sed aliquid (art. iii.) præter virtutes infusas, fidem, spem, charitatem, [110. art. 1.] habitudo quædam (art. iii. ad 3.) quæ præsupponitur in virtutibus istis sicut earum principium et radix ;" essentiam animæ tanquam subjectum occupat, non potentias, sed "ab ipsa" (art. iv. ad 1.) "effluunt virtutes in potentias animæ, per quas potentiæ moventur ad actus." Plur. vid. quæst. 113. de Justificatione. [t. xi. 253–255 ; 259, &c. ed. Antwerp. 1612. Comp. Concil. Trident. Sess. vi. Decr. de Justificatione, cap. vii. "Justificationis unica formalis causa est, justitia Dei ; non qua ipse justus est, sed qua nos justos facit, qua videlicet ab eo donati renovamur spiritu mentis nostræ, et non modo reputamur, sed vere justi nominati sumus ; justitiam in nobis recipientes unusquisque suam, secundum mensuram quam Spiritus Sanctus partitur singulis prout vult, et secundum propriam cujusque dispositionem et cooperationem." Ibid. can. xi. "Si quis dixerit, homines justificari vel sola imputatione justitiæ Christi, vel sola peccatorum remissione, exclusa gratia et caritate, quæ in cordibus eorum per Spiritum Sanctum diffundatur atque illis inhæreat, aut etiam gratiam, qua justificamur, esse tantum favorem Dei ; anathema sit."]

[2] [Concil. Trident. ubi supr. cap. 10.   "Mortificando membra carnis suæ, et exhibendo ea arma justitiæ in sanctificationem, per observationem mandatorum Dei et ecclesiæ, in ipsa justitia, per Christi gratiam accepta, cooperante fide bonis operibus, crescunt, atque magis justificantur : sicut

* Note *om.* D.

mentation whereof is merited by good works,[1] as good
works are made meritorious by it.[2] Wherefore, the first
receipt of grace is in their divinity [n] the first justification ;
the increase thereof, the second justification.[3] As grace
may be increased by the merit of good works ; so it may
be diminished by the demerit of sins venial ;[4] it may be
lost by mortal sin.[5] Inasmuch, therefore, as it is needful in
the one case to repair, in the other to recover, the loss which
is made ; the infusion of grace hath her sundry after-meals ;
for which [o] cause they make many ways to apply the infusion
of grace. It is applied unto infants [6] through baptism,
without either faith or works, and in them it really taketh
away original sin, and the punishment due unto it ; it is
applied unto infidels and wicked men in their first [p] justification through baptism, without works,[7] yet not without faith ;
and it taketh away both sin actual and original, together
with all whatsoever punishment eternal or temporal thereby
deserved.[8] Unto such as have attained the first justification,
that is to say, the first receipt of grace, it is applied further
by good works to the increase of former grace, which is the
second justification. If they work more and more, grace
doth more and more increase, and they are more and more
justified. To such as have diminished [q] it by venial sins, it
is applied by holy water, Ave Marias, crossings, papal saluta-

---

[n] in their divinity is E.   [o] the which E.   [p] the first E.   [q] diminish E

scriptum est, ' Qui justus est, justificetur adhuc.' " And can. xxiv. "Si
quis dixerit, justitiam acceptam non conservari, atque etiam non augeri
coram Deo per bona opera ; sed opera ipsa fructus solummodo et signa
esse justificationis adeptæ, non autem ipsius augendæ causam ; anathema
sit."]

[1] [Ibid. cap. xvi. "Bene operantibus usque in finem, et in Deo
sperantibus proponenda est vita æterna et tanquam gratia filiis Dei per
Christum Jesum misericorditer promissa, et tanquam merces ex ipsius
Dei promissione bonis ipsorum operibus et meritis fideliter reddenda."]

[2] [Ibid. "Cum ipse Christus Jesus, tanquam caput in membra, et
tanquam vitis in palmites, in ipsos justificatos jugiter virtutem influat,
quæ virtus bona eorum opera semper antecedit, comitatur et subsequitur,
et sine qua nullo pacto Deo grata et meritoria esse possent," &c.]

[3] [Catherinus, Dialog. de Justif. ad calc. Summ. Doctr. de Prædest.
Rom. 1550. p. 60.]

[4] [See in Aquinas (2 Summ. pars ii. qu. xxiv. art. 10 ; t. xi. pars ii.
p. 63. A. Antwerp, 1612.) with what qualification this must be taken.]

[5] [Id. ibid. art. 11, 12.]

[6] [Id. 3 Summ. qu. lxix. art. 6. (t. xii. 221.)]

[7] [Id. ibid. qu. lxviii. art. 5. fol. 219.]

[8] [Id. ibid. qu. lxix. art. 1, 2, 3. f. 220.]

tions,[1] and such like, which serve for reparations of grace
decayed. To such as have lost it through mortal sin, it is
applied by the sacrament (as they term it) of penance;
which sacrament hath force to confer grace anew,[2] yet in
such sort, that being so conferred, it hath not altogether so
much power[3] as at the first. For[r] it only cleanseth out
the stain or guilt of sin committed, and changeth the
punishment eternal into a temporal satisfactory punishment,
here, if time do serve, if not, hereafter to be endured, except
it be either[s] lightened by masses, works of charity, pilgrim-
ages, fasts, and such like; or else shortened by pardon for
term, or by plenary pardon quite removed and taken away.[4]
This is the mystery of the man of sin. This maze the
Church of Rome doth cause her followers to tread, when
they ask her the way of justification.[t] I cannot stand now
to unrip this building, and to sift it piece by piece; only I
will set a frame of apostolical erection by it in a few words,[u]

---

r first, for D. s either *om.* E. t to justification E
u pass it by in few words E.

[1] [Id. ibid. qu. lxxxvii. art. 3. fol. 292. "Triplici ratione aliqua
causant remissionem venialium peccatorum. Uno modo, in quantum
in eis infunditur gratia ;—et hoc modo . . . per omnia sacramenta
novæ legis . . . peccata venialia remittuntur. Secundo, in quantum
sunt cum aliquo motu detestationis peccatorum : et hoc modo confessio
generalis, tunsio pectoris, et oratio Dominica, operantur ad remissionem
venialium peccatorum. . . Tertio modo, in quantum sunt cum aliquo
motu reverentiæ in Deum, et ad res divinas ; et hoc modo benedictio
episcopalis, aspersio aquæ benedictæ, quælibet sacramentalis unctio,
oratio in ecclesia dedicata, et si aliqua sunt hujusmodi, operantur ad
remissionem venialium peccatorum."]

[2] [Conc. Trid. Sess. vi. Decr. de Justif. cap. xiv. "Qui ab accepta
justificationis gratia per peccatum exciderunt, rursus justificari poterunt,
cum excitante Deo, per pœnitentiæ sacramentum, merito Christi,
amissam gratiam recuperare procuraverint."]

[3] [Ibid. "Docendum est, Christiani hominis pœnitentiam post lapsum
multo aliam esse a baptismali, eaque contineri non modo cessationem a
peccatis, et eorum detestationem, aut cor contritum et humiliatum ;
verum etiam eorundem sacramentalem confessionem, saltem in voto, et
suo tempore faciendam, et sacerdotalem absolutionem ; itemque satisfactionem, per jejunia, eleemosynas, orationes, et alia vitæ spiritalis
exercitia, non quidem pro pœna æterna, quæ vel sacramento vel sacramenti voto una cum culpa remittitur, sed pro pœna temporali, quæ, ut
sacræ literæ docent, non semper, ut in baptismo fit, dimittitur illis, qui
gratiæ Dei, quam acceperunt, ingrati, Sp. Sanctum contristaverunt, et
templum Dei violare non sunt veriti." Comp. Sess. xiv. decr. de Pœnit.
cap. 9, et can. 13.]

[4] [Ibid. Sess. xxv. Decr. de Purgatorio ; et Decr. de Indulgentiis.
Comp. Aquin. in iv. Sent. dist. xx. qu. i. art. 3.]

that it [x] may befall Babylon, in presence [y] of that which God hath builded, as it [z] happened unto Dagon before the ark.

6. " Doubtless," saith the Apostle,[1] " I have counted all things loss,[a] and I do [b] judge them to be dung, that I may win Christ; and be found [c] in him, not having mine own righteousness, but that which is through the faith of Christ, the righteousness which is of God through faith." Whether they speak of the first or second justification, they make the essence of it [d] a divine quality inherent, they make it right-eousness which is in us. If it be in us, then it is [e] ours, as our souls are ours, though we have them from God, and can hold them no longer than pleaseth him; for if he with-draw the breath of our nostrils, we fall to dust: but the righteousness wherein we must be found, if we will be justified, is not our own; therefore we cannot be justified by any inherent quality. Christ hath merited righteousness for as many as are found in him. In him God findeth us, if we be faithful; for by faith we are incorporated into him.[f] Then, although in ourselves we be altogether sinful and unrighteous, yet even the man which in himself is impious,[g] full of iniquity, full of sin; him being found in Christ through faith, and having his sin in hatred [h] through repentance; him God beholdeth with a gracious eye, putteth away his sin by not imputing it, taketh quite away the punishment due thereunto, by pardoning it; and accepteth him in Jesus Christ, as perfectly righteous, as if he had fulfilled all that is [i] commanded him in the law: shall I say more perfectly righteous than if himself had fulfilled the whole law? I must take heed what I say: but the Apostle saith,[2] " God made him which knew no sin, to be sin for us; [k] that we might be made the righteousness of God in him." Such we are in the sight of God the Father, as is the very Son of God himself. Let it be counted folly, or phrensy, or fury, or [l] whatsoever. It is our wisdom, and our comfort; [m] we care for no knowledge in the world but this, that man hath sinned, and God hath suffered; that God hath made himself the sin [n] of men,[o] and that men are made the righteousness of God.

x that E.   y in the presence E.   z it *om*. E.   a lost E.
b I do *om*. E.   c to be found E.   d it *om*. ?   e it is E.   f Christ E.
g is impious in himself E.   h remitted E.   i was E.   k to be sin for us, who knew no sin E.   l or *om*. E.   m whatsoever, it is our comfort, and our wisdom E.   n son E.   o man E.

1 Phil. iii. 8, 9.   2 2 Cor. v. 21.

You see therefore that the church of Rome, in teaching justification by inherent grace, doth pervert the truth of Christ; and that by the hands of his [p] Apostles we have received otherwise than she teacheth. [q] Now concerning the righteousness of sanctification, we deny it not to be inherent; we grant, that unless [r] we work, we have it not; only we distinguish it as a thing in nature different from [s] the righteousness of justification : we are righteous the one way, by the faith of Abraham ; the other way, except we do the works of Abraham, we are not righteous. Of the one St. Paul,[1] "To him that worketh not, but believeth, faith is counted for righteousness." Of the other, St. John,[2] "Qui facit justitiam, justus est :—He is righteous which worketh righteousness." Of the one, St. Paul[3] doth prove by Abraham's example, that we have it of faith without works. Of the other, St. James[4] by Abraham's example, that by works we have it, and not only by faith. St. Paul doth plainly sever these two parts of Christian righteousness one from the other. For in the sixth to the Romans thus he writeth[5], "Being freed from sin, and made servants to [t] God, ye [u] have your fruit in holiness, and the end everlasting life." "Ye are made free from sin, and made servants unto God ;" this is the righteousness of justification : "Ye have your fruit in holiness ;" this is the righteousness of sanctification. By the one we are interested in the right of inheriting ; by the other we are brought to the actual possessing [x] of eternal bliss, and so the end of both is everlasting life.

7. The Prophet Habakkuk [y] doth here term the Jews "righteous men," not only because being justified by faith they were free from sin ; but also for that [z] they had their measure of fruit [a] in holiness. According to whose example of charitable judgment, which leaveth it to God to discern what men [b] are, and speaketh of them according to that which they do profess [c] themselves to be, although they be not holy [d] whom men do think, but whom God doth know indeed to be such ; yet let every Christian man know, that in Christian equity, he standeth bound so [e] to think and

p the Apostles E.   q D. begins the section here.   r without D.
s different in nature E.   t unto D.   u you D.   x possession E.
y Abakuk D.   z because E.   a fruits E.   b we E.   c they professt D
d holy men E.   e for E.

1 [Rom. iv. 5.]   2 [1 John iii. 7.]   3 [Rom. iv.]
4 [James ii.]   5 Rom. vi. 22.

speak of his brethren, as of men that have a measure in the fruit of holiness, and a right unto the titles wherewith God, in token of special favour and mercy, vouchsafeth to honour his chosen servants. So we see the Apostles of our Saviour Christ do use every where the name of *saints ;* so the prophet the name of *righteous.* But let us all endeavour to [f] be such as we desire to be termed : " *Reatus impii est pium nomen,*" saith Salvianus ; [1] "Godly names do not justify godless men." We are but upbraided, when we are honoured with names and titles whereunto our lives and manners are not suitable. If we have indeed [g] our fruit in holiness, notwithstanding we must note, that the more we abound therein, [h] the more need we have to crave that we may be strengthened and supported. Our very virtues may be snares unto us. The enemy that waiteth for all occasions to work our ruin, hath ever [i] found it harder to overthrow an humble sinner, than a proud saint. There is no man's case so dangerous as his, whom Satan hath persuaded that his own righteousness shall present him pure and blameless in the sight of God. If we could say, "we are [k] not guilty of any thing at all in our own [l] consciences," (we know ourselves far from this innocency, we cannot say, we know nothing by ourselves ; but if we could,) should we therefore plead not guilty in [m] the presence of our Judge, that sees further [n] into our hearts than we ourselves are able to see ? [o] If our hands did never offer violence to our brethren, a bloody thought doth prove us murderers before him : if we had never opened our mouths [p] to utter any scandalous, offensive, or hurtful word, the cry of our secret cogitations is heard in the ears of God. If we did not commit the evils which we do daily and hourly, either in deeds, words, or thoughts, [q] yet in the good things which we do, how many defects are there intermingled ! God, in that which is done, respecteth specially [r] the mind and intention of the doer. Cut off then all those things wherein we have regarded our own glory, those things which we [s] do to please men, or [t] to satisfy our own liking, those things which we do with any by-

---

[f] endeavour to *om.* E.   [g] indeed we have E.   [h] herein D.   [i] ever *om.* E.
[k] were E.   [l] own *om.* E.   [m] before E.   [n] farder D.   [o] ourselves
can do E.   [p] mouth E.   [q] If we did not commit the sins which daily
and hourly either in deed, word, or thoughts we do commit E.   [r] specially *om.* E.
[s] men E.   [t] and E.

[1] [De Gubern. Dei, lib. iv. p. 341. D ; in Bibl. Patr. Colon. t. v.
part. iii.]

respect,[u] not sincerely and purely for the love of God; and a small score will serve for the number of our righteous deeds. Let the holiest and best thing we do be considered. We are never better affected unto God than when we pray; yet when we pray, how are our affections many times distracted! How little reverence do we show to the grand majesty of that [x] God, unto whom we speak! How little remorse of our own miseries! How little taste of the sweet influence of his tender mercy [y] do we feel! Are we not as unwilling many times to begin, and as glad to make an end, as if God [z] in saying, "Call upon me," had [a] set us a very burdensome task?

It may seem somewhat extreme, which I will speak; therefore let every man [b] judge of it, even as his own heart shall tell him, and no otherwise; I will but only make a demand: If God should yield to us, not as unto Abraham, if fifty, forty, thirty, twenty, yea, or if ten good persons could be found in a city, for their sakes that [c] city should not be destroyed; but, if God [d] should make us an offer thus large, Search all the generations of men sithence the fall of your [e] father Adam, find one man, that hath done any [f] one action, which hath past from him [g] pure, without any stain or blemish at all; and for that one man's one only action, neither man nor angel shall feel the torments which are prepared for both: do you think that this ransom, to deliver men and angels, would be found [h] among the sons of men? The best things we do [i] have somewhat in them to be pardoned. How then can we do any thing meritorious, and [k] worthy to be rewarded? Indeed, God doth liberally promise whatsoever appertaineth to a blessed life, unto as many as sincerely keep his law, though they be not able exactly [l] to keep it. Wherefore, we acknowledge a dutiful necessity of doing well, but the meritorious dignity of well doing [m] we utterly renounce. We see how far we are from the perfect righteousness of the law; the little fruit which we have in holiness, it is, God knoweth,[n] corrupt and unsound: we put no confidence at all in it, we challenge nothing in the world for it, we dare not call God to a reckoning,[o] as if we had him in our debt-books: our continual suit to him is,

u by any respect E.　　x that *om*. E.　　y mercies E.　　z God *om*. E.
a he had set E.　　b one E.　　c this E.　　d an if he E.
f any *om*. E.　　g past him D.　　h could be found to be E.　　i which we do E.　　k or E.　　l exactly able E.　　m doing well E.　　n knowes D.
o to reckoning E.

and must be, to bear with our infirmities, to [p] pardon our offences.

8. But the people of whom the Prophet speaketh, were they all, or were the most part of them, such as had care to walk uprightly? did they thirst after righteousness? did they wish, did they long with the righteous Prophet,[1] "O that our ways were made so direct that we might keep thy statutes"? did they lament with the righteous Apostle,[2] "Miserable men, the good which we wish and purpose, and strive to do, we cannot"? No; the words of other prophets [q] concerning this people do shew the contrary. How grievously doth Esay mourn over them![3] "Ah sinful nation, people laden with iniquity, wicked seed, corrupt children!" All which notwithstanding, so wide are the bowels of his compassion enlarged, that he denieth us not, no not when we are [r] laden [s] with iniquity, leave to commune familiarly with him, liberty to crave and entreat, that what plagues soever we have deserved, we may not be in worse case than unbelievers, that we may not be hemmed in by pagans and infidels. Jerusalem is a sinful polluted city; but Jerusalem compared with Babylon is righteous. And shall the righteous be overborne, shall they be compassed about by the wicked? But the prophet doth not only complain; Lord, how cometh it to pass that thou handlest us so hardly, over [t] whom thy name is called, and bearest with heathen nations, that despise thee? no, he breaketh out through extremity of grief, and inferreth thus [u] violently, This proceeding is perverse; the righteous are thus handled, "therefore perverse judgment doth proceed."

9. Which illation containeth many things, whereof it were much better both for you to hear, and me to speak, if necessity did not draw me to another task.[x] Paul and Barnabas being requested[4] to preach the same things again which once they had preached, thought it their duties to satisfy the godly desires of men sincerely affected towards [y] the truth. Nor may it seem burdenous to me, or for you [z] unprofitable, that I follow their example, the like occasion unto theirs being offered me. When we had last the Epistle of St. Paul to the Hebrews in our hands [a], and of that

---

[p] and E.   [q] the other prophet E.   [r] were E.   [s] loden D.   [t] of E.
[u] thus *om*. E.   [x] stake D.   [y] to E.   [z] ye E.   [a] in hand E.

[1] [Psalm cxix. 5.]   [2] [Rom. vii. 19, 24.]
[3] [Isa. i. 4.]   [4] Acts xiii. 41-44.

epistle these words,[1] "In these last days he hath spoken
unto us by his Son;" after we had thence collected the
nature of the visible Church of Christ, and had defined it to
be a community of men [2] sanctified through the profession
of that truth which God hath taught the world by his Son;
and had declared, that the scope of Christian doctrine is the
comfort of them whose hearts are overcharged with the
burden of sin; and had proved that the doctrine professed
in the church of Rome doth bereave men of comfort, both
in their lives, and at [b] their deaths: the conclusion in the
end, whereunto we came,[c] was this; "The church of
Rome being in faith so corrupted, as she is, and refusing to
be reformed, as she doth, we are to sever ourselves from
her: the example of our fathers may not retain us in communion and fellowship [d] with that church, under hope that
we so continuing, might [e] be saved as well as they. God, I
doubt not, was merciful to save thousands of them, though
they lived in popish superstitions, inasmuch as they sinned
ignorantly: but the truth is now laid open [f] before our eyes."
The former part of this last sentence, namely, these words,
" I doubt not but *God was merciful to save thousands of our
fathers living in popish superstitions, inasmuch as they sinned
ignorantly:* " this sentence I beseech you to mark, and to
sift it with the strict [g] severity of austere judgment, that
if it be found as gold,[h] it may stand, suitable [i] to the
precious foundation whereupon it was then laid; for I
protest, that if it prove to [k] be hay or stubble, mine own
hand shall set fire to it.[l] Two questions have risen by
occasion of the [m] speech before alleged: the one, "Whether
our fathers, infected with popish errors and superstitions,
might [n] be saved:" the other, "Whether their ignorance be
a reasonable inducement to make us think that[o] they
might." We are therefore [p] to examine, first, what possibility, and [q] then, what probability there is, that God might
be merciful unto so many of our fathers.

[b] in E.　　　[c] the conclusion whereunto in thend we came of all D.　　　[d] and
fellowship *om.* E.　　[e] may E.　　[f] open *om.* E.　　[g] strict *om.* E.　　[h] to be
gold E.　　[i] be suitable E.　　[k] prove to *om.* E.　　[l] on it E.　　[m] this E.
[n] may E.　　[o] that *om.* E.　　[p] then E.　　[q] and *om.* E.

[1] * Heb. i. 2.
[2] * By sanctification, I mean a separation from others not professing
as they do.　For true holiness consisteth not in professing, but in obey-
ing the truth of Christ.

* Notes *om.* D.

10. So many of our fathers living in popish superstitions, yet by the mercy of God to be saved? No; this could not be: God hath spoken by his angel from heaven unto his people concerning Babylon (by Babylon we understand the church of Rome):[1] "Go out of her, my people, that ye be not partakers of her sins, and that ye receive not of her plagues."[r] For answer whereunto, first, I do not take these words to be meant only of temporal plagues, of the corporal death, sorrow, famine, and fire, whereunto God in his wrath had[s] condemned Babylon; and that to save his chosen people from these plagues, he saith, "Go out;" with like intent, as in the Gospel, speaking of Jerusalem's desolation, he saith,[2] "Let them that are in Judea flee unto the mountains, and them which are in the midst thereof depart out;" or, as in former times unto Lot,[3] "Arise, take thy wife and thy daughters which are here, lest thou be destroyed in the punishment of the city:" but forasmuch as here it is said, "Go out of Babylon, that ye be not partakers of her sins, and by consequence of her plagues;" plagues eternal being due to the sins of Babylon;[t] no doubt,[u] their everlasting destruction, which are partakers herein, is either principally meant, or necessarily implied in this sentence. How then was it possible for so many of our fathers to be saved, sith they were so far from departing out of Babylon, that they took her for their mother, and in her bosom yielded up the ghost?

11. First, the plagues[x] being threatened unto them that are partakers in the sins of Babylon, we can define nothing concerning our fathers out of this sentence; unless we shew what the sins of Babylon be, and who[y] they be that[z] are such partakers in[a] them, that their everlasting plagues are inevitable. The sins which may be common both to them of the church of Rome, and to[b] others departed thence, must be severed from this question. He which saith, "Depart out of Babylon, lest ye be partakers of her sins," sheweth plainly, that he meaneth such sins, as except we separate ourselves, we have no power in the world to avoid; such impieties, as by law[c] they have established, and

---

[r] that ye be not partaker of her plagues E.   [s] in wrath hath D.   [t] that ye be not . . . sins of Babylon, *om.* E.   [u] we doubt E.   [x] for the plagues E. [y] what E.   [z] which E.   [a] of E.   [b] to *om.* D.   [c] by their law E.

[1] Apoc. xviii. 4.   [2] Matt. xxiv. 16; S. Luke xxi. 21.
[3] Gen. xix. 15.

whereunto all that are among[d] them, either do indeed
assent, or else are by powerable means forced in show and
in[e] appearance to subject themselves. As for example, in
the church of Rome, it is maintained, that the same[1] credit
and reverence which[f] we give to the Scriptures of God,
ought also to be given to unwritten verities ; that the pope
is supreme head ministerial[2] over the universal church
militant ; that the bread in the Eucharist is transubstantiated[3] into Christ; that it is to be adored,[4] and to be
offered up unto God as a sacrifice propitiatory[5] for quick
and dead ; that images are to be worshipped, saints to be
called upon as intercessors,[6] and such like. Now, because

    [d] amongste D.   [e] in *om.* E.   [f] that E.

[1] [Conc. Trid. Sess. iv. Decr. de Canonicis Scripturis. "Ecclesia
. . . orthodoxorum Patrum exempla secuta, omnes libros tam Veteris
quam Novi Testamenti, cum utriusque unus Deus sit auctor, necnon
traditiones ipsas, tum ad fidem tum ad mores pertinentes, tanquam vel
ore tenus a Christo, vel a Sp. Sancto dictatas, et continua successione in
ecclesia catholica conservatas, pari pietatis affectu ac reverentia suscipit
ac veneratur." Conc. Hard. x. 22.]

[2] [Bulla Pii IV. super Profess. Fidei, (containing what is commonly
called Pope Pius' Creed, to which all ecclesiastical persons must
assent :) ibid. t. x. 201, a. "Sanctam catholicam et apostolicam
Romanam ecclesiam, omnium ecclesiarum matrem et magistram agnosco ; Romanoque Pontifici, beati Petri Apostolorum Principis successori,
ac Jesu Christi vicario, veram obedientiam spondeo ac juro."]

[3] [Conc. Trid. Sess. xiii. Can. 2. "Si quis dixerit in sacrosancto
Eucharistiæ sacramento remanere substantiam panis et vini una cum
corpore et sanguine Dom. nostri J. C. ; negaveritque mirabilem illam et
singularem conversionem totius substantiæ panis in corpus et totius
substantiæ vini in sanguinem, manentibus duntaxat speciebus panis et
vini, quam quidem conversionem catholica ecclesia aptissime transub-
stantiationem appellat ; anathema sit." t. x. 83.]

[4] [Ibid. can. 6. "Si quis dixerit, in sancto Eucharistiæ sacramento
Christum unigenitum Dei Filium non esse cultu latriæ, etiam externo,
adorandum ; atque ideo nec festiva peculiari celebritate venerandum,
neque in processionibus . . . solenniter circumgestandum ; vel non
publice, ut adoratur, populo proponendum ; et ejus adoratores esse
idololatras ; anathema sit." x. 84.]

[5] [Ibid. Sess. xxii. Decr. de Missa, cap. 2. "Quoniam in divino
hoc sacrificio, quod in missa peragitur, idem ille Christus continetur, et
incruente immolatur, qui in ara crucis semel seipsum cruente obtulit ;
docet sancta synodus, sacrificium istud vere propitiatorium esse . . .
Non solum pro fidelium vivorum peccatis, pœnis, satisfactionibus, et
aliis necessitatibus, sed et pro defunctis in Christo, nondum ad plenum
purgatis, rite, juxta Apostolorum traditionem, offertur." x. 127.]

[6] [Bulla Pii IV. ubi supr. "Constanter teneo . . . sanctos uno
cum Christo regnantes, venerandos atque invocandos esse : eosque
orationes Deo pro nobis offerre . . . Firmissime assero, imagines
Christi et Deiparæ semper Virginis, nec non aliorum sanctorum, haben-

some heresies do concern things only believed, as transubstantiating of[g] sacramental elements in the Eucharist; some concern things which are practised also[h] and put in ure, as adoration[i] of the elements transubstantiated : we must note that erroneously the practice of that is sometime received, whereof the doctrine which[k] teacheth it is not heretically maintained. They are all partakers in the maintenance of heresies, who by word or deed allow them, knowing them, although not knowing them to be heresies ; as also they, and that most dangerously of all others, who knowing heresy to be heresy, do notwithstanding, in worldly respects, make semblance of allowing that, which in heart and in[l] judgment they condemn : but heresy is heretically maintained, by such as obstinately hold it after wholesome admonition. Of the last sort, as also[m] of the next before, I make no doubt, but that their condemnation, without actual[n] repentance, is inevitable. Lest any man therefore should think, that in speaking of our fathers, I speak[o] indifferently of them all ; let my words, I beseech you, be well noted,[p] " I doubt not but God was merciful to save thousands of our fathers ; " which thing I will now by God's assistance set more plainly before your eyes.

12. Many are partakers of the error which are not of[q] the heresy of the church of Rome. The people following the conduct of their guides, and observing as they did, exactly that which was prescribed them,[r] thought they did God good service, when indeed they did dishonour him. This was their error : but the heresies[s] of the Church of Rome, their dogmatical positions opposite unto Christian truth, what one man among ten thousand did ever understand ? Of them, which understand Roman heresies, and allow them, all are not alike partakers in the action of allowing. Some allow them as the first founders and establishers of them ;[t] which crime toucheth none but their popes and councils : the people are clear and free[u] from this. Of them which maintain popish heresy[x] not as authors, but receivers of it from others, all maintain it not as Masters. In this are not the people partakers neither, but only their predicants

---

[g] the transubstantiation of the E. [h] also *om*. E. [i] the adoration E. [k] that E. [l] in *om*. E. [m] also *om*. E. [n] an actual E. [o] should speak E. [p] marked E. [q] in D. [r] them *om*. E. [s] heresy E. [t] of them *om*. D. [u] free and clear D. [x] heresies E. *and* them *for* it.

das et retinendas esse, atque eis debitum honorem ac venerationem impertiendam." x. 200.]

and their [y] schoolmen. Of them which have been partakers
in the [z] sin of teaching popish heresy, there is also a difference ; for they have not all been teachers of all popish
heresies. "Put a difference," saith St. Jude ;[1] "have
compassion upon some."   Shall we lap up all in one
condition ? shall we cast them all headlong, shall we plunge
them all in [a] that infernal and ever-flaming [b] lake ? them
that have been partakers in [c] the error [d] of Babylon, together
with them within [e] the heresy ? them which have been the
authors of heresy, with them that by terror and violence
have been forced to receive it ? them which have taught it,
with them [f] whose simplicity hath by sleights and conveyances of false teachers been seduced to believe it ? them
which have been partakers in one, with them which [g] have
been partakers in many ? them which in many, with them
which in all ?

13. Notwithstanding I grant, that although the condemnation of one [h] be more tolerable than another ;[i] yet
from the man that laboureth at the plough, to him that
sitteth in the Vatican ; to all partakers in the sins of
Babylon, our fathers, [k] though they did but erroneously
practise that which their guides did heretically teach ;[l] to
all without exception, plagues worldly [m] were due. The pit
is ordinarily the end, as well of the guide [n] in
blindness. But woe worth the hour wherein we were born,
except we might persuade [o] ourselves better things ; things
that accompany men's [p] salvation, even where we know that
worse and such as accompany condemnation are due. Then
must we shew some way how possibly they might escape.
What way is there for sinners to [q] escape the judgment of
God, but only by appealing unto the seat of his saving
mercy ? Which mercy we do not with Origen extend unto
devils and damned spirits. God hath mercy upon thousands,
but there be thousands also which be hardened.[r] Christ
hath therefore set the bounds, he hath fixed the limits of
his saving mercy within the compass of these two [s] terms.
In the third [t] of St. John's Gospel, mercy is restrained to

[y] their *om*. E.   [z] this E.   [a] into E.   [b] everlasting flaming E.
[c] of E.   [d] errors E.   [e] which are in E.   [f] those D.   [g] that D.
[h] them E.   [i] these E.   [k] to our fathers E.   [l] the guides . . . . taught E.
[m] worldly *om*. E.   [n] guide as of the guided E.   [o] promise E.   [p] which . . .
man's E.   [q] that sinners can find to E.   [r] he hardeneth E.   [s] two *om*. E.
[t] E. *inserts* In the third . . . . believers *between the two verses*.

[1] Ver. 22.

believers : [1] "God sent not his Son [u] to condemn the world, but that the world through him might be saved." [2] "He that believeth shall not be condemned : he that believeth not, is condemned already, because he believeth not in the Son of God." In the second of the Revelation, mercy is restrained to the penitent. For of Jezebel and her sectaries thus he speaketh : [3] "I gave her space to repent, and she repented not. Behold, I will cast her into a bed, and them that commit fornication with her into great affliction, except they repent them of their works ; and I will kill her children with death." Our hope therefore of the fathers is vain, if they were altogether faithless and impenitent.[x]

14. They be not all faithless that are either [y] weak in assenting to the truth, or stiff in maintaining things any way [z] opposite to the truth of Christian doctrine. But as many as hold the foundation which is precious, though they hold it but weakly, and as it were by [a] a slender thread, although they frame many base and unsuitable things upon it, things that cannot abide [b] the trial of the fire ; yet shall they pass the fiery [c] trial and be saved, which indeed have builded themselves upon the rock, which is the foundation of the Church. If then our fathers did not hold the foundation of faith, there is no doubt but they were faithless. If many of them held it, then is there herein [d] no impediment but that [e] many of them might be saved. Then let us see what the foundation of faith is, and whether we may think that thousands of our fathers living [f] in popish superstitions, did notwithstanding hold the foundation.

15. If the foundation of faith do import the general ground whereupon we rest when we do believe, the writings of the Evangelists and the Apostles are the foundation of Christian faith : "Credimus quia legimus," saith St. Jerome.[4] O that the church of Rome did as [5] soundly interpret those [g]

---

[u] own Son E.   [x] is, if they were not altogether faithless and impenitent E.
[y] either *om.* E.   [z] any way *om.* E.   [a] with E.   [b] byde D.   [c] fire D.
[d] therein E.   [e] that *om.* E.   [f] being E.   [g] these E.

---

[1] John iii. 17.   [2] John iii. 18.   [3] Rev. ii. 21-23.
[4] [Adv. Helvid. c. 19. t. ii. pars i. p. 226. ed. Vallarsii. Venet. 1767.]
[5] They misinterpret, not only by making false and corrupt glosses upon the Scripture, but also by forcing the old vulgar translation as the only authentical : howbeit, they refuse no book which is canonical, though they admit sundry which are not.*

* This note *om.* D.

fundamental writings whereupon we build our faith, as she doth willingly hold and embrace them !

16. But if the name Foundation [h] do note the principal thing which is believed, then is that the foundation of our faith which St. Paul hath unto Timothy : "God manifested in the flesh, justified in the Spirit," &c.: [1] that of Nathanael, "Thou art the Son of the living God ; thou art the king of Israel : " [2] that of the inhabitants of Samaria, "This is Christ the Saviour of the world : " he that directly denieth this, doth utterly raze [i] the very foundation of our faith.   I have proved heretofore, that although the church of Rome hath played the harlot worse than ever did Israel, yet are they not, as now the synagogue of the Jews, which plainly denieth [k] Christ Jesus, quite and clean excluded from the new covenant.   But as Samaria compared with Jerusalem is termed *Aholah*, a church or tabernacle of her own ; contrariwise, Jerusalem *Aholibah*, the resting place of the Lord : so, whatsoever we term the church of Rome, when we compare her to [1] reformed churches, still we put a difference, as then between Babylon and Samaria, so now between Rome and heathenish [m] assemblies.   Which opinion I must and will recall ; I must grant, and will, that the church of Rome, together with all her children, is clean excluded ; there is no difference in the world between our fathers and Saracens, Turks, or [n] Painims, if they did directly deny Christ crucified for the salvation of the world.

17. But how many millions of them are [o] known so to have ended their mortal [p] lives, that the drawing of their breath hath ceased with the uttering of this faith, "Christ my Saviour, my Redeemer Jesus ! "   And shall we say that such did not hold the foundation of Christian faith ? [q]

Answer is made, that this they might unfeignedly confess, and yet be far enough from salvation.   For behold, saith the Apostle, " I, Paul, say unto you, that if ye [r] be circumcised, Christ shall profit you nothing." [3]   Christ, in the work of man's salvation is alone : the Galatians were cast away by joining circumcision and other rites of the law with Christ : the church of Rome doth teach her children to join other things likewise with him ; therefore their faith, their belief, doth not profit them any thing at all.

[h] name of foundation E.   [i] raise D.   [k] deny E.   [l] with E.
[m] the heathenish E.   [n] and E.   [o] were E.   [p] mortal *om*. E.   [q] This sentence *om*. E.   [r] you D.   [s] the other E.

[1] 1 Tim. iii. 16.   [2] John i. 49 ; iv. 42.   [3] Gal. v. 2.

It is true, they[t] do indeed join other things with Christ; but how? Not in the work of redemption itself, which they grant that Christ alone hath performed sufficiently for the salvation of the whole world; but in the application of this inestimable treasure, that it may be effectual to their salvation: how demurely soever they confess that they seek remission of sins no otherwise than by the blood of Christ, using humbly the means appointed by him to apply the benefit of his holy blood; they teach, indeed, so many things pernicious to[u] Christian faith, in setting down the means whereof they speak, that the very foundation of faith which they hold, is thereby plainly overthrown,[1] and the force of the blood of Jesus Christ extinguished. We may therefore dispute with them, press them, urge[x] them even with as dangerous sequels as the Apostle doth the Galatians. But I demand, if some of those Galatians, heartily embracing the Gospel of Christ, sincere and sound in faith, this only[y] error excepted, had ended their lives before they were ever taught how perilous an opinion they held; shall we think that the damage of this error did so overweigh the benefit of their faith, that the mercy of God, his mercy,[z] might not save them? I grant they overthrew the very foundation of faith by consequent: doth not that so likewise which the[2]

---

[t] that they E.   [u] in E.   [x] disputing with them urge E.   [y] one only E.
[z] his mercy *om.* E.

[1] Plainly in all men's sight whose eyes God hath enlightened to behold his truth. For they which are in error are in darkness, and see not that which in light is plain. In that which they teach concerning the natures of Christ, they hold the same which Nestorius fully, the same which Eutyches about the proprieties of his nature.* [If taken in the full literal sense, it seems hardly possible that this note should be Hooker's, considering on the one hand his unvarying acknowledgment that the church of Rome is orthodox regarding the doctrine of the Incarnation; on the other hand his express condemnation of Nestorius and Eutyches. Comp. (e. g.) b. iii. c. i. 10; with b. v. c. xlii. 13; lii. 3, 4. It should be remembered that this sermon was not prepared by the author for the press, and that the Dublin copy of it has no notes at all.]

[2] The opinion of the Lutherans, though it be no direct denial of the foundation, may notwithstanding be damnable unto some; and I do not think but that in many respects it is less damnable, as at this day some maintain it, than it was in them which held it at first; as Luther and others, whom I had an eye unto in this speech. The question is not, whether an error with such and such circumstances; but simply, whether an error overthrowing the foundation, do exclude all possibility of salvation, if it be not recanted, and expressly repented of.*

* Note *om.* D.

Lutheran churches do at this day so stiffly and so fiercely[a] maintain? For mine[b] own part, I dare not hereupon[c] deny the possibility of their salvation, which have been the chiefest instruments of ours, albeit they carried to their grave a persuasion so greatly repugnant to the truth. Forasmuch therefore, as it may be said of the church of Rome, she hath yet "a little strength,"[1] she doth not directly deny the foundation of Christianity: I may, I trust without offence, persuade myself, that thousands of our fathers in former times, living and dying within her walls, have found mercy at the hands of God.

18. What although they repented not of their errors? God forbid that I should open my mouth to gainsay that which Christ himself hath spoken: "Except ye repent, ye shall all perish."[2] And if they did not repent, they perished. But withal note, that we have the benefit of a double repentance: the least sin which we commit in deed, word, or thought,[d] is death, without repentance. Yet how many things do escape us in every of these, which we do not know, how many, which we do not observe to be sins! and without the knowledge, without the observation of sin, there is no actual repentance. It cannot then be chosen, but that for as many as hold the foundation, and have all known sin and error[e] in hatred, the blessing of repentance for unknown sins and errors[f] is obtained at the hands of God, through the gracious mediation of Christ Jesus, for such suitors as cry with the prophet David, "Purge me, O Lord, from my secret sins."[3]

19. But we wash a wall of loam; we labour in vain; all this is nothing; it doth not prove, it cannot justify, that which we go about to maintain. Infidels and heathen men are not so godless, but that they may, no doubt, cry God mercy, and desire in general to have their sins forgiven them. To such as deny the foundation of faith, there can be no salvation, according to the ordinary course which God doth use in saving men, without a particular repentance of that error. The Galatians, thinking that except[g] they were circumcised they could not be saved, overthrew the foundation of faith directly: therefore if any of them did die so persuaded, whether before or after they were told of their

---

[a] firmly E.   [b] my D.   [c] here E.   [d] thought or word E.   [e] holden all sins and errors E.   [f] error D.   [g] unless E.

[1] [Apoc. iii. 8.]   [2] Luke xiii. 3.   [3] [Ps. xix. 12.]

error,[h] their case[i] is dreadful; there is no way with them but one, death and condemnation. For the Apostle speaketh nothing of men departed, but saith generally of all, "If ye be circumcised, Christ shall profit you nothing. Ye are abolished from Christ, whosoever are justified by the law; ye are fallen from grace."[1] Of them in the church of Rome the reason is the same. For whom Antichrist hath seduced, concerning them did not St. Paul speak long before, "That because[k] they received not the love of the truth,[l] that they might be saved; therefore God would send them strong delusions to believe lies, that all they might be damned which believed not the truth, but had pleasure in unrighteousness"?[2] And St. John, "All that dwell upon the earth shall worship him, whose names are not written in the Book of Life"?[3] Indeed many of them[m] in former times, as their books and writings do yet shew, held the foundation, to wit, salvation by Christ alone, and therefore might be saved. For[n] God hath always had a Church among them, which firmly kept his saving truth. As for such as hold with the church of Rome, that we cannot be saved by Christ alone without works; they do not only by a circle of consequence, but directly, deny the foundation of faith;[4] they hold it not, no not so much as by a slender[o] thread.

20. This, to my remembrance, being all that hath been as yet[p] opposed with any countenance or show of reason, I hope, if this be answered, the cause in question is at an end. Concerning general repentance, therefore: what? a murderer, a blasphemer, an unclean person, a Turk, a Jew, any sinner to escape the wrath of God by a general "God forgive me"?[q] Truly, it never came within my heart, that a general repentance doth serve for all sins or for all sinners:[r] it serveth

---

[h] errors E.   [i] end E.   [k] That because *om.* E.   word of truth E
[m] of them *om.* E.   [n] For *om.* E.   [o] slender *om.* E.   [p] as yet *om.* E.
[q] general repentance E.   [r] This clause *om.* E

[1] Gal. v. 2. 4.   [2] 2 Thess. ii. 10–12.   [3] Apoc. xiii. 8.
[4] [Penry, "M. Some laid out in his colours," &c. p. 29. "We hold, that to him which dieth a papist, let him do never so many good works, and build if it were possible ten thousand colleges or churches, the very gates and portcullis of God's mercy are quite shut up, and all those his glorious works, how sweet soever they may be to others, will prove but wrack and misery to himself. And in this point if either M. Hooker, M. Some, or all the reverend bishops of the land, do stand against us, it shall little dismay us: we say with their own Doctor, (but yet not altogether as he,) 'Instar mille,' (he saith *Platonis*, we say,) '*veritatis* calculus.'"]

only for the common oversights [s] of our sinful life, and for faults [t] which either we do not mark, or do not know that they are faults. Our fathers were actually penitent for sins, wherein they knew they displeased God: or else they come [u] not within the compass of my first speech. Again, that otherwise they could not be saved, than holding the foundation of Christian faith, we have not only affirmed, but proved. Why is it not then confessed, that thousands of our fathers, although they lived [x] in popish superstitions, might yet, by the mercy of God, be saved? First, if they had directly denied the very foundation [y] of Christianity, without repenting them particularly of that sin, he which saith, there could be no salvation for them, according to the ordinary course which God doth use in saving men, granteth plainly, or at the leastwise [z] closely insinuateth, that an extraordinary privilege of mercy might deliver their souls from hell; which is more than I required. Secondly, if the foundation be denied, it is denied by force [a] of some heresy which the church of Rome maintaineth. But how many were there amongst our fathers, who being seduced by the common error of that church, never knew the meaning of her heresies! So that if [b] all popish heretics did perish, thousands of them which lived in popish superstitions might be saved. Thirdly, seeing all that held popish heresies did not hold all the heresies of the pope; why might not thousands which were infected with other leaven, live and [c] die unsoured by [d] this, and so be saved? Fourthly, if they all had held [e] this heresy, many there were that held it no doubt only [f] in a general form of words, which a favourable interpreter [g] might expound in a sense differing far enough from the poisoned conceit of heresy. As for example; did they hold that we cannot be saved by Christ without works? [h] [1] We ourselves do, I think, all say as much, with this construction, salvation being taken as in that sentence, "Corde creditur ad justitiam, ore fit confessio ad salutem;" except infants, and men cut off upon the point of their con-

---

[s] oversight D.	[t] the faults F.	[u] fall E.	[x] which lived E.
[y] foundations E.	[z] at the least E.	[a] for fear E.	[b] although E.
[c] live and *om.* E.	[d] with E.	[e] all held E.	[f] but only E.
[g] interpretation E.	[h] good works E.		

[1] For this is the only thing alleged to prove the impossibility of their salvation: The church of Rome joineth works with Christ, which is a denial of the foundation, and unless we hold the foundation, we cannot be saved. *

* Note *om.* D.

version, of the rest none shall see God, but such as seek peace and holiness, though not as a cause of their salvation, yet as a way through [i] which they must walk that [k] will be saved. Did they hold, that without works we are not justified ? Take justification so that [l] it may also imply sanctification, and St. James doth say as much. [m] For except there be an ambiguity in some [n] term, St. Paul and St. James do contradict each other ; [o] which cannot be. Now, there is no ambiguity in the name either of faith or of works, both [p] being meant by them both in one and the same sense. Finding therefore that justification is spoken of by St. Paul without implying sanctification, when he proveth that a man is justified by faith without works ; finding likewise that justification doth sometimes imply sanctification also with it ; I suppose nothing more sound, [q] than so to interpret St. James as [r] speaking not in that sense, but in this.

21. [s] We have already shewed, that there are [t] two kinds of Christian righteousness : the one without us, which we have by imputation ; the other in us, which consisteth of faith, hope, charity, [u] and other Christian virtues ; and St. James doth prove that Abraham had not only the one, because the thing he [x] believed was imputed unto him for righteousness ; but also the other, because he offered up his son. God giveth us both the one justice and the other : the one by accepting us for righteous in Christ ; the other by working Christian righteousness in us. The proper and most immediate efficient cause in us of this latter, is, the spirit of adoption which [y] we have received into our hearts. That whereof it consisteth, where of it is really and formally made, are those infused virtues proper and particular unto saints ; which the Spirit, in that [z] very moment when first it is given of God, bringeth with it ; the effects thereof [a] are such actions as the Apostle doth call the fruits, the works, [b] the operations of the Spirit ; the difference of which [c] operations from the root whereof they spring, making it needful to put two kinds likewise of sanctifying righteousness, Habitual and Actual. Habitual, that holiness, wherewith our souls are inwardly endued, the same instant when first we begin to be the temples of

[i] through *om*. E.   [k] which E.   [l] as E.   [m] *Paragraph here in* D.
[n] the same E.   [o] each the other E.   [p] both *om*. E.   [q] nothing to be
more sound E.   [r] as *om*. E.   [s] *No paragraph* D.   [t] be E.   [u] and
charity E.   [x] he *om*. E.   [y] which *om*. E.   [z] the E.   [a] whereof E.
[b] fruits of works E.   [c] the which E.

the Holy Ghost; Actual, that holiness which afterward beauti-
fieth all the parts and actions of our life, the holiness for
which Enoch, Job, Zachary, Elizabeth, and other saints,
are in Scriptures [d] so highly commended.   If here it be
demanded, which of these we do first receive; I answer,
that the Spirit, the virtues of the Spirit, the habitual justice,
which is ingrafted, the external justice of Christ Jesus [e]
which is imputed, these we receive all at one and the same
time; whensoever we have any of these, we have all; they
go together.   Yet sith no man is justified except he believe,
and no man believeth except he have [f] faith, and no man
hath faith, unless [g] he have [h] received the Spirit of Adoption [i] forasmuch as these [k] do necessarily infer justification,
but [l] justification doth of necessity presuppose them; we
must needs hold that imputed righteousness, in dignity being
the chiefest, is notwithstanding in order the last [m] of all these,
but actual righteousness, which is the righteousness of good
works, succeedeth all, followeth after all, both in order and
in [n] time.   Which thing [o] being attentively marked, sheweth
plainly how the faith of true believers cannot be divorced
from hope and love; how faith is a part of sanctification,
and yet unto justification necessary; how faith is perfected
by good works, and yet no works of ours good without
faith: [p] finally, how our fathers might hold, We [q] are justified
by faith alone, and yet hold truly that without good [r] works
we are not justified.   Did they think that men do merit
rewards in heaven by the works they perform on earth? The
ancient Fathers [s] use *meriting* for *obtaining*, and in that
sense they of Wittenberg have in their Confession: "We
teach that good works commanded of God are necessarily to
be done, and that [t] by the free kindness of God they merit
their certain rewards.[1]   Others [u] therefore, speaking as our
fathers did, and we taking their speech in a sound meaning,

[d] the Scriptures E.   [e] Jesus Christ E.   [f] hath D.   [g] except E.
[h] hath E.   [i] hath faith *comes after* adoption E.   [k] they E.   [l] and E.
[m] to the last E.   [n] in *om.* E.   [o] thing *om.* E.   [p] and not works of ours
without faith E.   [q] that we E.   [r] good *om.* E.   [s] Fathers *om.* E.
[t] that *om.* E.   [u] Others *om.* E.

[1] [In Syntagm. Confess. pars ii. p. 106. Gen. 1654. "Docemus bona
opera divinitus præcepta necessario facienda esse, et *mereri* gratuita Dei
clementia sua quædam sive corporalia sive spiritualia præmia." This
confession was exhibited at the council of Trent, 1552, by the deputies
of the Duke of Wirtemberg.   It was drawn up by Brentius, (Sleidan, I.
22. p. 277. ed. Argent. 1559.) and had been approved by the Saxon
protestants.]

as we may take our fathers', and ought,[x] forasmuch as
their meaning is doubtful, and charity doth always interpret
doubtful things favourably ; what should induce us to think
that rather the damage of the worse[y] construction did light
upon them all, than that the blessing of the better was
granted unto thousands ?

Fifthly, if in the worst construction that can[z] be made,
they had generally all embraced it living, might not many of
them dying utterly renounce it ? Howsoever men, when
they sit at ease, do vainly tickle their own[a] hearts with the
wanton conceit of I know not what proportionable correspondence between their merits and their rewards, which, in
the trance of their high speculations, they dream that God
hath measured, weighed, and laid up, as it were, in bundles
for them ; notwithstanding we see by daily experience, in
a number even of them, that when the hour of death
approacheth, when they secretly hear themselves summoned
forthwith to appear, and stand at the bar of that[b] Judge,
whose brightness causeth the eyes of angels[c] themselves to
dazzle, all those[d] idle imaginations do then begin to hide
their faces ; to name merits then, is[e] to lay their souls upon
the rack, the memory of their own deeds is loathsome unto
them, they forsake all things wherein they have put any
trust and[f] confidence ; no staff to lean upon, no ease, no
rest, no comfort then, but only in Christ Jesus.[g]

22. Wherefore if this proposition were true, "To hold in
such wise, as the church of Rome doth, that we cannot be
saved by Christ alone without works, is directly to deny
the foundation of faith ;" I say, that if this proposition
were true, nevertheless so many ways I have shewed, whereby
we may hope that thousands of our fathers living[h] in popish
superstitions[i] might be saved.[1] But what[k] if it be not

---

[x] might E.	[y] worst E.	[z] may E.	[a] own *om.* E.	[b] the D.
[c] the angels E.	[d] these E.	[e] merits is then E.	[f] or E.	[g] Jesus Christ E.
	[h] which lived E.	[i] superstition E.	[k] what *om.* D.

[1] They may cease to put any confidence in works, and yet never
think, living in popish superstition, they did amiss. Pighius died
popish, and yet denied popery in the article of justification by works
long before his death. [See Bayle, art. Pighius. He died at Utrecht,
December 26, 1542 : having the same year published at Cologne,
"Controversiarum præcipuarum in comitiis Ratisponensibus tractatarum,
et quibus nunc potissimum exagitatur Christi fides et religio, diligens et
luculenta replicatio." In the 2nd Controversy, De Fide et Justificatione,
Sign. G. ii. is the following : "In illo iustificamur coram Deo, non in

true? What if neither that of the Galatians concerning circumcision, nor this of the church of Rome about ^m works, be
any direct denial of the foundation, as it is affirmed that
both are? I need not wade so far as to discuss this controversy, the matter which first was brought into question
being so cleared,ⁿ as I hope it is. Howbeit, because I
desire that the truth even in this ^o also may ^p receive light,
I will do mine ^q endeavour to set down somewhat more
plainly: first, the foundation of faith, what it is: secondly,
what it is directly to deny the foundation: thirdly, whether
they whom God hath chosen to be heirs of life, may
fall so far as directly to deny it: fourthly, whether the
Galatians did so by admitting the error about circumcision
and the law: last of all, whether the church of Rome, for
this one opinion of works, may be thought to do the like,
and thereupon to be no more a Christian church, than are
the assemblies of Turks or ^r Jews.

23. This word foundation being figuratively used, hath
always reference to somewhat which resembleth a material

^m by E.   ⁿ clear E.   ^o that E.   ^p should E.   ^q my D.   ^r and E.

nobis; non nostra sed illius justitia, quæ nobis cum illo jam communi-
cantibus imputatur. Propriæ justitiæ inopes, extra nos in illo docemur
justitiam quærere... Non nostra, sed Dei justitia justi efficimur in Christo.
Quo jure? amicitiæ, quæ communionem omnium inter amicos facit, juxta
vetus et celebratissimum proverbium: Christo insertis, conglutinatis, et
unitis, etiam sua nostra facit; suas divitias nobis communicat; suam justitiam inter Patris judicium et nostram injustitiam interponit, et sub ea,
velut sub umbone et clypeo, a divina, quam commeruimus, ira, nos abscon-
dit, tuetur, ac protegit; immo eandem nobis impertit, ac nostram facit,
qua tecti ornatique audacter et secure divino nos sistamus tribunali ac
judicio, justique non solum appareamus, sed etiam simus." Sign. G. iii.
"Justificat nos Deus Pater bonitate sua gratuita qua nos in Christo
complectitur: dum eidem insertos innocentia et justitia Christi nos
induit: quæ una ut vera et perfecta est, quæ Dei sustinere conspectum
potest, ita unam pro nobis sisti oportet tribunali divini judicii, et velut
causæ nostræ intercessorem eidem repræsentari." Ibid. et G. iv.
"Dissimulare non possumus, hanc vel primam doctrinæ Christianæ
partem obscuratam magis quam illustratam a scholasticis speciosis
plerisque quæstionibus et definitionibus, secundum quas nonnulli,
magno supercilio primam in omnibus auctoritatem sibi arrogantes, et de
omnibus facile pronunciantes, fortassis etiam nostram hanc damnarent
sententiam, qua propriam et quæ ex suis operibus esset coram Deo
justitiam derogamus omnibus Adæ filiis, et docuimus una Dei in Christo
niti nos posse justitia, una illa, justos esse coram Deo, destitutos
propria." It appears that he was censured in his own church as having
a tendency to the Calvinistic notion of justification: and accused of
Pelagianism both by Calvin and the Jansenists.]

building, as both the doctrine of the Christianity [s] [of Christ-
ianity] and the community of Christians do. By the masters
of civil policy nothing is so much inculcated, as that commonwealths are founded upon laws ; for that a multitude
cannot be compacted into one body otherwise than by a
common acceptation [t] of laws, whereby they are to be kept
in order.[1] (The ground of all civil laws is this : " No man
ought to be hurt or injured by another : " take away this
persuasion, and you [u] take away all laws ; [x] take away laws,
and what shall become of commonwealths ?) So it is in
our spiritual Christian community : I do not now [y] mean
that body mystical [2] whereof Christ is the only [z] head, that
building undiscernible by mortal eyes, wherein Christ is the
chief corner-stone : but I speak of the visible church ; the
foundation whereof is the doctrine [3] of [a] the Prophets and
Apostles profest. The mark whereunto their doctrine
tendeth, is pointed at in those [b] words of Peter unto Christ,
" Thou hast the words of eternal life : " in those of [c] Paul to
Timothy, " The holy Scriptures are able to make thee wise
unto salvation." It is the demand of nature itself,[d] " What
shall we do to have eternal life ? " [4] The desire of immortality and of [e] the knowledge of that whereby it may be
attained,[f] is so natural unto all men, that even they which [g]
are not persuaded that they shall, do [h] notwithstanding wish
that they might, know a way how to see no end of life. And
because natural means are not able still [i] to resist the force
of death, there is no people in the earth so savage, which
hath not devised some supernatural help or other, to fly
unto for aid and succour in extremities, against the enemies
of their lives.[k] A longing therefore to be saved, without
understanding the true way how, hath been the cause of all
the superstitions in the world. O that the miserable estate
of others, which wander in darkness, and wot not whither
they go, could give us understanding hearts, worthily to
esteem the riches of the mercies [l] of God towards us, before
whose eyes the doors of the kingdom of heaven are set wide

[s] that doctrine of laws E. [t] acception E. [u] ye E. [x] the laws E. [y] now om. E.
[z] only the E. [a] which E. [b] these E. [c] those words of E. [d] herself E.
[e] of om. E. [f] obtained E. [g] who E. [h] what they shall do D. [i] still om. E.
[k] laws E. [l] mercy E.

[1] " Vocata ad concionem multitudine, quæ coalescere in populi unius
corpus nulla re præterquam legibus poterat." Liv. de Romulo, lib. i.
[c. 8.]
[2] Ephes. i. 23 ; iv. 15. [3] Ephes. ii. 20.
[4] John vi. 68 ; 2 Tim. iii. 15.

open ! Should we not [m] offer violence unto it ? It offereth violence to us, and we gather strength to withstand it.

But I am besides my purpose when I fall to bewail the cold affection which we bear towards that whereby we should be saved; my purpose being only to set down what the ground of salvation is. The doctrine of the Gospel proposeth salvation as the end : and doth it not teach the way of attaining thereunto ? Yes,[n] the damsel possest [o] with a spirit of divination spake the truth : " These men are the servants of the most high God, which shew unto us the way of salvation : " " A new and living way, which Christ hath prepared for us through the vail, that is, his flesh ; "[1] salvation purchased by the death of Christ. (By this foundation the children of God, before the time of the written [p] law, were distinguished from the sons of men ; the reverend patriarchs both profest [q] it living, and spake expressly [2] of it at the hour of their death. It comforted Job [3] in the midst of grief ; it was afterwards likewise [r] the anchor-hold of all the righteous in Israel, from the writing of the law till the time of grace ; every prophet maketh mention of it. It was so [s] famously spoken of, about the time, when the coming of Christ to accomplish the promises, which were made long before,[t] drew near, that the sound thereof was heard even amongst the Gentiles. When he was come, as many as were his acknowledged that he was their salvation ; he, that long-expected hope of Israel ; he, that " seed, in whom all the nations of the world [u] should [x] be blest." [y] So that now his name is a name [z] of ruin, a name of death and condemnation, unto such as dream of a new Messias, to as many as look for salvation by any other than by him : (" For amongst men there is given no other name under heaven whereby we must be saved." [4]) Thus much St. Mark doth intimate by that which he putteth [a] in the very [b] front of his book, making his entrance with these words : " The beginning of the Gospel of Jesus Christ, the Son of God." His doctrine he termeth the Gospel, because it teacheth salvation ; the Gospel of Jesus Christ,[c] the Son of God, because it teacheth salvation by him. This is then the foundation, whereupon

---

[m] not *om.* E. [n] Yet E. [o] possessed D. [p] before the written E.
[q] possessed E. [r] likewise *om.* E. [s] so *om.* E. [t] before it E. [u] earth E.
[x] shall E. [y] blessed E. [z] he is a name E. [a] doth put E. [b] very
om. E. [c] Christ *om.* D.

[1] Acts xvi. 17 ; Heb. x. 20. [2] Gen. xlix.
[3] Job xix. [4] Acts iv. 12.

the frame of the Gospel is erected ; that very Jesus whom the
Virgin conceived of the Holy Ghost, whom Simeon embraced in his arms,[1] whom Pilate condemned, whom the
Jews crucified, whom the Apostles preached, he is Christ,
the Lord, the only Saviour of the world : "other foundation
can no man lay."[2] Thus I have briefly opened that principle in Christianity, which we call the foundation of our faith.
It followeth now that I declare unto you, what it is directly
to overthrow it. This will better appear,[d] if first[e] we understand, what it is to hold the foundation of faith.

24. There are which defend, that many of the Gentiles,
who never heard the name of Christ, held the foundation of
Christianity : and why? they acknowledged many of them
the providence of God, his infinite wisdom, strength, and[f]
power ; his goodness, and his mercy towards the children of
men ; that God hath judgment in store for the wicked, but
for the righteous that seeks[g] him rewards, &c. In this
which they confessed, that lieth covered which we believe ;
in the rudiments of their knowledge concerning God, the
foundation of our faith concerning Christ lieth secretly
wrapt[h] up, and is virtually contained : therefore they held
the foundation of faith, though they never heard[i] it. Might
we not with as good colour[k] of reason defend, that every
ploughman hath all the sciences, wherein philosophers have
excelled? For no man is ignorant of the [l] first principles,
which do virtually contain whatsoever by natural means
either[m] is or can be known. Yea, might we not with as
good[n] reason affirm, that a man may put three mighty oaks
wheresoever three acorns may be put? For virtually an
acorn is an oak. To avoid such paradoxes, we teach plainly,
that to hold the foundation is, in express terms to acknowledge it.

25. Now, because the foundation is an affirmative
proposition, they all overthrow it, who deny it ; they directly
overthrow it, who deny it directly ; and they overthrow it by
consequent, or indirectly, which hold any one assertion
whatsoever, whereupon the direct denial thereof may be
necessarily concluded. What is the question between the
Gentiles and us, but this, Whether salvation be by Christ?

d be better opened E.	e first *om.* E.	f and *om.* E.	g which serve E.
n wrapped D.	i had E.	k a colour E.	l their E.	m either *om.* E.
n great E.			

[1] Luke ii. 28. [2] 1 Cor. iii. 11.

What between the Jews and us, but this, Whether by this
Jesus, whom we call Christ, yea or no? This to be the
main point whereupon Christianity standeth, it is clear by
that one sentence of Festus concerning Paul's accusers:
"They brought no crime of such things as I supposed, but
had certain questions against him of their own [o] superstition,
and of one Jesus, which was dead, whom Paul affirmed to
be alive."[1] Where we see that Jesus, dead and raised for
the salvation of the world, is by Jews [p] denied, despised by
a Gentile, and by a Christian apostle maintained. The
Fathers therefore in the primitive church when they wrote;
Tertullian, the book which he calleth [q] Apologeticus; Minutius Felix, the book which he entitleth [r] Octavius; Arnobius,
his [s] seven books against the Gentiles; Chrysostom, his
orations against the Jews; Eusebius, his ten books of evangelical demonstration: they stood [t] in defence of Christianity [u] against them, by whom the foundation thereof was
directly denied. But the writings of the Fathers against
Novatians, Pelagians, and other heretics of the like note,
refel positions, whereby the foundation of Christian faith was
overthrown by consequent only. In the former sort of
writings the foundation is proved; in the latter, it is alleged
as a proof, which to men that had been known directly to
deny it, must needs have seemed a very beggarly kind of
disputing. All infidels therefore deny the foundation of
faith directly: by consequent, many a Christian man, yea
whole Christian churches, have [x] denied it, and do deny it at
this present day. Christian churches denying [y] the foundation of Christianity? Not [z] directly, for then they cease
to be Christian churches; but by consequent, in respect
whereof we condemn them as erroneous, although, for holding the foundation, we do and must hold them Christian.

26. We see what it is to hold the foundation; what
directly, and what by consequent, to deny it. The next
thing which followeth is, whether they whom God hath
chosen to obtain the glory of our Lord Jesus Christ, may,
being [a] once effectually called, and through faith truly justified,[b] afterwards fall so far, as directly to deny the foundation
which their hearts have before embraced with joy and
comfort in the Holy Ghost; for such is the faith, which

[o] own *om*. E.   [p] the Jews D.   [q] called E.   [r] entitled E.   [s] the E.   [t] stand E.
[u] the Christianity D.   [x] have *om*. E.   [y] denying *om*. E.
[z] Christianity, not D.   [a] being *om*. E.   [b] justified truly E.
                        [1] Acts xxv. 19.

indeed doth justify. Devils know the same things which we believe, and the minds of the most ungodly may be fully persuaded of the truth ; which knowledge in the one and persuasion[c] in the other, is sometimes termed faith, but equivocally, being indeed no such faith as that whereby a Christian man is justified. It is the spirit of adoption which worketh faith in us, in them not ; the things which we believe, are by us apprehended, not only as true, but also as good, and that to us : as good, they are not by them apprehended ; as true, they are. Whereupon followeth a third[d] difference ; the Christian man the more he increaseth in faith, the more his joy and comfort aboundeth : but they, the more sure they are of the truth, the more they quake and tremble at it. This begetteth another effect, wherein[e] the hearts of the one sort have a different disposition from the other. "Non ignoro plerosque conscientia meritorum, nihil se esse post[f] mortem magis optare quam credere ; malunt enim exstingui penitus, quam ad supplicia reparari."[1] I am not ignorant, saith Minutius, that there are too many,[g] who being conscious what they are to look for, do rather wish that they might, than think that they shall, cease to be,[h] when they cease to live ; because they hold it better that death should consume them unto nothing, than God receive them unto[i] punishment. So it is in other articles of faith, whereof wicked men think, no doubt, many times they are too true : on the contrary side, to the other, there is no grief nor[k] torment greater, than to feel their persuasion weak in things, whereof, when they are persuaded, they reap such comfort and joy of spirit : such is the faith whereby we are justified ; such, I mean, in respect of the quality. For touching the principal object of faith, longer than it holdeth that[l] foundation whereof we have spoken, it neither justifieth, nor is ; but ceaseth to be faith when it ceases to believe, that Jesus Christ is the only Saviour of the world. The cause of life spiritual in us, is Christ, not carnally or corporally inhabiting, but dwelling in the soul of man, as a thing which (when the mind apprehendeth it) is said to inhabit and[m] possess the mind. The mind conceiveth Christ by hearing the doctrine of Christianity. As the light of nature does cause the mind to apprehend those

[c] persuasion *om*. E.   [d] the third E.   [e] where E.   [f] per E.
[g] there be many E.   [h] to be *om*. E.   [i] into E.   [k] or E.   [l] the E.
[m] or E.

[1] Octav. c. 34.

truths which are merely rational; so that saving truth, which is far above the reach of human reason, cannot otherwise, than by the Spirit of the Almighty, be conceived. All these are implied, wheresoever any one [n] of them is mentioned as the cause of spiritual [o] life. Wherefore when we read,[p] that [1] the spirit is our life; or,[2] "the Word of our life;" or,[3] "Christ our life:" we are in every of these to understand, that our life is Christ, by the hearing of the Gospel apprehended as a Saviour, and assented unto by [q] the power of the Holy Ghost. The first intellectual conceit and comprehension of Christ so embraced, St. Peter calleth [4] the seed whereof we be new born: our first embracing of Christ, is our first reviving [5] from the state of death and condemnation. "He that hath the Son hath life," saith St. John,[6] and he that hath not the Son of God, hath not life." If therefore he which once hath the Son, may cease to have the Son, though it be but [r] a moment, he ceases for that moment to have life. But the life of them which live [s] by the Son of God [t] is everlasting, not only for that it shall be everlasting [7] in the world to come,[u] but because [8] as "Christ being raised from the dead dieth [x] no more, death hath no more power over him;" so the [y] justified man, being alive [z] to God in Jesus Christ our Lord, doth as necessarily from that time forward always live, as Christ, by whom he hath life, liveth always.[9]

I might, if I had not otherwhere largely done it already, shew by sundry [a] manifest and clear proofs, how the motions and operations of life are sometimes so undiscernible, and secret,[b] that they seem stone-dead, who notwithstanding are still alive unto God in Christ.

For as long as that abideth in us, which animateth, quickeneth, and giveth life, so long we live; and we know that the cause of our life [c] abideth in us for ever. If Christ, the fountain of life, may flit and leave the habitation where once he dwelleth, what shall become of his promise, "I am with

---

[n] one *om.* E.   [o] the spiritual E.   [p] if we have read E
[q] through E.   [r] for E.   [s] that D.   [t] which have the Son E.   [u] is everlasting in the world to come E.   [x] died E.   [y] the *om.* E.   [z] allied E·
[a] many and sundry E.   [b] so secret E.   [c] faith E.

[1] Rom. viii. 10.   [2] Phil. ii. 16.
[3] Col. iii. 4.   [4] 1 Pet. i. 23.
[5] Ephes. ii. 5.   [6] 1 John v. 12.
[7] 1 John v. 13.   Perpetuity of faith; Rom. vi. 10.
[8] [Should not "but" be omitted?]   [9] John xiv. 19.

you to the world's end?" If the seed of God, which
containeth Christ, may be first conceived and then cast
out; how doth St. Peter[1] term it immortal? How doth
St. John[2] affirm it abideth? If the Spirit, which is given to
cherish and preserve the seed of life, may be given and
taken away, how is the earnest[3] of our inheritance until
redemption; how doth it continue[4] with us for ever? If
therefore the man which is once just by faith, shall live by
faith, and live for ever, it followeth, that he which once
doth believe the foundation, must needs believe the foundation for ever. If he[d] believe it for ever, how can he ever
directly deny it?[5] Faith holding the direct affirmation;
the direct negation, so long as faith continueth, is excluded.

[e] But ye[f] will say, "That as he which to-day[g] is holy,
may, to-morrow forsake his holiness, and become impure;
as a friend may change his mind, and become[h] an enemy;
as hope may wither: so faith may die in the heart of man,
the Spirit may be quenched, Grace may be extinguished,
they which believe may be quite turned away from the
truth"

The[i] case[k] is clear, long experience hath made this manifest, it needs no proof. I grant we are apt, prone, and
ready, to forsake God;[6] but is God as ready to forsake
us? Our minds are changeable; is his so likewise?
Whom God hath justified, hath not Christ assured, that it is

---

[d] he *om.* D.   [*] *Object.* But E.   [f] you E.   [g] that is to-day E.
[h] be made E.   [i] *Sol.* The E.   [k] cause E.

[1] 1 Pet. i. 23.   [2] 1 John iii. 9.   [3] Ephes. i. 14.
[4] John xiv. 17.
[5] ["Mr. Miller in his madness denied it, and yet died faithful as I
hear." Anonymous note in the Dublin MS. of this sermon.]
[6] ["Bolton's end in despair, after persecution suffered in Queen
Mary's time." Ibid. Strype, Mem. iii. i. 576. "John Bolton, sometime of Reading, who lying in gaol for religion, grew mad, and in his
raving fits railed upon Queen Mary; who thereupon was cruelly
tormented in the said prison. Which Bolton becoming sober, and of a
better mind, Thackham took pity upon the man, because he seemed to
be of good religion, and . . . when by reason of the time, his very
friends durst not become surety for such a traitor and rank heretic, as
Bolton was then thought to be, he desired the mayor to take him alone
with Bolton, which the mayor gently granted. And so this poor man
was set at liberty and departed. But when the sessions came, Bolton
left Thackham to pay the forfeiture." It seems by a letter among
Strype's documents, Mem. iii. ii. 427, that this Bolton recanted so far
as to attend mass, and yet afterwards printed "a certain story of his
own great trouble and another's recanting." He was a silk weaver in
Long-lane, Smithfield.]

" his Father's will to give them a kingdom ? " Which kingdom,[1] notwithstanding, shall not [m] otherwise be [n] given them, than " [1] if they continue grounded and stablished in the faith, and be not moved away from the hope of the gospel ; " " [2] if they abide in love and holiness." Our Saviour therefore, when he spake of the sheep effectually called, and truly gathered into his fold,[3] " I give unto them eternal life, and they shall never perish, neither shall any pluck them out of my hands ; " in promising to save them, promised,[o] no doubt, to preserve them in that without the which there can be no salvation, as also from that whereby salvation is [p] irremediably [q] lost. Every error in things appertaining to [r] God is repugnant unto faith ; every fearful, cogitation, unto hope ; unto love every straggling inordinate desire ; unto holiness, every blemish whereby [s] either the inward thoughts of our minds, or the outward actions of our lives, are stained. But heresy, such as that of Ebion, Cerinthus, and others, against whom the Apostles were forced to bend themselves, both by word and also by writing ; that repining discouragement of heart which tempteth God, whereof we have Israel in the desert for a pattern ; coldness, such as that in the angel of Ephesus ; foul sins, known to be expressly against the first or the second table of the law, such as Noah, Manasses, David, Solomon, and Peter, committed : these are each in their kind so opposite to the former virtues, that they leave no place for salvation without an actual repentance. But infidelity, extreme despair, hatred of God and all godliness,[t] obduration in sin, cannot stand where there is the least [u] spark of faith, hope, love, or [x] sanctity ; even as cold in the lowest degree cannot be, where heat in the first [y] degree is found.

Whereupon I conclude, that although in the first kind, no man liveth that [z] sinneth not ; and in the second, as perfect as any do live, may sin : yet sith the man which is born of God hath a promise, that in him " the seed of God shall abide ; " [4] which seed is a sure preservative against the sins of [a] the third suit ; greater and clearer assurance we cannot

[1] Which kingdom *om.* E.   [m] it shall not E.   [n] be otherwise E.   [o] he promised E.   [p] whereby it is E.   [q] irrecoverably E.   [r] unto E.   [s] wherewith E.   [t] goodness E.   [u] but the least E.   [x] and E.   [y] highest E.   [z] which E.   [a] that are of E.

[1] Col. i. 23.   [2] 1 Tim. ii. 15.
[3] John x. 28.   [4] 1 John iii. 9.

have of anything, than of this, that from such sins God shall
preserve the righteous, as the apple of his eye, for ever.
Directly to deny the foundation of faith, is plain infidelity ;
where faith is entered, there infidelity is for ever excluded :
therefore by him which hath once sincerely believed in
Christ, the foundation of Christian faith can never be
directly denied. Did not Peter, did not Marcellinus,[1] did
not many others, both directly deny Christ after they [b] had
believed, and again believe after they had denied? No
doubt, as they may [c] confess in word,[d] whose condemnation
nevertheless is [e] their not believing (for example we have
Judas); so likewise, they may believe in heart, whose
condemnation, without repentance, is their not confessing.
Although therefore Peter and the rest, for whose faith Christ
had [f] prayed that it might not fail, did not by denial sin the
sin of infidelity, which is an inward abnegation of Christ
(for if they had done this, their faith had clearly failed):
yet, because they sinned notoriously and grievously, committing that which they knew to be so [g] expressly forbidden
by the law, which saith, " Thou shalt worship the Lord thy
God, and him only shalt thou serve : " necessary it was, that
he which purposed to save their souls, should, as he did,
touch their hearts with true unfeigned repentance, that his
mercy might restore them again to life, whom sin had made
the children of death and condemnation. Touching this
point, therefore, I hope I may safely set it [h] down, that if

[b] after that they E.　　[c] may *om*. E.　　[d] words E.　　[e] is nevertheless E.
[f] hath E.　　[g] so *om*. E.　　[h] it *om*. E.

[1] [Platin. Vitt. Pontiff. p. 39. Colon. Ubiorum. 1600. "Marcellinus pontifex" (A.D. 304) "ad sacrificia gentium ductus, cum minis
instarent carnifices, ut thura diis exhiberet, metu perterritus, deos
alienos adoravit. Habito deinde non ita multo post concilio clxxx.
episcoporum in Sinuessa urbe Campaniæ, eo et Marcellinus squalidus et
pulverulentus et cilicio indutus proficiscitur, petitque ut sibi pro incon-
stantia debita pœna tribuatur. Qui eum damnaret, in tanto concilio
nemo unus inventus est, cum dicerent omnes ea ferme ratione Petrum
peccasse, ac flendo peccati pœnam luisse. Rediit Romam Marcellinus
iratus, Diocletianum adiit hominemque increpat, qui se impulerit diis
gentium immolare. Ducitur ad martyrium Diocletiani jussu . . . .
Inter eundum vero Marcellum presbyterum admonet, ne corpus suum
sepulturæ traderet, quod diceret ob negatum Salvatorem se id nequaquam
mereri." This story is examined by Tillemont (among others) and
shewn to be incredible, Mem. t. v. p. 613. The Donatists in Africa
circulated such an account, which is mentioned by St. Augustin, contra
Lit. Petil. lib. ii. § 202. t. ix. 276; and rejected by him as unworthy
of notice, § 208. p. 280.]

the justified err, as he may, and never come to understand
his error, God doth save him through general repentance: but
if he fall into heresy, he calleth him[i] either at[k] one time
or other by actual repentance ; but from infidelity, which is
an inward direct denial of the foundation, preserveth[l]
him by special providence for ever.   Whereby we may
easily know what to think of those Galatians, whose hearts
were so possest with love[m] of the truth, that if it had been
possible, they would have plucked out their very[n] eyes, to
bestow upon their teachers.   It is true, that they were afterwards[o] greatly[1] changed, both in persuasion and affection ;
so that the Galatians, when St. Paul wrote unto them, were
not now the Galatians which they had been in former times,[p]
for that through error they wandered, although they were his
sheep.   I do not deny, but I[q] should deny, that they were
his sheep, if I should grant, that through error they perished.
It was a perilous opinion which they held, in them[r] which[s]
held it only as an error, because it overthroweth the foundation by consequent.   But in them which obstinately
maintained[t] it, I cannot think it less[u] than a damnable
heresy.

We must therefore put a difference between them which
err of ignorance, retaining nevertheless a mind desirous to
be instructed in the[x] truth, and them which, after the truth
is laid open, persist in stubborn[y] defence of their blindness.
Heretical defenders, froward and stiff-necked teachers of
circumcision, the blessed Apostle calleth[z] dogs : silly men,
that were seduced to think they taught the truth, he pitieth,
he taketh up in his arms, he lovingly embraceth, he kisseth,
and with more than fatherly tenderness doth so temper,
qualify, and[a] correct the speech he useth towards them, that

[i] him _om._ D.   [k] either at _om._ E.   [l] he preserveth E.   [m] the love E.
[n] very _om._ E.   [o] afterwards _om._ E.   [p] time E.   [q] but that I E.
[r] perilous even in them E.   [s] that E.   [t] maintain E.   [u] it is less D.
[x] the _om._ E.   [y] the stubborn E.   [z] calls E.   [a] and _om._ D.

[1] Howsoever men be changed, (for changed they may be, even the
best amongst men,) if they that have received, as it seemeth some of the
Galatians, which fell into error, had received, the gifts and graces of
God, which are called ἀμεταμέλητα, such as faith, hope, and charity
are, which God doth never take away from him to whom they are given,
as if it repented him to have given them ; if such might be so far
changed by error, as that the very root of faith should be quite
extinguished in them, and so their salvation utterly lost, it would shake
the hearts of the strongest and stoutest of us all.   See the contrary in
Beza's Observations upon the Harmony of Confessions.*

* This note _om._ D.

a man cannot easily discern, whether did most abound, the
love which he bare to their godly affection, or the grief which
the danger of their opinion bred him.[b] Their opinion was
dangerous ; was not theirs so [c] likewise who thought that [d]
the kingdom of Christ should be earthly ? was not theirs
which thought that [e] the gospel should be preached [f] only
to the Jews ? What more opposite to prophetical doctrine,
concerning the coming of Christ, than the one ? concerning
the catholic Church, than the other ? Yet they which had
these fancies, even when they had them, were not the worst
men in the world. The heresy of freewill was a millstone
about the Pelagians' neck ; [g] shall we therefore give sentence
of death inevitable [h] against all those Fathers in the Greek
church, which being mispersuaded, died in the error of freewill ? [1]

Of those [i] Galatians, therefore, which first were justified,[2]
and then deceived, as I can see no cause, why as many as
died before admonition might not by mercy be saved,[k][3]
even in error ; so I make no doubt, but as many as lived till
they were admonished, found the mercy of God effectual in
converting them from their error,[4] lest any one that is Christ's
should perish. Of this, as [l] I take it, there is no controversy :
only against the salvation of them which died, though before
admonition, yet in error, it is objected, that their opinion was
a very plain direct denial of the foundation. If Paul and
Barnabas had been so persuaded, they would haply have
used their [m] terms otherwise, speaking of the masters themselves, who did first set that error abroach, "certain of the
sect of the Pharisees which believed." [5] What difference

[F] [b] them E.   [e] theirs also E.   [d] that *om.* E.   [e] that *om.* E.   [f] only
should be preached E.   [g] necks D.   [h] inevitably E.   [i] these E.
[k] received E.   [l] as *om.* E.   [m] the E.

[1] [" They might err in freewill, yet not as Pelagius, who was enemy
to the grace of God." Anonymous note in D.]

[2] ["How were they justified, when their faith was subverted ? "
Ibid.]

[3] [" S. Paul saw they were turned to another gospel, therefore in a
damnable state." Note in D.]

[4] Error convicted, and afterwards maintained, is more than error ; for
although opinion be the same it was, in which respect I still call it error,
yet they are not now the same they were, when they are taught what
the truth is, and plainly taught.*

[5] Acts xv. 5. [" *Equivocally,* as the priests, John xii." Note in
D.]

* Note *om.* D.

was there between these Pharisees [n] and other, from whom
by a special description they are distinguished, but this?
They [o] which came to Antioch, teaching the necessity of
circumcision, were Christians; the other, enemies of Christianity. Why then should these be termed so distinctly
believers, if they did directly deny the foundation of our
belief; besides which, there was none [p] other thing, that
made the rest to be unbelievers? [q] We need go no further
than St. Paul's very reasoning against them, for proof of this
matter : [1] "Seeing ye [r] know God, or rather are known of
God, how turn you again unto impotent rudiments? [2] The
law engendereth servants, her children are in bondage : they
which are begotten by the gospel, are free. [3] Brethren, we
are not children of the servant, but of the free woman, and
will ye yet be under the law?" That they thought it unto
salvation necessary, for the Church of Christ to observe days,
and months, and times, and years, to keep the ceremonies
and the sacraments of the law, this was their error.[4] Yet
he which condemneth their error, confesseth notwithstanding,[s] that they knew God,[5] and were known of him; he
taketh not the honour from them to be termed sons begotten
of [t] the immortal seed of the gospel. Let the heaviest words
which [u] he useth be weighed; consider the drift of those
dreadful conclusions : [6] "If ye [x] be circumcised, Christ shall
profit you nothing : as many as are justified by the law, ye [y]
are fallen from Grace." It had been to no purpose in the
world so to urge them, had not the Apostle been persuaded,
that at the hearing of such sequels, "No benefit by Christ,"
"a defection from grace," their hearts would tremble and
quake within them : and why? because they [z] knew, that in
Christ, in grace,[a] their salvation lay, which is a plain [b] direct
acknowledgment of the foundation.

Lest I should herein seem to hold that which no one godly
and learned [c] hath done, let these words be considered,
which import as much as I affirm.[7] "Surely those brethren

[n] other Pharisees E.   [o] These E.   [p] no E.   [q] no believers E.
[r] you E.   [s] that notwithstanding E.   [t] by D.   [u] which *om.* D.
[x] you D.   [y] ye *om.* E.   [z] because that they E.   [a] and in grace E.
with a plain D.   [c] godly or learned E.

[1] Gal. iv. 9.   [2] Ver. 24.   [3] Ver. 31.   [4] Ver. 10.
[5] ["The elect among them all were to be reclaimed from that error."
Note in D.]
[6] Gal. v. 2, 4.
[7] Bucer. de Unit. Eccles. Servanda.* [The editor has not found in
         * This reference *om.* D.

which, in St. Paul's time, thought that God did lay a necessity
upon them to make choice of days and meats, spake as they
believed, and could not but in words condemn that liberty,
which they supposed to be brought in against the authority
of divine Scripture. Otherwise it had been needless for St.
Paul to admonish them, not to condemn such as eat, without scrupulosity, whatsoever was set before them. This error,
if ye weigh what it is of itself, did at once overthrow all
Scripture, whereby we are taught salvation by faith in Christ,
all that ever the prophets did foretell, all that ever the
Apostles did preach of Christ; it drew with it the denial of
Christ utterly: insomuch that[d] St. Paul complaineth, that
his labour was lost upon the Galatians,[e] unto whom this
error was obtruded; affirming that Christ, if so be they were
circumcised, should not profit them any thing at all. Yet
so far was St. Paul from striking their names out of Christ's
book, that he commanded others to entertain them, to accept
them with singular humanity, to use them like brethren; he
knew man's imbecility, he had a feeling of our blindness
which are mortal men, how great it is, and being sure that
they are the sons of God, whosoever be endued with his fear,
would not have them counted enemies of that whereunto they
could not as yet frame themselves to be friends, but did even
of[f] a very religious affection to the truth, unwittingly[g] reject
and resist[h] the truth. They acknowledged[1] Christ to be
their only and their[i] perfect Saviour, but saw not how repugnant their believing the[k] necessity of Mosaical ceremonies
was to their faith in Jesus Christ."

Hereunto[1] reply[m] is made, that if they had not directly
denied the foundation, they might have been saved; but
saved they could not be; therefore their opinion was, not
only by consequent, but directly, a denial of the foundation.
When the question was about the possibility of their salvation, their denying of the foundation was brought for proof[n]
that they could not be saved: now that the question is about
their denial,[o] the impossibility of their salvation is alleged to
prove they denied the foundation. Is there nothing which

---

[d] as D.   [e] spent upon the Galatians in vain D.   [f] ever upon E.
[g] willingly E.   [h] and resist om. E.   [i] their om. E.   [k] of D.
[1] Hereupon E.   [m] a reply E.   [n] to prove E.   [o] their denial of the
foundation E.

Bucer's works any tract with this title, and suspects that the name is
put erroneously for that of some other reformer.]
  [1] ["Not true." Note in D.]

excludeth men from salvation, but only the foundation of
faith denied? I should have thought, that beside [p] this,
many other things are death, except they be actually repented
of: as indeed this opinion of theirs was death,[q] unto as
many as, being given to understand [r] that to cleave thereunto
was to fall from Christ, did notwithstanding cleave unto it.
But of this enough. Wherefore I come to the last question,
" Whether the [s] doctrine of the Church of Rome, concerning
the necessity of works unto salvation, be a direct denial of
the foundation of [t] our faith?"

27. I seek not to obtrude unto you any private opinions [u]
of mine own. The best learned [1] in our profession are of
this judgment, that all the heresies and [x] corruptions of the
church of Rome do not prove her to deny the foundation
directly; if they did, they should prove[y] her simply to be no
Christian church. "But I suppose," saith one,[2] "that in
the papacy some church remaineth, a church crazed, or, if
you will, broken quite in pieces, forlorn, misshapen, yet
some church:" his reason is this, "Antichrist must sit in
the temple of God." Lest any man should think such sentences as this [z] to be true only in regard of them whom that
church is supposed to have kept by the special providence
of God, as it were, in the secret corners of his bosom, free
from infection, and as sound in the faith, as we trust, by his
mercy, we ourselves are; I permit it to your [a] wise considerations, whether it be not [b] more likely, that as phrensy,
though itself take away the use of reason, doth notwithstanding prove them reasonable creatures which have it, because
none can be frantic but they; so Antichristianity being the
bane and plain overthrow of Christianity, may nevertheless
argue the church wherein [c] Antichrist sitteth to be Christian.[3]
Neither have I ever [d] hitherto heard or read any one word

[p] besides E.   [q] except . . death om. E.   [r] understanding E.   [s] that
the E.   [t] the foundation of om. E.   [u] opinion E.   [x] heresies and om. E.
[y] grant E.   [z] these E.   [a] permit at your D.   [b] not om. E.   [c] where E.
[d] heretofore D.

[1] ["Who be they?" Ibid.]
[2] Calv. Ep. 104. [p. 126. ed. Gen. 1617. "Quod Ecclesiæ reliquias
manere in Papatu dico, non restringo ad electos, qui illic dispersi sunt,
sed ruinas dissipatæ Ecclesiæ illic extare intelligo. Ac ne mihi longis
rationibus disputandum sit, nos Pauli auctoritate contentos esse decet,
qui Antichristum in templo Dei sessurum pronunciat. Quanquam et
hoc rationibus satis validis me probasse puto, Ecclesiam licet semiruptam,
immo si lubet diruptam ac deformem, aliquam tamen manere in Papatu."
This is from a letter to Lælius Socinus, 9 Dec. 1549.]
[3] ["God's house a den of thieves." Note in D.]

alleged of force to warrant, that God doth otherwise than so
as hath been in the two next questions before declared,[e]
bind himself to keep his elect from worshipping the beast,
and from receiving his mark in their foreheads ; but he hath
preserved, and will preserve, them from receiving any deadly
wound at the hands of the man of sin, whose deceit hath
prevailed over none to death, but only such [f] as never loved
the truth, such as took pleasure [g] in unrighteousness : they in
all ages, whose hearts have delighted in the principal truth,
and whose souls have thirsted after righteousness, if they
received the mark of error, the mercy of God, even erring,
and dangerously erring, might save them ; if they received
the mark of heresy, the same mercy did, I doubt not, convert them.[1] How far Romish heresies may prevail over
God's elect, how many God hath kept from falling into them,
how many have been converted from them, is not the question now in hand : for if heaven had not received any one of
that coat for these thousand years, it may still be true,[2] that
the doctrine which at [h] this day they do profess, doth not
directly deny the foundation, and so prove them simply to
be no Christian church. One I have alleged, whose words,
in my ears, sound that way ; shall I add another, whose
speech is plainer ? [i] " I deny her not the name of a church,"
saith another,[3] " no more than to a man the name of a man,
as long as he liveth, what sickness soever he hath." His
reason is this : " Salvation in Jesus Christ, which is the mark
joineth the Head with the body, Jesus Christ with his [k]
Church, it [l] is so cut off by man's [m] merits, by the merits of

[e] before hath been declared E.   [f] unto such E.   [g] took a pleasure D.
[h] at *om.* E.   [i] plain E.   [k] the E.   [l] it *om.* E.   [m] many E.

[1] [" Giving Christian repentance, and knowledge of the truth necessary to salvation, 1 Tim. ii." Note in D.]

[2] [" They deny the sufficiency of the scriptures, which you make the
foundation." Ibid.]

[3] Morn. de Eccles. [c. 2. p. 32. ed. 1594. " Si de Christi officio, et
quærenda in Christo salute agatur, quo, tanquam jugulo, corpori caput,
Ecclesiæ Christus conjungitur : sic meritis hominum et sanctorum, indul-
gentiarum sordibus, et infinitis blasphemiarum machinis pars hæc doctrinæ labefactata est, ut jam e tenui filo vita ecclesiæ penderet, eoque
mox abrumpendo, (quæ fuit Artichristi in agendo sedulitas,) nisi tempore
Dominus, qui eum compescerent, servos suos emisisset. Quamdiu vel
tenui illud filum reliquum manet, Ecclesiæ nomen non denegamus, ut
nec ei qui morbo contabescit nomen hominis quamdiu vivit." The
author of this work was the Breton nobleman, Philip Mornay du Plessis,
leader of the more serious party among the French protestants : it was
first published, A.D. 1577.]

saints, by the pope's pardons, and such other wickedness, that the life of the Church holdeth by a very little [n] thread," yet still the life of the Church holdeth. A third hath these words : [1] "I acknowledge the church of Rome, even at this present day, for a church of Christ, such a church as Israel under [o] Jeroboam, yet a church." His reason is this : "Every man seeth, except he willingly hoodwink himself, that as always, so now, the church of Rome holdeth firmly and steadfastly the doctrine of truth concerning God, and the Person of our Lord Jesus Christ ; and baptizeth in the name of the Father, the Son, and the Holy Ghost ; confesseth and avoucheth Christ for [p] the only [2] Redeemer of the world, and the Judge that shall sit upon quick and dead, receiving true believers into endless joy, faithless and godless men being cast with Satan and his angels into flames unquenchable."

28. I may, and will, rein the question shorter than they do. Let the Pope take down his top, and captivate no more men's souls by his papal jurisdiction ; let him no longer count himself lord paramount over the princes of the earth,[q] no longer use[r] kings as his tenants[s] *paravaile;*[3] let his stately senate submit their necks to the yoke of Christ, and cease to dye their garments, like Edom, in blood ; let them, from the highest to the lowest, hate and forsake their idolatry,

---

[n] little *om.* E.   [o] did E.   [p] to be E.   [q] world E.   [r] hold E.
[s] servants E.

[1] Zanch. Præfat. de Relig. ["Nescio quo singulari Dei beneficio, hoc adhuc boni in Rom. ecclesia servari nemo non videt, nisi qui videre non vult ; quod nimirum, sicut semper, sic nunc etiam constans et firma in vera de Deo, deque personæ D. N. Jesu Christi doctrina persistit ; et baptizat in nomine Patris et Filii et Spiritus Sancti ; Christumque agnoscit ac prædicat pro unico mundi redemptore, futuroque vivorum et mortuorum judice, qui veros fideles secum in æternam vitam recepturus, incredulos autem et impios in æternum ignem cum Diabolo et angelis ejus ejecturus sit : quæ causa est, cur ecclesiam hanc pro ecclesia Christi etiamnum agnoscam : sed quali ? qualis et ab Osea aliisque Prophetis ecclesia Israelis sub Jeroboamo, et deinceps, fuisse describitur : nunquam enim resipuit a suis fornicationibus." Ad calc. Operis de Sacra Scriptura. t. viii. ed. 1605.]

[2] ["Not true altogether." Note in D.]

[3] [Blackstone's Commentaries, vol. ii. p. 60. ed. Coleridge. "If the King granted a manor to A, and he granted a portion of the land to B, . . . the King was styled Lord Paramount, A was both tenant and lord, or was a mesne lord ; and B was called tenant *paravail,* or the lowest tenant ; being he who was supposed to make *avail,* or profit, of the land. 2 Inst. 296."]

abjure all their errors and heresies, wherewith they have any
way perverted the truth; let them strip their church, till they
leave no polluted rag, but only this one about her; "By
Christ alone, without works,[1] we cannot be saved:" it is
enough for me, if I show, that the holding of this one thing
doth not prove the foundation of faith directly denied in the
Church of Rome.

29. Works are an addition to the foundation:[t] be it so,
what then? the foundation is not subverted by every kind
of addition: simply to add unto those fundamental words,
is not to mingle wine with puddle,[u] heaven with earth, things
polluted with the sanctified blood of Christ: of which crime
indict them, which[x] attribute those operations in whole or
in part to any creature, which in the work of our salvation
are wholly[y] peculiar unto Christ; and, if I open my mouth
to speak in their defence, if I hold my peace, and plead
not against them as long as breath is in[z] my body, let me
be[a] guilty of all the dishonour that ever hath been done
to the Son of God. But the more dreadful a thing it is to
deny salvation by Christ alone, the more slow and fearful I
am, except it be too too manifest[b] to lay a thing so grievous
unto any man's charge. Let us beware, lest if we make
too many ways of denying Christ, we scarce leave any way
for ourselves truly and soundly to confess him. Salvation
only by Christ is the true foundation whereupon indeed
Christianity standeth. But what if I say, ye[c] cannot be
saved only by Christ, without this addition, Christ believed
in heart, confessed with mouth, obeyed in life and conversation? Because I add, do I therefore deny that which
directly I did[d] affirm? There may be an additament of
explication, which overthroweth not, but proveth and concludeth the proposition whereunto it is annexed. He that[e]
saith, Peter was a chief Apostle, doth prove that Peter was
an Apostle: he which saith,[2] Our salvation is of the Lord,
through sanctification of the Spirit, and faith of the truth,

[t] to the foundation *om*. E. [u] water E. [x] that D. [y] wholly are E.
[z] within E. [a] be *om*. D. [b] to manifest E. [c] you E. [d] I did
directly E. [e] which E.

[1] ["Ambiguous, if they hold Christ's redemption without works to
be insufficient." Note in D. Dr. Todd states that "this note is not
easily decyphered, and ends imperfect, as if it had never been finished.
It seems to be, 'Ambiguous, if they hold workes, Christ's Redemption
without workes thus to be unsufficient or—'"]

[2] [2 Thess. ii. 13.]

proveth that our salvation is of the Lord. But if that which
is added, be such a privation as taketh away the very essence
of that whereunto it is adjoined,[f] then by sequel[g] it overthroweth. He which saith, Judas is a dead man, though in
word he grant[h] Judas to be a man, yet in effect he proveth
him by that very speech no man, because death depriveth
him of his being.[i] In like sort, he that should say, Our
election is of grace for our works' sake, should grant in
sound of words, but indeed by consequent deny, that our
election is of grace; for the grace which electeth us is no
grace,[1] if it elect us for our works' sake.

30. Now whereas the church of Rome addeth works, we
must note further, that the adding works[k][2] is not like the
adding of circumcision unto Christ. Christ came not to
abrogate and to take away[l] good works:[3] he did, to change
circumcision; for we see that in place thereof he hath substituted holy baptism. To say, ye cannot be saved by Christ
except ye be circumcised, is to add a thing excluded, a thing
not only not necessary to be kept, but necessary not to be
kept[4] by them that will be saved. On the other side, to say,
ye cannot be saved by Christ without works,[5] is to add things
not only not excluded, but commanded, as being in their[m]
place and in their kind necessary, and therefore subordinated
unto Christ, even[n] by Christ himself, by whom the web of
salvation is spun:[6] "Except your righteousness exceed the

---

[f] added E.	[g] by the sequel E.	[h] granteth E.	[i] of being E.
[k] adding of works E.	[l] and put away E.	[m] their *om.* D.	[n] even *om.* E.

[1] Rom. xi. 6.

[2] I deny not but that the church of Rome requireth some kinds of
works which she ought not to require at men's hands. But our question
is general about the adding of good works, not whether such or such
works be good. In this comparison it is enough to touch so much on
the matter in question between St. Paul and the Galatians, as inferreth
those conclusions. "Ye are fallen from grace; Christ can profit you
nothing:" which conclusions will follow upon circumcision and rites of
the law ceremonial, if they be required as things necessary to salvation.
This only was alleged against me: and need I touch more than was
alleged?[*]

[3] ["But to justify us by faith without the merit of good works." Note
n D.]

[4] ["The keeping of circumcision hindereth not salvation, but the
opinion of the necessity thereof." Ibid.]

[5] ["Ambiguous." Ibid.]

[6] [The words "web" and "spun" in D. are underlined, and upon
them written "tapinosis."]

[*] Note *om.* D.

righteousness of the Scribes and Pharisees, ye[o] shall not enter into the kingdom of heaven."[1] They were rigorous exacters of things not utterly to be neglected and left undone,[2] washings and tithings,[p] &c. As they were in these things,[q] so must we be in judgment and the love of God. Christ, in works ceremonial, giveth more liberty, in moral much less,[3] than they did. Works of righteousness therefore are not so repugnantly[4] added in the one proposition; as in the other circumcision is.

31. But we say, our salvation is by Christ alone; therefore howsoever, or whatsoever, we add unto Christ in the matter of salvation, we overthrow Christ. Our case were very hard, if this argument, so universally meant as it is proposed, were sound and good. We ourselves do not teach Christ alone, excluding our own faith,[5] unto justification; Christ alone, excluding our own works, unto sanctification; Christ alone, excluding the one or the other as[r] unnecessary unto salvation. It is a childish cavil wherewith in the matter of justification our adversaries do greatly please themselves, exclaiming, that we tread all Christian virtues under our[s] feet, and require nothing in Christians but faith; because we teach that faith alone justifieth : whereas we by this speech[t] never meant to exclude either hope and[u] charity from being always joined as inseparable mates with faith in the man that is justified; or works from being added as necessary duties, required at the hands of every justified man : but to shew that faith is the only hand which putteth on Christ unto justification; and Christ the only garment, which being so put on, covereth the shame of our defiled natures, hideth the imperfections of our works, preserveth us blameless in the sight of God, before whom otherwise the very[x] weakness of our faith were cause sufficient to make us culpable, yea, to shut us out[y] from the kingdom of heaven, where nothing that is not absolute can enter. That our dealing with them be not as childish as theirs with us; when we hear of salvation by Christ alone, considering that ("alone" is[z] an) exclusive particle, we are to note what it doth exclude, and where. If I say, "Such a judge

---

[o] you D.   [p] tithing E.   [q] things *om.* E.   [r] as *om.* E.   [s] our *om.* D.
[t] by this speech we E.   [u] or E.   [x] very *om.* E.   [y] out *om.* E.   [z] as E.

[1] Matt. v. 20.   [2] Luke xi. 39.   [3] Matt. v. 21.
[4] ["The merit of works is most repugnant." Note in D.]
[5] ["Sophistry." Note in D.]

only ought to determine such a cause," [a] all things incident unto the determination thereof, besides the person of the judge, as laws, depositions, evidences, &c. are not hereby excluded; persons are, yet not [b] from witnessing herein, or assisting, but only from determining and giving sentence. How then is our salvation wrought by Christ alone? is it our meaning, [c] that nothing is requisite to man's salvation, but Christ to save, and he to be saved quietly without any more to do? [d] No, we acknowledge no such foundation. [e] As we have received, so we teach that besides the bare and naked work, [1] wherein Christ, without any other associate, finished all the parts of our redemption, and purchased salvation himself alone; for conveyance of this eminent blessing unto us, many things are required, [f] as, to be known and chosen of God before the foundations of the world; in the world to be called, justified, sanctified; after we have left the world, to be received into [g] glory; Christ in every of these hath somewhat which he worketh alone. Through him, according to the eternal purpose of God before the foundation of the world, [2] born, crucified, buried, raised, &c., we were in a gracious acceptation [h] known unto God long before we were seen of men: God knew us, loved us, was kind towards us [i] in Christ Jesus, [k] in him we were elected to be heirs of life. Thus far God through Christ hath wrought in such sort alone, that ourselves are mere patients, working no more than dead and senseless matter, wood, or stone, or iron, doth in the artificer's hand, [l] no more than the clay, when the potter appointeth it to be framed for an honourable use; nay, not so much. For the matter whereupon the craftsman worketh he chooseth, being moved by [m] the fitness which is in it to serve his turn; in us no such thing. Touching the rest, that [n] which is laid for the foundation of our faith, importeth [o] further, that by him we be called, that we have redemption, remission of sins through his blood, health by his stripes; justice by him; that he doth sanctify his Church, and make it glorious to himself; that entrance into joy shall be given us by him; yea, all things by him alone. Howbeit, not so by him alone, as if in us, to our vocation, the hearing of the gospel; to our

---

[a] case E.   [b] are not excluded E.   [c] it is not one meaning E.   [d] ado? E.
[e] *This sentence om.* E   [f] are of necessity required E.   [g] unto E.
[h] acception E.   [i] to us E.   [k] Jesus Christ E.   [l] hands E.   [m] with D.
[n] that *om.* E.   [o] it importeth E.

[1] ["A base phrase." Note in D.]   [2] Eph. i. 11.

justification, faith; to our sanctification, the fruits of the spirit; to our entrance into rest, perseverance in hope, in faith, in holiness, were not necessary.

32. Then what is the fault of the church of Rome? Not that she requireth works at their hands that will be saved: but that she attributeth unto works a power of satisfying God for sin; and[p] a virtue to merit both grace here, and in heaven glory. That this overthroweth the foundation of faith, I grant willingly; that it is a direct[1] denial thereof, I utterly deny. What it is to hold, and what directly[2] to deny, the foundation of faith, I have already opened. Apply it particularly to this cause, and there needs no more ado. The thing which is handled, if the form under which it is handled be added thereunto, it sheweth the foundation of any doctrine whatsoever. Christ is the matter whereof the doctrine of the gospel treateth; and it treateth of Christ as of a Saviour. Salvation therefore by Christ is the foundation of Christianity: as for works, they are a thing subordinate, no otherwise necessary[q] than because our sanctification cannot[3] be accomplished without them. The doctrine concerning them is a thing builded upon the foundation; therefore the doctrine which addeth unto them power[r] of satisfying, or of meriting, addeth unto a thing subordinated, builded upon the foundation, not to[s][4] the very foundation itself; yet is the foundation consequently by this addition[t] overthrown, forasmuch as out of this addition it may negatively be[u] concluded, he which maketh any work good and acceptable in the sight of God, to proceed from the natural freedom of our will; he which giveth unto any good work[x] of ours the force of satisfying the wrath of God for sin, the power of meriting either earthly or heavenly rewards he which holdeth works going before our vocation, in congruity to merit our vocation; works following our first, to merit our second justification, and by condignity our last reward in the kingdom of heaven, pulleth up the doctrine of faith by the roots; for out of every of these the plain direct denial thereof may be necessarily concluded. Nor[y] this

[p] yea E. [q] necessary *om.* E. [r] the power E. [s] to *om.* D.
[t] by this addition consequently E. [u] be negatively E. [x] works E. [y] Not E

[1] "[All the controversy brought to a term." Note in D.]

[2] "All men take not 'directly' as he doth." Ibid.]

[3] "How is the sanctification of infants accomplished?" Ibid.]

[4] ["Merit addeth to the very foundation, as the papists themselves will confess." Ibid.]

only, but what other heresy is there which ᶻ doth not raze
the very foundation of faith by consequent? Howbeit, we
make a difference of heresies; accounting them in the next
degree to infidelity, which ᵃ directly deny any one thing to
be which is expressly acknowledged in the articles of our
belief; for out of any one article so denied, the denial of
the very foundation itself is straightway ᵇ inferred.¹ As for
example; if a man should say, "There is no catholic
Church," it followeth immediately hereupon,ᶜ that this Jesus
whom we call the Saviour, is not the Saviour of the world;
because all the prophets bear ᵈ witness, that the true Messias
should "shew light unto the Gentiles;"² that is to say,
gather such a Church as is catholic, not restrained any longer
unto one circumcised nation. In a ᵉ second rank we place
them, out of whose positions the denial of any of ᶠ the fore-
said articles may be with like facility concluded; such are ᵍ
they which have denied, either the divinity of Christ, with
Hebion, or with Marcion, his humanity; an example whereof may be that of Cassianus defending the incarnation of the
Son of God against Nestorius bishop of Antioch,³ which ʰ
held, that the Virgin, when she brought forth Christ, did
not bring forth the Son of God, but a sole and mere man.
Out of which heresy the denial of the articles of Christian ⁱ
faith he deduceth thus :⁴ "If thou dost deny our Lord

that E.　　ᵃ who D.　　ᵇ straightwaies D.　　ᶜ thereupon E.　　ᵈ bere
or bare D.　　ᵉ the E.　　ᶠ of *om.* E.　　ᵍ such as are E.　　ʰ who E.
the Christian E.

¹ "Hæc ratio ecclesiastici sacramenti et Catholicæ Fidei est, ut qui
partem divini sacramenti negat, partem non valeat confiteri. Ita enim
sibi connexa et concorporata sunt omnia, ut aliud sine alio stare non
possit, et qui unum ex omnibus denegaverit, alia ei omnia credidisse
non prosit." Cassian. lib. vi. de Incarnat. Dom. [c. 17.*]

² Acts xxvi. 23.

³ ["I think he was bishop of Constantinople." Ussher.]

⁴ Lib. vi. de Incar. Dom. cap. 17. ["Si negas Deum Dominum
Jesum Christum, necesse est ut Filium Dei denegans etiam Patrem
neges. Quia juxta ipsius Patris vocem, 'Qui non habet Filium, nec
Patrem habet; qui autem habet Filium et Patrem habet.' Negans ergo
genitum, etiam genitorem negas. Negans quoque Filium Dei in carne
natum, consequens est, ut etiam in spiritu natum neges, quia idem natus
in carne, qui prius natus in spiritu. Non credens ergo in carne editum,
necesse est etiam passum esse non credas. Non credens autem illius
passionem, quid reliquum est, nisi ut etiam resurrectionem neges? Quia
fides suscitati ex fide mortui est. Nec stare potest ratio resurrectionis,
nisi fides mortis ante præcesserit. Negans ergo passum et mortuum,
negas quoque ab inferis resurgentem. Consequens utique est, ut neges

* Note *om.* E.

Jesus Christ to be God,[k] in denying the Son, thou canst not choose but deny the Father; for, according to the voice of the Father himself, ' He that hath not the Son, hath not the Father.' Wherefore denying him that[l] is begotten, thou deniest him which doth beget. Again,[m] denying the Son of God to have been born in the flesh, how canst thou believe him to have suffered? believing not his passion, what remaineth, but that thou deny his resurrection? For we believe him not raised, except we first believe him dead : neither can the reason of his rising from the dead stand, without the faith of his death going before. The denial of his death and passion inferreth the denial of his rising from the depth.[n] Whereupon it followeth, that thou also deny his ascension into heaven : the Apostle affirming,[o] ' That he which ascended, did first descend.' So that, as much as lieth in thee, our Lord Jesus Christ hath neither risen from the depth,[p] nor is ascended into heaven, nor sitteth at the right hand of God the Father, neither shall he come at the day of final account, which is looked for, nor shall judge the quick and dead. And darest thou yet set foot in the Church? Canst thou think thyself a bishop, when thou hast denied all those things whereby thou didst [q] obtain a bishoply calling?" Nestorius confessed all the articles of the creed, but his opinion did imply the denial of every part of his confession. Heresies there are of a third[r] sort, such as the church of Rome maintaineth, which being[s] removed by a greater distance from the foundation, although indeed they overthrow it ; yet because of that weakness, which the philosopher noteth in men's capacities when he saith, that the common sort cannot see things which follow in reason, when they follow, as it were afar

---

[k] to be God *om.* E.   [l] which E.   [m] again *om.* E.   [n] from death D.
[o] affirmeth E.   [p] death D.   [q] dost E.   [r] the third E.   [s] be E.

---

etiam ascendentem : quia ascensio sine resurrectione esse non potuit. Et qui resurrexisse non creditur, necesse est nec ascendisse credatur : dicente Apostolo, ' Qui enim descendit, ipse est qui ascendit.' Ergo, quantum in te est, Dominus Jesus Christus neque ab inferis resurrexit, neque cœlum ascendit, neque ad dexteram Dei Patris sedet, neque ad illum qui expectatur examinationis ultimæ diem veniet, nec vivos nec mortuos judicabit." c. 18. " Intelligis itaque, O infelix et furiosa perversitas, evacuasse te penitus omnem symboli fidem, omnem spei sacramentique virtutem? Et in ecclesia insuper stare ausus es, et esse te acerdotem putas, cum illa omnia denegaveris, per quæ sacerdos esse cœpisti?" in Bibl. Patr. Colon. t. v. pars ii. p. 80.]

off by many deductions; therefore the repugnancy between [t] such heresy and the foundation is not so quickly nor [u] so easily found, but that an heretic of this, sooner than of the former kind, may directly grant, and consequently nevertheless deny, the foundation of faith.

33. If reason be suspected, trial will shew that the church of Rome doth no [x] otherwise, by teaching the doctrine she doth teach concerning works.[y]   Offer them the very fundamental words, and what one [z] man is there that will refuse to subscribe unto them? Can they directly grant, and deny directly [a] one and the very selfsame thing? Our own proceedings in disputing against their works satisfactory and meritorious do shew, not only that they hold, but that we acknowledge them to hold, the foundation, notwithstanding their opinion. For are not these our arguments against them? "Christ alone hath satisfied and appeased his Father's wrath : Christ hath merited salvation alone." We should do fondly to use such disputes, neither could we think to prevail by them, if that whereupon we ground, were a thing which we know they do not hold,[b] which we are assured they will not grant. Their very answers to all such reasons, as are in this controversy brought against them, will not permit us to doubt whether they hold the foundation or no. Can any man, which [c] hath read their books concerning this matter, be ignorant how they draw all their answers unto these heads? "That the remission of all our sins, the pardon of all whatsoever punishments thereby deserved, the rewards which God hath laid up in heaven, are by the blood of our Lord Jesus Christ purchased, and obtained sufficiently for all men : but for no man effectually for his benefit in particular, except the blood of Christ be applied particularly unto him by such means as God hath appointed it [d] to work by : That those means of themselves being but dead things, only the blood of Christ is that which putteth life, force, and efficacy in them to work, and to be available, each in his kind, to our salvation : Finally, that grace being purchased for us by the blood of Christ, and freely without any merit or desert at the first bestowed upon us, the good things which we do, after grace received, are [e] thereby made satisfactory and meritorious." Some of their sentences to this effect I must allege for mine own warrant.

[t] of E.   [u] or E.   [x] not D.   [y] good works E.   [z] one *om*. E.
[a] directly deny E.   [b] hold with D.   [c] that E.   [d] that E.   [e] be E.

If we desire to hear foreign judgments, we find in one this
confession : " He that could reckon how many the virtues
and merits of our Saviour Christ have[f] been, might likewise understand how many the benefits have been that
are come[g] unto us by him, forasmuch[h] as men are made
partakers of them all by the mean[i] of his passion : by him
is given unto us remission of our sins, grace, glory, liberty,
praise, [peace,] salvation, redemption, justification,[1] justice,
sanctification,[k] sacraments, merits, doctrine,[l] and all other
things which we [he] had, and were behoveful[m] for our
salvation." [2] In another we have these oppositions and
answers made unto them : " All grace is given by Christ
Jesus. True ; but not except Christ Jesus be applied.
He is the propitiation for our sins ;[n] by his stripes we are
healed ; he hath offered up himself[o] for us : all this [us
all : this?[p]] is true, but apply it. We put all satisfaction in the blood of Jesus Christ ; but we hold, that the
means which[q] Christ hath appointed for us in this case to
apply it, are our penal works." [3] Our countrymen in

[f] hath D. [g] are to come E. [h] for so much E. [i] means E. [k] satisfaction E. [l] doctrine *om.* E. [m] behooful D. [n] sin E. [o] himself
up E. [p] No stop in D. [q] of D.

[1] [The word "justification" is not either in the original or the English
translation.]

[2] Lewis of Granada, Medit. ch. last. 3. [" Of Prayer and Meditation. Wherein are contained fourteen devout Meditations for the
seven days of the week, both for the Mornings and Evenings. And in
them is treated of the consideration of the principal Mysteries of our
Faith. Written first in the Spanish tongue by the famous religious
Father, F. Lewis de Granada, Provincial of the holy order of Preachers
in the Province of Portugal." Paris 1582. fol. 317. The writer was
one of the most distinguished ascetic and devotional writers of Spain.
He was confessor to the Queen Regent of Portugal, and died 1588.
Biog. Univ.]

[3] Panigarola lett. 11. [" Disceptationes Calvinicæ a Joanne Tonso
Mediolan. Patritio in Latinum conversæ." Milan 1554. Discept. xi.
p. 272, 3. " 'Omnis gratia data est nobis per Christum Jesum :'
verum ; at per applicationem. 'Ipse est propitiatio pro peccatis nostris:'
verum ; at applica. 'Livore ejus sanati sumus :' at applica. 'Pro nobis
se obtulit :' at applica. . . . Omnem enim satisfactionem in sanguine
locamus ; sed applicationem hac in re tribuimus, quibus ipse tribuit
Christus, pœnalibus scilicet nostris operibus." Francis Panigarola was
one of the most distinguished preachers of Italy in the 16th century.
The work from which the above is translated was a course of lectures
against the Calvinists, addressed to Charles Emanuel, Duke of Savoy,
by whom Panigarola was made Bishop of Asti, A. D. 1587 : he died in
1594. See Tiraboschi, Storia della Letteratura Italiana, t. vii. part. i.
lib. iii. c. 6. No. 12–14.]

Rhemes make the like answer,[1] that they seek salvation no other way than by the blood of Christ; and that humbly they do use prayers, fasting,[r] alms, faith, charity, sacrifice, sacraments, priests, only as the means appointed by Christ, to apply the benefit of his holy blood unto them : touching our good works, that in their own natures they are not meritorious, nor answerable unto the joys of heaven; it cometh by the grace of Christ, and not of the work itself, that we have by well-doing a right to heaven, and deserve it worthily. If any man think that I seek to varnish their opinions, to set the better foot of a lame cause foremost; let him know, that since[s] I began throughly to understand their meaning, I have found their halting in this doctrine[t] greater than perhaps it seemeth to them which know not the deepness of Satan, as the blessed Divine speaketh.[2] For, although this be proof sufficient, that they do not directly deny the foundation of faith ; yet, if there were no other leaven in the whole lump of their doctrine but this, this were sufficient to prove, that their doctrine is not agreeable with[u] the foundation of Christian faith. The Pelagians, being over-great friends unto nature, made themselves enemies unto grace, for all their confessing, that men have their souls, and all the faculties thereof, their wills and the ability[x] of their wills, from God. And is not the church of Rome still an adversary unto Christ's merits, because of her acknowledging, that we have received the power of meriting by the blood of Christ ? Sir Thomas More setteth down the odds between us and the church of Rome in the matter of works thus : "Like as we grant them, that no good work of man is rewardable in heaven of his[y] own nature, but through the mere goodness of God, that list[z] to set so high a price upon so poor a thing ; and that this price God setteth through Christ's passion, and for that also that they be[a] his own works with us ; (for good works to God-ward worketh no man, without God work in

r fastings E.   s seyns D.   t in this doctrine om. E.   u unto E.
x all the ability E.   y its E.   z lists E.   a also they be E.

[1] Annot. in 1 John i. [v. 7. "Whether sins be remitted by prayers, by fasting, by alms, by faith, by charity, by sacrifice, by sacraments, or by the priests, (as the holy Scriptures do plainly attribute remission to every of these,) yet none of all these do otherwise remit, but in the force, by the virtue and merit, of Christ's blood : these being but the appointed means and instruments, by which Christ will have his holy blood to work effectually in us."]

[2] [Apoc. ii. 24.]

him :) and as we grant them also, that no man may be proud of his works, for his own [b] imperfect [c] working ; and for that in all that man may do, he can do no good,[d] but is a servant unprofitable, and doth but his bare duty : as we, I say, grant unto them these things, so this one thing or twain do they grant us again, that men are bound to work good works, if they have time and power ; and that whoso worketh in true faith most, shall be most rewarded : but then set they thereto, that all his rewards shall be given him for his faith alone, and nothing for his works at all, because his faith is the thing, they say, that forceth him to work well." [1] I see by this of sir Thomas More, how easy it is for men of great [e] capacity and judgment [f] to mistake things written or spoken, as well on one side as on another.[g] Their doctrine, as he thought, maketh the works [h] of man rewardable in the world to come through the mere [i] goodness of God, whom it pleaseth to set so high a price upon so poor a thing ; and ours, that a man doth receive that eternal and high reward, not for his works, but for his faith's sake, by which he worketh : whereas in truth our doctrine is no other than that which [k] we have learned at the feet of Christ ; namely, that God doth justify the believing man, yet not for the worthiness of his belief, but for his worthiness [l] which is believed ; God rewardeth abundantly every one which worketh, yet not for any meritorious dignity which is, or can be, in the work, but through his mere mercy, by whose commandment he worketh. Contrariwise, their doctrine is,[2] that as pure water of itself hath no savour, but if it pass through a sweet pipe, it taketh a pleasant smell of the

[b] own *om.* E. [c] unperfitt D. [d] do God no good E. [e] the greatest E. and judgment *om.* E. [f] as well on the one side as on the other E. [h] work E. mere *om.* E. [k] which *om.* E. [l] the worthiness of him E.

[1] In his Book of Consolation, [i. 11. Works, p. 1153, ed. 1557.]

[2] Panigarola, p. 264. ["Gratiam mereri non possumus (alioqui gratia non esset gratia, sed præmium : nam meritum sequeretur) gloriam autem possumus. Præterea (et in hoc summa consistit) opera nostra tanquam nostra, nunquam spiritalia et æterna bona merentur ; cum vero merentur, id contingit, quoniam ab anima proficiscuntur, quæ gratiam habet. Simili nempe ratione, qua ex aquæ puræ rivulo nullus odor afflatur ; sed si per odoratum canalem ea defluat, odorifera fit. Quare priusquam in gratia simus, res hujusmodi mereri non possumus ; sed ante justificationem a gratia longe absumus ; igitur ante justificationem non meremur : quo probato, consequens est, ut primam justificationem non mereamur, et primam gratiam mereri nunquam possumus. Atque ut rem absolvamus : opera nostra triplicia sunt, vel tribus modis considerare opera nostra possumus : tanquam quæ *idoneos reddunt,* quæ

pipe through which it passeth ; so, although before grace received, our works do neither satisfy nor merit ; yet after, they do both the one and the other.   Every virtuous action hath then power in such sort [m] to satisfy ; that if we ourselves commit no mortal sin, no heinous crime, whereupon to spend this treasure of satisfaction in our own behalf, it turneth to the benefit of other men's release, on whom it shall please the steward of the house of God to bestow it ; so that we may satisfy for ourselves and others, but merit only for ourselves.   In meriting, our actions do work with two hands : with the [n] one, they get their morning stipend, the increase of grace ; with the other, their evening hire, the everlasting crown of glory.   Indeed they teach, that our good works do not these things as they come from us, but as they come from grace in us ; which grace in us is another thing in their divinity, than is the mere goodness of God's mercy toward [o] us in Christ Jesus.

34. If it were not a strong deluding spirit which hath possession of their hearts ; were it possible but that they should see how plainly they do herein gainsay the very ground [p] of apostolic faith ? Is this that salvation by grace, whereof so plentiful mention is made in the sacred [q] Scriptures of God ? was this their meaning, which first taught the world to look for salvation only by Christ ? By grace, the Apostle saith, and by grace in such sort as a gift ; a thing that cometh not of ourselves, not of our works, lest any man should boast and say, "I have wrought out mine own salvation." [1] By grace they confess ; but by grace in such sort, that as many as wear the diadem of bliss, they wear nothing but what they have won. The Apostle, as if he had foreseen how the church of Rome would abuse the world in time by ambiguous terms, to declare in what sense the name of grace must be taken, when we make it the cause of our salvation, saith, "He saved us according to his mercy :" which mercy, although it exclude not the washing of our new birth, the renewing of our hearts by the Holy Ghost, the means, the

m sort *om.* E.   n the *om.* E.   o towards E.   p grounds D.
q sacred *om.* E

merentur, et quæ *satisfaciunt.*   Antequam simus in gratia, quod ad eam attinet, opera nostra ad eam obtinendam nos præparant, et reddunt idoneos.   Postquam vero gratiam obtinuimus, si pœnam tempore definitam, quæ reliqua est, spectemus, satisfaciunt ; si vero gloriam, merentur."]

[1] ["S. Paul commandeth us so to do."   Note in D.]

virtues, the duties, which God requireth at [r] their hands
which shall be saved; yet it is so repugnant unto merits, that
to say, we are saved for the worthiness of any thing which is
ours, is to deny we are saved by Grace. Grace bestoweth
freely; and therefore justly requireth the glory of that which
is bestowed. We deny the grace of our Lord Jesus Christ;
we imbase,[s] disannul, annihilate[t] the benefit of his bitter
passion, if we rest in those[u] proud imaginations, that life everlasting[x] is deservedly ours, that we merit it, and that we are
worthy of it.

35. Howbeit, considering how many virtuous and just men,
how many saints, how many martyrs, how many of the
ancient Fathers of the church, have had their sundry perilous
opinions; and among sundry of their[y] opinions this, that they
hoped to make God some part of amends for their sins, by
the voluntary punishments[z] which they laid upon themselves;
because by a consequent it may follow hereupon, that they
were injurious unto[a] Christ, shall we therefore make such
deadly epitaphs, and set them upon their graves, "They
denied the foundation of faith directly, they are damned,
there is no salvation for them"? St. Augustine hath said[b]
of himself, "Errare possum, hæreticus esse nolo." And,
except we put a difference between them that err, and them
that obstinately persist in error, how is it possible that ever
any man should hope to be saved? Surely, in this case, I
have no respect of any person alive or dead. Give me a
man, of what estate or condition soever, yea, a cardinal or a
pope, whom at[c] the extreme point of his life affliction hath
made to know himself; whose heart God hath touched with
true sorrow for all his sins, and filled with love toward the
Gospel of Christ; whose eyes are opened to see the truth,
and his mouth to renounce all heresy and error any way[d]
opposite thereunto, this one opinion of merits excepted;
which[e] he thinketh God will require at his hands, and
because he wanteth, therefore, trembleth, and is discouraged;
it may be I am forgetful, or[f] unskilful, not furnished with
things new and old, as a wise and[g] learned scribe should be,
nor able to allege that, whereunto, if it were alleged, he doth
bear a mind most willing to yield, and so to be recalled, as
well from this, as from other errors: and shall I think, because

---

[r] of E. [s] abuse E. [t] and annihilate E. adnichillate D. [u] these E.
[x] everlasting om. E. [y] of their om. D. [z] punishment D. [a] to D.
[b] saith E. [c] in E. [d] wise E. [e] which om. E. [f] and E.
[g] and om. E.

of this only error, that such a man toucheth not so much as
the hem of Christ's garment? If he do, wherefore should
not I have hope, that virtue may proceed from Christ to save
him? Because his error doth by consequent overthrow his
faith, shall I therefore cast him off, as one which hath utterly
cast off Christ? one which [h] holdeth not so much as by a
slender thread? No; I will not be afraid to say unto a
cardinal or to a pope [i] in this plight, Be of good comfort, we
have to do with a merciful God, ready to make the best of
that little [k] which we hold well, and not with a captious
sophister, which gathereth the worst out of every thing
wherein we err. Is there any reason that I should be
suspected, or you offended, for this speech? Let all affection
be laid aside; let the matter be indifferently [l] considered. [m]
Is it a dangerous thing to imagine, that such men may find
mercy? The hour may come, when we shall think it a blessed
thing to hear, that if our sins were as [n] the sins of the pope [o]
and cardinals, the bowels of the mercy of God are larger. I
do not propose unto you a pope with the neck of an emperor
under his foot; [p] a cardinal riding his horse to the bridle in
the blood of saints; but a pope or a cardinal sorrowful,
penitent, disrobed, stript, [q] not only of usurped power, but
also delivered and recalled from error and Antichrist, converted and lying prostrate at the feet [r] of Christ; and shall I
think that Christ will [s] spurn at him? shall [t] I cross and gainsay the merciful promises of God, generally made unto penitent sinners, by opposing the name of a pope or [u] cardinal?
What difference is there in the world between a pope and a
cardinal, and John a Style, [x][1] in this case? If we think it
impossible for them, after they be once come within that [y]
rank, to be afterwards touched with any such remorse, let
that be granted. The Apostle saith, " If I, or an angel from
heaven, preach unto you," &c. Let it be as likely, that
St. Paul or an angel from heaven should [z] preach heresy, as
that a pope or a [a] cardinal should be brought so far forth to
acknowledge the truth; yet if a pope or cardinal should,
what find we in their persons why they might not be saved?
It is not their [b] persons, you will say, but the error wherein I

---

[h] that E.   [i] pope or cardinal E.   [k] a little E.   [l] indifferently be E.
[m] *This sentence in marg.* E.   [n] as *om.* E.   [o] popes E.   [p] feet E.
[q] stripped E.   [r] foot E.   [s] shall E.   [t] and shall E.   [u] or of a E.
[x] John Stile D.   [y] the D.   [z] that Paul or an angel should D.   [a] a *om.* E.
[b] the E.

[1] [" John a Stile is not the son of perdition." Note in D.]

suppose them to die, which excludeth them from hope[c] of mercy; the opinion of merits doth take away all possibility of salvation from them. What although[d] they hold it only as an error? although they hold the truth soundly[e] and sincerely in all other parts of Christian faith? although they have in some measure all the virtues and graces of the Spirit, all other tokens of God's elect children in them? although they be far from having any proud presumptuous opinion, that they shall be saved for[f] the worthiness of their deeds? although the only thing which troubleth and molesteth them be but a little too much dejection, somewhat too great a fear, rising from an erroneous conceit that God will require a worthiness in them, which they are grieved to find wanting in themselves? although they be not obstinate in this persuasion? although they be willing, and would be glad to forsake it, if any one reason were brought sufficient to disprove it? although the only let, why they do not forsake it ere they die, be the ignorance of the mean[g] whereby[h] it might be disproved? although the cause why the ignorance in this point is not removed, be the want of knowledge in such as should be able, and are not, to remove it? Let me die, if ever it be proved, that simply an error doth exclude a pope or a cardinal, in such a case, utterly from hope of life. Surely, I must confess unto you, if it be an error to think,[i] that God may be merciful to save men even when they err,[1] my greatest comfort is my error; were it not for the love I bear unto this error, I would neither[k] wish to speak nor to live.

36. Wherefore to resume that mother-sentence, whereof I little thought that so much trouble would have grown, "I doubt not but God was merciful to save thousands of our fathers living in popish superstitions, inasmuch as they sinned ignorantly:" alas! what bloody matter is there contained in this sentence, that it should be an occasion of so many hard censures? Did I say, "That thousands of our fathers might be saved?" I have shewed which way it cannot be denied. Did I say, "I doubt it[1] not but they were saved?" I see no impiety in this persuasion, though I had no reason in the world[m] for it. Did I say, "Their

e the hope E.   d if E.   e truly E.   f by E.   g means E.
h by which E.   i to think om. E.   k never E.   l doubted E.
m in the world om. E.

1 ["In these things whereof the truth is necessary to be known." Note in D.]

ignorance doth make me hope they did find mercy, and so were saved ? " What doth hinder[n] salvation but sin ? Sins are not equal; and ignorance, though it do[o] not make sin to be no sin, yet seeing it did make their sin the less, why should it not make our hope concerning their life the greater ? We pity the most, and I[p] doubt not but God hath most compassion over them that sin for want of understanding. As much is confessed by sundry others, almost in the self-same words which I have used. It is but only my ill[q] hap, that the same sentences which favour[r] verity in other men's books, should seem to bolster heresy when they are once by me recited. If I be deceived in this point, not they, but the blessed Apostle hath deceived me.[1] What I said of others, the same he saith[s] of himself, "I obtained mercy,[2] for I did it ignorantly." Construe his words, and ye[t] cannot miscon-strue mine. I speak no otherwise, I meant no otherwise.[u]

37. Thus have I brought the question concerning our fathers at the length unto an end. Of whose estate, upon so fit an occasion as was offered me, handling the weighty causes of separation between the church of Rome and us, and the weak motives which commonly are[x] brought to retain men in that society; amongst which motives the example[y] of our fathers deceased is one; although I saw it convenient to utter that sentence which I did, to the end that all men might thereby understand, how untruly we are said to condemn as many as have been before us otherwise persuaded than we ourselves are : yet more than that one sentence I did not think it expedient to utter, judging it a great deal meeter for us to have regard to our own estate, than to sift over curiously what is become of other men ; and fearing, lest that such questions as this,[z] if voluntarily they should be too far waded in, might seem worthy of that rebuke which our Saviour thought needful in a case not unlike, "What is this unto thee ? "[3] When as[a] I was forced, much besides mine[b] expectation, to render a reason of my speech, I could not but yield at the call of

---

[n] hindereth E.   [o] doth E.   [p] I *om.* E.   [q] evil E.   [r] savour E.
[s] said E.   [t] you E.   [u] I spake no otherwise, I meant no otherwise than he did E.   [x] are commonly E.   [y] examples E.   [z] these E.   [a] as *om.* E.
[b] my D.

[1] ["The Apostle hath not deceived you, if [oft ?] you mistake his meaning." Note in D.]

[2] ["The Apostle obtained mercy to shew the truth which he perse-cuted in ignorance." Note in D.]

[3] [St. John xxi. 22.]

others, to [c] proceed as [d] duty bound me, for the fuller satisfaction of men's minds.[e] Wherein I have walked, as with
reverence, so with fear: with reverence, in regard of our fathers,
which lived in former times; not without fear, considering
them that are alive.

38. I am not ignorant how ready men are to feed and
sooth up themselves in evil. Shall I (will the man say, that
loveth the [f] present world more than he loveth Christ), shall
I incur the high displeasure of the mightiest upon earth?
shall I hazard my goods, endanger my estate,[g] put my life
in [h] jeopardy, rather than yield unto that which so many of
my fathers have [i] embraced, and yet found favour in the
sight of God? " Curse Meroz," saith the Lord, " curse her
inhabitants, because they help [k] not the Lord, they help [l]
him not against the mighty." [1] If I should not only not [m]
help the Lord against the mighty, but help to strengthen
them that are mighty against the Lord; worthily might I fall
under the burden of that curse, worthy I were to bear my
own judgment. But if the doctrine which I teach be a
flower gathered in the garden of the Lord, a part of the
saving truth of the Gospel, from whence notwithstanding
poisonous creatures do suck venom; I can but wish it were
otherwise, and content myself with the lot that hath befallen
me, the rather, because it hath not befallen me alone. St.
Paul did preach [n] a truth, and a comfortable truth, when
he taught, that the greater our misery is in respect of our
iniquities, the readier is the mercy of our [o] God for our
release, if we seek unto him; the more we have sinned,
the more praise, and glory,[p] and honour unto him that
pardoneth our sin. But mark what lewd collections were
made hereupon by some: [2] " Why then am I condemned
for a [q] sinner?" And, saith the Apostle, " as we are
blamed, and as some affirm that we say, ' Why do we not
evil that good may come of it?'" He was accused to
teach that which ill-disposed men did gather by his teaching, though it were clean not only beside,[r] but against
his meaning. The Apostle addeth, " Their condemnation
which thus do is just." I am not hasty to apply sentences
of condemnation: I wish from my heart their conversion,

[c] and E. [d] so far as E. [e] satisfying of minds E. [f] this D.
[g] state D. [h] myself into E. [i] have *om.* E. [k] helped E.
[l] helped E. [m] not *om.* D. [n] taught E. [o] our *om.* E. [p] glory and
praise D. [q] am I then ... as D. [r] besides E.

[1] Judges v. 23. [2] Rom. iii. 7, 8.

whosoever are thus perversely affected. For I must needs say, their case is fearful, their estate dangerous, which harden themselves, presuming on [s] the mercy of God towards others. It is true, that God is merciful, but let us beware of presumptuous sins. God delivered Jonah from the bottom of the sea ; will you therefore cast yourselves headlong from the tops of rocks, and say in your hearts, God shall deliver us ? He pitieth the blind that would gladly see ; but will God [t] pity him that may see, and hardeneth himself in blindness ? No ; Christ hath spoken too much unto you, for you [u] to claim the privilege of your fathers.

39. As for us that have handled this cause concerning the condition of our fathers, whether it be this thing or any other which we bring unto you, the counsel is good which the Wise Man giveth,[1] "Stand thou fast in thy sure understanding, in the way and knowledge of the Lord, and have but one manner of word, and follow the word of peace and righteousness." As a loose tooth is a great [x] grief unto him that eateth, so doth a wavering and unstable word, in speech that tendeth to instruction, offend. "Shall a wise man speak words of the wind,"[2] saith Eliphaz ; light, unconstant, unstable words ? Surely the wisest may speak words of the wind : such is the untoward constitution of our nature, that we neither do [y] so perfectly understand the way and knowledge of the Lord, nor so steadfastly embrace it, when it is understood ; nor so graciously utter it, when it is embraced ; nor so peaceably maintain it, when it is uttered ; but that the best of us are overtaken sometime through blindness, sometime through hastiness, sometime through impatience, sometime through other passions of the mind, whereunto (God doth know) we are too subject. We must therefore be contented both to pardon others, and to crave that others may [z] pardon us for such things. Let no man, which [a] speaketh as a man, think himself (whilest [b] he liveth) always freed from scapes and oversights in his speech. The things themselves which I have spoken unto you I hope [c] are sound, howsoever they have seemed otherwise unto some ; at whose hands if [d] I have, in that respect, received injury, I willingly forget it ; although, in truth, [e] considering the benefit which I have reaped by

[s] upon D.   [t] He E.   [u] for you *om.* E.   [x] great *om.* E.   [y] do neither E.   [z] must E.   [a] that E.   [b] whiles E.   [c] I hope *om.* E.   [d] it *om. and a period at* injury E.   [e] indeed E.

[1] [Ecclus. v. 10.]   [2] [Job xv. 2.]

this necessary search [f] of truth, I rather incline unto that of the Apostle,[1] "They have not injured me at all." I have cause to wish, and I do wish,[g] them as many blessings in the kingdom of heaven, as they have forced me to utter words and syllables in this cause; wherein I could not be more sparing in [h] speech than I have been. "It becometh no man," saith St. Jerome,[2] "to be patient in the crime of heresy." Patient, as I take it, we should be always, though the crime of heresy were intended; but silent in a thing of so great consequence, I could not, beloved, I durst not be; especially the love, which I bear to the truth in[i] Christ Jesus, being hereby somewhat called in question. Whereof I beseech them, in the meekness of Christ, that have been the first original cause, to consider that a watchman may cry "An enemy!" when indeed a friend cometh. In which case,[k] as I deem[l] such a watchman more worthy to be loved for his care, than misliked for his error; so I have judged it my own part in this case,[m] as much as in me lieth, to take away all suspicion of any unfriendly intent or meaning against the truth, from which, God doth know, my heart is free.

40. Now to you, beloved, which have heard these things, I will use no other words of admonition, than those which are offered me by St. James,[3] "My brethren, have not the faith of our glorious Lord Jesus Christ,[n] in respect of persons." Ye are not now to learn, that as of itself it is not hurtful, so neither should it be to any man[o] scandalous and offensive, in doubtful cases, to hear the different[p] judgment[q] of men. Be it that Cephas hath one interpretation, and Apollos hath another; that Paul is of this mind, and Barnabas of that; if this offend you, the fault is yours. Carry peaceable minds, and ye[r] may have comfort by this variety.

Now the God of peace give you peaceable minds, and turn it to your everlasting comfort.

f speech E.   g and I do wish om. E.   h of my E.   i of E.   k cause E.
l deny D.   m case om. E.   n Christ om. E.   o man om. E.
p indifferent E.   q judgments E.   r you E.

1 [Gal. iv. 12.]
2 [Contr. Joan. Ierosolym. § 2. t. ii. 409. C. ed. Vallars. "Nolo in suspicione hæreseos quenquam esse patientem; ne apud eos qui ignorant innocentiam ejus, dissimulatio conscientia judicetur, si taceat."]
3 James ii. 1.

PREFACE

THE REFORMATION OF THE LAWS

AND

ORDERS ECCLESIASTICAL

IN THE

CHURCH OF ENGLAND

THOUGH for no other cause, yet for this ; that posterity may know we have not loosely through silence permitted things to pass away as in a dream, there shall be for men's information extant thus much concerning the present state of the Church of God established amongst us, and their careful endeavour which would have upheld the same.[1] At your hands, beloved in our Lord and Saviour Jesus Christ, (for in him the love which we bear unto all that would but seem to be born of him, it is not the sea of your gall and bitterness that shall ever drown,) I have no great cause to look for other than the selfsame portion and lot, which your manner hath been hitherto to lay on them that concur not in opinion and sentence with you.[2] But our hope is, that

---

[1] [The same foreboding tone of thought is apparent in b. v. 79, 16.]

[2] [Christ. Letter, &c. p. 4. "May wee not trulie say, that under the shewe of inveighing against Puritanes, the chiefest pointes of popish blasphemie are many times and in many places by divers men not obscurelie broached, both in sermons and in writing . . . . and verelie such a thing offered itselfe unto our eyes, in reading your bookes, and we had not skill howe to judge otherwise of the handling of your penne and of the scope of your matter. Notwithstanding because rash judgement may prejudice honest travailes, and faithfull labourers may have their unadvised slippes, and we could not tell how zeale, love, or glorie, might carie a man of such towardlie and excellent giftes, in the first shewing of himselfe to the worlde ; or that an earnest striving and bending yourselfe in heate of disputation against the one side, might dazell your eyes, and draw your hand at unawares to farre and too favourable to the other side ; or else peradventure we might mistake your meaning, and so wee should doe you wrong against our willes.

the God of peace shall (notwithstanding man's nature too impatient of contumelious malediction) enable us quietly and even gladly to suffer all things, for that work sake which we covet to perform.

[2.] The wonderful zeal and fervour wherewith ye have withstood the received orders of this church, was the first thing which caused me to enter into consideration, whether (as all your published books and writings peremptorily maintain) every Christian man, fearing God, stand bound to join with you for the furtherance of that which ye term *the Lord's Discipline.* Wherein I must plainly confess unto you, that before I examined your sundry declarations in that behalf, it could not settle in my head to think, but that undoubtedly such numbers of otherwise right well affected and most religiously inclined minds had some marvellous reasonable inducements, which led them with so great earnestness that way. But when once, as near as my slender ability would serve, I had with travail and care performed that part of the Apostle's advice and counsel in such cases, whereby he willeth to " try all things," [1] and was come at the length so far, that there remained only the other clause to be satisfied, wherein he concludeth that " what good is must be held ;" there was in my poor under-standing no remedy, but to set down this as my final resolute persuasion : " Surely the present form of church-government which the laws of this land have established is such, as no law of God nor reason of man hath hitherto been alleged of force sufficient to prove they do ill, who to the uttermost of their power withstand the alteration thereof." Contrariwise, " The other, which instead of it

We thought it therefore our parte, in regarde of our dutie to the Church, and most agreeing to charitie, both for your credit and our ease, in all Christian love to intreat you, that as you tender the good estate of Christe's Church among us, and of thousands converted to the gospel, you would in like publike manner (but plainly and directlie) show unto us and all English protestants your owne true meaning, and how your wordes in divers thinges doe agree with the doctrine established among us." On which Hooker's note is, " That because they are loth to pre-judice honest travailes by rash judgment, and it might be they mistooke my meaning, they thought it fittest in charity, in great care of my credit, and in all Christian love, to set abroad their suspitions, and to give notise of alarm throughout hir majestie's dominions, till such time as my mind were explained unto them for satisfaction in their doubtes, wherby they might be the better furnished to satisfy others in my behalf."]

[1] [I Thess. v. 21.]

we are required to accept, is only by error and misconceit
named the ordinance of Jesus Christ, no one proof as yet
brought forth whereby it may clearly appear to be so in
very deed."

[3.] The explication of which two things I have here
thought good to offer into your own hands, heartily beseeching you even by the meekness of Jesus Christ, whom
I trust ye love ; that, as ye tender the peace and quietness
of this church, if there be in you that gracious humility
which hath ever been the crown and glory of a Christianly-
disposed mind, if your own souls, hearts, and consciences
(the sound integrity whereof can but hardly stand with the
refusal of truth in personal respects) be, as I doubt not but
they are, things most dear and precious unto you : "let not
the faith which ye have in our Lord Jesus Christ" be
blemished "with partialities ;"[1] regard not who it is which
speaketh, but weigh only what is spoken. Think not that
ye read the words of one who bendeth himself as an
adversary against the truth which ye have already embraced ; but the words of one who desireth even to
embrace together with you the selfsame truth, if it be the
truth ; and for that cause (for no other, God he knoweth)
hath undertaken the burdensome labour of this painful
kind of conference. For the plainer access whereunto, let
it be lawful for me to rip up to the very bottom, how and
by whom your discipline was planted, at such time as this
age we live in began to make first trial thereof.

II. [2] A founder it had, whom, for mine own part, I think
incomparably the wisest man that ever the French church
did enjoy, since the hour it enjoyed him. His bringing
up was in the study of the civil law. Divine knowledge he
gathered, not by hearing or reading so much, as by teaching
others. For, though thousands were debtors to him, as
touching knowledge in that kind ; yet he to none but only
to God, the author of that most blessed fountain, the Book
of Life, and of the admirable dexterity of wit, together with
the helps of other learning which were his guides : till
being occasioned to leave France, he fell at the length upon
Geneva ; which city the bishop and clergy thereof had a

[1] James ii. 1.
[2] [Compare the second chapter of Abp. Bancroft's Survey of the pretended Holy Discipline : in which a similar sketch is given of Calvin's
proceedings at Geneva.]

little before (as some do affirm) forsaken,[1] being of likelihood frighted with the people's sudden attempt for abolishment of Popish religion : the event of which enterprize they thought it not safe for themselves to wait for in that place. At the coming of Calvin thither,[2] the form of their civil regiment was popular, as it continueth at this day : neither king, nor duke, nor nobleman of any authority or power over them, but officers chosen by the people yearly out of themselves, to order all things with public consent.   For spiritual government, they had no laws at all agreed upon, but did what the pastors of their souls by persuasion could win them unto.   Calvin, being admitted one of their preachers, and a divinity reader amongst them, considered how dangerous it was that the whole estate of that church should hang still on so slender a thread, as the liking of an ignorant multitude is, if it have power to change whatsoever itself listeth.   Wherefore taking unto him two of the other ministers [3] for more countenance of the action, (albeit the rest were all against it,) they moved, and in the end persuaded [4] with much ado, the people to bind themselves by solemn oath, first never to admit the Papacy amongst them again ; and secondly, to live in obedience unto such orders concerning the exercise of their religion, and the form of their ecclesiastical government, as those their true and faithful ministers of God's word had agreeably to scripture set down for that end and purpose.

[2.] When these things began to be put in ure, the people also (what causes moving them thereunto, themselves best know) began to repent them of that they had done, and irefully to champ upon the bit they had taken into their mouths ; the rather, for that they grew by means of this innovation into dislike with some churches near about them,

---

[1] [Pierre de la Baume, of a noble family in France, was the last bishop acknowledged in Geneva. " Il partit à la mi-Juillet [1533] pour se ranger au party de Savoye contre la Ville." Besides the agitation occasioned by the new opinions, he was at the time engaged in a dispute with the Syndics regarding the judicial prerogative. Spon. Hist. de Genève, I. 344. Aug. 27, 1535, Protestantism was established by ordinance of the Syndics. ibid. p. 366.]

[2] [Aug. 1536. He was on his way to Basle or Strasburgh, but went round by Geneva on account of the war, and was persuaded by Farel to remain. Spon. II. p. 14.]

[3] [Farel and Couraut. Beza, Vit. Calv. prefixed to his works Gen. 1617 : from which most of these particulars are taken.]

[4] [20 July, 1537.]

the benefit of whose good friendship their state could not well lack.[1]

It was the manner of those times (whether through men's desire to enjoy alone the glory of their own enterprizes, or else because the quickness of their occasions required present dispatch; so it was,) that every particular church did that within itself, which some few of their own thought good, by whom the rest were all directed. Such number of churches then being, though free within themselves, yet small, common conference beforehand might have eased them of much after trouble.[2] But a greater inconvenience it bred, that every later endeavoured to be certain degrees more removed from conformity with the church of Rome, than the rest before had been:[3] whereupon grew marvellous great dissimilitudes, and by reason thereof, jealousies, heart-burnings, jars and discords amongst them. Which, notwithstanding, might have easily been prevented, if the orders, which each church did think fit and convenient for itself, had not so peremptorily been established under that high commanding form, which tendered them unto the people, as things everlastingly required by the law of that Lord of lords, against whose statutes there is no exception to be taken. For by this mean it came to pass, that one church could not but accuse and condemn another of disobedience to the will of Christ, in those things where manifest difference was between them: whereas the selfsame orders allowed, but yet established in

---

[1] ["Sous pretexte de conserver les libertez de la ville, et de ce qu'ils n'avoient pas voulu se conformer à l'usage de Berne pour la Communion, ils firent prononcer un arrêt au Conseil," &c. Spon. II. 18.]

[2] [Chr. Letter, p. 39. "You blame them, that in that troublesome time they wanted common conference." Hooker, MS. note. "No man blamed for those defects, which necessity casteth upon him."]

[3] [Chr. Letter, p. 43. "The Church of Rome favourablie admitted to be of the house of God; Calvin with the reformed churches full of faults, and *most of all they which indevoured to be most removed from conformitie with the Church of Rome.*"

Hooker, MS. note. "True. For are not your Anabaptists, Familists, Libertines, Arrians, and other like extreme reformers of popery grown by that very meanes hatefull to the whole world? Are not their heresies a thousand times more execrable and hatefull than popery?

"Is it then a matter heinous to looke awry upon any man which hath been earnest against the Pope? As earnest men that way as M. Calvin are nothing spared by you and yours in any such conflict. You honour Calvin as the father of discipline: this is the boil that will not be touched."]

more wary and suspense manner, as being to stand in force
till God should give the opportunity of some general
conference what might be best for every of them afterwards
to do ; this I say had both prevented all occasion of just
dislike which others might take, and reserved a greater
liberty unto the authors themselves of entering into farther
consultation afterwards. Which though never so necessary
they could not easily now admit, without some fear of
derogation from their credit : and therefore that which once
they had done, they became for ever after resolute to
maintain.

Calvin therefore and the other two his associates, stiffly
refusing to administer the holy Communion to such as would
not quietly, without contradiction and murmur, submit
themselves unto the orders which their solemn oath had
bound them to obey, were in that quarrel banished the
town.[1]

[3.] A few years after[2] (such was the levity of that people)
the places of one or two of their ministers being fallen void,
they were not before so willing to be rid of their learned
pastor, as now importunate to obtain him again from them
who had given him entertainment, and which were loath to
part with him, had not unresistable earnestness been used.
One of the town ministers, that saw in what manner the
people were bent for the revocation of Calvin, gave him
notice of their affection in this sort.[3] "The senate of two
hundred being assembled, they all crave Calvin. The next
day a general convocation ; they cry in like sort again all,
We will have Calvin, that good and learned man, Christ's
minister. This," saith he, "when I understood, I could
not choose but praise God, nor was I able to judge otherwise than that 'this was the Lord's doing, and that it was
marvellous in our eyes,' and that 'the stone which the builders

---

[1] [MS. note on Chr. Letter, p. 39. "De Calvino vere quod Tullius
de Q. Metel. 'De civitate decedere maluit quam de sententia.' Orat.
vol. iii. p. 151. Oratione pro Balbo." c. 5.]

[2] [1541, 1 May. Spon. II. 25.]

[3] Epist. Cal. 24, [p. 27, ed. Gen. 1617. "In crastinum Ducentorum
congregatur concilium, et omnes petunt Calvinum : congregatur et
generale sequenti die, itidem clamant omnes, Calvinum probum et
doctum virum Christi ministrum volumus. Quod cum intellexissem,
non potui non laudare Deum, aliterque [neque aliter ?] judicare, quam
quod a Domino es et factum istud, et esset mirabile in oculis nostris :
quodque lapidem quem reprobarant ædificantes in caput fieret anguli."
Bernard to Calvin. 6 Feb. 1541.]

refused, was now made the head of the corner.'"[1]   The other two[2] whom they had thrown out, (together with Calvin,) they were content should enjoy their exile.   Many causes might lead them to be more desirous of him.   First, his yielding unto them in one thing might happily put them in hope, that time would breed the like easiness of condescending further unto them.   For in his absence he had persuaded them, with whom he was able to prevail, that albeit himself did better like of common bread to be used in the Eucharist, yet the other they rather should accept, than cause any trouble in the Church about it.[3]   Again, they saw that the name of Calvin waxed every day greater abroad,[4] and that together with his fame, their infamy was spread, which had so rashly and childishly ejected him.   Besides, it was not unlikely but that his credit in the world might many ways stand the poor town in great stead : as the truth is, their minister's foreign estimation hitherto hath been the best stake in their hedge.   But whatsoever secret respects were likely to move them ; for contenting of their minds Calvin returned (as it had been another Tully) to his old home.

[4.]   He ripely considered how gross a thing it were for men of his quality, wise and grave men, to live with such a multitude, and to be tenants at will under them, as their ministers, both himself and others, had been.   For the remedy of which inconvenience, he gave them plainly to understand, that if he did become their teacher again, they must be content to admit a complete form of discipline, which both they and also their pastors should now be solemnly sworn to observe for ever after.   Of which discipline the main and principal parts were these :   A standing

---

[1] Luke xx. 17.   [Ps. cxviii. 22, 23.]

[2] [There seems to be a slight oversight here.   Farel and Couraut (not Viret) were the two ejected with Calvin in 1538.   Couraut died the same year.   (Calv. Ep. p. 10.)   Viret was before that time settled at Lausanne, but returned to Geneva for a time to assist Calvin in the new settlement, 1541 ; as did Farel from Neufchatel, where he had obtained an appointment.   Bayle, art. Viret. Spon. II. 19, 25.]

[3] [Calvinus bonos nonnullos ista mutatione usque adeo offensos, ut etiam a cœna sibi abstinendum putarent, serio monuit, ne ob istud ἀδιάφορον litem moverent."   Beza. Vit. Calv.]

[4] [By his theological lectures at Strasburgh ;   his settlement of the church there ;   his defence of the church itself of Geneva against Cardinal Sadolet ;   his Institutes, Commentary on the Romans, and Book on the Lord's Supper.]

ecclesiastical court to be established; perpetual judges in that court to be their ministers; others of the people to be annually chosen (twice so many in number as they) to be judges together with them in the same court: these two sorts to have the care of all men's manners, power of determining all kind of ecclesiastical causes, and authority to convent, to control, to punish, as far as with excommunication, whomsoever they should think worthy, none either small or great excepted.

This device I see not how the wisest at that time living could have bettered, if we duly consider what the present estate of Geneva did then require. For their bishop and his clergy being (as it is said) departed from them by moonlight, or howsoever, being departed; to choose in his room any other bishop, had been a thing altogether impossible. And for their ministers to seek that themselves alone might have coercive power over the whole church, would perhaps have been hardly construed at that time. But when so frank an offer was made, that for every one minister there should be two of the people to sit and give voice in the ecclesiastical consistory, what inconvenience could they easily find which themselves might not be able always to remedy?

Howbeit (as evermore the simpler sort, are even when they see no apparent cause, jealous notwithstanding over the secret intents and purposes of wiser men) this proposition of his did somewhat trouble them. Of the ministers themselves which had stayed behind in the city when Calvin was gone, some, upon knowledge of the people's earnest intent to recall him to his place again, had beforehand written their letters of submission, and assured him of their allegiance for ever after, if it should like him to hearken unto that public suit. But yet misdoubting what might happen, if this discipline did go forward; they objected against it the example of other reformed churches living quietly and orderly without it. Some of chiefest place and countenance amongst the laity professed with greater stomach their judgments, that such a discipline was little better than Popish tyranny disguised and tendered unto them under a new form.[1]

---

[1] [Capito, of Basle, writes thus to Farel in Calvin's Epist. p. 6. "Auditis, 'Tyranni esse voluistis in liberam ecclesiam, voluistis novum Pontificatum revocare.' Beza: Non deerant . . . . qui Papisticam tyrannidem sic revocari clamitarent."]

This sort, it may be,[1] had some fear, that the filling up of the seats in the consistory with so great a number of

---

[1] [Chr. Letter, p. 39. "After speaking of his restoring and re-establishing of discipline, you have in one place, 'Many things might lead them (to be more desirous of him.') And in another place, 'he rightelie considered,' &c. 'This devise I see not howe the wisest,' &c. Therefore we pray you to tell us how such 'might lead' and 'may bees,' such entring into his thought, and crosse comme ding that for his divise which he simply propounded as out of the scriptures of God, may not drop into your reader's heart such unheeded impressions, as may make him highly admire R. H. great gravitie and judicious wise-dome, and J. Calvin's carnall policie, fine hipocrisie and peremptorie follie." Hooker, MS. note. "Safer to discuss all the saincts in heaven than M. Calvin. Howe bold they are themselves with as great men as M. Calvin, namely, Chrysostome, Jerome, Ambroe, Austin. Calvin himself not hereby justifyed from censuring both the deedes and writings of men which went before him.—The acts of every present age most sincerely judged of by posterity. While men are living the judgment of their friends is perverted with love, the verdict of their enimies corrupt through envie.

"That Calvin's bitternes was a great cause to augment his troble. His nature from a child observed by his own parents, as Beza noteth, was propense to sharpe and severe reprehension where he thought any falt was." ('Destinabat eum pater ab initio theologiæ studiis, ad quæ ultro illum inclinare ex eo colligebat, quod in illa etiam tenera ætate mirum in modum religiosus esset, et severus omnium in suis sodalibus vitiorum censor.') And this not to be misliked in him.

"But his maner of dealing against them which were in deed bad men was that which wrought him self much woe, and did them no good. His frends saw this, as appeareth by his 95 Epist. unto Farellus. [N. suo more rescripsisse non infitiatus est Bucerus. Nam hoc unum causatus est cur mihi non recitaret, quia nollet mihi frustra stomachum movere. Hinc collige quantum amarulentiæ fuerit, quod ille judicavit pro sua prudentia non posse a me sine graviore offensione transmitti," p. 338.] "His own wordes declaring how in his sermons he handled and delt with his adversaries, Epist. 15." ["Ita ejus impietatem palam et aperte etiam pro concione sugillabam, ut nihilo minus aut ipsi aut aliis dubius esset sermo, quam si vel nominassem, vel digito demonstrassem." p. 19. On his death bed he thus expressed himself to the senators of Geneva: "Ultro certe agnosco me vobis hoc quoque nomine plurimum debere, quod vehementiam illam meam interdum immoderatam æquo animo tulistis." Beza.] "His usage of H. 8, hir M. father that now is. Such courses condemned by Beza in the fourth of his Epistles against one Adrian a Dutch minister, p. 42." ("Hoc certe non fuit vel prudentis vel boni etiam pastoris in illustrissimum illum Principem nominatim declamare.")

Id. note on p. 37. "Remember to make a comparison between Calvin and Beza, how different they were in naturall disposition, and yeat how linked in amity and concord, Calvin being of a stiff nature, Beza of a pliable, the one stern and severe, the other tractable and gentle. Both wise and discreet men. Whereby we see what it is for any one church or place of government to have two, one succeeding

laymen was but to please the minds of the people, to the
end they might think their own sway somewhat; but when
things came to trial of practice, their pastors' learning would
be at all times of force to over-persuade simple men, who
knowing the time of their own presidentship to be but short
would always stand in fear of their ministers' perpetual
authority : and among the ministers themselves, one being
so far in estimation above the rest, the voices of the rest
were likely to be given for the most part respectively, with
a kind of secret dependency and awe : so that in show a
marvellous indifferently composed senate ecclesiastical was
to govern, but in effect one only man should, as the spirit
and soul of the residue, do all in all.[1]   But what did these
vain surmises boot? Brought they were now to so straight
an issue, that of two things they must choose one : namely,
whether they would to their endless disgrace, with ridiculous
lightness dismiss him whose restitution they had in so
impotent manner desired; or else condescend unto that
demand, wherein he was resolute either to have it, or to
leave them.   They thought it better to be somewhat hardly
yoked at home, than for ever abroad discredited.   Wherefore in the end those orders were on all sides assented unto :
with no less alacrity of mind than cities unable to hold out
longer are wont to shew, when they take conditions such as
it liketh him to offer them which hath them in the narrow
straits of advantage.

[5.] Not many years were over-passed, before these twice-
sworn men adventured to give their last and hottest assault

another, and both in theire waies excellent, although unlike. For Beza
was one whom no man would displease, Calvin one whom no man
durst. His dependants both abroad and at home ; his intelligence from
forrein churches ; his correspondence every where with the chiefest ;
his industry in pursuing them which did at any time openly either withstand his proceedings or gainsay his opinions ; his booke intitled,
'contra Nebulonem quendam ;' his writing but of three lines in disgrace of any man as forcible as any proscription throughout all reformed
churches ; his rescripts and answeres of as great authority as decretall
epistles. His grace in preaching the meanest of all other guilts
in him," ['Facundiæ contemptor et verborum parcus.' Beza.] "yeat
even that way so had in honour and estimation, that an hearer of
his being asked wherfore he came not sometime to other men's
sermons as well as Calvin's, answered, That if Calvin and S. Paul
himself should preach both in one hower, he would leave S. Paul to
heare Calvin.   Zanch. tom. VII. Epist. ante Miscell."   This reference
is from the C. C. C. Transcript.]
   [1] Compare Bancroft, Survey, p. 20.]

to the fortress of the same discipline; childishly granting
by common consent of their whole senate, and that under
their town seal, a relaxation to one Bertelier, whom the
eldership had excommunicated:[1] further also decreeing,
with strange absurdity, that to the same senate it should
belong to give final judgment in matter of excommunication,
and to absolve whom it pleased them : clean contrary to their
own former deeds and oaths.   The report of which decree
being forthwith brought unto Calvin; "Before," saith he,
"this decree take place, either my blood or banishment
shall sign it."   Again, two days before the communion
should be celebrated, his speech was publickly to like effect :
"Kill me if ever this hand do reach forth the things that
are holy to them whom The Church hath judged despisers."[2]
Whereupon, for fear of tumult, the forenamed Bertelier was
by his friends advised for that time not to use the liberty
granted him by the senate, nor to present himself in the
church, till they saw somewhat further what would ensue.
After the communion quietly ministered, and some likelihood of peaceable ending of these troubles without any
more ado, that very day in the afternoon, besides all men's
expectation, concluding his ordinary sermon, he telleth
them, that because he neither had learned nor taught to
strive with such as are in authority, "therefore," saith he,
"the case so standing as now it doth, let me use these
words of the apostle unto you, 'I commend you unto God
and the word of his grace;'"[3] and so bade them heartily
all adieu.[4]

[6.] It sometimes cometh to pass, that the readiest way

---

[1] [Calv. Epist. p. 163.]

[2] ["Inter concionandum, elata voce ac manu, multa de sacris
mysteriis in eorum contemptores locutus : 'At ego, inquit, Chrysosto-
mum secutus vim quidem non opponam, sed ultro me potius occidi
facile patiar, quam hæc manus contemptoribus Dei, rite judicatis, sancta
Domini porrigat.'"   Beza.]

[3] [Acts xx. 32.]

[4] ["Locum illum insignem Actorum Apostolicorum forte tractans, in
quo Paulus Ecclesiæ Ephesinæ valedicit, testatus se eum non esse, qui
adversus magistratum pugnare sciret aut doceret, cætumque multis
verbis cohortatus, ut in ea quam audivisset doctrina perseveraret,
tandem, veluti postremam hanc concionem Genevæ habiturus, 'Et
quandoquidem, inquit, ita se res habent, liceat mihi quoque, fratres,
apud vos hæc Apostoli verba usurpare, Commendo vos Deo et sermoni
gratiæ ipsius :' quæ voces tum sceleratos illos mirifice perculerunt, tum
bonos etiam tanto magis serio officii admonuerunt."   Beza.]

which a wise man hath to conquer, is to fly. This voluntary and unexpected mention of sudden departure caused presently the senate (for according to their wonted manner they still continued only constant in unconstancy) to gather themselves together, and for a time to suspend their own decree, leaving things to proceed as before till they had heard the judgment of four Helvetian cities [1] concerning the matter which was in strife. This to have done at the first before they gave assent unto any order had shewed some wit and discretion in them : but now to do it was as much as to say in effect, that they would play their parts on a stage. Calvin therefore dispatcheth with all expedition his letters unto some principal pastor in every of those cities, craving earnestly at their hands, to respect this cause as a thing whereupon the whole state of religion and piety in that church did so much depend, that God and all good men were now inevitably certain to be trampled under foot, unless those four cities by their good means might be brought to give sentence with the ministers of Geneva, when the cause should be brought before them : yea so to give it, that two things it might effectually contain ; the one an absolute approbation of the discipline of Geneva as consonant unto the word of God, without any cautions, qualifications, ifs or ands ; the other an earnest admonition not to innovate or change the same. His vehement request herein as touching both points was satisfied. For albeit the said Helvetian churches did never as yet observe that discipline, nevertheless, the senate of Geneva having required their judgment concerning these three questions : First, " After what manner, by God's commandment, according to the scripture and unspotted religion, excommunication is to be exercised : " Secondly, " Whether it may not be exercised some other way than by the consistory : " Thirdly, " What the use of their churches was to do in this case : " [2] answer was returned from the said churches, " That they had heard already of those consistorial laws, and did acknowledge them to be *godly* ordinances *drawing towards* the prescript of the word of God ; for which cause they did not think it good for *the Church of Geneva* by innovation to

---

[1] [Zurich, Berne, Schaffhausen, Basle. See the letters from Calvin to Viret and Bullinger, and the case submitted to the Church of Zurich, with Bullinger's answer, in Calvin's Epistles, p. 163–171.]

[2] Epist. 166.

change the same, but rather to keep them as they were."[1]
Which answer, although not answering unto the former
demands, but respecting what Master Calvin had judged
requisite for them to answer, was notwithstanding accepted
without any further reply : in as much as they plainly saw,
that when stomach doth strive with wit, the match is not
equal. And so the heat of their former contentions began
to slake.

[7.] The present inhabitants of Geneva, I hope, will not
take it in evil part, that the faultiness of their people heretofore is by us so far forth laid open, as their own learned
guides and pastors have thought necessary to discover it
unto the world. For out of their books and writings it is
that I have collected this whole narration, to the end it
might thereby appear in what sort amongst them that
discipline was planted, for which so much contention is
raised amongst ourselves. The reason which moved Calvin
herein to be so earnest, was, as Beza himself testifieth,[2]
"For that he saw how needful these bridles were, to be put
in the jaws of that city." That which by wisdom he saw
to be requisite for that people, was by as great wisdom
compassed.

But wise men are men, and the truth is truth. That
which Calvin did for establishment of his discipline, seemeth
more commendable than that which he taught for the
countenancing of it established.[3] Nature worketh in us all

---

[1] [Bullinger to Calvin, Epist. p. 170. "Dudum audivisse nos de
legibus istius Ecclesiæ Consistorialibus, et agnoscere illas pias esse, et
accedere ad verbi Dei præscriptum : ideoque non videri admittendum
ut per innovationem mutentur." Calvin's own statement of the affair
may be found in his correspondence, p. 163–172.]

[2] "Quod eam urbem videret omnino his frænis indigere."

[3] [Chr. Letter, p. 42. "If such bold and bare affirmations may go
for payment, why may wee not as well heare and believe Maister
Harding, which calles all the whole and pure doctrine beleeved and
professed in England, A wicked new devise of Geneva?"

Hooker, MS. note. "Do not you yourself call the discipline which
they use in Geneva, a new found discipline? p. 45. If it be a new
found thing, and not found elsewhere till Geneva had erected it, yourself must say of discipline, It is a new devise of Geneva : except you
recant your opinion concerning the newnes of it. For all the world
doth know that the first practise thereof was in Geneva. You graunt-
ing it to be but a new found thing must either shew us some author
more ancient, or els acknowledge it as we do to have been there devised.
If you excuse the speech and say it is ironicall, you betray yourself to
be a favourer of that part, and confess yourself an egregious dissembler.

a love to our own counsels. The contradiction of others
is a fan to inflame that love. Our love set on fire to maintain that which once we have done, sharpeneth the wit to
dispute, to argue, and by all means to reason for it. Wherefore a marvel it were if a man of so great capacity, having
such incitements to make him desirous of all kind of
furtherances unto his cause, could espy in the whole
Scripture of God nothing which might breed at the least a
probable opinion of likelihood, that divine authority itself
was the same way somewhat inclinable. And all which the
wit even of Calvin was able from thence to draw, by sifting
the very utmost sentence and syllable, is no more than that
certain speeches there are which to him did seem to intimate
that all Christian churches ought to have their elderships
endued with power of excommunication, and that a part of
those elderships every where should be chosen out from
amongst the laity, after that form which himself had framed
Geneva unto. But what argument are ye able to shew,
whereby it was ever proved by Calvin, that any one sentence
of Scripture doth necessarily enforce these things, or the
rest wherein your opinion concurreth with his against the
orders of your own church?

[8.] We should be injurious unto virtue itself, if we did
derogate from them whom their industry hath made great.
Two things of principal moment there are which have
deservedly procured him honour throughout the world : the
one his exceeding pains in composing the Institutions of
Christian religion ; the other his no less industrious travails
for exposition of holy Scripture according unto the same
Institutions. In which two things whosoever they were that
after him bestowed their labour, he gained the advantage of

"Because the anti-Trinitarians doe say, that our doctrine of the
glorious and blessed Trinity is a wicked new devise of the Pope, will
you say that this may as well be believed as their speech which say that
sundry other things in the papacie are both new and wicked ? Although
I terme not their discipline wicked for mine owne part. Only I hold
it a new devise."

The passage referred to stands thus in p. 45 of the Chr. Letter: " Is
that new found discipline so nearlie seated with our English creed, that
such expert archers ayming at the one must needes hit the other ?" On
which Hooker's note is, " A new found discipline ! who is able to
endure such blasphemy ? You speake but in jest. Were it known
that you meane as you say, surely those wordes might cost you deare.
But they are incident into your part, and have in that respect their safe
conduct."]

prejudice against them, if they gainsayed ; and of glory above them, if they consented. His writings published after the question about that discipline was once begun omit not any the least occasion of extolling the use and singular necessity thereof. Of what account the Master of Sentences[1] was in the church of Rome, the same and more amongst the preachers of reformed churches Calvin had purchased ; so that the perfectest divines were judged they, which were skilfullest in Calvin's writings. His books almost the very canon to judge both doctrine and discipline by.[2] French churches, both under others abroad and at home in their own country, all cast according to that mould which Calvin had made. The church of Scotland in erecting the fabric of their reformation took the selfsame pattern. Till at length the discipline, which was at the first so weak, that without the staff of their approbation, who were not subject unto it themselves, it had not brought others under subjection, began now to challenge universal obedience,[3] and to enter into open conflict with those very churches, which in desperate extremity had been relievers of it.

[9.] To one of those churches which lived in most peaceable sort, and abounded as well with men for their learning in other professions singular, as also with divines whose equals were not elsewhere to be found, a church ordered by Gualter's discipline, and not by that which Geneva adoreth ; unto this church, the church of Heidelburg, there cometh one who craving leave to dispute publicly defendeth with open disdain of their government, that "to a minister with his eldership power is given by the law of God to ex-

---

[1] [Peter Lombard. A.D. 1141. See Cave, Hist. Lit. I. 667, and Heumann ap Brucker. Hist. Phil. III. 717. "Fastigium summum theologiæ scholasticæ assecutus illi ætati visus est, ejusque vestigiis insistere pulchrum duxit ipsius posteritas scholastica."]

[2] ["What should the world doe with the old musty doctors? Alleage scripture, and shew it alleaged in the sense that Calvin alloweth, and it is of more force in any man's defense, and to the proofe of any assertion, than if ten thousand Augustines, Jeromes, Chrysostomes, Cyprians, or whosoever els were brought foorth. Doe we not daily see that men are accused of heresie for holding that which the fathers held, and that they never are cleere, if they find not somewhat in Calvin to justify themselves?" MS. note of Hooker in the title-page of "A Christian Letter," &c.]

[3] ["Two things there are which trouble greatly these later times: one that the Church of Rome cannot, another that Geneva will not erre." MS. note of Hooker on Chr. Letter, p. 37.]

communicate whomsoever, yea even kings and princes themselves."[1] Here were the seeds sown of that controversy which sprang up between Beza and Erastus about the matter of excommunication, whether there ought to be in all churches an eldership having power to excommunicate, and a part of that eldership to be of necessity certain chosen out from amongst the laity for that purpose. In which disputation they have, as to me it seemeth, divided very equally the truth between them ; Beza most truly maintaining the necessity of excommunication, Erastus as truly the non-necessity of lay-elders to be ministers thereof.

[10.] Amongst ourselves, there was in King Edward's days some question moved by reason of a few men's scrupulosity[2] touching certain things. And beyond seas, of them which fled in the days of Queen Mary, some contenting themselves abroad with the use of their own servicebook at home authorized before their departure out of the realm, others liking better the Common Prayer-book of the Church of Geneva translated, those smaller contentions before begun were by this means somewhat increased.[3] Under the happy reign of her Majesty which now is, the greatest

---

[1] [" Accidit, ut Anglus quidam, qui propter rem vestiariam ex Anglia ferebatur excessisse, doctoris titulo cuperet insigniri, et de adiaphoris et vestibus disputationem proponeret. Hanc theologi admittere noluerunt, ne scilicet Anglos offenderent, ... ut autem nostræ res turbarentur, pro nihilo, ut videtur, duxerunt. Quare inter alias hanc thesin proposuit ; oportere in quavis recte constituta ecclesia hanc servari procurationem, in qua ministri cum suo delecto ad eam rem presbyterio ius teneant, quosvis peccantes, etiam Principes, excommunicandi." Erastus, Præf. Thesium. The dispute occurred A.D. 1568. But the work was not published till after Erastus' death, 1589 : the dispute having been quieted for the time by the interference of the Church of Zurich, and Frederic, Elector Palatine. Beza replied, 1590, by his tract " de vera Excommunicatione et Christiano Presbyterio :" in the Preface to which he charges the publisher of Erastus' work as follows, " An boni et pii homines auctores tibi fuerunt, ut clam ista excuderes? ut pro Londini, vel alterius in Anglia civitatis nomine, Presclavium fictitium supponeres?" And in a letter to Whitgift, (Strype, Whitg. III. 302,) he intimates the same : and Whitgift in his reply (II. 168) allows it, though disclaiming all connivance at the publication on his own part.]

[2] [See Strype, Cranm. I. 302-309. Mem. II. i. 350-354. Burnet, Reform. II. 282, III. 349-351. Wordsworth's Eccl. Biog. II. 437-440.]

[3] [See Strype, Grind. 13-16. Mem. II. 404-411. Burnet II. 612, and especially "Troubles at Frankfort," (of which book vid. Strype, An. II. i. 482,) in Phœnix II. 44, &c.]

matter awhile contended for was the wearing of the cap and
surplice,[1] till there came Admonitions [2] directed unto the
high court of Parliament, by men who concealing their
names thought it glory enough to discover their minds and
affections, which now were universally bent even against all
the orders and laws, wherein this church is found unconformable to the platform of Geneva.[3]   Concerning the

[1] [In the convocation of 1562, about half of the lower house were for
concession in these and one or two other points. (Strype, Ann. I. i.
499–506.) In 1564, complaints having been made from different
quarters of positive molestation given by the nonconformists, Archbishop
Parker endeavoured to enforce conformity, but was checked by the
interest of the Puritans with Lord Leicester ; so that he could not
obtain the royal sanction for the " Advertisements" then issued, (Str.
Parker, I. 300–345. Ann. I. ii. 125–175,) until the following year ;
when they occasioned several deprivations in the diocese of London.
(Parker I. 420–460. Grind. 142–146.) In 1567 this had led to the
establishment of conventicles, (Parker I. 478. Grind. 168,) and more
extensive reform began to be talked of, (Ann. I. ii. 349.) especially in
1570, at Cambridge, which caused Cartwright's expulsion (ibid. 372.)
In 1571, a bill of alterations was proposed in parliament, which
occasioning the Queen's interference, had the effect, as it should seem,
of preventing the adoption of the " Reformatio Legum Ecclesiasti-
carum," which the archbishop at the time had thoughts of, (An. II. i.
93–99. P. II. 62, 63.)]

[2] [The rejection of Mr. Strickland's bill abovementioned, by the
parliament of 1571, led to the immediate publication of the first
" Admonition to the Parliament." It was so eagerly read, that it went
through four editions before the end of 1572, (Parker II. 110,) in which
year Field and Wilcox were imprisoned for it. (Ann. II. i. 274.
Parker II. 139.)]

[3] [Bishop Cooper, Adm. to the People of England, p. 160, takes the
following view of the gradual advance of Puritanism. "At the beginning, some learned and godly preachers, for private respects in themselves, made strange to wear the surplice, cap, or tippet : but yet so that
they declared themselves to think the thing indifferent, and not to judge
evil of such as did use them." (He seems to mean Grindal, Sandys,
Parkhurst, Nowel, and others, 1562.) " Shortly after rose up other,"
(Sampson, Humfrey, Lever, Whittingham, &c.) " defending that they
were not things indifferent, but distained with antichristian idolatry,
and therefore not to be suffered in the Church. Not long after came
another sort," (Cartwright, Travers, Field, &c.) " affirming that those
matters touching apparel were but trifles, and not worthy contention in
the Church, but that there were greater things far of more weight and
importance, and indeed touching faith and religion, and therefore meet
to be altered in a church rightly reformed. As the Book of Common
Prayer, the administration of the Sacraments, the government of the
Church, the election of ministers, and a number of other like. Fourthly,
now break out another sort," (the Brownists,) " earnestly affirming, and
teaching, that we have no church, no bishops, no ministers, no sacraments ; and therefore that all that love Jesus Christ ought with all

Defender [1] of which Admonitions, all that I mean to say is but this : *there will come a time when three words uttered with charity and meekness shall receive a far more blessed reward than three thousand volumes written with disdainful sharpness of wit.* But the manner of men's writing must not alienate our hearts from the truth, if it appear they have the truth ; as the followers of the same defender do think he hath ; and in that persuasion they follow him, no otherwise than himself doth Calvin, Beza, and others, with the like persuasion that they in this cause had the truth. We being as fully persuaded otherwise, it resteth that some kind of trial be used to find out which part is in error.

III. The first mean whereby nature teacheth men to judge good from evil, as well in laws as in other things, is the force of their own discretion. Hereunto therefore St. Paul referreth oftentimes his own speech, to be considered of by them that heard him. " I speak as to them which have understanding, judge ye what I say." [2] Again afterward, " Judge in yourselves, is it comely that a woman pray uncovered ? " [3] The exercise of this kind of judgment our Saviour requireth in the Jews.[4] In them of Berea the Scripture commendeth it.[5] Finally, whatsoever we do, if our own secret judgment consent not unto it as fit and good to be done, the doing of it to us is sin, although the thing itself be allowable. St. Paul's rule therefore generally is, " Let every man in his own mind be fully persuaded of that thing which he either alloweth or doth." [6]

[2.] Some things are so familiar and plain, that truth from falsehood, and good from evil, is most easily discerned in them, even by men of no deep capacity. And of that nature, for the most part, are things absolutely unto all men's salvation

speed to separate themselves from our congregations, because our assemblies are profane, wicked, and antichristian. Thus have you heard of four degrees for the overthrow of the state of the Church of England. Now lastly of all come in these men, that make their whole direction against the living of bishops and other ecclesiastical ministers : that they should have no temporal lands or jurisdiction."]

[1] [Thomas Cartwright. Whitgift's Answer to the Admonition was sent to Parker, Oct. 21, 1572, (Str. Whitg. I. 86,) and replied to by T. C. early the next year. For Whitgift was far advanced in his Defence, June 4, 1573: (Park. II. 254:) and it was sent to Lord Burghley, 5 Feb. 157¾. Cartwright's 2nd Reply came out in two portions, 1575 and 1577.]

[2] 1 Cor. x. 15.　　　　[3] Ibid. xi. 13.　　　　[4] Luke xii. 56, 57.
[5] Acts xvii. 11.　　　　　　　　　[6] Rom. xiv. 5.

necessary, either to be held or denied, either to be done or avoided. For which cause St. Augustine [1] acknowledgeth, that they are not only set down, but also plainly set down in Scripture ; so that he which heareth or readeth may without any great difficulty understand. Other things also there are belonging (though in a lower degree of importance) unto the offices of Christian men : which, because they are more obscure, more intricate and hard to be judged of, therefore God hath appointed some to spend their whole time principally in the study of things divine, to the end that in these more doubtful cases their understanding might be a light to direct others. "If the understanding power or faculty of the soul be" (saith the grand physician [2]) "like unto bodily sight, not of equal sharpness in all, what can be more convenient than that, even as the dark-sighted man is directed by the clear about things visible ; so likewise in matters of deeper discourse the wise in heart do shew the simple where his way lieth ? " In our doubtful cases of law, what man is there who seeth not how requisite it is that professors of skill in that faculty be our directors ? So it is in all other kinds of knowledge. And even in this kind likewise the Lord hath himself appointed, that "the priest's lips should preserve knowledge, and that other men should seek the truth at his mouth, *because* he is the messenger of the Lord of hosts." [3] Gregory Nazianzen, offended at the people's too great presumption in controlling the judgment of them to whom in such cases they should have rather submitted their own, seeketh by earnest entreaty to stay them within their bounds : "Presume not ye that are sheep to make yourselves guides of them that should guide you ; neither seek ye to overskip the fold which they about you have pitched. It sufficeth for your part, if ye can well frame yourselves to be ordered. Take

---

[1] [De peccator. merit. et remiss. t. x. p. 59, where after mentioning a certain obscure subject, he adds, "Credo quod etiam hinc divinorum eloquiorum claissima auctoritas esset, si homo id sine dispendio promissæ salutis ignorare non posset." And t. x. p. 71, the marginal note is, "Scripturæ claræ in his quæ ad salutem necessariæ sunt."]

[2] Galen. de opt. docen. gen. [Εἰ δ᾽ ἔοτι μὲν, ὥσπερ ὀφθαλμὸς τῷ σώματι, τοιοῦτος ἐν τῇ ψυχῇ νοῦς, οὐ μὴν ἅπασί γε ὁμοίως ὀξὺς, ἐγχωρεῖ καθάπερ βλέπων ὀξύτερον ἐπάγει πρὸς τὸ θέαμα τὸν ἀμβλύτερον ὁρῶντα, κατὰ τὸν αὐτὸν τρόπον καὶ ἐπὶ τῶν νοημάτων, ὑπὸ τῶν φθασάντων ἰδεῖν ἐναργῶς τὸ νοητὸν ἐπάγεσθαι πρὸς τὴν θέασιν αὐτῆς τὸν ἀμβλύτατον. (qu. ἀμβλύτερον?) t. i. p. 8. Basil, 1538.]

[3] Mal. ii. 7.

not upon you to judge your judges, nor to make them subject to your laws who should be a law to you ; for God is not a God of sedition and confusion, but of order and of peace."[1]

[3.] But ye will say that if the guides of the people be blind, the common sort of men must not close up their own eyes and be led by the conduct of such :[2] if the priest be "partial in the law,"[3] the flock must not therefore depart from the ways of sincere truth, and in simplicity yield to be followers of him for his place sake and office over them. Which thing, though in itself most true, is in your defence notwithstanding weak ; because the matter wherein ye think that ye see, and imagine that your ways are sincere, is of far deeper consideration than any one amongst five hundred of you conceiveth. Let the vulgar sort amongst you know, that there is not the least branch of the cause wherein they are so resolute, but to the trial of it a great deal more appertaineth than their conceit doth reach unto. I write not this in disgrace of the simplest that way given, but I would gladly they knew the nature of that cause wherein they think themselves thoroughly instructed and are not ; by means whereof they daily run themselves, without feeling their own hazard, upon the dint of the apostles' sentence against "evil-speakers as touching things wherein they are ignorant."[4]

[4.] If it be granted a thing unlawful for private men, not called unto public consultation, to dispute which is the best state of civil polity,[5] (with a desire of bringing in some other kind, than that under which they already live, for of such disputes I take it his meaning was ;) if it be a thing confessed, that of such questions they cannot determine without rashness, inasmuch as a great part of them consisteth in

---

[1] Greg. Nazian. Orat. qua se excusat. [p. 37, of Musculus's Latin Version. Basil, 1550, or Opp. t. i. p. 154. Paris, 1609. Τὰ πρόβατα μὴ ποιμαίνετε τοὺς ποιμένας, μηδὲ ὑπὲρ τοὺς ἑαυτῶν ὅρους ἐπαίρεσθε· ἀρκεῖ γὰρ ὑμῖν, ἂν καλῶς ποιμαίνησθε· μὴ κρίνετε τοὺς κριτὰς, μηδὲ νομοθετεῖτε τοῖς νομόθεταις. Οὐ γάρ ἐστι Θεὸς ἀκαταστασίας καὶ ἀταξίας, ἀλλ' εἰρήνης καὶ τάξεως. The second clause is in the Latin, "neque super terminos *eorum* elevemini :" from which evidently Hooker translated.]

[2] Matt. xv. 14.   [3] Mal. ii. 9.

[4] Jude 10 ; 2 Pet. ii. 12.

[5] Calvin. Instit. lib. iv. cap. xx. § 8. ["Sane valde otiosum esset, quis potissmus sit politiæ in eo quo vivunt loco futurus status, a privatis hominibus disputari : quibus de constituenda re aliqua publica deliberare non licet."]

special circumstances, and for one kind as many reasons may be brought as for another; is there any reason in the world, why they should better judge what kind of regiment ecclesiastical is the fittest? For in the civil state more insight, and in those affairs more experience a great deal must needs be granted them, than in this they can possibly have. When they which write in defence of your discipline and commend it unto the Highest not in the least cunning manner, are forced notwithstanding to acknowledge "that with whom the truth is they know not,"[1] they are not certain; what certainty or knowledge can the multitude have thereof?

[5.] Weigh what doth move the common sort so much to favour this innovation, and it shall soon appear unto you, that the force of particular reasons which for your several opinions are alleged is a thing whereof the multitude never did nor could so consider as to be therewith wholly carried; but certain general inducements are used to make saleable your cause in gross; and when once men have cast a fancy towards it, any slight declaration of specialties will serve to lead forward men's inclinable and prepared minds.

[6.] The method of winning the people's affection unto a general liking of "the cause" (for so ye term it) hath been this. First, In the hearing of the multitude, the faults especially of higher callings are ripped up with marvellous exceeding severity and sharpness of reproof;[2] which being

[1] The Author of the Petition directed to her Majesty, p. 3. ["I do not now write either to pull down bishoprics, or erect presbyteries. With whom the truth is I will not determine, for I know not. What seemeth most probable and true to me, that I know. How the truth should come to light, that is the question." This writer was Penry. Bancr. Surv. 342.]

[2] ["A certain writer for reformation . . . writeth of noblemen and gentlemen . . . 'Whereof came,' saith he, 'this division of such personages from others, seeing all men came of one man and one woman? Was it for their lusty hawking and hunting? for their nimble dicing, and cunning carding? for their singing and dancing? for their open bragging and swearing? for their false fleering and flattering? for their subtle killing and stealing? for their cruel polling and pilling, &c. No, no, there was no such thing.' You would be glad then, I am sure, to know what thing it was: indeed the same author doth not conceal it: in effect it is (though it be delivered in better words) viz. that their rebellion and treason against their governors procured them that prerogative with the people: 'Because,' saith he, 'they revenged and delivered the oppressed people out of the hands of their governors who abused their authority, and wickedly, cruelly, and tyrannously ruled over them; the people of a grateful and thankful

oftentimes done begetteth a great good opinion of integrity, zeal, and holiness, to such constant reprovers of sin, as by likelihood would never be so much offended at that which is evil, unless themselves were singularly good.

[7.] The next thing hereunto is, to impute all faults and corruptions, wherewith the world aboundeth, unto the kind of ecclesiastical gorvernment established.[1] Wherein, as before by reproving faults they purchased unto themselves with the multitude a name to be virtuous; so by finding out this kind of cause they obtain to be judged wise above others : whereas in truth unto the form even of Jewish government, which the Lord himself (they all confess) did establish, with like show of reason they might impute those faults which the prophets condemn in the governors of that commonwealth, as to the English kind of regiment ecclesi-astical, (whereof also God himself though in another sort is author,) the stains and blemishes found in our state ; which springing from the root of human frailty and corruption, not only are, but have been always more or less, yea and (for any thing we know to the contrary) will be till the world's end complained of, what form of government soever take place.

[8.] Having gotten thus much sway in the hearts of men, a third step is to propose their own form of church-govern-ment, as the only sovereign remedy of all evils ; and to adorn it with all the glorious titles that may be. And the nature, as of men that have sick bodies, so likewise of the people in the crazedness of their minds possessed with dislike and discontentment at things present, is to imagine that any thing, the virtue whereof they hear commended, would help them; but that most, which they least have tried.

[9.] The fourth degree of inducement is by fashioning

mind gave them that estimation and honour.'" Bancr. Sur. p. 7, quoting "A Treatise of Obedience," p. 114, of which treatise, see Strype, An. I. i. 182, 185. It was written by Chr. Goodman against Q. Mary, and published at Geneva, 1558, with a recommendatory preface by Whittingham.]

[1] [" The necessity of the thing is many ways apparent, both in that it hath so plentiful warrant from God's own word . . . and also in that the gospel can take no root, nor have any free passage, for want of it : and the greatness of your fault appeareth by this ; that in so doing you are the cause of all the ignorance, atheism, schisms, treasons, popery, and ungodliness, that is to be found in this land." Pref. to Demonstr. of Discipline.]

the very notions and conceits of men's minds in such sort, that when they read the Scripture, they may think that every thing soundeth towards the advancement of that discipline, and to the utter disgrace of the contrary. Pythagoras, by bringing up his scholars in the speculative knowledge of numbers, made their conceits therein so strong, that when they came to the contemplation of things natural, they imagined that in every particular thing they even beheld as it were with their eyes, how the elements of number gave essence and being to the works of nature: a thing in reason impossible; which notwithstanding, through their misfashioned preconceit, appeared unto them no less certain, than if nature had written it in the very foreheads of all the creatures of God.[1] When they of the "Family of Love" have it once in their heads, that Christ doth not signify any one person, but a quality whereof many are partakers; that to be "raised" is nothing else but to be regenerated, or endued with the said quality; and that when separation of them which have it from them which have it not is here made, this is "judgment:" how plainly do they imagine that the Scripture every where speaketh in the favour of that sect?[2] And assuredly, the very

[1] Arist. Metaph, lib. i. cap. 5. ["It is no hard thing for a man that hath wit, and is strongly possest of an opinion, and resolute to maintain it, to find some places of scripture, which by good handling will be woed to cast a favourable countenance upon it. Pythagoras' Schollers having been bred up in the doctrine of numbers, when afterward they diverted upon the studies of nature, fancied in themselves somewhat in natural bodies like unto numbers, and thereupon fell into a conceit that numbers were the principles of them. So fares it with him that to the reading of Scripture comes fore-possest with some opinion." Hale's Golden Remains, p. 4, ed. 1658. See Diog. Laert. lib. viii. p. 220, ed. Pearson; Brucker, Hist. Phil. I. 1045, &c.]

[2] [The Family of Love, or Familists, as they are sometimes called, originated with Henry Nicholas of Amsterdam, and afterwards of Embden, about the middle of the 16th century: and may be considered as a kind of offshoot from the German Anabaptists. For their progress in England see Strype, Ann. II. i. 556, ii. 282. Grindal, 383, Whitg. I. 421, III. 158. Christopher Vitel, a joiner of Colchester, was one of their chief propagandists here. See "The displaying of an horrible sect of gross and wicked heretics, naming themselves the Family of Love: with the lives of the authors, &c. by J. R." (John Rogers,) "1578, London." This writer says that H. N. had then as many as 1000 followers in England. From the number of their tracts, (he quotes about a dozen,) and from the attention which they appear to have attracted at the time, he would seem to have much underrated their numbers. Vitel replied to this pamphlet, and Rogers rejoined in 1579.

cause which maketh the simple and ignorant to think they even see how the word of God runneth currently on your

Both his pamphlets are in Bp. Atterbury's collection, in the library of Christ Church, Oxford, E. 522, 525.) The same year an elaborate and scholarlike "Confutation of certain monstrous and horrible heresies taught by H. N." was published by J. Knewstubs, of Cambridge, afterwards one of the representatives of the Puritan Party at the Hampton-court conference. He states, p. 32, "By the doctrine of H. N. Christ is no one man, but an estate and condition in man, common unto so many as have [50.] received his doctrine that they are grown thereby to perfection." And, p. 36, "H. N. his Christ is not God, but an affection or disposition in man, which, if it were good, were yet no more but godliness, not God himself." Which statements he abundantly confirms by quotations from various tracts, but refers to one which he had not seen, as being reported to contain the fullest development of the new doctrine. That work is "An Introduction to the holy understanding of the Glass of Righteousness; set forth by H. N." No printer's name nor date is given. The following passage may be taken as a fair specimen of it. (c. 5. No. 28.) "Behold, this same holy being of God is the true life of the Holy Ghost, which heretofore God wrought among his people Israel, and likewise among the Gentiles that feared his name. . . . 29. This same being of God is indeed the right food of the soul, and bread of life, and is descended unto us from heaven for a life to the man: and was heretofore broken and distributed to *the people of Israel* and the disciples of Christ, to feed on in their souls. . . . 31. This same bread which is given unto them is the true meat offering of Christ, viz. His Body: and this cup which is poured forth unto them is the true shedding of His Blood, *the which is the outflowing of the holy word or Spirit* of Christ, upon all believers of Christ, to everlasting life. . . . 33. Behold, that same bread or Body of Christ is the Word that became flesh and it dwelt among them. . . . 34. *And the same is the New Testament,* which God in those days made and appointed with His people." Compare c. 18, No. 16, &c. And c. 22, 30. "Unto all that believed was the resurrection from the dead, and everlasting life, witnessed and promised through Jesus Christ. In sure and firm hope whereof the upright believers have rested in the Lord Jesus Christ, till the appearing of His coming, *which is now, in this day of the Love, revealed, out of the heavenly Being.* With which Jesus Christ the former believers of Christ, who were fallen asleep, rested, or died in Him, *are now also manifested in glory.* For Christ in the appearing of his coming *raiseth* his deceased from the dead, to the intent they should reign with Him over all his enemies, and *condemneth* all the ungodly who have not liked of him."

"I remember," (says Strype, Ann. II. i. 561, writing in 1725,) "a great admirer of this sect, within less than twenty years ago, told me, that there was then but one of the Family of Love alive, and he an old man." But their principles, unfortunately, were not extinct. "I have now before me the works, (or part of them,) of Henry Nicholas, the Father of the Family of Love: they were given to a friend of mine by a Quaker, with this encomium, that he believed he would not find one word amiss, or one superfluous, in the whole book, and commended it, as an excellent piece. It is not unlikely that he took it for a Quaker

side, is, that their minds are forestalled and their conceits perverted beforehand, by being taught, that an "elder" doth signify a layman admitted only to the office or rule of government in the Church ; a "doctor," one which may only teach, and neither preach nor administer the Sacraments ; a "deacon," one which hath charge of the alms-box, and of nothing else : that the "sceptre," the "rod," the "throne" and "kingdom" of Christ, are a form of regiment, only by pastors, elders, doctors, and deacons ;[1] that by mystical resemblance Mount Sion and Jerusalem are the churches which admit, Samaria and Babylon the churches which oppugn the same form of regiment. And in like sort they are taught to apply all things spoken of repairing the walls and decayed parts of the city and temple of God, by Esdras, Nehemias, and the rest ;[2] as if purposely the Holy Ghost had therein meant to foresignify, what the authors of Admonitions to the Parliament, of Supplications to the Council, of Petitions to her Majesty, and of such other-like writs, should either do or suffer in behalf of this their cause.

[10.] From hence they proceed to a higher point, which is the persuading of men credulous and over-capable of such pleasing errors, that it is the special illumination of the Holy Ghost, whereby they discern those things in the word, which others reading yet discern them not. "Dearly beloved," saith St. John, "give not credit unto every spirit."[3] There are but two ways whereby the Spirit leadeth men into all truth ; the one extraordinary, the

book ; for there is not his name at length, only H. N. to it ; and it has quite through the Quaker phyz and mien, that twins are not more alike. And though he directs it, To the Family of Love, yet an ignorant Quaker might take that for his own family, and apply it to the Quakers." Leslie's Works, II. 609, ed. 1721.]

[1] [" Having occasion to talk upon a time with an artisan of Kingston, about his refusal, after the purest fashion, to be examined upon his oath, because I saw how peart he was, and rapt out text upon text (full ignorantly, God knoweth,) I was so bold as to examine him in the second petition of the Lord's Prayer, demanding of him, what he thought was meant by this word, 'kingdom,' therein mentioned. Whereunto he made in effect this answer, without any staggering : ' We pray,' saith he, ' that our heavenly Father would at the last grant unto us, that we might have pastors, doctors, elders, and deacons in every parish, and so be governed by such elderships as Christ's holy discipline doth require.' " Bancroft, Survey, &c. c. 31.]

[2] T. C. Preface to 2d Reply, fol. 1. 2.]

[3] 1 John iv. 1.

other common; the one belonging but unto some few, the other extending itself unto all that are of God; the one, that which we call by a special divine excellency Revelation, the other Reason. If the Spirit by such revelation have discovered unto them the secrets of that discipline out of Scripture, they must profess themselves to be all (even men, women, and children) Prophets. Or if reason be the hand which the Spirit hath led them by; forasmuch as persuasions grounded upon reason are either weaker or stronger according to the force of those reasons whereupon the same are grounded, they must every of them from the greatest to the least be able for every several article to shew some special reason as strong as their persuasion therein is earnest. Otherwise how can it be but that some other sinews there are from which that overplus of strength in persuasion doth arise? Most sure it is, that when men's affections do frame their opinions, they are in defence of error more earnest a great deal, than (for the most part) sound believers in the maintenance of truth apprehended according to the nature of that evidence which scripture yieldeth : which being in some things plain, as in the principles of Christian doctrine ; in some things, as in these matters of discipline, more dark and doubtful; frameth correspondently that inward assent which God's most gracious Spirit worketh by it as by his effectual instrument. It is not therefore the fervent earnestness of their persuasion, but the soundness of those reasons whereupon the same is built, which must declare their opinions in these things to have been wrought by the Holy Ghost, and not by the fraud of that evil spirit, which is even in his illusions strong.[1]

[11.] After that the fancy of the common sort hath once thoroughly apprehended the Spirit to be author of their persuasions concerning discipline ; then is instilled into their hearts, that the same Spirit leading men into this opinion doth thereby seal them to be God's children; and that, as the state of the times now standeth, the most special token to know them that are God's own from others is an earnest affection that way. This hath bred high terms of separation between such and the rest of the world ; whereby the one sort are named The brethren, The godly, and so forth; the

---

[1] 2 Thess. ii. 11.

other, worldlings, time-servers, pleasers of men not of God, with such like.[1]

[12.] From hence, they are easily drawn on to think it exceeding necessary, for fear of quenching that good Spirit, to use all means whereby the same may be both strengthened in themselves, and made manifest unto others. This maketh them diligent hearers of such as are known that way to incline ; this maketh them eager to take and to seek all occasions of secret conference with such ; this maketh them glad to use such as counsellors and directors in all their dealings which are of weight, as contracts, testaments, and the like ; this maketh them, through an unweariable desire of receiving instruction from the masters of that company, to cast off the care of those very affairs which do most concern their estate, and to think that then they are like unto Mary, commendable for making choice of the better part. Finally, this is it which maketh them willing to charge, yea, oftentimes even to overcharge themselves, for such men's sustenance and relief, lest their zeal to the cause should any way be unwitnessed. For what is it which poor beguiled souls will not do through so powerful incitements ?

[13.] In which respect it is also noted, that most labour hath been bestowed to win and retain towards this cause them whose judgments are commonly weakest by reason of their sex.[2] And although not "women loden with

---

[1] [The 22d art. of Charge against Cartwright in 1590 is, "That from time to time, since his abode in Warwick, by his practice and dealing, he hath nourished a faction, and heartburning of one inhabitant there against another, severing them in his own and his followers' speeches, by the names of *The godly*, or *Brethren favouring sincerity*, and *The profane*." Fuller, C. H. b. ix. p. 200.]

[2] [For example : a copy of the Admonition to the Parliament, in the library of Christ Church, Oxford, has the following lines in MS. in the blank leaf at the beginning :

To Mrs. Catesbie my very frende.

Read and peruse this lytle booke
 with prayer to the Lorde
That all may yelde that therein looke
 to truthe with one accorde.
Whiche thoughe our troubles it hathe wrought
 it shall prevayle at laste,
And utterly confounde God's foes
 with his confoundinge blaste.
As Pope hath falne, so muste all popes,
 and popelinges every one,
So muste his lawes whereby he rulde,
 and God's worde stand alone.

sins "[1] as the apostle Saint Paul speaketh, but (as we verily esteem of them for the most part) women propense and inclinable to holiness be otherwise edified in good things, rather than carried away as captives into any kind of sin and evil, by such as enter into their houses with purpose to plant there a zeal and a love towards this kind of discipline: yet some occasion is hereby ministered for men to think, that if the cause which is thus furthered did gain by the soundness of proof whereupon it doth build itself, it would not most busily endeavour to prevail where least ability of judgment is: and therefore, that this so eminent industry in making proselytes more of that sex than of the other groweth, for that they are deemed apter to serve as instruments and helps in the cause. Apter they are through the eagerness of their affection, that maketh them, which way soever they take, diligent in drawing their husbands, children, servants, friends and allies the same way; apter through that natural inclination unto pity, which breedeth in them a greater readiness than in men to be bountiful towards their preachers who suffer want; apter through sundry opportunities, which they especially have, to procure encouragements for their brethren; finally, apter through a singular delight which they take in giving very large and particular intelligence, how all near about them stand affected as concerning the same cause.

[14.] But be they women or be they men, if once they have tasted of that cup, let any man of contrary opinion open his mouth to persuade them, they close up their ears, his reasons they weigh not, all is answered with rehearsal of the words of John, "'We are of God;

> Whiche is the scepter of the might
> of Christe our Lorde and Kynge,
> To whiche we must subject of right
> ourselves, and everye thinge.
> Yors in the Lorde,
> Io. Feilde.

Field is mentioned by Archb. Bancroft (Survey, &c. p. 42.) as one of the first planners of the Admonition. He was imprisoned the year it came out, (1572,) according to Strype, (Ann. II. i. 275,) for presenting a copy of it to the parliament. Bishop Sandys complained that when Field was in Newgate the people resorted to him "as in popery they were wont to run on pilgrimage." (Strype, Parker, II. 268.) He was a leader of the secret Puritan synod in 1580: and is constantly mentioned as one of the most busy and important among them.

See also Clarendon's Hist. of the Reb. I. 177, Oxford, 1819.]

[1] 2 Tim. iii. 6.

he that knoweth God heareth us:'[1] as for the rest, ye
are of the world; for this world's pomp and vanity it is
that ye speak, and the world, whose ye are, heareth you."
Which cloak sitteth no less fit on the back of their cause,
than of the Anabaptists, when the dignity, authority and
honour of God's magistrate is upheld against them. Shew
these eagerly-affected men their inability to judge of such
matters; their answer is, "God hath chosen the simple."[2]
Convince them of folly, and that so plainly, that very
children upbraid them with it; they have their bucklers
of like defence : "Christ's own apostle was accounted mad :
the best men evermore by the sentence of the world have
been judged to be out of their right minds."[3]

[15.] When instruction doth them no good, let them feel
but the least degree of most mercifully-tempered severity,[4]
they fasten on the head of the Lord's vicegerents here on
earth whatsoever they any where find uttered against the
cruelty of bloodthirsty men, and to themselves they draw
all the sentences which scripture hath in the favour of
innocency persecuted for the truth ; yea, they are of their
due and deserved sufferings no less proud, than those
ancient disturbers to whom Saint Augustine writeth, saying :[5]
"Martyrs rightly so named are they not which suffer for
their disorder, and for the ungodly breach they have made
of Christian unity, but which for righteousness' sake are
persecuted. For Agar also suffered persecution at the
hands of Sarah, wherein, she which did impose was holy,

---

[1] 1 John iv. 6.   [2] 1 Cor. i. 27.

[3] Acts xxvi. 24. Sap. v. 4. "We fools thought his life madness."
Merc. Tris. ad Æsculap. [lib. xv. fol. 43.] Οἱ ἐν γνώσει ὄντες οὔτε
τοῖς πολλοῖς ἀρέσκουσι, οὔτε οἱ πολλοὶ αὐτοῖς· μεμηνέναι δὲ δοκοῦσι, καὶ
γέλωτα ὀφλισκάνουσι. Vide Lactant. de Justit. lib. v. cap. 16.

[4] [This was written before either of the executions which took place
in Queen Elizabeth's reign for disturbances on puritanical grounds.
For Hooker's book was sent to Lord Burghley, March 13, 1592,
(Strype, Whitg. III. 300,) Barrow and Greenwood were condemned,
March 23, (ibid. II. 186,) Penry in May (ib. 176). Udall who had been
convicted was pardoned, at Whitgift's intercession, June 1592, (ib. 102.)]

[5] Aug. Ep. 50. [al. 185, § 9. t. II. 64⅖. "Veri martyres illi sunt,
de quibus Dominus ait, Beati qui persecutionem patiuntur propter
justitiam. Non ergo qui propter iniquitatem, et propter Christianæ
unitatis impiam divisionem, sed qui propter justitiam persecutionem
patiuntur, hi martyres veri sunt. Nam et Agar passa est persecutionem
a Sara, et illa erat sancta quæ faciebat, illa iniqua quæ patiebatur.
Et ipse Dominus cum latronibus crucifixus est : sed quos passio
jungebat, causa separabat."]

and she unrighteous which did bear the burden. In like sort, with thieves was the Lord himself crucified ; but they, who were matched in the pain which they suffered,[1] were in the cause of their sufferings disjoined." . . . "If that must needs be the true church which doth endure persecution, and not that which persecuteth, let them ask of the apostle what church Sarah did represent, when she held her maid in affliction. For even our mother which is free, the heavenly Jerusalem, that is to say, the true Church of God, was, as he doth affirm, prefigured in that very woman by whom the bondmaid was so sharply handled. Although, if all things be thoroughly scanned, she did in truth more persecute Sarah by proud resistance, than Sarah her by severity of punishment."

[16.] These are the paths wherein ye have walked that are of the ordinary sort of men ; these are the very steps ye have trodden, and the manifest degrees whereby ye are of your guides and directors trained up in that school : a custom of inuring your ears with reproof of faults especially in your governors ; an use to attribute those faults to the kind of spiritual regiment under which ye live ; boldness in warranting the force of their discipline for the cure of all such evils ; a slight of framing your conceits to imagine that Scripture every where favoureth that discipline ; persuasion that the cause why ye find it in Scripture is the illumination of the Spirit, that the same Spirit is a seal unto you of your nearness unto God, that ye are by all means to nourish and witness it in yourselves, and to strengthen on every side your minds against whatsoever might be of force to withdraw you from it.

IV. Wherefore to come unto you whose judgment is a lantern of direction for all the rest, you that frame thus the people's hearts, not altogether (as I willingly persuade myself) of a politic intent or purpose, but yourselves being first overborne with the weight of greater men's judgments : on your shoulders is laid the burden of upholding the cause by argument. For which purpose sentences out of the word

---

[1] [Ibid. § 11. "Si Ecclesia vera ipsa est, quæ persecutionem patitur, non quæ facit ; quærant ab Apostolo, quam Ecclesiam significabat Sara, quando persecutionem faciebat ancillæ. Liberam quippe matrem nostram, cœlestem Jerusalem, id est veram Dei Ecclesiam, in illa muliere dicit fuisse figuratam, quæ affligebat ancillam. Si autem melius discutiamus, magis illa persequebatur Saram superbiendo, quam illam Sara coercendo."]

of God ye allege divers : but so, that when the same are discussed, thus it always in a manner falleth out, that what things by virtue thereof ye urge upon us as altogether necessary, are found to be thence collected only by poor and marvellous slight conjectures. I need not give instance in any one sentence so alleged, for that I think the instance in any alleged otherwise a thing not easy to be given. A very strange thing sure it were, that such a discipline as ye speak of should be taught by Christ and his apostles in the word of God, and no church ever have found it out, nor received it till this present time ;[1] contrariwise, the government against which ye bend yourselves be observed every where throughout all generations and ages of the Christian world, no church ever perceiving the word of God to be against it. We require you to find out but one church upon the face of the whole earth, that hath been ordered by your discipline, or hath not been ordered by ours, that is to say, by episcopal regiment, sithence the time that the blessed Apostles were here conversant.

[2.] Many things out of antiquity ye bring, as if the purest times of the Church had observed the selfsame orders which you require ; and as though your desire were that the churches of old should be patterns for us to follow, and even glasses, wherein we might see the practice of that which by you is gathered out of Scripture. But the truth is, ye mean nothing less. All this is done for fashion's sake only : for ye complain of it as of an injury, that men should be willed to seek for examples and patterns of government in any of those times that have been before.[2] Ye plainly hold, that from the very Apostles' time till this present age, wherein yourselves imagine ye have found out a right pattern of sound discipline, there never was any time safe to be followed. Which thing ye thus endeavour to prove.

---

[1] [Bancroft, Sermon at St. Paul's Cross, 9 Feb. 158⅝, p. 10, 11, has the same affirmation and challenge almost in the same words. "A very strange matter if it were true, that Christ should erect a form of government for the ruling of his Church, to continue from his departure out of the world until his coming again ; and that the same should never be once thought of or put in practice for the space of 1500 years : or at the least (to take them at their best) that the government and kingdom of Christ should then be overthrown, when by all men's confessions the divinity of his Person, the virtue of his Priesthood, the power of his office as He is a Prophet, and the honour of his kingly Authority was so godly, so learnedly, and so mightily established."]

[2] T. C. lib. i. p. 97.

" Out of [1] Egesippus " ye say that " Eusebius [2] writeth," how
although "as long as the Apostles lived the Church did
remain a pure virgin, yet after the death of the Apostles, and
after they were once gone whom God vouchsafed to make
hearers of the divine wisdom with their own ears, the
placing of wicked error began to come into the Church.
Clement also in a certain place, to confirm that there was
corruption of doctrine immediately after the Apostles' time,
allegeth the proverb, ' That there are few sons like their
fathers.' [3] Socrates saith of the churches of Rome and
Alexandria,[4] the most famous churches in the Apostles'
times, that about the year 430, the Roman and Alexandrian
bishops, leaving the sacred function, were degenerate to a
secular rule or dominion." [5]   Hereupon ye conclude, that it
is not safe to fetch our government from any other than the
Apostles' times.

[3.] Wherein by the way it may be noted, that in proposing the Apostles' times as a pattern for the Church to
follow, though the desire of you all be one, the drift and
purpose of you all is not one.   The chiefest thing which
lay-reformers yawn for is, that the clergy may through conformity in state and condition be apostolical, poor as the
Apostles of Christ were poor.   In which one circumstance
if they imagine so great perfection, they must think that
church which hath such store of mendicant friars, a church
in that respect most happy.   Were it for the glory of God
and the good of his Church indeed that the clergy should be
left even as bare as the Apostles when they had neither
staff nor scrip ; that God, which should lay upon them the
condition of his Apostles, would I hope endue them with
the selfsame affection which was in that holy Apostle, whose
words concerning his own right virtuous contentment of

[1] [Id. ibid. and ii. 507–511.]
[2] Euseb. Hist. Eccles. lib. iii. cap. 32. iv. 22.   ['Ο αὐτὸς ἀνὴρ ἐπι-
λέγει, ὡς ἄρα μέχρι τῶν τότε χρόνων παρθένος καθαρὰ καὶ ἀδιάφθορος
ἔμεινεν ἡ ἐκκλησία, ἐν ἀδήλῳ που σκότει φωλευόντων εἰσέτι τότε, τῶν,
εἰ καί τινες ὑπῆρχον, παραφθείρειν ἐπιχειρούντων τὸν ὑγιῆ κανόνα τοῦ
σωτηρίου κηρύγματος.   And in b. iv. 22, he cites the very words of
Hegesipⁱ us, Διὰ τοῦτο ἐκάλουν τὴν ἐκκλησίαν παρθένον· οὔπω γὰρ
ἔφθαρτο ἀκοαῖς ματαίαις.   See Dr. Routh's note, Reliquiæ Sacræ,
i. 233.]
[3] Lib. Strom. somewhat after the beginning.   [Ed. Potter. t. i. 322.]
[4] Hist. Eccles. lib. vii. cap. 11.
[5] [Τῆς 'Ρωμαίων ἐπισκοπῆς, ὁμοίως τῇ 'Αλεξανδρέων, πέρα τῆς ἱερω-
σύνης, ἐπὶ δυναστείαν ἤδη πάλαι προελθούσης.]

heart, "as well how to want, as how to abound," [1] are a most fit episcopal emprese. The Church of Christ is a body mystical. A body cannot stand, unless the parts thereof be proportionable. Let it therefore be required on both parts, at the hands of the clergy, to be in meanness of state like the Apostles ; at the hand of the laity, to be as they were who lived under the Apostles : and in this reformation there will be, though little wisdom, yet some indifferency.

[4.] But your reformation which are of the clergy (if yet it displease you not that I should say ye are of the clergy [2]) seemeth to aim at a broader mark. Ye think that he which will perfectly reform must bring the form of church-discipline unto the state which then it was at. A thing neither possible, nor certain, nor absolutely convenient.

Concerning the first, what was used in the Apostles' times, the Scripture fully declareth not ; so that making their times the rule and canon of church-polity, ye make a rule, which being not possible to be fully known, is as impossible to be kept.

Again, sith the latter even of the Apostles' own times had that which in the former was not thought upon ; in this general proposing of the Apostolical times, there is no certainty which should be followed : especially seeing that ye give us great cause to doubt how far ye allow those times. [3] For albeit "the loover of antichristian building were not," ye say, as then "set up, yet the foundations thereof were secretly and under the ground laid in the Apostles' times : " [4] so that all other times ye plainly reject,

---

[1] Phil. iv. 12. [For the word emprese or impress see Shakespeare, Rich. II. act. III. sc. 1.]

[2] [T. C. iii. 219. "Those which were baptized in their beds were thereby made unapt to have any place among the clergy (*as they call them*)."]

[3] [Penry, Brief Discovery, &c. p. 20. "We know Diotrephes to have been in the Church even in the Apostles' times . . . and therefore we cannot greatly marvel, though even in their time there had been a divers government from this of the Lord's appointment, which we labour for. For even in the Apostles' time the mystery of iniquity began to work."]

[4] [T. C. i. 97. The word "loover" is also used, T. C. ii. 621. "How childishe is yt, after so long travaile to prove a bishop over the ministers off a diocese . . . in the ende to endevour to prove, that there may be superiorite? as if any man would denie this that graunted the other : and yt is *to set the fondacion upon the lover*." "Louver, (from *l'ouvert*, Fr. an opening :) an opening for the smoke to go out at

and the Apostles' own times ye approve with marvellous
great suspicion, leaving it intricate and doubtful, wherein we
are to keep ourselves unto the pattern of their times.

Thirdly, whereas it is the error of the common multitude
to consider only what hath been of old, and if the same
were well, to see whether still it continue; if not, to condemn that presently which is, and never to search upon
what ground or consideration the change might grow : such
rudeness cannot be in you so well borne with, whom
learning and judgment hath enabled much more soundly
to discern how far the times of the Church and the orders
thereof may alter without offence. True it is, the
ancienter,[1] the better ceremonies of religion are ; howbeit,
not absolutely true and without exception ; but true only
so far forth as those different ages do agree in the state of
those things, for which at the first those rites, orders, and
ceremonies, were instituted. In the Apostles' times that was
harmless, which being now revived would be scandalous ;
as their *oscula sancta*.[2] Those feasts of charity,[3] which

in the roof of a cottage : in the north of England, an opening at the
top of a dovecote. ' The ancient manner of building in Cornwall was,
to set hearths in the midst of rooms for chimneys, which vented the
smoke at a louver in the top.' Carew, Survey of Cornwall. And see
Spenser's F. Q. vi. x. 42." Todd's Johnson's Dict.]

[1] "Antiquitas ceremoniis atque fanis tantum sanctitatis tribuere
consuevit, quantum adstruxerit vetustatis." Arno. p. 746. The words
are from Minutius Felix, p. 4, line 30, ed. Elmenhorst. In many
former editions, and no doubt in that which Hooker used, the dialogue
of Minutius is ascribed to Arnobius.

[2] Rom. xvi. 16 ; 2 Cor. xiii. 12 ; 1 Thess. v. 26 ; 1 Pet. v. 14. In
their meetings to serve God, their manner was, in the end to salute one
another with a kiss ; using these words, " Peace be with you." For
which cause Tertullian doth call it, *signaculum orationis*, "the seal of
prayer." Lib. de Orat. [c. 14.]

[3] Epist. Jud. 12. Concerning which feasts, Saint Chrysostom saith,
"Statis diebus mensas faciebant communes, et peracta synaxi post
sacramentorum communionem inibant convivium, divitibus quidem cibos
afferentibus, pauperibus autem et qui nihil habebant etiam vocatis."
[Καθάπερ ἐπὶ τῶν τρισχιλίων τῶν ἐξ ἀρχῆς πιστευσάντων, κοινῇ πάντες
εἰστιῶντο καὶ κοινὰ πάντα ἐκέκτηντο, οὕτω καὶ τότε ὅτε ταῦτα ἔγραψεν ὁ
Ἀπόστολος ἐγίνετο, οὐχ οὕτω μὲν μετὰ ἀκριβείας, ὥσπερ δέ τις ἀπόρροια
τῆς κοινωνίας ἐκείνης ἐναπομείνασα καὶ εἰς τοὺς μετὰ ταῦτα κατέβη. Καὶ
ἐπειδὰν συνέβαινε τοὺς μὲν πένητας εἶναι, τοὺς δὲ πλουσίους, τὰ μὲν
ἑαυτῶν οὐ κατετίθεντο πάντα εἰς μέσον, κοινὰς δὲ ἐποιοῦντο τὰς τραπέζας
ἐν ἡμέραις νενομισμέναις, ὡς εἰκός, καὶ τῆς συνάξεως ἀπαρτισθείσης μετὰ
τὴν τῶν μυστηρίων κοινωνίαν ἐπὶ κοινὴν πάντες ᾔεσαν εὐωχίαν, τῶν μὲν
πλουτούντων φερόντων τὰ ἐδέσματα, τῶν δὲ πενομένων καὶ οὐδὲν ἐχόντων
ὑπ' αὐτῶν καλουμένων καὶ κοινῇ πάντων ἐστιωμένων. iii. 416.] In 1 Cor.

being instituted by the Apostles, were retained in the Church long after, are not now thought any where needful. What man is there of understanding, unto whom it is not manifest how the way of providing for the clergy by tithes, the device of almshouses for the poor, the sorting out of the people into their several parishes, together with sundry other things which the Apostles' times could not have, (being now established,) are much more convenient and fit for the Church of Christ, than if the same should be taken away for conformity's sake with the ancientest and first times?

[5.] The orders therefore, which were observed in the Apostles' times, are not to be urged as a rule universally either sufficient or necessary. If they be, nevertheless on your part it still remaineth to be better proved, that the form of discipline, which ye entitle apostolical, was in the Apostles' times exercised. For of this very thing ye fail even touching that which ye make most account of,[1] as being matter of substance in discipline, I mean the power of your lay-elders, and the difference of your doctors from the pastors in all churches. So that in sum, we may be bold to conclude, that besides these last times, which for insolency, pride, and egregious contempt of all good order, are the worst, there are none wherein ye can truly affirm, that the complete form of your discipline, or the substance thereof, was practised.

[6.] The evidence therefore of antiquity failing you, ye fly to the judgments of such learned men, as seem by their writings to be of opinion, that all Christian churches should receive your discipline, and abandon ours. Wherein, as ye heap up the names of a number of men not unworthy to be had in honour ; so there are a number whom when ye mention, although it serve you to purpose with the ignorant and vulgar sort, who measure by tale and not by weight, yet surely they who know what quality and value the men

---

xi. 17, Hom. xxvii. Of the same feasts, in like sort, Tertullian. "Cœna nostra de nomine rationem sui ostendit. Vocatur enim ἀγάπη, id quod est penes Græcos *dilectio*. " Quantiscunque sumptibus constet, lucrum est pietatis nomine facere sumptum." Apol. cap. 39.

[1] ["Tantum inter cæteros eminent Presbyteri isti non docentes, 'quantum lenta solent inter viburna cupressi:' tantumque præstare videntur reliquis, ut ipsorum nomine totus hic consessus Presbyterium dicatur. Quum igitur tota illa moles novæ disciplinæ . . . hoc uno fundamento nitatur . . . &c." Sutcliffe de Presbyt. p. 90.]

are of, will think ye draw very near the dregs. But were they all of as great account as the best and chiefest amongst them, with us notwithstanding neither are they, neither ought they to be of such reckoning, that their opinion or conjecture should cause the laws of the Church of England to give place. Much less when they neither do all agree in that opinion, and of them which are at agreement, the most part through a courteous inducement have followed one man as their guide, finally that one therein not unlikely to have swerved. If any one chance to say it is probable that in the Apostles' times there were lay-elders, or not to mislike the continuance of them in the Church, or to affirm that Bishops at the first were a name but not a power distinct from Presbyters, or to speak any thing in praise of those churches which are without episcopal regiment, or to reprove the fault of such as abuse that calling ; all these ye register for men persuaded as you are, that every Christian church standeth bound by the law of God to put down bishops, and in their rooms to elect an eldership so authorized as you would have it for the government of each parish. Deceived greatly they are therefore, who think that all they whose names are cited amongst the favourers of this cause, are on any such verdict agreed.[1]

[7.] Yet touching some material points of your discipline, a kind of agreement we grant there is amongst many divines of reformed churches abroad. For, first, to do as the Church of Geneva did the learned in some other churches must needs be the more willing, who having used in like manner not the slow and tedious help of proceeding by public authority, but the people's more quick endeavour for alteration, in such an exigent I see not well how they could have stayed to deliberate about any other regiment than that which already was devised to their hands, that which in like case had been taken, that which was easiest to be established without delay, that which was likeliest to content the people by reason of some kind of sway which it giveth them. When therefore the example of one church was thus at the first almost through a kind of constraint or necessity followed by many, their concurrence in persuasion about some material points belonging to the same polity is not strange. For we are not to marvel greatly, if they

[1] [Full evidence of this point may be seen in Whitgift's two works.]

which have all done the same thing, do easily embrace the
same opinion as concerning their own doings.

[8.] Besides, mark I beseech you that which Galen in
matter of philosophy noteth ;[1] for the like falleth out even
in questions of higher knowledge. It fareth many times
with men's opinions as with rumours and reports. " That
which a credible person telleth is easily thought probable
by such as are well persuaded of him. But if two, or three,
or four, agree all in the same tale, they judge it then to be
out of controversy, and so are many times overtaken for
want of due consideration ; either some common cause
leading them all into error, or one man's oversight deceiv-
ing many through their too much credulity and easiness of
belief." Though ten persons be brought to give testimony
in any cause, yet if the knowledge they have of the thing
whereunto they come as witnesses, appear to have grown
from some one amongst them, and to have spread itself
from hand to hand, they all are in force but as one testimony. Nor is it otherwise here where the daughter churches
do speak their mother's dialect ; here where so many sing
one song, by reason that he is the guide of the choir, concerning whose deserved authority amongst even the gravest
divines we have already spoken at large. Will ye ask what
should move so many learned to be followers of one man's
judgment, no necessity of argument forcing them thereunto ?
Your demand is answered by yourselves. Loth ye are to
think that they, whom ye judge to have attained as sound
knowledge in all points of doctrine as any since the
Apostles' time, should mistake in discipline.[2] Such is
naturally our affection, that whom in great things we

---

[1] Galen. clas. 2, lib. de cujusque Anim. Peccat. Notitia atque
Medeia. t. i. p. 366. Basil. 1538. [—μηδενὶ ψευδῶς συγκαταθέμενον
ἑαυτὸν, ὥσπερ ἑκάστης ἡμέρας ὁρῶ παμπόλλους τῶν φίλων, ἐνίους μὲν
ἑνὶ τῶν εἰπόντων ὁτιοῦν πιστεύσαντας· . . . . προπετῶς δὲ καὶ ὁ τρισὶν
ἢ τέσσαρσιν, ἄνευ τοῦ διορίσασθαι πότερον ἐνδέχεται πάντας αὐτοὺς
ἐκ μιᾶς αἰτίας κοινῆς ἀληθεύειν, ἢ ψεύδεσθαι πάντας ἐκ μιᾶς αἰτίας
κοινῆς.]

[2] Petition to the Queen's Majesty, p. 14.—[" It *may* be that they
who have attained to as sound knowledge in all points of doctrine as
any since the apostles' time should mistake in discipline. It *may* be
that they whom the Spirit of truth and wisdom hath directed in
expounding the Scriptures should be always forsaken of that Spirit
when they come to expound or speak of a text concerning discipline
. . . But . . . men not partial will still make scruples in these
matters."]

mightily admire, in them we are not persuaded willingly
that any thing should be amiss. The reason whereof is,
"for that as dead flies putrify the ointment of the apothecary,
so a little folly him that is in estimation for wisdom."[1] This
in every profession hath too much authorized the judgments
of a few. This with Germans hath caused Luther, and with
many other churches Calvin, to prevail in all things. Yet
are we not able to define, whether the wisdom of that God,
who setteth before us in holy Scripture so many admirable
patterns of virtue, and no one of them without somewhat
noted wherein they were culpable ; to the end, that to Him
alone it might always be acknowledged, "Thou only art
holy, thou only art just;"[2] might not permit those worthy
vessels of his glory to be in some things blemished with the
stain of human frailty, even for this cause, lest we should
esteem of any man above that which behoveth.

V. Notwithstanding, as though ye were able to say a
great deal more than hitherto your books have revealed
to the world, earnest challengers[3] ye are of trial by some
public disputation. Wherein if the thing ye crave be no
more than only leave to dispute openly about those matters
that are in question, the schools in universities (for any
thing I know) are open unto you. They have their yearly
acts and commencements, besides other disputations both
ordinary and upon occasion, wherein the several parts of
our own ecclesiastical discipline are oftentimes offered unto

---

[1] Eccles. x. 1.

[2] [ὅτι μόνος ὅσιος. Apoc. xv. 4. Σὺ μόνος Ἅγιος,—σὺ μόνος Κύριος.
Morning Hymn in Apost. Constit. vii. 4, used by our Church in the
Post-Communion.]

[3] ["Would to God that free conference in these matters might be
had. For howesoever learned and many they seeme to be, they should
and may in this realme finde inowe, to matche them, and shame them
to, if they hold on as they have begon." Address "to the godly
readers," prefixed to the first Admonition to the Parliament, p. 2.
See also "A View of Popish Abuses," subjoined to the 1st Admonition,
p. 18 ; and 2d Adm. p. 36 ; and Petition to the Queen's Maj. p. 3.
"There is a way devised and much commended by learned men, as a
notable mean to compound controversies, namely, private conferences
by advised writing, not extemporal speaking, the question agreed of.
The arguments, the answers, replies, and rejoinders set down, till both
parties had fully said, all by-matters laid aside. In fine the whole to
be published, that your Majesty, the honourable counsellors and Parliament may judge thereof." And Pref. to Dem. of Disc. "Venture
your bishopricks upon a disputation, and we will venture our lives :
take the challenge if you dare."]

that kind of examination; the learnedest of you have been of late years noted seldom or never absent from thence at the time of those greater assemblies; and the favour of proposing there in convenient sort whatsoever ye can object (which thing myself have known them to grant of scholastical courtesy unto strangers) neither hath (as I think) nor ever will (I presume) be denied you.

[2.] If your suit be to have some great extraordinary confluence, in expectation whereof the laws that already are should sleep and have no power over you, till in the hearing of thousands ye all did acknowledge your error and renounce the further prosecution of your cause : haply they whose authority is required unto the satisfying of your demand do think it both dangerous to admit such concourse of divided minds, and unmeet that laws, which being once solemnly established are to exact obedience of all men and to constrain thereunto, should so far stoop as to hold themselves in suspense from taking any effect upon you till some disputer can persuade you to be obedient.[1]   A law is the deed of the whole body politic, whereof if ye judge yourselves to be any part, then is the law even your deed also.   And were it reason in things of this quality to give men audience, pleading for the overthrow of that which their own very deed hath ratified?   Laws that have been approved may be (no man doubteth) again repealed, and to that end also disputed against, by the authors thereof themselves.   But this is when the whole doth deliberate what laws each part shall observe, and not when a part refuseth the laws which the whole hath orderly agreed upon.

[3.] Notwithstanding, forasmuch as the cause we maintain is (God be thanked) such as needeth not to shun any trial, might it please them on whose approbation the matter dependeth to condescend so far unto you in this behalf, I wish heartily that proof were made even by solemn conference in orderly and quiet sort, whether you would yourselves be satisfied, or else could by satisfying others draw them to your part.   Provided always, first, inasmuch as ye go about to destroy a thing which is in force, and to draw in that which hath not as yet been received ; to impose on us that which we think not ourselves bound

[1] [See in Strype, Ann. IV. 239, 240, a petition of Barrow for a conference, with Archbishop Whitgift's reasons against it.]

unto, and to overthrow those things whereof we are possessed; that therefore ye are not to claim in any such conference other than the plaintiff's or opponent's part, which must consist altogether in proof and confirmation of two things : the one, that our orders by you condemned we ought to abolish ; the other, that yours we are bound to accept in the stead thereof : secondly, because the questions in controversy between us are many, if once we descend unto particularities ; that for the easier and more orderly proceeding therein the most general be first discussed, nor any question left off, nor in each question the prosecution of any one argument given over and another taken in hand, till the issue whereunto by replies and answers both parts are come, be collected, read, and acknowledged as well on the one side as on the other to be the plain conclusion which they are grown unto : thirdly, for avoiding of the manifold inconveniences whereunto ordinary and extemporary disputes are subject ; as also because, if ye should singly dispute one by one as every man's own wit did best serve, it might be conceived by the rest that haply some other would have done more ; the chiefest of you do all agree in this action, that whom ye shall then choose your speaker, by him that which is publickly brought into disputation be acknowledged by all your consents not to be his allegation but yours, such as ye all are agreed upon, and have required him to deliver in all your names ; the true copy whereof being taken by a notary, that a reasonable time be allowed for return of answer unto you in the like form. Fourthly, whereas a number of conferences have been had in other causes with the less effectual success, by reason of partial and untrue reports published afterwards unto the world ; that to prevent this evil, there be at the first a solemn declaration made on both parts, of their agreement to have that very book and no other set abroad, wherein their present authorized notaries do write those things fully and only, which being written and there read, are by their own open testimony acknowledged to be their own. Other circumstances hereunto belonging, whether for the choice of time, place, and language, or for prevention of impertinent and needless speech, or to any end and purpose else — they may be thought on when occasion serveth.

In this sort to broach my private conceit for the ordering

of a public action I should be loth (albeit I do it not otherwise than under correction of them whose gravity and wisdom ought in such cases to overrule,) but that so venturous boldness I see is a thing now general ; and am thereby of good hope, that where all men are licensed to offend, no man will shew himself a sharp accuser.

VI. What success God may give unto any such kind of conference or disputation, we cannot tell. But of this we are right sure, that nature, Scripture,[1] and experience itself, have all taught the world to seek for the ending of contentions by submitting itself unto some judicial and definitive sentence, whereunto neither part that contendeth may under any pretence or colour refuse to stand. This must needs be effectual and strong. As for other means without this, they seldom prevail. I would therefore know, whether for the ending of these irksome strifes, wherein you and your followers do stand thus formally divided against the authorized guides of this church, and the rest of the people subject unto their charge ; whether I say ye be content to refer your cause to any other higher judgment than your own, or else intend to persist and proceed as ye have begun, till yourselves can be persuaded to condemn yourselves. If your determination be this, we can be but sorry that ye should deserve to be reckoned with such, of whom God himself pronounceth, " The way of peace they have not known."[2]

[2.] Ways of peaceable conclusion there are, but these two certain : the one, a sentence of judicial decision given by authority thereto appointed within ourselves ; the other the like kind of sentence given by a more universal authority. The former of which two ways God himself in the Law prescribeth, and his Spirit it was which directed the very first Christian churches in the world to use the latter.

The ordinance of God in the Law was this. " [3] If there arise a matter too hard for thee in judgment, between blood and blood, between plea, &c. then shalt thou arise, and go up unto the place which the Lord thy God shall choose ; and thou shalt come unto the priests of the Levites, and unto the judge that shall be in those days, and ask, and

---

[1] [Hebr. vi. 16. " An oath for confirmation is to them an end of all strife."]

[2] Rom. iii. 17.   [3] Deut. xvii. 8.

they shall shew thee the sentence of judgment, and thou shalt do according to that thing, which they of that place which the Lord hath chosen shew thee, and thou shalt observe to do according to all that they inform thee; according to the law which they shall teach thee, and according to the judgment which they shall tell thee, shalt thou do; thou shalt not decline from the thing which they shall shew thee to the right hand nor to the left. And that man that will do presumptuously, not hearkening unto the priest (that standeth before the Lord thy God to minister there) or unto the judge, that man shall die, and thou shalt take away evil from Israel."

When there grew in the Church of Christ a question, Whether the Gentiles believing might be saved, although they were not circumcised after the manner of Moses, nor did observe the rest of those legal rites and ceremonies whereunto the Jews were bound; after great dissension and disputation about it, their conclusion in the end was to have it determined by sentence at Jerusalem; which was accordingly done in a council there assembled for the same purpose.[1] Are ye able to allege any just and sufficient cause wherefore absolutely ye should not condescend in this controversy to have your judgments overruled by some such definitive sentence, whether it fall out to be given with or against you; that so these tedious contentions may cease?

[3.] Ye will perhaps make answer, that being persuaded already as touching the truth of your cause, ye are not to hearken unto any sentence, no not though Angels should define otherwise, as the blessed Apostle's own example teacheth[2]: again, that men, yea councils, may err; and that, unless the judgment given do satisfy your minds, unless it be such as ye can by no further argument oppugn, in a word, unless you perceive and acknowledge it yourselves consonant with God's word; to stand unto it not allowing it were to sin against your own consciences.

But consider I beseech you first as touching the Apostle, how that wherein he was so resolute and peremptory, our Lord Jesus Christ made manifest unto him even by intuitive revelation, wherein there was no possibility of error. That which you are persuaded of, ye have it no otherwise than by your own only probable collection, and therefore such

---

[1] Acts. xv.   [2] [Gal. i. 8.]

bold asseverations as in him were admirable, should in your mouths but argue rashness. God was not ignorant that the priests and judges, whose sentence in matters of controversy he ordained should stand, both might and oftentimes would be deceived in their judgment. Howbeit, better it was in the eye of His understanding, that sometime an erroneous sentence definitive should prevail, till the same authority perceiving such oversight, might afterwards correct or reverse it, than that strifes should have respite to grow, and not come speedily unto some end.

Neither wish we that men should do any thing which in their hearts they are persuaded they ought not to do, but this persuasion ought (we say) to be fully settled in their hearts ; that in litigious and controversed causes of such quality, the will of God is to have them do whatsoever the sentence of judicial and final decision shall determine, yea, though it seem in their private opinion to swerve utterly from that which is right: as no doubt many times the sentence amongst the Jews did seem unto one part or other contending, and yet in this case, God did then allow them to do that which in their private judgment it seemed, yea and perhaps truly seemed, that the law did disallow. For if God be not the author of confusion but of peace, then can he not be the author of our refusal, but of our contentment, to stand unto some definitive sentence ; without which almost impossible it is that either we should avoid confusion, or ever hope to attain peace. To small purpose had the council of Jerusalem been assembled, if once their determination being set down, men might afterwards have defended their former opinions. When therefore they had given their definitive sentence, all controversy was at an end. Things were disputed before they came to be determined ; men afterwards were not to dispute any longer, but to obey. The sentence of judgment finished their strife, which their disputes before judgment could not do. This was ground sufficient for any reasonable man's conscience to build the duty of obedience upon, whatsoever his own opinion were as touching the matter before in question. So full of wilfulness and self-liking is our nature, that without some definitive sentence, which being given may stand, and a necessity of silence on both sides afterward imposed, small hope there is that strifes thus far prosecuted will in short time quietly end.

[4.] Now it were in vain to ask you, whether ye could be

content that the sentence of any court already erected
should be so far authorized, as that among the Jews
established by God himself, for the determining of all
controversies : " That man which will do presumptuously,
not hearkening unto the priest that standeth before the
Lord to minister there, nor unto the judge, let him die."
Ye have given us already to understand, what your opinion
is in part concerning her sacred majesty's court of high
commission ; the nature whereof is the same with that
amongst the Jews,[1] albeit the power be not so great.   The
other way happily may like you better, because Master Beza,
in his last book save one[2] written about these matters,
professeth himself to be now weary of such combats and
encounters, whether by word or writing, inasmuch as he
findeth that " controversies thereby are made but " brawls ;"
and therefore wisheth " that in some common lawful assembly
of churches all these strifes may at once be decided."

[5.] Shall there be in the meanwhile no " doings "?   Yes.
There are the weightier matters of the law, judgment, and
" mercy, and fidelity."[3]   These things we ought to do ; and
these things, while we contend about less, we leave undone.
Happier are they whom the Lord when he cometh, shall
find doing in these things, than disputing about " doctors,
elders, and deacons."   Or if there be no remedy but somewhat
needs ye must do which may tend to the setting forward of
your discipline ; do that which wise men, who think some
statute of the realm more fit to be repealed than to stand in
force, are accustomed to do before they come to parliament
where the place of enacting is ; that is to say, spend the
time in re-examining more duly your cause, and in more
throughly considering of that which ye labour to overthrow.
As for the orders which are established, sith equity and
reason, the law of nature, God and man, do all favour that

---

[1] [See George Cranmer's notes on B. vi.]

[2] Præf. Tract. de Excom. et Presbyt. ["Ab illis peto, . . . ut me
jampridem istarum concertationum pertæsum, quibus in rixas evadere
potius quam mitigari, nedum extingui controversias apparet, non inviti
patiantur vel partes istas minus occupatis aliis fratribus relinquere, si
fuerit opus, obeundas ; vel tacitum expectare, donec aut Ecclesiæ suæ
sic domi et foris vexatæ precibus hoc tribuat Dominus, ut lites omnes
istæ communi aliquo legitimo ecclesiarum conventu decidantur ; vel
mihi denique septuagesimum primum jam annum in terris peregrinanti
portus ille beatæ et perennis quietis, ad quem totus anhelo, per clemen-
tissimi Servatoris mei misericordiam patefiat."]

[3] Matt. xxiii. 23.

which is in being, till orderly judgment of decision be given against it ; it is but justice to exact of you, and perverseness in you it should be to deny, thereunto your willing obedience.

[6.] Not that I judge it a thing allowable for men to observe those laws which in their hearts they are steadfastly persuaded to be against the law of God : but your persuasion in this case ye are all bound for the time to suspend ; and in otherwise doing, ye offend against God by troubling his Church without any just or necessary cause. Be it that there are some reasons inducing you to think hardly of our laws. Are those reasons demonstrative, are they necessary, or but mere probabilities only ? An argument necessary and demonstrative is such, as being proposed unto any man and understood, the mind cannot choose but inwardly assent. Any one such reason dischargeth, I grant, the conscience, and setteth it at full liberty. For the public approbation given by the body of this whole church unto those things which are established, doth make it but probable that they are good. And therefore unto a necessary proof that they are not good it must give place. But if the skilfullest amongst you can shew that all the books ye have hitherto written be able to afford any one argument of this nature, let the instance be given. As for probabilities, what thing was there ever set down so agreeable with sound reason, but some probable show against it might be made ? Is it meet that when publicly things are received, and have taken place, general obedience thereunto should cease to be exacted, in case this or that private person, led with some probable conceit, should make open protestation, " I Peter or John disallow them, and pronounce them nought " ? In which case your answer will be, that concerning the laws of our church, they are not only condemned in the opinion of "a private man, but of thousands," yea and even " of those amongst which divers are in public charge and authority." [1] As though when public consent of the whole hath established any thing, every man's judgment being thereunto compared were not private, howsoever his calling be to some kind of public charge. So that of peace and quietness there is not any way possible, unless the probable voice of every entire society or body politic overrule all private of like nature in

[1] T. C. lib. iii. p. 181.

*E 201

the same body. Which thing effectually proveth, that God, being author of peace and not of confusion in the church, must needs be author of those men's peaceable resolutions, who concerning these things have determined with themselves to think and do as the church they are of decreeth, till they see necessary cause enforcing them to the contrary.

VII. Nor is mine own intent any other in these several books of discourse, than to make it appear unto you, that for the ecclesiastical laws of this land, we are led by great reason to observe them, and ye by no necessity bound to impugn them. It is no part of my secret meaning to draw you hereby into hatred, or to set upon the face of this cause any fairer glass than the naked truth doth afford; but my whole endeavour is to resolve the conscience, and to shew as near as I can what in this controversy the heart is to think, if it will follow the light of sound and sincere judgment, without either cloud of prejudice, or mist of passionate affection.

[2.] Wherefore seeing that laws and ordinances in particular, whether such as we observe, or such as yourselves would have established;—when the mind doth sift and examine them, it must needs have often recourse to a number of doubts and questions about the nature, kinds, and qualities of laws in general; whereof unless it be thoroughly informed, there will appear no certainty to stay our persuasion upon: I have for that cause set down in the first place an introduction on both sides needful to be considered: declaring therein what law is, how different kinds of laws there are, and what force they are of according unto each kind.

[3.] This done, because ye suppose the laws for which ye strive are found in Scripture, but those not against which ye strive; and upon this surmise are drawn to hold it as the very main pillar of your whole cause, "That Scripture ought to be the only rule of all our actions," and consequently that the church-orders which we observe being not commanded in Scripture, are offensive and displeasant unto God: I have spent the second Book in sifting of this point, which standeth with you for the first and chiefest principle whereon ye build.

[4.] Whereunto the next in degree is, That as God will have always a Church upon earth, while the world doth continue, and that Church stand in need of government; of which government it behoveth Himself to be both the Author and

Teacher: so it cannot stand with duty that man should ever presume in any wise to change and alter the same; and therefore "that in Scripture there must of necessity be found some particular form of Polity Ecclesiastical, the Laws whereof admit not any kind of alteration."

[5.] The first three Books being thus ended, the fourth proceedeth from the general grounds and foundations of your cause unto your general accusations against us, as having in the orders of our church (for so you pretend) "corrupted the right form of church-polity with manifold popish rites and ceremonies, which certain reformed churches have banished from amongst them, and have thereby given us such example as" (you think) "we ought to follow." This your assertion hath herein drawn us to make search, whether these be just exceptions against the customs of our church, when ye plead that they are the same which the church of Rome hath, or that they are not the same which some other reformed churches have devised.

[6.] Of those four Books which remain and are bestowed about the specialties of that cause which lieth in controversy, the first examineth the causes by you alleged, wherefore the public duties of Christian religion, as our prayers, our Sacraments, and the rest, should not be ordered in such sort as with us they are; nor that power, whereby the persons of men are consecrated unto the ministry, be disposed of in such manner as the laws of this church do allow. The second and third are concerning the power of jurisdiction: the one, whether laymen, such as your governing elders are, ought in all congregations for ever to be invested with that power; the other, whether bishops may have that power over other pastors, and therewithal that honour, which with us they have? And because besides the power of order which all consecrated persons have, and the power of jurisdiction which neither they all nor they only have, there is a third power, a power of ecclesiastical dominion, communicable, as we think, unto persons not ecclesiastical, and most fit to be restrained unto the Prince or Sovereign commander over the whole body politic: the eighth Book we have allotted unto this question, and have sifted therein your objections against those preeminences royal which thereunto appertain.

[7.] Thus have I laid before you the brief of these my travails, and presented unto your view the limbs of that cause litigious between us : the whole entire body whereof being thus compact, it shall be no troublesome thing for any man to find each particular controversy's resting-place, and the coherence it hath with those things, either on which it dependeth, or which depend on it.

VIII. The case so standing therefore, my brethren, as it doth, the wisdom of governors ye must not blame, in that they further also forecasting the manifold strange and dangerous innovations which are more than likely to follow if your discipline should take place, have for that cause thought it hitherto a part of their duty to withstand your endeavours that way. The rather, for that they have seen already some small beginnings of the fruits thereof, in them who concurring with you in judgment about the necessity of that discipline, have adventured without more ado to separate themselves from the rest of the Church, and to put your speculations in execution.[1] These men's hastiness the warier sort of you doth not commend ; ye wish they had held themselves longer in, and not so dangerously flown abroad before the feathers of the cause had been grown ; their error with merciful terms ye reprove, naming them,

---

[1] [See Strype, Whitg. II. 191 ; Ann. IV. 127, 136, 187–196, 197, 202, 239, 246. Bancroft, Survey, &c. 340–349. The head of this separation was Robert Browne. See his "Treatise of Reformation without tarrying for any, and of the wickedness of those Preachers, which will not reform themselves and their charge, because they will tarry till the Magistrate command and compel them." Prefixed to "A Book which sheweth the Life and Manners of all true Christians." (Bodl. 4°. B. 8. Th. Seld.) Middleburgh, 1582. Also (Bodl. 4°. Crymes, 744.) "Greenwood's Answer to Giffard," (who had written a short Treatise against the Donatists of England,) and in the same volume, 2. "A collection of certain slanderous Articles given out by the Bishops ;" and 3. "A Collection of certain Letters and Conferences lately passed betwixt certain Preachers and two Prisoners in the Fleet," (Barrow and Greenwood,) all 1590. In this latter, p. 7, we find the following portion of a dialogue between Barrow and Sperin, a Puritan minister. "Bar. 'Trow you, are none wicked in all the land, with whom you stand one body ? for all are of your church. Will you justify also all the parishes of England ?' Sper. 'I will justify all those parishes that have preaching ministers.' Bar. 'And what think you of those that have unpreaching ministers ?' Sper. '*I think not such to be true churches.*' (Mr. Sperin was here requested to set down this under his hand, but would not.") In "An Answer to M. Cartwright's Letter for joining with the English Churches," (which letter is subjoined in the same pamphlet, Bodl. 4°. S. 58. Th.) we read, p. 12, "Another proof is, as though it were granted him, "*That where a preaching minister is, there is a church.*"]

in great commiseration of mind, your "poor brethren."[1]
They on the contrary side more bitterly accuse you as their
"false brethren;" and against you they plead, saying:
"From your breasts it is that we have sucked those things,
which when ye delivered unto us ye termed that heavenly,
sincere, and wholesome milk of God's word,[2] howsoever ye
now abhor as poison that which the virtue thereof hath
wrought and brought forth in us. You sometime our
companions, guides and familiars, with whom we have had
most sweet consultations,[3] are now become our professed
adversaries, because we think the statute-congregations in
England to be no true Christian churches;[4] because we
have severed ourselves from them; and because without
their leave and license that are in civil authority, we have
secretly framed our own churches according to the platform
of the word of God. For of that point between you and us
there is no controversy. Alas! what would ye have us to
do? At such time as ye were content to accept us in the
number of your own, your teachings we heard, we read your
writings: and though we would, yet able we are not to
forget with what zeal ye have ever professed, that in the
English congregations (for so many of them as be ordered
according unto their own laws) the very public service of
God is fraught as touching matter with heaps of intolerable
pollutions, and as concerning form, borrowed from the shop
of Antichrist; hateful both ways in the eyes of the Most
Holy; the kind of their government by bishops and
archbishops antichristian; that discipline which Christ hath

[1] (Penry, Preface to "A Brief Discovery," (after speaking of Donatism,) "If any of our poor brethren be carried away, to think otherwise
of the congregations of England, which enjoy the word truly preached
and the right administration of the sacraments: we cease not to pray
that the Lord would reform their judgments. But woe be unto our
bishops, which are the cause of this their stumbling, and maintainers of
their error. For the poor brethren do hold nothing in this point, but
that which the learned fathers, as M. Bancroft calleth them, have
decreed."]

[2] 1 Pet. ii. 2.   [3] Psalm lv. 13.

[4] [See the opinions charged on Barrow and Greenwood before the
court of high commission, Nov. 1587, in Paule's Life of Whitgift;
Wordsworth, E. B. IV. 356. One of them is, "That all the precise,
which refuse the ceremonies of the Church, and yet preach in the same
Church, strain at a gnat and swallow a camel; and are close hypocrites,
and walk in a left-handed policy: as Master Cartwright, Wiggington,
&c." See the notes on Cranmer's letter to Hooker, vol. ii. book v.
appendix 2.]

'essentially tied,' that is to say, so united unto his Church, that we cannot account it really to be his Church which hath not in it the same discipline, that very discipline no less there despised, than in the highest throne of Antichrist ; [1] all such parts of the word of God as do any way concern that discipline no less unsoundly taught and interpreted by all authorized English pastors, than by Antichrist's factors themselves ; at baptism crossing, at the supper of the Lord kneeling, at both, a number of other the most notorious badges of antichristian recognizance usual. Being moved with these and the like your effectual discourses, whereunto we gave most attentive ear, till they entered even into our souls, and were as fire within our bosoms ; we thought we might hereof be bold to conclude, that sith no such antichristian synagogue may be accounted a true church of Christ, you by accusing all congregations ordered according to the laws of England as antichristian, did mean to condemn those congregations, as not being any of them worthy the name of a true Christian church. Ye tell us now it is not your meaning. But what meant your often threatenings of them, who professing themselves the inhabitants of Mount Sion, were too loth to depart wholly as they should out of Babylon ? Whereat our hearts being fearfully troubled, we durst not, we durst not continue longer so near her confines, lest her plagues might suddenly overtake us, before we did cease to be partakers with her

---

[1] Pref. against Dr. Bancr. [Pref. to "a Briefe Discovery of the Untruthes and Slanders (against the true government of the Church of Christ) contained in a Sermon, preached the 8 of Februarie, 1588, by D. Bancroft, and since that time set forth in print, with additions by the said Author." By Penry, 1590. The passage referred to is, "The visible Church of God, wheresoever it be, hath the power of binding and loosing annexed unto it, as our Saviour Christ teacheth us, Matth. 18, which authority is so essentially tied unto the visible Church, that wheresoever this power is to be found, there the Church of Christ is also visible, and wheresoever there is a visible Church, there this authority cannot be denied to be . . . Now the reader cannot be ignorant, that our bishops will never grant that the visible congregations in England ought to have this power of binding and loosing . . . The crime therefore of schism, and Donatism, which M. Bancroft and the prelates would fasten upon us, doth justly cleave unto themselves . . . It shall be proved in the end, that they are the schismatics and not we. It shall appear that they are growing to make a body of their own, wherewith the Church of God in a while (if they hold on their course) can have no more to do, than in times past it had with the schismatical Donatists."]

sins : for so we could not choose but acknowledge with grief that we were, when, they doing evil, we by our presence in their assemblies seemed to like thereof, or at leastwise not so earnestly to dislike, as became men heartily zealous of God's glory. For adventuring to erect the discipline of Christ without the leave of the Christian magistrate, haply ye may condemn us as fools, in that we hazard thereby our estates and persons further than you which are that way more wise think necessary : but of any offence or sin therein committed against God, with what conscience can you accuse us, when your own positions are, that the things we observe should every of them be dearer unto us than ten thousand lives ; that they are the peremptory commandments of God ; that no mortal man can dispense with them, and that the magistrate grievously sinneth in not constraining thereunto ? Will ye blame any man for doing that of his own accord, which all men should be compelled to do that are not willing of themselves ? When God commandeth, shall we answer that we will obey, if so be Cæsar will grant us leave ? Is discipline an ecclesiastical matter or a civil? If an ecclesiastical, it must of necessity belong to the duty of the minister. And the minister (you say) holdeth all his authority of doing whatsoever belongeth unto the spiritual charge of the house of God even immediately from God himself, without dependency upon any magistrate. Whereupon it followeth, as we suppose, that the hearts of the people being willing to be under the sceptre of Christ, the minister of God, into whose hands the Lord himself hath put that sceptre, is without all excuse if thereby he guide them not. Nor do we find that hitherto greatly ye have disliked those churches abroad, where the people with direction of their godly ministers have even against the will of the magistrate brought in either the doctrine or discipline of Jesus Christ. For which cause we must now think the very same thing of you, which our Saviour did sometime utter concerning falsehearted Scribes and Pharisees, ' they say, and do not.' " [1] Thus the foolish Barrowist deriveth his schism by way of conclusion, as to him it seemeth, directly and plainly out of your principles. Him therefore we leave to be satisfied by you from whom he hath sprung.

[2.] And if such by your own acknowledgment be persons dangerous, although as yet the alterations which they have

[1] Matt. xxiii. 3.

made are of small and tender growth ; the changes likely
to ensue throughout all states and vocations within this
land, in case your desire should take place, must be thought
upon.

First concerning the supreme power of the Highest,
they are no small prerogatives, which now thereunto belonging the form of your discipline will constrain it to
resign ; as in the last book of this treatise we have shewed
at large.[1]

Again it may justly be feared whether our English nobility,
when the matter came in trial, would contentedly suffer
themselves to be always at the call, and to stand to the
sentence of a number of mean persons assisted with the
presence of their poor teacher,[2] a man (as sometimes it
happeneth) though better able to speak, yet little or no whit
apter to judge, than the rest : from whom, be their dealings
never so absurd, (unless it be by way of complaint to a
synod,) no appeal may be made unto any one of higher
power, inasmuch as the order of your discipline admitteth
no standing inequality of courts, no spiritual judge to have
any ordinary superior on earth, but as many supremacies as
there are parishes and several congregations.

[3.] Neither is it altogether without cause that so many
do fear the overthrow of all learning as a threatened sequel
of this your intended discipline. For if "the world's
preservation" depend upon "the multitude of the wise ;"[3]

---

[1] [From this it would seem that the whole treatise was in a manner
finished before 1594, when this preface was published.]

[2] [Sutcliffe de Presbyt, 134. "Legibus nostris antiquatis, et hominibus doctis ab Ecclesiæ clavo (quam secundum leges et divinas et hu-
manas administrant) dimotis, presbyteri se ad rem accingent, Deus
bone, quales et quanti homines ! accedent primo Pastores quidam (si
quales apud nos sunt scire cupiatis) adolescentuli plerique novi, rerum
imperiti, cui pueros male credideris, aut unum servulum ; qui seipsos
vix regunt, tantum abest ut principes regere possint. Aderunt etiam
(τὸ ἐπὶ τῇ φακῇ μύρον) Presbyteri, viri bene barbati et tetrici, quorum
plurimæ sunt species : eorum enim nonnulli artifices sunt, ut fabri, qui
nobis arte Vulcania disciplinam excudent : coqui etiam aderunt, ut
aliquid sit in presbyterio insipido condimenti : sutores, ut pugnantes
presbyterorum sententias sarciant : sine cæmentariis, arx hæc presbyter-
alis ædificari non potest : adjungentur præterea aliquot agricolarum et
mercatorum centuriæ : pharmacopolæ vero non recte desiderabuntur,
multo enim illis opus erit helleboro. Atque istis ita constitutis et con-
sarcinatis, quis non presbyterium istiusmodi omnibus archiepiscopis,
episcopis, et reliquis ecclesiæ Anglicanæ moderatoribus præferat ?"]

[3] Sap. vi. 24.

and of that sort the number hereafter be not likely to wax
over-great, "when" (that wherewith the son of Sirach
professeth himself at the heart grieved) "men of understanding are" already so "little set by:"[1] how should
their minds whom the love of so precious a jewel filleth
with secret jealousy even in regard of the least things which
may any way hinder the flourishing estate thereof, choose
but misdoubt lest this discipline, which always you match
with divine doctrine as her natural and true sister, be found
unto all kinds of knowledge a step-mother;[2] seeing that
the greatest worldly hopes, which are proposed unto the
chiefest kind of learning, we seek utterly to extirpate as
weeds, and have grounded your platform on such proposi-
tions as do after a sort undermine those most renowned
habitations, where through the goodness of Almighty God all
commendable arts and sciences are with exceeding great
industry hitherto (and so may they for ever continue) studied,
proceeded in, and professed?[3]   To charge you as purposely
bent to the overthrow of that, wherein so many of you have
attained no small perfection, were injurious.   Only therefore
I wish that yourselves did well consider, how opposite
certain of your positions are unto the state of collegiate
societies, whereon the two universities consist.   Those
degrees which their statutes bind them to take are by your
laws taken away;[4] yourselves who have sought them ye
so excuse, as that ye would have men to think ye judge them
not allowable, but tolerable only, and to be borne with, for
some help which ye find in them unto the furtherance of

[1] Ecclus. xxvi. 28.

[2] ["By studying in corners, many melancholy model-makers, and
church-cobblers may be made, but not one sound divine: for scholars
profit by mutual conference, disputation, exercise, mutual emulation
and example, as much as by hearing and reading: but those helps they
lose that teach in corners.   There is but small hope that they would
make learned men, or semblant that they mean any such matter, when
taking away the livings of the clergy, and hope of reward from the
learned, they turn men up to live upon pensions, and to stand to the
courtesy of unlettered elders and deacons, that think crusts too good
for learned men."   Sutcliffe, False Semblant, &c. 134.]

[3] [Technical words, for the three degrees academical in the several
faculties: including the faculty of arts; for masters of arts are all,
properly speaking, professors or readers.]

[4] [Adm. 16.   "The titles of oure universitie, doctors, and bachelors
of divinitie, are not only for vayn glory sought and graunted, but there
they are the names of course, conferred rather by the prophane judgments
of them that know not what office of the Church they belong to," &c.]

your purposes, till the corrupt estate of the Church may be better reformed.   Your laws forbidding ecclesiastical persons utterly the exercise of civil power must needs deprive the heads and masters in the same colleges of all such authority as now they exercise, either at home, by punishing the faults of those, who not as children to their parents by the law of nature, but altogether by civil authority are subject unto them ; or abroad by keeping courts amongst their tenants. Your laws making permanent inequality amongst ministers a thing repugnant to the word of God, enforce those colleges, the seniors whereof are all or any part of them ministers under the government of a master in the same vocation, to choose as oft as they meet together a new president.   For if so ye judge it necessary to do in synods, for the avoiding of permanent inequality amongst ministers, the same cause must needs even in these collegiate assemblies enforce the like.   Except peradventure ye mean to avoid all such absurdities, by dissolving those corporations, and by bringing the universities unto the form of the school of Geneva. Which thing men the rather are inclined to look for, inasmuch as the ministry, whereinto their founders with singular providence have by the same statutes appointed them necessarily to enter at a certain time, your laws bind them much more necessarily to forbear, till some parish abroad call for them.[1]

[4.] Your opinion concerning the law civil is that the knowledge thereof might be spared, as a thing which this land doth not need.[2]   Professors in that kind being few, ye are the bolder to spurn at them, and not to dissemble your minds as concerning their removal : in whose studies although myself have not much been conversant, nevertheless exceeding great cause I see there is to wish that thereunto more encouragement were given ; as well for the singular treasures of wisdom therein contained, as also for the great use we have thereof, both in decision of certain kinds of

---

[1] [Decl. of Disc. transl. by T. C. p. 155.]

[2] Humb. Motion to the L. L. p. 50.   [" As for the canon law, it is no way hurtful, but good for the state of this realm, if it were abolished : being, as hereafter will appear, not necessary but dangerous to the state. . . As for the maintaining of civilians, as the law already maketh no great necessity of them, having little other way to set them on work, but by the canon law : if such men's studies were converted another way to more profit, in the Church and commonwealth, little or no loss or inconvenience would follow."]

causes arising daily within ourselves, and especially for
commerce with nations abroad, whereunto that knowledge
is most requisite. The reasons wherewith ye would persuade
that Scripture is the only rule to frame all our actions by,
are in every respect as effectual for proof that the same is
the only law whereby to determine all our civil controversies.
And then what doth let, but that as those men may have
their desire, who frankly broach it already that the work of
reformation will never be perfect, till the law of Jesus Christ
be received alone`; so pleaders and counsellors may bring
their books of the common law, and bestow them as the
students of curious and needless arts[1] did theirs in the
Apostles' time? I leave them to scan how far those words
of yours may reach, wherein ye declare that, whereas now
many houses lie waste through inordinate suits of law, "this
one thing will shew the excellency of discipline for the
wealth of the realm, and quiet of subjects; that the Church
is to censure such a party who is apparently troublesome
and contentious, and without *reasonable cause* upon a mere
will and stomach doth vex and molest his brother, and
trouble the country."[2] For mine own part I do not see
but that it might very well agree with your principles, if your
discipline were fully planted, even to send out your writs of
surcease unto all courts of England besides, for the most
things handled in them.[3]

---

[1] Acts xix. 19.   [2] Humb. Motion, p. 74.

[3] [Bp. Cooper, Adm. to the people of England, (1588,) p. 86.
"The canon law must be utterly taken away, with all offices to the
same belonging . . . The use and study of the civil law will be utterly
overthrown. For the civilians in this realm live not by the use of the
civil law, but by the offices of the canon law, and such things as are
within the compass thereof. And if you take those offices and functions
away, and those matters wherewith they deal in the canon law, you
must needs take away the hope of reward, and by that means their
whole study." Sutcliffe, Remonstrance to the Demonstr. of Disc. p. 41.
"That which is needless, is unlawful. All courts of record, as chancery
and common-pleas, &c. shall be found needless, if the consistory of
presbyters and elders were set up : which is only needful in the church
or congregation of the faithful brethren, because they may determine
all matters wherein any breach of charity may be ; as the admonitioner
saith : *Ergo*, all courts of record, as chancery, common pleas, &c. by
their reason will be found unlawful :" and see p. 178, where, Udall
having said, "Governors of the Church may not meddle but in matters
ecclesiastical only, . . . in deciding of controversies, in doctrine and
manners, as far as appertaineth to the conscience," Sutcliffe remarks;
"This one limit of authority will carry all causes (though most civil in

[5.] A great deal further I might proceed and descend lower. But forasmuch as against all these and the like difficulties your answer is,[1] that we ought to search what things are consonant to God's will, not which be most for our own ease; and therefore that your discipline being (for such is your error) the absolute commandment of Almighty God, it must be received although the world by receiving it should be clean turned upside down; herein lieth the greatest danger of all. For whereas the name of divine authority is used to countenance these things, which are not the commandments of God, but your own erroneous collections; on him ye must father whatsoever ye shall afterwards be led, either to do in withstanding the adversaries of your cause, or to think in maintenance of your doings. And what this may be, God doth know. In such kinds of error the mind once imagining itself to seek the execution of God's will, laboureth forthwith to remove both things and persons which any way hinder it from taking place; and in such cases if any strange or new thing seem requisite to be done, a strange and new opinion concerning the lawfulness thereof is withal received and broached under countenance of divine authority.

[6.] One example[2] herein may serve for many, to shew that false opinions, touching the will of God to have things done, are wont to bring forth mighty and violent practices against the hinderances of them; and those practices new opinions more pernicious than the first, yea most extremely sometimes opposite to that which the first did seem to intend. Where the people took upon them the reformation of the Church by casting out Popish superstition, they having received from their pastors a general instruction "that whatsoever the heavenly Father hath not planted

their nature and practice) out of all courts in the land unto their elderships. First, the chancery, that decideth matters of controversy by conscience, is clearly dammed up, and may go pick paigles" (i. e. cowslips). "And are any other civil courts in better case? No verily: for can any controversy be betwixt man and man, but it 'appertaineth to conscience,' to give the matter contended for unto him to whom of right it is due?" See also "False Semblant," &c. p. 132, 133.]

[1] Counterp. p. 108. ["His" (Cosins's) "first reasons are drawn from the inconveniences, which he thinketh will come into the Church by this means; as requiring rather (like a civilian not a divine) what is safe, than what is according to God his will."]

[2] [See Abp. Whitgift's Exhortation prefixed to the Answer to the Admonition. 1st ed. p. 13–16.]

must be rooted out,"[1] proceeded in some foreign places so far that down went oratories and the very temples of God themselves. For as they chanced to take the compass of their commission stricter or larger, so their dealings were accordingly more or less moderate. Amongst others there sprang up presently one kind of men, with whose zeal and forwardness the rest being compared were thought to be marvellous cold and dull. These grounding themselves on rules more general; that whatsoever the law of Christ commandeth not, thereof Antichrist is the author: and that whatsoever Antichrist or his adherents did in the world, the true professors of Christ are to undo; found out many things more than others had done, the extirpation whereof was in their conceit as necessary as of any thing before removed. Hereupon they secretly made their doleful complaints every where as they went,[2] that albeit the world did begin to profess some dislike of that which was evil in the kingdom of darkness, yet fruits worthy of a true repentance were not seen; and that if men did repent as they ought, they must endeavour to purge the earth of all manner evil, to the end there might follow a new world afterward, wherein righteousness only should dwell. Private repentance they said must appear by every man's fashioning his own life contrary unto the customs and orders of this present world, both in greater things and in less. To this

[1] Matt. xv. 13. [See Brandt. Hist. of the Reform. in the Low Countries: B. ii. and vii.]

[2] Guy de Brés contre l'Erreur des Anabaptistes, p. 3. ["La racine, source, et fondement des Anabaptistes ou Rebaptisez de nostre temps: avec tres ample refutation des arguments principaux, par lesquels ils ont accoustumé de troubler l'Eglise de nosiee Seigneur Jesus Christ, et seduire les simples. Le tout reduit en trois livres, par Guy de Brés. Chez Pierre de S. Andre, MDXCV," small 4to. pp. 903, no place of publication mentioned. The author was a pastor at Lille and Valenciennes, and with Saravia and three or four others was a principal author of "A Confession of Faith of the Reformed Churches of the Low Countries, 1561 or 1562," adopted by the States of Holland in 1622. "The said Saravia says in a certain letter, which I myself have seen, that 'Guido de Brés communicated this Confession to such ministers as he could find, desiring them to correct what they thought amiss in it; so that it was not to be considered as one man's work; but that none who were concerned in it ever designed it for a rule of faith to others, but only for a scriptural proof of what they themselves believed.'" Brandt's Hist. of the Reform. in the Low Countries, Eng. Transl. I. 142. De Brés was hanged at Valenciennes by the government of Philip II, in 1567. Ibid. p. 250. Anabaptism began by his account in Lower Saxony, about 1521.]

purpose they had always in their mouths those greater things, charity, faith, the true fear of God, the cross, the mortification of the flesh.[1] All their exhortations were to set light of the things in this world, to count riches and honours vanity, and in token thereof not only to seek neither, but if men were possessors of both, even to cast away the one and resign the other, that all men might see their unfeigned conversion unto Christ.[2] They were solicitors of men to fasts,[3] to often meditations of heavenly things, and as it were conferences in secret with God by prayers, not framed according to the frozen manner of the world, but expressing such fervent desires as might even force God to hearken unto them. Where they found men in diet, attire, furniture of house, or any other way, observers of civility and decent order, such they reproved as being carnally and earthly minded. Every word otherwise than severely and sadly uttered seemed to pierce like a sword through them.[4] If any man were pleasant, their manner was presently with deep sighs to repeat those words of our Saviour Christ, "Woe be to you which now laugh, for ye shall lament."[5] So great was their delight to be always in trouble, that such as did quietly lead their lives, they judged of all other men to be in most dangerous case. They so much affected to cross the ordinary custom in every thing, that when other men's use was to put on better attire, they would be sure to shew themselves openly abroad in worse : the ordinary names of the days in the week they thought it a kind of profaneness to use, and therefore accustomed themselves to make no other distinction than by numbers, the First, Second, Third day.[6]

[7.] From this they proceeded unto public reformation, first ecclesiastical, and then civil. Touching the former, they boldly avouched that themselves only had the truth, which thing upon peril of their lives they would at all times defend ; and that since the Apostles lived, the same was never before in all points sincerely taught.[7] Wherefore that things might again be brought to that ancient integrity which Jesus Christ by his word requireth, they began to control the ministers of the gospel for attributing so much force and virtue unto the scriptures of God read, whereas the truth was, that when the word is said to engender faith

---

[1] p. 4.   [2] p. 16.   [3] p. 118, 119.   [4] p. 116, 120.
[5] Luke vi. 25.   [6] p. 117.   [7] p. 40.

in the heart, and to convert the soul of man, or to work any such spiritual divine effect, these speeches are not thereunto appliable as it is read or preached, but as it is ingrafted in us by the power of the Holy Ghost opening the eyes of our understanding, and so revealing the mysteries of God, according to that which Jeremy promised before should be, saying, "I will put my law in their inward parts, and I will write it in their hearts."[1] The Book of God they notwithstanding for the most part so admired, that other disputation against their opinions than only by allegation of Scripture they would not hear; besides it they thought no other writings in the world should be studied; insomuch as one of their great prophets exhorting them to cast away all respects unto human writings, so far to his motion they condescended, that as many as had any books save the Holy Bible in their custody, they brought and set them publicly on fire.[2] When they and their Bibles were alone together, what strange fantastical opinion soever at any time entered into their heads, their use was to think the Spirit taught it them. Their phrensies concerning our Saviour's incarnation, the state of souls departed, and such-like,[3] are things needless to be rehearsed. And forasmuch as they were of the same suite with those of whom the Apostle speaketh, saying, "They are still learning, but never attain to the knowledge of truth,"[4] it was no marvel to see them every day broach some new thing, not heard of before. Which restless levity they did interpret to be their growing to spiritual perfection, and a proceeding from faith to faith.[5] The differences amongst them grew by this mean in a manner infinite, so that scarcely was there found any one of them, the forge of whose brain was not possessed with some special mystery. Whereupon, although their mutual contentions[6] were most fiercely prosecuted amongst themselves, yet when they came to defend the cause common to them all against the adversaries of their faction, they had ways to lick one another whole; the sounder in his own persuasion excusing *the dear brethren*,[7] which were not so far enlightened, and professing a charitable hope of the mercy of God towards them notwithstanding their swerving from him in some things. Their own ministers

---

[1] Jer. xxxi. 33. [De Brés, p. 81, 92.] [2] p. 27. [and 702.]
[3] [De Brés, l. ii. and iii.] [4] 2 Tim. iii. 7, p. 65.
[5] p. 66. [6] p. 135. [7] p. 25.

they highly magnified as men whose vocation was from God;[1] the rest their manner was to term disdainfully Scribes and Pharisees,[2] to account their calling a human creature, and to detain the people as much as might be from hearing them.   As touching Sacraments,[3] Baptism administered in the Church of Rome they judged to be but an execrable mockery and no baptism; both because the ministers thereof in the Papacy are wicked idolaters, lewd persons, thieves and murderers, cursed creatures, ignorant beasts; and also for that to baptize is a proper action belonging unto none but the Church of Christ, whereas Rome is Antichrist's synagogue.   The custom of using godfathers and godmothers at christenings they scorned.[4]   Baptizing of infants, although confessed by themselves to have been continued ever sithence the very Apostles' own times, yet they altogether condemned; partly because sundry errors are of no less antiquity;[5] and partly for that there is no commandment in the gospel of Christ which saith, "Baptize infants;"[6] but he contrariwise in saying, "Go preach and baptize," doth appoint that the minister of baptism shall in that action first administer doctrine, and then baptism; as also in saying, "Whosoever doth believe and is baptized," he appointeth that the party to whom baptism is administered shall first believe and then be baptized; to the end that believing may go before this sacrament in the receiver, no otherwise than preaching in the giver; sith equally in both,[7] the law of Christ declareth not only what things are required, but also in what order they are required.   The Eucharist they received (pretending our Lord and Saviour's example) after supper; and for avoiding all those impieties which have been grounded upon the mystical words of Christ, "This is my body, this is my blood," they thought it not safe to mention either body or blood in that sacrament, but rather to abrogate both, and to use no words but these, "Take, eat, declare the death of our Lord: Drink, shew forth our Lord's death."[8]   In rites and ceremonies their profession was hatred of all conformity with the church of Rome: for which cause they would rather endure any torment than observe the solemn festivals which others did, inasmuch as Antichrist (they said) was the first inventor of them[9]

[8.] The pretended end of their civil reformation was that Christ might have dominion over all; that all crowns and sceptres might be thrown down at his feet; that no other might reign over Christian men but he, no regiment keep them in awe but his discipline, amongst them no sword at all to be carried besides his, the sword of spiritual excommunication. For this cause they laboured with all their might in overturning the seats of magistracy,[1] because Christ hath said, "Kings of nations;"[2] in abolishing the execution of justice,[3] because Christ hath said, "Resist not evil;" in forbidding oaths, the necessary means of judicial trial,[4] because Christ hath said, "Swear not at all:" finally, in bringing in community of goods,[5] because Christ by his Apostles hath given the world such example, to the end that men might excel one another not in wealth the pillar of secular authority, but in virtue.

[9.] These men at the first were only pitied in their error, and not much withstood by any; the great humility, zeal, and devotion, which appeared to be in them, was in all men's opinion a pledge of their harmless meaning The hardest that men of sound understanding conceived of them was but this, "O quam honesta voluntate miseri errant! With how good a meaning these poor souls do evil!"[6] Luther made request unto Frederick duke of Saxony,[7] that within his dominion they might be favourably dealt with and spared, for that (their error exempted) they seemed otherwise right good men. By means of which merciful toleration they gathered strength, much more than was safe for the state of the commonwealth wherein they lived. They had their secret corner-meetings and assemblies in the night, the people flocked unto them by thousands.[8]

[10.] The means whereby they both allured and retained so great multitudes were most effectual: first, a wonderful show of zeal towards God, wherewith they seemed to be even rapt in every thing they spake: secondly, a hatred of sin, and a singular love of integrity, which men did think to be much more than ordinary in them, by reason of the custom which they had to fill the ears of the people with invectives against their authorized guides, as well spiritual

---

[1] p. 841.   [2] [Luke xxii. 25.]   [3] p. 833.   [4] p. 849.   [5] p. 40.
[6] Lactant. de Justit. lib. v. c. 19. [p. 480. ed. Oxon. 1684.]
[7] p. 6.   [8] p. 4, 20, 41, 42.

as civil: thirdly, the bountiful relief wherewith they eased
the broken estate of such needy creatures, as were in that
respect the more apt to be drawn away:[1] fourthly, a tender
compassion which they were thought to take upon the
miseries of the common sort, over whose heads their manner
was even to pour down showers of tears, in complaining
that no respect was had unto them, that their goods were
devoured by wicked cormorants, their persons had in
contempt, all liberty both temporal and spiritual taken
from them,[2] that it was high time for God now to hear
their groans, and to send them deliverance: lastly, a cunning
sleight which they had to stroke and smooth up the minds
of their followers, as well by appropriating unto them all
the favourable titles, the good words, and the gracious
promises in Scripture; as also by casting the contrary
always on the heads of such as were severed from that
retinue. Whereupon the people's common acclamation
unto such deceivers was, "These are verily the men of
God, these are his true and sincere prophets."[3] If any
such prophet or man of God did suffer by order of law
condign and deserved punishment, were it for felony,
rebellion, murder, or what else, the people, (so strangely
were their hearts enchanted,) as though blessed Saint
Stephen had been again martyred, did lament that God
took away his most dear servants from them.[4]

[11.] In all these things being fully persuaded, that what
they did, it was obedience to the will of God, and that all
men should do the like; there remained, after speculation,
practice, whereby the whole world thereunto (if it were
possible) might be framed. This they saw could not be
done but with mighty opposition and resistance; against
which to strengthen themselves, they secretly entered into
league of association.[5] And peradventure considering,
that although they were many, yet long wars would in time
waste them out; they began to think whether it might not
be that God would have them do, for their speedy and
mighty increase, the same which sometime God's own
chosen people, the people of Israel, did. Glad and fain
they were to have it so; which very desire was itself apt to
breed both an opinion of possibility, and a willingness to
gather arguments of likelihood, that so God himself would
have it. Nothing more clear unto their seeming, than that

[1] p. 55.   [2] p. 6, 7.   [3] p. 7.   [4] p. 27.   [5] p. 6.

a new Jerusalem being often spoken of in Scripture, they undoubtedly were themselves that new Jerusalem, and the old did by way of a certain figurative resemblance signify what they should both be and do. Here they drew in a sea of matter, by applying all things unto their own company, which are any where spoken concerning divine favours and benefits bestowed upon the old commonwealth of Israel: concluding that as Israel was delivered out of Egypt, so they spiritually out of the Egypt of this world's servile thraldom unto sin and superstition; as Israel was to root out the idolatrous nations, and to plant instead of them a people which feared God; so the same Lord's good will and pleasure was now, that these new Israelites should, under the conduct of other Joshuas, Samsons, and Gideons, perform a work no less miraculous in casting out violently the wicked from the earth, and establishing the kingdom of Christ with perfect liberty: and therefore, as the cause why the children of Israel took unto one man many wives, might be lest the casualties of war should any way hinder the promise of God concerning their multitude from taking effect in them; so it was not unlike that for the necessary propagation of Christ's kingdom under the Gospel the Lord was content to allow as much.

[12.] Now whatsoever they did in such sort collect out of Scripture, when they came to justify or persuade it unto others, all was the heavenly Father's appointment, his commandment, his will and charge. Which thing is the very point, in regard whereof I have gathered this declaration. For my purpose herein is to shew, that when the minds of men are once erroneously persuaded that it is the will of God to have those things done which they fancy, their opinions are as thorns in their sides, never suffering them to take rest till they have brought their speculations into practice. The lets and impediments of which practice their restless desire and study to remove leadeth them every day forth by the hand into other more dangerous opinions, sometimes quite and clean contrary to their first pretended meanings: so as what will grow out of such errors as go masked under the cloak of divine authority, impossible it is that ever the wit of man should imagine, till time have brought forth the fruits of them: for which cause it behoveth wisdom to fear the sequels thereof, even beyond all apparent cause of fear. These men, in whose mouths at the first sounded nothing but only mortification of the flesh, were come at the length to think they might lawfully have their six or seven wives apiece; they which at the first thought judgment and justice itself to be merciless cruelty, accounted at the length their own hands sanctified with being embrued in Christian blood; they who at the first were wont to beat down all dominion, and to urge against poor constables, "Kings of nations;" had at the length both consuls and kings of their own erection amongst themselves: finally, they which could not brook at the first that any man should seek, no not by law, the recovery of goods injuriously taken or withheld from him, were grown at the last to think they could not offer unto God more acceptable sacrifice, than by turning their adversaries clean out of house and home, and by enriching themselves with all kind of spoil and pillage; which thing being laid to their charge, they had in a readiness their answer,[1] that now the time was come, when according to our Saviour's promise, "the meek ones must inherit the earth;"[2] and that their title hereunto was the same which the righteous Israelites had unto the goods of the wicked Egyptians.[3]

[13.] Wherefore sith the world hath had in these men so fresh experience, how dangerous such active errors are, it must not offend you though touching the sequel of your present mispersuasions much more be doubted, than your own intents and purposes do haply aim at. And yet your words already are somewhat, when ye affirm, that your Pastors, Doctors, Elders, and Deacons, ought to be in this Church of England, "whether her Majesty and our state will or no;"[4] when for the animating of your confederates ye publish the musters which ye have made of your own bands, and proclaim them to amount I know not to how many thousands;[5] when ye threaten, that sith neither your

---

[1] p. 41. [2] Matt. v. 5. [3] Exod. xi. 2.
[4] Mart. in his third Libel.
[5] [Second Adm. p. 59, (misprint for 65,) ed. 1617. "We beseech you to pity this case, and to provide for it; it is the case already of many a thousand in this land; yea, it is the case of as many as seek the Lord aright, and desire to have his own orders restored. Great troubles will come of it, if it be not provided for; even the same God that hath stirred me, a man unknown, to speak, though those poor men which are locked up in Newgate, neither do, nor can be suffered to speak, will daily stir up more."

Str. Whitg. II. 18. (from a MS.) "One of our late libellers" [marg. Martyn] "braggeth of 100,000 hands: and wisheth the parliament to

suits to the parliament, nor supplications to our convocation-house, neither your defences by writing, nor challenges of disputation in behalf of that cause are able to prevail, we must blame ourselves, if to bring in discipline some such means hereafter be used as shall cause all our hearts to ache.[1] "That things doubtful are to be construed in the better part," is a principle not safe to be followed in matters concerning the public state of a commonweal. But how-soever these and the like speeches be accounted as arrows

bring in this reformation though it be by withstanding the Queen's Majesty."

Ibid. 191. In 1592, the Barrowists "were reckoned to amount to 20,000 by Sir W. Raleigh, in a speech of his in the last parliament."

"You are too broad with Martin's brood, for he hath 100,000 that will set their hands to his articles, and shew the Queen." Pap with an Hatchet. (This pamphlet was either by Thomas Nash or John Lyly.)

"Let the magistrate once consider what pestilent and dangerous beasts these wretches" (the Bishops) "are unto the civil state. For either by their own confession they are the bishops of the Devil, (and so by that means will be the undoing of the state, if they be continued therein,) or else their places ought to be in this commonwealth *whether her Majesty and our State will or no, because they are not* (as they say) *the Bishops of man.* Are they then the Bishops of God ? that is, have they such a calling as the Apostles, Evangelists, &c. had ? that is, such a calling as ought lawfully to be in a Christian commonwealth (unless the magistrate would injury the Church, yea, maim, deform, and make a monster of the Church) whether the magistrate will or no." Ha' ye any Work for a Cooper ? p. 28.

And in the Epitome, against Dr. Bridges, having quoted a passage from Bp. Aylmer's "Harborough for faithful Subjects," in which the Bishop had commended "those that in King Henry VIII. days would not grant him that his proclamations should have the force of a statute," Penry proceeds, "I assure you, brother John, you have spoken many things worthy the noting, and I would our parliament men would mark this action done in K. Hen. VIII. days, and follow it in bringing in reformation, and putting down Lord Bishops, with all other points of superstition. They may in your judgment not only do any thing against their King's or Queen's mind (that is behovefull to the honour of God and the good of the commonwealth) but even withstand the proceedings of their sovereign."]

[1] *Demonstr.* in the Pref. ["We have sought to advance the cause of God, by humble suit to the parliament, by supplication to your convocation house, by writing in defence of it, and by challenging to dispute for it : seeing none of these means used by us have prevailed, if it come in by that means, which will make all your hearts to ache, blame yourselves : for it must prevail, maugre the malice of all that stand against it ; or such a judgment must overtake this land, as shall cause the ears that hear thereof to tingle, and make us be a by word to all that pass by us."]

idly shot at random, without either eye had to any mark, or
regard to their lighting-place ; hath not your longing desire
for the practice of your discipline brought the matter already
unto this demurrer amongst you, whether the people and
their godly pastors that way affected ought not to make
separation from the rest, and to begin the exercise of
discipline without the license of civil powers, which license
they have sought for, and are not heard? Upon which
question as ye have now divided yourselves, the warier sort
of you taking the one part, and the forwarder in zeal the
other ; so in case these earnest ones should prevail, what
other sequel can any wise man imagine but this, that having
first resolved that attempts for discipline without superiors
are lawful, it will follow in the next place to be disputed
what may be attempted against superiors which will not
have the sceptre of that discipline to rule over them? Yea
even by you which have stayed yourselves from running
headlong with the other sort, somewhat notwithstanding
there hath been done without the leave or liking of your
lawful superiors, for the exercise of a part of your discipline
amongst the clergy thereunto addicted.[1] And lest examination of principal parties therein should bring those things to
light, which might hinder and let your proceedings ; behold,
for a bar against that impediment, one opinion ye have newly
added unto the rest even upon this occasion, an opinion to
exempt you from taking oaths which may turn to the
molestation of your brethren in that cause.[2] The next
neighbour opinion whereunto when occasion requireth may
follow, for dispensation with oaths already taken, if they
afterwards be found to import a necessity of detecting aught

[1] [In 1567, some of the ministers who had been silenced by the
bishops for nonconformity began to set up separate assemblies, using
the Geneva Prayer Book. Strype, Parker, I. 478-483. In 1577, the
same party, by their "use or rather abuse" (Bishop Cox to Burghley,
in Str. Ann. II. ii. 611.) of prophesyings, caused the inhibition of
those exercises, (Queen's letter to the Bishop of Lincoln, ibid. 612.)
and the suspension of Archbishop Grindal. (Grind. 342.) In 1585,
they are charged with having established synods and classes in various
counties, with reordination, unauthorized fast-days, and other schismatical acts. (Articles against Cartwright, in Fuller, C. H. IX. 200,
201, 202.) comp. in Strype's Whitg. III. 244-256, the bill exhibited
against them in the Star Chamber.]
[2] [This seems to have been first started, in a formal and public way,
by Cartwright and others, when cited before the ecclesiastical commission in 1590. Strype, Whitg. II. 19, 26, 28-32.]

which may bring such good men into trouble or damage, whatsoever the cause be.[1] O merciful God, what man's wit is there able to sound the depth of those dangerous and fearful evils, whereinto our weak and impotent nature is inclinable to sink itself, rather than to shew an acknowledgment of error in that which once we have unadvisedly taken upon us to defend, against the stream as it were of a contrary public resolution!

[14.] Wherefore if we any thing respect their error, who being persuaded even as you are have gone further upon that persuasion than you allow; if we regard the present state of the highest governor placed over us, if the quality and disposition of our nobles, if the orders and laws of our famous universities, if the profession of the civil or the practice of the common law amongst us, if the mischiefs whereinto even before our eyes so many others have fallen headlong from no less plausible and fair beginnings than yours are : there is in every of these considerations most just cause to fear lest our hastiness to embrace a thing of so perilous consequence should cause posterity to feel those evils, which as yet are more easy for us to prevent than they would be for them to remedy.

IX. The best and safest way for you therefore, my dear brethren, is, to call your deeds past to a new reckoning, to re-examine the cause ye have taken in hand, and to try it even point by point, argument by argument, with all the diligent exactness ye can ; to lay aside the gall of that bitterness wherein your minds have hitherto over-abounded, and with meekness to search the truth. Think ye are men, deem it not impossible for you to err ; sift unpartially your own hearts, whether it be force of reason or vehemency of affection, which hath bred and still doth feed these opinions in you. If truth do any where manifest itself, seek not to smother it with glosing delusions, acknowledge the greatness thereof, and think it your best victory when the same doth prevail over you.

[2.] That ye have been earnest in speaking or writing

---

[1] [The 31st article tendered to Cartwright (Fuller, ubi sup.) contains this clause, "That they should all teach . . . that it is not lawful to take any oath, whereby a man may be driven to discover any thing penal to himself or to his brother ; especially if he be persuaded the matter to be lawful, for which the punishment is like to be inflicted : or having taken it in this case, need not discover the very truth."]

again and again the contrary way, shall be no blemish or
discredit at all unto you. Amongst so many so huge volumes
as the infinite pains of St. Augustine have brought forth,
what one hath gotten him greater love, commendation and
honour, than the book[1] wherein he carefully collecteth
his own oversights, and sincerely condemneth them? Many
speeches there are of Job's whereby his wisdom and other
virtues may appear; but the glory of an ingenuous mind he
hath purchased by these words only, "[2] Behold, I will lay
mine hand on my mouth; I have spoken once, yet will I
not therefore maintain argument; yea twice, howbeit for
that cause further I will not proceed."

[3.] Far more comfort it were for us (so small is the joy
we take in these strifes) to labour under the same yoke, as
men that look for the same eternal reward of their labours,
to be joined with you in bands of indissoluble love and
amity, to live as if our persons being many our souls were
but one, rather than in such dismembered sort to spend our
few and wretched days in a tedious prosecuting of wearisome
contentions: the end whereof, if they have not some speedy
end, will be heavy even on both sides. Brought already we
are even to that estate which Gregory Nazianzen mournfully
describeth, saying,[3] "My mind leadeth me" (sith there is
no other remedy) "to fly and to convey myself into some
corner out of sight, where I may scape from this cloudy
tempest of maliciousness, whereby all parts are entered
into a deadly war amongst themselves, and that little
remnant of love which was, is now consumed to nothing.

---

[1] [viz. "Retractationum."]   [2] Job xl. 4, 5.
[3] Greg. Naz. in Apol. [p. 33, sq. ed. Par. 1609. ἀγαπητὸν, ὁρῶντα
τοὺς ἄλλους ἄνω καὶ κάτω φερομένους τε καὶ ταρασσομένους, φυγόντα
φυγῇ ἐκ τοῦ μέσου, ὑπὸ σκέπην ἀναχωρήσαντα, λαθεῖν τοῦ Πονηροῦ τὴν
ζάλην καὶ τὴν σκοτόμαιναν· ἡνίκα πολεμεῖ μὲν ἀλλήλοις τὰ μέλη, οἴχεται
δὲ τῆς ἀγάπης εἴ τι καὶ ἦν λείψανον. . . . . . . Πάντες δὲ ἐσμὲν εὐσεβεῖς,
ἐξ ἑνὸς μόνου, τοῦ καταγινώσκειν ἄλλων ἀσέβειαν . . . θηρούμεν δὲ τὰς
ἀλλήλων ἁμαρτίας, οὐκ ἵνα θρηνήσωμεν, ἀλλ' ἵνα ὀνειδίσωμεν . . . . . 'Εκ
δὲ τούτων, ὡς τὸ εἰκὸς, μισούμεθα μὲν ἐν τοῖς ἔθνεσι· καὶ, ὁ τούτου
χαλεπώτερον, οὐδὲ εἰπεῖν ἔχομεν, ὡς οὐ δικαίως· διαβεβλήμεθα δὲ καὶ
τῶν ἡμετέρων τοῖς ἐπιεικεστέροις· οὐδὲν γὰρ θαυμαστὸν, εἰ τοῖς πλείοσιν,
οἳ μόλις ἄν τι καὶ τῶν καλῶν ἀποδέχοιντο· τεκταίνουσι δὲ ἐπὶ τῶν
νώτων ἡμῶν οἱ ἁμαρτωλοί, καὶ ἃ κατ' ἀλλήλων ἐπινοοῦμεν, κατὰ πάντων
ἔχουσι· καὶ γεγόναμεν θέατρον καινὸν . . . . . . Ταῦτα ἡμῖν ὁ πρὸς
ἀλλήλους πόλεμος· ταῦτα οἱ λίαν ὑπὲρ τοῦ ἀγαθοῦ καὶ πρᾴου μαχόμενοι.
Hooker appears to have translated from Musculus' Latin, p. 18, 19.]

The only godliness we glory in, is to find out somewhat whereby we may judge others to be ungodly. Each other's faults we observe as a matter of exprobration and not of grief. By these means we are grown hateful in the eyes of the heathens themselves, and (which woundeth us the more deeply) able we are not to deny but that we have deserved their hatred. With the better sort of our own our fame and credit is clean lost. The less we are to marvel if they judge vilely of us, who although we did well would hardly allow thereof. On our backs they also build that are lewd, and what we object one against another, the same they use to the utter scorn and disgrace of us all. This we have gained by our mutual home-dissensions. This we are worthily rewarded with, which are more forward to strive than becometh men of virtuous and mild disposition."

[4.] But our trust in the Almighty is, that with us contentions are now at their highest float, and that the day will come (for what cause of despair is there?) when the passions of former enmity being allayed, we shall with ten times redoubled tokens of our unfeignedly reconciled love, shew ourselves each towards other the same which Joseph and the brethren of Joseph were at the time of their interview in Egypt. Our comfortable expectation and most thirsty desire whereof what man soever amongst you shall any way help to satisfy, (as we truly hope there is no one amongst you but some way or other will,) the blessings of the God of peace, both in this world and in the world to come, be upon him moe than the stars of the firmament in number.

WHAT THINGS ARE HANDLED IN THE BOOKS FOLLOWING.

Book the First, concerning Laws in general.

The Second, of the use of Divine Law contained in Scripture : whether that be the only Law which ought to serve for our direction in all things without exception.

The Third, of Laws concerning Ecclesiastical Polity: whether the form thereof be in Scripture so set down, that no addition or change is lawful.

The Fourth, of general exceptions taken against the Laws of our Polity, as being popish, and banished out of certain reformed churches.

The Fifth, of our Laws that concern the public religious duties of the Church, and the manner of bestowing that Power of Order, whih enableth men in sandry degrees and callings to execute the same.

The Sixth, of the Power of Jurisdiction, which the reformed platform claimeth unto lay-elders, with others.

The Seventh, of the Power of Jurisdiction, and the honour which is annexed thereunto in Bishops.

The Eighth, of the power of Ecclesiastical Dominion or Supreme Authority, which with us the highest governor or Prince hath, as well in regard of domestical Jurisdictions, as of that other foreignly claimed by the Bishop of Rome.

OF THE

L A W S

OF

ECCLESIASTICAL POLITY

———

THE FIRST BOOK

CONCERNING LAWS AND THEIR SEVERAL KINDS IN GENERAL

———

THE MATTER CONTAINED IN THIS FIRST BOOK

1 [Of this title it may be not improper to remark, that it by no means conveys the same idea with the phrase commonly substituted for it, Hooker's Ecclesiastical Polity. It does not profess to deliver a complete scheme or system, but only to contain a methodized course of observations on those portions of Church government, which seemed at the time most to require discussion.]

147

I. HE that goeth about to persuade a multitude, that they are not so well governed as they ought to be, shall never want attentive and favourable hearers; because they know the manifold defects whereunto every kind of regiment is subject, but the secret lets and difficulties, which in public proceedings are innumerable and inevitable, they have not ordinarily the judgment to consider. And because such as openly reprove supposed disorders of state are taken for principal friends to the common benefit of all, and for men that carry singular freedom of mind; under this fair and plausible colour whatsoever they utter passeth for good and current. That which wanteth in the weight of their speech, is supplied by the aptness of men's minds to accept and believe it. Whereas on the other side, if we maintain things that are established, we have not only to strive with a number of heavy prejudices deeply rooted in the hearts of men, who think that herein we serve the time, and speak in favour of the present state, because thereby we either hold or seek preferment; but also to bear such exceptions as minds so averted beforehand usually take against that which they are loth should be poured into them.

[2.] Albeit therefore much of that we are to speak in this present cause may seem to a number perhaps tedious, perhaps obscure, dark, and intricate; (for many talk of the truth, which never sounded the depth from whence it springeth; and therefore when they are led thereunto they are soon weary, as men drawn from those beaten paths wherewith they have been inured;) yet this may not so far prevail as to cut off that which the matter itself requireth, howsoever the nice humour of some be therewith pleased or no. They unto whom we shall seem tedious are in no wise injuried by us, because it is in their own hands to spare that labour which they are not willing to endure. And if any complain of obscurity, they must consider, that in these matters it cometh no otherwise to pass than in sundry the works both of art and also of nature, where that which hath greatest force in the very things we see is notwithstanding itself oftentimes not seen. The stateliness of houses, the goodliness of trees, when we behold them delighteth the eye; but that foundation which beareth up the one, that root which ministereth unto the other nourishment and life, is in the bosom of the earth concealed ; and if there be at any time occasion to search into it, such labour is then more necessary than pleasant, both to them which undertake it and for the lookers-on. In like manner, the use and benefit of good laws all that live under them may enjoy with delight and comfort, albeit the grounds and first original causes from whence they have sprung be unknown, as to the greatest part of men they are. But when they who withdraw their obedience pretend that the laws which they should obey are corrupt and vicious ; for better examination of their quality it behoveth the very foundation and root, the highest wellspring and fountain of them to be discovered. Which because we are not oftentimes accustomed to do, when we do it the pains we take are more needful a great deal than acceptable, and the matters which we handle seem by reason of newness (till the mind grow better acquainted with them) dark, intricate, and unfamiliar. For as much help whereof as may be in this case, I have endeavoured throughout the body of this whole discourse, that every former part might give strength unto all that follow, and every later bring some light unto all before. So that if the judgments of men do but hold themselves in suspense as touching these first more general meditations, till in order they have perused the rest that ensue ; what may seem dark at the first will afterwards be found more plain, even as the later particular decisions will appear I doubt not more strong, when the other have been read before.

[3.] The Laws of the Church, whereby for so many ages together we have been guided in the exercise of Christian religion and the service of the true God, our rites, customs, and orders of ecclesiastical government, are called in question : we are accused as men that will not have Christ Jesus to rule over them, but have wilfully cast his statutes behind their backs, hating to be reformed and made subject unto the sceptre of his discipline. Behold therefore we offer the laws whereby we live unto the general trial and judgment of the whole world ; heartily beseeching Almighty God, whom we desire to serve according to his own will, that both we and others (all kind of partial affection being clean laid aside) may have eyes to see and hearts to embrace the things that in his sight are most acceptable.

And because the point about which we strive is the quality of our laws, our first entrance hereinto cannot better be made, than with consideration of the nature of law in general, and of that law which giveth life unto all the rest, which are commendable, just, and good; namely the law whereby the Eternal himself doth work. Proceeding from hence to the law, first of Nature, then of Scripture, we shall have the easier access unto those things which come after to be debated, concerning the particular cause and question which we have in hand.

II. All things that are, have some operation not violent or casual. Neither doth any thing ever begin to exercise the same, without some fore-conceived end for which it worketh. And the end which it worketh for is not obtained, unless the work be also fit to obtain it by. For unto every end every operation will not serve. That which doth assign unto each thing the kind, that which doth moderate the force and power, that which doth appoint the form and measure, of working, the same we term a Law. So that no certain end could ever be attained, unless the actions whereby it is attained were regular; that is to say, made suitable, fit and correspondent unto their end, by some canon, rule or law. Which thing doth first take place in the works even of God himself.

[2.] All things therefore do work after a sort according to law: all other things according to a law, whereof some superior, unto whom they are subject, is author; only the works and operations of God have him both for their worker, and for the law whereby they are wrought. The being of God is a kind of law to his working; for that perfection which God is, giveth perfection to that he doth. Those natural, necessary, and internal operations of God, the Generation of the Son, the Proceeding of the Spirit, are without the compass of my present intent: which is to touch only such operations as have their beginning and being by a voluntary purpose, wherewith God hath eternally decreed when and how they should be. Which eternal decree is that we term an eternal law.

Dangerous it were for the feeble brain of man to wade far into the doings of the Most High; whom although to know be life, and joy to make mention of his name; yet our soundest knowledge is to know that we know him not as indeed he is, neither can know him: and our safest eloquence concerning him is our silence, when we confess without confession that his glory is inexplicable, his greatness above our capacity and reach.[1] He is above, and we upon earth; therefore it behoveth our words to be wary and few.[2]

Our God is one, or rather very Oneness, and mere unity, having nothing but itself in itself, and not consisting (as all things do besides God) of many things. In which essential Unity of God a Trinity personal nevertheless subsisteth, after a manner far exceeding the possibility of man's conceit. The works which outwardly are of God, they are in such sort of him being one, that each Person hath in them somewhat peculiar and proper. For being Three, and they all subsisting in the essence of one Deity; from the Father, by the Son, through the Spirit, all things are. That which the Son doth hear of the Father, and which the Spirit doth receive of the Father and the Son, the same we have at the hands of the Spirit as being the last, and therefore the nearest unto us in order, although in power the same with the second and the first.[3]

[3.] The wise and learned among the very heathens themselves have all acknowledged some First Cause, whereupon originally the being of all things dependeth. Neither have they otherwise spoken of that cause than as an Agent, which knowing what and why it worketh, observeth in working a most exact order or law. Thus much is signified by that which Homer mentioneth, Διὸς δ' ἐτελείετο βουλή.[4] Thus much acknowledged by Mercurius Trismegistus, Τὸν πάντα κόσμον ἐποίησεν ὁ δημιουργὸς οὐ χερσὶν ἀλλὰ λόγῳ.[5] Thus much confest by Anaxagoras and Plato, terming the Maker of the world an *intellectual* Worker.[6] Finally the Stoics,

[1] ["De quo nihil dici et exprimi mortalium potis est significatione verborum: qui, ut intelligaris, tacendum est; atque, ut per umbram te possit errans investigare suspicio, nihil est omnino mutiendum." Arnob. adv. Gentes, I. 31. See Davison on Prophecy, p. 672, first ed.]

[2] [Eccles. v. 2.]

[3] John xvi. 13–15. [ὅταν δὲ ἔλθῃ ἐκεῖνος, τὸ Πνεῦμα τῆς ἀληθείας, ὁδηγήσει ὑμᾶς εἰς πᾶσαν τὴν ἀλήθειαν· οὐ γὰρ λαλήσει ἀφ' ἑαυτοῦ, ἀλλ' ὅσα ἂν ἀκούσῃ λαλήσει, ... 'Εκεῖνος ἐμὲ δοξάσει, ὅτι ἐκ τοῦ ἐμοῦ λήψεται, καὶ ἀναγγελεῖ ὑμῖν. Πάντα, ὅσα ἔχει ὁ Πατὴρ, ἐμά ἐστι· διὰ τοῦτο εἶπον, ὅτι ἐκ τοῦ ἐμοῦ λήψεται, καὶ ἀναγγελεῖ ὑμῖν. And c. xiv. 15. πάντα, ἃ ἤκουσα παρὰ τοῦ Πατρός μου, ἐγνώρισα ὑμῖν.]

[4] Jupiter's *counsel* was accomplished. [Il. A. 5.]

[5] [C 7. § 1.] The Creator made the whole world not with hands, but by *reason*.

[6] Stob. in Eclog. Phys. [This seems to refer to the following: 'Αναξαγόρας, νοῦν κόσμον ποιῶν [κοσμοποιῶν] τὸν Θεόν. Stob. ed. Canter. p. 2. Πλάτων . . . "νοῦς ὁ Θεός . . . τούτου δὲ πατρὸς καὶ ποιητοῦ, τὰ ἄλλα θεῖα ἔγγονα." . . . Ibid. p. 5.]

although imagining the first cause of all things to be fire, held nevertheless, that the same fire having art, did ὁδῷ βαδίζειν ἐπὶ γενέσει κόσμου.[1] They all confess therefore in the working of that first cause, that Counsel is used, Reason followed, a Way observed; that is to say, constant Order and Law is kept; whereof itself must needs be author unto itself. Otherwise it should have some worthier and higher to direct it, and so could not itself be the first. Being the first, it can have no other than itself to be the author of that law which it willingly worketh by.

God therefore is a law both to himself, and to all other things besides. To himself he is a law in all those things, whereof our Saviour speaketh, saying, "My Father worketh as yet, so I."[2] God worketh nothing without cause. All those things which are done by him have some end for which they are done; and the end for which they are done is a reason of his will to do them. His will had not inclined to create woman, but that he saw it could not be well if she were not created. *Non est bonum*, "It is not good man should be alone; therefore let us make a helper for him."[3] That and nothing else is done by God, which to leave undone were not so good.

If therefore it be demanded, why God having power and ability infinite, the effects notwithstanding of that power are all so limited as we see they are: the reason hereof is the end which he hath proposed, and the law whereby his wisdom hath stinted the effects of his power in such sort, that it doth not work infinitely, but correspondently unto that end for which it worketh, even "all things χρηστῶς,[4] in most decent and comely sort," all things in Measure, Number, and Weight.

[4.] The general end of God's external working is the exercise of his most glorious and most abundant virtue. Which abundance doth shew itself in variety, and for that cause this variety is oftentimes in Scripture exprest by the name of *riches.*[5] "The Lord hath made all things for his own sake."[6] Not that any thing is made to be beneficial

---

[1] Proceed by a certain and a set *Way* in the making of the world. [οἱ Στοικοὶ νοερὸν θεὸν ἀποφαίνονται, πῦρ τεχνικὸν, ὁδῷ βάδιζον ἐπὶ γενέσει κόσμου. Ibid. 5.]

[2] John v. 17.   [3] Gen. ii. 18.   [4] Sap. viii. 1; xi. 20.

[5] Ephes. i. 7; Phil. iv. 19; Col. ii. 3.

[6] Prov. xvi. 4.

unto him, but all things for him to shew beneficence and grace in them.

The particular drift of every act proceeding externally from God we are not able to discern, and therefore cannot always give the proper and certain reason of his works. Howbeit undoubtedly a proper and certain reason there is of every finite work of God, inasmuch as there is a law imposed upon it; which if there were not, it should be infinite, even as the worker himself is.

[5.] They err therefore who think that of the will of God to do this or that there is no reason besides his will. Many times no reason known to us; but that there is no reason thereof I judge it most unreasonable to imagine, inasmuch as he worketh all things κατὰ τὴν βουλὴν τοῦ θελήματος αὐτοῦ, not only according to his own will, but "the Counsel of his own will." [1]   And whatsoever is done with counsel or wise resolution hath of necessity some reason why it should be done, albeit that reason be to us in some things so secret, that it forceth the wit of man to stand, as the blessed Apostle himself doth, amazed thereat: [2] "O the depth of the riches both of the wisdom and knowledge of God! how unsearchable are his judgments," &c.   That law eternal which God himself hath made to himself, and thereby worketh all things whereof he is the cause and author; that law in the admirable frame whereof shineth with most perfect beauty the countenance of that wisdom which hath testified concerning herself," [3] "The Lord possessed me in the beginning of his way, even before his works of old I was set up;" that law, which hath been the pattern to make, and is the card to guide the world by; that law which hath been of God and with God everlastingly; that law, the author and observer whereof is one only God to be blessed for ever: how should either men or angels be able perfectly to behold?   The book of this law we are neither able nor worthy to open and look into.   That little thereof which we darkly apprehend we admire, the rest with religious ignorance we humbly and meekly adore.

[6.] Seeing therefore that according to this law He worketh, "of whom, through whom, and for whom, are all things;" [4] although there seem unto us confusion and disorder in the affairs of this present world: "Tamen

---

[1] Ephes. i. 11.   [2] Rom. xi. 33.
[3] Prov. viii. 22.   [4] Rom. xi. 36.

quoniam bonus mundum rector temperat, recte fieri cuncta ne dubites:"[1] "let no man doubt but that every thing is well done, because the world is ruled by so good a guide," as transgresseth not His own law: than which nothing can be more absolute, perfect, and just.

The law whereby He worketh is eternal, and therefore can have no show or colour of mutability: for which cause, a part of that law being opened in the promises which God hath made (because his promises are nothing else but declarations what God will do for the good of men) touching those promises the Apostle hath witnessed, that God may as possibly "deny himself"[2] and not be God, as fail to perform them. And concerning the counsel of God, he termeth it likewise a thing "unchangeable;"[3] the counsel of God, and that law of God whereof now we speak, being one.

Nor is the freedom of the will of God any whit abated, let, or hindered, by means of this; because the imposition of this law upon himself is his own free and voluntary act.

This law therefore we may name eternal, being "that order which God before all ages hath set down with himself, for himself to do all things by."

III. I am not ignorant that by "law eternal" the learned for the most part do understand the order, not which God hath eternally purposed himself in all his works to observe, but rather that which with himself he hath set down as expedient to be kept by all his creatures, according to the several conditions wherewith he hath endued them. They who thus are accustomed to speak apply the name of Law unto that only rule of working which superior authority imposeth; whereas we somewhat more enlarging the sense thereof term any kind of rule or canon, whereby actions are framed, a law. Now that law which, as it is laid up in the bosom of God, they call Eternal, receiveth according unto the different kinds of things which are subject unto it different and sundry kinds of names. That part of it which ordereth natural agents we call usually Nature's law; that which Angels do clearly behold and without any swerving observe is a law Celestial and heavenly; the law of Reason, that which bindeth creatures reasonable in this world, and

---

[1] Boet. lib. iv. de Consol. Philos. [p. 105, ed. Lugd. Bat. 1656.] pros. 5.

[2] 2 Tim. ii. 13.

[3] Heb. vi. 17.

with which by reason they may most plainly perceive themselves bound; that which bindeth then., and is not known
but by special revelation from God, Divine law; Human
law, that which out of the law either of reason or of God
men probably gathering to be expedient, they make it a law.
All things therefore, which are as they ought to be, are conformed unto *this second law eternal;* and even those things
which to this eternal law are not conformable are notwithstanding in some sort ordered by *the first eternal law.* For
what good or evil is there under the sun, what action
correspondent or repugnant unto the law which God hath
imposed upon his creatures, but in or upon it God doth
work according to the law which himself hath eternally purposed to keep; that is to say, the *first law eternal?* So
that a twofold law eternal being thus made, it is not hard to
conceive how they both take place in all things.[1]

[2.] Wherefore to come to the law of nature: albeit
thereby we sometimes mean that manner of working which
God hath set for each created thing to keep; yet forasmuch
as those things are termed most properly natural agents,
which keep the law of their kind unwittingly, as the heavens
and elements of the world, which can do no otherwise than
they do; and forasmuch as we give unto intellectual natures
the name of Voluntary agents, that so we may distinguish
them from the other; expedient it will be, that we sever the
law of nature observed by the one from that which the other
is tied unto. Touching the former, their strict keeping of
one tenure, statute, and law, is spoken of by all, but hath in
it more than men have as yet attained to know, or perhaps
ever shall attain, seeing the travail of wading herein is given

---

[1] "Id omne, quod in rebus creatis fit, est materia legis æternæ.'
Th. I. 1, 2. q. 93, art. 4, 5, 6. [Thom. Aquin. Opp. xi. 202.] "Nullo
modo aliquid legibus summi Creatoris ordinationique subtrahitur, a quo
pax universitatis administratur." August. de Civit. Dei, lib. xix. cap.
12. [t. VII. 556.] Immo et peccatum, quatenus a Deo juste permittitur,
cadit in legem æternam. Etiam legi æternæ subjicitur peccatum,
quatenus voluntaria legis transgressio pœnale quoddam incommodum
animæ inserit, juxta illud Augustini, "Jussisti Domine, et sic est, ut
pœna sua sibi sit omnis animus inordinatus." Confes. lib. i. cap. 12.
[t. I. 77.] Nec male scholastici, "Quemadmodum," inquiunt, "videmus res naturales contingentes, hoc ipso quod a fine particulari suo
atque adeo a lege æterna exorbitant, in eandem legem æternam incidere,
quatenus consequuntur alium finem a lege etiam æterna ipsis in casu
particulari constitutum; sic verisimile est homines, etiam cum peccant
et desciscunt a lege æterna ut præcipiente, reincidere in ordinem æternæ
legis ut punientis."

of God to the sons of men,[1] that perceiving how much the least thing in the world hath in it more than the wisest are able to reach unto, they may by this means learn humility. Moses, in describing the work of creation, attributeth speech unto God: "God said, Let there be light: let there be a firmament: let the waters under the heaven be gathered together into one place: let the earth bring forth: let there be lights in the firmament of heaven." Was this only the intent of Moses, to signify the infinite greatness of God's power by the easiness of his accomplishing such effects, without travail pain, or labour? Surely it seemeth that Moses had herein besides this a further purpose, namely, first to teach that God did not work as a necessary but a voluntary agent, intending beforehand and decreeing with himself that which did outwardly proceed from him: secondly, to shew that God did then institute a law natural to be observed by creatures, and therefore according to the manner of laws, the institution thereof is described, as being established by solemn injunction. His commanding those things to be which are, and to be in such sort as they are, to keep that tenure and course which they do, importeth the establishment of nature's law. This world's first creation, and the preservation since of things created, what is it but only so far forth a manifestation by execution, what the eternal law of God is concerning things natural? And as it cometh to pass in a kingdom rightly ordered, that after a law is once published, it presently takes effect far and wide, all states framing themselves thereunto; even so let us think it fareth in the natural course of the world: since the time that God did first proclaim the edicts of his law upon it, heaven and earth have hearkened unto his voice, and their labour hath been to do his will: He "made a law for the

---

[1] [Eccles. III. 9, 10. "I have seen the travail which God hath given to the sons of men to be exercised in it. He hath made every thing beautiful in his time: also he hath set the world in their heart, so that no man can find out the work that God maketh from the beginning to the end."
Compare the use which Lord Bacon has made of the same text, Advancement of Learning, b. ii. "Knowledges are as pyramids, whereof history is the basis. So of natural philosophy, the basis is natural history; the stage next the basis is physic; the stage next the vertical point is metaphysic. As for the vertical point, *Opus, quod operatur Deus a principio usque ad finem*, the summary law of nature, we know not whether man's inquiry can attain unto it." Works, I. p. 104, 8vo. London, 1803.]

rain;"[1] He gave his "decree unto the sea, that the waters should not pass his commandment."[2] Now if nature should intermit her course, and leave altogether though it were but for a while the observation of her own laws; if those principal and mother elements of the world, whereof all things in this lower world are made, should lose the qualities which now they have; if the frame of that heavenly arch erected over our heads should loosen and dissolve itself; if celestial spheres should forget their wonted motions, and by irregular volubility turn themselves any way as it might happen; if the prince of the lights of heaven, which now as a giant doth run his unwearied course,[3] should as it were through a languishing faintness begin to stand and to rest himself; if the moon should wander from her beaten way, the times and seasons of the year blend themselves by disordered and confused mixture, the winds breathe out their last gasp, the clouds yield no rain, the earth be defeated of heavenly influence, the fruits of the earth pine away as children at the withered breasts of their mother no longer able to yield them relief:[4] what would become of man himself, whom these things now do all serve? See we not plainly that obedience of creatures unto the law of nature is the stay of the whole world?

[3.] Notwithstanding with nature it cometh sometimes to

---

[1] [Job xxviii. 26.]   [2] [Jer. v. 22.]   [3] Psalm xix. 5.
[4] [Hooker seems to have had in his mind the following passage:
"Postquam esse nomen in terris Christianæ religionis occœpit, quidnam inusitatum, quid incognitum, quid contra leges principaliter institutas aut sensit aut passa est rerum ipsa quæ dicitur appellaturque Natura? Nunquid in contrarias qualitates prima illa elementa mutata sunt, ex quibus res omnes consensum est esse concretas? Nunquid machinæ hujus, et molis, qua universi tegimur et continemur inclusi, parte est in aliqua relaxata aut dissoluta constructio? Nunquid vertigo hæc mundi, primogenii motus moderamen excedens, aut tardius repere, aut præcipiti cœpit volubilitate raptari? Nunquid ab occiduis partibus attollere se astra, atque in ortus fieri signorum cœpta est inclinatio? Nunquid ipse syderum sol princeps, cujus omnia luce vestiuntur atque animantur, calore exarsit, intepuit, atque in contrarios habitus moderaminis soliti temperamenta corrupit? Nunquid luna desivit redintegrare seipsam, atque in veteres formas, novellarum semper restitutione, traducere? Nunquid frigora, nunquid calores, nunquid tepores medii, inæqualium temporum confusionibus occiderunt? Nunquid longos habere dies bruma, et revocare tardissimas luces nox cœpit æstatis? Nunquid suas animas expiraverunt venti? emortuisque flaminibus neque cœlum coarctatur in nubila, nec madidari ex imbribus arva suescunt? Commendata semina tellus recusat accipere? aut frondescere arbores nolunt?" Arnob. adv. Gent. I. 2.]

pass as with art. Let Phidias have rude and obstinate stuff to carve, though his art do that it should, his work will lack that beauty which otherwise in fitter matter it might have had. He that striketh an instrument with skill may cause notwithstanding a very unpleasant sound, if the string whereon he striketh chance to be uncapable of harmony. In the matter whereof things natural consist, that of Theophrastus taketh place, Πολὺ τὸ οὐχ ὑπακοῦον οὐδὲ δεχόμενον τὸ εὖ.[1] "Much of it is oftentimes such as will by no means yield to receive that impression which were best and most perfect." Which defect in the matter of things natural, they who gave themselves unto the contemplation of nature amongst the heathen observed often : but the true original cause thereof, divine malediction, laid for the sin of man upon these creatures which God had made for the use of man, this being an article of that saving truth which God hath revealed unto his Church, was above the reach of their merely natural capacity and understanding. But howsoever these swervings are now and then incident into the course of nature, nevertheless so constantly the laws of nature are by natural agents observed, that no man denieth but those things which nature worketh are wrought, either always or for the most part, after one and the same manner.[2]

[4.] If here it be demanded what that is which keepeth nature in obedience to her own law, we must have recourse to that higher law whereof we have already spoken, and because all other laws do thereon depend, from thence we must borrow so much as shall need for brief resolution in this point. Although we are not of opinion therefore, as some are, that nature in working hath before her certain exemplary draughts or patterns, which subsisting in the bosom of the Highest, and being thence discovered, she fixeth her eye upon them, as travellers by sea upon the pole-star of the world, and that according thereunto she guideth her hand to work by imitation : although we rather embrace the oracle of Hippocrates,[3] that "each thing both

---

[1] Theophrast. in Metaph. [p. 271, l. 10, ed. Basil, 1541.]

[2] Arist. Rhet. i. cap. 39. [ἢ γὰρ αἰεὶ, ἢ ὡς ἐπιτοπολὺ ὡσαύτως ἀποβαίνει.]

[3] Τὴν πεπρωμένην μοίρην ἕκαστον ἐκπληροῖ καὶ ἐπὶ τὸ μεῖζον καὶ ἐπὶ τὸ μεῖον . . . ἃ πρήσσουσιν οὐκ οἴδασιν, ἃ δὲ πρήσσουσι δοκέουσιν εἰδέναι, καί θ' ἃ μὲν ὁρῶσι οὐ γινώσκουσι. [p. 342, 48. ed. Genev. 1657. It need hardly be observed, that the beginning of the sentence alludes to Plato's doctrine.]

in small and in great fulfilleth the task which destiny hath set down ;" and concerning the manner of executing and fulfilling the same, "what they do they know not, yet is it in show and appearance as though they did know what they do; and the truth is they do not discern the things which they look on:" nevertheless, forasmuch as the works of nature are no less exact, than if she did both behold and study how to express some absolute shape or mirror always present before her ; yea, such her dexterity and skill appeareth, that no intellectual creature in the world were able by capacity to do that which nature doth without capacity and knowledge ; it cannot be but nature hath some director of infinite knowledge to guide her in all her ways. Who the guide of nature, but only the God of nature? "In Him we live, move, and are."[1] Those things which nature is said to do, are by divine art performed, using nature as an instrument ; nor is there any such art or knowledge divine in nature herself working, but in the Guide of nature's work.

Whereas therefore things natural which are not in the number of voluntary agents, (for of such only we now speak, and of no other,) do so necessarily observe their certain laws, that as long as they keep those forms[2] which give them their being, they cannot possibly be apt or inclinable to do otherwise than they do; seeing the kinds of their operations are both constantly and exactly framed according to the several ends for which they serve, they themselves in the meanwhile, though doing that which is fit, yet knowing neither what they do, nor why: it followeth that all which they do in this sort proceedeth originally from some such agent, as knoweth, appointeth, holdeth up, and even actually frameth the same.

The manner of this divine efficiency, being far above us, we are no more able to conceive by our reason, than creatures unreasonable by their sense are able to apprehend after what manner we dispose and order the course of our affairs. Only thus much is discerned, that the natural generation and process of all things receiveth order of pro-

---

[1] Acts xvii. 28.
[2] Form in other creatures is a thing proportionable unto the soul in living creatures. Sensible it is not, nor otherwise discernible than only by effects. According to the diversity of inward forms, things of the world are distinguished into their kinds.

ceeding from the settled stability of divine understanding. This appointeth unto them their kinds of working; the disposition whereof in the purity of God's own knowledge and will is rightly termed by the name of Providence. The same being referred unto the things themselves here disposed by it, was wont by the ancient to be called natural Destiny. That law, the performance whereof we behold in things natural, is as it were an authentical or an original draught written in the bosom of God himself; whose Spirit being to execute the same useth every particular nature, every mere natural agent, only as an instrument created at the beginning, and ever since the beginning used, to work his own will and pleasure withal. Nature therefore is nothing else but God's instrument:[1] in the course whereof Dionysius perceiving some sudden disturbance is said to have cried out, "Aut Deus naturæ patitur, aut mundi machina dissolvetur:"[2] "either God doth suffer impediment, and is by a greater than himself hindered; or if that be impossible, then hath he determined to make a present dissolution of the world; the execution of that law beginning now to stand still, without which the world cannot stand."

This workman, whose servitor nature is, being in truth but only one, the heathens imagining to be moe, gave him in the sky the name of Jupiter, in the air the name of Juno, in the water the name of Neptune, in the earth the name of Vesta and sometimes of Ceres, the name of Apollo in the sun, in the moon the name of Diana, the name of Æolus and divers others in the winds; and to conclude, even so many guides of nature they dreamed of, as they saw there were kinds of things natural in the world. These they honoured, as having power to work or cease accordingly as men deserved of them. But unto us there is one only[3] Guide of all agents natural, and he both the Creator and

---

[1] Vide Thom. in Compend. Theol. cap. 3. "Omne quod movetur ab aliquo est quasi instrumentum quoddam primi moventis. Ridiculum est autem, etiam apud indoctos, ponere, instrumentum moveri non ab aliquo principali agente." [t. xvii. fol. 10.]

[2] [Vid. Breviar. Roman. 9 Oct. "Dionysius . . . unus ex Areopagitis . . . cum adhuc in Gentilitatis errore versaretur, eo die quo Christus Dominus cruci affixus est, solem præter naturam defecisse animadvertens, exclamasse traditur: 'aut Deus,' &c." Suidas (in Dionysio) makes him say, Ἡ τὸ θεῖον πάσχει, ἢ τῷ πάσχοντι συμπάσχει. Michael Syngelus in Encomio; Ὁ ἄγνωστος, ἔφη, σαρκὶ πάσχει Θεός. Apud Opp. S. Dionys. II. 213. See also, p. 91, 253-259.]

[3] [Suggested by 1 Cor. viii. 6. ἡμῖν εἷς Θεὸς, ὁ Πατήρ.]

the Worker of all in all, alone to be blessed, adored and honoured by all for ever.

[5.] That which hitherto hath been spoken concerneth natural agents considered in themselves. But we must further remember also, (which thing to touch in a word shall suffice,) that as in this respect they have their law, which law directeth them in the means whereby they tend to their own perfection : so likewise another law there is, which toucheth them as they are sociable parts united into one body ; a law which bindeth them each to serve unto other's good, and all to prefer the good of the whole before whatsoever their own particular ; as we plainly see they do, when things natural in that regard forget their ordinary natural wont ; that which is heavy mounting sometime upwards of its own accord, and forsaking the centre of the earth which to itself is most natural, even as if it did hear itself commanded to let go the good it privately wisheth, and to relieve the present distress of nature in common.

IV. But now that we may lift up our eyes (as it were) from the footstool to the throne of God, and leaving these natural, consider a little the state of heavenly and divine creatures : touching Angels, which are spirits [1] immaterial and intellectual, the glorious inhabitants of those sacred palaces, where nothing but light and blessed immortality, no shadow of matter for tears, discontentments, griefs, and uncomfortable passions to work upon, but all joy, tranquillity, and peace, even for ever and ever doth dwell : as in number and order they are huge, mighty, and royal armies,[2] so likewise in perfection of obedience unto that law, which the Highest, whom they adore, love, and imitate, hath imposed upon them, such observants they are thereof, that our Saviour himself being to set down the perfect idea of that which we are to pray and wish for on earth, did not teach to pray or wish for more than only that here it might be with us, as with them it is in heaven.[3] God which moveth mere natural agents as an efficient only, doth otherwise move intellectual creatures, and especially his holy angels : for beholding the face of God,[4] in admiration of so great excellency they all adore him ; and being rapt with the love of his beauty, they cleave inseparably for ever unto

[1] Psalm civ. 4 ; Heb. i. 7 ; Ephes. iii. 10.
[2] Dan. vii. 10 ; Matt. xxvi. 53 ; Heb. xii. 22 ; Luke ii. 13.
[3] Matt. vi. 10.   [4] Matt. xviii. 10.

him.   Desire to resemble him in goodness maketh them
unweariable and even unsatiable in their longing to do by
all means all manner good unto all the creatures of God,[1]
but especially unto the children of men : [2] in the countenance of whose nature, looking downward, they behold themselves beneath themselves ; even as upward, in God, beneath
whom themselves are, they see that character which is no
where but in themselves and us resembled.   Thus far even
the paynims have approached ; thus far they have seen into
the doings of the angels of God ; Orpheus confessing, that
"the fiery throne of God is attended on by those most
industrious angels, careful how all things are performed
amongst men ; " [3] and the Mirror of human wisdom plainly
teaching, that God moveth angels, even as that thing doth
stir man's heart, which is thereunto presented amiable.[4]
Angelical actions may therefore be reduced unto these three
general kinds : first, most delectable love arising from the
visible apprehension of the purity, glory, and beauty of
God, invisible saving only unto spirits that are pure : [5]
secondly, adoration grounded upon the evidence of the
greatness of God, on whom they see how all things depend ; [6]
thirdly, imitation,[7] bred by the presence of his exemplary
goodness, who ceaseth not before them daily to fill heaven

---

[1] [" How oft do they their silver bowers leave,
       To come to succour us, that succour want !
  How oft do they with golden pinions cleave
       The flitting skies, like flying pursuivant,
       Against foul fiends to aid us militant !
  They for us fight, they watch and duly ward,
       And their bright squadrons round about us plant,
       And all for love, and nothing for reward—
  O why should heavenly God to men have such regard ? "
                                   Fairy Queen, II. viii. 2.

The three first books of the Fairy Queen were published 1590.   Spenser
died 1598.]

[2] Psalm xci. 11, 12 ; Luke xv. 7 ; Heb. i. 14 ; Acts x. 3 ; Dan. ix.
23 ; Matt. xviii. 10 ; Dan. iv. 13.

[3] Σῷ δὲ θρόνῳ πυρόεντι παρεστᾶσιν πολύμοχθοι
    Ἄγγελοι, οἷσι μέμηλε βροτοῖς ὡς πάντα τελεῖται.
         [Fragm. iii. ex Clem. Alex. Strom. V. p. 824, 8.]

[4] Arist. Metaph. l. xii. c. 7. [" Movet ut amatum : moto vero, alia
moventur." Ap. Thom. Aquin. t. IV. fol. 159, ed. Venet. 1593.]

[5] Job xxxviii. 7 ; Matt. xviii. 10.

[6] Psalm cxlviii. 2 ; Heb i. 6 ; Isa. vi. 3.

[7] This is intimated wheresoever we find them termed "the sons of
God," as Job i. 6, and xxxviii. 7.

and earth with the rich treasures of most free and undeserved grace.

[2.] Of angels, we are not to consider only what they are and do in regard of their own being, but that also which concerneth them as they are linked into a kind of corporation amongst themselves, and of society or fellowship with men. Consider angels each of them severally in himself, and their law is that which the prophet David mentioneth, "All ye his angels praise him."[1] Consider the angels of God associated, and their law is that which disposeth them as an army, one in order and degree above another.[2] Consider finally the angels as having with us that communion which the apostle to the Hebrews noteth, and in regard whereof angels have not disdained to profess themselves our "fellow-servants;" from hence there springeth up a third law, which bindeth them to works of ministerial employment.[3] Every of which their several functions are by them performed with joy.

[3.] A part of the angels of God notwithstanding (we know) have fallen,[4] and that their fall hath been through the voluntary breach of that law, which did require at their hands continuance in the exercise of their high and admirable virtue. Impossible it was that ever their will should change or incline to remit any part of their duty, without some object having force to avert their conceit from God, and to draw it another way; and that before they attained that high perfection of bliss, wherein now the elect angels[5] are without possibility of falling. Of any thing more than of God they could not by any means like, as long as whatsoever they knew besides God they apprehended it not in itself without dependency upon God; because so long God must needs seem infinitely better than any thing which they so could apprehend. Things beneath them could not in such sort be presented unto their eyes, but that therein they must needs see always how those things did depend on God. It seemeth therefore that there was no other way for angels to sin, but by reflex of their understanding upon themselves; when being held with admiration of their own sublimity and honour, the memory of their subordination unto God and their dependency on him was drowned in

[1] Ps. cxlviii. 2.   [2] Luke ii. 13; Matt. xxvi. 53.
[3] Heb. xii. 22; Apoc. xxii. 9.   [4] 2 Pet. ii. 4; Jude 6.
[5] [1 Tim. v. 21.]

this conceit ; whereupon their adoration, love, and imitation
of God could not choose but be also interrupted. The fall
of angels therefore was pride.[1] Since their fall, their practices have been the clean contrary unto those before mentioned.[2] For being dispersed, some in the air, some on the
earth, some in the water, some among the minerals, dens,
and caves, that are under the earth ; they have by all means
laboured to effect a universal rebellion against the laws, and
as far as in them lieth utter destruction of the works of God.
These wicked spirits the heathens honoured instead of gods,
both generally under the name of *dii inferi*, " gods infernal ;"
and particularly, some in oracles, some in idols, some as
household gods, some as nymphs : in a word, no foul and
wicked spirit which was not one way or other honoured of
men as God, till such time as light appeared in the world
and dissolved the works of the Devil. Thus much therefore
may suffice for angels, the next unto whom in degree are
men.

V. God alone excepted, who actually and everlastingly is
whatsoever he may be, and which cannot hereafter be that
which now he is not ;[3] all other things besides are somewhat in possibility, which as yet they are not in act. And
for this cause there is in all things an appetite or desire,
whereby they incline to something which they may be ;
and when they are it, they shall be perfecter than now
they are. All which perfections are contained under the
general name of Goodness. And because there is not in
the world any thing whereby another may not some way
be made the perfecter, therefore all things that are, are
good.

---

[1] [" But pride, impatient of long resting peace,
　　　Did puff them up with greedy bold ambition,
　　　That they gan cast their state how to increase
　　　Above the fortune of their first condition,
　　　And sit in God's own seat without commission :
　　　The brightest angel, even the child of light,
　　　Drew millions more against their God to fight."
　　　　　Spenser's Hymn on Heavenly Love, published 1596.]

[2] John viii. 44 ; 1 Peter v. 8 ; Apoc. ix. 11 ; Gen. iii. 15 ; 1 Chron.
xxi. 1 ; Job i. 7 and ii. 2 ; John xiii. 27 ; Acts v. 3 ; Apoc. xx. 8.

[3] [" Let him know, that I have considered, *that God only is what he
would be ;* and that I am by his grace become now so like him, as to be
pleased with what pleaseth him." Walton's Life of Herbert, p. 321.
ed. 1675.]

[2.] Again, sith there can be no goodness desired which proceedeth not from God himself, as from the supreme cause of all things; and every effect doth after a sort contain, at leastwise resemble, the cause from which it proceedeth : all things in the world are said in some sort to seek the highest, and to covet more or less the participation of God himself.[1] Yet this doth no where so much appear as it doth in man, because there are so many kinds of perfections which man seeketh. The first degree of goodness is that general perfection which all things do seek, in desiring the continuance of their being. All things therefore coveting as much as may be to be like unto God in being ever, that which cannot hereunto attain personally doth seek to continue itself another way, that is by offspring and propagation. The next degree of goodness is that which each thing coveteth by affecting resemblance with God in the constancy and excellency of those operations which belong unto their kind. The immutability of God they strive unto, by working either always or for the most part after one and the same manner; his absolute exactness they imitate, by tending unto that which is most exquisite in every particular. Hence have arisen a number of axioms in philosophy,[2] shewing how "the works of nature do always aim at that which cannot be bettered."

[3.] These two kinds of goodness rehearsed are so nearly united to the things themselves which desire them, that we scarcely perceive the appetite to stir in reaching forth her hand towards them. But the desire of those perfections which grow externally is more apparent; especially of such as are not expressly desired unless they be first known, or such as are not for any other cause than for knowledge itself desired. Concerning perfections in this kind; that by proceeding in the knowledge of truth, and by growing in the exercise of virtue, man amongst the creatures of this inferior world aspireth to the greatest conformity with God; this is not only known unto us, whom he himself hath so instructed,[3] but even they do acknowledge, who amongst

---

[1] Πάντα γὰρ ἐκείνου ὀρέγεται. Arist. de An. lib. ii. cap. 4. [Opp. I. 390. ed. Lugd. 1590.]

[2] Ἐν τοῖς φύσει δεῖ τὸ βέλτιον, ἐὰν ἐνδέχηται ὑπάρχειν, μᾶλλον· ἡ φύσις ἀεὶ ποιεῖ τῶν ἐνδεχομένων τὸ βέλτιστον. Arist. 2. de cœl. cap. 5. [t. i. p. 283.]

[3] Matt. v. 48; Sap. vii. 27.

men are not judged the nearest unto him. With Plato
what one thing more usual, than to excite men unto love
of wisdom, by shewing how much wise men are thereby
exalted above men; how knowledge doth raise them up
into heaven; how it maketh them, though not gods, yet as
gods, high, admirable, and divine? And Mercurius Trismegistus speaking of the virtues of a righteous soul,[1] "Such
spirits" (saith he) "are never cloyed with praising and
speaking well of all men, with doing good unto every one
by word and deed, because they study to frame themselves
according to *the pattern* of the Father of spirits."

VI. In the matter of knowledge, there is between the
angels of God and the children of men this difference:
angels already have full and complete knowledge in the
highest degree that can be imparted unto them; men, if we
view them in their spring, are at the first without understanding or knowledge at all.[2] Nevertheless from this utter
vacuity they grow by degrees, till they come at length to be
even as the angels themselves are. That which agreeth to
the one now, the other shall attain unto in the end; they are
not so far disjoined and severed, but that they come at
length to meet. The soul of man being therefore at the
first as a book, wherein nothing is and yet all things may
be imprinted; we are to search by what steps and degrees
it riseth unto perfection of knowledge.

[2.] Unto that which hath been already set down concerning natural agents this we must add, that albeit therein we
have comprised as well creatures living as void of life, if
they be in degree of nature beneath men; nevertheless a
difference we must observe between those natural agents
that work altogether unwittingly, and those which have
though weak yet some understanding what they do, as
fishes, fowls, and beasts have. Beasts are in sensible
capacity as ripe even as men themselves, perhaps more
ripe. For as stones, though in dignity of nature inferior
unto plants, yet exceed them in firmness of strength or
durability of being; and plants, though beneath the excellency of creatures endued with sense, yet exceed them in
the faculty of vegetation and of fertility: so beasts, though

---

[1] ʽΗ δὲ τοιαύτη ψυχὴ κόρον οὐδέποτε ἔχει ὑμνοῦσα εὐφημοῦσά τε πάντας
ἀνθρώπους, καὶ λόγοις καὶ ἔργοις πάντας [πάντως] εὐποιοῦσα, μιμουμένη
αὐτῆς τὸν πατέρα. [c. 10. § 21.] lib. iv. f. 12.

[2] Vide Isa. vii. 16.

otherwise behind men, may notwithstanding in actions of sense and fancy go beyond them ; because the endeavours of nature, when it hath a higher perfection to seek, are in lower the more remiss, not esteeming thereof so much as those things do, which have no better proposed unto them.

[3.] The soul of man therefore being capable of a more divine perfection, hath (besides the faculties of growing unto sensible knowledge which is common unto us with beasts) a further ability, whereof in them there is no show at all, the ability of reaching higher than unto sensible things.[1] Till we grow to some ripeness of years, the soul of man doth only store itself with conceits of things of inferior and more open quality, which afterwards do serve as instruments unto that which is greater; in the meanwhile above the reach of meaner creatures it ascendeth not. When once it comprehendeth any thing above this, as the differences of time, affirmations, negations, and contradictions in speech, we then count it to have some use of natural reason. Whereunto if afterwards there might be added the right helps of true art and learning (which helps, I must plainly confess, this age of the world, carrying the name of a learned age, doth neither much know nor greatly regard), there would undoubtedly be almost as great difference in maturity of judgment between men therewith inured, and that which now men are, as between men that are now and innocents. Which speech if any condemn, as being over hyperbolical, let them consider but this one thing : no art is at the first finding out so perfect as industry may after make it; yet the very first man that to any purpose knew the way we speak of [2] and followed it, hath alone thereby performed more very near in all parts of natural knowledge, than sithence in any one part thereof the whole world besides hath done.

[4.] In the poverty of that other new devised aid [3] two

---

[1] Ὁ δὲ ἄνθρωπος εἰς τὸν οὐρανὸν ἀναβαίνει, καὶ μετρεῖ αὐτὸν, καὶ οἶδε ποῖα μὲν ἐστιν αὐτῷ [leg. αὐτοῦ] ὑψηλὰ, ποῖα δὲ ταπεινὰ, καὶ τὰ ἄλλα πάντα ἀκριβῶς μανθάνει. Καὶ τὸ πάντων μεῖζον, οὐδὲ τὴν γῆν καταλιπὼν ἄνω γίνεται. Merc. Tris. [c. 10. fin.] lib. iv. f. 12.

[2] Aristotelical Demonstration.

[3] Ramistry. [Peter Ramus was born in Picardy, 1515. He was a kind of self-taught person, who rose to eminence in the university of Paris. In 1543, he published "Institutiones Dialecticæ," and about the same time "Animadversiones Aristotelicæ." He was silenced after disputation, but allowed the next year to lecture in Rhetoric, and in

things there are notwithstanding singular. Of marvellous
quick dispatch it is, and doth shew them that have it as
much almost in three days, as if it dwell threescore years
with them. Again, because the curiosity of man's wit doth
many times with peril wade farther in the search of things
than were convenient ; the same is thereby restrained unto
such generalities as every where offering themselves are
apparent unto men of the weakest conceit that need be. So
as following the rules and precepts thereof, we may define
it to be, an Art which teacheth the way of speedy discourse,
and restraineth the mind of man that it may not wax over-
wise.

[5.] Education and instruction are the means, the one by
use, the other by precept, to make our natural faculty of
reason both the better and the sooner able to judge rightly
between truth and error, good and evil. But at what time
a man may be said to have attained so far forth the use of
reason, as sufficeth to make him capable of those Laws,
whereby he is then bound to guide his actions ; this is a
great deal more easy for common sense to discern, than for

1552 was made Professor of Eloquence and Philosophy, probably
through the Cardinal of Lorraine's influence. In 1562 he was ejected,
and continued more or less unsettled till 1572, when he lost his life in
the massacre of St. Bartholomew. (Brucker, Hist. Phil. v. 548-585.
Lips. 1766.) Strype, Ann. III. i. 500, says, " About this time (1585)
and somewhat before, another great contest arose in both universities,
concerning the two philosophers, Aristotle and Ramus, then chiefly
read, and which of them was rather to be studied." See also Ann. II.
ii. 405. (1580.) "Everard Digby had writ somewhat dialogue-wise
against Ramus's *Unica Methodus,* which in those times prevailed much ;
and perhaps brought into that college (St. John's, Cambridge) to be
read ; the rather, Ramus being a protestant as well as a learned man."
His institutes of Logic, expanded and illustrated, may be seen in
Milton's Prose Works, by Symmons, VI. 195-353. He seems to have
fallen into the common error of confounding rhetorical arrangement
with logic. Of the value of his theory the following was Bacon's
opinion : " De Unica Methodo, et dichotomiis perpetuis nihil attinet
dicere : fuit enim nubecula quædam doctrinæ, quæ cito transiit ; res
simul et levis et scientiis damnosissima. Etenim hujusmodi homines,
cum methodi suæ legibus res torqueant, et quæcumque in dichotomias
illas non apte cadunt, aut omittant, aut præter naturam inflectant, hoc
efficiunt, ut quasi nuclei et grana scientiarum exsiliant, ipsi aridas
tantum et desertas siliquas stringant." Further on in the same chapter
he specifies Ramus as the patron of the method alluded to. De Augm.
Scient. VI. 2. In his Impetus Philosophici, c. 2, he says, "Nullum
mihi commercium cum hoc ignorantiæ latibulo, perniciosissima literarum
tinea, compendiorum patre," &c. Works, IX. 304. 8°. Lond. 1803.
Andrew Melvin was a pupil of Ramus. Zouch's Walton, II. 134.]

any man by skill and learning to determine; even as it is not in philosophers, who best know the nature both of fire and of gold, to teach what degree of the one will serve to purify the other, so well as the artisan who doth this by fire discerneth by sense when the fire hath that degree of heat which sufficeth for his purpose.

VII. By reason man attaineth unto the knowledge of things that are and are not sensible. It resteth therefore that we search how man attaineth unto the knowledge of such things unsensible as are to be known that they may be done. Seeing then that nothing can move unless there be some end, the desire whereof provoketh unto motion; how should that divine power of the soul, that "spirit of our mind," [1] as the Apostle termeth it, ever stir itself unto action, unless it have also the like spur? The end for which we are moved to work, is sometimes the goodness which we conceive of the very working itself, without any further respect at all; and the cause that procureth action is the mere desire of action, no other good besides being thereby intended. Of certain turbulent wits it is said, "Illis quieta movere magna merces videbatur:" [2] they thought the very disturbance of things established an hire sufficient to set them on work. Sometimes that which we do is referred to a further end, without the desire whereof we would leave the same undone; as in their actions that gave alms to purchase thereby the praise of men. [3]

[2.] Man in perfection of nature being made according to the likeness of his Maker resembleth him also in the manner of working; so that whatsoever we work as men, the same we do wittingly work and freely; neither are we according to the manner of natural agents any way so tied, but that it is in our power to leave the things we do undone. The good which either is gotten by doing, or which consisteth in the very doing itself, causeth not action, unless apprehending it as good we so like and desire it: that we do unto any such end, the same we choose and prefer before the leaving of it undone. Choice there is not, unless the thing which we take be so in our power that we might have refused and left it. If fire consume the stubble, it chooseth not so to do, because the nature thereof is such that it can do no other. To choose is to will one thing

---

[1] Eph. iv. 23.   [2] Sallust. [Cat. 21.]   [3] Matt. vi. 2.

before another. And to will is to bend our souls to the
having or doing of that which they see to be good. Goodness is seen with the eye of the understanding. And the
light of that eye, is reason. So that two principal fountains
there are of human action, Knowledge and Will; which
Will, in things tending towards any end, is termed Choice.[1]
Concerning Knowledge, "Behold, (saith Moses,[2]) I have
set before you this day good and evil, life and death."
Concerning Will, he addeth immediately, "Choose life;"
that is to say, the things that tend unto life, them choose.

[3.] But of one thing we must have special care, as being
a matter of no small moment; and that is, how the Will,
properly and strictly taken, as it is of things which are
referred unto the end that man desireth, differeth greatly
from that inferior natural desire which we call Appetite.
The object of Appetite is whatsoever sensible good may be
wished for; the object of Will is that good which Reason
doth lead us to seek. Affections, as joy, and grief, and fear,
and anger, with such like, being as it were the sundry
fashions and forms of Appetite, can neither rise at the conceit
of a thing indifferent, nor yet choose but rise at the sight of
some things. Wherefore it is not altogether in our power,
whether we will be stirred with affections or no: whereas
actions which issue from the disposition of the Will are in
the power thereof to be performed or stayed. Finally,
Appetite is the Will's solicitor, and the Will is Appetite's
controller; what we covet according to the one by the other
we often reject; neither is any other desire termed properly
Will, but that where Reason and Understanding, or the show
of Reason, prescribeth the thing desired.

It may be therefore a question, whether those operations
of men are to be counted voluntary, wherein that good which
is sensible provoketh Appetite, and Appetite causeth action,
Reason being never called to counsel; as when we eat or
drink, and betake ourselves unto rest, and such like The
truth is, that such actions in men having attained to the use
of Reason are voluntary For as the authority of higher
powers hath force even in those things, which are done
without their privity, and are of so mean reckoning that to
acquaint them therewith it needeth not; in like sort, voluntarily we are said to do that also, which the Will if it listed
might hinder from being done, although about the doing

---

[1] [See Arist. Eth. III. 2, 3. VI. 2.]   [2] Deut. xxx. 19.

thereof we do not expressly use our reason or understanding, and so immediately apply our wills thereunto. In cases therefore of such facility, the Will doth yield her assent as it were with a kind of silence, by not dissenting; in which respect her force is not so apparent as in express mandates or prohibitions, especially upon advice and consultation going before.

[4.] Where understanding therefore needeth, in those things Reason is the director of man's Will by discovering in action what is good. For the Laws of well-doing are the dictates of right Reason. Children, which are not as yet come unto those years whereat they may have; again, innocents, which are excluded by natural defect from ever having; thirdly, madmen, which for the present cannot possibly have the use of right Reason to guide themselves, have for their guide the Reason that guideth other men, which are tutors over them to seek and to procure their good for them. In the rest there is that light of Reason, whereby good may be known from evil, and which discovering the same rightly is termed right.

[5.] The Will notwithstanding doth not incline to have or do that which Reason teacheth to be good, unless the same do also teach it to be possible. For albeit the Appetite, being more general, may wish any thing which seemeth good, be it never so impossible;[1] yet for such things the reasonable Will of man doth never seek. Let Reason teach impossibility in any thing, and the Will of man doth let it go; a thing impossible it doth not affect, the impossibility thereof being manifest.

[6.] There is in the Will of man naturally that freedom, whereby it is apt to take or refuse any particular object whatsoever being presented unto it.[2] Whereupon it followeth,

---

[1] O mihi præteritos referat si Jupiter annos! [Virg. Æn. viii. 560.]

[2] [Chr. Letter, p. 11. "Heere we pray your helpe to teach us, how will is *apt* (as you say) freelie to take or refuse anie particular object whatsoever, and that reason by diligence is able to find out any good concerning us: if it be true that the Church of England professeth, that without the preventing and helping grace of God, we can will and doe nothing pleasing to God."

Hooker, MS note. "There are certaine wordes, as Nature, Reason, Will, and such like, which wheresoever you find named, you suspect them presently as bugs wordes,* because what they mean you do not

---

[* "These are bugs words." Beaum. and Fletch. Tamer tamed, Act I. Sc. 3.]

that there is no particular object so good, but it may have
the show of some difficulty or unpleasant quality annexed
to it, in respect whereof the Will may shrink and decline it ;
contrariwise (for so things are blended) there is no particular evil which hath not some appearance of goodness
whereby to insinuate itself. For evil as evil cannot be
desired : [1] if that be desired which is evil, the cause is the
goodness which is or seemeth to be joined with it. Goodness doth not move by being, but by being apparent ; and
therefore many things are neglected which are most precious,
only because the value of them lieth hid. Sensible Goodness
is most apparent, near, and present ; which causeth the
Appetite to be therewith strongly provoked. Now pursuit
and refusal in the Will do follow, the one the affirmation
the other the negation of goodness, which the understanding
apprehendeth,[2] grounding itself upon sense, unless some
higher Reason do chance to teach the contrary. And if
Reason have taught it rightly to be good, yet not so

indeed as you ought apprehend. You have heard that man's Nature is
corrupt, his Reason blind, his Will perverse. Whereupon under coulour
of condemning corrupt Nature, you condemn Nature, and so in the
rest."

"Vide Hilarium, p. 31." (Ed. Basil ; 1570 ; p. 822. ed. Bened.)
"Vide et Philon. p. 33." (Ed. Paris, 1552.) "et Dionys. p. 338."
(Par. 1562.)

"Voluntas hominis natura sua non ligatur, sed vi vitiositatis quæ
naturæ accessit.

"Apt', originaliter apta, *able*. Ratio divinis instructa auxiliis potest
omne bonum necessarium invenire, destituta nullum. Habet tamen
omne bonum satis quidem in se quo probare se possit homini sedulo
diligenterque attendenti. Sed nostra nos alio segnities avertit, donec
studium virtutis Spiritus Sanctus excitat. Vide Cyprianum de sua
conversione." (Ad Donatum, Opp. p. 3. ed. Fell.) "Item ea quæ
Sapientia de se profitetur in libro Proverbiorum atque alibi. Est itaque
segnis humana ratio propter summam bonarum rerum investigandarum
difficultatem. Eam difficultatem tollit lumen divinæ gratiæ. Hinc
alacres efficimur, alioqui a labore ad libidinem proclives. Habet virtus
vitio et plura et fortiora quæ hominem alliciant. Sed ea latent maximam
partem hominum. Quid ita? Quia Ratio, quæ est oculus mentis, alto
in nobis somno sepulta jacet otiose. At excitata et illuminata Sancti
Spiritus virtute omnia dijudicat, et quæ prius ignota fastidio fuerunt, ea
nunc perspecta modis omnibus amplectenda decernit."]

[1] [Εἰ δέ τις ἐπὶ κακίαν ὁρμᾷ, πρῶτον μὲν οὐχ ὡς ἐπὶ κακίαν αὐτὴν
ὁρμήσει, ἀλλ' ὡς ἐπ' ἀγαθόν. Paulo post : Ἀδύνατον γὰρ ὁρμᾶν ἐπὶ κακὰ
βουλόμενον ἔχειν αὐτὰ, οὔτε ἐλπίδι ἀγαθοῦ οὔτε φόβῳ μείζονος κακοῦ.
Alcin. de Dog. Plat. [c. 38. ed. Oxon. 1667.]

[2] [Arist. Eth. Nic. VI. 2. Ὅπερ ἐν διανοίᾳ κατάφασις καὶ ἀπόφασις,
τοῦτο ἐν ὀρέξει δίωξις καὶ φυγή.]

apparently that the mind receiveth it with utter impossibility of being otherwise, still there is place left for the Will to take or leave. Whereas therefore amongst so many things as are to be done, there are so few, the goodness whereof Reason in such sort doth or easily can discover, we are not to marvel at the choice of evil even then when the contrary is probably known. Hereby it cometh to pass that custom inuring the mind by long practice, and so leaving there a sensible impression, prevaileth more than reasonable persuasion what way soever. Reason therefore may rightly discern the thing which is good, and yet the Will of man not incline itself thereunto, as oft as the prejudice of sensible experience doth oversway.

[7.] Nor let any man think that this doth make any thing for the just excuse of iniquity. For there was never sin committed, wherein a less good was not preferred before a greater, and that wilfully; which cannot be done without the singular disgrace of Nature, and the utter disturbance of that divine order, whereby the pre-eminence of chiefest acceptation is by the best things worthily challenged. There is not that good which concerneth us, but it hath evidence enough for itself, if Reason were diligent to search it out. Through neglect thereof, abused we are with the show of that which is not; sometimes the subtilty of Satan inveigling us as it did Eve,[1] sometimes the hastiness of our Wills preventing the more considerate advice of sound Reason, as in the Apostles,[2] when they no sooner saw what they liked not, but they forthwith were desirous of fire from heaven; sometimes the very custom of evil making the heart obdurate against whatsoever instructions to the contrary, as in them over whom our Saviour spake weeping,[3] "O Jerusalem, how often, and thou wouldest not!" Still therefore that wherewith we stand blameable, and can no way excuse it, is, In doing evil, we prefer a less good before a greater, the greatness whereof is by reason investigable and may be known. The search of knowledge is a thing painful; and the painfulness of knowledge is that which maketh the Will so hardly inclinable thereunto. The root hereof, divine malediction; whereby the instruments[4] being weakened

---

[1] 2 Cor. xi. 3.   [2] Luke ix. 54.   [3] Matt. xxiii. 37.
[4] "A corruptible body is heavy unto the soul, and the earthly mansion keepeth down the mind that is full of cares. And hardly can we discern the things that are upon earth, and with great labour find we

wherewithal the soul (especially in reasoning) doth work, it preferreth rest in ignorance before wearisome labour to know. For a spur of diligence therefore we have a natural thirst after knowledge ingrafted in us. But by reason of that original weakness in the instruments, without which the understanding part is not able in this world by discourse to work, the very conceit of painfulness is as a bridle to stay us. For which cause the Apostle, who knew right well that the weariness of the flesh is an heavy clog to the Will, striketh mightily upon this key, "Awake thou that sleepest; Cast off all which presseth down; Watch; Labour; Strive to go forward, and to grow in knowledge." [1]

VIII. Wherefore to return to our former intent of discovering the natural way, whereby rules have been found out concerning that goodness wherewith the Will of man ought to be moved in human actions; as every thing naturally and necessarily doth desire the utmost good and greatest perfection whereof Nature hath made it capable, even so man. Our felicity therefore being the object and accomplishment of our desire, we cannot choose but wish and covet it. All particular things which are subject unto action, the Will doth so far forth incline unto, as Reason judgeth them the better for us, and consequently the more available to our bliss. If Reason err, we fall into evil, and are so far forth deprived of the general perfection we seek. Seeing therefore that for the framing of men's actions the knowledge of good from evil is necessary, it only resteth that we search how this may be had. Neither must we suppose that there needeth one rule to know the good and another the evil by. [2] For he that knoweth what is straight doth even thereby discern what is crooked, because the absence of straightness in bodies capable thereof is crookedness. Goodness in actions is like unto straightness; wherefore that which is done well we term *right*. For as the straight way is most acceptable to him that travelleth, because by it he cometh soonest to his journey's end; so in action, that which doth lie the evenest between us and the

out the things which are before us. Who can then seek out the things that are in heaven?" Sap. ix. 15, 16.

[1] Eph. v. 14; Heb. xii. 1, 12; 1 Cor. xvi. 13; Prov. ii. 4; Luke xiii. 24.

[2] Τῷ εὐθεῖ καὶ αὐτὸ καὶ τὸ καμπύλον γινώσκομεν· κριτὴς γὰρ ἀμφοῖν ὁ κανών. Arist. de An. lib. i. [cap. 3. t. 85.]

end we desire must needs be the fittest for our use. Besides
which fitness for use, there is also in rectitude, beauty; as
contrariwise in obliquity, deformity. And that which is
good in the actions of men, doth not only delight as profitable, but as amiable also. In which consideration the
Grecians most divinely have given to the active perfection
of men a name expressing both beauty and goodness,[1] because goodness in ordinary speech is for the most part
applied only to that which is beneficial. But we in the name
of goodness do here imply both.

[2.] And of discerning goodness there are but these two
ways ; the one the knowledge of the causes whereby it is
made such ; the other the observation of those signs and
tokens, which being annexed always unto goodness, argue
that where they are found, there also goodness is, although
we know not the cause by force whereof it is there. The
former of these is the most sure and infallible way, but so
hard that all shun it, and had rather walk as men do in the
dark by haphazard, than tread so long and intricate mazes
for knowledge' sake. As therefore physicians are many
times forced to leave such methods of curing as themselves
know to be the fittest, and being overruled by their patients'
impatiency are fain to try the best they can, in taking that
way of cure which the cured will yield unto ; in like sort,
considering how the case doth stand with this present age
full of tongue and weak of brain, behold we yield to the
stream thereof ; into the causes of goodness we will not
make any curious or deep inquiry; to touch them now and
then it shall be sufficient, when they are so near at hand
that easily they may be conceived without any far-removed
discourse : that way we are contented to prove, which being
the worse in itself, is notwithstanding now by reason of
common imbecility the fitter and likelier to be brooked.[2]

[3.] Signs and tokens to know good by are of sundry
kinds ; some more certain and some less. The most certain
token of evident goodness is, if the general persuasion of
all men do so account it. And therefore a common received
error is never utterly overthrown, till such time as we go
from signs unto causes, and shew some manifest root or
fountain thereof common unto all, whereby it may clearly

---

[1] Καλοκἀγαθία.
[2] [Arist. Eth. Nic. I. 4, 5. ed. Cardwell : Ἴσως οὖν ἡμῖν γε ἀρκτέον
ἀπὸ τῶν ἡμῖν γνωρίμων.]

appear how it hath come to pass that so many have been overseen. In which case surmises and slight probabilities will not serve, because the universal consent of men is the perfectest and strongest in this kind, which comprehendeth only the signs and tokens of goodness. Things casual do vary, and that which a man doth but chance to think well of cannot still have the like hap. Wherefore although we know not the cause, yet thus much we may know ; that some necessary cause there is, whensoever the judgments of all men generally or for the most part run one and the same way, especially in matters of natural discourse. For of things necessarily and naturally done there is no more affirmed but this, " They keep either always or for the most part one tenure." [1] The general and perpetual voice of men is as the sentence of God himself. For that which all men have at all times learned, Nature herself must needs have taught ; [2] and God being the author of Nature, her voice is but his instrument. By her from Him we receive whatsoever in such sort we learn. Infinite duties there are, the goodness whereof is by this rule sufficiently manifested, although we had no other warrant besides to approve them. The Apostle St. Paul having speech concerning the heathen saith of them, [3] " They are a law unto themselves." His meaning is, that by force of the light of Reason, wherewith God illuminateth every one which cometh into the world,

---

[1] Ἢ ἀεὶ ἢ ὡς ἐπὶ τὸ πολὺ ὡσαύτως ἀποβαίνει. Arist. Rhet. l. i. [c. 10.]

[2] "Non potest error contingere ubi omnes idem [ita] opinantur." Monticat. in 1. Polit. [p. 3,] "Quicquid in omnibus individuis unius speciei communiter inest, id causam communem habeat oportet, quæ est eorum individuorum species et natura." Idem. "Quod a tota aliqua specie fit, universalis particularisque naturæ fit instinctu." [" Meminisse debemus vaticinium illud, Quod a tota aliqua animalium specie fit, quia universalis particularisque fit instinctu, verum existere."] Ficin. de Christ. Rel. [cap. 1.] " Si proficere cupis, primo firme id verum puta, quod sana mens omnium hominum attestatur." Cusa in Compend. cap. 1. [D. Nicolai de Cusa Cardinalis, utriusque juris Doctoris, omnique philosophia incomparabilis viri Opera. Basil. 1565. Compendium ; Directio Veritatis, p. 239. See Cave Hist. Lit. t. I. App. 130.] "Non licet naturale universaleque hominum judicium falsum vanumque existimare." Teles. [Bernardi Telesii, Consentini, de Rerum Natura juxta propria principia Libri ix, Neapoli 1586. On this writer's method of philosophizing see a dissertation in Bacon's works, ix. 332.] Ὅ γὰρ πᾶσι δοκεῖ, τοῦτο εἶναι φάμεν. Ὁ δὲ ἀναιρῶν ταύτην τὴν πίστιν οὐ πάνυ πιστότερα ἐρεῖ. Arist. Eth. lib. x. cap. 2.

[3] Rom. ii. 14.

men being enabled to know truth from falsehood, and good from evil, do thereby learn in many things what the will of God is ; which will himself not revealing by any extra-ordinary means unto them, but they by natural discourse attaining the knowledge thereof, seem the makers of those Laws which indeed are his, and they but only the finders of them out.

[4.] A law therefore generally taken, is a directive rule unto goodness of operation. The rule of divine operations outward, is the definitive appointment of God's own wisdom set down within himself. The rule of natural agents that work by simple necessity, is the determination of the wisdom of God, known to God himself the principal Director of them, but not unto them that are directed to execute the same. The rule of natural agents which work after a sort of their own accord, as the beasts do, is the judgment of com-mon sense or fancy concerning the sensible goodness of those objects wherewith they are moved. The rule of ghostly or immaterial natures, as spirits and angels, is their intuitive intellectual judgment concerning the amiable beauty and high goodness of that object, which with unspeakable joy and delight doth set them on work. The rule of voluntary agents on earth is the sentence that Reason giveth concern-ing the goodness of those things which they are to do. And the sentences which Reason giveth are some more some less general, before it come to define in particular actions what is good.

[5.] The main principles of Reason are in themselves apparent. For to make nothing evident of itself unto man's understanding were to take away all possibility of knowing any thing. And herein that of Theophrastus is true, " They that seek a reason of all things do utterly overthrow Reason." [1] In every kind of knowledge some such grounds there are, as that being proposed the mind doth presently embrace them as free from all possibility of error, clear and manifest without proof. In which kind axioms or principles more general are such as this, " that the greater good is to be chosen before the less." If therefore it should be de-manded what reason there is, why the Will of Man, which doth necessarily shun harm and covet whatsoever is pleasant and sweet, should be commanded to count the pleasures of

[1] Ἁπάντων ζητοῦντες λόγον, ἀναιροῦσι λόγον. Theoph. in Metaph. [p. 270. 23.]

sin gall, and notwithstanding the bitter accidents wherewith virtuous actions are compassed, yet still to rejoice and delight in them : surely this could never stand with Reason, but that wisdom thus prescribing groundeth her laws upon an infallible rule of comparison ; which is, ' That small difficulties when exceeding great good is sure to ensue, and on the other side momentary benefits when the hurt which they draw after them is unspeakable, are not at all to be respected.' This rule is the ground whereupon the wisdom of the Apostle buildeth a law, enjoining patience unto himself ;[1] " The present lightness of our affliction worketh unto us even with abundance upon abundance an eternal weight of glory ; while we look not on the things which are seen, but on the things which are not seen : for the things which are seen are temporal, but the things which are not seen are eternal : " therefore Christianity to be embraced, whatsoever calamities in those times it was accompanied withal. Upon the same ground our Saviour proveth the law most reasonable, that doth forbid those crimes which men for gain's sake fall into. " For a man to win the world if it be with the loss of his soul, what benefit or good is it ? "[2] Axioms less general, yet so manifest that they need no further proof, are such as these, ' God to be worshipped ;' ' parents to be honoured ;' ' others to be used by us as we ourselves would be by them.' Such things, as soon as they are alleged, all men acknowledge to be good ; they require no proof or further discourse to be assured of their goodness.

Notwithstanding whatsoever such principle there is, it was at the first found out by discourse, and drawn from out of the very bowels of heaven and earth. For we are to note, that things in the world are to us discernible, not only so far forth as serveth for our vital preservation, but further also in a twofold higher respect. For first if all other uses were utterly taken away, yet the mind of man being by nature speculative and delighted with contemplation in itself, they were to be known even for mere knowledge and understanding's sake. Yea further besides this, the knowledge of every the least thing in the whole world hath in it a second peculiar benefit unto us, inasmuch as it serveth to minister rules, canons, and laws, for men to direct those actions by which we properly term human. This did the very heathens themselves obscurely insinuate,

[1] 2 Cor. iv. 17.　　　　　　[2] Matt. xvi. 26.

by making *Themis*, which we call *Jus*, or Right, to be the daughter of heaven and earth.[1]

[6.] We know things either as they are in themselves, or as they are in mutual relation one to another. The knowledge of that which man is in reference unto himself, and other things in relation unto man, I may justly term the mother of all those principles, which are as it were edicts, statutes, and decrees, in that Law of Nature, whereby human actions are framed. First therefore having observed that the best things, where they are not hindered, do still produce the best operations, (for which cause, where many things are to concur unto one effect, the best is in all congruity of reason to guide the residue, that it prevailing most, the work principally done by it may have greatest perfection:) when hereupon we come to observe in ourselves, of what excellency our souls are in comparison of our bodies, and the diviner part in relation unto the baser of our souls; seeing that all these concur in producing human actions, it cannot be well unless the chiefest do command and direct the rest.[2] The soul then ought to conduct the body, and the spirit of our minds[3] the soul. This is therefore the first Law, whereby the highest power of the mind requireth general obedience at the hands of all the rest concurring with it unto action.

[7.] Touching the several grand mandates, which being imposed by the understanding faculty of the mind must be obeyed by the will of Man, they are by the same method found out, whether they import our duty towards God or towards man.

Touching the one, I may not here stand to open, by what degrees of discourse the minds even of mere natural men have attained to know, not only that there is a God, but also what power, force, wisdom, and other properties that God hath, and how all things depend on him. This being therefore presupposed, from that known relation which God hath unto us as unto children,[4] and unto all good things as unto effects whereof himself is the principal cause,[5] these axioms and laws natural concerning our duty

---

[1] [Hesiod. Theog. 126, 133, 135.]

[2] Arist. Pol. i. cap. 5.

[3] [Eph. iv. 23.]

[4] Οὐδεὶς Θεὸς δύσνους ἀνθρώποις. Plat. in Theæt. [t. i. 151. ed. Serrani.]

[5] Ὅ τε γὰρ Θεὸς δοκεῖ τὸ αἴτιον πᾶσιν εἶναι καὶ ἀρχή τις. Arist. Metaph. lib. i. cap. 2. [t. ii. 485.]

have arisen, 'that in all things we go about his aid is by
prayer to be craved:'[1] 'that he cannot have sufficient
honour done unto him, but the utmost of that we can do
to honour him we must;'[2] which is in effect the same that
we read,[3] "Thou shalt love the Lord thy God with all thy
heart, with all thy soul, and with all thy mind:' which
Law our Saviour doth term[4] "The first and the great
commandment."

Touching the next, which as our Saviour addeth is "like
unto this," (he meaneth in amplitude and largeness, inasmuch as it is the root out of which all Laws of duty to
men-ward have grown, as out of the former all offices of
religion towards God,) the like natural inducement hath
brought men to know that it is their duty no less to love
others than themselves. For seeing those things which are
equal must needs all have one measure; if I cannot but
wish to receive all good, even as much at every man's hand
as any man can wish unto his own soul, how should I look
to have any part of my desire herein satisfied, unless myself
be careful to satisfy the like desire which is undoubtedly in
other men, we all being of one and the same nature? To
have any thing offered them repugnant to this desire must
needs in all respects grieve them as much as me: so that if
I do harm I must look to suffer; there being no reason
that others should shew greater measure of love to me
than they have by me shewed unto them. My desire
therefore to be loved of my equals in nature as much as
possible may be, imposeth upon me a natural duty of
bearing to them-ward fully the like affection. From which
relation of equality between ourselves and them that are as
ourselves, what several rules and canons natural Reason
hath drawn for direction of life no man is ignorant; as
namely, "That because we would take no harm, we must
therefore do none;" "That sith we would not be in any
thing extremely dealt with, we must ourselves avoid all
extremity in our dealings;" "that from all violence and
wrong we are utterly to abstain;"[5] with such like; which

---

[1] Ἀλλ', ὦ Σώκρατες, τοῦτό γε δὴ πάντες, ὅσοι καὶ κατὰ βραχὺ σωφρο-
σύνης μετέχουσιν, ἐπὶ πάσῃ ὁρμῇ καὶ σμικροῦ καὶ μεγάλου πράγματος
Θεὸν ἀεί που καλοῦσι.   Plat. in Tim. [t. iii. 27.]

[2] Arist. Ethic. lib. iii. cap. ult.

[3] Deut. vi. 5.   [4] Matt. xxii. 38.

[5] "Quod quis in se approbat, in alio reprobare non posse." L. *in*

further to wade in would be tedious, and to our present purpose not altogether so necessary, seeing that on these two general heads already mentioned all other specialties are dependent.[1]

[8.] Wherefore the natural measure whereby to judge our doings, is the sentence of Reason, determining and setting down what is good to be done. Which sentence is either mandatory, shewing what must be done; or else permissive, declaring only what may be done; or thirdly admonitory, opening what is the most convenient for us to do. The first taketh place, where the comparison doth stand altogether between doing and not doing of one thing which in itself is absolutely good or evil; as it had been for Joseph[2] to yield or not to yield to the impotent desire of his lewd mistress, the one evil the other good simply. The second is, when of divers things evil, all being not evitable, we are permitted to take one; which one saving only in case of so great urgency were not otherwise to be taken; as in the matter of divorce amongst the Jews.[3] The last, when of divers things good, one is principal and most eminent; as in their act who sold their possessions and laid the price at the Apostles' feet;[4] which possessions they might have retained unto themselves without sin: again, in the Apostle St. Paul's own choice[5] to maintain himself by his own labour; whereas in living by the Church's maintenance, as others did, there had been no offence committed.[6] In Goodness therefore there is a latitude or extent, whereby it cometh to pass that even of good actions some are better than other some; whereas otherwise one man could not excel another, but all should be either absolutely good, as hitting jump that indivisible point or centre wherein goodness consisteth; or else missing it they should be excluded out of the number of well-doers. Degrees of well-doing there could be none, except perhaps

---

arenam, C. de inof. test. [Cod. Just. p. 254. ed. Lugd. 1553.] "Quod quisque juris in alium statuerit, ipsum quoque eodem uti debere." L. *quod quisque.* [Digest. lib. ii. tit. 2. tom. 1. p. 60. Lugd. 1552.] "Ab omni penitus injuria atque vi abstinendum." L. i. sect. 1. *Quod vi, aut clam.* [Ibid. lib. xliii. tit. 23. tom. 3. p. 335.]

[1] "On these two commandments hangeth the whole Law." Matt. xxii. 40.

[2] Gen. xxxix. 9.

[3] Mark x. 4.

[4] Acts iv. 37; v. 4.

[5] 2 Thess. iii. 8.

[6] [See note, b. ii. c. 8. § 5.]

in the seldomness and oftenness of doing well. But the nature of Goodness being thus ample, a Law is properly that which Reason in such sort defineth to be good that it must be done. And the Law of Reason or human Nature is that which men by discourse of natural Reason have rightly found out themselves to be all for ever bound unto in their actions.

[9.] Laws of Reason have these marks to be known by. Such as keep them resemble most lively in their voluntary actions that very manner of working which Nature herself doth necessarily observe in the course of the whole world. The works of Nature are all behoveful, beautiful, without superfluity or defect; even so theirs, if they be framed according to that which the Law of Reason teacheth. Secondly, those Laws are investigable by Reason, without the help of Revelation supernatural and divine. Finally, in such sort they are investigable, that the knowledge of them is general, the world hath always been acquainted with them; according to that which one in Sophocles observeth concerning a branch of this Law, " It is no child of to-day's or yesterday's birth, but hath been no man knoweth how long sithence."[1] It is not agreed upon by one, or two, or few, but by all. Which we may not so understand, as if every particular man in the whole world did know and confess whatsoever the Law of Reason doth contain; but this Law is such that being proposed no man can reject it as unreasonable and unjust. Again, there is nothing in it but any man (having natural perfection of wit and ripeness of judgment) may by labour and travail find out. And to conclude, the general principles thereof are such, as it is not easy to find men ignorant of them. Law rational therefore, which men commonly use to call the Law of Nature, meaning thereby the Law which human Nature knoweth itself in reason universally bound unto, which also for that cause may be termed most fitly the Law of Reason; this Law, I say, comprehendeth all those things which men by the light of their natural understanding evidently know, or at leastwise may know, to be beseeming or unbeseeming, virtuous or vicious, good or evil for them to do.

[10.] Now although it be true, which some have

---

[1] Οὐ γάρ τι νῦν γε κἀχθὲς, ἀλλ᾽ ἀεί ποτε
Ζῇ τοῦτο, κοὐδεὶς οἶδεν ἐξ ὅτου ᾿φάνη.
Soph. Antig. [v. 456.]

said,[1] that "whatsoever is done amiss, the Law of Nature and Reason thereby is transgressed," because even those offences which are by their special qualities breaches of supernatural laws, do also, for that they are generally evil, violate in general that principle of Reason, which willeth universally to fly from evil: yet do we not therefore so far extend the Law of Reason, as to contain in it all manner laws whereunto reasonable creatures are bound, but (as hath been shewed) we restrain it to those only duties, which all men by force of natural wit either do or might understand to be such duties as concern all men. "Certain half-waking men there are" (as Saint Augustine noteth[2]), "who neither altogether asleep in folly, nor yet throughly awake in the light of true understanding, have thought that there is not at all any thing just and righteous in itself; but look wherewith nations are inured, the same they take to be right and just. Whereupon their conclusion is, that seeing each sort of people hath a different kind of right from other, and that which is right of its own nature must be everywhere one and the same, therefore in itself there is nothing right. These good folk," saith he, ("that I may not trouble their wits with rehearsal of too many things), have not looked so far into the world as to perceive that, 'Do as thou wouldst be done unto,' is a sentence which all nations under heaven are agreed upon. Refer this sentence to the love of God, and it extinguisheth all heinous crimes; refer it to the love of thy neighbour, and all grievous wrongs it banisheth out of the world." Wherefore as touching the Law of Reason, this was (it seemeth) Saint Augustine's judgment: namely, that there are in it some things which stand as principles universally agreed upon; and that out

---

[1] Th. 1. 2. q. 94. art. 3. [tom. xi. 204.] "Omnia peccata sunt in universum contra rationem et naturæ legem." Aug de Civit. Dei, l. xii. cap. 1. "Omne vitium naturæ nocet, ac per hoc contra naturam est." [tom. vii. 301.]

[2] De Doctr. Christ. l. iii. c. 14. [tom iii. 51. "Quidam dormitantes, ut ita dicam, qui neque alto somno stultitiæ sopiebantur, nec in sapientiæ lucem poterant evigilare, putaverunt nullam esse justitiam per se ipsam, sed unicuique genti consuetudinem suam justam videri; quæ cum sit diversa omnibus gentibus, debeat autem incommutabilis manere justitia, fieri manifestum, nullam usquam esse justitiam. Non intellexerunt, (ne multa commemorem,) 'Quod tibi fieri non vis, alii ne feceris,' nullo modo posse ulla eorum gentili diversitate variari. Quæ sententia cum refertur ad dilectionem Dei, omnia flagitia moriuntur; cum ad proximi, omnia facinora."]

of those principles, which are in themselves evident, the greatest moral duties we owe towards God or man may without any great difficulty be concluded.

[11.] If then it be here demanded, by what means it should come to pass (the greatest part of the Law moral being so easy for all men to know) that so many thousands of men notwithstanding have been ignorant even of principal moral duties, not imagining the breach of them to be sin : I deny not but lewd and wicked custom, beginning perhaps at the first amongst few, afterwards spreading into greater multitudes, and so continuing from time to time, may be of force even in plain things to smother the light of natural understanding; because men will not bend their wits to examine whether things wherewith they have been accustomed be good or evil. For example's sake, that grosser kind of heathenish idolatry, whereby they worshipped the very works of their own hands, was an absurdity to reason so palpable, that the Prophet David comparing idols and idolaters together maketh almost no odds between them, but the one in a manner as much without wit and sense as the other; "They that make them are like unto them, and so are all that trust in them."[1] That wherein an idolater doth seem so absurd and foolish is by the Wise Man thus exprest,[2] "He is not ashamed to speak unto that which hath no life, he calleth on him that is weak for health, he prayeth for life unto him which is dead, of him which hath no experience he requireth help, for his journey he sueth to him which is not able to go, for gain and work and success in his affairs he seeketh furtherance of him that hath no manner of power." The cause of which senseless stupidity is afterwards imputed to custom.[3] "When a father mourned grievously for his son that was taken away suddenly, he made an image for him that was once dead, whom now he worshippeth as a god, ordaining to his servants ceremonies and sacrifices. Thus by process of time this wicked custom prevailed, and was kept as a law;" the authority of rulers, the ambition of craftsmen, and such like means thrusting forward the ignorant, and increasing their superstition.

Unto this which the Wise Man hath spoken somewhat besides may be added. For whatsoever we have hitherto taught, or shall hereafter, concerning the force of man's

---

[1] Psalm cxxxv. 18.   [2] Wisd. xiii. 17.
[3] Wisd. xiv. 15, 16.

natural understanding, this we always desire withal to be understood; that there is no kind of faculty or power in man or any other creature, which can rightly perform the functions allotted to it, without perpetual aid and concurrence of that Supreme Cause of all things.   The benefit whereof as oft as we cause God in his justice to withdraw, there can no other thing follow than that which the Apostle noteth, even men endued with the light of reason to walk notwithstand-ing[1] "in the vanity of their mind, having their cogitations darkened, and being strangers from the life of God through the ignorance which is in them, because of the hardness of their hearts."   And this cause is mentioned by the prophet Esay,[2] speaking of the ignorance of idolaters, who see not how the manifest Law of Reason condemneth their gross iniquity and sin.   "They have not in them," saith he, "so much wit as to think, 'Shall I bow to the stock of a tree? All knowledge and understanding is taken from them; for God hath shut their eyes that they cannot see."

That which we say in this case of idolatry serveth for all other things, wherein the like kind of general blindness hath prevailed against the manifest Laws of Reason.   Within the compass of which laws we do not only comprehend what-soever may be easily known to belong to the duty of all men, but even whatsoever may possibly be known to be of that quality, so that the same be by *necessary* consequence deduced out of clear and manifest principles.   For if once we descend unto probable collections what is convenient for men, we are then in the territory where free and arbitrary determinations, the territory where Human Laws take place; which laws are after to be considered.

IX. Now the due observation of this Law which Reason teacheth us cannot but be effectual unto their great good that observe the same.   For we see the whole world and each part thereof so compacted, that as long as each thing performeth only that work which is natural unto it, it thereby preserveth both other things and also itself. Contrariwise, let any principal thing, as the sun, the moon, any one of the heavens or elements, but once cease or fail, or swerve, and who doth not easily conceive that the sequel thereof would be ruin both to itself and whatsoever dependeth on it?   And is it possible, that Man being not only the noblest creature in the world, but even a very world

---

[1] Ephes. iv. 17, 18.   [2] Isa. xliv. 18, 19.

in himself, his transgressing the Law of his Nature should draw no manner of harm after it? Yes,[1] "tribulation and anguish unto every soul that doeth evil." Good doth follow unto all things by observing the course of their nature, and on the contrary side evil by not observing it; but not unto natural agents that good which we call Reward, not that evil which we properly term Punishment. The reason whereof is, because amongst creatures in this world, only Man's observation of the Law of his Nature is Righteousness, only Man's transgression Sin. And the reason of this is the difference in his manner of observing or transgressing the Law of his Nature. He doth not otherwise than voluntarily the one or the other. What we do against our wills, or constrainedly, we are not properly said to do it, because the motive cause of doing it is not in ourselves, but carrieth us, as if the wind should drive a feather in the air, we no whit furthering that whereby we are driven. In such cases therefore the evil which is done moveth compassion; men are pitied for it, as being rather miserable in such respect than culpable. Some things are likewise done by man, though not through outward force and impulsion, though not against yet without their wills; as in alienation of mind, or any the like inevitable utter absence of wit and judgment. For which cause, no man did ever think the hurtful actions of furious men and innocents to be punishable. Again, some things we do neither against nor without, and yet not simply and merely with our wills, but with our wills in such sort moved, that albeit there be no impossibility but that we might, nevertheless we are not so easily able to do otherwise. In this consideration one evil deed is made more pardonable than another. Finally, that which we do being evil, is notwithstanding by so much more pardonable, by how much the exigence of so doing or the difficulty of doing otherwise is greater; unless this necessity or difficulty have originally risen from ourselves. It is no excuse therefore unto him, who being drunk committeth incest, and allegeth that his wits were not his own; inasmuch as himself might have chosen whether his wits should by that mean have been taken from him. Now rewards and punishments do always presuppose something willingly done well or ill; without which respect though we may sometimes receive good or harm, yet then the one is only a benefit and not a

[1] Rom. ii. 9.

reward, the other simply an hurt not a punishment. From the sundry dispositions of man's Will, which is the root of all his actions, there groweth variety in the sequel of rewards and punishments, which are by these and the like rules measured: 'Take away the will, and all acts are equal: That which we do not, and would do, is commonly accepted as done.'[1] By these and the like rules men's actions are determined of and judged, whether they be in their own nature rewardable or punishable.

[2.] Rewards and punishments are not received, but at the hands of such as being above us have power to examine and judge our deeds. How men come to have this authority one over another in external actions, we shall more diligently examine in that which followeth. But for this present, so much all do acknowledge, that sith every man's heart and conscience doth in good or evil, even secretly committed and known to none but itself, either like or disallow itself, and accordingly either rejoice, very nature exulting (as it were) in certain hope of reward, or else grieve (as it were) in a sense of future punishment; neither of which can in this case be looked for from any other, saving only from Him who discerneth and judgeth the very secrets of all hearts: therefore He is the only rewarder and revenger of all such actions; although not of such actions only, but of all whereby the Law of Nature is broken whereof Himself is author. For which cause, the Roman laws, called The Laws of the Twelve Tables, requiring offices of inward affection which the eye of man cannot reach unto, threaten the neglecters of them with none but divine punishment.[2]

X. That which hitherto we have set down is (I hope) sufficient to shew their brutishness, which imagine that religion and virtue are only as men will account of them; that we might make as much account, if we would, of the contrary, without any harm unto ourselves, and that in nature they are as indifferent one as the other. We see then how nature itself teacheth laws and statutes to live by. The laws which have been hitherto mentioned do bind men absolutely even as they are men, although they have never

---

[1] "Voluntate sublata, omnem actum parem esse." L. *fœdissimam*, c. *de adult*. [Cod. Justin. 968.] "Bonam voluntatem plerumque pro facto reputari." L. *si quis in testament*. [Ibid. 732.]

[2] "Divos caste adeunto, pietatem adhibento: qui secus faxit, Deus ipse vindex erit." [Cic. de Leg. II. 8.]

any settled fellowship, never any solemn agreement amongst themselves what to do or not to do.[1] But forasmuch as we are not by ourselves sufficient to furnish ourselves with competent store of things needful for such a life as our nature doth desire, a life fit for the dignity of man; therefore to supply those defects and imperfections which are in us living single and solely by ourselves, we are naturally induced to seek communion and fellowship with others. This was the cause of men's uniting themselves at the first in politic Societies, which societies could not be without Government, nor Government without a distinct kind of Law from that which hath been already declared. Two foundations there are which bear up public societies; the one, a natural inclination, whereby all men desire sociable life and fellowship; the other, an order expressly or secretly agreed upon touching the manner of their union in living together. The latter is that which we call the Law of a Commonweal, the very soul of a politic body, the parts whereof are by law animated, held together, and set on work in such actions, as the common good requireth. Laws politic, ordained for external order and regiment amongst men, are never framed as they should be, unless presuming the will of man to be inwardly obstinate, rebellious, and averse from all obedience unto the sacred laws of his nature; in a word, unless presuming man to be in regard of his depraved mind little better than a wild beast, they do accordingly provide notwithstanding so to frame his outward actions, that they be no hinderance unto the common good for which societies are instituted : unless they do this, they are not perfect. It resteth therefore that we consider how nature findeth out such laws of government as serve to direct even nature depraved to a right end.

[2.] All men desire to lead in this world a happy life. That life is led most happily, wherein all virtue is exercised without impediment or let. The Apostle,[2] in exhorting men to contentment although they have in this world no more than very bare food and raiment, giveth us thereby to understand that those are even the lowest of things necessary; that if we should be stripped of all those things

---

[1] Ἔστι γὰρ, ὃ μαντεύονταί τι πάντες φύσει κοινὸν δίκαιον καὶ ἄδικον, κἂν μηδεμία κοινωνία πρὸς ἀλλήλους ᾖ μηδὲ συνθήκη. Arist. Rhet. i. [c. 13.]
[2] 1 Tim. vi. 8.

without which we might possibly be, yet these must be left; that destitution in these is such an impediment, as till it be removed suffereth not the mind of man to admit any other care. For this cause, first God assigned Adam maintenance of life, and then appointed him a law to observe.[1] For this cause, after men began to grow to a number, the first thing we read they gave themselves unto was the tilling of the earth and the feeding of cattle. Having by this mean whereon to live, the principal actions of their life afterward are noted by the exercise of their religion.[2] True it is, that the kingdom of God must be the first thing in our purposes and desires.[3] But inasmuch as righteous life presupposeth life; inasmuch as to live virtuously it is impossible except we live; therefore the first impediment, which naturally we endeavour to remove, is penury and want of things without which we cannot live. Unto life many implements are necessary; more, if we seek (as all men naturally do) such a life as hath in it joy, comfort, delight, and pleasure. To this end we see how quickly sundry arts mechanical were found out, in the very prime of the world.[4] As things of greatest necessity are always first provided for, so things of greatest dignity are most accounted of by all such as judge rightly. Although therefore riches be a thing which every man wisheth, yet no man of judgment can esteem it better to be rich, than wise, virtuous, and religious. If we be both or either of these, it is not because we are so born. For into the world we come as empty of the one as of the other, as naked in mind as we are in body. Both which necessities of man had at the first no other helps and supplies than only domestical; such as that which the Prophet implieth, saying, "Can a mother forget her child?"[5] such as that which the Apostle mentioneth, saying, "He that careth not for his own is worse than an infidel;"[6] such as that concerning Abraham, "Abraham will command his sons and his household after him, that they keep the way of the Lord."[7]

[3.] But neither that which we learn of ourselves nor that which others teach us can prevail, where wickedness and malice have taken deep root. If therefore when there was but as yet one only family in the world, no means of instruction human or divine could prevent effusion of blood;[8]

---

[1] Gen. i. 29; ii. 17. [2] Gen. iv. 2, 26. [3] Matt. vi. 33.
[4] Gen. iv. 20, 21, 22. [5] Isa. xlix. 15. [6] 1 Tim. v. 8.
[7] Gen. xviii. 19. [8] Gen. iv. 8.

how could it be chosen but that when families were multiplied and increased upon earth, after separation each providing for itself, envy, strife, contention and violence must
grow amongst them? For hath not Nature furnished man
with wit and valour, as it were with armour, which may be
used as well unto extreme evil as good? Yea, were they not
used by the rest of the world unto evil; unto the contrary
only by Seth, Enoch, and those few the rest in that line?[1]
We all make complaint of the iniquity of our times: not
unjustly; for the days are evil. But compare them with those
times wherein there were no civil societies, with those times
wherein there was as yet no manner of public regiment established, with those times wherein there were not above eight
persons righteous living upon the face of the earth;[2] and
we have surely good cause to think that God hath blessed
us exceedingly, and hath made us behold most happy days.

[4.] To take away all such mutual grievances, injuries,
and wrongs, there was no way but only by growing unto
composition and agreement amongst themselves, by ordaining some kind of government public, and by yielding
themselves subject thereunto; that unto whom they granted
authority to rule and govern, by them the peace, tranquillity,
and happy estate of the rest might be procured. Men
always knew that when force and injury was offered they
might be defenders of themselves; they knew that howsoever men may seek their own commodity, yet if this were
done with injury unto others it was not to be suffered, but
by all men and by all good means to be withstood; finally
they knew that no man might in reason take upon him to
determine his own right, and according to his own determination proceed in maintenance thereof, inasmuch as every
man is towards himself and them whom he greatly affecteth
partial; and therefore that strifes and troubles would be
endless, except they gave their common consent all to be
ordered by some whom they should agree upon: without
which consent there were no reason that one man should
take upon him to be lord or judge over another; because,
although there be according to the opinion of some very
great and judicious men a kind of natural right in the
noble, wise, and virtuous, to govern them which are of
servile disposition;[3] nevertheless for manifestation of this

---

[1] Gen. vi. 5; Gen. v.   [2] 2 Pet. ii. 5.
[3] Arist. Polit. lib. iii. et iv.

their right, and men's more peaceable contentment on both sides, the assent of them who are to be governed seemeth necessary.

To fathers within their private families Nature hath given a supreme power ; for which cause we see throughout the world even from the foundation thereof, all men have ever been taken as lords and lawful kings in their own houses. Howbeit over a whole grand multitude having no such dependency upon any one, and consisting of so many families as every politic society in the world doth, impossible it is that any should have complete lawful power, but by consent of men, or immediate appointment of God ; because not having the natural superiority of fathers, their power must needs be either usurped, and then unlawful ; or, if lawful, then either granted or consented unto by them over whom they exercise the same, or else given extraordinarily from God, unto whom all the world is subject. It is no improbable opinion therefore which the arch-philosopher was of, that as the chiefest person in every household was always as it were a king, so when numbers of households joined themselves in civil society together, kings were the first kind of governors amongst them.[1] Which is also (as it seemeth) the reason why the name of Father continued still in them, who of fathers were made rulers ; as also the ancient custom of governors to do as Melchisedec, and being kings to exercise the office of priests, which fathers did at the first, grew perhaps by the same occasion.

Howbeit not this the only kind of regiment that hath been received in the world. The inconveniences of one kind have caused sundry other to be devised. So that in a word all public regiment of what kind soever seemeth evidently to have risen from deliberate advice, consultation, and composition between men, judging it convenient and behoveful ; there being no impossibility in nature considered by itself, but that men might have lived without any public regiment. Howbeit, the corruption of our nature being presupposed, we may not deny but that the Law of Nature doth now require of necessity some kind of regiment ; so that to bring things unto the first course they were in, and utterly to take away all kind of public government in the world, were apparently to overturn the whole world.

[5.] The case of man's nature standing therefore as it

[1] Arist. Polit. lib. i. cap. 2 Vide et Platonem in 3. de Legibus [t. ii. 680.]

doth, some kind of regiment the Law of Nature doth require ; yet the kinds thereof being many, Nature tieth not to any one, but leaveth the choice as a thing arbitrary. At the first when some certain kind of regiment was once approved, it may be that nothing was then further thought upon for the manner of governing, but all permitted unto their wisdom and discretion which were to rule ;[1] till by experience they found this for all parts very inconvenient, so as the thing which they had devised for a remedy did indeed but increase the sore which it should have cured. They saw that to live by one man's will became the cause of all men's misery. This constrained them to come unto laws, wherein all men might see their duties beforehand, and know the penalties of transgressing them. If things be simply good or evil, and withal universally so acknowledged, there needs no new law to be made for such things.[2] The first kind therefore of things appointed by laws human containeth whatsoever being in itself naturally good or evil, is notwithstanding more secret than that it can be discerned by every man's present conceit, without some deeper discourse and judgment. In which discourse because there is difficulty and possibility many ways to err, unless such things were set down by laws, many would be ignorant of their duties which now are not, and many that know what they should do would nevertheless dissemble it, and to excuse themselves pretend ignorance and simplicity, which now they cannot.[3]

[6.] And because the greatest part of men are such as prefer their own private good before all things, even that good which is sensual before whatsoever is most divine ; and for that the labour of doing good, together with the pleasure arising from the contrary, doth make men for the most part slower to the one and proner to the other, than

---

[1] "Cum premeretur initio multitudo ab iis qui majores opes habebant, ad unum aliquem confugiebant virtute præstantem, qui cum prohiberet injuria tenuiores, æquitate constituenda summos cum infimis pari jure retinebat. Cum id minus contingeret, leges sunt inventæ." Cic. Offic. lib. ii. [c. 12.]

[2] Τὸ γονέας τιμᾷν καὶ φίλους εὐποιεῖν καὶ τοῖς εὐεργέταις χάριν ἀποδιδόναι, ταῦτα καὶ τὰ τούτοις ὅμοια οὐ προστάττουσι τοῖς ἀνθρώποις οἱ γεγραμμένοι νόμοι ποιεῖν, ἀλλ' εὐθὺς ἀγράφῳ καὶ κοινῷ νόμῳ νομίζεται. Arist. Rhet. ad Alex. [c. 2.]

[3] "Tanta est enim vis voluptatum, ut. et ignorantiam protelet in occasionem, et conscientiam corrumpat in dissimulationem." Tertull. ib. de Spectacul. [c. 1.]

that duty prescribed them by law can prevail sufficiently with them : therefore unto laws that men do make for the benefit of men it hath seemed always needful to add rewards, which may more allure unto good than any hardness deterreth from it, and punishments, which may more deter from evil than any sweetness thereto allureth. Wherein as the generality is natural, *virtue rewardable and vice punishable ;* so the particular determination of the reward or punishment belongeth unto them by whom laws are made. Theft is naturally punishable, but the kind of punishment is positive, and such lawful as men shall think with discretion convenient by law to appoint.

[7.] In laws, that which is natural bindeth universally, that which is positive not so. To let go those kind of positive laws which men impose upon themselves, as by vow unto God, contract with men, or such like ; somewhat it will make unto our purpose, a little more fully to consider what things are incident unto the making of the positive laws for the government of them that live united in public society. Laws do not only teach what is good, but they enjoin it, they have in them a certain constraining force. And to constrain men unto any thing inconvenient doth seem unreasonable. Most requisite therefore it is that to devise laws which all men shall be forced to obey none but wise men be admitted. Laws are matters of principal consequence ; men of common capacity and but ordinary judgment are not able (for how should they ?) to discern what things are fittest for each kind and state of regiment. We cannot be ignorant how much our obedience unto laws dependeth upon this point. Let a man though never so justly oppose himself unto them that are disordered in their ways, and what one amongst them commonly doth not stomach at such contradiction, storm at reproof, and hate such as would reform them ? Notwithstanding even they which brook it worst that men should tell them of their duties, when they are told the same by a law, think very well and reasonably of it. For why ? They presume that the law doth speak with all indifferency ; that the law hath no side-respect to their persons ; that the law is as it were an oracle proceeded from wisdom and understanding.[1]

[8.] Howbeit laws do not take their constraining force from the quality of such as devise them, but from that power

[1] [Arist. Eth. Nic. x. c. ix. 12.]

which doth give them the strength of laws. That which we spake before concerning the power of government must here be applied unto the power of making laws whereby to govern ; which power God hath over all : and by the natural law, whereunto he hath made all subject. the lawful power of making laws to command whole politic societies of men belongeth so properly unto the same entire societies, that for any prince or potentate of what kind soever upon earth to exercise the same of himself, and not either by express commission immediately and personally received from God, or else by authority derived at the first from their consent upon whose persons they impose laws, it is no better than mere tyranny.

Laws they are not therefore which public approbation hath not made so. But approbation not only they give who personally declare their assent by voice sign or act, but also when others do it in their names by right originally at the least derived from them. As in parliaments, councils, and the like assemblies, although we be not personally ourselves present, notwithstanding our assent is by reason of others agents there in our behalf. And what we do by others, no reason but that it should stand as our deed, no less effectually to bind us than if ourselves had done it in person. In many things assent is given, they that give it not imagining they do so, because the manner of their assenting is not apparent. As for example, when an absolute monarch commandeth his subjects that which seemeth good in his own discretion, hath not his edict the force of a law whether they approve or dislike it ? Again, that which hath been received long sithence and is by custom now established, we keep as a law which we may not transgress ; yet what consent was ever thereunto sought or required at our hands ?

Of this point therefore we are to note, that sith men naturally have no full and perfect power to command whole politic multitudes of men, therefore utterly without our consent we could in such sort be at no man's commandment living. And to be commanded we do consent, when that society whereof we are part hath at any time before consented, without revoking the same after by the like universal agreement. Wherefore as any man's deed past is good as long as himself continueth ; so the act of a public society of men done five hundred years sithence standeth as theirs who presently are of the same societies, because corporations are immortal ; we were then alive in our predecessors, and they in their successors do live still. Laws therefore human, of what kind soever, are available by consent.

[9.] If here it be demanded how it cometh to pass that this being common unto all laws which are made, there should be found even in good laws so great variety as there is ; we must note the reason hereof to be the sundry particular ends, whereunto the different disposition of that subject or matter, for which laws are provided, causeth them to have a special respect in making laws. A law there is mentioned amongst the Grecians whereof Pittacus is reported to have been author ; and by that law it was agreed, that he which being overcome with drink did then strike any man, should suffer punishment double as much as if he had done the same being sober.[1] No man could ever have thought this reasonable, that had intended thereby only to punish the injury committed according to the gravity of the fact : for who knoweth not that harm advisedly done is naturally less pardonable, and therefore worthy of the sharper punishment ? But forasmuch as none did so usually this way offend as men in that case, which they wittingly fell into, even because they would be so much the more freely outrageous ; it was for their public good where such disorder was grown to frame a positive law for remedy thereof accordingly. To this appertain those known laws of making laws ; as that law-makers must have an eye to the place where, and to the men amongst whom ; that one kind of laws cannot serve for all kinds of regiment ; that where the multitude beareth sway, laws that shall tend unto preservation of that state must make common smaller offices to go by lot, for fear of strife and division likely to arise ; by reason that ordinary qualities sufficing for discharge of such offices, they could not but by many be desired, and so with danger contended for, and not missed without grudge and discontentment, whereas at an uncertain lot none can find themselves grieved, on whomsoever it lighteth ; contrariwise the greatest, whereof but few are capable, to pass by popular election, that neither the people may envy such as have those honours, inasmuch as themselves bestow them, and that the chiefest may be kindled with desire to exercise all parts of rare and beneficial virtue, knowing they

[1] Arist. Polit. lib. ii. cap. ult.

shall not lose their labour by growing in fame and estimation amongst the people : if the helm of chief government
be in the hands of a few of the wealthiest, that then laws
providing for continuance thereof must make the punishment of contumely and wrong offered unto any of the
common sort sharp and grievous, that so the evil may be
prevented whereby the rich are most likely to bring themselves into hatred with the people, who are not wont to take
so great offence when they are excluded from honours and
offices as when their persons are contumeliously trodden
upon. In other kinds of regiment the like is observed concerning the difference of positive laws, which to be every
where the same is impossible and against their nature.

[10.] Now as the learned in the laws [1] of this land
observe, that our statutes sometimes are only the affirmation
or ratification of that which by common law was held
before; so here it is not to be omitted that generally all
laws human, which are made for the ordering of politic
societies, be either such as establish some duty whereunto
all men by the law of reason did before stand bound ; or
else such as make that a duty now which before was none.
The one sort we may for distinction's sake call " mixedly,"
and the other " merely" human. That which plain or
necessary reason bindeth men unto may be in sundry considerations expedient to be ratified by human law. For
example, if confusion of blood in marriage, the liberty of
having many wives at once, or any other the like corrupt
and unreasonable custom doth happen to have prevailed
far, and to have gotten the upper hand of right reason with
the greatest part ; so that no way is left to rectify such foul
disorder without prescribing by law the same things which
reason necessarily *doth* enforce but is not *perceived* that so
it doth ; or if many be grown unto that which the Apostle
did lament in some, concerning whom he writeth, saying,
that "even what things they naturally know, in those very

---

[1] Staundf. Preface to the Pleas of the Crown. ["Citavi non pauca e
Bractono et Britono, vetustis legum scriptoribus, hoc nimirum consilio :
ut cum leges coronæ magna ex parte jure statutario constant, ponatur
ante legentis oculos commune jus, quod fuit ante ea statuta condita.
Nam ea res maxime conducit recte interpretandis statutis. Id enim
intelligenti statim occurrunt mala quæ commune jus contraxit. Per-
videt autem ille quotæ illorum malorum parti medetur, et quotæ non ;
et sitne hujusmodi statutum novatum jus per se, an nihil aliud quam
communis juris affirmatio." Ed. 1574.]

things as beasts void of reason they corrupted themselves;"[1] or if there be no such special accident, yet forasmuch as the common sort are led by the sway of their sensual desires, and therefore do more shun sin for the sensible evils which follow it amongst men, than for any kind of sentence which reason doth pronounce against it:[2] this very thing is cause sufficient why duties belonging unto each kind of virtue, albeit the Law of Reason teach them, should notwithstanding be prescribed even by human law. Which law in this case we term *mixed*, because the matter whereunto it bindeth is the same which reason necessarily doth require at our hands, and from the Law of Reason it differeth in the manner of binding only. For whereas men before stood bound in conscience to do as the Law of Reason teacheth, they are now by virtue of human law become constrainable, and if they outwardly transgress, punishable. As for laws which are *merely* human, the matter of them is any thing which reason doth but probably teach to be fit and convenient; so that till such time as law hath passed amongst men about it, of itself it bindeth no man. One example whereof may be this. Lands are by human law in some places after the owner's decease divided unto all his children, in some all descendeth to the eldest son. If the Law of Reason did necessarily require but the one of these two to be done, they which by law have received the other should be subject to that heavy sentence, which denounceth against all that decree wicked, unjust, and unreasonable things, *woe*.[3] Whereas now whichsoever be received there is no Law of Reason transgressed ; because there is probable reason why either of them may be expedient, and for either of them more than probable reason there is not to be found.

[11.] Laws whether mixedly or merely human are made by politic societies ; some, only as those societies are civilly united ; some, as they are spiritually joined and make such a body as we call the Church. Of laws human in this latter kind we are to speak in the third book following. Let it therefore suffice thus far to have touched the force wherewith Almighty God hath graciously endued our nature, and thereby enabled the same to find out both those laws which all men generally are for ever bound to observe, and

---

[1] Jude 10.
[2] [Arist. Eth. Nic. X. 10. Οἱ πολλοὶ ἀνάγκῃ μᾶλλον ἢ λόγῳ πειθαρχοῦσι, καὶ ζημίαις ἢ τῷ καλῷ.] [3] Isaiah x. 1.

also such as are most fit for their behoof, who lead their lives in any ordered state of government.

[12.] Now besides that law which simply concerneth men as men, and that which belongeth unto them as they are men linked with others in some form of politic society, there is a third kind of law which toucheth all such several bodies politic, so far forth as one of them hath public commerce with another. And this third is the Law of Nations. Between men and beasts there is no possibility of sociable communion, because the well-spring of that communion is a natural delight which man hath to transfuse from himself into others, and to receive from others into himself especially those things wherein the excellency of his kind doth most consist. The chiefest instrument of human communion therefore is speech, because thereby we impart mutually one to another the conceits of our reasonable understanding.[1] And for that cause seeing beasts are not hereof capable, forasmuch as with them we can use no such conference, they being in degree, although above other creatures on earth to whom nature hath denied sense, yet lower than to be sociable companions of man to whom nature hath given reason; it is of Adam said that amongst the beasts "he found not for himself any meet companion."[2] Civil society doth more content the nature of man than any private kind of solitary living, because in society this good of mutual participation is so much larger than otherwise. Herewith notwithstanding we are not satisfied, but we covet (if it might be) to have a kind of society and fellowship even with all mankind. Which thing Socrates intending to signify professed himself a citizen, not of this or that commonwealth, but of the world.[3] And an effect of that very natural desire in us (a manifest token that we wish after a sort an universal fellowship with all men) appeareth by the wonderful delight men have, some to visit foreign countries, some to discover nations not heard of in former ages, we all to know the affairs and dealings of other people, yea to be in league of amity with them : and this not only for traffick's sake, or to the end that when many are confederated each may make other the more strong, but for such cause also as moved the Queen of Saba to visit

---

[1] Arist. Polit. i. cap. 2. [2] Gen. ii. 20.

[3] Cic. Tusc. v. [c. 37.] et i. de Legib. [c. 12.]

Solomon;[1] and in a word, because nature doth presume
that how many men there are in the world, so many gods
as it were there are, or at leastwise such they should be
towards men.

[13.] Touching laws which are to serve men in this
behalf; even as those Laws of Reason, which (man retaining his original integrity) had been sufficient to direct
each particular person in all his affairs and duties, are
not sufficient but require the access of other laws, now
that man and his offspring are grown thus corrupt and
sinful; again, as those laws of polity and regiment, which
would have served men living in public society together
with that harmless disposition which then they should
have had, are not able now to serve, when men's iniquity
is so hardly restrained within any tolerable bounds: in
like manner, the national laws of natural commerce between societies of that former and better quality might
have been other than now, when nations are so prone to
offer violence, injury, and wrong. Hereupon hath grown
in every of these three kinds that distinction between
Primary and Secondary laws; the one grounded upon
sincere, the other built upon depraved nature. Primary
laws of nations are such as concern embassage, such as
belong to the courteous entertainment of foreigners and
strangers, such as serve for commodious traffick, and the
like. Secondary laws in the same kind are such as this
present unquiet world is most familiarly acquainted with;
I mean laws of arms, which yet are much better known
than kept. But what matter the Law of Nations doth
contain I omit to search.

The strength and virtue of that law is such that no
particular nation can lawfully prejudice the same by any
their several laws and ordinances, more than a man by
his private resolutions the law of the whole commonwealth
or state wherein he liveth. For as civil law, being the
act of the whole body politic, doth therefore overrule
each several part of the same body; so there is no reason
that any one commonwealth of itself should to the prejudice of another annihilate that whereupon the whole
world hath agreed. For which cause, the Lacedæmonians
forbidding all access of strangers into their coasts, are in
that respect both by Josephus and Theodoret deservedly

[1] 1 Kings x. 1 ; 2 Chron. ix. 1 ; Matt. xii. 42 ; Luke xi. 31.

blamed,[1] as being enemies to that hospitality which for common humanity's sake all the nations on earth should embrace.

[14.] Now as there is great cause of communion, and consequently of laws for the maintenance of communion, amongst nations; so amongst nations Christian the like in regard even of Christianity hath been always judged needful.

And in this kind of correspondence amongst nations the force of general councils doth stand. For as one and the same law divine, whereof in the next place we are to speak, is unto all Christian churches a rule for the chiefest things; by means whereof they all in that respect make one church, as having all but "one Lord, one faith, and one baptism:"[2] so the urgent necessity of mutual communion for preservation of our unity in these things, as also for order in some other things convenient to be every where uniformly kept, maketh it requisite that the Church of God here on earth have her laws of spiritual commerce between Christian nations; laws by virtue whereof all churches may enjoy freely the use of those reverend, religious, and sacred consultations, which are termed Councils General. A thing whereof God's own blessed Spirit was the author;[3] a thing practised by the holy Apostles themselves; a thing always afterward kept and observed throughout the world; a thing never otherwise than most highly esteemed of, till pride, ambition, and tyranny began by factious and vile endeavours to abuse that divine invention unto the furtherance of wicked purposes. But as the just authority of civil courts and parliaments is not therefore to be abolished, because sometime there is cunning used to frame them according to the private intents of men over potent in the commonwealth; so the grievous abuse which hath been of councils should rather cause men to study how so gracious a thing may again be reduced to that first perfection, than in regard of stains and blemishes sithence growing be held for ever in extreme disgrace.

To speak of this matter as the cause requireth would require very long discourse. All I will presently say is this: whether it be for the finding out of any thing where-

---

[1] Joseph. lib. ii. contra Apion. [c. 36.] Theod. lib. ix. de sanand. Græc. Aff. [p. 611, t. iv. ed. Par. 1642.]

[2] Ephes. iv. 5.   [3] Acts xv. 28.

unto divine law bindeth us, but yet in such sort that men are not thereof on all sides resolved; or for the setting down of some uniform judgment to stand touching such things, as being neither way matters of necessity, are notwithstanding offensive and scandalous when there is open opposition about them; be it for the ending of strifes touching matters of Christian belief, wherein the one part may seem to have probable cause of dissenting from the other; or be it concerning matters of polity, order, and regiment in the church; I nothing doubt but that Christian men should much better frame themselves to those heavenly precepts, which our Lord and Saviour with so great instancy gave [1] as concerning peace and unity, if we did all concur in desire to have the use of ancient councils again renewed, rather than these proceedings continued, which either make all contentions endless, or bring them to one only determination, and that of all other the worst, which is by sword.

[15.] It followeth therefore that a new foundation being laid, we now adjoin hereunto that which cometh in the next place to be spoken of; namely, wherefore God hath himself by Scripture made known such laws as serve for direction of men.

XI. All things, (God only excepted,) besides the nature which they have in themselves, receive externally some perfection from other things, as hath been shewed. Insomuch as there is in the whole world no one thing great or small, but either in respect of knowledge or of use it may unto our perfection add somewhat. And whatsoever such perfection there is which our nature may acquire, the same we properly term our Good; our Sovereign Good or Blessedness, that wherein the highest degree of all our perfection consisteth, that which being once attained unto there can rest nothing further to be desired; and therefore with it our souls are fully content and satisfied, in that they have they rejoice, and thirst for no more. Wherefore of good things desired some are such that for themselves we covet them not, but only because they serve as instruments unto that for which we are to seek: of this sort are riches. Another kind there is, which although we desire for itself, as health, and virtue, and knowledge, nevertheless they are not the last mark whereat we aim, but have their further end where-

[1] John xiv. 27.

unto they are referred, so as in them we are not satisfied as having attained the utmost we may, but our desires do still proceed. These things are linked and as it were chained one to another; we labour to eat, and we eat to live, and we live to do good, and the good which we do is as seed sown with reference to a future harvest.[1] But we must come at length to some pause. For, if every thing were to be desired for some other without any stint, there could be no certain end proposed unto our actions, we should go on we know not whither; yea, whatsoever we do were in vain, or rather nothing at all were possible to be done. For as to take away the first efficient of our being were to annihilate utterly our persons, so we cannot remove the last final cause of our working, but we shall cause whatsoever we work to cease. Therefore something there must be desired for itself simply and for no other. That is simply for itself desirable, unto the nature whereof it is opposite and re-pugnant to be desired with relation unto any other. The ox and the ass desire their food, neither propose they unto themselves any end wherefore; so that of them this is desired for itself; but why? By reason of their imper-fection which cannot otherwise desire it; whereas that which is desired simply for itself, the excellency thereof is such as permitteth it not in any sort to be referred to a further end.

[2.] Now that which man doth desire with reference to a further end, the same he desireth in such measure as is unto that end convenient; but what he coveteth as good in itself, towards that his desire is ever infinite. So that unless the last good of all, which is desired altogether for itself, be also infinite, we do evil in making it our end; even as they who placed their felicity in wealth or honour or pleasure or any thing here attained; because in desiring any thing as our final perfection which is not so, we do amiss.[2] Nothing may be infinitely desired but that good which indeed is infinite: for the better the more desirable; that therefore most desirable wherein there is infinity of goodness: so that if any thing desirable may be infinite,

---

[1] "He that soweth to the Spirit shall of the Spirit reap life ever-lasting." Gal. vi. 8.

[2] Vide Arist. Ethic. lib. x. c. 10. [c. 7.] et Metaph. l. xii. c. 6. ["Est aliquid, quod non motum movet; quod æternum, et substantia, et actus est."] et c. 4, ["Præter hæc item [est] cuncta movens, tanquam omnium primum."] et c. 30.

that must needs be the highest of all things that are
desired. No good is infinite but only God; therefore
He our felicity and bliss. Moreover, desire tendeth unto
union with that it desireth. If then in him we be blessed,
it is by force of participation and conjunction with Him.
Again, it is not the possession of any good thing can make
them happy which have it, unless they enjoy the thing
wherewith they are possessed. Then are we happy therefore when fully we enjoy God, as an object wherein the
powers of our souls are satisfied even with everlasting
delight: so that although we be men, yet by being unto
God united we live as it were the life of God.

[3.] Happiness therefore is that estate whereby we attain,
so far as possibly may be attained, the full possession of
that which simply for itself is to be desired, and containeth
in it after an eminent sort the contentation of our desires,
the highest degree of all our perfection. Of such perfection
capable we are not in this life. For while we are in the
world, subject we are unto sundry imperfections,[1] griefs of
body, defects of mind; yea the best things we do are
painful, and the exercise of them grievous, being continued
without intermission; so as in those very actions whereby
we are especially perfected in this life we are not able to
persist; forced we are with very weariness, and that often,
to interrupt them: which tediousness cannot fall into those
operations that are in the state of bliss, when our union
with God is complete. Complete union with him must be
according unto every power and faculty of our minds apt to
receive so glorious an object. Capable we are of God both
by understanding and will: by understanding, as He is that
sovereign Truth which comprehendeth the rich treasures of
all wisdom; by will, as He is that sea of Goodness whereof
whoso tasteth shall thirst no more. As the will doth now
work upon that object by desire, which is as it were a
motion towards the end as yet unobtained; so likewise
upon the same hereafter received it shall work also by love.
"Appetitus inhiantis fit amor fruentis," saith St. Augustine:

---

[1] Μόνον, ὦ 'Ασκληπιε, τὸ ὄνομα τοῦ ἀγαθοῦ ἐν ἀνθρώποις, τὸ δε ἔργον
οὐδαμοῦ. . . . Τὸ μὴ λίαν κακὸν, ἐνθάδε τὸ ἀγαθόν ἐστι. Τὸ δὲ ἐνθάδε
ἀγαθόν, μόριον τοῦ κακοῦ τὸ ἐλάχιστον. 'Αδύνατον οὖν τὸ ἀγαθὸν ἐνθάδε
καθαρεύειν τῆς κακίας. . . . Κᾀγὼ δὲ χάριν ἔχω τῷ Θεῷ τῷ εἰς νοῦν μοι
βαλόντι περὶ τῆς γνώσεως τοῦ ἀγαθοῦ, ὅτι ἀδύνατόν ἐστιν αὐτὸ ἐν τῷ
κόσμῳ εἶναι· ὁ γὰρ κόσμος πλήρωμά ἐστι τῆς κακίας, ὁ δὲ Θεὸς τοῦ ἀγαθοῦ,
ἢ τὸ ἀγαθὸν τοῦ Θεοῦ.   Merc. Tris. [lib. vi. f. 14.]

"The longing disposition of them that thirst is changed into the sweet affection of them that taste and are replenished."[1]   Whereas we now love the thing that is good, but good especially in respect of benefit unto us ; we shall then love the thing that is good, only or principally for the goodness of beauty in itself. The soul being in this sort, as it is active, perfected by love of that infinite good, shall, as it is receptive, be also perfected with those supernatural passions of joy, peace, and delight. All this endless and everlasting.[2] Which perpetuity, in regard whereof our blessedness is termed "a crown which withereth not,"[3] doth neither depend upon the nature of the thing itself, nor proceed from any natural necessity that our souls should so exercise themselves for ever in beholding and loving God, but from the will of God, which doth both freely perfect our nature in so high a degree, and continue it so perfected. Under Man, no creature in the world is capable of felicity and bliss. First, because their chiefest perfection consisteth in that which is best for them, but not in that which is simply best, as ours doth. Secondly, because whatsoever external perfection they tend unto, it is not better than themselves, as ours is. How just occasion have we therefore even in this respect with the Prophet to admire the goodness of God ? "Lord, what is man, that thou shouldst exalt him above the works of thy hands,"[4] so far as to make thyself the inheritance of his rest and the substance of his felicity ?

[4.] Now if men had not naturally this desire to be happy, how were it possible that all men should have it ? All men have. Therefore this desire in man is natural. It is not in our power not to do the same ; how should it then be in our power to do it coldly or remissly ? So that our desire being natural is also in that degree of earnestness whereunto nothing can be added. And is it probable that God should frame the hearts of all men so desirous of that which no man may obtain ? It is an axiom of Nature that natural desire cannot utterly be frustrate.[5] This desire

[1] Aug. de Trin. lib. ix. c. ult. [Verbatim, "Appetitus, quo inhiatur rei cognoscendæ, fit amor cognitæ." viii. 888.]
[2] "The just shall go into life everlasting." Matt. xxv. [46.] "They shall be as the angels of God." Matt. xxii. [30.]
[3] 2 Tim. iv. 8 ; 1 Pet. v. 4.   [4] Psalm viii. 4.
[5] Comment. in Proœm. ii. Metaph. ["Si comprehensio esset impossibilis, tunc desiderium esset otiosum : et concessum est ab om-

of ours being natural should be frustrate, if that which may satisfy the same were a thing impossible for man to aspire unto. Man doth seek a triple perfection:[1] first a sensual, consisting in those things which very life itself requireth either as necessary supplements, or as beauties and ornaments thereof; then an intellectual, consisting in those things which none underneath man is either capable of or acquainted with; lastly a spiritual and divine, consisting in those things whereunto we tend by supernatural means here, but cannot here attain unto them. They who make the first of these three the scope of their whole life, are said by the Apostle[2] to have no god but only their belly, to be earthly-minded men. Unto the second they bend themselves, who seek especially to excel in all such knowledge and virtue as doth most commend men. To this branch belongeth the law of moral and civil perfection. That there is somewhat higher than either of these two, no other proof doth need than the very process of man's desire, which being natural should be frustrate, if there were not some farther thing wherein it might rest at the length contented, which in the former it cannot do. For man doth not seem to rest satisfied, either with fruition of that wherewith his life is preserved, or with performance of such actions as advance him most deservedly in estimation; but doth further covet, yea oftentimes manifestly pursue with great sedulity and earnestness, that which cannot stand him in any stead for vital use; that which exceedeth the reach of sense; yea somewhat above capacity of reason, somewhat divine and heavenly, which with hidden exultation it rather surmiseth than conceiveth; somewhat it seeketh, and what that is directly it knoweth not, yet very intentive desire thereof doth so incite it, that all other known delights and pleasures are laid aside, they give place to the search of this but only suspected desire. If the soul of man did serve only to give him being in this life, then things appertaining unto this life would content him, as we see they do other creatures; which creatures enjoying what they live by seek no further, but in this contentation do shew a kind of acknowledgment that there is no higher good which doth any way belong unto them. With us it is otherwise. For although the

nibus, quod nulla res est otiosa in fundamento naturæ et creaturæ." t. viii. p. 14, ed. Venet. 1552.]

[1] [Arist. Eth. Nic. I. v. 2.]   [2] Phil. iii. 19.

beauties, riches, honours, sciences, virtues, and perfections of all men living, were in the present possession of one; yet somewhat beyond and above all this there would still be sought and earnestly thirsted for. So that Nature even in this life doth plainly claim and call for a more divine perfection than either of these two that have been mentioned.

[5.] This last and highest estate of perfection whereof we speak is received of men in the nature of a Reward.[1] Rewards do always presuppose such duties performed as are rewardable. Our natural means therefore unto blessed-ness are our works; nor is it possible that Nature should ever find any other way to salvation than only this. But examine the works which we do, and since the first found-ation of the world what one can say, My ways are pure? Seeing then all flesh is guilty of that for which God hath threatened eternally to punish, what possibility is there this way to be saved? There resteth therefore either no way unto salvation, or if any, then surely a way which is super-natural, a way which could never have entered into the heart of man as much as once to conceive or imagine, if God himself had not revealed it extraordinarily. For which cause we term it the Mystery or secret way of salvation. And therefore St. Ambrose in this matter appealeth justly from man to God,[2] "Cœli mysterium doceat me Deus, qui condidit, non homo qui seipsum ignoravit:—Let God himself that made me, let not man that knows not himself, be my instructor concerning the mystical way to heaven." "When men of excellent wit," saith Lactantius, "had wholly betaken themselves unto study, after farewell bidden unto all kind as well of private as public action, they spared no labour that might be spent in the search of truth; holding it a thing of much more price to seek and to find out the reason of all affairs as well divine as human, than to stick fast in the toil of piling up riches and gather-ing together heaps of honours. Howbeit, they both did fail of their purpose, and got not as much as to quit their charges; because truth which is the secret of the Most High God, whose proper handy-work all things are, cannot

---

[1] "Rejoice and be glad, for great is your reward in heaven." Matt. v. 12. "Summa merces est ut ipso perfruamur." Aug. de Doct. Christ. cap. 6. [I. 32. t. iii. 16.]

[2] Ambros. contra Sym. [Ep. 18, § 7. t. ii. 835.]

be compassed with that wit and those senses which are our own. For God and man should be very near neighbours, if man's cogitations were able to take a survey of the counsels and appointments of that Majesty everlasting. Which being utterly impossible, that the eye of man by itself should look into the bosom of divine Reason ; God did not suffer him being desirous of the light of wisdom to stray any longer up and down, and with bootless expense of travel to wander in darkness that had no passage to get out by. His eyes at the length God did open, and bestow upon him the knowledge of the truth by way of Donative, to the end that man might both be clearly convicted of folly, and being through error out of the way, have the path that leadeth unto immortality laid plain before him." [1] Thus far Lactantius Firmianus, to shew that God himself is the teacher of the truth, whereby is made known the supernatural way of salvation and law for them to live in that shall be saved. In the natural path of everlasting life the first beginning is that ability of doing good, which God in the day of man's creation endued him with ; from hence obedience unto the will of his Creator, absolute righteousness and integrity in all his actions ; and last of all the justice of God rewarding the worthiness of his deserts with the crown of eternal glory. Had Adam continued in his first estate, this had been the way of life unto him and all his posterity. Wherein I confess notwithstanding with the wittiest of the school-divines,[2] " That if we speak of

---

[1] " Magno et excellenti ingenio viri, cum se doctrinæ penitus dedissent, quicquid laboris poterat impendi (contemptis omnibus et privatis et publicis actionibus) ad inquirendæ veritatis studium contulerunt, existimantes multo esse præclarius humanarum divinarumque rerum investigare ac scire rationem, quam struendis opibus aut cumulandis honoribus inhærere. Sed neque adepti sunt id quod volebant, et operam simul atque industriam perdiderunt : quia veritas, id est arcanum summi Dei qui fecit omnia, ingenio ac propriis sensibus non potest comprehendi. Alioqui nihil inter Deum hominemque distaret, si consilia et dispositiones illius majestatis æternæ cogitatio assequeretur humana. Quod quia fieri non potuit ut homini per seipsum ratio divina notesceret, non est passus hominem Deus lumen sapientiæ requirentem diutius aberrare, ac sine ullo laboris effectu vagari per tenebras inextricabiles. Aperuit oculos ejus aliquando, et notionem veritatis munus suum fecit, ut et humanam sapientiam nullam esse monstraret, et erranti ac vago viam consequendæ immortalitatis ostenderet." Lactant. lib. i. cap. 1.

[2] Scot. lib. iv. Sent. dist. 49, 6. " Loquendo de stricta justitia, Deus nulli nostrum propter quæcunque merita est debitor perfectionis reddendæ tam intensæ, propter immoderatum excessum illius perfectionis ultra illa merita. Sed esto quod ex liberalitate sua deter-

strict justice, God could no way have been bound to requite man's labours in so large and ample a manner as human felicity doth import; inasmuch as the dignity of this exceedeth so far the other's value. But be it that God of his great liberality had determined in lieu of man's endeavours to bestow the same, by the rule of that justice which best beseemeth him, namely, the justice of one that requireth nothing mincingly, but all with pressed and heaped and even over-enlarged measure ; yet could it never hereupon necessarily be gathered, that such justice should add to the nature of that reward the property of everlasting continuance ; sith possession of bliss, though it should be but for a moment, were an abundant retribution." But we are not now to enter into this consideration, how gracious and bountiful our good God might still appear in so rewarding the sons of men, albeit they should exactly perform whatsoever duty their nature bindeth them unto. Howsoever God did propose this reward, we that were to be rewarded must have done that which is required at our hands ; we failing in the one, it were in nature an impossibility that the other should be looked for. The light of nature is never able to find out any way of obtaining the reward of bliss, but by performing exactly the duties and works of righteousness.

[6.] From salvation therefore and life all flesh being excluded this way, behold how the wisdom of God hath revealed a way mystical and supernatural, a way directing unto the same end of life by a course which groundeth itself upon the guiltiness of sin, and through sin desert of condemnation and death. For in this way the first thing is the tender compassion of God respecting us drowned and swallowed up in misery ; the next is redemption out of the same by the precious death and merit of a mighty Saviour, which hath witnessed of himself, saying,[1] " I am the way," the way that leadeth us from misery into bliss. This supernatural way had God in himself prepared before all worlds. The way of supernatural duty which to us he hath pre-

---

minasset meritis conferre actum tam perfectum tanquam præmium, tali quidem justitia qualis decet eum, scilicet supererogantis in præmiis : tamen non sequitur ex hoc necessario, quod per illam justitiam sit reddenda perfectio perennis tanquam præmium, imo abundans fieret retributio in beatitudine unius momenti." [p. 168. Venet. 1598.]

[1] John xiv. 6.

scribed, our Saviour in the Gospel of St. John doth note, terming it by an excellency, The Work of God,[1] "This is the work of God, that ye believe in him whom he hath sent." Not that God doth require nothing unto happiness at the hands of men saving only a naked belief (for hope and charity we may not exclude [2]) ; but that without belief all other things are as nothing, and it the ground of those other divine virtues.

Concerning Faith, the principal object whereof is that eternal Verity which hath discovered the treasures of hidden wisdom in Christ; concerning Hope, the highest object whereof is that everlasting Goodness which in Christ doth quicken the dead ; concerning Charity, the final object whereof is that incomprehensible Beauty which shineth in the countenance of Christ the Son of the living God : concerning these virtues, the first of which beginning here with a weak apprehension of things not seen, endeth with the intuitive vision of God in the world to come ; the second beginning here with a trembling expectation of things far removed and as yet but only heard of, endeth with real and actual fruition of that which no tongue can express ; the third beginning here with a weak inclination of heart towards him unto whom we are not able to approach, endeth with endless union, the mystery whereof is higher than the reach of the thoughts of men ; concerning that Faith, Hope, and Charity, without which there can be no salvation, was there ever any mention made saving only in that law which God himself hath from heaven revealed ? There is not in the world a syllable muttered with certain truth concerning any of these three, more than hath been supernaturally received from the mouth of the eternal God.

Laws therefore concerning these things are supernatural, both in respect of the manner of delivering them, which is divine ; and also in regard of the things delivered, which are such as have not in nature any cause from which they flow,

---

[1] John vi. 29.

[2] [Chr. Letter, p. 13. " Tell us . . . whether you thinke that *not faith alone*, but faith, hope, and love, be the formall cause of our righteousness."

Hooker, MS. note. " Is faith then the formall cause of justification ? And faith alone a cause in this kind ? Who hath taught you this doctrine ? Have you been tampering so long with Pastors, Doctors, Elders, Deacons ; that the first principles of your religion are now to learn ? "]

but were by the voluntary appointment of God ordained besides the course of nature, to rectify nature's obliquity withal.

XII. When supernatural duties are necessarily exacted, natural are not rejected as needless. The law of God therefore is, though principally delivered for instruction in the one, yet fraught with precepts of the other also. The Scripture is fraught even with laws of Nature; insomuch that Gratian[1] defining Natural Right, (whereby is meant the right which exacteth those general duties that concern men naturally even as they are men,) termeth "Natural Right, that which the Books of the Law and the Gospel do contain." Neither is it vain that the Scripture aboundeth with so great store of laws in this kind: for they are either such as we of ourselves could not easily have found out, and then the benefit is not small to have them readily set down to our hands; or if they be so clear and manifest that no man endued with reason can lightly be ignorant of them, yet the Spirit as it were borrowing them from the school of Nature, as serving to prove things less manifest, and to induce a persuasion of somewhat which were in itself more hard and dark, unless it should in such sort be cleared, the very applying of them unto cases particular is not without most singular use and profit many ways for men's instruction. Besides, be they plain of themselves or obscure, the evidence of God's own testimony added to the natural assent of reason concerning the certainty of them, doth not a little comfort and confirm the same.

[2.] Wherefore inasmuch as our actions are conversant about things beset with many circumstances, which cause men of sundry wits to be also of sundry judgment concerning that which ought to be done; requisite it cannot but seem the rule of divine law should herein help our imbecility, that we might the more infallibly understand what is good and what evil. The first principles of the Law of Nature are easy; hard it were to find men ignorant of them. But concerning the duty which Nature's law doth require at the hands of men in a number of things particular, so far hath the natural understanding even of sundry whole nations been darkened, that they have not discerned no not gross iniquity to be sin.[2] Again, being so prone as we are to fawn upon

---

[1] "Jus naturale est, quod in Lege et Evangelio continetur."   p. 1, d. 1. [Corp. Jur. Can. p. 2. Lugd. 1584.]

[2] Joseph. lib. secundo contra Apion. [c. 37.]   "Lacedæmonii quo-

ourselves, and to be ignorant as much as may be of our own deformities, without the feeling sense whereof we are most wretched ; even so much the more, because not knowing them we cannot so much as desire to have them taken away ; how should our festered sores be cured, but that God hath delivered a law as sharp as the two-edged sword, piercing the very closest and most unsearchable corners of the heart,[1] which the Law of Nature can hardly, human laws by no means possible, reach unto ? Hereby we know even secret concupiscence to be sin, and are made fearful to offend though it be but in a wandering cogitation. Finally, of those things which are for direction of all the parts of our life needful, and not impossible to be discerned by the light of Nature itself ; are there not many which few men's natural capacity, and some which no man's, hath been able to find out ? They are, saith St. Augustine,[2] but a few, and they endued with great ripeness of wit and judgment, free from all such affairs as might trouble their meditations, instructed in the sharpest and the subtilest points of learning, who have, and that very hardly, been able to find out but only the immortality of the soul. The resurrection of the flesh what man did ever at any time dream of, having not heard it otherwise than from the school of Nature ? Whereby it appeareth how much we are bound to yield unto our Creator the Father of all mercy eternal thanks, for that he

modo non sunt ob inhospitalitatem reprehendendi, fœdumque neglectum nuptiarum ? Elienses vero et Thebani ob coitum cum masculis plane impudentem et contra naturam, quem recte et utiliter exercere putabant ? Cumque hæc omnino perpetrarunt, etiam suis legibus miscuere." Vid. Th. I, 2, q. 94, 4, 5, 6. "Lex naturæ sic corrupta fuit apud Germanos, ut latrocinium non reputarent peccatum." [t. xi. 204.] August. (aut quisquis auctor est) lib. de quæst. Nov. et Vet. Test. "Quis nesciat quid bonæ vitæ conveniat, aut ignoret quia quod sibi fieri non vult aliis minime debeat facere ? At vero ubi naturalis lex evanuit oppressa consuetudine delinquendi, tunc oportuit manifestari scriptis, ut Dei judicium omnes audirent [legem manifestari, ut in Judæis omnes homines audirent :] non quod penitus obliterata est, sed quia maxima ejus auctoritate carebant, idololatriæ studebatur, timor Dei in terris non erat, fornicatio operabatur, circa rem proximi avida erat concupiscentia. Data [danda] ergo lex erat, ut et quæ sciebantur auctoritatem haberent, et quæ latere cœperant manifestarentur." Quæst. iv. [t. iii. App. 44.]

[1] Heb. iv. 12.

[2] ["Humanis argumentationibus hæc invenire conantes, vix pauci magno præditi ingenio, abundantes otio, doctrinisque subtilissimis eruditi, ad indagandam solius animæ immortalitatem pervenire potue-runt." De Trin. lib. xiii. c. 12. tom. viii. 935.]

hath delivered his law unto the world, a law wherein so many things are laid open, clear, and manifest, as a light which otherwise would have been buried in darkness, not without the hazard, or rather not with the hazard but with the certain loss, of infinite thousands of souls most undoubtedly now saved.

[3.] We see, therefore, that our sovereign good is desired naturally; that God the author of that natural desire had appointed natural means whereby to fulfil it; that man having utterly disabled his nature unto those means hath had other revealed from God, and hath received from heaven a law to teach him how that which is desired naturally must now supernaturally be attained. Finally, we see that because those latter exclude not the former quite and clean as unnecessary, therefore together with such supernatural duties as could not possibly have been otherwise known to the world, the same law that teacheth them, teacheth also with them such natural duties as could not by light of Nature easily have been known.

XIII. In the first age of the world God gave laws unto our fathers, and by reason of the number of their days their memories served instead of books; whereof the manifold imperfections and defects being known to God, he mercifully relieved the same by often putting them in mind of that whereof it behoved them to be specially mindful. In which respect we see how many times one thing hath been iterated unto sundry even of the best and wisest among them. After that the lives of men were shortened, means more durable to preserve the laws of God from oblivion and corruption grew in use, not without precise direction from God himself. First therefore of Moses it is said, that he "wrote all the words of God;"[1] not by his own private motion and device: for God taketh this act to himself,[2] "I have written." Furthermore, were not the Prophets following commanded also to do the like? Unto the holy evangelist St. John, how often express charge is given, "Scribe," "Write these things."[3] Concerning the rest of our Lord's disciples, the words of St. Augustine are,[4] "Quicquid ille de suis factis et dictis nos legere voluit, hoc scribendum illis tanquam suis manibus imperavit."

[1] Exod. xxiv. 4.   [2] Hos. viii. 12. [and Exod. xxiv. 12.]
[3] Apoc. i. 11; xiv. 13.
[4] Aug. lib. i. de Cons. Evang. cap. ult. [t. iii. pars 2. p. 26.]

[2.] Now, although we do not deny it to be a matter
merely accidental unto the law of God to be written;
although writing be not that which addeth authority and
strength thereunto; finally, though his laws do require at
our hands the same obedience howsoever they be delivered;
his providence notwithstanding which hath made principal
choice of this way to deliver them, who seeth not what
cause we have to admire and magnify? The singular benefit
that hath grown unto the world, by receiving the laws of
God even by his own appointment committed unto writing,
we are not able to esteem as the value thereof deserveth.
When the question therefore is, whether we be now to seek
for any revealed law of God otherwhere than only in the
sacred Scripture; whether we do now stand bound in the
sight of God to yield to traditions urged by the Church of
Rome the same obedience and reverence we do to his
written law, honouring equally and adoring both as divine:
our answer is, No. They that so earnestly plead for the
authority of tradition, as if nothing were more safely conveyed than that which spreadeth itself by report, and
descendeth by relation of former generations unto the ages
that succeed, are not all of them (surely a miracle it were if
they should be) so simple as thus to persuade themselves;
howsoever, if the simple were so persuaded, they could be
content perhaps very well to enjoy the benefit, as they
account it, of that common error. What hazard the truth is
in when it passeth through the hands of report, how maimed
and deformed it becometh, they are not, they cannot
possibly be ignorant. Let them that are indeed of this
mind consider but only that little of things divine, which the [1]
heathen have in such sort received. How miserable had
the state of the Church of God been long ere this, if wanting the sacred Scripture we had no record of his laws, but
only the memory of man receiving the same by report and
relation from his predecessors?

[3.] By Scripture it hath in the wisdom of God seemed

[1] I mean those historical matters concerning the ancient state of the
first world, the deluge, the sons of Noah, the children of Israel's
deliverance out of Egypt, the life and doings of Moses their captain,
with such like : the certain truth whereof delivered in Holy Scripture
is of the heathen which had them only by report so intermingled with
fabulous vanities, that the most which remaineth in them to be seen is
the show of dark and obscure steps, where some part of the truth hath
gone.

meet to deliver unto the world much but personally expedient to be practised of certain men; many deep and profound points of doctrine, as being the main original ground whereupon the precepts of duty depend; many prophecies, the clear performance whereof might confirm the world in belief of things unseen; many histories to serve as looking-glasses to behold the mercy, the truth, the righteousness of God towards all that faithfully serve, obey, and honour him; yea many entire meditations of piety, to be as patterns and precedents in cases of like nature; many things needful for explication, many for application unto particular occasions, such as the providence of God from time to time hath taken to have the several books of his holy ordinance written. Be it then that together with the principal necessary laws of God there are sundry other things written, whereof we might haply be ignorant and yet be saved: what? shall we hereupon think them needless? shall we esteem them as riotous branches wherewith we sometimes behold most pleasant vines overgrown? Surely no more than we judge our hands or our eyes superfluous, or what part soever, which if our bodies did want, we might notwithstanding any such defect retain still the complete being of men. As therefore a complete man is neither destitute of any part necessary, and hath some parts whereof though the want could not deprive him of his essence, yet to have them standeth him in singular stead in respect of the special uses for which they serve; in like sort all those writings which contain in them the Law of God, all those venerable books of Scripture, all those sacred tomes and volumes of Holy Writ; they are with such absolute perfection framed, that in them there neither wanteth any thing the lack whereof might deprive us of life, nor any thing in such wise aboundeth, that as being superfluous, unfruitful, and altogether needless, we should think it no loss or danger at all if we did want it.

XIV. Although the Scripture of God therefore be stored with infinite variety of matter in all kinds, although it abound with all sorts of laws, yet the principal intent of Scripture is to deliver the laws of duties supernatural. Oftentimes it hath been in very solemn manner disputed, whether all things necessary unto salvation be necessarily set down in the Holy Scriptures or no.[1] If we define that necessary

[1] "Utrum cognitio supernaturalis necessaria viatori sit sufficienter

unto salvation, whereby the way to salvation is in any sort made more plain, apparent, and easy to be known; then is there no part of true philosophy, no art of account, no kind of science rightly so called, but the Scripture must contain it. If only those things be necessary, as surely none else are, without the knowledge and practice whereof it is not the will and pleasure of God to make any ordinary grant of salvation; it may be notwithstanding and oftentimes hath been demanded, how the books of Holy Scripture contain in them all necessary things, when of things necessary the very chiefest is to know what books we are bound to esteem holy; which point is confessed impossible for the Scripture itself to teach. Whereunto we may answer with truth, that there is not in the world any art or science, which proposing unto itself an end (as every one doth some end or other) hath been therefore thought defective, if it have not delivered simply whatsoever is needful to the same end; but all kinds of knowledge have their certain bounds and limits; each of them presupposeth many necessary things learned in other sciences and known beforehand. He that should take upon him to teach men how to be eloquent in pleading causes, must needs deliver unto them whatsoever precepts are requisite unto that end; otherwise he doth not the thing which he taketh upon him. Seeing then no man can plead eloquently unless he be able first to speak; it followeth that ability of speech is in this case a thing most necessary. Notwithstanding every man would think it ridiculous, that he which undertaketh by writing to instruct an orator should therefore deliver all the precepts of grammar; because his profession is to deliver precepts necessary unto eloquent speech, yet so that they which are to receive them be taught beforehand so much of that which is thereunto necessary, as comprehendeth the skill of speaking. In like sort, albeit Scripture do profess to contain in it all things that are necessary unto salvation; yet the meaning cannot be simply of all things which are necessary, but all things that are necessary in some certain kind or form; as all things which are necessary, and either could not at all or could not easily be known by the light of natural discourse; all things which are necessary to be known that we may be saved; but known with presupposal of knowledge

tradita in sacra Scriptura?" This question proposed by Scotus is affirmatively concluded. [In Sent. lib. i. p. 10, D. et Resp. p. 2, K.]

concerning certain principles whereof it receiveth us already persuaded, and then instructeth us in all the residue that are necessary. In the number of these principles one is the sacred authority of Scripture. Being therefore persuaded by other means that these Scriptures are the oracles of God, themselves do then teach us the rest, and lay before us all the duties which God requireth at our hands as necessary unto salvation.

[2.] Further, there hath been some doubt likewise, whether *containing in Scripture* do import express setting down in plain terms, or else *comprehending* in such sort that by reason we may from thence conclude all things which are necessary. Against the former of these two constructions instance hath sundry ways been given. For our belief in the Trinity, the co-eternity of the Son of God with his Father, the proceeding of the Spirit from the Father and the Son, the duty of baptizing infants : these with such other principal points, the necessity whereof is by none denied, are notwithstanding in Scripture no where to be found by express literal mention, only deduced they are out of Scripture by collection. This kind of comprehension in Scripture being therefore received, still there is doubt how far we are to proceed by collection, before the full and complete measure of things necessary be made up. For let us not think that as long as the world doth endure the wit of man shall be able to sound the bottom of that which may be concluded out of the Scripture; especially if "things contained by collection" do so far extend, as to draw in whatsoever may be at any time out of Scripture but probably and conjecturally surmised. But let *necessary* collection be made requisite, and we may boldly deny, that of all those things which at this day are with so great necessity urged upon this church under the name of reformed church-discipline, there is any one which their books hitherto have made manifest to be contained in the Scripture. Let them if they can allege but one properly belonging to their cause, and not common to them and us, and shew the deduction thereof out of Scripture to be necessary.

[3.] It hath been already shewed how all things necessary unto salvation in such sort as before we have maintained must needs be possible for men to know ; and that many things are in such sort necessary, the knowledge whereof is by the light of Nature impossible to be attained. Whereupon it followeth that either all flesh is excluded from possibility of salvation, which to think were most barbarous; or else that God hath by supernatural means revealed the way of life so far forth as doth suffice For this cause God hath so many times and ways spoken to the sons of men. Neither hath he by speech only, but by writing also, instructed and taught his Church. The cause of writing hath been to the end that things by him revealed unto the world might have the longer continuance, and the greater certainty of assurance, by how much that which standeth on record hath in both those respects pre-eminence above that which passeth from hand to hand, and hath no pens but the tongues, no books but the ears of men to record it. The several books of Scripture having had each some several occasion and particular purpose which caused them to be written, the contents thereof are according to the exigence of that special end whereunto they are intended. Hereupon it groweth that every book of Holy Scripture doth take out of all kinds of truth, natural,[1] historical,[2] foreign,[3] supernatural,[4] so much as the matter handled requireth.

Now forasmuch as there hath been reason alleged sufficient to conclude, that all things necessary unto salvation must be made known, and that God himself hath therefore revealed his will, because otherwise men could not have known so much as is necessary; his surceasing to speak to the world, since the publishing of the Gospel of Jesus Christ and the delivery of the same in writing, is unto us a manifest token that the way of salvation is now sufficiently opened, and that we need no other means for our full instruction than God hath already furnished us withal.

[4.] The main drift of the whole New Testament is that which St. John setteth down as the purpose of his own history; [5] "These things are written, that ye might believe that Jesus is Christ the Son of God, and that in believing ye might have life through his name." The drift of the Old that which the Apostle mentioneth to Timothy, [6] "The Holy Scriptures are able to make thee wise unto Salvation." So that the general end both of Old and New is one; the difference between them consisting in this, that the Old did make wise by teaching salvation through Christ that should come, the New by teaching that Christ the Saviour is come,

---

[1] Eph. v. 29.   [2] 2 Tim. iii. 8.   [3] Tit. i. 12.
[4] 2 Pet. ii. 4.   [5] John xx. 31.   [6] 2 Tim. iii. 15.

and that Jesus whom the Jews did crucify, and whom God did raise again from the dead, is he. When the Apostle therefore affirmeth unto Timothy, that the Old was able to make him wise to salvation, it was not his meaning that the Old alone can do this unto us which live sithence the publication of the New. For he speaketh with presupposal of the doctrine of Christ known also unto Timothy; and therefore first it is said, [1] "Continue thou in those things which thou hast learned and art persuaded, knowing of whom thou hast been taught them." Again, those Scriptures he granteth were able to make him wise to salvation; but he addeth, [2] "through the faith which is in Christ." Wherefore without the doctrine of the New Testament teaching that Christ hath wrought the redemption of the world, which redemption the Old did foreshew he should work, it is not the former alone which can on our behalf perform so much as the Apostle doth avouch, who presupposeth this when he magnifieth that so highly. And as his words concerning the books of ancient Scripture do not take place but with presupposal of the Gospel of Christ embraced; so our own words also, when we extol the complete sufficiency of the whole entire body of the Scripture, must in like sort be understood with this caution, that the benefit of nature's light be not thought excluded as unnecessary, because the necessity of a diviner light is magnified.

[5.] There is in Scripture therefore no defect, but that any man, what place or calling soever he hold in the Church of God, may have thereby the light of his natural understanding so perfected, that the one being relieved by the other, there can want no part of needful instruction unto any good work which God himself requireth, be it natural or supernatural, belonging simply unto men as men, or unto men as they are united in whatsoever kind of society. It sufficeth therefore that Nature and Scripture do serve in such full sort, that they both jointly and not severally either of them be so complete, that unto everlasting felicity we need not the knowledge of any thing more than these two may easily furnish our minds with on all sides; [3] and there-

---

[1] 2 Tim. iii. 14.   [2] Verse 15.

[3] [Christ. Letter, p. 7. "Although you exclude traditions as a part of supernaturall trueth, yet you infer that the light of nature teacheth some knowledge naturall whiche is necessarie to salvation." And p. 8. "What scripture approveth such a saying, . . that cases and matters of

fore they which add traditions, as a part of supernatural necessary truth, have not the truth, but are in error. For they only plead, that whatsoever God revealeth as necessary for all Christian men to do or believe, the same we ought to embrace, whether we have received it by writing or otherwise; which no man denieth : when that which they should confirm, who claim so great reverence unto traditions, is, that the same traditions are necessarily to be acknowledged divine and holy. For we do not reject them only because they are not in the Scripture, but because they are neither in Scripture, nor can otherwise sufficiently by any reason be proved to be of God. That which is of God, and may be evidently proved to be so, we deny not but it hath in his kind, although unwritten, yet the selfsame force and authority with the written laws of God. It is by ours acknowledged, "that the Apostles did in every church institute and ordain some rites and customs serving for the seemliness of church-regiment, which rites and customs they have not committed unto writing." [1] Those rites and customs being known to be apostolical, and having the nature of things changeable, were no less to be accounted of in the Church than other things of the like degree; that is to say, capable in like sort of alteration, although set down in the Apostles' writings. For both being known to be apostolical, it is not the manner of delivering them unto the Church, but the author from whom they proceed, which doth give them their force and credit.

XV. Laws being imposed either by each man upon himself, or by a public society upon the particulars thereof, or by all the nations of men upon every several society, or by the Lord himself upon any or every of these; there is not amongst these four kinds any one but containeth sundry both natural and positive laws. Impossible it is but that

salvation bee determinable by any other lawe then of holy Scripture." Hooker, MS. note. "Remember here to show the use of the law of nature in handling matters of religion. Are there not cases of salvation wherein a man may have controversie with infidels which believe not the Scriptures? And even with them which believe Scripture the law of nature notwithstanding is not without force, that any man to whom it is alleaged can cast it of as a thing impertinent."]

[1] [Whitakerus adversus Bellarmin. quæst. 6, cap. 6. "Fatemur Apostolos in singulis ecclesiis ritus aliquos atque consuetudines, ordinis et decori causa, sanxisse, non autem scripsisse : quia hi ritus non fuerunt perpetui futuri, sed liberi, qui pro commodo et temporum ratione mutari possent." Bellarmin. Opp. I. 372. quæst. 6, cap. 6. Genev. 1610.]

they should fall into a number of gross errors, who only take such laws for positive as have been made or invented of men, and holding this position hold also, that all positive and none but positive laws are mutable. Laws natural do always bind; laws positive not so, but only after they have been expressly and wittingly imposed. Laws positive there are in every of those kinds before mentioned. As in the first kind the promises which we have passed unto men, and the vows we have made unto God; for these are laws which we tie ourselves unto, and till we have so tied ourselves they bind us not. Laws positive in the second kind are such as the civil constitutions peculiar unto each particular commonweal. In the third kind the law of heraldry in war is positive: and in the last all the judicials which God gave unto the people of Israel to observe. And although no laws but positive be mutable, yet all are not mutable which be positive. Positive laws are either permanent or else changeable, according as the matter itself is concerning which they were first made. Whether God or man be the maker of them, alteration they so far forth admit, as the matter doth exact.

[2.] Laws that concern supernatural duties are all positive,[1] and either concern men supernaturally as men, or else as parts of a supernatural society, which society we call the Church. To concern men as men supernaturally is to concern them as duties which belong of necessity to all, and yet could not have been known by any to belong unto them, unless God had opened them himself, inasmuch as they do not depend upon any natural ground at all out of which they may be deduced, but are appointed of God to supply the defect of those natural ways of salvation, by which we are not now able to attain thereunto. The Church being a supernatural society doth differ from natural societies in this, that the persons unto whom we associate ourselves, in

---

[1] [To prevent any misapplication of this principle, it may be useful to compare Butler's Analogy, p. ii. c. I. § 2 ; where moral precepts and duties are contrasted with positive in a manner which may at first appear inconsistent with Hooker's language. But the appearance of discrepancy will perhaps be removed, if it is considered that Hooker opposes the term Positive to Natural, in regard of our ability or inability to *obtain the knowledge* of a law without express revelation : Butler on the other hand opposes Positive to Moral, in regard of our ability or inability to *discern the reasonableness* of a law *made known* to us by revelation or otherwise.]

the one are men simply considered as men, but they to whom we be joined in the other, are God, Angels, and holy men. Again the Church being both a society and a society super-natural, although as it is a society it have the selfsame original grounds which other politic societies have, namely, the natural inclination which all men have unto sociable life, and consent to some certain bond of association, which bond is the law that appointeth what kind of order they shall be associated in : yet unto the Church as it is a society supernatural this is peculiar, that part of the bond of their association which belong to the Church of God must be a law supernatural, which God himself hath revealed concern-ing the kind of worship which his people shall do unto him. The substance of the service of God therefore, so far forth as it hath in it any thing more than the Law of Reason doth teach, may not be invented of men, as it is amongst the heathens,[1] but must be received from God himself, as always it hath been in the Church, saving only when the Church hath been forgetful of her duty.

[3.] Wherefore to end with a general rule concerning all the laws which God hath tied men unto : those laws divine that belong, whether naturally or supernaturally, either to men as men, or to men as they live in politic society, or to men as they are of that politic society which is the Church, without any further respect had unto any such variable accident as the state of men and of societies of men and of the Church itself in this world is subject unto ; all laws that so belong unto men, they belong for ever, yea although they be Positive Laws, unless being positive God himself which made them alter them. The reason is, because the subject or matter of laws in general is thus far forth constant : which matter is that for the ordering whereof laws were instituted, and being instituted are not changeable without cause, neither can they have cause of change, when that which gave them their first institution remaineth for ever one and the same. On the other side, laws that were made for men or societies or churches, in regard of their being such as they do not always continue, but may perhaps be clean otherwise a while after, and so may require to be otherwise ordered than before ; the laws of God himself which are of this nature, no man endued with common sense will ever deny to be of a

---

[1] " Their fear towards me was taught by the precept of men." Isa. xxix. 13.

different constitution from the former, in respect of the one's constancy and the mutability of the other. And this doth seem to have been the very cause why St. John doth so peculiarly term the doctrine that teacheth salvation by Jesus Christ, [1]*Evangelium æternum*, "an eternal Gospel;" because there can be no reason wherefore the publishing thereof should be taken away, and any other instead of it proclaimed, as long as the world doth continue: whereas the whole law of rites and ceremonies, although delivered with so great solemnity, is notwithstanding clean abrogated, inasmuch as it had but temporary cause of God's ordaining it.

[4.] But that we may at length conclude this first general introduction unto the nature and original birth, as of all other laws, so likewise of those which the sacred Scripture containeth, concerning the Author whereof even infidels have confessed that He can neither err nor deceive: [2] albeit about things easy and manifest unto all men by common sense there needeth no higher consultation; because as a man whose wisdom is in weighty affairs admired would take it in some disdain to have his counsel solemnly asked about a toy, so the meanness of some things is such, that to search the Scripture of God for the ordering of them were to derogate from the reverend authority and dignity of the Scripture, no less than they do by whom Scriptures are in ordinary talk very idly applied unto vain and childish trifles: yet better it were to be superstitious than profane; to take from thence our direction even in all things great or small, than to wade through matters of principal weight and moment, without ever caring what the law of God hath either for or against our designs. Concerning the custom of the very Painims, thus much Strabo witnesseth: "Men that are civil do lead their lives after one common law appointing them what to do. For that otherwise a multitude should with harmony amongst themselves concur in the doing of one thing, (for this is civilly to live,) or that they should in any sort manage community of life, it is not possible. Now laws or statutes are of two sorts. For they are either received from gods, or else from men. And our ancient predecessors

---

[1] Apoc. xiv. 6.

[2] Κομιδῇ ἄρα ὁ Θεὸς ἁπλοῦν καὶ ἀληθὲς ἔν τε ἔργῳ καὶ ἐν λόγῳ, καὶ οὔτε αὐτὸς μεθίσταται οὔτε ἄλλους ἐξαπατᾷ, οὔτε κατὰ φαντασίας οὔτε κατὰ λόγους οὔτε κατὰ σημείων πομπὰς, οὔθ' ὕπαρ οὐδ' ὄναρ. Plat. in fine 2 Polit.

did surely most honour and reverence that which was from the gods; for which cause consultation with oracles was a thing very usual and frequent in their times." [1] Did they make so much account of the voice of their gods, which in truth were no gods : and shall we neglect the precious benefit of conference with those oracles of the true and living God, whereof so great store is left to the Church, and whereunto there is so free, so plain, and so easy access for all men? "By thy commandments" [2] (this was David's confession unto God) "thou hast made me wiser than mine enemies." Again, "I have had more understanding than all my teachers, because thy testimonies are my meditations." What pains would not they have bestowed in the study of these books, who travelled sea and land to gain the treasure of some few days' talk with men whose wisdom the world did make any reckoning of? That little which some of the heathens did chance to hear, concerning such matter as the sacred Scripture plentifully containeth, they did in wonderful sort affect; their speeches [3] as oft as they make mention thereof are strange, and such as themselves could not utter as they did other things, but still acknowledged that their wits, which did every where else conquer hardness, were with profoundness here over-matched. Wherefore seeing that God hath endued us with sense, to the end that we might perceive such things as this present life doth need; and with reason, lest that which sense cannot reach unto, being both now and also in regard of a future estate hereafter necessary to be known, should lie obscure; finally, with the heavenly support of prophetical revelation, which doth open those hidden mysteries that reason could never have been able to find out, [4] or to have known the necessity of them unto our everlasting good : use we the precious gifts of God unto his glory and honour that gave them, seeking by all means to know what the will of our God is; what righteous before

---

[1] Πολιτικοὶ ὄντες ἀπὸ προστάγματος κοινοῦ ζῶσιν. Ἄλλως γὰρ οὐχ οἷόν τε τοὺς πολλοὺς ἕν τι κατὰ ταὐτὸ ποιεῖν ἡρμοσμένως ἀλλήλοις (ὅπερ ἦν τὸ πολιτεύεσθαι), καὶ ἄλλως πως νέμειν βίον κοινόν. Τὸ δὲ πρόσταγμα διττόν· ἢ γὰρ παρὰ θεῶν ἢ παρὰ ἀνθρώπων. Καὶ οἵ γε ἀρχαῖοι τὸ παρὰ τῶν θεῶν ἐπρέσβευον μᾶλλον καὶ ἐσέμνυνον· καὶ διὰ τοῦτο καὶ ὁ χρηστηρια-ζόμενος ἦν τότε πολύς. Strab. Geogr. lib. xvi. [c. 38. t. vi p. 361, Lips. 1811.]

[2] Psalm cxix. 98.   [3] Vide Orphei Carmina.

[4] Ὧν γὰρ ὁ νοῦς ἀπολείπεται, πρὸς ταῦθ' ἡ προφητεία φθάνει. Philo de Mos. [lib. ii. in init. p. 655, Paris 1640.]

him ; in his sight what holy, perfect, and good, that we may
truly and faithfully do it.

XVI. Thus far therefore we have endeavoured in part to
open, of what nature and force laws are, according unto their
several kinds ; the law which God with himself hath eternally
set down to follow in his own works ; the law which he hath
made for his creatures to keep; the law of natural and
necessary agents ; the law which angels in heaven obey; the
law whereunto by the light of reason men find themselves
bound in that they are men ; the law which they make by
composition for multitudes and politic societies of men to be
guided by; the law which belongeth unto each nation ; the law
that concerneth the fellowship of all ; and lastly the law which
God himself hath supernaturally revealed.   It might peradventure have been more popular and more plausible to vulgar
ears, if this first discourse had been spent in extolling the force
of laws, in shewing the great necessity of them when they are
good, and in aggravating their offence by whom public laws
are injuriously traduced.   But forasmuch as with such kind
of matter the passions of men are rather stirred one way or
other, than their knowledge any way set forward unto the
trial of that whereof there is doubt made ; I have therefore
turned aside from that beaten path, and chosen though a less
easy yet a more profitable way in regard of the end we propose.   Lest therefore any man should marvel whereunto all
these things tend, the drift and purpose of all is this, even to
shew in what manner, as every good and perfect gift, so this
very gift of good and perfect laws is derived from the Father
of lights ; [1] to teach men a reason why just and reasonable
laws are of so great force, of so great use in the world ; and
to inform their minds with some method of reducing the
laws whereof there is present controversy unto their first
original causes, that so it may be in every particular ordinance
thereby the better discerned, whether the same be reasonable,
just, and righteous, or no.   Is there any thing which can either
be thoroughly understood or soundly judged of, till the very
first causes and principles from which originally it springeth
be made manifest?   If all parts of knowledge have beed
thought by wise men to be then most orderly delivered anu
proceeded in, when they are drawn to their first original ;[2]

---

[1] James i. 17.
[2] Arist. Phys. lib. i. cap. 1. [τὸ εἰδέναι καὶ τὸ ἐπίστασθαι συμβαίνι.
περὶ πάσας τὰς μεθόδους, ὧν εἰσιν ἀρχαὶ ἢ αἴτια ἢ στοιχεῖα, ἐκ τοῦ ταῦτα

seeing that our whole question concerneth the quality of
ecclesiastical laws, let it not seem a labour superfluous that
in the entrance thereunto all these several kinds of laws have
been considered, inasmuch as they all concur as principles,
they all have their forcible operations therein, although not
all in like apparent and manifest manner. By means
whereof it cometh to pass that the force which they have
is not observed of many.

[2.] Easier a great deal it is for men by law to be taught
what they ought to do, than instructed how to judge as they
should do of law : the one being a thing which belongeth
generally unto all, the other such as none but the wiser and
more judicious sort can perform. Yea, the wisest are always
touching this point the readiest to acknowledge, that soundly
to judge of a law is the weightiest thing which any man can
take upon him.[1] But if we will give judgment of the laws
under which we live ; first let that law eternal be always
before our eyes, as being of principal force and moment to
breed in religious minds a dutiful estimation of all laws, the
use and benefit whereof we see ; because there can be no
doubt but that laws apparently good are (as it were) things
copied out of the very tables of that high everlasting law ;
even as the book of that law hath said concerning itself, " By
me kings reign, and " by me "princes decree justice."[2] Not as
if men did behold that book and accordingly frame their laws ;
but because it worketh in them, because it discovereth and (as
it were) readeth itself to the world by them, when the laws
which they make are righteous. Furthermore, although we
perceive not the goodness of laws made, nevertheless sith
things in themselves may have that which we peradventure
discern not, should not this breed a fear in our hearts how
we speak or judge in the worse part concerning that, the unadvised disgrace whereof may be no mean dishonour to Him
towards whom we profess all submission and awe? Surely
there must be very manifest iniquity in laws, against which
we shall be able to justify our contumelious invectives. The
chiefest root whereof, when we use them without cause, is
ignorance how laws inferior are derived from that supreme
or highest law.

γνωρίζειν· τότε γὰρ οἰόμεθα γιγνώσκειν ἕκαστον, ὅταν τὰ αἴτια γνωρίσωμεν
τὰ πρῶτα, καὶ τὰς ἀρχὰς τὰς πρώτας, καὶ μεχρὶ τῶν στοιχείων.]

[1] Arist. Ethic. x. [c. 10.] Τὸ κρῖναι ὀρθῶς μέγιστον. Intelligit de
legum qualitate judicium.   [2] Prov. viii. 15.

[3.] The first that receive impression from thence are natural agents. The law of whose operations might be haply thought less pertinent, when the question is about laws for human actions, but that in those very actions which most spiritually and supernaturally concern men, the rules and axioms of natural operations have their force. What can be more immediate to our salvation than our persuasion concerning the law [1] of Christ towards his Church? What greater assurance of love towards his Church, than the knowledge of that mystical union, whereby the Church is become as near unto Christ as any one part of his flesh is unto other? That the Church being in such sort his he must needs protect it, what proof more strong than if a manifest law so require, which law it is not possible for Christ to violate? And what other law doth the Apostle for this allege, but such as is both common unto Christ with us, and unto us with other things natural; "No man hateth his own flesh, but doth love and cherish it?" [2] The axioms of that law therefore, whereby natural agents are guided, have their use in the moral, yea, even in the spiritual actions of men, and consequently in all laws belonging unto men howsoever.

[4.] Neither are the Angels themselves so far severed from us in their kind and manner of working, but that between the law of their heavenly operations and the actions of men in this our state of mortality such correspondence there is, as maketh it expedient to know in some sort the one for the other's more perfect direction. Would Angels acknowledge themselves "fellow-servants" [3] with the sons of men, but that both having one Lord, there must be some kind of law which is one and the same to both, whereunto their obedience being perfecter is to our weaker both a pattern and a spur? Or would the Apostles, speaking of that which belongeth unto saints as they are linked together in the bond of spiritual society, [4] so often make mention how Angels therewith are delighted, if in things publicly done by the Church we are not somewhat to respect what the Angels of

[1] [The context leads to the suspicion that Hooker wrote "the *love* of Christ." But the original edition reads "law," and the list of errata at the end, which is carefully made, as appears, by the author himself, offers no correction: neither does Dr. Spenser's edition, at least the reprint of it in 1632.]

[2] Ephes. v. 29.   [3] Apoc. xix. 10.

[4] 1 Pet. i. 12; Ephes. iii. 10; 1 Tim. v. 21.

heaven do ? Yea, so far hath the Apostle Saint Paul proceeded, as to signify,[1] that even about the outward orders of
the Church which serve but for comeliness, some regard is
to be had of Angels, who best like us when we are most like
unto them in all parts of decent demeanour. So that the
law of Angels we cannot judge altogether impertinent unto
the affairs of the Church of God.

[5.] Our largeness of speech how men do find out what
things reason bindeth them of necessity to observe, and
what it guideth them to choose in things which are left as
arbitrary ; the care we have had to declare the different
nature of laws which severally concern all men, from such
as belong unto men either civilly or spiritually associated,
such as pertain to the fellowship which nations, or which
Christian nations, have amongst themselves, and in the last
place such as concerning every or any of these God himself
hath revealed by his Holy Word : all serveth but to make
manifest, that as the actions of men are of sundry distinct
kinds, so the laws thereof must accordingly be distinguished.
There are in men operations, some natural, some rational,
some supernatural, some politic, some finally ecclesiastical :
which if we measure not each by his own proper law, whereas the things themselves are so different, there will be in our
understanding and judgment of them confusion.

As that first error sheweth, whereon our opposites in this
cause have grounded themselves.   For as they rightly maintain that God must be glorified in all things, and that the
actions of men cannot tend unto his glory unless they be
framed after his law ; so it is their error to think that the
only law which God hath appointed unto men in that behalf
is the sacred Scripture. By that which we work naturally,
as when we breathe, sleep, move, we set forth the glory of
God as natural agents do,[2] albeit we have no express purpose
to make that our end, nor any advised determination therein
to follow a law, but do that we do (for the most part) not
as much as thinking thereon.   In reasonable and moral
actions another law taketh place ; a law by the observation
whereof[3] we glorify God in such sort, as no creature else
under man is able to do ; because other creatures have not
judgment to examine the quality of that which is done by
them, and therefore in that they do they neither can accuse
nor approve themselves.   Men do both, as the Apostle

---

[1] 1 Cor. xi. 10.   [2] Psalm cxlviii. 7, 8, 9.   [3] Rom. i. 21.

teacheth; yea, those men which have no written law of God
to shew what is good or evil, carry written in their hearts the
universal law of mankind, the Law of Reason, whereby they
judge as by a rule which God hath given unto all men for
that purpose.[1] The law of reason doth somewhat direct
men how to honour God as their Creator; but how to glorify
God in such sort as is required, to the end he may be an
everlasting Saviour, this we are taught by divine law, which
law both ascertaineth the truth and supplieth unto us the
want of that other law. So that in moral actions, divine
law helpeth exceedingly the law of reason to guide man's
life; but in supernatural it alone guideth.

Proceed we further; let us place man in some public
society with others, whether civil or spiritual; and in this
case there is no remedy but we must add yet a further law.
For although even here likewise the laws of nature and
reason be of necessary use, yet somewhat over and besides
them is necessary, namely human and positive law, together
with that law which is of commerce between grand societies,
the law of nations, and of nations Christian. For which
cause the law of God hath likewise said, "Let every soul be
subject to the higher powers."[2] The public power of all
societies is above every soul contained in the same societies.
And the principal use of that power is to give laws unto all
that are under it; which laws in such case we must obey,
unless there be reason shewed which may necessarily enforce
that the Law of Reason or of God doth enjoin the contrary.
Because except our own private and but probable resolutions
be by the law of public determinations overruled, we take
away all possibility of sociable life in the world. A plainer
example whereof than ourselves we cannot have. How
cometh it to pass that we are at this present day so rent
with mutual contentions, and that the Church is so much
troubled about the polity of the Church? No doubt if men
had been willing to learn how many laws their actions in
this life are subject unto, and what the true force of each
law is, all these controversies might have died the very day
they were first brought forth.

[6.] It is both commonly said, and truly, that the best men
otherwise are not always the best in regard of society. The
reason whereof is, for that the law of men's actions is one,
if they be respected only as men; and another, when they

[1] Rom. ii. 15.   [2] Rom. xiii. 1.

are considered as parts of a politic body. Many men there are, than whom nothing is more commendable when they are singled; and yet in society with others none less fit to answer the duties which are looked for at their hands.[1] Yea, I am persuaded, that of them with whom in this cause we strive, there are whose betters amongst men would be hardly found, if they did not live amongst men, but in some wilderness by themselves. The cause of which their disposition so unframable unto societies wherein they live, is, for that they discern not aright what place and force these several kinds of laws ought to have in all their actions. Is their question either concerning the regiment of the Church in general, or about conformity between one church and another, or of ceremonies, offices, powers, jurisdictions in our own church? Of all these things they judge by that rule which they frame to themselves with some show of probability, and what seemeth in that sort convenient, the same they think themselves bound to practise; the same by all means they labour mightily to uphold; whatsoever any law of man to the contrary hath determined they weigh it not. Thus by following the law of private reason, where the law of public should take place, they breed disturbance.

[7.] For the better inuring therefore of men's minds with the true distinction of laws, and of their several force according to the different kind and quality of our actions, it shall not peradventure be amiss to shew in some one example how they all take place. To seek no further, let but that be considered, than which there is not any thing more familiar unto us, our food.

What things are food and what are not we judge naturally by sense;[2] neither need we any other law to be our director in that behalf than the selfsame which is common unto us with beasts.

But when we come to consider of food, as of a benefit which God of his bounteous goodness hath provided for all things living;[3] the law of Reason doth here require the duty of thankfulness at our hands, towards him at whose hands we have it. And lest appetite in the use of food should lead us beyond that which is meet, we owe in this case obedience to that law of Reason, which teacheth mediocrity in meats

---

[1] Πολλοὶ γὰρ ἐν μὲν τοῖς οἰκείοις τῇ ἀρετῇ δύνανται χρῆσθαι, ἐν δὲ τοῖς πρὸς ἕτερον ἀδυνατοῦσι.   Arist. Ethic. lib. v. cap. 3.

[2] Job xxxiv. 3.   [3] Psalm cxlv. 15, 16.

and drinks. The same things divine law teacheth also, as at large we have shewed it doth all parts of moral duty, whereunto we all of necessity stand bound, in regard of the life to come.[1]

[1] [Chr. Letter, p. 13. "If from sound and sincere virtues (as you say) full joy and felicitie ariseth, and that we all of necessitie stand bound unto all partes of morall duetie in regarde of life to come, and God requireth more at the handes of men unto happines, then such a naked beleefe, as Christ calleth the worke of God : alas what shall we poore sinful wretches doe, &c." Hooker, MS. note, "Repent, and believe." And again, Chr. Letter, ibid. "Tell us . . . whether there bee not other sufficient causes to induce a Christian to godlines and honestie of life, such as is the glorie of God our Father ; his great mercies in Christ ; his love to us ; example to others, but that we must do it to merit or to make perfitt that which Christ hath done for us." Hooker, MS. note. "Your godfathers and godmothers have much to answere unto God for not seeing you better catechised.

"A thing necessarie as you graunt that by good workes we shold seeke God's glory, shew ourselves thankfull for his mercyes in Christ, answer his loving kindnes towardes us, and give other men good example. If then these things be necessarie unto eternall life, and workes necessarily to be done for these ends, how should workes bee but necessary unto the last end, seing the next and neerest cannot be attained without them ?

"And is there neither heaven nor hell, neither reward nor punishment hereafter, to be respected here in the leading of our lives ? When thapostle doth deterre from sinne, are his arguments only these ? only these his reasons when he stirreth unto workes of righteousnes ?

"See Euseb. Emisenus where he speaketh of Dorcas hir garments made for the poor." (De Init. Quadrag. Bibl. Patr. Colon. 1618, v. 551. "'Orationibus,' inquit, 'et eleemosynis purgantur peccata ;' per utramque ergo rem, sed maxime per eleemosynam, Dei misericordia requirenda est. Oportet itaque ut sibi res utraque consentiat : illa rogat, hæc impetrat ; illa quodammodo judicis audientiam deprecatur, hæc gratiam promeretur ; illa ostium pulsat, hæc aperit ; illa prodit desiderium, hæc desiderii procurat effectum : illa supplicat, sed supplicantem ista commendat. Sic laudabilis Tabitha, quæ in Actibus Apostolorum interpretata dicitur Dorcas, in operibus bonis vitæ diem claudens, evolante anima corpus relinquens, cum jam omnibus et operationis et vitæ renuntiasset officiis, flentes accurrunt viduæ, pauperes adgregantur tunicas et vestes quas faciebat illis Dorcas cœlo ostendentes, conveniunt Deum : testimonia meritorum clamant ; defuncta operatrice, vox operum bona : quæ in sæculo gesserat consequuntur animam in aliud sæculum ; consequuntur et revolvuntur ; reditque de loco mortis ad vitam præstitam. Itaque indumenta pauperculis hic ostenduntur, illic operantur ; hic adhuc præbent usum, illic jam tribuunt præmium : quam mira et pretiosa merita largitatis ! Hic adhuc utentium algentes humeros calefaciebant, etiam illic largitricis animam refrigerabant. Unde et nos, charissimi, animas nostras morti obnoxias piis operibus suscitemus. Dabunt absque dubio æternam vitam, quæ aliquoties etiam temporariam reddiderunt." Who was author of this Homily is uncertain : evidently not Eusebius of Emesa. It might be Salvian,

But of certain kinds of food the Jews sometimes had, and we ourselves likewise have, a mystical, religious, and supernatural use, they of their paschal lamb and oblations, we of our bread and wine in the Eucharist; which use none but divine law could institute.

Now as we live in civil society, the state of the commonwealth wherein we live both may and doth require certain laws concerning food; [1] which laws, saving only that we are members of the commonwealth where they are of force, we should not need to respect as rules of action, whereas now in their place and kind they must be respected and obeyed.

Yea, the selfsame matter is also a subject wherein sometime ecclesiastical laws have place; so that unless we will be authors of confusion in the Church, our private discretion, which otherwise might guide us a contrary way, must here submit itself to be that way guided, which the public judgment of the Church hath thought better. In which case that of Zonaras concerning fasts may be remembered. "Fastings are good, but let good things be done in good and convenient manner. He that transgresseth in his fasting the orders of the holy fathers," the positive laws of the Church of Christ, must be plainly told, "that good things do lose the grace of their goodness, when in good sort they are not performed." [2]

Eucherius of Lyons, or some other Father of the Gallican Church in the fourth or fifth century. See Cave, Hist. Lit. i. 157, and E. P. B. vi.)

On this whole subject Hooker says, "Looke S. Augustin's booke, 'De Fide et Operibus.'" (of which the following is a specimen : "Hoc est enim evangelizare Christum, non tantum dicere quæ sunt credenda de Christo, sed etiam quæ observanda ei qui accedit ad compagem corporis Christi ; immo vero cuncta dicere quæ sunt credenda de Christo, non solum cujus sit filius, unde secundum divinitatem, unde secundum carnem genitus, quæ perpessus et quare, quæ sit virtus resurrectionis ejus, quod donum Spiritus promisit dederitque fidelibus ; sed etiam qualia membra, quibus sit caput, quærat, instituat, diligat, liberet, atque ad æternam vitam honoremque perducat. Hæc cum dicuntur, aliquando brevius atque constrictius, aliquando latius et uberius, Christus evangelizatur ; et tamen non solum quod ad fidem, verum etiam quod ad mores fidelium pertinet, non prætermittitur." t. vi 172, F. c. ix. see also c. x.–xiv.)]

[1] See 5 Eliz. c. 5. § 14, 15; 27 Eliz. c. 11 ; 35 Eliz. c. 7. § 22.]

[2] [Καλὸν μὲν ἡ νηστεία· τὰ δὲ καλὰ καλῶς γινέσθω. Εἰ δέ τις θεσμοὺς ἀποστολικοὺς ἢ πατέρων ἁγίων παραβαίνων νηστεύει, ἀκούσεται] ὅτι οὐ καλὸν τὸ καλὸν, ὅταν μὴ καλῶς γίνηται. Zonar. in Can. Apost. 66. p. 34. [ap. Beverig. Synod. t. i. p. 43. Probably Hooker has here respect to the schismatical fasts which were practised by many of the Puritans.]

And as here men's private fancies must give place to the higher judgment of that Church which is in authority a mother over them ; so the very actions of whole churches have in regard of commerce and fellowship with other churches been subject to laws concerning food, the contrary unto which laws had else been thought more convenient for them to observe ; as by that order of abstinence from strangled and blood [1] may appear ; an order grounded upon that fellowship which the churches of the Gentiles had with the Jews.

Thus we see how even one and the selfsame thing is under divers considerations conveyed through many laws ; and that to measure by any one kind of law all the actions of men were to confound the admirable order, wherein God hath disposed all laws, each as in nature, so in degree, distinct from other.

[8.] Wherefore that here we may briefly end : of Law there can be no less acknowledged, than that her seat is the bosom of God, her voice the harmony of the world : all things in heaven and earth do her homage, the very least as feeling her care, and the greatest as not exempted from her power : both Angels and men and creatures of what condition soever, though each in different sort and manner, yet all with uniform consent, admiring her as the mother of their peace and joy.

[1] Acts xv. 20.

THE SECOND BOOK

CONCERNING THEIR FIRST POSITION WHO URGE REFORM-
ATION IN THE CHURCH OF ENGLAND: NAMELY, THAT
SCRIPTURE IS THE ONLY RULE OF ALL THINGS WHICH
IN THIS LIFE MAY BE DONE BY MEN

THE MATTER CONTAINED IN THIS SECOND BOOK

I. An answer to their first proof brought out of Scripture, Prov. ii. 9.
II. To their second, 1 Cor. x. 31.
III. To their third, 1 Tim. iv. 5.
IV. To their fourth, Rom. xiv. 23.
V. To their proofs out of Fathers, who dispute negatively from
    authority of Holy Scripture.
VI. To their proof by the Scripture's custom of disputing from divine
    authority negatively.
VII. An examination of their opinion concerning the force of arguments
    taken from human authority for the ordering of men's actions and
    persuasions.
VIII. A declaration what the truth is in this matter.

I. As that which in the title hath been proposed for the
matter whereof we treat, is only the ecclesiastical law whereby we are governed; so neither is it my purpose to maintain any other thing than that which therein truth and
reason shall approve. For concerning the dealings of men
who admin ster government, and unto whom the execution of
that law belongeth; they have their Judge who sitteth in
heaven, and before whose tribunal-seat they are accountable
for whatsoever abuse or corruption, which (being worthily
misliked in this church) the want either of care or of conscience in them hath bred. We are no patrons of those
things therefore, the best defence whereof is speedy redress
and amendment. That which is of God we defend, to
the utmost of that ability which he hath given; that
which is otherwise, let it wither even in the root from
whence it hath sprung.[1] Wherefore all these abuses being
severed and set apart, which rise from the corruption
of men and not from the laws themselves; come we
to those things which in the very whole entire form of
our church polity have been (as we persuade ourselves)

[1] [Acts v. 38, 39.]

233

injuriously blamed by them, who endeavour to overthrow
the same, and instead thereof to establish a much worse;
only through a strong misconceit they have, that the
same is grounded on divine authority.

Now whether it be that through an earnest longing desire
to see things brought to a peaceable end, I do but imagine
the matters whereof we contend to be fewer than indeed
they are; or else for that in truth they are fewer when they
come to be discussed by reason, than otherwise they seem
when by heat of contention they are divided into many
slips, and of every branch an heap is made: surely, as now
we have drawn them together, choosing out those things
which are requisite to be severally all discussed, and
omitting such mean specialties as are likely (without any
great labour) to fall afterwards of themselves; I know no
cause why either the number or the length of these controversies should diminish our hope of seeing them end
with concord and love on all sides; which of his infinite
love and goodness the Father of all peace and unity grant.

[2.] Unto which scope that our endeavour may the more
directly tend, it seemeth fittest that first those things be
examined, which are as seeds from whence the rest that
ensue have grown. And of such the most general is that
wherewith we are here to make our entrance: a question
not moved (I think) any where in other churches, and
therefore in ours the more likely to be soon (I trust)
determined. The rather, for that it hath grown from no
other root, than only a desire to enlarge the necessary use
of the Word of God; which desire hath begotten an error
enlarging it further than (as we are persuaded) soundness of
truth will bear. For whereas God hath left sundry kinds of
laws unto men, and by all those laws the actions of men are
in some sort directed; they hold that one only law, the
Scripture, must be the rule to direct in all things, even so
far as to the "taking up of a rush or straw."[1]   About

---

[1] T. C. l. ii. p. 59, 60. [The words are (p. 59,) "When he seeth
that St. Paul speaketh here of civil, private, and indifferent actions,
as of eating this or that kind of meat (than which there can be nothing
more indifferent) he might easily have seen that the sentence of the
Apostle reacheth even to his case, of taking up a straw." Which refers
to Whitg. Def. 85. "It is not true that whatsoever cannot be proved
in the word of God is not of faith, for then to take up a straw . . .
were against faith, and so deadly sin, because it is not found in the Law
of God." Again, T. C. ii. 60. "Seemeth it so strange a thing unto

which point there should not need any question to grow, and that which is grown might presently end, if they did yield but to these two restraints : the first is, not to extend the actions whereof they speak so low as that instance doth import of taking up a straw, but rather keep themselves at the least within the compass of moral actions, actions which have in them vice or virtue : the second, not to exact at our hands for every action the knowledge of some place of Scripture out of which we stand bound to deduce it, as by divers testimonies they seek to enforce ; but rather as the truth is, so to acknowledge, that it sufficeth if such actions be framed according to the law of Reason ; the general axioms, rules, and principles of which law being so frequent in Holy Scripture, there is no let but in that regard even out of Scripture such duties may be deduced by some kind of consequence, (as by long circuit of deduction it may be that even all truth out of any truth may be concluded,[1]) howbeit no man bound in such sort to deduce all his actions out of Scripture, as if either the place be to him unknown whereon they may be concluded, or the reference unto that place not presently considered of, the action shall in that respect be condemned as unlawful. In this we dissent, and this we are presently to examine.

[3.] In all parts of knowledge rightly so termed things most general are most strong. Thus it must be, inasmuch as the certainty of our persuasion touching particulars dependeth altogether upon the credit of those generalities out of which they grow. Albeit therefore every cause admit not such infallible evidence of proof, as leaveth no possibility of doubt or scruple behind it ; yet they who claim the general assent of the whole world unto that which they teach, and do not fear to give very hard and heavy sentence upon as many as refuse to embrace the same, must have special regard that their first foundations and grounds be more than slender probabilities. This whole question which hath been moved about the kind of church regiment, we could not but for our own resolution's sake endeavour

him that a man should not take up a straw but for some purpose, and for some good purpose ? " &c.]

[1] [So Bishop Butler, Analogy, part 1, ch. vii. " Things seemingly the most insignificant imaginable are perpetually observed to be necessary conditions to other things of the greatest importance ; so that any one thing whatever may, for ought we know to the contrary, be a necessary condition to any other." p. 182. ed. 1736.]

to unrip and sift; following therein as near as we might the conduct of that judicial method which serveth best for invention of truth. By means whereof, having found this the head theorem of all their discourses, who plead for the change of ecclesiastical government in England, namely, "That the Scripture of God is in such sort the rule of human actions, that simply whatsoever we do and are not by it directed thereunto, the same is sin;" we hold it necessary that the proofs hereof be weighed. Be they of weight sufficient or otherwise, it is not ours to judge and determine; only what difficulties there are which as yet withhold our assent, till we be further and better satisfied, I hope no indifferent amongst them will scorn or refuse to hear.

[4.] First therefore whereas they allege, "That Wisdom" doth teach men "every good way;"[1] and have thereupon inferred that no way is good in any kind of action unless wisdom do by Scripture lead unto it; see they not plainly how they restrain the manifold ways which wisdom hath to teach men by unto one only way of teaching, which is by Scripture? The bounds of wisdom are large, and within them much is contained. Wisdom was Adam's instructor in Paradise; wisdom endued the fathers who lived before the law with the knowledge of holy things; by the wisdom of the law of God David attained to excel others in understanding;[2] and Solomon likewise to excel David by the selfsame wisdom of God teaching him many things besides the law. The ways of well-doing are in number even as many as are the kinds of voluntary actions; so that whatsoever we do in this world and may do it ill, we shew ourselves therein by well-doing to be wise. Now if wisdom did teach men by Scripture not only all the ways that are right and good in some certain kind, according to that of St. Paul[3] concerning the use of Scripture, but did simply

---

[1] T. C. l. i. p. 20. "I say, that the word of God containeth whatsoever things can fall into any part of man's life. For so Solomon saith in the second chapter of the Proverbs, 'My son, if thou receive my words, &c. then thou shalt understand justice, and judgment, and equity, and every good way.'" [In T. C. literally it is, "The word of God containeth the direction of all things pertaining to the Church, yea, of whatsoever things can fall into any part of man's life." (p. 14.)]

[2] Psalm cxix. 99.

[3] 2 Tim. iii. 16. "The whole Scripture is given by inspiration of God, and is profitable to teach, to improve, to correct, and to instruct

without any manner of exception, restraint, or distinction,
teach every way of doing well; there is no Art but Scripture
should teach it, because every art doth teach the way how
to do something or other well. To teach men therefore
wisdom professeth, and to teach them every good way; but
not every good way by one way of teaching. Whatsoever
either men on earth or the Angels of heaven do know, it is
as a drop of that unemptiable fountain of wisdom; which
wisdom hath diversely imparted her treasures unto the
world. As her ways are of sundry kinds, so her manner of
teaching is not merely one and the same. Some things she
openeth by the sacred books of Scripture; some things by
the glorious works of Nature: with some things she inspireth
them from above by spiritual influence; in some things she
leadeth and traineth them only by worldly experience and
practice. We may not so in any one special kind admire
her, that we disgrace her in any other; but let all her ways
be according unto their place and degree adored.

II. That "all things be done to the glory of God,"[1] the
blessed Apostle (it is true) exhorteth. The glory of God is
the admirable excellency of that virtue divine, which being
made manifest, causeth men and Angels to extol his greatness, and in regard thereof to fear him. By "being
glorified" it is not meant that he doth receive any augmentation of glory at our hands, but his name we glorify when
we testify our acknowledgment of his glory. Which albeit
we most effectually do by the virtue of obedience; nevertheless it may be perhaps a question, whether St. Paul did
mean that we sin as oft as ever we go about any thing,
without an express intent and purpose to obey God therein.
He saith of himself, "I do in all things please all men,

in righteousness, that the man of God may be absolute, being made
perfect unto all good works." He meaneth all and only those good
works, which belong unto us as we are men of God, and which unto
salvation are necessary. Or if we understand by *men of God*, God's
ministers, there is not required in them an universal skill of every good
work or way, but an ability to teach whatsoever men are bound to do
that they may be saved. And with this kind of knowledge the
Scripture sufficeth to furnish them as touching matter.

[1] T. C. l. i. p. 26. [14.] "St. Paul saith, 'That whether we eat or
drink, or whatsoever we do, we must do it to the glory of God.' But
no man can glorify God in any thing but by obedience; and there is no
obedience but in respect of the commandment and word of God:
therefore it followeth that the word of God directeth a man in all his
actions."

seeking not mine own commodity but" rather the good "of many, that they may be saved."[1]   Shall it hereupon be thought that St. Paul did not move either hand or foot, but with express intent even thereby to further the common salvation of men ?   We move, we sleep, we take the cup at the hand of our friend, a number of things we oftentimes do, only to satisfy some natural desire, without present, express, and actual reference unto any commandment of God.   Unto his glory even these things are done which we naturally perform, and not only that which morally and spiritually we do.   For by every effect proceeding from the most concealed instincts of nature His power is made manifest.   But it doth not therefore follow that of necessity we shall sin, unless we expressly intend this in every such particular.

[2.] But be it a thing which requireth no more than only our general presupposed willingness to please God in all things, or be it a matter wherein we cannot so glorify the name of God as we should without an actual intent to do him in that particular some special obedience ; yet for any thing there is in this sentence alleged to the contrary, God may be glorified by obedience, and obeyed by performance of his will, and his will be performed with an actual intelligent desire to fulfil that law which maketh known what his will is, although no special clause or sentence of Scripture be in every such action set before men's eyes to warrant it.   For Scripture is not the only law whereby God hath opened his will touching all things that may be done, but there are other kinds of laws which notify the will of God, as in the former book hath been proved at large : nor is there any law of God, whereunto he doth not account our obedience his glory.   "Do therefore all things unto the glory of God (saith the Apostle), be inoffensive both to Jews and Grecians and the Church of God ; even as I please all men in all things, not seeking mine own commodity, but many's, that they may be saved."   In the least thing done disobediently towards God, or offensively against the good of men, whose benefit we ought to seek for as for our own, we plainly shew that we do not acknowledge God to be such as indeed he is, and consequently that we glorify him not.   This the blessed Apostle teacheth ; but doth any Apostle teach, that we cannot glorify God

[1] Cor. x. 33.

otherwise, than only in doing what we find that God in Scripture commandeth us to do?

[3.] The churches dispersed amongst the heathen in the east part of the world are by the Apostle St. Peter exhorted to have their "conversation honest amongst the Gentiles, that they which speak evil of them as of evil-doers might by the good works which they should see glorify God in the day of visitation."[1] As long as that which Christians did was good, and no way subject unto just reproof, their virtuous conversation was a mean to work the heathen's conversion unto Christ. Seeing therefore this had been a thing altogether impossible, but that infidels themselves did discern, in matters of life and conversation, when believers did well and when otherwise, when they glorified their heavenly Father and when not; it followeth that some things wherein God is glorified may be some other way known than only by the sacred Scripture; of which Scripture the Gentiles being utterly ignorant did notwithstanding judge rightly of the quality of Christian men's actions. Most certain it is that nothing but only sin doth dishonour God. So that to glorify him in all things is to do nothing whereby the name of God may be blasphemed;[2] nothing whereby the salvation of Jew or Grecian or any in the Church of Christ may be let or hindered;[3] nothing whereby his law is transgressed.[4] But the question is, whether only Scripture do shew whatsoever God is glorified in?

III. And though meats and drinks be said to be sanctified by the word of God and by prayer,[5] yet neither is this a reason sufficient to prove, that by Scripture we must of necessity be directed in every light and common thing which is incident into any part of man's life. Only it sheweth that unto us the Word, that is to say the Gospel of Christ, having not delivered any such difference of things clean and unclean, as the Law of Moses did unto the Jews, there is no cause but that we may use indifferently all things, as long as we do not (like swine) take the benefit of them without a thankful acknowledgment of His liberality and goodness

[1] I Pet. ii. 12.   [2] Rom. ii. 24.
[3] I Cor. x. 32.   [4] Rom. ii. 23.
[5] "And that which St. Paul said of meats and drinks, that they are sanctified unto us by the word of God, the same is to be understanded of all things else whatsoever we have the use of." T. C. l. i. p. 26.
[14.]

by whose providence they are enjoyed. And therefore the Apostle gave warning beforehand to take heed of such as should enjoin to "abstain from meats, which God hath created to be received with thanksgiving by them which believe and know the truth. For every creature of God is good, and nothing to be refused, if it be received with thanksgiving, because it is sanctified by the Word of God and prayer." [1] The Gospel, by not making many things unclean, as the Law did, hath sanctified those things generally to all, which particularly each man unto himself must sanctify by a reverend and holy use. Which will hardly be drawn so far as to serve their purpose, who have imagined the Word in such sort to sanctify all things, that neither food can be tasted, nor raiment put on, nor in the world any thing done, but this deed must needs be sin in them which do not first know it appointed unto them by Scripture before they do it.

IV. But to come unto that which of all other things in Scripture is most stood upon; that place of St. Paul they say is "of all other most clear, where speaking of those things which are called indifferent, in the end he concludeth, That 'whatsoever is not of faith is sin.' But faith is not but in respect of the Word of God. Therefore whatsoever is not done by the Word of God is sin." Whereunto we answer, that albeit the name of Faith being properly and strictly taken, it must needs have reference unto some uttered word as the object of belief: nevertheless sith the ground of credit is the credibility of things credited; and things are made credible, either by the known condition and quality of the utterer, [2] or by the manifest likelihood of truth which they have in themselves; hereupon it riseth that whatsoever we are persuaded of, the same we are generally said to believe. In which generality the object of Faith may not so narrowly be restrained, as if the same did extend no further than to the only Scriptures of God. "Though," saith our Saviour, "ye believe not me, believe my works, that ye may know and believe that the Father is in me and I in him." [3] "The other disciples said unto Thomas, We have seen the Lord;" but his answer unto them was, "Except I see in his hands the print of the nails, and put my finger into them, I will not believe." [4]

---

[1] 1 Tim. iv. 3, 4.　　[2] Psalm xix. 8 ; Apoc. iii. 14 ; 2 Cor. i. 18.
[3] John x. 38.　　　　　　　　　　　　[4] John xx. 25.

Can there be any thing more plain than that which by these two sentences appeareth, namely, that there may be a certain belief grounded upon other assurance than Scripture : any thing more clear, than that we are said not only to believe the things which we know by another's relation, but even whatsoever we are certainly persuaded of, whether it be by reason or by sense?

[2.] Forasmuch therefore as it is granted that St. Paul doth mean nothing else by Faith, but only "a full persuasion that that which we do is well done;"[1] against which kind of faith or persuasion as St. Paul doth count it sin to enterprise any thing, so likewise "some of the very heathen have taught,[2] as Tully, 'That nothing ought to be done whereof thou doubtest whether it be right or wrong;'[3] whereby it appeareth that even those which had no knowledge of the word of God did see much of the equity of this which the Apostle requireth of a Christian man;" I hope we shall not seem altogether unnecessarily to doubt of the soundness of their opinion, who think simply that nothing but only the word of God can give us assurance in any thing we are to do, and resolve us that we do well. For might not the Jews have been fully persuaded that they did well to think (if they had so thought) that in Christ God the Father was, although the only ground of this their faith had been the wonderful works they saw him do? Might not, yea, did not Thomas fully in the end persuade himself, that he did well to think that body which now was raised to be the same which had been crucified? That which gave Thomas this assurance was his sense; "Thomas, because

---

[1] "And if any will say that St. Paul meaneth there a full πληροφορίαν and persuasion that that which he doth is well done, I grant it. But from whence can that spring but from faith? How can we persuade and assure ourselves that we do well, but whereas we have the word of God for our warrant?" T. C. l. i. p. 27. [14.]

[2] "What also that some even of those heathen men have taught, that nothing ought to be done whereof thou doubtest whether it be right or wrong. Whereby it appeareth that even those which had no knowledge of the word of God did see much of the equity of this which the Apostle requireth of a Christian man : and that the chiefest difference is, that where they sent men for the difference of good and evil to the light of Reason, in such things the Apostle sendeth them to the school of Christ in his word, which only is able through faith to give them assurance and resolution in their doings." T. C. l. ii. p. 60.

[3] [De Offic. i. 9. "Bene præcipiunt, qui vetant quidquam agere, quod dubites æquum sit an iniquum."]

thou hast seen, thou believest," saith our Saviour.[1] What
Scripture had Tully for his assurance? Yet I nothing
doubt but that they who allege him think he did well to set
down in writing a thing so consonant unto truth. Finally,
we all believe that the Scriptures of God are sacred, and
that they have proceeded from God; ourselves we assure
that we do right well in so believing. We have for this
point a demonstration sound and infallible. But it is not
the word of God which doth or possibly can assure us, that
we do well to think it his word. For if any one book of
Scripture did give testimony to all, yet still that Scripture
which giveth credit to the rest would require another Scripture to give credit unto it, neither could we ever come unto
any pause whereon to rest our assurance this way; so that
unless beside Scripture there were something which might
assure us that we do well, we could not think we do well,
no not in being assured that Scripture is a sacred and holy
rule of well-doing.

[3.] On which determination we might be contented to
stay ourselves without further proceeding herein, but that
we are drawn on into larger speech by reason of their so
great earnestness, who beat more and more upon these last
alleged words, as being of all other most pregnant.

Whereas therefore they still argue, "That wheresoever
faith is wanting, there is sin;" and, "in every action not
commanded faith is wanting;" *ergo*, "in every action not
commanded, there is sin:"[2] I would demand of them first,
forasmuch as the nature of things indifferent is neither to be
commanded nor forbidden, but left free and arbitrary; how
there can be any thing indifferent, if for want of faith sin be
committed when any thing not commanded is done. So
that of necessity they must add somewhat, and at leastwise
thus set it down: in every action not commanded of God
or permitted with approbation, faith is wanting, and for
want of faith there is sin.

[4.] The next thing we are to inquire is, What those
things be which God permitteth with approbation, and how
we may know them to be so permitted. When there are
unto one end sundry means; as for example, for the sustenance of our bodies many kinds of food, many sorts of
raiment to clothe our nakedness, and so in other things
of like condition: here the end itself being necessary, but

---

[1] John xx. 29.   [2] T. C. l. ii. p. 58.

not so any one mean thereunto; necessary that our bodies should be both fed and clothed, howbeit no one kind of food or raiment necessary; therefore we hold these things free in their own nature and indifferent. The choice is left to our own discretion, except a principal bond of some higher duty remove the indifferency that such things have in themselves. Their indifferency is removed, if either we take away our own liberty, as Ananias did,[1] for whom to have sold or held his possessions it was indifferent, till his solemn vow and promise unto God had strictly bound him one only way; or if God himself have precisely abridged the same, by restraining us unto or by barring us from some one or more things of many, which otherwise were in themselves altogether indifferent. Many fashions of priestly attire there were, whereof Aaron and his sons might have had their free choice without sin, but that God expressly tied them unto one.[2] All meats indifferent unto the Jew, were it not that God by name excepted some, as swine's flesh.[3] Impossible therefore it is we should otherwise think, than that what things God doth neither command nor forbid, the same he permitteth with approbation either to be done or left undone. "All things are lawful unto me," saith the Apostle,[4] speaking as it seemeth in the person of the Christian gentile for maintenance of liberty in things indifferent; whereunto his answer is, that nevertheless "all things are not expedient;" in things indifferent there is a choice, they are not always equally expedient.

[5.] Now in things although not commanded of God yet lawful because they are permitted, the question is, what light shall shew us the conveniency which one hath above another. For answer, their final determination is, that [5] " Whereas the heathen did send men for the difference of good and evil to the light of Reason, in such things the Apostle sendeth us to the school of Christ in his word, which only is able through faith to give us assurance and resolution in our doings." Which word *only*, is utterly without possibility of ever being proved. For what if it were true concerning things indifferent, that unless the word of the Lord had determined of the free use of them, there could have been no lawful use of them at all: which notwithstanding is untrue; because it is not the Scripture's setting down such

---

[1] Acts v. 4.   [2] Exod. xxviii. 4, 43; xxxix.   [3] Lev. xi.
[4] 1 Cor. vi. 12.   [5] [T. C. ii. 60.]

things as indifferent, but their not setting down as necessary,
that doth make them to be indifferent : yet this to our
present purpose serveth nothing at all. We inquire not now,
whether any thing be free to be used which Scripture hath
not set down as free : but concerning things known and
acknowledged to be indifferent, whether particularly in
choosing any one of them before another we sin, if any thing
but Scripture direct us in this our choice. When many
meats are set before me, all are indifferent, none unlawful,
I take one as most convenient. If Scripture require me so
to do, then is not the thing indifferent, because I must do
what Scripture requireth. They are all indifferent, I might
take any, Scripture doth not require of me to make any
special choice of one : I do notwithstanding make choice of
one, my discretion teaching me so to do. A hard case, that
hereupon I should be justly condemned of sin. Nor let any
man think that following the judgment of natural discretion
in such cases we can have no assurance that we please God.
For to the Author and God of our nature, how shall any
operation proceeding in natural sort be in that respect
unacceptable? The nature which himself hath given to
work by he cannot but be delighted with, when we exercise
the same any way without commandment of his to the
contrary.

[6.] My desire is to make this cause so manifest, that if it
were possible, no doubt or scruple concerning the same
might remain in any man's cogitation. Some truths there
are, the verity whereof time doth alter : as it is now true that
Christ is risen from the dead ; which thing was not true at
such time as Christ was living on earth, and had not suffered.
It would be known therefore, whether this which they teach
concerning the sinful stain of all actions not commanded of
God, be a truth that doth now appertain unto us only, or a
perpetual truth, in such sort that from the first beginning of
the world unto the last consummation thereof, it neither
hath been nor can be otherwise. I see not how they can
restrain this unto any particular time, how they can think it
true now and not always true, that in every action not commanded there is for want of faith sin. Then let them cast
back their eyes unto former generations of men, and mark
what was done in the prime of the world. Seth, Enoch,
Noah, Sem, Abraham, Job, and the rest that lived before
any syllable of the law of God was written, did they not sin

as much as we do in every action not commanded? That which God is unto us by his sacred word, the same he was unto them by such like means as Eliphaz in Job describeth.[1] If therefore we sin in every action which the Scripture commandeth us not, it followeth that they did the like in all such actions as were not by revelation from heaven exacted at their hands. Unless God from heaven did by vision still shew them what to do, they might do nothing, not eat, not drink, not sleep, not move.

[7.] Yea, but even as in darkness candlelight may serve to guide men's steps, which to use in the day were madness ; so when God had once delivered his law in writing, it may be they are of opinion that then it must needs be sin for men to do any thing which was not there commanded them to do, whatsoever they might do before. Let this be granted, and it shall hereupon plainly ensue, either that the light of Scripture once shining in the world, all other light of Nature is therewith in such sort drowned, that now we need it not, neither may we longer use it ; or if it stand us in any stead, yet as Aristotle speaketh of men whom Nature hath framed for the state of servitude, saying, " They have reason so far forth as to conceive when others direct them,[2] but little or none in directing themselves by themselves ; " so likewise our natural capacity and judgment must serve us only for the right understanding of that which the sacred Scripture teacheth. Had the Prophets who succeeded Moses, or the blessed Apostles which followed them, been settled in this persuasion, never would they have taken so great pains in gathering together natural arguments, thereby to teach the faithful their duties. To use unto them any other motive than *Scriptum est,* "Thus it is written," had been to teach them other grounds of their actions than Scripture ; which I grant they alleged commonly, but not only. Only Scripture they should have alleged, had they been thus persuaded, that so far forth we do sin as we do any thing otherwise directed than by Scripture. St. Augustine was resolute in points of Christianity to credit none, how godly and learned soever he were, unless he confirmed his sentence by the Scriptures, *or by some reason not*

---

[1] Job. iv. 12. [" A thing was secretly brought to me, and mine ear received a little thereof ; in thoughts from the visions of the night, when deep sleep falleth on men," &c.]

[2] Arist. Pol, i. c. 5. [ὁ κοινωνῶν λόγου τόσουτον ὅσον αἰσθάνεσθαι ἀλλὰ μὴ ἔχειν.]

contrary to them.[1] Let them therefore with St. Augustine
reject and condemn that which is not grounded either on the
Scripture, or on some reason not contrary to Scripture, and
we are ready to give them our hands in token of friendly
consent with them.

V. But against this it may be objected, and is, That
the Fathers do nothing more usually in their books, than
draw arguments from the Scripture negatively in reproof of
that which is evil; "Scriptures teach it not, avoid it therefore;" these disputes with the Fathers are ordinary, neither
is it hard to shew that the Prophets themselves have so
reasoned. Which arguments being sound and good, it
should seem that it cannot be unsound or evil to hold still
the same assertion against which hitherto we have disputed.
For if it stand with reason thus to argue, "such a thing is
not taught us in Scripture, therefore we may not receive or
allow it;" how should it seem unreasonable to think, that
whatsoever we may lawfully do, the Scripture by commanding it must make it lawful? But how far such arguments
do reach, it shall the better appear by considering the
matter wherein they have been urged.

[2.] First therefore this we constantly deny, that of so many
testimonies as they are able to produce for the strength of
negative arguments, any one doth generally (which is the
point in question) condemn either all opinions as false, or
all actions as unlawful, which the Scripture teacheth us not.
The most that can be collected out of them is only that in
some cases a negative argument taken from Scripture is
strong, whereof no man endued with judgment can doubt.
But doth the strength of some negative argument prove this
kind of negative argument strong, by force whereof all things
are denied which Scripture affirmeth not, or all things which
Scripture prescribeth not condemned? The question be-

---

[1] August. Ep. 19. [al. 82. t. ii. 190. "Ego enim fateor caritati
tuæ," (he is writing to St. Jerome) "solis eis Scripturarum libris, qui
jam canonici appellantur, didici hunc timorem honoremque deferre, ut
nullum eorum auctorem scribendo aliquid errasse firmissime credam.
Ac si aliquid in eis offendero literis quod videatur contrarium veritati,
nihil aliud, quam vel mendosum esse codicem, vel interpretem non
assecutum esse quod dictum est, vel me minime intellexisse, non am-
bigam. Alios autem ita lego, ut quantalibet sanctitate doctrinaque præ-
polleant, non ideo verum putem, quia ipsi ita senserunt, sed quia mihi
vel per illos auctores canonicos, vel probabili ratione, quod a vero non
abhorreat persuadere potuerunt."]

tween us is concerning matter of action, what things are lawful or unlawful for men to do. The sentences alleged out of the Fathers are as peremptory and as large in every respect for matter of opinion as of action : which argueth that in truth they never meant any otherwise to tie the one than the other unto Scripture, both being thereunto equally tied, as far as each is required in the same kind of necessity unto salvation. If therefore it be not unlawful to know and with full persuasion to believe much more than Scripture alone doth teach; if it be against all sense and reason to condemn the knowledge of so many arts and sciences as are otherwise learned than in Holy Scripture, notwithstanding the manifest speeches of ancient Catholic Fathers, which seem to close up within the bosom thereof all manner good and lawful knowledge ; wherefore should their words be thought more effectual to shew that we may not in deeds and practice, than they are to prove that in speculation and knowledge we ought not to go any farther than the Scripture? Which Scripture being given to teach matters of belief no less than of action, the Fathers must needs be and are even as plain against credit besides the relation, as against practice without the injunction of the Scripture.

[3.] St. Augustine hath said,[1] "Whether it be question of Christ, or whether it be question of his Church, or of what thing soever the question be ; I say not, if we, but if an angel from heaven shall tell us any thing beside that you have received in the Scripture under the Law and the Gospel, let him be accursed."[2] In like sort Tertullian,[3] "We may not give ourselves this liberty to bring in any thing of our will, nor choose any thing that other men

[1] Aug. cont. Liter. Petil. lib. iii. c. 6. [t. ix. 301. "Sive de Christo, sive de ejus Ecclesia, sive de quacunque alia re quæ pertinet ad fidem vitamque vestram,—non dicam nos, nequaquam comparandi ei qui dixit, 'Licet si nos,' sed omnino quod secutus adjecit,—Si angelus de cœlo vobis annunciaverit præter quam quod in Scripturis legalibus et evangelicis accepistis, anathema sit."]

[2] T. C. l. ii. p. 80. "Augustine saith, Whether it be question of Christ, or whether it be question of his Church, &c. And lest the answerer should restrain the general saying of Augustine unto the Doctrine of the Gospel, so that he would thereby shut out the Discipline ; " [Here T. C. alleges the passage ascribed to St. Cyprian, quoted by Hooker in the next note ;] " even Tertullian himself, before he was imbrued with the heresy of Montanus, giveth testimony unto the discipline in these words, 'We may not give ourselves,' &c."

[3] Tertull. de Præscript. [c. 6. "Nobis vero nihil ex nostro arbitrio inducere licet, sed nec eligere quod aliquis de arbitrio suo induxerit.

bring in of their will; we have the Apostles themselves for authors, which themselves brought nothing of their own will, but the discipline which they received of Christ they delivered faithfully unto the people." In which place the name of Discipline importeth not as they who allege it would fain have it construed, but as any man who noteth the circumstance of the place and the occasion of uttering the words will easily acknowledge, even the selfsame thing it signifieth which the name of Doctrine doth, and as well might the one as the other there have been used. To help them farther, doth not St. Jerome[1] after the selfsame manner dispute, " We believe it not, because we read it not?" Yea, " We ought not so much as to know the things which the Book of the Law containeth not," saith St. Hilary. Shall we hereupon then conclude, that we may not take knowledge of or give credit unto any thing, which sense or experience or report or art doth propose, unless we find the same in Scripture? No; it is too plain that so far to extend their speeches is to wrest them against their true intent and meaning. To urge any thing upon the Church, requiring thereunto that religious assent of Christian belief, wherewith the words of the holy prophets are received; to urge any thing as part of that supernatural and celestially revealed truth which God hath taught, and not to shew it in Scripture; this did the ancient Fathers evermore think unlawful, impious, execrable. And thus, as their speeches were meant, so by us they must be restrained.

[4.] As for those alleged words of Cyprian,[2] "The Christian Religion shall find, that out of this Scripture rules of all doctrines have sprung, and that from hence doth spring and hither doth return whatsoever the ecclesiastical discipline doth contain:" surely this place would never have been

Apostolos Domini habemus auctores, qui nec ipsi quicquam ex suo arbitrio, quod inducerent, elegerunt : sed acceptam a Christo disciplinam fideliter nationibus adsignaverunt."]

[1] Hieron. contra Helvid. [" Ut hæc quæ scripta sunt non negamus, ita ea quæ non sunt scripta renuimus. Natum Deum esse de virgine credimus, quia legimus : Mariam nupsisse post partum non credimus, quia non legimus." t. ii. 13.] Hilar. in Ps. cxxxii. [§ 6. pag. 463. " Quæ libro legis non continentur, ea nec nosse debemus." He is speaking of an apocryphal tradition, that the angels supposed by some to be mentioned in Genesis vi. 1, 4, used to haunt Mount Hermon especially.]

[2] " Let him hear what Cyprian saith, The Christian religion (saith he) shall find, that," &c. T. C. l. ii. p. 80.

brought forth in this cause, if it had been but once read over in the author himself out of whom it is cited. For the words are uttered concerning that one principal commandment of love ; in the honour whereof he speaketh after this sort: [1] "Surely this commandment containeth the Law and the Prophets, and in this one word is the abridgment of all the volumes of Scripture : this nature and reason and the authority of thy word, O Lord, doth proclaim ; this we have heard out of thy mouth ; herein the perfection of all religion doth consist. This is the first commandment and the last : this being written in the Book of Life is (as it were) an everlasting lesson both to Men and Angels. Let Christian religion read this one word, and meditate upon this commandment, and out of this Scripture it shall find the rules of all learning to have sprung, and from hence to have risen and hither to return whatsoever the ecclesiastical discipline containeth, and that in all things it is vain and bootless which charity confirmeth not." Was this a sentence (trow you) of so great force to prove that Scripture is the only rule of all the actions of men ? Might they not hereby even as well prove, that one commandment of Scripture is the only rule of all things, and so exclude the rest of the Scripture, as now they do all means beside Scripture ? But thus it fareth, when too much desire of contradiction causeth our speech rather to pass by number than to stay for weight.

[5.] Well, but Tertullian doth in this case speak yet more

[1] "Vere hoc mandatum legem complectitur et prophetas, et in hoc verbo omnium Scripturarum volumina coarctantur. Hoc natura, hoc ratio, hoc, Domine, verbi tui clamat auctoritas, hoc ex ore tuo audivimus, hic invenit consummationem omnis religio. Primum est hoc mandatum et ultimatum, hoc in libro vitæ conscriptum indeficientem et hominibus et angelis exhibit lectionem. Legat hoc unum verbum et in hoc mandato meditetur Christiana religio, et inveniet ex *hac* Scriptura omnium doctrinarum regulas emanasse, et hinc nasci et huc reverti quicquid ecclesiastica continet disciplina, et in omnibus irritum esse et frivolum quicquid dilectio non confirmat." [Arnold. Carnotens. de Baptismo Christi, ad calc. S. Cyprian. ed. Fell. page 33. Udall in his Demonstration of Discipline having quoted the same passage, Sutcliffe, Remonstrance to the Demonstration, page 17, meets it with the following, which occurs just before in the same tract : " Magister bone, libenter te audio, et cum adversaris mihi, etiam in plagis et doloribus intelligo disciplinam, nec latet me, *te docente*, ad siccandas corruptionum mearum putredines prodesse cauterium, et mundare cicatrices veteres salem *disciplinæ* tuæ, Evangelio tuo medente infusum. . . . You see, that which he first called Doctrine, he after, ἐξηγητικῶς, calleth Discipline."]

plainly :[1]   " The Scripture," saith he, " denieth what it noteth not ; " which are indeed the words of Tertullian.[2] But what? the Scripture reckoneth up the kings of Israel, and amongst those kings David ; the Scripture reckoneth up the sons of David, and amongst those sons Solomon.   To prove that amongst the kings of Israel there was no David but only one, no Solomon but one in the sons of David ; Tertullian's argument will fitly prove.   For inasmuch as the Scripture did propose to reckon up all, if there were more it would have named them.   In this case " the Scripture doth deny the thing it noteth not."   Howbeit I could not but think that man to do me some piece of manifest injury, which would hereby fasten upon me a general opinion, as if I did think the Scripture to deny the very reign of King Henry the Eighth, because it no where noteth that any such King did reign.   Tertullian's speech is probable concerning such matter as he there speaketh of.   " There was," saith Tertullian, " no second Lamech like to him that had two wives ; the Scripture denieth what it noteth not."   As therefore it noteth one such to have been in that age of the world ; so had there been more, it would by likelihood as well have noted many as one.   What infer we now hereupon ?   " There was no second Lamech ; the Scripture denieth what it noteth not."   Were it consonant unto reason to divorce these two sentences, the former of which doth shew how the latter is restrained, and not marking the former to conclude by the latter of them, that simply whatsoever any man at this day doth think true is by the Scripture denied, unless it be there affirmed to be true?   I wonder that a cause so weak and feeble hath been so much persisted in.

[6.] But to come unto those their sentences wherein matters of action are more apparently touched : the name of Tertullian is as before so here again pretended ;[3]   who

---

[1] Tertull. lib. de Monog. [c. 4. " Semel vim passa institutio Dei per Lamechum, constitit postea in finem usque gentis illius. Secundus Lamech nullus extitit, quomodo duabus maritatus. Negat Scriptura quod non notat." p. 671.]

[2] " And in another place Tertullian saith, That the Scripture denieth that which it noteth not." T. C. l. ii. p. 81.

[3] T. C. l. ii. p. 80. " And that in indifferent things it is not enough that they be not against the word, but that they be according to the word, it may appear by other places, where he saith, ' That whatsoever pleaseth not the Lord, displeaseth him, and with hurt is received,'" lib. ii. ad Uxorem.

writing unto his wife two books, and exhorting her in the
one to live a widow, in case God before her should take him
unto his mercy; and in the other, if she did marry, yet not
to join herself to an infidel, as in those times some widows
Christian had done for the advancement of their estate in
this present world, he urgeth very earnestly St. Paul's words,
"only in the Lord:"[1] whereupon he demandeth of them
that think they may do the contrary, what Scripture they
can shew where God hath dispensed and granted license to
do against that which the blessed Apostle so strictly doth
enjoin: and because in defence it might perhaps be replied,
"Seeing God doth will that couples which are married
when both are infidels, if either party chance to be after
converted unto Christianity, this should not make separation between them, as long as the unconverted was willing
to retain the other on whom the grace of Christ had
shined; wherefore then should that let the making of
marriage, which doth not dissolve marriage being made?"
after great reasons shewed why God doth in converts being
married allow continuance with infidels, and yet disallow
that the faithful when they are free should enter into bonds
of wedlock with such, concludeth in the end concerning
those women that so marry, "They that please not the
Lord do even thereby offend the Lord; they do even
thereby throw themselves into evil;"[2] that is to say,
while they please him not by marrying in him, they do that
whereby they incur his displeasure; they make an offer of
themselves into the service of that enemy with whose
servants they link themselves in so near a bond. What
one syllable is there in all this prejudicial any way to that
which we hold? For the words of Tertullian as they are by
them alleged are two ways misunderstood; both in the

[1] 1 Cor. vii. 39. Ad Uxor. l. ii. c. 2. ["Cum dicit, Tantum in
Domino, jam non suadet, sed excerte jubet. . . . Igitur cum quædam
istis diebus nuptias suas de Ecclesia tolleret, id est, Gentili conjunge-
retur; idque ab aliis retro factum recordarer; miratus aut ipsarum
petulantiam, aut consiliariorum prævaricationem, quod nulla Scriptura
ejus facti licentiam proferrent, ' Nunquid,' inquam, 'de illo capitulo
sibi blandiuntur, primæ ad Corinthios, ubi scriptum est, Siquis frater
infidelem habet uxorem, et illa matrimonio consentit, ne dimittat eam,'
&c. Hanc monitionem forsan fidelibus injunctis simpliciter intelli-
gendam putent, (etiam infidelibus nubere licere,) qui ita interpretantur."
p. 198.]
[2] "Quæ Domino non placent, utique Dominum offendunt, utique
Malo se inferunt." [Tertull. ad Uxor. lib. ii. c. 7.]

former part, where that is extended generally to "all things" in the neuter gender, which he speaketh in the feminine gender of women's persons; and in the latter, where "received with hurt" is put instead of "wilful incurring that which is evil." And so in sum Tertullian doth neither mean nor say as is pretended, "Whatsoever pleaseth not the Lord displeaseth him, and with hurt is received;" but, "Those women that please not the Lord" by their kind of marrying "do even thereby offend the Lord, they do even thereby throw themselves into evil."

[7.] Somewhat more show there is in a second place of Tertullian, which notwithstanding when we have examined it will be found as the rest are.[1] The Roman emperor's custom was at certain solemn times to bestow on his soldiers a donative; which donative they received wearing garlands upon their heads. There were in the time of the emperors Severus and Antoninus[2] many, who being soldiers had been converted unto Christ, and notwithstanding continued still in that military course of life. In which number, one man there was amongst all the rest, who at such a time coming to the tribune of the army to receive his donative, came but with a garland in his hand, and not in such sort as others did. The tribune offended hereat demandeth what this great singularity should mean. To whom the soldier, *Christianus sum*, "I am a Christian." Many there were so besides him which yet did otherwise at that time; whereupon grew a question, whether a Christian soldier might herein do as the unchristian did, and wear as they wore. Many of them which were very sound in Christian

---

[1] T. C. l. ii. p. 81.   " And to come yet nearer, where he disputeth against the wearing of crown or garland, (which is indifferent of itself,) to those which objecting asked, where the Scripture saith that a man might not wear a crown, he answereth by asking, where the Scripture saith that they may wear. And unto them replying that 'it is permitted which is not forbidden,' he answereth, that 'it is forbidden which is not permitted.' Whereby appeareth that the argument of the Scriptures negatively holdeth not only in the doctrine and ecclesiastical discipline, but even in matters arbitrary, and variable by the advice of the Church. Where it is not enough that they be not forbidden, unless there be some word which doth permit the use of them; it is not enough that the Scripture speaketh not against them, unless it speak for them; and finally, where it displeaseth the Lord which pleaseth him not : we [one] must of necessity have the word of his mouth to declare his pleasure."

[2] [Caracalla.]

belief did rather commend the zeal of this man than approve his action.

Tertullian was at the same time a Montanist, and an enemy unto the Church for condemning that prophetical spirit which Montanus and his followers did boast they had received, as if in them Christ had performed his last promise ; as if to them he had sent the Spirit that should be their perfecter and final instructor in the mysteries of Christian truth. Which exulceration of mind made him apt to take all occasions of contradiction. Wherefore in honour of that action, and to gall their minds who did not so much commend it, he wrote his book *De Corona Militis*, not dissembling the stomach wherewith he wrote it. For first, the man he commendeth as " one more constant than the rest of his brethren, who presumed," saith he, "that they might well enough serve two Lords." [1] Afterwards choler somewhat more rising with him, he addeth, " It doth even remain that they should also devise how to rid themselves of his martyrdoms, towards the prophecies of whose Holy Spirit they have already shewed their disdain. They mutter that their good and long peace is now in hazard. I doubt not but some of them send the Scriptures before, truss up bag and baggage, make themselves in a readiness that they may fly from city to city. For that is the only point of the Gospel which they are careful not to forget. I know even their pastors very well what men they are ; in peace lions, harts in time of trouble and fear." [2] " Now these men," saith Tertullian, " they must be answered where we do find it written in Scripture that a Christian man may not wear a garland." [3]

And as men's speeches uttered in heat of distempered affection have oftentimes much more eagerness than weight, so he that shall mark the proofs alleged and the answers to

[1] Tert. de Coron. Milit. c. 1. [" Dei miles cæteris constantior fratribus, qui se duobus dominis servire non posse præsumpserat, solus libero capite, coronamento in manu otioso." The reading before Pamelius was " servire posse præsumpserant."]

[2] [" Plane superest ut etiam martyria recusare meditentur, qui prophetias ejusdem Sp. Sancti respuerunt. Mussitant denique tam bonam et longam sibi pacem periclitari. Nec dubio quosdam Scripturas emigrare, sarcinas expedire, fugæ accingi de civitate in civitatem. Nullam enim aliam Evangelii memoriam curant. Novi et pastores eorum in pace leones, in prœlio cervos." p. 205.]

[3] [" Quatenus illud opponunt, Ubi autem prohibemur coronari ? hanc magis localem substantiam causæ præsentis aggrediar." ibid.]

things objected in that book will now and then perhaps espy
the like imbecility. Such is that argument whereby they
that wore on their heads garlands are charged as trans-
gressors of nature's law,[1] and guilty of sacrilege against God
the Lord of nature, inasmuch as flowers in such sort worn
can neither be smelt nor seen well by those that wear them ;
and God made flowers sweet and beautiful, that being seen
and smelt unto they might so delight. Neither doth Tertullian bewray this weakness in striking only, but also in
repelling their strokes with whom he contendeth. They ask,
saith he, "What Scripture is there which doth teach that we
should not be crowned ? And what Scripture is there which
doth teach that we should? For in requiring on the contrary part the aid of Scripture, they do give sentence beforehand that their part ought also by Scripture to be aided."[2]
Which answer is of no great force. There is no necessity,
that if I confess I ought not to do that which the Scripture
forbiddeth me, I should thereby acknowledge myself bound
to do nothing which the Scripture commandeth me not.
For many inducements besides Scripture may lead me to
that, which if Scripture be against, they all give place and
are of no value, yet otherwise are strong and effectual to
persuade.

Which thing himself well enough understanding, and
being not ignorant that Scripture in many things doth
neither command nor forbid, but use silence ; his resolution
in fine is, that in the church a number of things are strictly
observed, whereof no law of Scripture maketh mention one
way or other ;[3] that of things once received and confirmed

---

[1] [Ibid. c. 5. "In capite quis sapor floris ? quis coronæ sensus,
nisi vinculi tantum ? quia neque color cernitur, neque odor ducitur, nec
teneritas commendatur. Tam contra naturam est florem capite sectari,
quam cibum aure, quam sonum nare. Omne autem quod contra
naturam est monstri meretur notam penes omnes, penes nos vero etiam
elogium sacrilegii, in Deum naturæ Dominum et auctorem."]

[2] [Ibid. c. 2. "Facile est statim exigere, ubi scriptum sit, ne coronemur ? At enim ubi scriptum est, ut coronemur ? Expostulantes
enim Scripturæ patrocinium in parte diversa, præjudicant suæ quoque
parti Scripturæ patrocinium adesse debere. Nam si ideo dicetur coronari licere, quia non prohibeat Scriptura, æque retorquebitur ideo
coronari non licere, quia Scriptura non jubeat."]

[3] [Ibid. c. 3. "Etiam in traditionis obtentu exigenda est, inquis,
auctoritas scripta. Ergo quæramus an et traditio non scripta non
debeat recipi ? Plane negabimus recipiendam, si nulla exempla præju-
dicent aliarum observationum, quas sine ullius Scripturæ instrumento,
solius traditionis titulo, exinde consuetudinis patrocinio vindicamus."]

by use long usage is a law sufficient; that in civil affairs,
when there is no other law, custom itself doth stand for
law;[1] that inasmuch as law doth stand upon reason, to
allege reason serveth as well as to cite Scripture;[2] that
whatsoever is reasonable, the same is lawful whosoever is
author of it; that the authority of custom is great;[3] finally,
that the custom of Christians was then and had been a long
time not to wear garlands, and therefore that undoubtedly
they did offend who presumed to violate such a custom by
not observing that thing, the very inveterate observation
whereof was a law sufficient to bind all men to observe it,
unless they could shew some higher law, some law of
Scripture, to the contrary.[4] This presupposed, it may
stand then very well with strength and soundness of
reason, even thus to answer, "Whereas they ask what
Scripture forbiddeth them to wear a garland; we are in this
case rather to demand what Scripture commandeth them.
They cannot here allege that it is permitted which is not
forbidden them: no, that is forbidden them which is not
permitted." For long-received custom forbidding them
to do as they did, (if so be it did forbid them,)
there was no excuse in the world to justify their act,
unless in the Scripture they could shew some law, that did
license them thus to break a received custom.

He then instances in the customs of interrogatories in baptism, of trine
immersion, and several other Church usages.]

[1] [Ibid. c. 4. "His igitur exemplis renunciatum erit, posse etiam
non scriptam traditionem in observatione defendi, confirmatam consuetudine. . . . Consuetudo autem etiam in civilibus rebus pro lege
suscipitur, cum deficit lex."]

[2] [Ibid. "Nec differt, Scriptura an ratione consistat, quando et
legem ratio commendet. Porro si lex ratione constat, lex erit omne
quod jam ratione constiterit *a quocunque productum*."]

[3] [Ibid. "Hanc (rationem divinam) nunc expostula, salvo traditionis
respectu, *quocunque traditore censetur:* nec auctorem respicias, sed
auctoritatem: et inprimis consuetudinis ipsius, quæ propterea colenda
est, ne non sit rationis interpres, ut si hanc Deus dederit, tunc discas,
curnam observanda sit tibi consuetudo."]

[4] [Ibid. c. 2. "Neminem dico fidelium coronam capite nosse alias,
extra tempus tentationis ejusmodi. Omnes ita observant a catechu-
menis usque ad confessores et martyres, vel negatores. Viderint, unde
auctoritas moris, de qua cum maxime quæritur. Porro cum quæritur
cur quid observetur, observari interim constat. Ergo nec nullum nec
incertum videri potest delictum, quod committitur in observationem suo
jam nomine vindicandam, et satis auctoratam consensus patrocinio."
and c. 3, Habentes observationem inveteratam, quæ præveniendo
statum facit."]

Now whereas in all the books of Tertullian besides there is not so much found as in that one, to prove not only that we may do but that we ought to do sundry things which the Scripture commandeth not; out of that very book these sentences are brought to make us believe that Tertullian was of a clean contrary mind. We cannot therefore hereupon yield; we cannot grant, that hereby is made manifest the argument of Scripture negatively to be of force, not only in doctrine and ecclesiastical discipline, but even in matters arbitrary. For Tertullian doth plainly hold even in that book, that neither the matter which he entreateth of was arbitrary but necessary, inasmuch as the received custom of the Church did tie and bind them not to wear garlands as the heathens did; yea and further also he reckoneth up particularly a number of things, whereof he expressly concludeth, "Harum et aliarum ejusmodi disciplinarum si legem expostules Scripturarum, nullam invenies;"[1] which is as much as if he had said in express words, "Many things there are which concern the discipline of the Church and the duties of men, which to abrogate and take away the Scripture negatively urged may not in any case persuade us, but they must be observed, yea, although no Scripture be found which required any such thing." Tertullian therefore undoubtedly doth not in this book shew himself to be of the same mind with them by whom his name is pretended.

VI. [2] But sith the sacred Scriptures themselves afford oftentimes such arguments as are taken from divine authority

[1] Ibid. c. 4.
[2] T. C. l. ii. p. 48. "It is not hard to shew that the Prophets have reasoned negatively. As when in the person of the Lord the Prophet saith, *Whereof I have not spoken,* Jer. xix. 5. *And which never entered into my heart,* Jer. vii. 31. And where he condemneth them because they have not asked counsel at the mouth of the Lord, Isai. xxx. 2. And it may be shewed that the same kind of argument hath been used in things which are not of the substance of salvation or damnation, and whereof there was no commandment to the contrary, (as in the former there was. Levit. xviii. 21 ; and xx. 3 ; Deut. xvii. 16.) In Joshua the children of Israel are charged by the Prophet that they asked not counsel at the mouth of the Lord, when they entered into covenant with the Gibeonites, Joshua ix. 14. And yet that covenant was not made contrary unto any commandment of God. Moreover, we read that when David had taken this counsel, to build a temple unto the Lord, albeit the Lord had revealed before in his word that there should be such a standing-place, where the ark of the covenant and the service should have a certain abiding; and albeit there was no word of God

both one way and the other; "The Lord hath commanded, therefore it must be;" and again in like sort, "He hath not, therefore it must be;" some certainty concerning this point seemeth requisite to be set down.

God himself can neither possibly err, nor lead into error. For this cause his testimonies, whatsoever he affirmeth, are always truth and most infallible certainty.[1]

Yea, further, because the things that proceed from him are perfect without any manner of defect or maim; it cannot be but that the words of his mouth are absolute, and lack nothing which they should have for performance of that thing whereunto they tend. Whereupon it followeth, that the end being known whereunto he directeth his speech, the argument even negatively is evermore strong and forcible concerning those things that are apparently requisite unto the same end. As for example: God intending to set down sundry times that which in Angels is most excellent, hath not any where spoken so highly of them as he hath of our Lord and Saviour Jesus Christ; therefore they are not in dignity equal unto him. It is the Apostle St. Paul's argument.[2]

[2.] The purpose of God was to teach his people, both unto whom they should offer sacrifice, and what sacrifice was to be offered. To burn their sons in fire unto Baal he did not command them, he spake no such thing, neither came it into his mind; therefore this they ought not to have done. Which argument the Prophet Jeremy useth more than once, as being so effectual and strong, that although the thing he reproveth were not only commanded but forbidden them,[3] and that expressly; yet the Prophet chooseth rather to charge them with the fault of making a

which forbade David to build the temple; yet the Lord (with commendation of his good affection and zeal he had to the advancement of his glory) concludeth against David's resolution to build the temple with this reason, namely, that he had given no commandment of this who should build it. 1 Chron. xvii. 6." [The first part of this extract, from "It is not hard" to "Isai. xxx. 2." is from T. C. i. 13, 14. The parenthesis ("As in the former. . . . Deut. xvii. 16.") seems to be a note of Hooker's. The latter part from "Moreover" is from T. C. ii. 49.]

[1] [1 John i. 5. "God is light, and there is in him no darkness at all." Heb. vi. 18. "It is impossible that God should lie." Numb. xxiii. 19. "God is not as man that he should lie."]

[2] [Heb. i. 5-13; ii. 5-8.]

[3] Levit. xviii. 21; xx. 3; Deut. xviii. 10.

law unto themselves, than with the crime of transgressing a law which God had made.[1] For when the Lord hath once himself precisely set down a form of executing that wherein we are to serve him; the fault appeareth greater to do that which we are not, than not to do that which we are commanded. In this we seem to charge the law of God with hardness only, in that with foolishness: in this we shew ourselves weak and unapt to be doers of his will, in that we take upon us to be controllers of his wisdom; in this we fail to perform the thing which God seeth meet, convenient, and good, in that we presume to see what is meet and convenient better than God himself. In those actions therefore the whole form whereof God hath of purpose set down to be observed, we may not otherwise do than exactly as he hath prescribed; in such things negative arguments are strong.

[3.] Again, with a negative argument David is pressed concerning the purpose he had to build a temple unto the Lord; "Thus saith the Lord, Thou shalt not build me a house to dwell in. Wheresoever I have walked with all Israel, spake I one word to any of the judges of Israel, whom I commanded to feed my people, saying Why have ye not built me an house?"[2] The Jews urged with a negative argument touching the aid which they sought at the hands of the King of Egypt; "Woe to those rebellious children, saith the Lord, which walk forth to go down into Egypt, and have not asked counsel at my mouth; to strengthen themselves with the strength of Pharaoh."[3] Finally, the league of Joshua with the Gibeonites is likewise with a negative argument touched. It was not as it should be: and why? the Lord gave them not that advice; "They sought not counsel at the mouth of the Lord."[4]

By the virtue of which examples if any man shall suppose the force of negative arguments approved, when they are taken from Scripture in such sort as we in this question are pressed therewith, they greatly deceive themselves. For unto which of all these was it said that they had done amiss, in purposing to do or in doing any thing at all which "the Scripture" commanded them not? Our question is, Whether all be sin which is done without direction by Scripture, and not, Whether the Israelites did at any time

---

[1] [See Whitgift, Defence, &c. p. 78.]
[2] 1 Chron. xvii. 6.   [3] Isaiah xxx. 1, 2.   [4] Josh. ix. 14.

amiss by following their own minds without asking counsel of God. No, it was that people's singular privilege, a favour which God vouchsafed them above the rest of the world, that in the affairs of their estate which were not determinable one way or other by the Scripture, himself gave them extraordinarily direction and counsel as oft as they sought it at his hands. Thus God did first by speech unto Moses, after by Urim and Thummim unto priests, lastly by dreams and visions unto prophets, from whom in such cases they were to receive the answer of God.

Concerning Joshua therefore, thus spake the Lord unto Moses, saying, " He shall stand before Eleazar the priest, who shall ask counsel for him by the judgment of Urim before the Lord ; " [1] whereof had Joshua been mindful, the fraud of the Gibeonites could not so smoothly have passed unespied till there was no help.

The Jews had prophets to have resolved them from the mouth of God himself whether Egyptian aids should profit them, yea or no ; but they thought themselves wise enough, and him unworthy to be of their counsel. In this respect therefore was their reproof though sharp yet just, albeit there had been no charge precisely given them that they should always take heed of Egypt.

But as for David, to think that he did evil in determining to build God a temple, because there was in Scripture no commandment that he should build it, were very injurious : the purpose of his heart was religious and godly, the act most worthy of honour and renown ; neither could Nathan choose but admire his virtuous intent, exhort him to go forward, and beseech God to prosper him therein. [2] But God saw the endless troubles which David should be subject unto during the whole time of his regiment, and therefore gave charge to defer so good a work till the days of tranquillity and peace, wherein it might without interruption be performed. David supposed that it could not stand with the duty which he owed unto God, to set himself in a house of cedar-trees, and to behold the ark of the Lord's covenant unsettled. This opinion the Lord abateth, by causing Nathan to shew him plainly, that it should be no more imputed unto him for a fault than it had been unto the Judges of Israel before him, his case being the same which

[1] Numb. xxvii. 21. [2] 1 Chron. xvii. 2.

theirs was, their times not more unquiet than his, not more unfit for such an action.

Wherefore concerning the force of negative arguments so taken from the authority of Scripture as by us they are denied, there is in all this less than nothing.

[4.] And touching that which unto this purpose is borrowed from the controversy sometime handled between M. Harding[1] and the worthiest divine that Christendom hath bred for the space of some hundreds of years,[2] who being brought up together in one University,[3] it fell out in them which was spoken of two others, "They learned in the same that which in contrary camps they did practise:"[4] of these two the one objecting that with us arguments taken from authority negatively are over common,

---

[1] T. C. l. ii. p. 50. "M. Harding reproacheth the Bishop of Salisbury with this kind of reasoning; unto whom the Bishop answereth, 'The argument of authority negatively is taken to be good, whensoever proof is taken of God's word; and is used not only by us, but also by many of the Catholic Fathers.' A little after he sheweth the reason why the argument of authority of the Scripture negatively is good; namely, 'For that the word of God is perfect.' In another place unto M. Harding casting him in the teeth with negative arguments, he allegeth places out of Irenæus, Chrysostom, Leo, which reasoned negatively of the authority of the Scriptures. The places which he allegeth be very full and plain in generality, without any such restraints as the answerer imagineth; as they are there to be seen."

[2] [Vaghan in his life of Dr. Thos. Jackson, prefixed to his (Jackson's) works, p. 8, says of him, "I shall willingly associate him to those other worthies, his predecessors in the same college, (all living at the same time :) to the invaluable Bishop Jewel, *Theologorum quos orbis Christianus per aliquot annorum centenarios produxit maximo :* as grave Bishop Godwin hath described him. To the famous Mr. Hooker, who for his solid writings was sirnamed, The Judicious, and entitled by the same, *Theologorum Oxonium ;* 'The Oxford of Divines :' as one calls Athens, 'The Greece of Greece itself.' To the learned Dr. Reinolds, who managed the government of the same college with the like care, honour and integrity, although not with the same austerities" as Dr. Jackson. Bishop Godwin borrowed the expression referred to (De Præsul. Angl. p. 354, ed. 1743,) from Hooker ; and adds concerning him, that he was "*a magno Theologo Literarum Oxonium appellatus.*"]

[3] [According to Camden, they were bred in the same grammar school also. "Out of this town's school" (he is speaking of Barnstaple) "there issued two right learned men and most renowned divines, John Jewell Bishop of Sarisbury, and T. Hardinge." Britannia, transl. by Holland, p. 208.]

[4] Vell. Paterc. "Jugurtha ac Marius sub eodem Africano militantes, in iisdem castris didicere quæ postea in contrariis facerent." [l. ii. c. 9.]

the Bishop's answer hereunto is, that [1] " This kind of argument is thought to be good, whensoever proof is taken of God's word ; and is used not only by us, but also by St. Paul, and by many of the Catholic Fathers. St. Paul saith, God said not unto Abraham, ' In thy seeds all the nations of the earth shall be blessed ;' but, ' In thy seed, which is Christ ;' and thereof he thought he made a good argument.[2] Likewise, saith Origen, 'The bread which the Lord gave unto his disciples, saying unto them, Take and eat, he deferred not, nor commanded to be reserved till the next day.' [3] Such arguments Origen and other learned Fathers thought to stand for good, whatsoever misliking Master Harding hath found in them. This kind of proof is thought to hold in God's commandments, for that they be full and perfect : and God hath specially charged us, that we should neither put to them nor take from them ; and therefore it seemeth good unto them that have learned of Christ, *Unus est magister vester, Christus*,[4] and have heard the voice of God the Father from heaven, *Ipsum audite*.[5] But unto them that add to the word of God what them listeth, and make God's will subject unto their will, and break God's commandments for their own tradition's sake, unto them it seemeth not good."

Again, the English Apology alleging the example of the Greeks, how they have neither private masses, nor mangled sacraments, nor purgatories, nor pardons ; it pleaseth Master Harding to jest out the matter, to use the help of his wits where strength of truth failed him, and to answer with scoffing at negatives. The Bishop's defence in this case is,[6] " The ancient learned Fathers having to deal with impudent heretics, that in defence of their errors avouched the judgment of all the old bishops and doctors that had been before them, and the general consent of the primitive and whole universal Church, and that with as good regard of truth and as faithfully as you do now ; the better to discover the shameless boldness and nakedness of their doctrine, were oftentimes likewise forced to use the negative, and so to drive the same heretics, as we do you, to prove their affirm-

---

[1] [Reply to M. Harding's Answer.] Art. i. Divis. 29. [p. 51, ed. 1611.]   [2] Gal. iii. 16.
[3] Orig. in Levit. Hom. 5. [t. ii. 211. ed. Bened.]
[4] Matt. xxiii. 8. 10.   [5] Matt. xvii. 5.
[6] Defens. par. v. cap. 15, divis. 1.

atives, which thing to do it was never possible. The ancient father Irenæus thus stayed himself, as we do, by the negative,[1] 'Hoc neque Prophetæ prædicaverunt, neque Dominus docuit, neque Apostoli tradiderunt;' 'This thing neither did the Prophets publish, nor our Lord teach, nor the Apostles deliver.' By a like negative Chrysostom saith,[2] 'This tree neither Paul planted, nor Apollos watered, nor God increased.' In like sort Leo saith,[3] 'What needeth it to believe that thing that neither the Law hath taught, nor the Prophets have spoken, nor the Gospel hath preached, nor the Apostles have delivered?' And again,[4] 'How are the new devices brought in that our Fathers never knew?' St. Augustine, having reckoned up a great number of the Bishops of Rome, by a general negative saith thus;[5] 'In all this order of succession of bishops there is not one bishop found that was a Donatist.' St. Gregory being himself a Bishop of Rome, and writing against the title of *Universal Bishop*, saith thus,[6] 'None of all my predecessors ever consented to use this ungodly title; no Bishop of Rome ever took upon him this name of singularity.' By such negatives, M. Harding, we reprove the vanity and novelty of your religion; we tell you, none of the catholic ancient learned Fathers either Greek or Latin, ever used either your private mass, or your half communion, or your barbarous unknown prayers. Paul never planted them, Apollos never watered them, God never increased them; they are of yourselves, they are not of God.'

In all this there is not a syllable which any way crosseth us. For concerning arguments negative even taken from human authority, they are here proved to be in some cases

---

[1] Lib. i. cap. 1.

[2] De incomp. nat. Dei, Hom. 3. t. vi. 403. ["Hanc arborem non Paulus plantavit, non Apollos rigavit, non Deus auxit."]

[3] Epist. xciii. c. 12. [p. 167, ed. Paris, 1639. "Quid opus est in cor admittere quod lex non docuit, quod prophetia non cecinit, quod Evangelii veritas non prædicavit, quod Apostolica doctrina non tradidit?"]

[4] Epist. xcvii. c. 5. ["Quomodo . . . nova inducuntur, quæ nostri nunquam sensere majores?" Quoted by S. Leo from S. Ambrose, de Incarn. Dom. c. 6.]

[5] Epist. clxv. [al. 53. t. ii. 121. "In hoc ordine successionis nullus Donatista episcopus invenitur."]

[6] Lib. iv. Ep. 32. ["Nemo decessorum meorum hoc tam profano vocabulo uti consensit: nullus Romanorum Pontificum hoc singularitatis nomen assumpsit."]

very strong and forcible. They are not in our estimation idle reproofs, when the authors of needless innovations are opposed with such negatives as that of Leo, "How are these new devices brought in which our Fathers never knew?" When their grave and reverend superiors do reckon up unto them as Augustine did unto the Donatists, large catalogues of Fathers wondered at for their wisdom, piety, and learning,[1] amongst whom for so many ages before us no one did ever so think of the Church's affairs as now the world doth begin to be persuaded; surely by us they are not taught to take exception hereat, because such arguments are negative. Much less when the like are taken from the sacred authority of Scripture, if the matter itself do bear them. For in truth the question is not, whether an argument from Scripture negatively may be good, but whether it be so generally good, that in all actions men may urge it. The Fathers I grant do use very general and large terms, even as Hiero the king did in speaking of Archimedes, "From henceforward whatsoever Archimedes "speaketh, it must be believed."[2] His meaning was not that Archimedes could simply in nothing be deceived, but that he had in such sort approved his skill, that he seemed worthy of credit for ever after in matters appertaining unto the science he was skilful in. In speaking thus largely it is presumed that men's speeches will be taken according to the matter whereof they speak. Let any man therefore that carrieth indifferency of judgment peruse the bishop's

---

[1] [St. Aug. Ep. 53. (al. 165.) § 2. "Si ordo episcoporum sibi succedentium considerandus est, quanto certius et vere salubriter ab ipso Petro numeramus, cui totius Ecclesiæ figuram gerenti Dominus ait, 'Super hanc petram ædificabo Ecclesiam meam, et portæ inferorum non vincent eam.' Petro enim successit Linus ; Lino, Clemens ; Clementi, Anacletus ; Anacleto, Evaristus ; Evaristo, Alexander ; Alexandro, Sixtus ; Sixto, Telesphorus ; Telesphoro, Iginus ; Igino, Anicetus ; Aniceto, Pius ; Pio, Soter ; Soteri, Eleutherius ; Eleutherio, Victor ; Victori, Zephirinus ; Zephirino, Calixtus ; Calixto, Urbanus ; Urbano, Pontianus ; Pontiano, Antherus ; Anthero, Fabianus ; Fabiano, Cornelius ; Cornelio, Lucius ; Lucio, Stephanus ; Stephano, Xystus ; Xysto, Dionysius ; Dionysio, Felix ; Felici, Eutychianus ; Eutychiano, Gaius ; Gaio, Marcellinus ; Marcellino, Marcellus ; Marcello, Eusebius ; Eusebio, Miltiades ; Miltiadi, Sylvester ; Sylvestro, Marcus ; Marco, Julius ; Julio, Liberius ; Liberio, Damasus ; Damaso, Siricius ; Siricio, Anastasius. In hoc ordine successionis nullus Donatista Episcopus invenitur."]

[2] [Proclus in Euclid. II. 3. Montucla, Hist. des Mathématiques, I. 230.]

speeches, and consider well of those negatives concerning Scripture, which he produceth out of Irenæus, Chrysostom, and Leo ;[1] which three are chosen from among the residue, because the sentences of the others (even as one of theirs also) do make for defence of negative arguments taken from human authority, and not from divine only. They mention no more restraint in the one than in the other ; yet I think themselves will not hereby judge, that the Fathers took both to be strong, without restraint unto any special kind of matter wherein they held such arguments forcible. Nor doth the bishop either say or prove any more, than that an argument in some kinds of matter may be good, although taken negatively from Scripture.

VII. An earnest desire to draw all things under the determination of bare and naked Scripture hath caused here much pains to be taken in abating the estimation and credit of man. Which if we labour to maintain as far as truth and reason will bear, let not any think that we travel about a matter not greatly needful. For the scope of all their pleading against man's authority is, to overthrow such orders, laws, and constitutions in the Church, as depending thereupon if they should therefore be taken away, would peradventure leave neither face nor memory of Church to continue long in the world, the world especially being such as now it is. That which they have in this case spoken I would for brevity's sake let pass, but that the drift of their speech being so dangerous, their words are not to be neglected.

[2.] Wherefore to say that simply an argument taken from

---

[1] [St. Irenæus, I. 1. 15, (after a minute exposition of the Valentinian doctrine of Æons ;) Τοιαύτης δὲ τῆς ὑποθέσεως αὐτῶν οὔσης, ἣν οὔτε Προφῆται ἐκήρυξαν, οὔτε ὁ Κύριος ἐδίδαξεν, οὔτε Ἀπόστολοι παρέδωκαν, ἣν περὶ τῶν ὅλων αὐχοῦσι πλεῖον τῶν ἄλλων ἐγνωκέναι, ἐξ ἀγράφων ἀναγινώσκοντες, καὶ τὸ δὴ λεγόμενον, ἐξ ἄμμου σχοινία πλέκειν ἐπιτηδεύοντες· ἀξιοπίστως προσαρμόζειν πειρῶνται τοῖς εἰρημένοις ἤτοι παραβολὰς κυριακὰς, ἢ ῥήσεις προφητικὰς, ἢ λόγους Ἀποστολικοὺς, ἵνα τὸ πλάσμα αὐτῶν μὴ ἀμάρτυρον εἶναι δοκῇ.

St. Chrysostom, VI. p. 402, 3, (speaking of one of the most offensive modifications of Arianism ;) Ἡ τῶν Ἀνομοίων ἐρημωθεῖσα ψυχὴ, καὶ τῆς ἀπὸ τῶν γραφῶν ἐπιμελείας οὐκ ἀπολαύσασα, οἴκοθεν καὶ παρ' ἑαυτῆς τὴν ἀγρίαν ταύτην καὶ ἀνήμερον ἐξέβρασεν αἵρεσιν· τοῦτο γὰρ τὸ δένδρον οὐ Παῦλος ἐφύτευσεν, οὐκ Ἀπολλὼς ἐπότισεν, οὐχ ὁ θεὸς ηὔξησεν· ἀλλ' ἐφύτευσε μὲν λογισμῶν ἄκαιρος περιεργία, ἐπότισε δὲ ἀπονοίας τῦφος, ηὔξησε δὲ φιλοδοξίας ἔρως.

St. Leo, as before, Ep. xciii. c. 12.]

man's authority doth hold no way, "neither affirmatively nor negatively,"[1] is hard. By a man's authority we here understand the force which his word hath for the assurance of another's mind that buildeth upon it ; as the Apostle somewhat did upon their report of the house of Chloe ;[2] and the Samaritans in a matter of far greater moment upon the report of a simple woman. For so it is said in St. John's Gospel, "Many of the Samaritans of that city believed in him for the saying of the woman, which testified, He hath told me all things that ever I did."[3]

The strength of man's authority is affirmatively such that the weightiest affairs in the world depend thereon. In judgment and justice are not hereupon proceedings grounded? Saith not the Law that "in the mouth of two or three witnesses every word shall be confirmed?"[4] This the law of God would not say, if there were in a man's testimony no force at all to prove any thing.

And if it be admitted that in matter of fact there is some credit to be given to the testimony of man, but not in matter of opinion and judgment ; we see the contrary both acknowledged and universally practised also throughout the world. The sentences of wise and expert men were never but highly esteemed. Let the title of a man's right be called in question ; are we not bold to rely and build upon the judgment of such as are famous for their skill in the laws of this land? In matter of state the weight many times of some one man's authority is thought reason sufficient, even to sway over whole nations.

And this not only "with the simpler sort ;" but the learneder and wiser we are, the more such arguments in some cases prevail with us. The reason why the simpler sort are moved with authority is the conscience of their own ignorance ; whereby it cometh to pass that having learned men in admiration, they rather fear to dislike them than

---

[1] T. C. lib. i. p. 25. [13.] "When the question is of the authority of a man, it holdeth neither affirmatively nor negatively. The reason is, because the infirmity of man can neither attain to the perfection of any thing whereby he might speak all things that are to be spoken of it, neither yet be free from error in those things which he speaketh or giveth out. And therefore this argument neither affirmatively nor negatively compelleth the hearer, but only induceth him to some liking or disliking of that for which it is brought, and is rather for an orator to persuade the simpler sort than for a disputer to enforce him that is learned."

[2] 1 Cor. i. 11.   [3] iv. 39.   [4] Deut. xix. 15 ; Matt. xviii. 16.

know wherefore they should allow and follow their judgments. Contrariwise with them that are skilful authority is
much more strong and forcible; because they only are able
to discern how just cause there is why to some men's
authority so much should be attributed. For which cause
the name of Hippocrates (no doubt) were more effectual to
persuade even such men as Galen himself, than to move a
silly empiric. So that the very selfsame argument in this
kind which doth but induce the vulgar sort to like, may
constrain the wiser to yield. And therefore not orators
only with the people, but even the very profoundest disputers
in all faculties have hereby often with the best learned
prevailed most.

As for arguments taken from human authority and that
negatively; for example sake, if we should think the
assembling of the people of God together by the sound of a
bell, the presenting of infants at the holy font by such as
commonly we call their godfathers, or any other the like
received custom, to be impious, because some men of whom
we think very reverently have in their books and writings no
where mentioned or taught that such things should be in
the Church; this reasoning were subject unto just reproof,
it were but feeble, weak, and unsound. Notwithstanding
even negatively an argument from human authority may be
strong, as namely thus: The Chronicles of England mention
no more than only six kings bearing the name of Edward
since the time of the last conquest; therefore it cannot be
there should be more. So that if the question be of the
authority of a man's testimony, we cannot simply avouch
either that affirmatively it doth not any way hold; or that
it hath only force to induce the simpler sort, and not to
constrain men of understanding and ripe judgment to yield
assent; or that negatively it hath in it no strength at all.
For unto every of these the contrary is most plain.

[3.] Neither doth that which is alleged concerning the
infirmity of men overthrow or disprove this. Men are
blinded with ignorance and error; many things may escape
them, and in many things they may be deceived; yea, those
things which they do know they may either forget, or upon
sundry indirect considerations let pass; and although themselves do not err, yet may they through malice or vanity
even of purpose deceive others. Howbeit infinite cases
there are wherein all these impediments and lets are so

manifestly excluded, that there is no show or colour whereby any such exception may be taken, but that the testimony
of man will stand as a ground of infallible assurance. That
there is a city of Rome, that Pius Quintus and Gregory the
Thirteenth and others have been Popes of Rome, I suppose
we are certainly enough persuaded. The ground of our
persuasion, who never saw the place nor persons before-
named, can be nothing but man's testimony. Will any man
here notwithstanding allege those mentioned human infirmities, as reasons why these things should be mistrusted or
doubted of?

Yea, that which is more, utterly to infringe the force and
strength of man's testimony were to shake the very fortress
of God's truth. For whatsoever we believe concerning
salvation by Christ, although the Scripture be therein the
ground of our belief ; yet the authority of man is, if we mark
it, the key which openeth the door of entrance into the
knowledge of the Scripture. The Scripture could not teach
us the things that are of God, unless we did credit men
who have taught us that the words of Scripture do signify
those things. Some way therefore, notwithstanding man's
infirmity, yet his authority may enforce assent.

[4.] Upon better advice and deliberation so much is perceived, and at the length confest ; that arguments taken
from the authority of men may not only so far forth as hath
been declared but further also be of some force in "human
sciences ; " which force be it never so small, doth shew that
they are not utterly naught. But in "matters divine" it is
still maintained stiffly, that they have no manner force at
all.[1] Howbeit, the very selfsame reason, which causeth to

---

[1] T. C. lib. ii. p. 19. "Although that kind of argument of authority
of men is good neither in human nor divine sciences ; yet it hath some
small force in human sciences, (forasmuch as naturally, and in that he is
a man, he may come to some ripeness of judgment in those sciences,)
which in divine matters hath no force at all ; as of him which naturally,
and as he is a man, can no more judge of them than a blind man of
colours. Yea so far is it from drawing credit, if it be barely spoken
without reason and testimony of Scripture, that it carrieth also a suspicion
of untruth whatsoever proceedeth from him ; which the Apostle did well
note, when, to signify a thing corruptly spoken, and against the truth,
he saith, that 'it is spoken according to man,' Rom. iii. He saith not,
'as a wicked and lying man,' but simply 'as a man.' And although
this corruption be reformed in many, yet for so much as in whom the
knowledge of the truth is most advanced there remaineth both ignorance
and disordered affections 'whereof either of them turneth him from

yield that they are of some force in the one, will at the length constrain also to acknowledge that they are not in the other altogether unforcible. For if the natural strength of man's wit may by experience and study attain unto such ripeness in the knowledge of things human, that men in this respect may presume to build somewhat upon their judgment; what reason have we to think but that even in matters divine, the like wits furnished with necessary helps, exercised in Scripture with like diligence, and assisted with the grace of Almighty God, may grow unto so much perfection of knowledge, that men shall have just cause, when any thing pertinent unto faith and religion is doubted of, the more willingly to incline their minds towards that which the sentence of so grave, wise, and learned in that faculty shall judge most sound? For the controversy is of the weight of such men's judgments. Let it therefore be suspected; let it be taken as gross, corrupt, repugnant unto the truth, whatsoever concerning things divine above nature shall at any time be spoken as out of the mouths of mere natural men, which have not the eyes wherewith heavenly things are discerned. For this we contend not. But whom God hath endued with principal gifts to aspire unto knowledge by; whose exercises, labours, and divine studies he hath so blessed that the world for their great and rare skill that way hath them in singular admiration; may we reject even their judgment likewise, as being utterly of no moment? For mine own part, I dare not so lightly esteem of the Church, and of the principal pillars therein.

[5.] The truth is, that the mind of man desireth evermore to know the truth according to the most infallible certainty which the nature of things can yield. The greatest assurance generally with all men is that which we have by plain aspect and intuitive beholding. Where we cannot attain unto this, there what appeareth to be true by strong and invincible demonstration, such as wherein it is not by any way possible to be deceived, thereunto the mind doth necessarily assent, neither is it in the choice thereof to do otherwise. And in case these both do fail, then which way greatest probability leadeth, thither the mind doth evermore incline. Scripture with Christian men being received as the Word of God; that

speaking of the truth), no man's authority, with the Church especially and those that are called and persuaded of the authority of the Word of God, can bring any assurance unto the conscience."

for which we have probable, yea, that which we have necessary reason for, yea, that which we see with our eyes, is not thought so sure as that which the Scripture of God teacheth; because we hold that his speech revealeth there what himself seeth, and therefore the strongest proof of all, and the most necessarily assented unto by us (which do thus receive the Scripture) is the Scripture. Now it is not required nor can be exacted at our hands, that we should yield unto any thing other assent, than such as doth answer the evidence which is to be had of that we assent unto. For which cause even in matters divine, concerning some things we may lawfully doubt and suspend our judgment, inclining neither to one side nor other; as namely touching the time of the fall both of man and angels: of some things we may very well retain an opinion that they are probable and not unlikely to be true, as when we hold that men have their souls rather by creation than propagation, or that the Mother of our Lord lived always in the state of virginity as well after his birth as before (for of these two the one, her virginity before, is a thing which of necessity we must believe; the other, her continuance in the same state always, hath more likelihood of truth than the contrary); finally in all things then are our consciences best resolved, and in a most agreeable sort unto God and nature settled, when they are so far persuaded as those grounds of persuasion which are to be had will bear.

Which thing I do so much the rather set down, for that I see how a number of souls are for want of right information in this point oftentimes grievously vexed. When bare and unbuilded conclusions are put into their minds, they finding not themselves to have thereof any great certainty, imagine that this proceedeth only from lack of faith, and that the Spirit of God doth not work in them as it doth in true believers; by this means their hearts are much troubled, they fall into anguish and perplexity: whereas the truth is, that how bold and confident soever we may be in words, when it cometh to the point of trial, such as the evidence is which the truth hath either in itself or through proof, such is the heart's assent thereunto; neither can it be stronger, being grounded as it should be.

I grant that proof derived from the authority of man's judgment is not able to work that assurance which doth grow by a stronger proof; and therefore although ten thousand general councils would set down one and the same definitive sentence concerning any point of religion whatsoever, yet one demonstrative reason alleged, or one manifest testimony cited from the mouth of God himself to the contrary, could not choose but overweigh them all ; inasmuch as for them to have been deceived it is not impossible ; it is, that demonstrative reason or testimony divine should deceive. Howbeit in defect of proof infallible, because the mind doth rather follow probable persuasions than approve the things that have in them no likelihood of truth at all ; surely if a question concerning matter of doctrine were proposed, and on the one side no kind of proof appearing, there should on the other be alleged and shewed that so a number of the learnedest divines in the world have ever thought ; although it did not appear what reason or what Scripture led them to be of that judgment, yet to their very bare judgment somewhat a reasonable man would attribute, notwithstanding the common imbecilities which are incident into our nature.

[6.] And whereas it is thought, that especially with "the Church, and those that are called and persuaded of the authority of the Word of God, man's authority" with them especially "should not prevail ;" it must and doth prevail even with them, yea with them especially, as far as equity requireth ; and farther we maintain it not.[1] For men to be

---

[1] T. C. lib. ii. p. 21. "Of divers sentences of the Fathers themselves (whereby some have likened them to brute beasts without reason which suffer themselves to be led by the judgment and authority of others, some have preferred the judgment of one simple rude man alleging reason unto companies of learned men) I will content myself at this time with two or three sentences. Irenæus saith, Whatsoever is to be shewed in the Scripture cannot be shewed but out of the Scriptures themselves. lib. iii. cap. 12. Jerome saith, 'No man be he never so holy or eloquent hath any authority after the Apostles :' in Ps. lxxxvi. Augustine saith, 'That he will believe none, how godly and learned soever he be, unless he confirm his sentence by the Scriptures, or by some reason not contrary to them.' Ep. 18." [al. 82. t. ii. p. 190.] "And in another place, Hear this, the Lord saith : Hear not this, Donatus saith, Rogatus saith, Vincentius saith, Hilarius saith, Ambrose saith, Augustine saith, but hearken unto this, The Lord saith. Ep. 48." [al. 93. c. 6. Opp. t. ii. p. 239. It may be questioned whether this place is at all relevant to Cartwright's purpose. *Glorificatum est nomen meum in gentibus, dicit Dominus.* Audi, *dicit Dominus;* non, dicit Donatus, aut Rogatus, aut Vincentius, aut Hilarius, aut Ambrosius, aut Augustinus ; sed, *dicit Dominus;* cum legitur, *Et benedicentur in eo omnes tribus terræ. . . . Et replebitur gloria ejus omnis terra, fiat, fiat.* Et tu sedes Cartennis, et cum decem Rogatistis, qui remansistis, dicis, *Non fiat, non fiat.*] 'And again, having to do with an Arian, he affirmeth that neither he

tied and led by authority, as it were with a kind of captivity of judgment, and though there be reason to the contrary not to listen unto it, but to follow like beasts the first in the herd, they know not nor care not whither, this were brutish. Again, that authority of men should prevail with men either against or above Reason, is no part of our belief. "Companies of learned men" be they never so great and reverend are to yield unto Reason ; the weight whereof is no whit prejudiced by the simplicity of his person which doth allege it, but being found to be sound and good, the bare opinion of men to the contrary must of necessity stoop and give place.

Irenæus,[1] writing against Marcion, which held one God author of the Old Testament and another of the New, to prove that the Apostles preached the same God which was known before to the Jews, he copiously allegeth sundry their sermons and speeches uttered concerning that matter and recorded in Scripture. And lest any should be wearied with such store of allegations, in the end he concludeth, "While we labour for these demonstrations out of Scripture,

ought to bring forth the Council of Nice, nor the other the Council of Arimine, thereby to bring prejudice each to other ; neither ought the Arian to be holden by the authority of the one nor himself by the authority of the other, but by the Scriptures, which are witnesses proper to neither but common to both matter with matter, cause with cause, reason with reason, ought to be debated. Cont. Max. Arian. l. iii. c. 14." [al. lib. ii. c. 14. § 3. t. viii. 704. Nec nunc ego Nicænum, nec tu debes Ariminense tanquam præjudicaturus proferre concilium. Nec ego hujus auctoritate, nec tu illius detineris. Scripturarum auctoritatibus, non quorumque propriis, sed utrisque communibus testibus, res cum re, causa cum causa, ratio cum ratione concertet.] "And in another place against Petilian the Donatist he saith, Let not these words be heard between us, I say, You say ; let us hear this, Thus saith the Lord. And by and by speaking of the Scriptures he saith, There let us seek the Church, there let us try the cause. De Unit. Eccles. cap. 5." [cap. 2, 3. Inter nos et Donatistas quæstio est, ubi sit hoc corpus : i.e. ubi sit Ecclesia. Quid ergo facturi sumus? in verbis nostris eam quæsituri ; an in verbis capitis sui, Domini nostri Jesu Christi? Puto, quod in illius potius verbis eam quærere debemus, qui Veritas est, et optime novit corpus suum . . . . In verbis nostris Ecclesiam quæri nolumus . . . . c. 5. Non audiamus, "Hæc dicis, hoc dico," sed audiamus, "Hæc dicit Dominus." Sunt certe libri Dominici, quorum auctoritati utrique consentimus, utrique cedimus, utrique servimus : ibi quæramus Ecclesiam, ibi discutiamus causam nostram.] "Hereby [here] it is manifest, that the argument of the authority of man affirmatively is nothing worth.

[1] [P. 230. ed. Grabe. "Nobis autem conlaborantibus his ostensionibus quæ ex Scripturis sunt, et quæ multifarie dicta sunt breviter et compendiose annuntiantibus, et tu cum magnanimitate attende eis, et non longiloquium puta ; hoc intelligens : quoniam," &c.]

and do summarily declare the things which many ways have been spoken, be contented quietly to hear, and do not think my speech tedious : Quoniam ostensiones quæ sunt in Scripturis non possunt ostendi nisi ex ipsis Scripturis; Because demonstrations that are in Scripture may not otherwise be shewed than by citing them out of the Scriptures themselves where they are." Which words make so little unto the purpose, that they seem as it were offended at him which hath called them thus solemnly forth to say nothing.

And concerning the verdict of Jerome ;[1] if no man, be he never so well learned, have after the Apostles any authority to publish new doctrine as from heaven, and to require the world's assent as unto truth received by prophetical revelation ; doth this prejudice the credit of learned men's judgments in opening that truth, which by being conversant in the Apostles' writings they have themselves from thence learned?

St. Augustine exhorteth not to hear men, but to hearken what God speaketh. His purpose is not (I think) that we should stop our ears against his own exhortation, and therefore he cannot mean simply that audience should altogether be denied unto men, but either that if men speak one thing and God himself teach another, then he not they to be obeyed ; or if they both speak the same thing, yet then also man's speech unworthy of hearing, not simply, but in comparison of that which proceedeth from the mouth of God.

"Yea, but we doubt what the will of God is." Are we in this case forbidden to hear what men of judgment think it to be ? If not, then this allegation also might very well have been spared.

In that ancient strife which was between the catholic Fathers and Arians, Donatists, and others of like perverse and froward disposition, as long as to Fathers or councils alleged on the one side the like by the contrary side were opposed, impossible it was that ever the question should by this means grow unto any issue or end. The Scripture they

---

[1] [viii. 127. C. sup. Psalm 86. v. 6. " ' Dominus narrabit in scriptura populorum et principum, horum qui fuerunt in ea.' ' Principum : ' hoc est, Apostolorum et Evangelistarum. ' Horum qui fuerunt in ea.' Videte quid dicat : ' Qui fuerunt,' non ' qui sunt : ' ut exceptis Apostolis, quodcunque aliud postea dicetur, abscindatur : non habeat postea auctoritatem. Quamvis ergo sanctus sit aliquis post Apostolos, quamvis disertus sit, non habet auctoritatem."]

both believed; the Scripture they knew could not give sentence on both sides; by Scripture the controversy between them was such as might be determined. In this case what madness was it with such kinds of proofs to nourish their contention, when there were such effectual means to end all controversy that was between them! Hereby therefore it doth not as yet appear, that an argument of authority of man affirmatively is in matters divine nothing worth.

Which opinion being once inserted into the minds of the vulgar sort, what it may grow unto God knoweth. Thus much we see, it hath already made thousands so headstrong even in gross and palpable errors, that a man whose capacity will scarce serve him to utter five words in sensible manner blusheth not in any doubt concerning matter of Scripture to think his own bare *Yea* as good as the *Nay* of all the wise, grave, and learned judgments that are in the whole world: which insolency must be repressed, or it will be the very bane of Christian religion.

[7.] Our Lord's disciples marking what speech he uttered unto them, and at the same time calling to mind a common opinion held by the Scribes, between which opinion and the words of their Master it seemed unto them that there was some contradiction, which they could not themselves answer with full satisfaction of their own minds; the doubt they propose to our Saviour, saying, " Why then say the Scribes that Elias must first come?"[1] They knew that the Scribes did err greatly, and that many ways even in matters of their own profession. They notwithstanding thought the judgment of the very Scribes in matters divine to be of some value; some probability they thought there was that Elias should come, inasmuch as the Scribes said it. Now no truth can contradict any truth; desirous therefore they were to be taught how both might stand together; that which they knew could not be false, because Christ spake it; and this which to them did seem true, only because the Scribes had said it. For the Scripture, from whence the Scribes did gather it, was not then in their heads. We do not find that our Saviour reproved them of error for thinking the judgment of the Scribes to be worth the objecting, for esteeming it to be of any moment or value in matters concerning God.

[8.] We cannot therefore be persuaded that the will of God is, we should so far reject the authority of men as to

---

[1] [St. Matt. xvii. 10.]

reckon it nothing.   No, it may be a question, whether they
that urge us unto this be themselves so persuaded indeed.[1]
Men do sometimes bewray that by deeds, which to confess
they are hardly drawn.   Mark then if this be not general
with all men for the most part : when the judgments of
learned men are alleged against them, what do they but
either elevate their credit, or oppose unto them the judgments of others as learned ?   Which thing doth argue that
all men acknowledge in them some force and weight, for
which they are loath the cause they maintain should be so
much weakened as their testimony is available.   Again, what
reason is there why alleging testimonies as proofs, men give
them some title of credit, honour, and estimation, wh m
they allege, unless beforehand it be sufficiently known who
they are ; what reason hereof but only a common ingrafted
persuasion, that in some men there may be found such
qualities as are able to countervail those exceptions which
might be taken against them, and that such men's authority
is not lightly to be shaken off ?

[9.]   Shall I add further, that the force of arguments
drawn from the authority of Scripture itself, as Scriptures
commonly are alleged, shall (being sifted) be found to
depend upon the strength of this so much despised and
debased authority of man ?   Surely it doth, and that oftener
than we are aware of.   For although Scripture be of God,
and therefore the proof which is taken from thence must
needs be of all other most invincible ; yet this strength it
hath not, unless it avouch the selfsame thing for which it is
brought.   If there be either undeniable appearance that so
it doth, or reason such as cannot deceive, then Scripture-
proof (no doubt) in strength and value exceedeth all.   But
for the most part, even such as are readiest to cite for one
thing five hundred sentences of holy Scripture ; what warrant
have they, that any one of them doth mean the thing for
which it is alleged ?   Is not their surest ground most com-

---

[1]   [Christ. Letter, p. 8.   "We pray you to explane your owne meaning,
whether you thinke that there be anie naturall light, teaching knowledge
of things necessarie to salvation, which knowledge is not contayned in
holy Scripture."   Hooker MS. note.   "They are matters of salvation I
think which you handle in this booke.   If therefore determinable only
by Scripture, why presse you me so often with humane authorities?
Why alleage you the Articles of Religion as the voice of the Church
against me ?   Why cite you so many commentaries, bookes and sermons,
partly of Bishops partly of others ? "]

monly, either some probable conjecture of their own, or the judgment of others taking those Scriptures as they do ? Which notwithstanding to mean otherwise than they take them, it is not still altogether impossible. So that now and then they ground themselves on human authority, even when they most pretend divine. Thus it fareth even clean throughout the whole controversy about that discipline which is so earnestly urged and laboured for. Scriptures are plentifully alleged to prove that the whole Christian world for ever ought to embrace it. Hereupon men term it, *The Discipline of God.* Howbeit examine, sift and resolve their alleged proofs, till you come to the very root from whence they spring, the heart wherein their strength lieth ; and it shall clearly appear unto any man of judgment, that the most which can be inferred upon such plenty of divine testimonies is only this, That *some things* which they maintain, as far as *some men* can *probably conjecture*, do *seem* to have been out of Scripture *not absurdly* gathered. Is this a warrant sufficient for any man's conscience to build such proceedings upon, as have been and are put in ure for the stablishment of that cause ?

[10.] But to conclude, I would gladly understand how it cometh to pass, that they which so peremptorily do maintain that human authority is nothing worth are in the cause which they favour so careful to have the common sort of men persuaded, that the wisest, the godliest, and the best learned in all Christendom are that way given, seeing they judge this to make nothing in the world for them. Again how cometh it to pass they cannot abide that authority should be alleged on the other side, if there be no force at all in authorities on one side or other ? Wherefore labour they to strip their adversaries of such furniture as doth not help ? Why take they such needless pains to furnish also their own cause with the like ? If it be void and to no purpose that the names of men are so frequent in their books, what did move them to bring them in, or doth to suffer them there remaining ? Ignorant I am not how this is salved, "They do it not but after the truth made manifest first by Reason or by Scripture : they do it not but to control the enemies of the truth, who bear themselves bold upon human authority making not for them but against them rather."[1] Which answers are

[1] "If at any time it happened unto Augustine (as it did against the Donatists and others) to allege the authority of the ancient Fathers which

nothing: for in what place or upon what consideration soever it be they do it, were it in their own opinion of no force being done, they would undoubtedly refrain to do it.

VIII. But to the end it may more plainly appear what we are to judge of their sentences, and of the cause itself wherein they are alleged ; first, it may not well be denied, that all actions of men endued with the use of reason are generally either good or evil. For although it be granted that no action is properly termed good or evil unless it be voluntary ; yet this can be no let to our former assertion, That all actions of men endued with the use of reason are generally either good or evil ; because even those things are done voluntarily by us which other creatures do naturally, inasmuch as we might stay our doing of them if we would. Beasts naturally do take their food and rest when it offereth itself unto them. If men did so too, and could not do otherwise of themselves, there were no place for any such reproof as that of our Saviour Christ unto his disciples,[1] "Could ye not watch with me one hour ? " That which is voluntarily performed in things tending to the end, if it be well done, must needs be done with deliberate consideration of some reasonable cause wherefore we rather should do it than not. Whereupon it seemeth, that in such actions only those are said to be good or evil which are capable of deliberation : so that many things being hourly done by men, wherein they need not use with themselves any manner of consultation at all, it may perhaps hereby seem that well or ill-doing belongeth only to our weightier affairs, and to those deeds which are of such great importance that they require advice. But thus to determine were perilous, and peradventure unsound also. I do rather incline to think, that seeing all the unforced actions of men are voluntary, and all voluntary actions tending to the end have choice, and all choice presupposeth the knowledge of some cause wherefore we make it : where the reasonable cause of such actions so readily offereth itself that it needeth not to be sought for ; in those things though we do not deliberate, yet they are of their

had been before him ; yet this was not done before he had laid a sure foundation of his cause in the Scriptures, and that also being provoked by the adversaries of the truth, who bare themselves high of some council, or of some man of name that had favoured that part." T. C. lib. ii p. 22.

[1] Matt. xxvi. 40.

nature apt to be deliberated on, in regard of the will, which may incline either way, and would not any one way bend itself, if there were not some apparent motive to lead it. Deliberation actual we use, when there is doubt what we should incline our wills unto. Where no doubt is, deliberation is not excluded as impertinent unto the thing, but as needless in regard of the agent, which seeth already what to resolve upon. It hath no apparent absurdity therefore in it to think, that all actions of men endued with the use of reason are generally either good or evil.

[2.] Whatsoever is good, the same is also approved of God : and according unto the sundry degrees of goodness, the kinds of divine approbation are in like sort multiplied. Some things are good, yet in so mean a degree of goodness, that men are only not disproved nor disallowed of God for them. "No man hateth his own flesh." [1] "If ye do good unto them that do so to you, the very publicans themselves do as much." [2] "They are worse than infidels that have no care to provide for their own." [3] In actions of this sort, the very light of Nature alone may discover that which is so far forth in the sight of God allowable.

[3.] Some things in such sort are allowed, that they be also required as necessary unto salvation, by way of direct immediate and proper necessity final ; so that without performance of them we cannot by ordinary course be saved, nor by any means be excluded from life observing them. In actions of this kind our chiefest direction is from Scripture, for Nature is no sufficient teacher what we should do that we may attain unto life everlasting. The unsufficiency of the light of Nature is by the light of Scripture so fully and so perfectly herein supplied, that further light than this hath added there doth not need unto that end.

[4.] Finally some things, although not so required of necessity that to leave them undone excludeth from salvation, are notwithstanding of so great dignity and acceptation with God, that most ample reward in heaven is laid up for them. Hereof we have no commandment either in Nature or Scripture which doth exact them at our hands ; yet those motives there are in both which draw most effectually our minds unto them. In this kind there is not the least action but it doth somewhat make to the accessory augmentation of our bliss. For which cause

[1] Ephes. v. 29.　　　[2] Matt. v. 46.　　　[3] 1 Tim. v. 8.

our Saviour doth plainly witness, that there shall not be as much as a cup of cold water bestowed for his sake without reward.[1]   Hereupon dependeth whatsoever difference there is between the states of saints in glory ; hither we refer whatsoever belongeth unto the highest perfection of man by way of service towards God ; hereunto that fervour and first love of Christians did bend itself, causing them to sell their possessions, and lay down the price at the blessed Apostles' feet.[2]   Hereat St. Paul undoubtedly did aim in so far abridging his own liberty, and exceeding that which the bond of necessary and enjoined duty tied him unto.[3]

[5.] Wherefore seeing that in all these several kind of actions there can be nothing possibly evil which God approveth ; and that he approveth much more than he doth command ;[4] and that his very commandments in

---

[1] Matt. x. 42.   [2] Acts iv. 34, 35.   [3] 1 Thess. ii. 7, 9.
[4] [Chr. Letter, p. 15.   "Whether we may not justly judge, that in thus speaking you sow the seede of that doctrine which leadeth men to those arrogant workes of supererogation."

Hooker, MS. note.   "Did God command Paul not to marry, or not to receyve his daily maintenance from the Church ?   He refrained both without commandment, but not without approbation from God.   Yea, he himself doth counsell that which he doth not command, and they that followed his counsell did well, although they did it not by way of necessary obedience, but of voluntarie choice.

"Was the sale of Ananias his land allowed in God's sight ?   I hope you will graunt it was, sith the Holy Ghost commendeth sundry others which did the like.   His purpose in selling was good, but his fraud irreligious and wicked in withholding the price which he pretended to give whole.   Yeat did not God command Ananias or the rest to make any such sale.   For then how should Peter have said it was free for Ananias to have reteined it in his handes ?   God did therefore approve what he did not command in that action.

"Had not the Law as well free offerings, which were approved, as necessary, which were commanded, of God ?

"If I should ask, have you sinned in not setting your name to your book, I am very sure you will answere, no, but that you have done what God alloweth.   Yeat hath not God I think commaunded that you should conceale your name : and so you have shewed yourself heere a Papist by doing a work of supererogation, if every thing done and not commanded be such a work.   The like might be said although you had put your name thereto.   For the case is like in all workes indifferent.   But as for supererogation in poperie, it belongeth unto satisfactory actions, and not unto meritorious.   Whereas therefore with them workes not commanded are chiefly meritorious, and in merit no supererogation held, you do ill to say that he which maketh any thing not commanded allow able establisheth workes of supererogation.'

Chr. Letter, p. 15.   " You appeare to us to scatter the prophane graines of poperie."

some kind, as namely his precepts comprehended in the law of nature, may be otherwise known than only by Scripture ; and that to do them, howsoever we know them, must needs be acceptable in his sight :[1] let them with whom we have hitherto disputed consider well, how it can stand with reason to make the bare mandate of sacred Scripture the only rule of all good and evil in the actions of mortal men. The testimonies of God are true the testimonies of God are perfect, the testimonies of God are all sufficient unto that end for which they were given. Therefore accordingly we do receive them, we do not think that in them God hath omitted anything needful unto his purpose, and left his intent to be accomplished by our devisings. What the Scripture purposeth, the same in all points it doth perform.

Howbeit that here we swerve not in judgment, one thing especially we must observe, namely that the absolute perfection of Scripture is seen by relation unto that end whereto it tendeth. And even hereby it cometh to pass, that first such as imagine the general and main drift of the body of sacred Scripture not to be so large as it is, nor that God did thereby intend to deliver, as in truth he doth, a full instruction in all things unto salvation necessary, the knowledge whereof man by nature could not otherwise in this life attain unto : they are by this very mean induced either still to look for new revelations from heaven, or else dangerously to add to the word of God uncertain tradition, that so the doctrine of man's salvation may be complete ; which doctrine we constantly hold in all respects without any such thing added to be so complete, that we utterly refuse as much as once to acquaint ourselves with any thing further. Whatsoever to make up the doctrine of man's salvation is added, as in supply of the Scripture's unsufficiency, we reject it. Scripture purposing this, hath perfectly and fully done it.

Again the scope and purpose of God in delivering the

Hooker, MS. note. " It is not I that scatter, but you that gather more than ever was let fall."]

[1] [Hooker, MS. note on Chr. Letter, p. 14. " De imperfectione bonorum operum vide Hier. contra Lucifer. cap. 6." (p. 142, D. "Conveniat unusquisque cor suum, et in omni vita inveniet, quam rarum sit fidelem animam inveniri, ut nihil ob gloriæ cupiditatem, nihil ob rumusculos hominum faciat, &c.") "and Genebrard. in Symb. Athanas. p. 306."]

Holy Scripture such as do take more largely than behoveth, they on the contrary side, racking and stretching it further than by him was meant, are drawn into sundry as great inconveniences. These pretending the Scripture's perfection infer thereupon, that in Scripture all things lawful to be done must needs be contained. We count those things perfect which want nothing requisite for the end whereto they were instituted. As therefore God created every part and particle of man exactly perfect, that is to say in all points sufficient unto that use for which he appointed it; so the Scripture, yea every sentence thereof, is perfect, and wanteth nothing requisite unto that purpose for which God delivered the same. So that if hereupon we conclude, that because the Scripture is perfect, therefore all things lawful to be done are comprehended in the Scripture; we may even as well conclude so of every sentence, as of the whole sum and body thereof, unless we first of all prove that it was the drift, scope, and purpose of Almighty God in Holy Scripture to comprise all things which man may practise.

[6.] But admit this, and mark, I beseech you, what would follow. God in delivering Scripture to his Church should clean have abrogated amongst them the law of nature: which is an infallible knowledge imprinted in the minds of all the children of men, whereby both general principles for directing of human actions are comprehended, and conclusions derived from them; upon which conclusions groweth in particularity the choice of good and evil in the daily affairs of this life. Admit this, and what shall the Scripture be but a snare and a torment to weak consciences, filling them with infinite perplexities, scrupulosities, doubts insoluble, and extreme despairs?[1] Not that the Scripture itself doth cause any such thing, (for it tendeth to the clean contrary, and the fruit thereof is resolute assurance and certainty in that it teacheth,) but the necessities of this life urging men to do that which the light of nature, common discretion and judgment of itself directeth them unto; on the other side, this doctrine teaching them that so to do were to sin against their own

---

[1] " Where this doctrine is accused of bringing men to despair, it hath wrong. For when doubting is the way to despair, against which this doctrine offereth the remedy, it must need be that it bringeth comfort and joy to the conscience of man." T. C. lib. ii. p. 61.

souls, and that they put forth their hands to iniquity
whatsoever they go about and have not first the sacred
Scripture of God for direction; how can it choose but
bring the simple a thousand times to their wits' end: how
can it choose but vex and amaze them? For in every
action of common life to find out some sentence clearly
and infallibly setting before our eyes what we ought to do,
(seem we in Scripture never so expert,) would trouble us
more than we are aware. In weak and tender minds we
little know what misery this strict opinion would breed,
besides the stops it would make in the whole course of all
men's lives and actions. Make all things sin which we do
by direction of nature's light, and by the rule of common
discretion, without thinking at all upon Scripture; admit
this position, and parents shall cause their children to sin,
as oft as they cause them to do any thing, before they
come to years of capacity and be ripe for knowledge in the
Scripture: admit this, and it shall not be with masters as
it was with him in the Gospel, but servants being commanded to go [1] shall stand still, till they have their errand
warranted unto them by Scripture. Which as it standeth
with Christian duty in some cases, so in common affairs to
require it were most unfit.

[7.] Two opinions therefore there are concerning sufficiency of Holy Scripture, each extremely opposite unto
the other, and both repugnant unto truth. The schools of
Rome teach Scripture to be so unsufficient, as if, except
traditions were added, it did not contain all revealed and
supernatural truth, which absolutely is necessary for the
children of men in this life to know that they may in the
next be saved. Others justly condemning this opinion
grow likewise unto a dangerous extremity, as if Scripture
did not only contain all things in that kind necessary, but
all things simply, and in such sort that to do any thing
according to any other law were not only unnecessary but
even opposite unto salvation, unlawful and sinful. Whatsoever is spoken of God or things appertaining to God
otherwise than as the truth is; though it seem an honour,
it is an injury. And as incredible praises given unto men
do often abate and impair the credit of their deserved
commendation; so we must likewise take great heed, lest
in attributing unto Scripture more than it can have, the

[1] Luke vii. 8.

incredibility of that do cause even those things which indeed it hath most abundantly to be less reverently esteemed. I therefore leave it to themselves to consider, whether they have in this first point or not overshot themselves ; which God doth know is quickly done, even when our meaning is most sincere, as I am verily persuaded theirs in this case was.

THE THIRD BOOK

CONCERNING THEIR SECOND ASSERTION, THAT IN SCRIP-
TURE THERE MUST BE OF NECESSITY CONTAINED A FORM
OF CHURCH POLITY, THE LAWS WHEREOF MAY IN NOWISE
BE ALTERED

THE MATTER CONTAINED IN THIS THIRD BOOK

I. What the Church is, and in what respect Laws of Polity are thereunto
   necessarily required.

II. Whether it be necessary that some particular Form of Church Polity
    be set down in Scripture, sith the things that belong particularly
    to any such Form are not of necessity to Salvation.

III. That matters of Church Polity are different from matters of Faith
     and Salvation, and that they themselves so teach which are our
     reprovers for so teaching.

IV. That hereby we take not from Scripture any thing which thereunto
    with the soundness of truth may be given.

V. Their meaning who first urged against the Polity of the Church of
   England, that nothing ought to be established in the Church more
   than is commanded by the Word of God.

VI. How great injury men by so thinking should offer unto all the
    Churches of God.

VII. A shift notwithstanding to maintain it, by interpreting *commanded*,
     as though it were meant that greater things only ought to be
     found set down in Scripture particularly, and lesser framed by
     the general rules of Scripture.

VIII. Another device to defend the same, by expounding *commanded*,
      as if it did signify *grounded* on Scripture, and were opposed to
      things found out by light of natural reason only.

IX. How Laws for the Polity of the Church may be made by the advice
    of men, and how those Laws being not repugnant to the Word
    of God, are approved in his sight.

X. That neither God's being the Author of Laws, nor yet his committing of them to Scripture, is any reason sufficient to prove that
   they admit no addition or change.

XI. Whether Christ must needs intend Laws unchangeable altogether,
    or have forbidden any where to make any other Law than himself
    did deliver.

I. ALBEIT the substance of those controversies whereinto
we have begun to wade be rather of outward things appertaining to the Church of Christ, than of any thing wherein the
nature and being of the Church consisteth, yet because the
subject or matter which this position concerneth is, *A Form
of Church Government* or *Church Polity*, it therefore behoveth

us so far forth to consider the nature of the Church, as is
requisite for men's more clear and plain understanding in
what respect Laws of Polity or Government are necessary
thereunto.

[2.] That Church of Christ, which we properly term his
body mystical, can be but one; neither can that one be
sensibly discerned by any man, inasmuch as the parts thereof
are some in heaven already with Christ, and the rest that are
on earth (albeit their natural persons be visible) we do not
discern under this property, whereby they are truly and infallibly of that body. Only our minds by intellectual conceit
are able to apprehend, that such a real body there is, a
body collective, because it containeth an huge multitude; a
body mystical, because the mystery of their conjunction is
removed altogether from sense. Whatsoever we read in
Scripture concerning the endless love and the saving mercy
which God sheweth towards his Church, the only proper
subject thereof is this Church. Concerning this flock it is
that our Lord and Saviour hath promised, "I give unto
them eternal life, and they shall never perish, neither shall
any pluck them out of my hands."[1] They who are of this
society have such marks and notes of distinction from all
others, as are not object unto our sense; only unto God,
who seeth their hearts and understandeth all their secret
cogitations, unto him they are clear and manifest. All men
knew Nathanael to be an Israelite. But our Saviour piercing
deeper giveth further testimony of him than men could
have done with such certainty as he did, " Behold indeed
an Israelite in whom is no guile."[2] If we profess, as Peter
did,[3] that we love the Lord, and profess it in the hearing of
men, charity is prone to believe all things, and therefore
charitable men are likely to think we do so, as long as they
see no proof to the contrary. But that our love is sound
and sincere, that it cometh from " a pure heart and a good
conscience and a faith unfeigned,"[4] who can pronounce,
saving only the Searcher of all men's hearts, who alone
intuitively doth know in this kind who are His?

[3.] And as those everlasting promises of love, mercy, and
blessedness belong to the mystical Church; even so on the
other side when we read of any duty which the Church of
God is bound unto, the Church whom this doth concern

---

[1] John x. 28.
John xxi. 15.

[2] John i. 47.
[4] Tim. i. 5.

is a sensibly known company. And this visible Church in like sort is but one, continued from the first beginning of the world to the last end. Which company being divided into two moieties, the one before, the other since the coming of Christ ; that part, which since the coming of Christ partly hath embraced and partly shall hereafter embrace the Christian religion, we term as by a more proper n me the Church of Christ. And therefore the Apostle affirmeth plainly of all men Christian,[1] that be they Jews or Gentiles, bond or free, they are all incorporated into one company, they all make but *one body*.[2] The unity of which visible body and Church of Christ consisteth in that uniformity which all several persons thereunto belonging have, by reason of that *one Lord* whose servants they all profess themselves, that *one Faith* which they all acknowledge, that *one Baptism* wherewith they are all initiated.[3]

[4.] The visible Church of Jesus Christ is therefore one, in outward profession of those things, which supernaturally appertain to the very essence of Christianity, and are necessarily required in every particular Christian man. "Let all the house of Israel know for certainty," saith Peter, "that God hath made him both Lord and Christ, even this Jesus whom you have crucified."[4] Christians therefore they are not, which call not him their Master and Lord.[5] And from hence it came that first at Antioch, and afterwards throughout the whole world, all that are of the Church visible were called Christians even amongst the heathen. Which name unto them was precious and glorious, but in the estimation of the rest of the world even Christ Jesus himself was execrable ;[6] for whose sake all men were so likewise which did acknowledge him to be their Lord. This himself did foresee, and therefore armed his Church,

---

[1] Cor. xii. 13.

[2] " That he might reconcile both unto God in one body." Ephes. ii. 16. "That the Gentiles should be inheritors also, and of the same body." Ephes. iii. 6. Vide Th. p. 3. q. 7. art. 3. [should it not be "q. 8. art. 3"?]

[3] [Ephes. iv. 5.]   [4] Acts ii. 36.   [5] John xiii. 13 ; Col. iii. 24 ; iv. 1.

[6] 1 Cor. i. 23. Vide et Tacitum, lib. Annal. xv. [c. 44] "Nero quæsitissimis pœnis affecit quos per flagitia invisos vulgus Christianos appellabat. Auctor nominis ejus Christus, qui Tiberio imperitante per procuratorem Pontium Pilatum supplicio affectus erat. Repressaque in præsens exitiabilis superstitio rursus erumpebat, non modo per Judæam, originem ejus mali, sed per urbem etiam, quo cuncta undique atrocia aut pudenda confluunt celebranturque."

to the end they might sustain it without discomfort. "All these things they will do unto you for my name's sake ; yea, the time shall come, that whosoever killeth you will think that he doth God good service."[1] "These things I tell you, that when the hour shall come, ye may then call to mind how I told you beforehand of them."[2]

[5.] But our naming of Jesus Christ the Lord is not enough to prove us Christians, unless we also embrace that faith, which Christ hath published unto the world. To shew that the angel of Pergamus continued in Christianity, behold how the Spirit of Christ speaketh, "Thou keepest my name, and thou hast not denied my faith."[3] Concerning which faith "the rule thereof," saith Tertullian, "is one alone, immovable, and no way possible to be better framed anew."[4] What rule that is he sheweth by rehearsing those few articles of Christian belief. And before Tertullian, Ireney ; "The Church though scattered through the whole world unto the utmost borders of the earth, hath from the Apostles and their disciples received belief."[5] The parts of which belief he also reciteth, in substance the very same with Tertullian, and thereupon inferreth, "This faith the Church being spread far and wide preserveth as if one house did contain them: these things it equally embraceth, as though it had even one soul, one heart, and no more : it publisheth teacheth and delivereth these things with uniform consent, as if God had given it but one only tongue wherewith to speak. He which amongst the guides of the Church is best able to speak uttereth no more than this, and less than this the most simple doth not utter," when they make profession of their faith.

[6.] Now although we know the Christian faith and allow of it, yet in this respect we are but entering ; entered we

---

[1] John xv. 21.   [2] John xvi. 2. 4.   [3] Apoc. ii. 13.
[4] Tertull. de Virgin. Veland. [c. 1. "Regula quidem fidei una omnino est, sola immobilis et irreformabilis."]
[5] Iren advers. Hæres. lib. i. cap. 2. et 3. ['Η μὲν ἐκκλησία, καίπερ καθ' ὅλης τῆς οἰκουμένης ἕως περάτων τῆς γῆς διεσπαρμένη, παρὰ δὲ τῶν Ἀποστόλων καὶ τῶν ἐκείνων μαθητῶν παραλαβοῦσα τὴν . . . πίστιν . . .
And c. iii. Ταύτην τὴν πίστιν, ὡς προέφαμεν, ἡ ἐκκλησία, καίπερ ἐν ὅλῳ τῷ κόσμῳ διεσπαρμένη, ἐπιμελῶς φυλάσσει, ὡς ἕνα οἶκον οἰκοῦσα· καὶ ὁμοίως πιστεύει τούτοις, ὡς μίαν ψυχὴν καὶ τὴν αὐτὴν ἔχουσα καρδίαν· καὶ συμφώνως ταῦτα κηρύσσει καὶ διδάσκει καὶ παραδίδωσιν, ὡς ἓν στόμα κεκτημένη . . . καὶ οὔτε ὁ πάνυ δυνατὸς ἐν λόγῳ τῶν ἐν ταῖς ἐκκλησίαις προεστώτων ἕτερα τούτων ἐρεῖ . . . οὔτε ὁ ἀσθενὴς ἐν τῷ λόγῳ ἐλαττώσει τὴν παράδοσιν.]

are not into the visible Church before our admittance by
the door of Baptism. Wherefore immediately upon the
acknowledgment of Christian faith, the Eunuch (we see)
was baptized by Philip,[1] Paul by Ananias.[2] by Peter an
huge multitude containing three thousand souls,[3] which
being once baptized were reckoned in the number of souls
added to the visible Church.

[7.] As for those virtues that belong unto moral righteousness and honesty of life, we do not mention them, because
they are not proper unto Christian men, as they are Christian,
but do concern them as they are men.   True it is, the want
of these virtues excludeth from salvation.[4]   So doth much
more the absence of inward belief of heart ; so doth despair
and lack of hope ; so emptiness of Christian love and
charity.   But we speak now of the visible Church, whose
children are signed with this mark, "One Lord, one Faith,
one Baptism."   In whomsoever these things are, the Church
doth acknowledge them for her children ; them only she
holdeth for aliens and strangers, in whom these things are
not found.   For want of these it is that Saracens, Jews,

---

[1] Acts viii. 38.   [2] Acts xxii. 16.   [3] Acts ii. 41.

[4] [Chr. Letter, p. 8. "Whether you mean . . . that morall virtues
are any where rightlie taught but in holy Scripture : *or that wheresoever
they be taught, they be of such necessitie, that the wante of them exclude
from salvation, and what Scripture approveth such a saying?*"

Hooker, MS. note. "A doctrine which would well have pleased
Caligula, Nero, and such other monsters to heare. Had thapostles
taught this it might have advanced them happily to honour. The contrary doctrine hath cost many saints and martyrs their lives."

Ibid. p. 13. "The very cause why good workes cannot justify is for
that evell workes do exclude from salvation : And the most righteous
in some things offend. Vid. Philon. p. 205." (εἰ γὰρ βουληθείη ὁ θεὸς
δικάσαι τῷ θνητῷ χωρὶς ἐλέου, τὴν καταδικάζουσαν ψῆφον οἴσει, μηδενὸς
ἀνθρώπων τὸν ἀπὸ γενέσεως μέχρι τελευτῆς βίον ἄπταιστον ἐξ ἑαυτοῦ
δραμόντος, ἀλλὰ τοῦ μὲν ἑκουσίοις, τοῦ δὲ ἀκουσίοις χρησαμένου τοῖς ἐν
ποσὶν ὀλισθήμασιν.)

And again, ibid. "The workes of heathen men not acceptable *propter pravum agendi principium.* Vide Eucher." ("Licet dicere, Philo-
sophiæ alios nomen usurpasse, nos vitam. Etenim, qualia ab his dari
possunt præcepta vivendi? Causam nesciunt : ignorantes enim Deum, et
statim ab exordio justitiæ declinantes, consequenti in cætera feruntur
errore. Sic fit postea, ut studiorum talium finis sit vanitas. Siqui apud
illos honestiora definiunt, huic jactantiæ deserviunt, huic laborant : ita
apud eos non est vacua vitiis abstinentia vitiorum." Epist. ad Valerian.
in Bibl. Patr. Colon. 1618. t. iv. p. 777.)

And again, ibid. "Morall workes done in faith, hope and charitie
are accepted and rewarded with God, the want thereof punished with
eternal death. Noe fornicator, adulterer, &c."]

and Infidels are excluded out of the bounds of the Church. Others we may not deny to be of the visible Church, as long as these things are not wanting in them. For apparent it is, that all men are of necessity either Christians or not Christians. If by external profession they be Christians, then are they of the visible Church of Christ; and Christians by external profession they are all, whose mark of recogniz· ance hath in it those things which we have mentioned, yea, although they be impious idolaters, wicked heretics, persons excommunicable, yea, and cast out for notorious improbity. Such withal we deny not to be the imps and limbs of Satan, even as long as they continue such.

[8.] Is it then possible, that the selfsame men should belong both to the synagogue of Satan and to the Church of Jesus Christ? Unto that Church which is his mystical body, not possible; because that body consisteth of none but only true Israelites, true sons of Abraham, true servants and saints of God. Howbeit of the visible body and Church of Jesus Christ those may be and oftentimes are, in respect of the main parts of their outward profession, who in regard of their inward disposition of mind, yea, of external convers· ation, yea, even of some parts of their very profession, are most worthily both hateful in the sight of God himself, and in the eyes of the sounder part of the visible Church most execrable. Our Saviour therefore compareth the kingdom of heaven to a net, whereunto all which cometh neither is nor seemeth fish:[1] his Church he compareth unto a field, where tares manifestly known and seen by all men do grow intermingled with good corn,[2] and even so shall continue till the final consummation of the world. God hath had ever and ever shall have some Church visible upon earth. When the people of God worshipped the calf in the wilder· ness;[3] when they adored the brazen serpent;[4] when they served the gods of nations; when they bowed their knees to Baal;[5] when they burnt incense and offered sacrifice unto idols:[6] true it is, the wrath of God was most fiercely inflamed against them, their prophets justly condemned them, as an adulterous seed[7] and a wicked generation miscreants, which had forsaken the living God,[8] and of him were likewise forsaken,[9] in respect of that singular mercy

---

[1] Matt. xiii. 47.   [2] Matt. xiii. 24.   [3] Exod. xxxii; Ps. cvi. 19, 20.
[4] 2 Kings xviii. 4.   [5] Jer. xi. 13.   [6] 2 Kings xxii. 17.   [7] Isa. lvii. 3.
[8] Isa. i. 4.   [9] Isa. lx. 15.

wherewith he kindly and lovingly embraced his favourite children. Howbeit retaining the law of God and the holy seal of his covenant, the sheep of his visible flock they continued even in the depth of their disobedience and rebellion.[1] Wherefore not only *amongst* them God always had his Church, because he had thousands which never bowed their knees to Baal;[2] but whose knees were bowed unto Baal, even they were also of the visible Church of God. Nor did the Prophet so complain, as if that Church had been quite and clean extinguished; but he took it as though there had not been remaining in the world any besides himself, that carried a true and an upright heart towards God with care to serve him according unto his holy will.

[9.] For lack of diligent observing the difference, first between the Church of God mystical and visible, then between the visible sound and corrupted, sometimes more, sometimes less, the oversights are neither few nor light that have been committed. This deceiveth them, and nothing else, who think that in the time of the first world the family of Noah did contain all that were of the visible Church of God. From hence it grew, and from no other cause in the world, that the African bishops in the council of Carthage,[3] knowing how the administration of baptism belongeth only to the Church of Christ, and supposing that heretics which were apparently severed from the sound believing Church could not possibly be of the Church of Jesus Christ, thought it utterly against reason, that baptism administered by men of corrupt belief should be accounted as a sacrament. And therefore in maintenance of rebaptization their arguments are built upon the fore-alleged ground,[4] "That heretics are not at all any part of the Church of Christ. Our Saviour founded his Church on a rock, and not upon heresy.[5] Power of baptizing he gave to his Apostles, unto heretics he gave it not.[6] Wherefore they that are without the Church, and oppose themselves against Christ, do but scatter his sheep and flock, without the Church baptize they cannot." Again, "Are heretics Christians or are they not? If they

---

[1] Jer. xiii. 11.   [2] 1 Kings xix. 18.   [3] [A. D. 256.]
[4] Fortunat. in Concil. Car. ["Jesus Christus, Dominus et Deus noster, Dei Patris et Creatoris Filius, super petram ædificavit Ecclesiam suam, non super hæresin; et potestatem baptizandi Episcopis dedit, non hæreticis. Quare qui extra Ecclesiam sunt, et contra Christum stantes oves ejus et gregem spargunt, baptizare foris non possunt." t. i. 233. ed. Fell.]
[5] Matt. vii. 24; xvi. 18.   [6] Matt. xxviii. 19.

be Christians, wherefore remain they not in God's Church?
If they be no Christians, how make they Christians? Or
to what purpose shall those words of the Lord serve:
'He which is not with me is against me;' and, 'He
which gathereth not with me scattereth?'[1] Wherefore
evident it is, that upon misbegotten children and the brood
of Antichrist without rebaptization the Holy Ghost cannot
descend."[2] But none in this case so earnest as Cyprian:[3]
" I know no baptism but one, and that in the Church only;
none without the Church, where he that doth cast out the
Devil hath the Devil; he doth examine about belief whose
lips and words do breathe forth a canker; the faithless doth
offer the articles of faith; a wicked creature forgiveth
wickedness; in the name of Christ Antichrist si_neth;
he which is cursed of God blesseth; a dead carrion pro-
miseth life; a man unpeaceable giveth peace; a blasphemer
calleth upon the name of God; a profane person doth
exercise priesthood; a sacrilegious wretch doth prepare
the altar; and in the neck of all these that evil also
cometh, the Eucharist a very bishop of the Devil doth presume to consecrate." All this was true, but not sufficient
to prove that heretics were in no sort any part of the visible
Church of Christ, and consequently their baptism no
baptism. This opinion was therefore afterwards both condemned by a better advised council,[4] and also revoked by
the chiefest of the authors thereof themselves.

[1] Matt. xii. 30.

[2] Secundinus in eodem Concil. [ibid. p. 234. " Hæretici Christiani
sunt, an non? Si Christiani sunt, cur in Ecclesia Dei non sunt? Si
Christiani non sunt, quomodo Christianos faciunt? aut quo pertinebit
sermo Domini dicentis, Qui non est mecum adversus me est, et qui non
mecum colligit spargit? Unde constat, super filios alienos et soboles
Antichristi Spiritum Sanctum per manus impositionem tantummodo non
posse descendere."]

[3] [Not Cyprian, but another Cæcilius, Bishop of Bilta in Mauritania,
ibid. 230. " Ego unum baptisma in Ecclesia sola scio, et extra Ecclesiam nullum. Hic erit unum, ubi spes vera est et fides certa. Sic enim
scriptum est: 'Una fides, una spes, unum baptisma,' non apud hæreticos, ubi spes nulla est, et fides falsa, ubi omnia per mendacium aguntur,
ubi exorcizat dæmoniacus; sacramentum interrogat cujus os et verba
cancer emittunt; fidem dat infidelis; veniam delictorum tribuit sceler-
atus; in nomine Christi tingit Antichristus; benedicit a Deo maledictus;
vitam pollicetur mortuus; pacem dat impacificus; Deum invocat blas-
phemus; sacerdotium administrat prophanus; ponit altare sacrilegus.
Ad hæc omnia accedit et illud malum, ut antistites Diaboli audeant
Eucharistiam facere."]

[4] In Concilio Niceno. Vide Hieron. Dial. adv. Lucifer. [ii. 146.

[10.] What is but only the selfsame error and misconceit, wherewith others being at this day likewise possessed, they ask us where our Church did lurk, in what cave of the earth it slept for so many hundreds of years together before the birth of Martin Luther? As if we were of opinion that Luther did erect a new Church of Christ. No, the Church of Christ which was from the beginning is and continueth unto the end : of which Church all parts have not been always equally sincere and sound. In the days of Abia it plainly appeareth that Judah was by many degrees more free from pollution than Israel, as that solemn oration sheweth wherein he pleadeth for the one against the other in this wise : [1] "O Jeroboam and all Israel hear you me : have ye not driven away the priests of the Lord, the sons of Aaron and the Levites, and have made you priests like the people of nations? Whosoever cometh to consecrate with a young bullock and seven rams, the same may be a priest of them that are no gods. But we belong unto the Lord our God and have not forsaken him ; and the priests the sons of Aaron minister unto the Lord every morning and every evening burnt-offerings and sweet incense, and the bread is set in order upon the pure table, and the candlestick of gold with the lamps thereof to burn every evening ; for we keep the watch of the Lord our God, but ye have forsaken

The genuine canons of the council of Nice contain no express general enactment on this point : only the 8th canon exempts the Novatians from rebaptization, the 19th imposes it on the followers of Paul of Samosata. The principle however, for which Hooker contends, is plainly implied in these two enactments. See Routh, Scriptorum Ecclesiasticorum Opuscula, p. 359, 366. The 7th canon of Constantinople is more express : but its genuineness is doubted : however it may safely be appealed to for the practice of the orthodox church in that age, ibid. 379, 450. The passage from St. Jerome is as follows : "Conatus est beatus Cyprianus contritos lacus fugere, nec bibere de aqua aliena ; et idcirco hæreticorum baptisma reprobans, ad Stephanum tunc Romanæ urbis Episcopum, qui a beato Petro vigesimus sextus fuit, super hac re Africanam synodum direxit : sed conatus ejus frustra fuit. Denique illi ipsi episcopi, qui rebaptizandos hæreticos cum eo statuerant, ad antiquam consuetudinem revoluti, novum emisere decretum." (But see the viiith canon of the council of Arles, (A.D. 314.) as quoted by Dr. Routh, Reliquiæ Sacræ, III. 137. and his note there, which seems to prove that St. Jerome did not mean a formal repeal of St. Cyprian's rule, but a discontinuance of it in practice, sanctioned as we know by St. Augustin, who was Jerome's contemporary.) And p. 147, A. "Synodus quoque Nicæna . . . omnes hæreticos suscepit, exceptis Pauli Samosateni discipulis."]

[1] 2 Chron. xiii. 4, 9, 10, 11.

him."[1]   In St. Paul's time the integrity of Rome was
famous; Corinth many ways reproved; they of Galatia
much more out of square.[2]   In St. John's time Ephesus
and Smyrna in far better state than Thyatira and Pergamus
were.[3]   We hope therefore that to reform ourselves if at
any time we have done amiss, is not to sever ourselves from
the Church we were of before. In the Church we were,
and we are so still. Other difference between our estate before and now we know none but only such as we see in Judah;
which having sometime been idolatrous became afterwards
more soundly religious by renouncing idolatry and superstition. If Ephraim "be joined unto idols," the counsel of
the Prophet is, "Let him alone."   "If Israel play the
harlot, let not Judah sin."[4]   "If it seem evil unto you,"
saith Joshua,[5] "to serve the Lord, choose you this day
whom you will serve; whether the gods whom your fathers
served beyond the flood, or the gods of the Amorites in
whose land ye dwell: but I and mine house will serve the
Lord." The indisposition therefore of the Church of Rome
to reform herself must be no stay unto us from performing
our duty to God; even as desire of retaining conformity
with them could be no excuse if we did not perform that
duty.

Notwithstanding so far as lawfully we may, we have held
and do hold fellowship with them. For even as the Apostle
doth say of Israel that they are in one respect enemies but
in another beloved of God;[6] in like sort with Rome we
dare not communicate concerning sundry her gross and
grievous abominations, yet touching those main parts of
Christian truth wherein they constantly still persist, we

---

[1] [See the conclusion of Hooker's first Sermon on part of St. Jude.]

[2] [Rom. i. 8; 1 Cor. i. iii.-vi. ; Gal. i. 6.]

[3] Apoc. ii. Vide S. Hieron. [ubi sup. 146. Apostolis adhuc in seculo
aperstitibus, adhuc apud Judæam Christi sanguine recenti, phantasma
Domini corpus asserebatur: Galatas ad observationem legis traductos
Apostolus iterum parturit: Corinthios resurrectionem carnis non cre-
dentes pluribus argumentis ad verum iter trahere conatur. . . . Plurimi
(hæreticorum) vivente adhuc Joanne Apostolo eruperunt. . . . Angelo
Ephesi deserta charitas imputatur: in angelo Pergamenæ Ecclesiæ,
idolothytorum esus, et Nicolaitarum doctrina reprehenditur: item apud
angelum Thiatyrorum, Hiezabel Prophetissa, et simulacrorum escæ,
et fornicationes increpantur. Et tamen omnes hos ad pœnitentiam
Dominus hortatur . . . non autem cogeret pœnitere, si non esset
pœnitentibus veniam concessurus."]

[4] Hos. iv. 17, 15.   [5] Josh. xxiv. 15.   [6] Rom. xi. 28.

gladly acknowledge them to be of the family of Jesus
Christ; and our hearty prayer unto God Almighty is, that
being conjoined so far forth with them, they may at the
length (if it be his will) so yield to frame and reform themselves, that no distraction remain in any thing, but that
we "all may with one heart and one mouth glorify God
the Father of our Lord and Saviour,"[1] whose Church we
are.

As there are which make the Church of Rome utterly no
Church at all, by reason of so many, so grievous errors in
their doctrines; so we have them amongst us, who under
pretence of imagined corruptions in our discipline do give
even as hard a judgment of the Church of England itself.[2]

[11.] But whatsoever either the one sort or the other
teach, we must acknowledge even heretics themselves to be,
though a maimed part, yet a part of the visible Church. If
an infidel should pursue to death an heretic professing
Christianity, only for Christian profession's sake, could we
deny unto him the honour of martyrdom? Yet this honour
all men know to be proper unto the Church. Heretics
therefore are not utterly cut off from the visible Church of
Christ.

If the Fathers do any where, as oftentimes they do, make
the true visible Church of Christ and heretical companies
opposite; they are to be construed as separating heretics,
not altogether from the company of believers, but from the
fellowship of sound believers. For where professed unbelief is, there can be no visible Church of Christ; there
may be, where sound belief wanteth. Infidels being clean
without the Church deny directly and utterly reject the very
principles of Christianity; which heretics embrace, and err
only by misconstruction: whereupon their opinions, although
repugnant indeed to the principles of Christian faith, are
notwithstanding by them held otherwise, and maintained as
most consonant thereunto. Wherefore being Christians in
regard of the general truth of Christ which they openly profess, yet they are by the Fathers every where spoken of as
men clean excluded out of the right believing Church, by
reason of their particular errors, for which all that are of a
sound belief must needs condemn them.

[12.] In this consideration, the answer of Calvin unto

---

[1] Rom. xv. 6.   [2] [See Pref. c. viii. 1.]

Farel concerning the children of Popish parents doth seem crazed.[1] "Whereas," saith he, "you ask our judgment about a matter, whereof there is doubt amongst you, whether ministers of our order professing the pure doctrine of the Gospel may lawfully admit unto baptism an infant whose father is a stranger unto our Churches, and whose mother hath fallen from us unto the Papacy, so that both the parents are popish : thus we have thought good to answer; namely, that it is an absurd thing for us to baptize them which cannot be reckoned members of our body. And sith Papists' children are such, we see not how it should be lawful to minister baptism unto them." Sounder a great deal is the answer of the ecclesiastical college of Geneva unto Knox, who having signified unto them, that himself did not think it lawful to baptize bastards or the children of idolaters (he meaneth Papists) or of persons excommunicate, till either the parents had by repentance submitted themselves unto the Church, or else their children being grown unto the years of understanding should come and sue for their own baptism : "For thus thinking," saith he, "I am thought to be over-severe, and that not only by them which are popish, but even in their judgments also who think themselves maintainers of the truth."[2] Master Knox's oversight herein they controlled. Their sentence was, "Wheresoever the profession of Christianity hath not utterly perished and been extinct, infants are beguiled of their right, if the common seal be denied them."[3] Which conclusion in itself is sound, although it seemeth the ground is but weak whereupon they built it. For the reason which

---

[1] Calvin. Epist. 149. [p. 173. ed. Genev. 1617. "Rogas, liceatne ordinis nostri ministris, qui puram evangelii doctrinam profitentur, ad baptismum admittere infantem, cujus pater ab ecclesiis nostris alienus est, mater vero ad Papatum defecit, ita ut parentes ambo sint Papistæ : ita respondendum censuimus; absurdum esse ut eos baptizemus, qui corporis nostri membra censeri nequeunt. Quum in hoc ordine sint Papistarum liberi, quomodo baptismum illis administrare liceat, non videmus."]

[2] Epist. 283. [Ibid. p. 441. "An ad baptismum admitti debeant spurii, idololatrarum et excommunicatorum filii, priusquam vel parentes per resipiscentiam sese subdiderint Ecclesiæ, vel ii qui ex hujusmodi prognati sunt, baptismum petere possint. Quia nego, plus æquo severus judicor, non a solis Papisticis, verum etiam ab iis qui sibi veritatis patroni videntur."]

[3] Epist. 285. [Ibid. p. 442. "Ubicunque non prorsus intercidit, vel extincta fuit Christianismi professio, fraudantur jure suo infantes, si a communi symbolo arcentur."]

they yield of their sentence, is this; "The promise which
God doth make to the faithful concerning their seed
reacheth unto a thousand generations; it resteth not only
in the first degree of descent. Infants therefore whose
great-grandfathers have been holy and godly, do in that
respect belong to the body of the Church, although the
fathers and grandfathers of whom they descend have been
apostates : because the tenure of the grace of God which
did adopt them three hundred years ago and more in their
ancient predecessors, cannot with justice be defeated and
broken off by their parents' impiety coming between."[1]
By which reason of theirs although it seem that all the
world may be baptized, inasmuch as no man living is a
thousand descents removed from Adam himself, yet we
mean not at this time either to uphold or to overthrow it :
only their alleged conclusion we embrace, so it be construed
in this sort; "That forasmuch as men remain in the
visible Church, till they utterly renounce the profession of
Christianity, we may not deny unto infants their right by
withholding from them the public sign of holy baptism,
if they be born where the outward acknowledgment of
Christianity is not clean gone and extinguished." For
being in such sort born, their parents are within the Church,
and therefore their birth doth give them interest and right
in baptism.

[13.] Albeit not every error and fault, yet heresies and
crimes which are not actually repented of and forsaken,
exclude quite and clean from that salvation which belongeth
unto the mystical body of Christ; yea, they also make a
separation from the visible sound Church of Christ;
altogether from the visible Church neither the one nor the
other doth sever. As for the act of excommunication, it
neither shutteth out from the mystical, nor clean from the
visible, but only from fellowship with the visible in holy
duties. With what congruity then doth the Church of

---

[1] [Calv. ubi supra. "Imprimis expendere convenit, quos Deus sua
voce ad baptismum invitet. Promissio autem non sobolem tantum cujusque
fidelium in primo gradu comprehendit, sed in mille generationes extend-
itur. . . . Nobis ergo minime dubium est, quin soboles ex piis et sanctis
atavis progenita, quamvis apostatæ fuerint avi et parentes, ad Ecclesiæ
tamen corpus pertineant. . . . Quia iniquum est, cum Deus ante annos
trecentos vel plures adoptione sua eos dignatus fuerit, ut quæ deinde
secuta est parentum impietas cælestis gratiæ cursum abrumpat." The
former letter was dated 1553, this 1559.]

Rome deny, that her enemies, whom she holdeth always for heretics, do at all appertain to the Church of Christ; when her own do freely grant, that albeit the Pope (as they say) cannot teach heresy nor propound error, he may notwithstanding himself worship idols, think amiss concerning matters of faith,[1] yea, give himself unto acts diabolical, even being Pope? How exclude they us from being any part of the Church of Christ under the colour and pretence of heresy, when they cannot but grant it possible even for him to be as touching his own personal persuasion heretical,[2] who in their opinion not only is of the Church, but holdeth the chief place of authority over the same? But of these things we are not now to dispute. That which already we have set down, is for our present purpose sufficient.

[14.] By the Church therefore in this question we understand no other than only the visible Church. For preservation of Christianity there is not any thing more needful, than that such as are of the visible Church have mutual fellowship and society one with another. In which consideration, as the main body of the sea being one, yet within divers precincts hath divers names; so the Catholic Church is in like sort divided into a number of distinct Societies, every of which is termed a Church within itself. In this sense the Church is always a visible society of men; not an assembly, but a Society. For although the name of the Church be given unto Christian assemblies, although any multitude of Christian men congregated may be termed by the name of a Church, yet assemblies properly are rather things that belong to a Church. Men are assembled for performance of public actions; which actions being ended, the assembly dissolveth itself and is no longer in being, whereas the Church which was assembled doth no less continue afterwards than before. "Where but three are, and they of the

---

[1] [Harding ap. Jewel. Def. of Apol. 632. ed. 1611. "The Pope may err by personal error, in his own private judgment, as a man; and as a particular Doctor in his own opinion: yet as he is Pope . . . in public judgment, in deliberation, and definitive sentence, he never erreth nor ever erred."]

[2] [Alphonsus de Castro de Hær. i. 4, ap. Jewel. 633. "Non dubitamus an hæreticum esse, et Papam esse, coire in unum possint. . . . Non enim credo aliquem esse adeo impudentem Papæ assentatorem, ut ei tribuere hoc velit, ut nec errare, nec in interpretatione sacrarum literarum hallucinari possit." This passage was omitted in the later editions of the work. See Laud's Conf. with Fisher, p. 263, 264. ed. 1639.]

laity also (saith Tertullian), yet there is a Church;"[1] that is to say, a Christian assembly. But a Church, as now we are to understand it, is a Society; that is, a number of men belonging unto some Christian fellowship, the place and limits whereof are certain. That wherein they have communion is the public exercise of such duties as those mentioned in the Apostles' Acts, "instruction, breaking of bread and prayer."[2] As therefore they that are of the mystical body of Christ have those inward graces and virtues, whereby they differ from all others, which are not of the same body; again, whosoever appertain to the visible body of the Church, they have also the notes of external profession, whereby the world knoweth what they are: after the same manner even the several societies of Christian men, unto every of which the name of a Church is given with addition betokening severalty, as the Church of Rome, Corinth, Ephesus, England, and so the rest, must be endued with correspondent general properties belonging unto them as they are public Christian societies. And of such properties common unto all societies Christian, it may not be denied that one of the very chiefest is Ecclesiastical Polity.

Which word I therefore the rather use, because the name of Government, as commonly men understand it in ordinary speech, doth not comprise the largeness of that whereunto in this question it is applied. For when we speak of Government, what doth the greatest part conceive thereby, but only the exercise of superiority peculiar unto Rulers and Guides of others? To our purpose therefore the name of Church-Polity will better serve, because it containeth both government and also whatsoever besides belongeth to the ordering of the Church in public. Neither is any thing in this degree more necessary than Church-Polity, which is a form of ordering the public spiritual affairs of the Church of God.

II. But we must note, that he which affirmeth speech to be necessary among all men throughout the world, doth not thereby import that all men must necessarily speak one kind of language. Even so the necessity of polity and regiment in all Churches may be held without holding any one certain form to be necessary in them all. Nor is it

---

[1] Tertull. Exhort. ad Castit. [c. 7.] "Ubi tres, Ecclesia est, licet Laici."

[2] Acts ii. 42.

possible that any form of polity, much less of polity ecclesiastical, should be good, unless God himself be author of it.[1] "Those things that are not of God" (saith Tertullian), "they can have no other than God's adversary for their author." Be it whatsoever in the Church of God, if it be not of God, we hate it. Of God it must be; either as those things sometime were, which God supernaturally revealed, and so delivered them unto Moses for government of the commonwealth of Israel; or else as those things which men find out by help of that light which God hath given them unto that end.[2] The very Law of Nature itself, which no man can deny but God hath instituted, is not of God, unless that be of God whereof God is the author as well this latter way as the former. But forasmuch as no form of Church-Polity is thought by them to be lawful, or to be of God, unless God be so the author of it that it be also set down in Scripture; they should tell us plainly, whether their meaning be that it must be there set down in whole or in part. For if wholly, let them shew what one form of Polity ever was so. Their own to be so taken out of Scripture they will not affirm; neither deny they that in part even this which they so much oppugn is also from thence taken. Again they should tell us, whether only that be taken out of Scripture, which is actually and particularly there set down; or else that also which the general principles and rules of Scripture potentially contain. The one way they cannot as much as pretend, that all the parts of their own discipline are in Scripture: and the other way their mouths are stopped, when they would plead against all other forms besides their own; seeing the general principles are such as do not particularly prescribe any one, but sundry may equally be consonant unto the general axioms of the Scripture.

[2.] But to give them some larger scope and not to close them up in these straits: let their allegations be considered, wherewith they earnestly bend themselves against all which deny it necessary that any one complete form of church polity should be in Scripture. First therefore whereas it hath been told them [3] that matters of faith, and in general matters

---

[1] Tertull. de habitu mul. [c. 8.] "Æmuli sint necesse est, quæ Dei non sunt."

[2] Rom. ii. 15. "Ille legis hujus inventor, disceptator, lator." Cic. iii. de Repub. [ap. Lact. vi. 8. and Opp. vii. 906. Ed. Ernesti.]

[3] [In Whitgift's Answer to the Admon. 20, 21. See Def. 76, &c.]

necessary unto Salvation, are of a different nature from
ceremonies, order, and the kind of church government ; and
that the one is necessary to be expressly contained in the
word of God, or else manifestly collected out of the same,
the other not so ; that it is necessary not to receive the one,
unless there be something in Scripture for them ; the other
free, if nothing against them may thence be alleged : although
there do not appear any just or reasonable cause to reject
or dislike of this, nevertheless as it is not easy to speak to
the contentation of minds exulcerated in themselves, but
that somewhat there will be always which displeaseth ; so
herein for two things we are reproved. [1] The first is *mis-
distinguishing*, because matters of discipline and church
government are (as they say) " matters necessary to salvation
and of faith," whereas we put a difference between the one
and the other. Our second fault is, *injurious dealing* with
the Scripture of God, as if it contained only " the principal
points of religion, some rude and unfashioned matter of
building the Church, but had left out that which belongeth

[1] Two things misliked ; the one, that we distinguish matters of discipline or church government from matters of faith and necessary unto
salvation : the other, that we are injurious to the Scripture of God in
abridging the large and rich contents thereof. Their words are these :
" You which distinguish between these, and say, that matters of faith
and necessary unto salvation may not be tolerated in the Church, unless
they be expressly contained in the word of God, or manifestly gathered ;
but that ceremonies, order, discipline, government in the Church, may
not be received against the word of God, and consequently may be
received if there be no word against them, although there be none for
them : you (I say) distinguishing or dividing after this sort do prove
yourself an evil divider. As though matters of discipline and a kind of
government were not matters necessary to salvation and of faith." [This
sentence (" as though . . . of faith ") is transposed by Hooker to this
place, from where it occurs in T. C. a few lines above.] " It is no
small injury which you do unto the word of God to pin it in so narrow
room, as that it should be able to direct us but in the principal points of
our religion ; or as though the substance of religion, or some rude and
unfashioned matter of building of the Church were uttered in them ; and
those things were left out that should pertain to the form and fashion of
it ; or as if there were in the Scriptures only to cover the Church's
nakedness, and not also chains and bracelets and rings and other jewels
to adorn her and set her out ; or that, to conclude there were sufficient
to quench her thirst and kill her hunger, but not to minister unto her a
more liberal and (as it were) a more delicious and dainty diet. These
things you seem to say, when you say, that matters necessary to Salvation
and of Faith are contained in Scripture ; especially when you oppose these
things to Ceremonies, Order, Discipline, and Government." T. C. lib. i.
p. 26. [14.]

unto the form and fashion of it ; as if there were in the Scripture no more than only to cover the Church's naked-ness, and not chains, bracelets, rings, jewels, to adorn her ; sufficient to quench her thirst, to kill her hunger, but not to minister a more liberal, and (as it were) a more delicious and dainty diet." In which case [1] our apology shall not need to be ve y long.

III. The mixture of those things by speech which by nature are divided, is the mother of all error. To take away therefore that error which confusion breedeth, dis-tinction is requisite. Rightly to distinguish is by conceit of mind to sever things different in nature, and to discern wherein they differ. So that if we imagine a difference where there is none, because we distinguish where we should not, it may not be denied that we misdistinguish. The only trial whether we do so, yea or no, dependeth upon com-parison between our conceit and the nature of things conceived.

[2.] Touching matters belonging unto the Church of Christ this we conceive, that they are not of one suit. Some things are *merely* of faith, which things it doth suffice that we know and believe ; some things not only to be known but done, because they concern the action of men. Articles about the Trinity are matters of *mere* faith, and must be believed. Precepts concerning the works of charity are matters of action ; which to know, unless they be practised, is not enough. This being so clear to all men's understand-ing, I somewhat marvel that they especially should think it absurd to oppose Church-government, a plain matter of action, unto matters of faith, who know that themselves divide the Gospel into Doctrine and Discipline.[2] For if matters of discipline be rightly by them distinguished from matters of doctrine, why not matters of government by us as reasonably set against matters of faith ? Do not they under doctrine comprehend the same which we intend by matter of faith ? Do not they under discipline comprise the regiment of the Church ? When they blame that in us which themselves follow, they give men great cause to

---

[1] [cause ?]

[2] T. C. l. ii. p. I. "We offer to shew the Discipline to be a part of the Gospel." And again, p. 5. "I speak of the Discipline as of a part of the Gospel." If the Discipline be one part of the Gospel, what other part can they assign but Doctrine to answer in division to the Discipline ? [See also lib. i. p. 32.]

doubt that some other thing than judgment doth guide their speech.

[3.] What the Church of God standeth bound to know or do, the same in part nature teacheth. And because nature can teach them but only in part, neither so fully as is requisite for man's salvation, nor so easily as to make the way plain and expedite enough that many may come to the knowledge of it, and so be saved ; therefore in Scripture hath God both collected the most necessary things that the school of nature teacheth unto that end, and revealeth also whatsoever we neither could with safety be ignorant of, nor at all be instructed in but by supernatural revelation from him. So that Scripture containing all things that are in this kind any way needful for the Church, and the principal of the other sort, this is the next thing wherewith we are charged as with an error : we teach that whatsoever is unto salvation termed *necessary* by way of excellency, whatsoever it standeth all men upon to know or do that they may be saved, whatsoever there is whereof it may truly be said, "This not to believe is eternal death and damnation," or, "This every soul that will live must duly observe;" of which sort the articles of Christian faith and the sacraments of the Church of Christ are : all such things if Scripture did not comprehend, the Church of God should not be able to measure out the length and the breadth of that way wherein for ever she is to walk, heretics and schismatics never ceasing some to abridge, some to enlarge, all to pervert and obscure the same. But as for those things that are accessory hereunto, those things that so belong to the way of salvation, as to alter them is no otherwise to change that way, than a path is changed by altering only the uppermost face thereof ; which be it laid with gravel, or set with grass, or paved with stone, remaineth still the same path ; in such things because discretion may teach the Church what is convenient, we hold not the Church further tied herein unto Scripture, than that against Scripture nothing be admitted in the Church, lest that path which ought always to be kept even, do thereby come to be overgrown with brambles and thorns.

[4.] If this be unsound, wherein doth the point of unsoundness lie ? It is not that we make some things *necessary*, some things *accessory* and appendent only : for our Lord and Saviour himself doth make that difference, by terming judgment and mercy and fidelity with other things of like nature,

"the greater and weightier matters of the law." [1] Is it then
in that we account ceremonies (wherein we do not comprise
sacraments, or any other the like sustained duties in the
exercise of religion, but only such external rites as are usually
annexed unto church actions), is it an oversight that we
reckon these things and matters [2] of government in the
number of things accessory, not things necessary in such
sort as hath been declared? Let them which therefore think
us blameable consider well their own words.   Do they not
plainly compare the one unto garments which cover the
body of the Church ; the other unto rings, bracelets, and
jewels, that only adorn it ; the one to that food which the
Church doth live by, the other to that which maketh her
diet liberal, dainty, and more delicious? [3]   Is dainty fare a
thing necessary to the sustenance, or to the clothing of the
body rich attire ?   If not, how can they urge the necessity
of that which themselves resemble by things not necessary?
or by what construction shall any man living be able to
make those comparisons true, holding that distinction
untrue, which putteth a difference between things of external
regiment in the Church and things necessary unto salvation?

IV. Now as it can be to nature no injury that of her we
say the same which diligent beholders of her works have
observed ; namely, that she provideth for all living creatures
nourishment which may suffice ; that she bringeth forth no
kind of creature whereto she is wanting in that which is
needful : [4] although we do not so far magnify her exceeding

---

[1] Matt. xxiii. 23.

[2] The government of the Church of Christ granted by Fenner himself
to be thought a matter of great moment, yet not of the substance of
religion. Against D. Bridges, pag. 121 : if it be Fenner which was the
author of that book. ["A Defence of the Ecclesiastical Discipline
ordayned of God to be used in His Church, against a Reply of Maister
Bridges to 'a briefe and plain Declaration' of it, which was printed an.
1584." 4°. 1588, p. 120, 121.   "Our Saviour is sayde, with charge and
commaundement that they should be observed, to have delivered to His
Disciples such things, as for the space of fourtie days He declared unto
them concerning His kingdome.   A part whereof (it hathe bin alreadie
shewed) must needes be understoode to have bin of the governement of
His Church, which necessarilie *dependeth on* His kingdome."]

[3] ["Mirum videri debet . . . doctrina evangelica tanquam bona
valetudine contentos, de disciplina, qua eandem tueantur, ac vires simul et
colorem acquirant, non esse solicitos." Eccl. Disc. fol. 2.   Medicis con-
tenta, qui salutem procurassent, aliptas ad colorem et vires acquirendas
non adhibuit." fol. 3.]

[4] Arist. Pol. lib. i. c. 8 et Plato in Menex. [t. ii. 237. E. ed. Serrani.

bounty, as to affirm that she bringeth into the world the
sons of men adorned with gorgeous attire, or maketh costly
buildings to spring up out of the earth for them : so I trust
that to mention what the Scripture of God leaveth unto the
Church's discretion in some things, is not in any thing to
impair the honour which the Church of God yieldeth to the
sacred Scripture's perfection. Wherein seeing that no more
is by us maintained, than only that Scripture must needs
teach the Church whatsoever is in such sort necessary as
hath been set down ; and that it is no more disgrace for
Scripture to have left a number of other things free to be
ordered at the discretion of the Church, than for nature to
have left it unto the wit of man to devise his own attire, and
not to look for it as the beasts of the field have theirs : if
neither this can import, nor any other proof sufficient be
brought forth, that we either will at any time or ever did
affirm the sacred Scripture to comprehend no more than
only those bare necessaries ; if we acknowledge that as well
for particular application to special occasions, as also in
other manifold respects, infinite treasures of wisdom are
over and besides abundantly to be found in the Holy
Scripture ; yea that scarcely there is any noble part of
knowledge, worthy the mind of man, but from thence it
may have some direction and light; yea, that although
there be no necessity it should of purpose prescribe any
one particular form of church government, yet touching the
manner of governing in general the precepts that Scripture
setteth down are not few, and the examples many which it
proposeth for all church governors even in particularities to
follow ; yea, that those things finally which are of principal
weight in the very particular form of church polity (although
not that form which they imagine, but that which we against
them uphold) are in the selfsame Scriptures contained : if
all this be willingly granted by us which are accused to pin
the word of God in so narrow room, as that it should be
able to direct us but in principal points of our religion ; or
as though the substance of religion or some rude and unfashioned matter of building the Church were uttered in
them, and those things left out that should pertain to the
form and fashion of it ; let the cause of the accused be
referred to the accuser's own conscience, and let that judge

πᾶν γὰρ τὸ τεκὸν τροφὴν ἔχει ἐπιτηδείαν ᾧ ἂν τέκῃ.]   Arist. lib. iii. de
Animal. c. 4, 5.

whether this accusation be deserved where it hath been laid.

V. But so easy it is for every man living to err, and so hard to wrest from any man's mouth the plain acknowledgment of error, that what hath been once inconsiderately defended, the same is commonly persisted in, as long as wit by whetting itself is able to find out any shift, be it never so sleight, whereby to escape out of the hands of present contradiction. So that it cometh herein to pass with men unadvisedly fallen into error, as with them whose state hath no ground to uphold it, but only the help which by subtile conveyance they draw out of casual events arising from day to day, till at length they be clean spent. They which first gave out, that "nothing ought to be established in the Church which is not commanded by the word of God," thought this principle plainly warranted by the manifest words of the Law,[1] "Ye shall put nothing unto the word which I command you, neither shall you take aught therefrom, that ye may keep the commandments of the Lord your God, which I command you." Wherefore having an eye to a number of rites and orders in the Church of England, as marrying with a ring, crossing in the one sacrament, kneeling at the other, observing of festival days more than only that which is called the Lord's day, enjoining abstinence at certain times from some kinds of meat, churching of women after childbirth, degrees taken by divines in universities, sundry church offices, dignities, and callings, for which they found no commandment in the Holy Scripture, they thought by the one only stroke of that axiom to have cut them off. But that which they took for an oracle being sifted was repelled. True it is concerning the word of God, whether it be by misconstruction of the sense or by falsification of the words, wittingly to endeavour that any thing may seem divine which is not, or any thing not seem which is, were plainly to abuse, and even to falsify divine evidence ; which injury offered but unto men, is most worthily counted heinous. Which point I wish they did well observe, with whom nothing is more familiar than to plead in these causes, "the law of God," "the word of

---

[1] "Whatsoever I command you, take heed you do it." "Thou shalt put nothing thereto, nor take aught therefrom." Deut. iv. 2. and xii. 32. [Adm. p. 3. See also Answ. 59, 60, 61. T. C. i. 21, 22. Eccl. Disc. fol. 5.]

the Lord;" who notwithstanding when they come to allege
what word and what law they mean, their common ordinary
practice is to quote by-speeches in some historical narration
or other, and to urge them as if they were written in most
exact form of law. What is to add to the law of God if
this be not? When that which the word of God doth but
deliver historically, we construe without any warrant as if it
were legally meant, and so urge it further than we can prove
that it was intended; do we not add to the laws of God,
and make them in number seem more than they are? It
standeth us upon to be careful in this case. For the
sentence of God is heavy against them that wittingly shall
presume thus to use the Scripture.[1]

VI. But let that which they do hereby intend be granted
them; let it once stand as consonant to reason, that because
we are forbidden to add to the law of God any thing, or to
take aught from it, therefore we may not for matters of the
Church make any law more than is already set down in
Scripture: who seeth not what sentence it shall enforce us
to give against all Churches in the world, inasmuch as there
is not one, but hath had many things established in it,
which though the Scripture did never command, yet for us
to condemn were rashness? Let the Church of God even
in the time of our Saviour Christ serve for example unto all
the rest. In their domestical celebration of the passover,
which supper they divided (as it were) into two courses:
what Scripture did give commandment that between the
first and the second he that was chief should put off the
residue of his garments, and keeping on his feast-robe[2]
only wash the feet of them that were with him? What
Scripture did command them never to lift up their hands
unwashed in prayer unto God? which custom Aristeas (be
the credit of the author more or less) sheweth wherefore
they did so religiously observe.[3] What Scripture did
command the Jews every festival-day to fast till the sixth
hour? the custom both mentioned by Josephus in the

---

[1] [Rev. xxii. 18.]

[2] John xiii. Cœnatorium: de quo Matt xxii. 12. Ibi de Cœnatorio
nuptiali.

[3] [De LXX Interpretibus, ad calc. Josephi, Colon. 1691, p. 33.
ἐπεꝛώτησαν δὲ καὶ τοῦτο· τίνος χάριν ἀπονιζόμενοι τὰς χεῖρας, τὸ τηνι-
καῦτα εὔχονται; διεσάφουν δὲ, ὅτι μαρτύριόν ἐστι τοῦ μηδὲν εἰργάσθαι
κακόν· πᾶσα γὰρ ἐνέργεια διὰ τῶν χειρῶν γίνεται.]

history of his own life,[1] and by the words of Peter signified.[2] Tedious it were to rip up all such things as were in that church established, yea by Christ himself and by his Apos le observed, though not commanded any where in Scripture.

VII. Well, yet a gloss there is to colour that paradox, and notwithstanding all this, still to make it appear in show not to be altogether unreasonable. And therefore till further reply come, the cause is held by a feeble distinction ; that the commandments of God being either general or special, although there be no express word for every thing in specialty, yet there are general commandments for all things, to the end, that even such cases as are not in Scripture particularly mentioned, might not be left to any to order at their pleasure, only with caution that nothing be done against the word of God : and that for this cause the Apostle hath set down in Scripture four general rules, requiring such things alone to be received in the Church as do best and nearest agree with the same rules, that so all things in the Church may be appointed, not only *not against*, but *by* and *according to* the word of God. The rules are these, " Nothing scandalous or offensive unto any, especially unto the Church of God ; " [3] " All things in order and with seemliness ; " [4] " All unto edification ; " [5] finally, " All to the glory of God." [6] Of which kind how many might be gathered out of the Scripture, if it were necessary to take so much pains ? Which rules they that urge, minding thereby to prove that nothing may be done in the Church but what Scripture commandeth, must needs hold that they tie the Church of Christ no otherwise than only because we find them there set down by the finger of the Holy Ghost. So that unless the Apostle by writing had delivered those rules to the Church, we should by observing them have sinned, as now by not observing them.

[2.] In the Church of the Jews is it not granted,[7] that the appointment for the hour for daily sacrifices ; the building of synagogues throughout the land to hear the word of God

---

[1] [c. 54. τὴν σύνοδον διέλυσεν ἐπελθοῦσα ἕκτη ὥρα, καθ᾽ ἣν τοῖς σάββασιν ἀριστοποιεῖσθαι νόμιμόν ἐστιν ἡμῖν. cf. Acts x. 9.]

[2] [Acts ii. 15.] [3] 1 Cor. x. 32. [4] 1 Cor. xiv. 40.

[5] 1 Cor. xiv. 26.

[6] Rom. xiv. 6, 7. [and 1 Cor. x. 31 ; see T. C. i. 27.]

[7] T. C. lib. i. p. 35. [21.]

and to pray in, when they came not up to Jerusalem, the erecting of pulpits and chairs to teach in, the order of burial, the rites of marriage, with such-like, being matters appertaining to the Church, yet are not any where prescribed in the law, but were by the Church's discretion instituted? What then shall we think? Did they hereby add to the law, and so displease God by that which they did? None so hardly persuaded of them. Doth their law deliver unto them the selfsame general rules of the Apostle, that framing thereby their orders they might in that respect clear themselves from doing amiss? St. Paul would then of likelihood have cited them out of the Law, which we see he doth not. The truth is, they are rules and canons of that law which is written in all men's hearts ; the Church had for ever no less than now stood bound to observe them, whether the Apostle had mentioned them or no.

Seeing therefore those canons do bind as they are edicts of nature, which the Jews observing as yet unwritten, and thereby framing such church orders as in their law were not prescribed, are notwithstanding in that respect unculpable : it followeth that sundry things may be lawfully done in the Church, so as they be not done against the Scripture, although no Scripture do command them, but the Church only following the light of reason judge them to be in discretion meet.

[3.] Secondly, unto our purpose and for the question in hand, whether the commandments of God in Scripture be general or special, it skilleth not : for if being particularly applied they have in regard of such particulars a force constraining us to take some one certain thing of many, and to leave the rest ; whereby it would come to pass, that any other particular but that one being established, the general rules themselves in that case would be broken ; then is it utterly impossible that God should leave any thing great or small free for the Church to establish or not.

[4.] Thirdly, if so be they shall grant, as they cannot otherwise do, that these rules are no such laws as require any one particular thing to be done, but serve rather to direct the Church in all things which she doth ; so that free and lawful it is to devise any ceremony, to receive any order, and to authorize any kind of regiment, no special commandment being thereby violated, and the same being thought such by them, to whom the judgment thereof

appertaineth, as that it is not scandalous, but decent,
tending unto edification, and setting forth the glory of God;
that is to say, agreeable unto the general rules of Holy
Scripture: this doth them no good in the world for the
furtherance of their purpose.   That which should make for
them must prove that men ought not to make laws for
church regiment, but only keep those laws which in Scripture they find made.   The plain intent of the Book of
Ecclesiastical Discipline[1] is to shew that men may not
devise laws of church government, but are bound for ever
to use and to execute only those which God himself hath
already devised and delivered in the Scripture.   The selfsame drift the Admonitioners also had, in urging that
nothing ought to be done in the Church according unto
any law of man's devising, but all according to that which
God in his word hath commanded.   Which not remembering, they gather out of Scripture general rules to be followed
in making laws; and so in effect they plainly grant that we
ourselves may lawfully make laws for the Church, and are
not bound out of Scripture only to take laws already made,
as they meant who first alleged that principle whereof we
speak.   One particular platform it is which they respected,
and which they laboured thereby to force upon all Churches;
whereas these general rules do not let but that there may
well enough be sundry.   It is the particular order established
in the Church of England, which thereby they did intend
to alter, as being not commanded of God; whereas unto
those general rules they know we do not defend that we
may hold any thing unconformable.   Obscure it is not what
meaning they had, who first gave out that grand axiom;
and according unto that meaning it doth prevail far and
wide with the favourers of that part.   Demand of them,
wherefore they conform not themselves unto the order of
our Church, and in every particular their answer for the
most part is, "We find no such thing commanded in the
word:" whereby they plainly require some special commandment for that which is exacted at their hands; neither
are they content to have matters of the Church examined
by general rules and canons.

[5.] As therefore in controversies between us and the
Church of Rome, that which they practise is many times
even according to the very grossness of that which the

---

[1] [By Travers, Geneva 1580.]

vulgar sort conceiveth ; when that which they teach to
maintain it is so nice and subtile that hold can very hardly
be taken thereupon ; in which cases we should do the
Church of God small benefit by disputing with them
according unto the finest points of their dark conveyances,
and suffering that sense of their doctrine to go uncontrolled,
wherein by the common sort it is ordinarily received and
practised : so considering what disturbance hath grown in
the Church amongst ourselves, and how the authors thereof
do commonly build altogether on this as a sure foundation,
"Nothing ought to be established in the Church which in
the word of God is not commanded ;" were it reason that
we should suffer the same to pass without controlment in
that current meeting whereby every where it prevaileth, and
stay till some strange construction were made thereof, which
no man would lightly have thought on but being driven
thereunto for a shift ?

VIII. The last refuge in maintaining this position is thus
to construe it, "Nothing ought to be established in the
Church, but that which is commanded in the word of
God ;" that is to say, all church orders must be "grounded
upon the word of God ;"[1] in such sort grounded upon the
word, not that being found out by some "star, or light of
reason, or learning, or other help," they may be received, so
they be not against the word of God ; but according at
leastwise unto the general rules of Scripture they must be
made. Which is in effect as much as to say, "We know
not what to say well in defence of this position ; and therefore lest we should say it is false, there is no remedy but to
say that in some sense or other it may be true, if we could
tell how."

[2.] First, that scholy had need of a very favourable
reader and a tractable, that should think it plain construction, when to be *commanded in the Word* and *grounded
upon the Word* are made all one. If when a man may live
in the state of matrimony, seeking that good thereby which
nature principally desireth,[2] he make rather choice of a
contrary life in regard of St. Paul's judgment ;[3] that which
he doth is manifestly *grounded* upon the word of God, yet
not *commanded* in his word, because without breach of any
commandment he might do otherwise.

[3.] Secondly, whereas no man in justice and reason can

---

[1] [T. C. ii. 56.]   [2] Arist. Pol. i. 2.   [3] 1 Cor. vii. 8, 26.

be reproved for those actions which are framed according
unto that known will of God, whereby they are to be
judged ; and the will of God which we are to judge our
actions by, no sound divine in the world ever denied to be
in part made manifest even by light of nature, and not by
Scripture alone : if the Church being directed by the former
of these two (which God hath given who gave the other,
that man might in different sort be guided by them both),
if the Church I say do approve and establish that which
thereby it judgeth meet, and findeth not repugnant to any
word or syllable of holy Scripture ; who shall warrant our
presumptuous boldness controlling herein the Church of
Christ ?

[4.] But so it is, the name of the light of nature is made
hateful with men ; the "star of reason and learning," and
all other such like helps, beginneth no otherwise to be
thought of than if it were an unlucky comet ; or as if God
had so accursed it, that it should never shine or give light
in things concerning our duty any way towards him, but be
esteemed as that star in the Revelation [1] called Wormwood,
which being fallen from heaven, maketh rivers and waters in
which it falleth so bitter, that men tasting them die thereof.
A number there are, who think they cannot admire as they
ought the power and authority of the word of God, if in
things divine they should attribute any force to man's
reason.   For which cause they never use reason so willingly
as to disgrace reason.   Their usual and common discourses
are unto this effect.   First, "the natural man perceiveth not
the things of the Spirit of God ; for they are foolishness
unto him : neither can he know them, because they are
spiritually discerned." [2]   Secondly, it is not for nothing that
St. Paul giveth charge to "beware of philosophy," [3] that is
to say, such knowledge as men by natural reason attain unto.
Thirdly, consider them that have from time to time opposed
themselves against the Gospel of Christ, and most troubled
the Church with heresy.   Have they not always been great
admirers of human reason ?   Hath their deep and profound
skill in secular learning made them the more obedient to the
truth, and not armed them rather against it ?   Fourthly, they
that fear God will remember how heavy his sentences are in
this case : " I will destroy the wisdom of the wise, and will cast
away the understanding of the prudent.   Where is the wise ?

[1] Apoc. viii. 10.   [2] 1 Cor. ii. 14.   Col. ii. 8.

where is the scribe? where is the disputer of this world?
hath not God made the wisdom of this world foolishness?
Seeing the world by wisdom knew not God in the wisdom
of God, it pleased God by the foolishness of preaching to
save believers."[1] Fifthly, the word of God in itself is
absolute, exact, and perfect. The word of God is a two-
edged sword;[2] as for the weapons of natural reason, they
are as the armour of Saul,[3] rather cumbersome about the
soldier of Christ than needful. They are not of force to do
that which the Apostles of Christ did by the power of the
Holy Ghost: "My preaching," therefore saith Paul, "hath
not been in the enticing speech of man's wisdom, but in
plain evidence of the Spirit and of power, that your faith
might not be in the wisdom of men, but in the power of
God."[4] Sixthly, if I believe the Gospel, there needeth no
reasoning about it to persuade me; if I do not believe, it
must be the Spirit of God and not the reason of man that
shall convert my heart unto him. By these and the like
disputes an opinion hath spread itself very far in the world,
as if the way to be ripe in faith were to be raw in wit and
judgment; as if Reason were an enemy unto Religion,
childish Simplicity the mother of ghostly and divine
Wisdom.

[5.] The cause why such declamations prevail so greatly,
is, for that men suffer themselves in two respects to be de-
luded: one is, that the wisdom of man being debased either
in comparison with that of God, or in regard of some special
thing exceeding the reach and compass thereof, it seemeth
to them (not marking so much) as if simply it were condemned: another, that learning, knowledge, or wisdom,
falsely so termed, usurping a name whereof they are not
worthy, and being under that name controlled; their reproof
is by so much the more easily misapplied, and through
equivocation wrested against those things whereunto so
precious names do properly and of right belong This,
duly observed, doth to the former allegations itself make
sufficient answer. Howbeit, for all men's plainer and fuller
satisfaction:

[6.] First, Concerning the inability of reason to search
out and to judge of things divine, if they be such as those
properties of God and those duties of men towards him

---

[1] i Cor. i. 19. [2] [Heb. iv. 12.]
[3] [1 Sam. xvii. 39.] [4] i Cor. ii. 4.

which may be conceived by attentive consideration of heaven and earth; we know that of mere natural men the Apostle testifieth,[1] how they knew both God, and the Law of God. Other things of God there be which are neither so found, nor though they be shewed can ever be approved without the *special* operation of God's good grace and Spirit. Of such things sometime spake the Apostle St. Paul, declaring how Christ had called him to be a witness of his death and resurrection from the dead, according to that which the Prophets and Moses had foreshewed. Festus, a mere natural man, an infidel, a Roman, one whose ears were unacquainted with such matter, heard him, but could not reach unto that whereof he spake; the suffering and the rising of Christ from the dead he rejecteth as idle superstitious fancies not worth the hearing.[2] The Apostle that knew them by the Spirit, and spake of them with power of the Holy Ghost, seemed in his eyes but learnedly mad.[3] Which example maketh manifest what elsewhere the same Apostle teacheth, namely, that nature hath need of grace,[4] whereunto I hope we are not opposite, by holding that grace hath use of nature.

[7.] Secondly, Philosophy we are warned to take heed of: not that philosophy, which is true and sound knowledge attained by natural discourse of reason; but that philosophy, which to bolster heresy or error casteth a fradulent show of reason upon things which are indeed unreasonable, and by that mean as by a stratagem spoileth the simple which are not able to withstand such cunning. "Take heed lest any spoil you through philosophy and vain deceit."[5] He that exhorteth to beware of an enemy's policy doth not give counsel to be impolitic, but rather to use all provident foresight and circumspection, lest our simplicity be overreached by cunning sleights. The way not to be inveigled by them that are so guileful through skill, is thoroughly to be instructed in that which maketh skilful against guile, and to be armed with that true and sincere philosophy, which doth teach, against that deceitful and vain, which spoileth.

[8.] Thirdly, But many great philosophers have been very unsound in belief. And many sound in belief, have been also great philosophers. Could secular knowledge bring the one sort unto the love of Christian faith? Nor Christian faith the other sort out of love with secular knowledge. The

---

[1] Rom. i. 21. 32.   [2] Acts xxv. 19.   [3] Acts xxvi. 24.
[4] 1 Cor. ii. 14.   [5] Col. ii. 8.

harm that heretics did, they did it unto such as were unable
to discern between sound and deceitful reasoning; and the
remedy against it was ever the skill which the ancient Fathers
had to descry and discover such deceit. Insomuch that
Cresconius the heretic complained greatly of St. Augustine,
as being too full of logical subtilties.[1] Heresy prevaileth
only by a counterfeit show of reason; whereby notwithstanding it becometh invincible, unless it be convicted of
fraud by manifest remonstrance clearly true and unable to
be withstood. When therefore the Apostle requireth ability
to convict heretics,[2] can we think he judgeth it a thing unlawful, and not rather needful, to use the principal instrument
of their conviction, the light of reason? It may not be
denied but that in the Fathers' writings there are sundry
sharp invectives against heretics, even for their very philoso-
phical reasonings. The cause whereof Tertullian confesseth
not to have been any dislike conceived against the kind of
such reasonings, but the end.[3] "We may," saith he, "even
in matters of God be made wiser by reasons drawn from the

[1] [S. Aug. contr. Crescon. i. 16. t. ix. 397. "Quid est aliud Dialectica, quam peritia disputandi? Quod ideo aperiendum putavi, quia
etiam ipsam mihi objicere voluisti, quasi 'Christianæ non congruat
veritati, et ideo me doctores vestri, velut hominem dialecticum, merito
fugiendum potius et cavendum, quam refellendum revincendumque
censuerint.' Quod cum tibi non persuaserint, nam te adversus nos
etiam scribendo disputare non piguit, tu tamen in me dialecticam
criminatus es, quo falleres imperitos, eosque laudares qui disputando
mecum congredi noluerant. Sed tu videlicet non dialectica uteris, cum
contra nos scribis?"]

[2] Tit. i. 9, 11.

[3] Tert. de Resur. Carnis, [c. 3. "Est quidem et de communibus
sensibus sapere in Dei rebus, sed in testimonium veri, non in adju-
torium falsi; quod sit secundum divinam, non contra divinam dispositionem. Quædam enim et natura nota sunt, ut immortalitas animæ
penes plures, ut Deus noster penes omnes. Utar ergo et sententia
Platonis alicujus pronunciantis, 'Omnis anima immortalis.' Utar et
conscientia populi, contestantis Deum Deorum . . . At cum aiunt,
'Mortuum quod mortuum,' et, 'Vive dum vivis,' et, 'Post mortem
omnia finiuntur, etiam ipsa:' tunc meminero, et cor vulgi cinerem a
Deo deputatum, et ipsam sapientiam sæculi stultitiam pronunciatam.
Tunc si et hæreticus ad vulgi vitia, vel sæculi ingenia confugerit,
'Discede,' dicam, 'ab ethnico, hæretice; etsi unum estis omnes qui
Deum fingitis; dum hoc tamen in Christi nomine facis, dum Christianus
tibi videris, alius ab ethnico es. Redde illi suos sensus, quia nec ille
de tuis instruitur. Quid cæco duci inniteris, si vides? Quid vestiris a
mundo, si Christum induisti? Quid alieno uteris clypeo, si ab Apostolo
armatus es? Ille potius a te discat carnis resurrectionem confiteri,
quam tu ab illo diffiteri.'"]

public persuasions, which are grafted in men's minds: so
they be used to further the truth, not to bolster error; so
they make with, not against, that which God hath determined.
For there are some things even known by nature, as the
immortality of the soul unto many, our God unto all. I
will therefore myself also use the sentence of some such as
Plato, pronouncing every soul immortal. I myself too will
use the secret acknowledgment of the commonalty, bearing
record of the God of gods. But when I hear men allege,
'That which is dead is dead;' and, 'While thou art alive be
alive ,' and, 'After death an end of all, even of death itself:'
then will I call to mind both that the heart of the people
with God is accounted dust,[1] and that the very wisdom of
the world is pronounced folly.[2] If then an heretic fly also
unto such vicious popular and secular conceits, my answer
unto him shall be, 'Thou heretic, avoid the heathen;
although in this ye be one, that ye both belie God, yet thou
that doest this under the name of Christ, differest from the
heathen, in that thou seemest to thyself a Christian. Leave
him therefore his conceits, seeing that neither will he learn
thine. Why dost thou having sight trust to a blind guide;
thou which hast put on Christ take raiment of him that is
naked? If the Apostle have armed thee, why dost thou
borrow a stranger's shield? Let him rather learn of thee to
acknowledge, than thou of him to renounce the resurrection
of the flesh.'" In a word, the Catholic Fathers did good
unto all by that knowledge, whereby heretics hindering the
truth in many, might have furthered therewith themselves,
but that obstinately following their own ambitious or otherwise corrupted affections, instead of framing their wills to
maintain that which reason taught, they bent their wits to
find how reason might seem to teach that which their wills
were set to maintain. For which cause the Apostle saith of
them justly, that they are for the most part αὐτοκατάκριτοι,
men condemned even in and of themselves.[3] For though
they be not all persuaded that it is truth which they withstand, yet that to be error which they uphold they might
undoubtedly the sooner a great deal attain to know, but that
their study is more to defend what once they have stood in,
than to find out sincerely and simply what truth they ought
to persist in for ever.

---

[1] [Isai. xliv. 20.]   [2] [1 Cor. iii. 19.]   [3] Tit. iii. 11.

[9.] Fourthly, There is in the world no kind of knowledge, whereby any part of truth is seen, but we justly account it precious ; yea, that principal truth, in comparison whereof all other knowledge is vile, may receive from it some kind of light ; whether it be that Egyptian and Chaldean wisdom mathematical, wherewith Moses and Daniel were furnished ;[1] or that natural, moral, and civil wisdom, wherein Solomon excelled all men ;[2] or that rational and oratorial wisdom of the Grecians, which the Apostle St. Paul brought from Tarsus ; or that Judaical, which he learned in Jerusalem sitting at the feet of Gamaliel :[3] to detract from the dignity thereof were to injury[4] even God himself, who being that light which none can approach unto, hath sent out these lights whereof we are capable, even as so many sparkles resembling the bright fountain from which they rise.

But there are that bear the title of wise men and scribes and great disputers of the world, and are nothing in deed less than what in show they most appear. These being wholly addicted unto their own wills, use their wit, their learning, and all the wisdom they have, to maintain that which their obstinate hearts are delighted with, esteeming in the frantic error of their minds the greatest madness in the world to be wisdom, and the highest wisdom foolishness. Such were both Jews and Grecians, which professed the one sort legal, and the other secular skill, neither enduring to be taught the mystery of Christ : unto the glory of whose most blessed name, whoso study to use both their reason and all other gifts, as well which nature as which grace hath endued them with, let them never doubt but that the same God who is to destroy and confound utterly that wisdom falsely so named in others, doth make reckoning of them as of true Scribes, Scribes by wisdom instructed to the kingdom of heaven,[5] not Scribes against that kingdom hardened in a vain opinion of wisdom ; which in the end being proved folly, must needs perish, true understanding, knowledge, judgment and reason continuing for evermore.

[1] Acts vii. 22 ; Dan. i. 17.
[2] 1 Kings iv. 29, 30. [3] Acts xxii. 3.
[4] ["To injury, v. for 'to injure.' 'Those that are in authority, and princes themselves, ought to take great heed how they *injury* any man by word or deed, and whom they *injury*.' Danet's Comines. lib. iii." Nare's Glossary.
"I am strangely *injured* by the Archbishop." Hugh Broughton in Strype's Whitg. iii. 367.] [5] Matt. xiii. 52.

[10.] Fifthly, Unto the word of God, being in respect of that end for which God ordained it perfect, exact, and absolute in itself, we do not add reason as a supplement of any maim or defect therein, but as a necessary instrument, without which we could not reap by the Scripture's perfection that fruit and benefit which it yieldeth. "The word of God is a twoedged sword,"[1] but in the hands of reasonable men; and reason as the weapon that slew Goliath, if they be as David was that use it. Touching the Apostles, He which gave them from above such power for miraculous confirmation of that which they taught, endued them also with wisdom from above to teach that which they so did confirm. Our Saviour made choice of twelve simple and unlearned men, that the greater their lack of natural wisdom was, the more admirable that might appear which God supernaturally endued them with from heaven. Such therefore as knew the poor and silly estate wherein they had lived, could not but wonder to hear the wisdom of their speech, and be so much the more attentive unto their teaching. They studied for no tongue, they spake with all; of themselves they were rude, and knew not so much as how to premeditate; the Spirit gave them speech and eloquent utterance.

But because with St. Paul it was otherwise than with the rest, inasmuch as he never conversed with Christ upon earth as they did; and his education had been scholastical altogether, which theirs was not; hereby occasion was taken by certain malignants, secretly to undermine his great authority in the Church of Christ, as though the gospel had been taught him by others than by Christ himself, and as if the cause of the Gentiles' conversion and belief through his means had been the learning and skill which he had by being conversant in their books; which thing made them so willing to hear him, and him so able to persuade them; whereas the rest of the Apostles prevailed, because God was with them, and by miracle from heaven confirmed his word in their mouths. They were mighty in *deeds :* as for him, being absent, his writings had some force; in presence, his power not like unto theirs. In sum, concerning his preaching, their very byword was, λόγος ἐξουθενημένος, *addle speech, empty talk :*[2] his writings full of great words, but in the power of miraculous operations his presence not like the rest of the Apostles.

---

[1] Heb. iv.   [2] 2 Cor. x. 10.

Hereupon it riseth that St. Paul was so often driven to make his apologies. Hereupon it riseth that whatsoever time he had spent in the study of human learning, he maketh earnest protestation to them of Corinth, that the gospel which he had preached amongst them did not by other means prevail with them, than with others the same gospel taught by the rest of the Apostles of Christ. "My preaching," saith he, "hath not been in the persuasive speeches of human wisdom, but in demonstration of the Spirit and of power : that your faith may not be in the wisdom of men, but in the power of God." [1] What is it which the Apostle doth here deny? Is it denied that his speech amongst them had been *persuasive*? No : for of him the sacred history plainly testifieth, that for the space of a year and a half he spake in their synagogue every Sabbath, and *persuaded* both Jews and Grecians. [2] How then is the speech of men made persuasive? Surely there can be but two ways to bring this to pass, the one human, the other divine. Either St. Paul did *only* by art and natural industry cause his own speech to be credited ; or else God by miracle did authorize it, and so bring credit thereunto, as to the speech of the rest of the Apostles. Of which two, the former he utterly denieth. For why? if the preaching of the rest had been effectual by miracle, his *only* by force of his own learning ; so great inequality between him and the other Apostles in this thing had been enough to subvert their faith. For might they not with reason have thought, that if he were sent of God as well as they, God would not have furnished them and not him with the power of the Holy Ghost? Might not a great part of them being simple haply have feared, lest their assent had been cunningly gotten unto his doctrine, rather through the weakness of their own wits than the certainty of that truth which he had taught them? How unequal had it been that all believers through the preaching of other Apostles should have their faith strongly built upon the evidence of God's own miraculous approbation, and they whom he had converted should have their persuasion built only upon his skill and wisdom who persuaded them?

As therefore calling from men may authorize us to teach, although it could not authorize him to teach as other Apostles did : so although the wisdom of man had not been sufficient to enable him such a teacher as the rest of the Apostles were,

---

[1] 1 Cor. ii. 4, 5.   [2] Acts xviii. 4, 11.

unless God's miracles had strengthened both the one and the other's doctrine ; yet unto our ability both of teaching and learning the truth of Christ, as we are but mere Christian men, it is not a little which the wisdom of man may add.[1]

[11.] Sixthly, Yea, whatsoever our hearts be to God and to his truth, believe we or be we as yet faithless, for our conversion or confirmation the force of natural reason is great. The force whereof unto those effects is nothing without grace. What then ? To our purpose it is sufficient, that whosoever doth serve, honour, and obey God, whosoever believeth in Him, that man would no more do this than innocents and infants do, but for the light of natural reason that shineth in him, and maketh him apt to apprehend those things of God, which being by grace discovered, are effectual to persuade reasonable minds and none other, that honour, obedience, and credit, belong of right unto God. No man cometh unto God to offer him sacrifice, to pour out supplica-

---

[1] [Chr. Letter, p. 43. "In all your bookes, although we finde manie good things, manie trueths and fine points bravely handled, yet in all your discourse, for the most parte, Aristotle the patriarch of philosophers (with divers other humane writers) and the ingenuous schoolemen, almost in all points have some finger : reason is highlie sett up against Holie Scripture, and reading against preaching."

Hooker, MS. note. "If Aristotle and the schoolmen be such perilous creatures, you must needes think yourself an happie man, whome God hath so fairely blest from too much knowledg in them.

"Remember heer S. Jerome's Epistle in his own defense." (To Magnus, t. II. 326. He pleads precedent, scriptural and ecclesiastical, for his use of profane learning.) "Forget not Picus Mirandula's judgment of the schoolemen ;" (Opp. i. 79. "Ut a nostris, ad quos postremo philosophia pervenit, nunc exordiar ; est in Joanne Scoto vegetum quiddam atque discussum, in Thoma solidum et æquabile, in Ægidio tersum et exactum, in Francisco acre et acutum, in Alberto priscum, amplum, et grande, in Henrico, ut mihi visum est, semper sublime et venerandum.") "Beza's judgment of Aristotle." (For his opinion of the use of logic, see Epist. 67.) "As also Calvin's judgment of philosophie. Epist. 90, ad Bucerum," (p. 110. "Et philosophia præclarum est Dei donum ; et qui omnibus sæculis extiterunt docti viri, eos Deus ipse excitavit, ut adveri notitiam mundo prælucerent.")

Again, Chr. Letter, ibid. "Shall we doe you wronge to suspect . . . that you esteeme the preaching and writing of all the reverend Fathers of our Church, and the bookes of holy Scripture to bee at the least of no greater moment than Aristotle and the schoolemen ?"

Hooker, MS. note: "I think of the Scripture of God as reverently as the best of the purified crew in the world. I except not any, no not the founders themselves and captaines of that faction. In which mind I hope by the grace of Almighty God that I shall both live and die."]

tions and prayers before him, or to do him any service, which doth not first believe him both to be, and to be a rewarder of them who in such sort seek unto him.[1] Let men be taught this either by revelation from heaven, or by instruction upon earth ; by labour, study, and meditation, or by the only secret inspiration of the Holy Ghost ; whatsoever the mean be they know it by, if the knowledge thereof were possible without discourse of natural reason, why should none be found capable thereof but only men ; nor men till such time as they come unto ripe and full ability to work by reasonable understanding ? The whole drift of the Scripture of God, what it is but only to teach Theology ? Theology, what is it but the science of things divine ? What science can be attained unto without the help of natural discourse and reason ? "Judge you of that which I speak,"[2] saith the Apostle. In vain it were to speak any thing of God, but that by reason men are able somewhat to judge of that they hear, and by discourse to discern how consonant it is to truth.

[12.] Scripture indeed teacheth things above nature, things which our reason by itself could not reach unto. Yet those things also we believe, knowing by reason that the Scripture is the word of God. In the presence of Festus a Roman, and of King Agrippa a Jew, St. Paul omitting the one, who neither knew the Jew's religion, nor the books whereby they were taught it, speaks unto the other of things foreshewed by Moses and the Prophets and performed in Jesus Christ ; intending thereby to prove himself so unjustly accused, that unless his judges did condemn both Moses and the Prophets, him they could not choose but acquit, who taught only that fulfilled, which they so long since had foretold. His cause was easy to be discerned ; what was done their eyes were witnesses ; what Moses and the Prophets did speak their books could quickly shew ; it was no hard thing for him to compare them, which knew the one, and believed the other. "King Agrippa, believest thou the Prophets ? I know thou dost."[3] The question is how the books of the Prophets came to be credited of King Agrippa. For what with him did authorize the Prophets, the like with us doth cause the rest of the Scripture of God to be of credit.

[13.] Because we maintain that in Scripture we are taught all things necessary unto salvation ; hereupon very childishly it is by some demanded, what Scripture can teach us the

[1] Heb. xi. 6.   [2] 1 Cor. x. 15.   [3] Acts xxvi. 27.

sacred authority of the Scripture, upon the knowledge whereof our whole faith and salvation dependeth? As though there were any kind of science in the world which leadeth men into knowledge without presupposing a number of things already known. No science doth make known the first principles whereon it buildeth, but they are always either taken as plain and manifest in themselves, or as proved and granted already, some former knowledge having made them evident. Scripture teacheth all supernatural revealed truth, without the knowledge whereof salvation cannot be attained. The main principle whereupon our belief of all things therein contained dependeth, is, that the Scriptures are the oracles of God himself. This in itself we cannot say is evident. For then all men that hear it would acknowledge it in heart, as they do when they hear that "every whole is more than any part of that whole," because this in itself is evident. The other we know that all do not acknowledge when they hear it. There must be therefore some former knowledge presupposed which doth herein assure the hearts of all believers. Scripture teacheth us that saving truth which God hath discovered unto the world by revelation, and it presumeth us taught otherwise that itself is divine and sacred.

[14.] The question then being by what means we are taught this; some answer that to learn it we have no other way than only tradition; as namely that so we believe because both we from our predecessors and they from theirs have so received. But is this enough? That which all men's experience teacheth them may not in any wise be denied. And by experience we all know, that the first outward motive leading men so to esteem of the Scripture is the authority of God's Church.[1] For when we know the whole Church of God hath that opinion of the Scripture, we

---

[1] [Chr. Letter, p. 9, 10. "Have we not here good cause to suspect the underpropping of a popish principle concerning the Churches authoritie above the Holie Scripture, to the disgrace of the English Church?"

Hooker, MS. note. "You have already done your best to make a jarre between nature and Scripture. Your next endeavour is to doe the mae betweene Scripture and the Church. Your delight in conflicts doth rrlike you dreame of them where they are not."

Again, Christ. Letter, p. 10. "We pray you to expound, either by experience or otherwise; Whether the worde of God was received in the world, and beleeved by men, by the virtue and authoritie of the witnesses, either Prophets or Apostles, or the holy Church; or that such were not esteemed for the wordes sake."

judge it even at the first an impudent thing for any man bred and brought up in the Church to be of a contrary mind without cause.   Afterwards the more we bestow our labour in reading or hearing the mysteries thereof, the more we find that the thing itself doth answer our received opinion concerning it.   So that the former inducement prevailing somewhat with us before, doth now much more prevail, when the very thing hath ministered farther reason.   If infidels or atheists chance at any time to call it in question, this giveth us occasion to sift what reason there is, whereby the testimony of the Church concerning Scripture, and our own persuasion which Scripture itself hath confirmed, may be proved a truth infallible.   In which case the ancient Fathers being often constrained to shew, what warrant they had so much to rely upon the Scriptures, endeavoured still to maintain the authority of the books of God by arguments such as unbelievers themselves must needs think reasonable, if they judged thereof as they should.   Neither is it a thing impossible or greatly hard, even by such kind of proofs so to manifest and clear that point, that no man living shall be able to deny it, without denying some apparent principle such as all men acknowledge to be true.

Wherefore if I believe the Gospel, yet is reason of singular use, for that it confirmeth me in this my belief the more : if I do not as yet believe, nevertheless to bring me to the number of believers except reason did somewhat help, and were an instrument which God doth use unto such purposes, what should it boot to dispute with infidels or godless persons for their conversion and persuasion in that point ?

[15.] Neither can I think that when grave and learned men do sometime hold, that of this principle there is no proof but by the testimony of the Spirit, which assureth our hearts therein, it is their meaning to exclude utterly all force which any kind of reason may have in that behalf ; but I rather incline to interpret such their speeches, as if they had more

Hooker, MS. note.   " I am sorie to see you in the groundes and elements of your religion so sclenderly instructed.

" Fides nititur authoritate docentis.   Docens autem confirmatam habet authoritatem personæ virtute miraculorum.   Id quod omnino necessarium est propter ea quæ docet supra et præter naturalem rationem : qua omnis probatio argumentosa nititur, quæ fidem facit.   Atque hoc Apostolus de se testatur, cum efficacem fuisse sermonem suum asserit non vi humanæ persuasionis, sed assistentis Spiritus ad opera miraculosa perficienda.   Vide Tertull. cont. Gent. p. 637."]

expressly set down, that other motives and inducements, be they never so strong and consonant unto reason, are notwithstanding uneffectual of themselves to work faith concerning this principle, if the special grace of the Holy Ghost concur not to the enlightening of our minds. For otherwise I doubt not but men of wisdom and judgment will grant, that the Church, in this point especially, is furnished with reason, to stop the mouths of her impious adversaries; and that as it were altogether bootless to allege against them what the Spirit hath taught us, so likewise that even to our ownselves it needeth caution and explication how the testimony of the Spirit may be discerned, by what means it may be known; lest men think that the Spirit of God doth testify those things which the spirit of error suggesteth. The operations of the Spirit, especially these ordinary which be common unto all true Christian men, are as we know things secret and undiscernible even to the very soul where they are, because their nature is of another and an higher kind than that they can be by us perceived in this life. Wherefore albeit the Spirit lead us into all truth and direct us in all goodness yet because these workings of the Spirit in us are so privy and secret, we therefore stand on a plainer ground, when we gather by reason from the quality of things believed or done, that the Spirit of God hath directed us in both, than if we settle ourselves to believe or to do any certain particular thing, as being moved thereto by the Spirit.

[16.] But of this enough. To go from the books of Scripture to the sense and meaning thereof: because the sentences which are by the Apostles recited out of the Psalms,[1] to prove the resurrection of Jesus Christ, did not prove it, if so be the Prophet David meant them of himself; this exposition therefore they plainly disprove, and shew by manifest reason, that of David the words of David could not possibly be meant. Exclude the use of natural reasoning about the sense of Holy Scripture concerning the articles of our faith, and then that the Scripture doth concern the articles of our faith who can assure us? That, which by right exposition buildeth up Christian faith, being misconstrued breedeth error: between true and false construction, the difference reason must shew. Can Christian men perform that which Peter requireth at their hands; is it possible they should both believe and be able, without the use of reason, to render "a reason of

---

[1] Acts xiii. 36; ii. 34.

their belief,"[1] a reason sound and sufficient to answer them that demand it, be they of the same faith with us or enemies thereunto? may we cause our faith without reason to appear reasonable in the eyes of men? This being required even of learners in the school of Christ, the duty of their teachers in bringing them unto such ripeness must needs be somewhat more, than only to read the sentences of Scripture, and then paraphrastically to scholy them; to vary them with sundry forms of speech, without arguing or disputing about any thing which they contain. This method of teaching may commend itself unto the world by that easiness and facility which is in it: but a law or a pattern it is not, as some do imagine, for all men to follow that will do good in the Church of Christ.

[17.] Our Lord and Saviour himself did hope by disputation to do some good, yea by disputation not only of but against, the truth, albeit with purpose for the truth. That Christ should be the son of David was truth; yet against this truth our Lord in the gospel objecteth, "If Christ be the son of David, how doth David call him Lord?"[2] There is as yet no way known how to dispute, or to determine of things disputed, without the use of natural reason.

If we please to add unto Christ their example, who followed him as near in all things as they could; the sermon of Paul and Barnabas set down in the Acts,[3] where the people would have offered unto them sacrifice; in that sermon what is there but only natural reason to disprove their act? "O men, why do you these things? We are men even subject to the selfsame passions with you: we preach unto you to leave these vanities and to turn to the living God, the God that hath not left himself without witness, in that he hath done good to the world, giving rain and fruitful seasons, filling our heart with joy and gladness."

Neither did they only use reason in winning such unto Christian belief as were yet thereto unconverted, but with believers themselves they followed the selfsame course. In that great and solemn assembly of believing Jews how doth Peter prove that the Gentiles were partakers of the grace of God as well as they, but by reason drawn from those effects, which were apparently known amongst them? "God which

<hr>

[1] 1 Pet. iii. 15.   [2] Matt. xxii. 43.   [3] Acts xiv. 15.

knoweth hearts hath borne them witness in giving unto them the Holy Ghost as unto us." [1]

The light therefore, which the star of natural reason and wisdom casteth, is too bright to be obscured by the mist of a word or two uttered to diminish that opinion which justly hath been received concerning the force and virtue thereof, even in matters that touch most nearly the principal duties of men and the glory of the eternal God.

[18.] In all which hitherto hath been spoken touching the force and use of man's reason in things divine, I must crave that I be not so understood or construed, as if any such thing by virtue thereof could be done without the aid and assistance of God's most blessed Spirit. The thing we have handled according to the question moved about it ; which question is, whether the light of reason be so pernicious, that in devising laws for the Church men ought not by it to search what may be fit and convenient. For this cause therefore we have endeavoured to make it appear, how in the nature of reason itself there is no impediment, but that the selfsame Spirit, which revealeth the things that God hath set down in his law, may also be thought to aid and direct men in finding out by the light of reason what laws are expedient to be made for the guiding of his Church, over and besides them that are in Scripture. Herein therefore we agree with those men, by whom human laws are defined to be ordinances, which such as have lawful authority given them for that purpose do probably draw from the laws of nature and God, by discourse of reason aided with the influence of divine grace. And for that cause, it is not said amiss touching ecclesiastical canons, that "by instinct of the Holy Ghost they have been made, and consecrated by the reverend acceptation of all the world." [2]

IX. Laws for the Church are not made as they should be, unless the makers follow such direction as they ought to be guided by : wherein that Scripture standeth not the Church of God in any stead, or serveth nothing at all to direct, but may be let pass as needless to be consulted with, we judge

---

[1] Acts xv. 8.
[2] Violatores. 25. q. i. [Decret. Gratian. caus. xxv. quæst. i. c. 6. in Corp. Jur. Canon. Paris. 1618. p. 313. "Violatores canonum voluntari graviter a sanctis patribus judicantur, et a Sancto Spiritu (instinctu cujus, et dono dictati sunt) damnantur."]

it profane, impious, and irreligious to think. For although it were in vain to make laws which the Scripture hath already made, because what we are already there commanded to do, on our parts there resteth nothing but only that it be executed ; yet because both in that which we are commanded, it concerneth the duty of the Church by law to provide, that the looseness and slackness of men may not cause the commandments of God to be unexecuted ; and a number of things there are for which the Scripture hath not provided by any law, but left them unto the careful discretion of the Church ; we are to search how the Church in these cases may be well directed to make that provision by laws which is most convenient and fit. And what is so in these cases, partly Scripture and partly reason must teach to discern. Scripture comprehending examples and laws, laws some natural and some positive : examples there neither are for all cases which require laws to be made, and when there are, they can but direct as precedents only. Natural laws direct in such sort, that in all things we must for ever do according unto them ; Positive so, that against them in no case we may do any thing, as long as the will of God is that they should remain in force. Howbeit when Scripture doth yield us precedents, how far forth they are to be followed ; when it giveth natural laws, what particular order is thereunto most agreeable ; when positive, which way to make laws unrepugnant unto them ; yea though all these should want, yet what kind of ordinances would be most for that good of the Church which is aimed at, all this must be by reason found out. And therefore, "to refuse the conduct of the light of nature," saith St. Augustine, "is not folly alone but accompanied with impiety."[1]

[2.] The greatest amongst the school-divines studying how to set down by exact definition the nature of an human law (of which nature all the Church's constitutions are) found not which way better to do it than in these words : "Out of the precepts of the law of nature, as out of certain common and undemonstrable principles, man's reason doth necessarily proceed unto certain more particular determinations ; which particular determinations being found out according unto the reason of man, they have the names of

---

[1] "Luminis naturalis ducatum repellere non modo stultum est sed et impium." August. lib. iv. de Trin. cap. 6. [The editor has not been able to verify this quotation.]

human laws, so that such other conditions be therein kept as the making of laws doth require,"[1] that is, if they whose authority is thereunto required do establish and publish them as laws. And the truth is, that all our controversy in this cause concerning the orders of the Church is, what particulars the Church may appoint. That which doth find them out is the force of man's reason. That which doth guide and direct his reason is first the general law of nature; which law of nature and the moral law of Scripture are in the substance of law all one. But because there are also in Scripture a number of laws particular and positive, which being in force may not by any law of man be violated; we are in making laws to have thereunto an especial eye. As for example, it might perhaps seem reasonable unto the Church of God, following the general laws concerning the nature of marriage, to ordain in particular that cousin-germans shall not marry. Which law notwithstanding ought not to be received in the Church, if there should be in Scripture a law particular to the contrary, forbidding utterly the bonds of marriage to be so far forth abridged. The same Thomas therefore whose definition of human laws we mentioned before, doth add thereunto this caution concerning the rule and canon whereby to make them:[2] *human laws are measures* in respect of men whose actions they must direct; howbeit such measures they are, as have also their higher rules to be measured by, *which rules are two, the law of God, and the law of nature.* So that laws human must be made according to the general laws of nature, and without contradiction unto any positive law in Scripture. Otherwise they are ill made.

[3.] Unto laws thus made and received by a whole church, they which live within the bosom of that church must not think it a matter indifferent either to yield or not to yield obedience. Is it a small offence to despise the

---

[1] Tho. Aqui. 1, 2. q. 91, art. 3. [t. xi. p. i. 199]   "Ex præceptis legis naturalis, quasi ex quibusdam principiis communibus et indemonstrabilibus, necesse est quod ratio humana procedat ad aliqua magis particulariter disponenda. Et istæ particulares dispositiones adinventæ secundum rationem humanam dicuntur *leges humanæ*, observatis aliis conditionibus quæ pertinent ad rationem legis."

[2] Quæst. 95. Art. 3. [t. xi. p. i. 206. "Lex humana . . . est quædam regula, vel mensura regulata, vel mensurata quadam superiori mensura; quæ quidem est duplex, scil. divina lex, et lex naturæ, ut ex supradictis patet."]

Church of God?[1] "My son keep thy father's command-ment," saith Solomon, "and forget not thy mother's in-struction: bind them both always about thine heart."[2] It doth not stand with the duty which we owe to our heavenly Father, that to the ordinances of our mother the Church we should shew ourselves disobedient. Let us not say we keep the commandments of the one, when we break the law of the other: for unless we observe both, we obey neither. And what doth let but that we may observe both, when they are not the one to the other in any sort repugnant? For of such laws only we speak, as being made in form and manner already declared, can have in them no contradiction unto the laws of Almighty God. Yea that which is more, the laws thus made God himself doth in such sort authorize, that to despise them is to despise in them Him. It is a loose and licentious opinion which the Anabaptists have embraced, holding that a Christian man's liberty is lost, and the soul which Christ hath redeemed unto himself in-juriously drawn into servitude under the yoke of human power, if any law be now imposed besides the Gospel of Jesus Christ: in obedience whereunto the Spirit of God and not the constraint of man is to lead us, according to that of the blessed Apostle, " Such as are led by the Spirit of God they are the sons of God,"[3] and not such as live in thraldom unto men. Their judgment is therefore that the Church of Christ should admit no law-makers but the Evangelists. The author of that which causeth another thing to be, is author of that thing also which thereby is caused. The light of natural understanding, wit, and reason, is from God; he it is which thereby doth illuminate every man entering into the world.[4] If there proceed from us any thing after-wards corrupt and naught, the mother thereof is our own darkness, neither doth it proceed from any such cause whereof God is the author. He is the author of all that we think or do by virtue of that light, which himself hath given. And therefore the laws which the very heathens did gather to direct their actions by, so far forth as they proceeded from the light of nature, God himself doth acknowledge to[5] have proceeded even from himself, and that he was the writer of them in the tables of their hearts. How much more then he the author of those laws, which have been

---

[1] Cor. xi. 22. [2] Prov. vi. 20. [3] Rom. viii. 14.
[4] John i. 9. [5] Rom. i. 19; ii. 15.

made by his saints, endued further with the heavenly grace of his Spirit, and directed as much as might be with such instructions as his sacred word doth yield! Surely if we have unto those laws that dutiful regard which their dignity doth require, it will not greatly need that we should be exhorted to live in obedience unto them. If they have God himself for their author, contempt which is offered unto them cannot choose but redound unto him. The safest and unto God the most acceptable way of framing our lives therefore is, with all humility, lowliness, and singleness of heart, to study, which way our willing obedience both unto God and man may be yielded even to the utmost of that which is due.

X. Touching the mutability of laws that concern the regiment and polity of the Church; changed they are, when either altogether abrogated, or in part repealed, or augmented with farther additions. Wherein we are to note, that this question about the changing of laws concerneth only such laws as are positive, and do make that now good or evil by being commanded or forbidden, which otherwise of itself were not simply the one or the other. Unto such laws it is expressly sometimes added, how long they are to continue in force. If this be no where exprest, then have we no light to direct our judgments concerning the changeableness or immutability of them, but by considering the nature and quality of such laws. The nature of every law must be judged of by the end for which it was made, and by the aptness of things therein prescribed unto the same end. It may so fall out that the reason why some laws of God were given is neither opened nor possible to be gathered by wit of man. As why God should forbid Adam that one tree, there was no way for Adam ever to have certainly understood. And at Adam's ignorance of this point Satan took advantage, urging the more securely a false cause because the true was unto Adam unknown. Why the Jews were forbidden to plough their ground with an ox and an ass, why to clothe themselves with mingled attire of wool and linen,[1] both it was unto them and to us it remaineth obscure. Such laws perhaps cannot be abrogated saving only by whom they were made: because the intent of them being known unto none but the author, he alone can judge how long it is

[1] Deut. xxii. 10, 11. [Spencer (de Legg. Hebræor. lib. ii. c. 31, 33.) conjectures, but without direct evidence, that these were prohibitions of Sabæan ceremonies.]

requisite they should endure. But if the reason why things
were instituted may be known, and being known do appear
manifestly to be of perpetual necessity; then are those
things also perpetual, unless they cease to be effectual unto
that purpose for which they were at the first instituted.
Because when a thing doth cease to be available unto the
end which gave it being, the continuance of it must then of
necessity appear superfluous. And of this we cannot be
ignorant, how sometimes that hath done great good, which
afterwards, when time hath changed the ancient course of
things, doth grow to be either very hurtful, or not so greatly
profitable and necessary. If therefore the end for which a
law provideth be perpetually necessary, and the way whereby
it provideth perpetually also most apt, no doubt but that
every such law ought for ever to remain unchangeable.

[2.] Whether God be the author of laws by authorizing
that power of men whereby they are made, or by delivering
them made immediately from himself, by word only, or in
writing also, or howsoever; notwithstanding the authority of
their Maker, the mutability of that end for which they are
made doth also make them changeable. The law of
ceremonies came from God: Moses had commandment
to commit it unto the sacred records of Scripture, where
it continueth even unto this very day and hour: in
force still, as the Jew surmiseth, because God himself was
author of it, and for us to abolish what he hath established
were presumption most intolerable. But (that which they
in the blindness of their obdurate hearts are not able to
discern) sith the end for which that law was ordained is now
fulfilled, past and gone; how should it but cease any longer
to be, which hath no longer any cause of being in force as
before? "That which necessity of some special time doth
cause to be enjoined bindeth no longer than during that
time, but doth afterwards become free."[1]

Which thing is also plain even by that law which the
Apostles assembled at the council of Jerusalem did from
thence deliver unto the Church of Christ, the preface whereof
to authorize it was, "To the Holy Ghost and to us it hath
seemed good:"[2] which style they did not use as matching

---

[1] "Quod pro necessitate temporis statutum est, cessante necessitate,
debet cessare pariter quod urgebat." i. q. 1. Quod pro necessit. [i.e.
Decr. Gratiani, pars 1. causa 1. qu. 1. c. 41. in Corp. Jur. Canon
116.]
[2] Acts xv. 28.

themselves in power with the Holy Ghost, but as testifying the Holy Ghost to be the author, and themselves but only utterers of that decree. This law therefore to h ive proceeded from God as the author thereof no faithful man will deny. It was of God, not only because God gave them the power whereby they might make laws, but for that it proceeded even from the holy motion and suggestion of that secret divine Spirit, whose sentence they did but only pronounce. Notwithstanding, as the law of ceremonies delivered unto the Jews, so this very law which the Gentiles received from the mouth of the Holy Ghost, is in like respect abrogated by decease of the end for which it was given.

[3.] But such as do not stick at this point, such as grant that what hath been instituted upon any special cause needeth not to be observed,[1] that cause ceasing, do notwithstanding herein fail; they judge the laws of God only by the author and main end for which they were made, so that for us to change that which he hath established, they hold it execrable pride and presumption, if so be the end and purpose for which God by that mean provideth be permanent. And upon this they ground those ample disputes concerning orders and offices, which being by him appointed for the government of his Church, if it be necessary always that the Church of Christ be governed, then doth the end for which God provided remain still; and therefore in those means which he by law did establish as being fittest unto that end, for us to alter any thing is to lift up ourselves against God, and as it were to countermand him. Wherein they mark not that laws are instruments to rule by, and that instruments are not only to be framed according unto the general end for which they are provided, but even according unto that very particular, which riseth out of the matter whereon they have

---

[1] Counterp. p. 8. [Cosin in his "Answer to the Abstract," had produced the change of time in celebrating the Eucharist, from the evening after supper, to the morning before the first meal, as an instance of the authority left with the Church to vary matters of discipline. The author of the Counter-poison replies, "As it is a mere circumstance of time, so the alteration hath ground in the Scripture, because one and the same time is not always kept. Acts iii. 42 ; xx. 7, 11, &c. Neither can that be said to be according to the institution, which *being done upon a particular cause* (as all divines agree) *should not be observed where that cause ceaseth*." T. C. ii. 465. "Neither any man, nor all men in the world, could have put down the temporal ministeries of Apostles, Evangelists, &c. which the Lord ordained, unless the Lord himself had withdrawn them."]

to work. The end wherefore laws were made may be permanent, and those laws nevertheless require some alteration,
if there be any unfitness in the means which they prescribe as
tending unto that end and purpose. As for example, a law
that to bridle theft doth punish thieves with a quadruple
restitution hath an end which will continue as long as the
world itself continueth. Theft will be always, and will
always need to be bridled. But that the mean which this
law provideth for that end,[1] namely the punishment of
quadruple restitution, that this will be always sufficient to
bridle and restrain that kind of enormity no man can
warrant. Insufficiency of laws doth sometimes come by
want of judgment in the makers. Which cause cannot fall
into any law termed properly and immediately divine, as it
may and doth into human laws often. But that which hath
been once most sufficient may wax otherwise by alteration
of time and place; that punishment which hath been sometime forcible to bridle sin may grow afterwards too weak and
feeble.

[4.] In a word, we plainly perceive by the difference of
those three laws which the Jews received at the hands of
God, the moral, ceremonial, and judicial, that if the end for
which and the matter according whereunto God maketh his
laws continue always one and the same, his laws also do the
like; for which cause the moral law cannot be altered:
secondly, that whether the matter whereon laws are made
continue or continue not, if their end have once ceased,
they cease also to be of force; as in the law ceremonial it
fareth: finally, that albeit the end continue, as in that law
of theft specified and in a great part of those ancient
judicials it doth; yet forasmuch as there is not in all
respects the same subject or matter remaining for which
they were first instituted, even this is sufficient cause of
change: and therefore laws, though both ordained of God
himself, and the end for which they were ordained continuing, may notwithstanding cease, if by alterations of persons
or times they be found insufficient to attain unto that end.
In which respect why may we not presume that God doth
even call for such change or alteration as the very condition
of things themselves doth make necessary?

[5.] They which do therefore plead the authority of the
law-maker as an argument, wherefore it should not be lawful

[1] [Exod. xxii. 1 ; 2 Sam. xii. 6.]

to change that which he hath instituted, and will have this the cause why all the ordinances of our Saviour are immutable ; they which urge the wisdom of God as a proof, that whatsoever laws he hath made they ought to stand, unless himself from heaven proclaim them disannulled, because it is not in man to correct the ordinance of God ; may know, if it please them to take notice thereof, that we are far from presuming to think that men can better any thing which God hath done, even as we are from thinking that men should presume to undo some things of men, which God doth know they cannot better.　God never ordained any thing that could be bettered.　Yet many things he hath that have been changed, and that for the better.　That which succeedeth as better now when change is requisite, had been worse when that which now is changed was instituted. Otherwise God had not then left this to choose that, neither would now reject that to choose this, were it not for some new-grown occasion making that which hath been better worse.　In this case therefore men do not presume to change God's ordinance, but they yield thereunto requiring itself to be changed.

[6.] Against this it is objected, that to abrogate or innovate the Gospel of Christ if men or angels should attempt, it were most heinous and cruel sacrilege.　And the Gospel (as they say) containeth not only doctrine instructing men how they should believe, but also precepts concerning the regiment of the Church.　Discipline therefore is "a part of the Gospel,"[1] and God being the author of the whole Gospel, as well of discipline as of doctrine, it cannot be but that both of them "have a common cause."　So that as we are to believe for ever the articles of evangelical doctrine, so the precepts of discipline we are in like sort bound for ever to observe.

[7.] Touching points of doctrine, as for example, the Unity of God, the Trinity of Persons, salvation by Christ, the resurrection of the body, life everlasting, the judgment to come, and such like, they have been since the first hour

---

[1] "We offer to shew the discipline to be a part of the Gospel, and therefore to have a common cause ; so that in the repulse of the discipline the Gospel receives a check."　And again, "I speak of the discipline as of a part of the Gospel, and therefore neither under nor above the Gospel, but the Gospel."　T. C. lib. ii. p. 1, 4. [These latter words are in p. 5, but in p. 4 are the following : "The discipline being, as it is propounded, and offered to be proved, a part of the Gospel, must needs arm the Lord against the refuser."]

that there was a Church in the world, and till the last they must be believed. But as for matters of regiment, they are for the most part of another nature. To make new articles of faith and doctrine no man thinketh it lawful ; new laws of government what commonwealth or church is there which maketh not either at one time or another ? " The rule of faith,"[1] saith Tertullian, " is but one, and that alone immoveable and impossible to be framed or cast anew." The law of outward order and polity not so.[2] There is no reason in the world wherefore we should esteem it as necessary always to do, as always to believe, the same things ; seeing every man knoweth that the matter of faith is constant, the matter contrariwise of action daily changeable, especially the matter of action belonging unto church polity. Neither can I find that men of soundest judgment have any otherwise taught, than that articles of belief and things which all men must of necessity do to the end that they may be saved, are either expressly set down in Scripture or else plainly thereby to be gathered. But touching things which belong to discipline and outward polity, the Church hath authority to make canons, laws, and decrees, even as we read that in the Apostles' times it did.[3] Which kind of laws (forasmuch as they are not in themselves necessary to salvation) may after they are made be also changed as the difference of times or places shall require. Yea, it is not denied I am sure by themselves, that certain things in discipline are of that nature, as they may be varied by times, places, persons, and other the like circumstances. Whereupon I demand, are those changeable points of discipline commanded in the word of God or no ? If they be not commanded and yet may be received in the Church, how can their former position stand, condemning all things in the Church which in the word are not commanded ? If they be commanded and yet may suffer change, how can this latter

[1] Tert. de Veland. Virg. c. I.

[2] Mart. [i.e. Peter Martyr] in I Sam. xiv. [" Positum sit, licere Ecclesiæ scribere sibi aut canones, aut leges, aut decreta, aut sanctiones, aut quocunque ea velis nomine appellari. Est enim Ecclesia cœtus, et regi debet verbo Dei, præsertim quod attinet ad salutem ipsius, et cultum Dei. Sed sunt alia, quæ tantum pertinent ad externam disciplinam. . . . Istarum legum finis esse debet ædificatio et εὐταξία. Quoniam autem necessariæ non sunt, pro temporum et locorum ratione mutari possunt."]

[3] Acts xv.

stand, affirming all things immutable which are commanded
of God? Their distinction touching matters of substance
and of circumstance, though true, will not serve. For be
they great things or be they small, if God have commanded
them in the Gospel, and his commanding them in the
Gospel do make them unchangeable, there is no reason we
should more change the one than we may the other. If the
authority of the maker do prove unchangeableness in the
laws which God hath made, then must all laws which he
hath made be necessarily for ever permanent, though they
be but of circumstance only and not of substance. I
therefore conclude, that neither God's being author of laws
for government of his Church, nor his committing them unto
Scripture, is any reason sufficient wherefore all churches
should for ever be bound to keep them without change.

[8.] But of one thing we are here to give them warning
by the way. For whereas in this discourse we have oftentimes profest that many parts of discipline or church polity
are delivered in Scripture, they may perhaps imagine that
we are driven to confess their discipline to be delivered in
Scripture, and that having no other means to avoid it, we
are fain to argue for the changeableness of laws ordained
even by God himself, as if otherwise theirs of necessity
should take place, and that under which we live be
abandoned. There is no remedy therefore but to abate
this error in them, and directly to let them know, that if
they fall into any such conceit, they do but a little flatter
their own cause. As for us, we think in no respect so highly
of it. Our persuasion is, that no age ever had knowledge
of it but only ours; that they which defend it devised it;
that neither Christ nor his Apostles at any time taught it,
but the contrary. If therefore we did seek to maintain that
which most advantageth our own cause, the very best way
for us and the strongest against them were to hold even as
they do, that in Scripture there must needs be found some
particular form of church polity which God hath instituted,
and which for that very cause belongeth to all churches, to
all times.[1] But with any such partial eye to respect our

---

[1] "Disciplina est Christianæ Ecclesiæ Politia, a Deo ejus recte
administrandæ causa constituta, ac propterea ex ejus verbo petenda, et
ob eandem causam omnium ecclesiarum communis et omnium temporum." Lib. de Eccles. Discip. in Anal. [See also p. 9, Cartwright's Translation.]

selves, and by cunning to make those things seem the truest which are the fittest to serve our purpose, is a thing which we neither like nor mean to follow. Wherefore that which we take to be generally true concerning the mutability of laws, the same we have plainly delivered, as being persuaded of nothing more than we are of this, that whether it be in matter of speculation or of practice, no untruth[1] can possibly avail the patron and defender long, and that things most truly are likewise most behovefully spoken.

XI. This we hold and grant for truth, that those very laws which of their own nature are changeable, be notwithstanding uncapable of change, if he which gave them, being of authority so to do, forbid absolutely to change them; neither may they admit alteration against the will of such a law-maker. Albeit therefore we do not find any cause why of right there should be necessarily an immutable form set down in holy Scripture; nevertheless if indeed there have been at any time a church polity so set down, the change whereof the sacred Scripture doth forbid, surely for men to alter those laws which God for perpetuity hath established were presumption most intolerable

[2.] To prove therefore that the will of Christ was to establish laws so permanent and immutable that in any sort to alter them cannot but highly offend God, thus they reason. First,[2] if Moses, being but a servant in the house

[1] Ἐοίκασιν οὖν οἱ ἀληθεῖς τῶν λόγων οὐ μόνον πρὸς τὸ εἰδέναι χρησιμώτατοι εἶναι, ἀλλὰ καὶ πρὸς τὸν βίον. Συνῳδοὶ γὰρ ὄντες ἔργοις, πιστεύονται. Arist. Ethic. lib. x. cap. 1.

[2] Heb. iii. 6. "Either that commendation of the son before the servant is a false testimony, or the son ordained a permanent government in the Church. If permanent, then not to be changed. What then do they, that [not only] hold it may be changed at the magistrate's pleasure, but advise the magistrate by his positive laws to proclaim, that it is his will, that if there shall be a church within his dominions, he will maim and deform the same?" M. M. [Martin Marprelate, "Ha' ye any work for a Cooper?"] p. 16 "He that was as faithful as Moses, left as clear instruction for the government of the Church: but Christ was as faithful as Moses: Ergo." Demonst. of Discip. cap. i. [p. 3. See also Theses Martinianæ, 5th Thesis. "If Christ did not ordain a church government which at the pleasure of man cannot be changed, then he is inferior unto Moses: for the government placed by him might no man alter, and thereto might no man add any thing. Heb. iii. 2, 3." Eccl. Disc. fol. 7. "Ne illum aliqua parte prophetici muneris spoliemus, aut servum, quantumvis fidelem, unigenito Filio, et tanquam Eliezerum Isaaco in paterna domo præferamus." Counterpoison, p. 9. Penry's Appellation to the High Court of Parliament, p. 18.]

of God, did therein establish laws of government for perpetuity, laws which they that were of the household might
not alter; shall we admit into our thoughts, that the Son
of God hath in providing for this his household declared
himself less faithful than Moses? Moses delivering unto
the Jews such laws as were durable, if those be changeable
which Christ hath delivered unto us, we are not able to
avoid it, but (that which to think were heinous impiety) we
of necessity must confess even the Son of God himself to
have been less faithful than Moses. Which argument shall
need no touchstone to try it by but some other of the like
making. Moses erected in the wilderness a tabernacle
which was moveable from place to place; Solomon a sump-
tuous and stately temple which was not moveable: therefore Solomon was faithfuller than Moses, which no man
endued with reason will think. And yet by this reason
it doth plainly follow.

He that will see how faithful the one or the other was,
must compare the things which they both did unto the
charge which God gave each of them. The Apostle in
making comparison between our Saviour and Moses attributeth faithfulness unto both, and maketh this difference
between them; Moses *in*, but Christ *over* the house of
God; Moses in that house which was *his by charge and commission*, though to govern it, yet to govern it *as a servant;*
but Christ over this house as being *his own entire possession*.

[3.] Our Lord and Saviour doth make protestation, " I
have given unto them the words which thou gavest me."[1]
Faithful therefore he was, and concealed not any part of his
Father's will. But did any part of that will require the
immutability of laws concerning church polity? They
answer, Yea. For else God should less favour us than the
Jews.[2] God would not have their church guided by any
laws but his own. And seeing this did so continue even till
Christ, now to ease God of that care, or rather to deprive
the Church of his patronage, what reason have we? Surely
none to derogate any thing from the ancient love which
God hath borne to his Church. An heathen philosopher[3]

---

[1] John xvii. 8.
[2] " Either God hath left a prescript form of government now, or else
he is less careful under the New Testament than under the Old."
Demonst. of Dis. cap. i.   [T. C. i. 62. ap. Whitg. Def. 304.]
[3] [Philemon, Fragm. Incert. xliii. ed. Cler.—

there is, who considering how many things beasts have
which men have not, how naked in comparison of them,
how impotent, and how much less able we are to shift for
ourselves a long time after we enter into this world, re-
piningly concluded hereupon, that nature being a careful
mother for them, is towards us a hard-hearted stepdame.
No, we may not measure the affection of our gracious God
towards his by such differences. For even herein shineth
his wisdom, that though the ways of his providence be
many, yet the end which he bringeth all at the length unto
is one and the selfsame.

[4.] But if such kind of reasoning were good, might we
not even as directly conclude the very same concerning
laws of secular regiment? Their own words are these : "In
the ancient church of the Jews, God did command and
Moses commit unto writing all things pertinent as well
to the civil as to the ecclesiastical state." [1] God gave them
laws of civil regiment, and would not permit their commonweal to be governed by any other laws than his own. Doth
God less regard our temporal estate in this world, or
provide for it worse than for theirs? To us notwithstanding
he hath not as to them delivered any particular form of
temporal regiment, unless perhaps we think, as some do,
that the grafting of the Gentiles [2] and their incorporating
into Israel [3] doth import that we ought to be subject unto
the rites and laws of their whole polity. We see then how
weak such disputes are, and how smally they make to this
purpose.

[5.] That Christ did not mean to set down particular
positive laws for all things in such sort as Moses did, the

πολύ γ' ἐστὶ πάντων ζῷον ἀθλιώτατον
ἄνθρωπος, εἴ τις ἐξετάζοι κατὰ τρόπον.
τὸν γὰρ βίον περίεργον εἰς τὰ πάντ' ἔχων,
ἀπορεῖ τὰ πλεῖστα διὰ τέλους, πονεῖ τ' ἀεί.
καὶ τοῖς μὲν ἄλλοις πᾶσιν ἡ γῆ θηρίοις
ἑκοῦσα παρέχει τὴν καθ' ἡμέραν τροφήν,
αὐτὴ πορίζουσ', οὐ λαβοῦσα· πάνυ μόλις
ὥσπερ τὸ κατὰ χρέος κεφάλαιον ἐκτίει
τὸ σπέρμα, τοὺς τόκους ἀνευρίσκουσ' ἀεὶ
πρόφασίν τιν' αὐχμὸν, ἢ πάγην, ἵν' ἀποστερῇ.]

---

[1] Ecclesiast. Disc. lib. i. [fol. 5. "In vetere ecclesia Judæorum
omnia quæ ad regendum non modo civilem sed etiam ecclesiasticum
statum [pertinent] . . . diligenter descripta sunt, et a Deo præcepta, a
Mose literis commendata."]

[2] Rom. xi. 17.   [3] Ephes. ii. 12-16.

M 201

very different manner of delivering the laws of Moses and
the laws of Christ doth plainly shew. Moses had commandment to gather the ordinances of God together distinctly, and orderly to set them down according unto their
several kinds, for each public duty and office the laws that
belong thereto, as appeareth in the books themselves,
written of purpose for that end. Contrariwise the laws of
Christ we find rather mentioned by occasion in the writings
of the Apostles, than any solemn thing directly written to
comprehend them in legal sort.

[6.] Again, the positive laws which Moses gave, they
were given for the greatest part with restraint to the land of
Jewry: "Behold," saith Moses, "I have taught you ordinances and laws, as the Lord my God commanded me, that
ye should do even so within the land whither ye go to
possess it."[1] Which laws and ordinances positively he
plainly distinguisheth afterward from the laws of the Two
Tables which were moral.[2] "The Lord spake unto you
out of the midst of the fire; ye heard the voice of the words,
but saw no similitude, only a voice. Then he declared
unto you his Covenant which he commanded you to do, the
Ten Commandments, and wrote them upon two tables of
stone. And the Lord commanded me that same time, that
I should teach you ordinances and laws which ye should
observe in the land whither ye go to possess it." The same
difference is again set down in the next chapter following.
For rehearsal being made of the Ten Commandments, it
followeth immediately,[3] "These words the Lord spake unto
all your multitude in the mount out of the midst of the fire,
the cloud, and the darkness, with a great voice, and added
no more; and wrote them upon two tables of stone, and
delivered them unto me." But concerning other laws, the
people give their consent to receive them at the hands of
Moses:[4] "Go thou near, and hear all that the Lord our
God saith, and declare thou unto us all that the Lord our
God saith unto thee, and we will hear it and do it." The
people's alacrity herein God highly commendeth with most
effectual and hearty speech:[5] "I have heard the voice
of the words of this people; they have spoken well. O
that there were such an heart in them to fear me, and
to keep all my commandments always, that it might go well

---

[1] Deut. iv. 5.   [2] Deut. iv. 12-14.   [3] Deut. v. 22.
[4] Deut. v. 27.   [5] Deut. v. 28-31.

with them and with their children for ever ! Go, say unto
them, 'Return you to your tents ;' but stand thou here with
me, and I will tell thee all the commandments and the
ordinances and the laws which thou shalt teach them, that
they may do them in the land which I have given them
to possess." From this latter kind the former are plainly
distinguished in many things. They were not both at one
time delivered, neither both after one sort, nor to one end.
The former uttered by the voice of God himself in the
hearing of six hundred thousand men ; the former written
with the finger of God ; the former termed by the name of a
Covenant ; the former given to be kept without either
mention of time how long, or of place where. On the
other side, the latter given after, and neither written by God
himself, nor given unto the whole multitude immediately
from God, but unto Moses, and from him to them both
by word and writing ; the latter termed Ceremonies, Judgments, Ordinances, but no where Covenants ; finally, the
observation of the latter restrained unto the land where God
would establish them to inhabit.

The laws positive are not framed without regard had to
the place and persons for the which they are made. If
therefore Almighty God in framing their laws had an eye
unto the nature of that people, and to the country where
they were to dwell ; if these peculiar and proper considerations were respected in the making of their laws, and must
be also regarded in the positive laws of all other nations
besides : then seeing that nations are not all alike, surely the
giving of one kind of positive laws unto one only people,
without any liberty to alter them, is but a slender proof,
that therefore one kind should in like sort be given to serve
everlastingly for all

[7.] But that which most of all maketh for the clearing
of this point is, that the Jews,[1] who had laws so particularly
determining and so fully instructing them in all affairs what
to do, were notwithstanding continually inured with causes
exorbitant, and such as their laws had not provided for.

---

[1] "Whereas you say, that they (the Jews) had nothing but what was
determined by the law, and we have many things undetermined and left
to the order of the Church ; I will offer, for one that you shall bring
that we have left to the order of the Church, to shew you that they had
twenty which were undecided by the express word of God." T. C. lib.
i. p. 35. [22.]

And in this point much more is granted us than we ask, namely, that for one thing which we have left to the order of the Church, they had twenty which were undecided by the express word of God; and that as their ceremonies and sacraments were multiplied above ours, even so grew the number of those cases which were not determined by any express word. So that if we may devise one law, they by this reason might devise twenty; and if their devising so many were not forbidden, shall their example prove us forbidden to devise as much as one law for the ordering of the Church? We might not devise no not one, if their example did prove that our Saviour had utterly forbidden all alteration of his laws; inasmuch as there can be no law devised, but needs it must either take away from his, or add thereunto more or less, and so make some kind of alteration. But of this so large a grant we are content not to take advantage. Men are oftentimes in a sudden passion more liberal than they would be if they had leisure to take advice. And therefore so bountiful words of course and frank speeches we are contented to let pass, without turning them unto advantage with too much rigour.

[8.] It may be they had rather be listened unto, when they commend the kings of Israel "which attempted nothing in the government of the Church without the express word of God;"[1] and when they urge[2] that God left nothing in his word "undescribed," whether it concerned the worship of God or outward polity, nothing unset down, and therefore charged them strictly to keep themselves unto that, without any alteration. Howbeit, seeing it cannot be denied, but that many things there did belong unto the course of their public affairs, wherein they had no express word at all to show precisely what they should do; the difference between their condition and ours in these cases will bring some light unto the truth of this present controversy. Before the fact of the son of Shelomith, there was no law which did appoint any certain punishment for blasphemers.[3] That wretched creature b ing therefore deprehended in that impiety, was held in ward, till the mind of the Lord were known con-

---

[1] T. C. in the table to his second book.
[2] "If he will needs separate the worship of God from the external polity, yet as the Lord set forth the one, so he left nothing undescribed in the other." T. C. lib. ii. p. 446.
[3] Levit. xxiv. 12.

cerning his case. The like practice is also mentioned upon occasion of a breach of the Sabbath day. They find a poor silly creature gathering sticks in the wilderness, they bring him unto Moses and Aaron and all the congregation, they lay him in hold, because it was not declared what should be done with him, till God had said unto Moses, "This man shall die the death."[1] The law required to keep the Sabbath; but for the breach of the Sabbath what punishment should be inflicted it did not appoint. Such occasions as these are rare. And for such things as do fall scarce once in many ages of men, it did suffice to take such order as was requisite when they fell. But if the case were such as being not already determined by law were notwithstanding likely oftentimes to come in question, it gave occasion of adding laws that were not before. Thus it fell out in the case of those men polluted,[2] and of the daughters of Zelophehad,[3] whose causes Moses having brought before the Lord, received laws to serve for the like in time to come. The Jews to this end had the Oracle of God, they had the Prophets: and by such means God himself instructed them from heaven what to do, in all things that did greatly concern their state and were not already set down in the Law. Shall we then hereupon argue even against our own experience and knowledge? Shall we seek to persuade men that of necessity it is with us as it was with them; that because God is ours in all respects as much as theirs, therefore either no such way of direction hath been at any time, or if it hath been it doth still continue in the Church; or if the same do not continue, that yet it must be at the least supplied by some such mean as pleaseth us to account of equal force? A more dutiful and religious way for us were to admire the wisdom of God, which shineth in the beautiful variety of all things, but most in the manifold and yet harmonious dissimilitude of those ways, whereby his Church upon earth is guided from age to age, throughout all generations of men.

[9.] The Jews were necessarily to continue till the coming of Christ in the flesh, and the gathering of nations unto him. So much the promise made unto Abraham[4] did import. So much the prophecy of Jacob at the hour of his death did foreshew.[5] Upon the safety therefore of their

---

[1] Numb. xv. 33–35.   [2] Numb. ix.   [3] Numb. xxvii.
[4] Gen. xviii. 18.   [5] Gen. xlix. 10.

very outward state and condition for so long, the after good of the whole world and the salvation of all did depend. Unto their so long safety, for two things it was necessary to provide ; namely, the preservation of their state against foreign resistance, and the continuance of their peace within themselves.

Touching the one, as they received the promise of God to be the rock of their defence, against which whoso did violently rush should but bruise and batter themselves ; so likewise they had his commandment in all their affairs that way to seek direction and counsel from him.   Men's consultations are always perilous.   And it falleth out many times that after long deliberation those things are by their wit even resolved on, which by trial are found most opposite to public safety.   It is no impossible thing for states, be they never so well established, yet by oversight in some one act or treaty between them and their potent opposites utterly to cast away themselves for ever.   Wherefore lest it should so fall out to them upon whom so much did depend, they were not permitted to enter into war, nor conclude any league of peace, nor to wade through any act of moment between them and foreign states, unless the Oracle of God or his Prophets were first consulted with.

And lest domestical disturbance should waste them within themselves, because there was nothing unto this purpose more effectual, than if the authority of their laws and governors were such, as none might presume to take exception against it, or to shew disobedience unto it, without incurring the hatred and detestation of all men that had any spark of the fear of God ; therefore he gave them even their positive laws from heaven, and as oft as occasion required chose in like sort rulers also to lead and govern them. Notwithstanding some desperately impious there were, which adventured to try what harm it could bring upon them, if they did attempt to be authors of confusion, and to resist both governors and laws.   Against such monsters God maintained his own by fearful execution of extraordinary judgment upon them.

By which means it came to pass, that although they were a people infested and mightily hated of all others throughout the world, although by nature hard-hearted, querulous, wrathful, and impatient of rest and quietness ; yet was there nothing of force either one way or other to work the ruin

and subversion of their state, till the time before-mentioned
was expired. Thus we see that there was not no cause of
dissimilitude in these things between that one only people
before Christ, and the kingdoms of the world since.

[10.] And whereas it is further alleged [1] that albeit "in
civil matters and things pertaining to this present life God
hath used a greater particularity with them than amongst us,
framing laws according to the quality of that people and
country; yet the leaving of us at greater liberty in things
civil is so far from proving the like liberty in things pertaining to the kingdom of heaven, that it rather proves a straiter
bond. For even as when the Lord would have his favour
more appear by temporal blessings of this life towards the
people under the Law than towards us, he gave also politic
laws most exactly, whereby they might both most easily
come into and most steadfastly remain in possession of
those earthly benefits: even so at this time, wherein he
would not have his favour so much esteemed by those
outward commodities, it is required, that as his care in
prescribing laws for that purpose hath somewhat fallen in
leaving them to men's consultations which may be deceived,
so his care for conduct and government of the life to come
should (if it were possible) rise, in leaving less to the order
of men than in times past." These are but weak and feeble
disputes for the inference of that conclusion which is
intended. For saving only in such consideration as hath
been shewed, there is no cause wherefore we should think
God more desirous to manifest his favour by tempo al
blessings towards them than towards us. Godliness had
unto them, and it hath also unto us, the promises both of
this life and the life to come. That the care of God hath
fallen in earthly things, and therefore should rise as much
in heavenly; that more is left unto men's consultations in
the one, and therefore less must be granted in the other;
that God, having used a greater particularity with them
than with us for matters pertaining unto this life, is to make
us amends by the more exact delivery of laws for government of the life to come: these are proportions, whereof if
there be any rule, we must plainly confess that which truth
is, we know it not. God which spake unto them by his
Prophets, hath unto us by his only-begotten Son; those
mysteries of grace and salvation which were but darkly

[1] T. C. lib. ii. p. 440.

disclosed unto them, have unto us most clearly shined. Such differences between them and us the Apostles of Christ have well acquainted us withal. But as for matter belonging to the outward conduct or government of the Church, seeing that even in sense it is manifest that our Lord and Saviour hath not by positive laws descended so far into particularities with us as Moses with them, neither doth by extraordinary means, oracles, and prophets, direct us as them he did in those things which rising daily by new occasions are of necessity to be provided for; doth it not hereupon rather follow, that although not to them, yet to us there should be freedom and liberty granted to make laws?

[11.] Yea, but the Apostle St. Paul doth fearfully charge Timothy,[1] even "in the sight of God who quickeneth all, and of Jesus Christ who witnessed that famous confession before Pontius Pilate,[2] to keep what was commanded him safe and sound till the appearance of our Lord Jesus Christ."[3] This doth exclude all liberty of changing the laws of Christ, whether by abrogation or addition or howsoever. For in Timothy the whole Church of Christ receiveth charge concerning her duty; and that charge is to keep the Apostle's commandment; and his commandment did contain the laws that concerned church government; and those laws he straitly requireth to be observed without breach or blame, till the appearance of our Lord Jesus Christ.

In Scripture we grant every one man's lesson to be the

---

[1] [See Eccl. Disc. fol. 10. "Sed universum hunc locum de disciplina a Deo profecta, et prophetica immobili atque perpetua, et omnium ecclesiarum communi, gravissima illa Pauli ad Timotheum de eadem conservanda obtestatione concludamus. Qui quum discipulum suum omnem domus Dei, quæ est Ecclesia, administrandæ rationem docuisset, 'Denuncio,' inquit, 'tibi, in conspectu Dei illius qui vivificat omnia, et Jesu Christi, qui præclaram illam confessionem Pontio Pilato professus est, ut hæc mandata sine labe et sine reprehensione custodias usque ad apparitionem Domini nostri Jesu Christi:' &c. quæ gravissimis verbis Apostolus persecutus est. Unde primo colligimus, disciplinæ quam ea epistola Paulus tradidisset, Deum omnipotentem auctorem esse, et Servatorem nostrum Jesum Christum: ut qui ejusdem violatæ ultores et vindices significantur. Tum constantem esse atque immutabilem, quæ nulla hominum neque gratia variari, neque auctoritate frangi debeat: cum non solum ἐντολὴ καὶ παραγγελία appelletur, sed jubeatur etiam ἄσπιλος καὶ ἀνεπίληπτος conservari. Postremo non certi alicujus temporis præceptum esse, sed perpetuum, et quod ad omnia Ecclesiæ tempora pertineat: quum tam diserte præceptum sit, ut usque in adventum Domini nostri Jesu Christi conservetur."]

[2] John xviii. 36, 37.   [3] 1 Tim. iv. 13, 14.

common instruction of all men, so far forth as their cases are like; and that religiously to keep the Apostle's commandments in whatsoever they may concern us we all stand bound. But touching that commandment which Timothy was charged with, we swerve undoubtedly from the Apostle's precise meaning, if we extend it so largely, that the arms thereof shall reach unto all things which were commanded him by the Apostle. The very words themselves do restrain themselves unto some one especial commandment among many. And therefore it is not said, "Keep the ordinances, laws, and constitutions, which thou hast received;" but τὴν ἐντολὴν, that great commandment, which doth principally concern thee and thy calling;" that commandment which Christ did so often inculcate unto Peter;[1] that commandment unto the careful discharge whereof they of Ephesus are exhorted, "Attend to yourselves, and to all the flock wherein the Holy Ghost hath placed you Bishops, to feed the Church of God, which he hath purchased by his own blood;"[2] finally that commandment which unto the same Timothy is by the same Apostle even in the same form and manner afterwards again urged, "I charge thee in the sight of God and the Lord Jesus Christ, which will judge the quick and dead at his appearance and in his kingdom, *preach the word of God.*"[3] When Timothy was instituted into that office, then was the credit and trust of this duty committed unto his faithful care. The doctrine of the Gospel was then given him, "as the precious talent or treasure of Jesus Christ;"[4] then received he for performance of this duty "the special gift of the Holy Ghost."[5] "To keep this commandment immaculate and blameless" was to teach the Gospel of Christ without mixture of corrupt and unsound doctrine, such as a number did even in those times intermingle with the mysteries of Christian belief. "Till the appearance of Christ to keep it so," doth not import the time wherein it should be kept, but rather the time whereunto the final reward for keeping it was reserved: according to that of St. Paul concerning himself, "I have kept the faith; for the residue there is laid up for me a crown of righteousness, which the Lord the righteous shall in that day render unto me."[6] If they that

---

[1] John xxi. 15.
[2] Acts xx. 28.
[3] 2 Tim. iv. 1.
[4] 1 Tim. vi. 20. τὴν παρακαταθήκην.
[5] 1 Tim. iv. 14.
[6] 2 Tim. iv. 7, 8.

labour in this harvest should respect but the present fruit of their painful travel, a poor encouragement it were unto them to continue therein all the days of their life. But their reward is great in heaven ; the crown of righteousness which shall be given them in that day is honourable. The fruit of their industry then shall they reap with full content ment and satisfaction, but not till then. Wherein the greatness of their reward is abundantly sufficient to counter-vail the tediousness of their expectation. Wherefore till then, they that are in labour must rest in hope. "O Timothy, keep that which is committed unto thy charge ; that great commandment which thou hast received keep, till the appearance of our Lord Jesus Christ."

In which sense although we judge the Apostle's words to have been uttered, yet hereunto we do not require them to yield, that think any other construction more sound. If therefore it be rejected, and theirs esteemed more probable which hold, that the last words do import perpetual observ-ation of the Apostle's commandment imposed necessarily for ever upon the militant Church of Christ ; let them withal consider, that then his commandment cannot so largely be taken, as to comprehend whatsoever the Apostle did command Timothy. For themselves do not all bind the Church unto some things whereof Timothy received charge, as namely unto that precept concerning the choice of widows.[1] So as they cannot hereby maintain that all things positively commanded concerning the affairs of the Church were commanded for perpetuity. And we do not deny that certain things were commanded to be though positive yet perpetual in the Church.

[12.] They should not therefore urge against us places that seem to forbid change, but rather such as set down some measure of alteration, which measure if we have exceeded, then might they therewith charge us justly : whereas now they themselves both granting, and also using liberty to change, cannot in reason dispute absolutely against all change. Christ delivered no inconvenient or unmeet laws : sundry of ours they hold inconvenient : therefore such laws they cannot possibly hold to be Christ's : being not his, they must of necessity grant them added unto his. Yet certain of those very laws so added they them-selves do not judge unlawful ; as they plainly confess both

[1] [1 Tim. v. 9. See T. C. i. 153. al. 191. Whitg. Def. 693.]

in matter of prescript attire and of rites appertaining to burial. Their own protestations are, that they plead against the inconvenience not the unlawfulness of popish apparel;[1] and against the inconvenience not the unlawfulness of ceremonies in burial. Therefore they hold it a thing not unlawful to add to the laws of Jesus Christ; and so consequently they yield that no law of Christ forbiddeth addition unto church laws.

[13.] The judgment of Calvin being alleged[2] against them, to whom of all men they attribute most;[3] whereas his words be plain, that for ceremonies and external discipline the Church hath power to make laws: the answer which hereunto they make is, that indefinitely the speech is true, and that so it was meant by him; namely, that some things belonging unto external discipline and ceremonies are in the power and arbitrement of the Church; but neither was it meant, neither is it true generally, that all external discipline

[1] "My reasons do never conclude the unlawfulness of these ceremonies of burial, but the inconvenience and inexpedience of them." T. C. lib. iii. p. 241. And in the table. "Of the inconvenience, not of the unlawfulness, of popish apparel and ceremonies in burial."

[2] [By Archbishop Whitgift: see Answer, p. 25-29, and Def. 109-113. The passage from Calvin is the following: "Quia Dominus . . . quicquid ad salutem necessarium erat, sacris suis oraculis tum fideliter complexus est, tum perspicue enarravit, in his solus magister est audiendus. Quia autem in externa disciplina et ceremoniis non voluit sigillatim praescribere quid sequi debeamus, quod istud pendere a temporum conditione praevideret, neque judicaret unam saeculis omnibus formam convenire, confugere hic oportet ad generales, quas dedit, regulas; ut ad eas exigantur, quaecunque ad ordinem et decorum praecipi necessitas Ecclesiae postulabit." Instit. c. xiii. § 31. ed. 1550, or lib. iv. c. x. § 30, according to the present arrangement. All Whitgift's quotations from the Institution specify *chapter* and *section* only. The division of the work into books first took place in the edition of 1559: and Whitgift used an earlier copy. See Def. 391, 508.]

[3] "Upon the indefinite speaking of M. Calvin, saying, 'ceremonies and external discipline,' without adding 'all' or 'some,' you go about subtilly to make men believe, that M. Calvin had placed the whole external discipline in the power and arbitrement of the Church. For if all external discipline were arbitrary, and in the choice of the Church, excommunication also (which is a part of it) might be cast away; which I think you will not say." And in the very next words before: "Where you would give to understand that ceremonies and external discipline are not prescribed particularly by the word of God, and therefore left to the order of the Church: you must understand that all external discipline is not left to the order of the Church, being particularly prescribed in the Scriptures: no more than all ceremonies are left to the order of the Church, as the Sacrament of Baptism, and Supper of the Lord." T. C. lib. i. p. 32. [and 33. al. 19. Whitgf. Def. 111.]

and all ceremonies are left to the order of the Church, inasmuch as the sacraments of Baptism and the Supper of the Lord are ceremonies, which yet the Church may not therefore abrogate.   Again, Excommunication is a part of external discipline, which might also be cast away, if all external discipline were arbitrary and in the choice of the Church.

By which their answer it doth appear, that touching the names of ceremony and external discipline they gladly would have us so understood, as if we did herein contain a great deal more than we do.   The fault which we find with them is, that they overmuch abridge the Church of her power in these things.   Whereupon they recharge us, as if in these things we gave the Church a liberty which hath no limits or bounds;   as if all things which the name of discipline containeth were at the Church's free choice;   so that we might either have church governors and government or want them, either retain or reject church censures as we list.   They wonder at us, as at men which think it so indifferent what the Church doth in matter of ceremonies, that it may be feared lest we judge the very Sacraments themselves to be held at the Church's pleasure.

No, the name of ceremonies we do not use in so large a meaning as to bring Sacraments within the compass and reach thereof, although things belonging unto the outward form and seemly administration of them are contained in that name, even as we use it.   For the name of ceremonies we use as they themselves do, when they speak after this sort : " The doctrine and discipline of the Church, as the weightiest things, ought especially to be looked unto ; but the ceremonies also, as mint and cummin, ought not to be neglected." [1]   Besides, in the matter of external discipline or regiment itself, we do not deny but there are some things whereto the church is bound till the world's end.   So as the question is only how far the bounds of the Church's liberty do reach.   We hold, that the power which the Church hath lawfully to make laws and orders for itself doth extend unto sundry things of ecclesiastical jurisdiction, and such other matters, whereto their opinion is that the Church's authority and power doth not reach.   Whereas therefore in disputing against us about this point, they take their compass a great deal wider than the truth of things can afford ; producing

[1] T. C. lib. iii. p. 171.

reasons and arguments by way of generality, to prove that Christ hath set down all things belonging any way unto the form of ordering his Church, and hath absolutely forbidden change by addition or diminution, great or small : (for so their manner of disputing is :) we are constrained to make our defence, by shewing that Christ hath not deprived his Church so far of all liberty in making orders and laws for itself, and that they themselves do not think he hath so done. For are they able to shew that all particular customs, rites, and orders of reformed churches have been appointed by Christ himself? No : they grant that in matter of circumstance they alter that which they have received,[1] but in things of substance they keep the laws of Christ without change. If we say the same in our own behalf (which surely we may do with a great deal more truth) then must they cancel all that hath been before alleged, and begin to inquire afresh, whether we retain the laws that Christ hath delivered concerning matters of substance, yea or no. For our constant persuasion in this point is as theirs, that we have no where altered the laws of Christ farther than in such particularities only as have the nature of things changeable according to the difference of times, places, persons, and other the like circumstances. Christ hath commanded prayers to be made, sacraments to be ministered, his Church to be carefully taught and guided. Concerning every of these somewhat Christ hath commanded which must be kept till the world's end. On the contrary side, in every of them somewhat there may be added, as the Church s all judge it expedient. So that if they will speak to purpose, all which hitherto hath been disputed of they must give over, and stand upon such particulars only as they can shew we have either added or abrogated otherwise than we ought, in the matter of church polity. Whatsoever Christ hath commanded for ever to be kept in his Church, the same we take not upon us to abrogate ; and whatsoever our laws have thereunto added besides, of such quality we hope it is as no law of Christ doth any where condemn.

[14.] Wherefore that all may be laid together and gathered

---

[1] "We deny not but certain things are left to the order of the Church, because they are of the nature of those which are varied by times, places, persons, and other circumstances, and so could not at once be set down and established for ever." T. C. lib. i. p. 27. [15.]

into a narrow room : First, so far forth as the Church is the mystical body of Christ and his invisible spouse, it needeth no external polity. That very part of the law divine which teacheth faith and works of righteousness is itself alone sufficient for the Church of God in that respect. But as the Church is a visible society and body politic, laws of polity it cannot want.[1]

[15.] Secondly : Whereas therefore it cometh in the second place to be inquired, what laws are fittest and best for the Church ; they who first embraced that rigorous and strict opinion, which depriveth the Church of liberty to make any kind of law for herself, inclined as it should seem thereunto, for that they imagined all things which the Church doth without commandment of Holy Scripture subject to that reproof which the Scripture itself useth in certain cases[2] when divine authority ought alone to be followed. Hereupon they thought it enough for the cancelling of any kind of order whatsoever, to say, "The word of God teacheth it not, it is a device of the brain of man, away with it therefore out of the Church."[3] St. Augustine was of another mind, who speaking of fasts on the Sunday saith,[4] "That he which would choose out that day to fast on, should give thereby no small offence to the Church of God, which had received a contrary custom. For in these things, whereof the Scripture appointeth no certainty, the use of the people of God or the ordinances of our fathers must serve for a law. In which case if we will dispute, and condemn one sort by another's custom, it will be but matter of endless contention ; where, forasmuch as the labour of reasoning shall hardly beat into men's heads any certain or necessary truth, surely it standeth us upon to take heed, lest with the tempest of strife the brightness of charity and love be darkened."

If all things must be commanded of God which may be practised of his Church, I would know what commandment

---

[1] [See above, ch. i.]   [2] Isa. xxix. 14 ; Col. ii. 22.

[3] [See above, ch. ii. 1.]

[4] August. Ep. 86. [al. 36. t. ii. 68. "Quisquis hunc diem jejunio decernendum putaverit, . . . non parvo scandalo erit Ecclesiæ : nec immerito. In his enim rebus de quibus nihil certi statuit Scriptura divina, mos populi Dei, vel instituta majorum pro lege tenenda sunt. De quibus si disputare voluerimus, et ex aliorum consuetudine alios improbare, orietur interminata luctatio : quæ labore sermocinationis cum certa documenta nulla veritatis insinuet, utique cavendum est, ne tempestate contentionis serenitatem caritatis obnubilet."

the Gileadites had to erect that altar which is spoken of in
the book of Joshua.[1] Did not congruity of reason induce
them thereunto, and suffice for defence of their fact? I
would know what commandment the women of Israel had
yearly to mourn and lament in the memory of Jephthah's
daughter;[2] what commandment the Jews had to celebrate
their feast of Dedication, never spoken of in the law, yet
solemnized even by our Saviour himself;[3] what commandment finally they had for the ceremony of odours used about
the bodies of the dead, after which custom notwithstanding
(sith it was their custom) our Lord was contented that his
own most precious body should be entombed.[4] Wherefore
to reject all orders of the Church which men have established, is to think worse of the laws of men in this respect,
than either the judgment of wise men alloweth, or the law
of God itself will bear.

[16.] Howbeit they which had once taken upon them to
condemn all things done in the Church and not commanded
of God to be done, saw it was necessary for them (continuing in defence of this their opinion) to hold that needs there
must be in Scripture set down a complete particular form of
church polity, a form prescribing how all the affairs of the
Church must be ordered, a form in no respect lawful to be
altered by mortal men.[5] For reformation of which oversight and error in them, there were that thought it a part of
Christian love and charity to instruct them better,[6] and to
open unto them the difference between matters of perpetual
necessity to all men's salvation, and matters of ecclesiastical
polity: the one both fully and plainly taught in holy Scripture, the other not necessary to be in such sort there
prescribed; the one not capable of any diminution or
augmentation at all by men, the other apt to admit both.
Hereupon the authors of the former opinion were presently

---

[1] Josh. xxii. 10.   [2] Judges xi. 40.   [3] John x. 22.
[4] John xix. 40.
[5] [1 Admon. to the Parl. fol. 1. ap. Whitg. Def. 76. "Seeing that
nothing in this mortal life is more diligently to be sought for, and carefully to be looked unto, than the restitution of true religion, and reformation of God's Church: it shall be your parts (dearly beloved) in this
present parliament assembled, as much as in you lieth to promote the
same, and to employ your whole labour and study not only in abandon-
ing all popish remnants both in ceremonies and regiment, but also in
bringing in and placing in God's Church those things only, which the
Lord himself in his word commandeth."]
[6] [Vide Whitgift's Answer to the Admonition, p. 20-29.]

seconded by other wittier and better learned,[1] who being
loth that the form of church polity which they sought to
bring in should be otherwise than in the highest degree
accounted of, took [2] first an exception against the difference
between church polity and matters of necessity unto salvation;[3] secondly, against the restraint of Scripture, which
they say receiveth injury at our hands, when we teach that
it teacheth not as well matters of polity as of faith and
salvation.[4] Thirdly, Constrained hereby we have been therefore both to maintain that distinction, as a thing not only
true in itself, but by them likewise so acknowledged, though
unawares;[5] Fourthly, and to make manifest that from
Scripture we offer not to derogate the least thing that truth
thereunto doth claim, inasmuch as by us it is willingly confest, that the Scripture of God is a storehouse abounding
with inestimable treasures of wisdom and knowledge in
many kinds, over and above things in this one kind barely
necessary; yea, even that matters of ecclesiastical polity are
not therein omitted, but taught also, albeit not so taught as
those other things before-mentioned.[6] For so perfectly are
those things taught, that nothing can ever need to be added,
nothing ever cease to be necessary; these on the contrary
side, as being of a far other nature and quality, not so strictly
nor everlastingly commanded in Scripture, but that unto the
complete form of church polity much may be requisite
which the Scripture teacheth not, and much which it hath
taught become unrequisite, sometime because we need not
use it, sometime also because we cannot.   In which respect
for mine own part, although I see that certain reformed
churches, the Scottish especially and French, have not that
which best agreeth with the sacred Scripture,[7] I mean the

----

[1] [By this it should seem that Hooker did not consider Cartwright
himself as one of the authors of the Admonition]
[2] [See above, ch. ii. 2.]   [3] [T. C. 1 Reply, p. 14.]
[4] [T. C. ibid.]   [5] [In ch. iii.]   [6] [In ch. iv.]
[7] [Saravia, De diversis Ministrorum Gradibus, Prol. ad Lect. "De
hoc novo Ecclesiæ regendæ modo idem censeo, quod alii de Episcoporum regimine judicant; nempe quod sit humanus et ferendus, ubi
alius melior obtineri non potest: et contra ille qui improbatur tanquam
humanus mihi videtur esse divinus; utpote qui tam in Veteri quam in
Novo Testamento a Deo sit institutus." Sutcliffe, False Semblant of
counterfeit Discipline detected, p. 8. "We say, that so much as Christ
hath appointed to be observed, as that there be pastors to teach, and a
certain government, and such like discipline, is diligently to be kept.
Where He hath left it free, there the governors of the Church, *i. e.*

government that is by Bishops, inasmuch as both those churches are fallen under a different kind of regiment; which to remedy it is for the one altogether too late, and too soon for the other during their present affliction and trouble:[1] this their defect and imperfection I had rather lament in such case than exagitate, considering that men oftentimes without any fault of their own may be driven to want that kind of polity or regiment which is best, and to content themselves with that, which either the irremediable error of former times, or the necessity of the present hath cast upon them.

[17.] Fifthly, Now because that position first-mentioned, which holdeth it necessary that all things which the Church may lawfully do in her own regiment be commanded in holy Scripture, hath by the later defenders thereof been greatly qualified; who, though perceiving it to be over-extreme, are notwithstanding loth to acknowledge any oversight therein, and therefore labour what they may to salve it by construction; we have for the more perspicuity delivered what was thereby meant at the first:[2] sixthly, how injurious a thing it were unto all the churches of God for men to hold it in that meaning:[3] seventhly, and how imperfect their interpretations are who so much labour to help it, either by dividing commandments of Scripture into two kinds, and so defending that all things must be commanded, if not in special yet in general precepts;[4] eighthly, or by taking it as meant, that in case the Church do devise any new order, she ought therein to follow the direction of Scripture only, and not any starlight of man's reason.[5] Ninthly, both which evasions being cut off, we have in the next place declared after what sort the Church may lawfully frame to herself laws of polity, and in what reckoning such positive laws both are with God and should be with men.[6] Tenthly, further_

Christian princes and bishops may set orders and see the same executed: and the orders appointed by Christ, and canons and customs of the Church, we call ecclesiastical discipline: and this we account to be changeable so far forth as is not by Christ commanded to be kept."]

[1] [The first part of Hooker's work was licensed to the press, March 9, 1592-3. The affliction meant is therefore the civil war in France, not the secession from protestantism of Henry IV.: which was not made known till after June that year. Davila, lib. xiii. p. 697, comp. d. 692. Venice, 1692.]

[2] [In ch. v.]   [3] [In ch. vi.]   [4] [In ch. vii.]
[5] [In ch. viii.]   [6] [In ch. ix.]

more, because to abridge the liberty of the Church in this
behalf, it hath been made a thing very odious, that when
God himself hath devised some certain laws and committed
them to sacred Scripture, man by abrogation, addition, or
any way, should presume to alter and change them ; it was
of necessity to be examined, whether the authority of God
in making, or his care in committing those his laws unto
Scripture, be sufficient arguments to prove that God doth in
no case allow they should suffer any such kind of change.[1]
Eleventhly, the last refuge for proof that divine laws or
Christian church polity may not be altered by extinguishment of any old or addition of new in that kind, is partly a
marvellous strange discourse, that Christ (unless he should
shew himself not so faithful as Moses, or not so wise as
Lycurgus and Solon[2]) must needs have set down in holy
Scripture some certain complete and unchangeable form of
polity ;[3] and partly a coloured show of some evidence where
change of that sort of laws may seem expressly forbidden,
although in truth nothing less be done.[4]

[18.] I might have added hereunto their more familiar
and popular disputes, as, The Church is a city, yea, the city
of the great King ; and the life of a city is polity : The
Church is the house of the living God ; and what house can
there be without some order for the government of it ? In
the royal house of a prince there must be officers for government, such as not any servant in the house but the prince
whose the house is shall judge convenient. So the house of
God must have orders for the government of it, such as not
any of the household but God himself hath appointed. It
cannot stand with the love and wisdom of God to leave such
order untaken as is necessary for the due government of his
Church. The numbers, degrees, orders, and attire of
Solomon's servants, did shew his wisdom ; therefore he
which is greater than Solomon hath not failed to leave in his
house such orders for government thereof, as may serve to
be a looking-glass for his providence, care, and wisdom, to

[1] [In ch. x.]
[2] " Nisi reip. suæ statum omnem constituerit, magistratus ordinarit,
singulorum munera potestatemque descripserit, quæ judiciorum forique
ratio habenda, quomodo civium finiendæ lites : non solum minus
Ecclesiæ Christianæ providit quam Moses olim Judaicæ, sed quam a
Lycurgo, Solone, Numa, civitatibus suis prospectum sit." Lib. de
Ecclesiast. Discip. [fol. 8, or p. 10 of T. C.'s translation.]
[3] [In ch. xi. 1–8.]   [4] [Ch. xi. 9.]

be seen in.[1] That little spark of the light of nature which remaineth in us may serve us for the affairs of this life. " But as in all other matters concerning the kingdom of heaven, so principally in this which concerneth the very government of that kingdom, needful it is we should be taught of God. As long as men are persuaded of any order that it is only of men, they presume of their own understanding, and they think to devise another not only as good, but better than that which they have received. By severity of punishment this presumption and curiosity may be restrained. But that cannot work such cheerful obedience as is yielded where the conscience hath respect to God as the author of laws and orders. This was it which countenanced the laws of Moses, made concerning outward polity for the administration of holy things. The like some lawgivers of the heathens did pretend, but falsely; yet wisely discerning the use of this persuasion. For the better obedience' sake therefore it was expedient that God should be author of the polity of his Church."

[19.] But to what issue doth all this come ? A man would think that they which hold out with such discourses were of nothing more fully persuaded than of this, that the Scripture hath set down a complete form of church polity, universal, perpetual, altogether unchangeable. For so it would follow, if the premises were sound and strong to such effect as is pretended. Notwithstanding, they which have thus formally maintained argument in defence of the first oversight, are by the very evidence of truth themselves constrained to make this in effect their conclusion, that the Scripture of God hath many things concerning church polity; that of those many some are of greater weight, some of less; that what hath been urged as touching immutability of laws, it extendeth in truth no farther than only to laws wherein things of greater

---

[1] [Eccl. Disc. fol. 143. "Christianæ Ecclesiæ, tanquam domus Dei (ut a Paulo appellatur) οἰκονομίαν qui attentius et accuratius consideraverit, animadvertet profecto incredibilem quandam illam in omnibus ejus partibus et divinam sapientiam, ac tanto quidem illa Salomonis in sacra historia magis admirabilem, quanto sapientior Salomone fuerit qui omnem hujus domus ordinem rationemque descripsit. Sive enim ministrorum ordines, sive accubitus, sive varium pro cujusque dignitate ornatum et habitum consideremus, quod ad Ecclesiæ non modo salutem conservandam, sed etiam dignitatem illustrandam ornandamque aut prudenter excogitari, aut cum judicio atque ratione disponi collocarique potuerit : quid in hac οἰκονομίᾳ requiratur ? "]

moment are prescribed. Now those things of greater moment, what are they? Forsooth,[1] "doctors, pastors, lay-elders, elderships compounded of these three ; synods, consisting of many elderships ; deacons, women-church-servants or widows ; free consent of the people unto actions of greatest moment, after they be by churches or synods orderly resolved." All "this form" of polity (if yet we may term that a form of building, when men have laid a few rafters together, and those not all of the soundest neither) but howsoever, all this form they conclude is prescribed in such sort, that to add to it any thing as of like importance (for so I think they mean) or to abrogate of it any thing at all, is unlawful. In which resolution if they will firmly and constantly persist, I see not but that concerning the points which hitherto have been disputed of, they must agree that they have molested the Church with needless opposition, and henceforward as we said before betake themselves wholly unto the trial of particulars, whether every of those things which they esteem as principal, be either so esteemed of, or at all established for perpetuity in holy Scripture ; and whether any particular thing in our church polity be received other than the Scripture alloweth of, either in greater things or in smaller.

[20.] The matters wherein church polity is conversant are the public religious duties of the Church, as the administration of the word and sacraments, prayers, spiritual censures, and the like. To these the Church standeth always bound. Laws of polity, are laws which appoint in what manner these duties shall be performed.

In performance whereof because all that are of the Church cannot jointly and equally work, the first thing in polity required is a difference of persons in the Church, without which difference those functions cannot in orderly sort be executed. Hereupon we hold that God's clergy are a state, which hath been and will be, as long as there is a Church upon earth, necessary by the plain word of God himself ; a state whereunto the rest of God's people must be subject as touching things that appertain to their soul's health. For where polity is, it cannot but appoint some to be leaders of others, and some to be led by others. "If the blind lead the blind, they both perish."[2] It is with the clergy, if their

---

[1] The Defence of Godly Ministers against D. Bridges, p. 133.
[2] Luke vi. 39.

persons be respected, even as it is with other men ; their
quality many times far beneath that which the dignity of
their place requireth. Howbeit according to the order of
polity, they being the "lights of the world," [1] others (though
better and wiser) must that way be subject unto them.

Again, forasmuch as where the clergy are any great multitude, order doth necessarily require that by degrees they
be distinguished ; we hold there have ever been and ever
ought to be in such case at leastwise two sorts of ecclesiastical persons, the one subordinate unto the other ; as to
the Apostles in the beginning, and to the Bishops always
since, we find plainly both in Scripture and in all
ecclesiastical records, other ministers of the word and
sacraments have been.

Moreover, it cannot enter into any man's conceit to think
it lawful, that every man which listeth should take upon him
charge in the Church ; and therefore a solemn admittance is
of such necessity, that without it there can be no church
polity.

A number of particularities there are, which make for the
more convenient being of these principal and perpetual
parts in ecclesiastical polity, but yet are not of such constant
use and necessity in God's Church. Of this kind are, times
and places appointed for the exercise of religion ; specialties
belonging to the public solemnity of the word, the sacraments, and prayer ; the enlargement or abridgment of
functions ministerial depending upon those two principals
before-mentioned ; to conclude, even whatsoever doth by
way of formality and circumstance concern any public action
of the Church. Now although that which the Scripture
hath of things in the former kind be for ever permanent :
yet in the latter both much of that which the Scripture
teacheth is not always needful ; and much the Church of
God shall always need which the Scripture teacheth not.

So as the form of polity by them set down for perpetuity
is three ways faulty : faulty in omitting some things which
in Scripture are of that nature, as namely the difference that
ought to be of pastors when they grow to any great multitude : faulty in requiring doctors, deacons, widows, and such
like, as things of perpetual necessity by the law of God,
which in truth are nothing less : faulty also in urging some
things by Scripture immutable, as their lay-elders, which the

[1] Matt. v. 14.

Scripture neither maketh immutable nor at all teacheth, for any thing either we can as yet find or they have hitherto been able to prove. But hereof more in the books that follow.

[21.] As for those marvellous discourses whereby they adventure to argue that God must needs have done the thing which they imagine was to be done; I must confess I have often wondered at their exceeding boldness herein. When the question is whether God have delivered in Scripture (as they affirm he hath) a complete, particular, immutable form of church polity, why take they that other both presumptuous and superfluous labour to prove he should have done it; there being no way in this case to prove the deed of God, saving only by producing that evidence wherein he hath done it? But if there be no such thing apparent upon record, they do as if one should demand a legacy by force and virtue of some written testament, wherein there being no such thing specified, he pleadeth that there it must needs be, and bringeth arguments from the love or goodwill which always the testator bore him; imagining, that these or the like proofs will convict a testament to have that in it which other men can no where by reading find. In matters which concern the actions of God, the most dutiful way on our part is to search what God hath done, and with meekness to admire that, rather than to dispute what he in congruity of reason ought to do. The ways which he hath whereby to do all things for the greatest good of his Church are more in number than we can search, other in nature than that we should presume to determine which of many should be the fittest for him to choose, till such time as we see he hath chosen of many some one; which one we then may boldly conclude to be the fittest, because he hath taken it before the rest. When we do otherwise, surely we exceed our bounds; who and where we are we forget; and therefore needful it is that our pride in such cases be controlled, and our disputes beaten back with those demands of the blessed Apostle, "How unsearchable are his judgments, and his ways past finding out! Who hath known the mind of the Lord, or who was his counsellor?"[1]

[1] Rom. xi. 33, 34.

THE FOURTH BOOK

CONCERNING THEIR THIRD ASSERTION, THAT OUR FORM OF
CHURCH POLITY IS CORRUPTED WITH POPISH ORDERS,
RITES, AND CEREMONIES, BANISHED OUT OF CERTAIN
REFORMED CHURCHES, WHOSE EXAMPLE THEREIN WE
OUGHT TO HAVE FOLLOWED

THE MATTER CONTAINED IN THIS FOURTH BOOK

I. Such was the ancient simplicity and softness of spirit which sometimes prevailed in the world, that they whose words were even as oracles amongst men, seemed evermore loth to give sentence against any thing publicly received in the Church of God, except it were wonderful apparently evil; for that they did not so much incline to that severity which delighteth to reprove the least things it seeth amiss, as to that charity which is unwilling to behold any thing that duty bindeth it to reprove. The state of this present age, wherein zeal hath drowned charity, and skill meekness, will not now suffer any man to marvel, whatsoever he shall hear reproved by whomsoever. Those rites and ceremonies of the Church therefore, which are the selfsame now that they were when holy and virtuous men maintained them against profane and deriding adversaries, her own children have at this day in derision. Whether justly or no, it shall then appear, when all things are heard which they have to allege against the outward received orders of this church. Which inasmuch as themselves do compare unto "mint and cummin,"[1] granting them to be no part of those things which in the matter of polity are weightier, we hope that for small things their strife will neither be earnest nor long.

[2.] The sifting of that which is objected against the orders of the Church in particular, doth not belong unto this place. Here we are to discuss only those general exceptions, which have been taken at any time against them.

First therefore to the end that their nature and the use whereunto they serve may plainly appear, and so afterwards their quality the better be discerned; we are to note, that in every grand or main public duty which God requireth at the hands of his Church, there is, besides that matter and form wherein the essence thereof consisteth, a certain outward fashion whereby the same is in decent sort administered. The substance of all religious actions is delivered from God himself in few words. For example's sake in the sacraments.[2] "Unto the element let the word be added,

---

[1] Matt. xxiii. 23. "The doctrine and discipline of the Church, as the weightiest things, ought especially to be looked unto: but the ceremonies also, as 'mint and cummin,' ought not to be neglected." T. C. l. iii. p. 171.

[2] [In Joan. Tract. 80. § 3. t. iii. pars ii. 703. "'Jam vos mundi estis propter verbum quod locutus sum vobis.' Quare non ait, 'mundi

and they both do make a sacrament," saith St. Augustine. Baptism is given by the element of water, and that prescript form of words which the Church of Christ doth use; the sacrament of the body and blood of Christ is administered in the elements of bread and wine, if those mystical words be added thereunto. But the due and decent form of administering those holy sacraments doth require a great deal more.

[3.] The end which is aimed at in setting down the outward form of all religious actions is the edification of the Church. Now men are edified, when either their understanding is taught somewhat whereof in such actions it behoveth all men to consider, or when their hearts are moved with any affection suitable thereunto; when their minds are in any sort stirred up unto that reverence, devotion, attention, and due regard, which in those cases seemeth requisite. Because therefore unto this purpose not only speech but sundry sensible means besides have always been thought necessary, and especially those means which being object to the eye, the liveliest and the most apprehensive sense of all other, have in that respect seemed the fittest to make a deep and a strong impression: from hence have risen not only a number of prayers, readings, questionings, exhortings, but even of visible signs also; which being used in performance of holy actions, are undoubtedly most effectual to open such matter, as men when they know and remember carefully, must needs be a great deal the better informed to what effect such duties serve. We must not think but that there is some ground of reason even in nature, whereby it cometh to pass that no nation under heaven either doth or ever did suffer public actions which are of weight, whether they be civil and temporal or else spiritual and sacred, to pass without some visible solemnity: the very strangeness whereof and difference from that which is common, doth cause popular eyes to observe and to mark the same. Words, both because they are common, and do not so strongly move the fancy of man, are for the most part but slightly heard: and therefore with singular wisdom it hath been provided, that

estis propter baptismum quo loti estis,' nisi quia et in aqua verbum mundat? Detrahe verbum, et quid est aqua nisi aqua? Accedit verbum ad elementum, et fit sacramentum, etiam ipsum tanquam visibile verbum."]

the deeds of men which are made in the presence of
witnesses should pass not only with words, but also
with certain sensible actions, the memory whereof is
far more easy and durable than the memory of speech
can be.

The things which so long experience of all ages hath
confirmed and made profitable, let not us presume to
condemn as follies and toys, because we sometimes know
not the cause and reason of them. A wit disposed to
scorn whatsoever it doth not conceive, might ask wherefore
Abraham should say to his servant, " Put thy hand under
my thigh and swear : "[1] was it not sufficient for his servant
to shew the religion of an oath by naming the Lord God
of heaven and earth, unless that strange ceremony were
added ? In contracts, bargains, and conveyances, a man's
word is a token sufficient to express his will. Yet "this
was the ancient manner in Israel concerning redeeming
and exchanging, to establish all things ; a man did pluck
off his shoe and give it his neighbour ; and this was a sure
witness in Israel."[2] Amongst the Romans in their making
of a bondman free, was it not wondered wherefore so great
ado should be made ? The master to present his slave in
some court, to take him by the hand, and not only to say
in the hearing of the public magistrate, " I will that this
man become free," but after these solemn words uttered, to
strike him on the cheek, to turn him round, the hair of his
head to be shaved off, the magistrate to touch him thrice
with a rod, in the end a cap and a white garment to
be given him. To what purpose all this circumstance ?[3]
Amongst the Hebrews how strange and in outward appearance almost against reason, that he which was minded
to make himself a perpetual servant, should not only testify
so much in the presence of the judge, but for a visible
token thereof have also his ear bored through with an
awle ![4] It were an infinite labour to prosecute these
things so far as they might be exemplified both in civil and
religious actions. For in both they have their necessary
use and force. "The sensible things which religion hath
hallowed, are resemblances framed according to things

---

[1] Gen. xxiv. 2. [2] Ruth iv. 7.
[3] [See Persius, Sat. V. 75, &c. Festus, voc. "manumitti." Isidor.
Orig. ix. 4.]
[4] Exod. xxi. 6.

spiritually understood, whereunto they serve as a hand to lead, and a way to direct."[1]

[4.] And whereas it may peradventure be objected, that to add to religious duties such rites and ceremonies as are significant, is to institute new Sacraments;[2] sure I am they will not say that Numa Pompilius did ordain a sacrament, a significant ceremony he did ordain, in commanding the priests "to execute the work of their divine service with their hands as far as to the fingers covered; thereby signifying that fidelity must be defended, and that men's right hands are the sacred seat thereof."[3]   Again we are also to put them in mind, that themselves do not hold all significant ceremonies for sacraments, insomuch as imposition of hands they deny to be a sacrament, and yet they give thereunto a forcible signification; for concerning it their words are these: "The party ordained by this ceremony was put in mind of his separation to the work of the Lord, that remembering himself to be taken as it were with the hand of God from amongst others, this might teach him not to account himself now his own, nor to do what himself listeth, but to consider that God hath set him about a work, which if he will discharge and accomplish, he may at the hands of God assure himself of reward; and if otherwise, of revenge."[4]   Touching significant ceremonies, some of them are sacraments, some as sacraments only. Sacraments are those which are signs and tokens of some general promised grace, which always really descendeth from God unto the soul that duly receiveth them; other significant tokens are only as Sacraments, yet no Sacra-

---

[1] Τὰ μὲν αἰσθητῶς ἱερὰ τῶν νοητῶν ἀπεικονίσματα, καὶ ἐπ' αὐτὰ χειραγωγία καὶ ὁδός.   Dionys. p. 121. [de Eccl. Hierarch. c. 2. No. 3. § 2. t. i. 255. Antverp. 1634.]

[2] [See Beza's Letter to Grindall in Adm. 5.   "They sinned righte greevously, as often as they brought any Sacramentalles (that is to say, any ceremonies to import signification of spiritual things) into the Church of God."]

[3] "Manu ad digitos usque involuta rem divinam facere, significantes fidem tutandam, sedemque ejus etiam in dextris sacratam esse."   Liv. lib. i. [c. 21.]

[4] Eccles. disc. fol. 51. ["Designatus hac ceremonia monebatur se ad opus Domini separari, et e reliquo populo ad illam procurationem Dei ipsius manu quasi decerpi atque delibari: ut jam non amplius se sui juris esse sciret, ut agat quod velit, sed a Deo ad opus suum adhibitum, cujus illum perfecti atque absoluti remunerato rem, contempti autem et neglecti ultorem atque vindicem habiturus esset."]

ments: which is not our distinction, but theirs. For concerning the Apostles' imposition of hands these are their own words; "manuum signum hoc et quasi Sacramentum usurparunt;" "they used this sign, or as it were sacrament."[1]

II. Concerning rites and ceremonies there may be fault, either in the kind or in the number and multitude of them. The first thing blamed about the kind of ours is, that in many things we have departed from the ancient simplicity of Christ and his Apostles; we have embraced more outward stateliness, we have those orders in the exercise of religion, which they who best pleased God and served him most devoutly never had. For it is out of doubt that the first state of things was best, that in the prime of Christian religion faith was soundest, the Scriptures of God were then best understood by all men, all parts of godliness did then most abound; and therefore it must needs follow, that customs, laws, and ordinances devised since are not so good for the Church of Christ, but the best way is to cut off later inventions, and to reduce things unto the ancient state wherein at the first they were.[2] Which rule or canon we hold to be either uncertain or at leastwise unsufficient, if not both.[3]

[2.] For in case it be certain, hard it cannot be for them to shew us, where we shall find it so exactly set down, that we may say without all controversy, "these were the orders of the Apostles' times, these wholly and only, neither fewer nor more than these." True it is that many things of this nature be alluded unto, yea many things declared, and many things necessarily collected out of the Apostles' writings. But is it necessary that all the orders of the Church which were then in use should be contained in their books? Surely no. For if the tenor of their writings be well observed, it shall unto any man easily appear, that no more of them are there touched than were needful to be spoken of, sometimes by one occasion and sometimes by another. Will they allow then of any other records besides? Well assured I am they are far enough from acknowledging that the Church ought to keep any thing as apostolical, which is not found in the Apostles' writings, in what other records soever it be found. And therefore

---

[1] Fol. 52.   [2] Lib. Eccles. Disc. et T. C. lib. iii. p. 181.
[3] [See before, Preface, iv. 4.]

whereas St. Augustine affirmeth that those things which the whole Church of Christ doth hold, may well be thought to be apostolical although they be not found written;[1] this his judgment they utterly condemn. I will not here stand in defence of St. Augustine's opinion, which is, that such things are indeed apostolical, but yet with this exception; unless the decree of some general council have haply caused them to be received:[2] for of positive laws and orders received throughout the whole Christian world, St. Augustine could imagine no other fountain save these two. But to let pass St. Augustine; they who condemn him herein must needs confess it a very uncertain thing what the orders of the Church were in the Apostles' times, seeing the Scriptures do not mention them all, and other records thereof besides they utterly reject. So that in tying the Church to the orders of the Apostles' times, they tie it to a marvellous uncertain rule; unless they require the observation of no orders but only those which are known to be apostolical by the Apostles' own writings. But then is not this their rule of such sufficiency, that we should use it as a touchstone to try the orders of the Church by for ever.

[3.] Our end ought always to be the same; our ways and means thereunto not so. The glory of God and the good of his Church was the thing which the Apostles aimed at, and therefore ought to be the mark whereat we also level. But seeing those rites and orders may be at one time more which at another are less available unto that purpose, what reason is there in these things to urge the state of one only age as a pattern for all to follow? It is not I am right sure their meaning, that we should now assemble our people to serve God in close and secret meetings; or that common brooks or rivers should be used for places of baptism; or

---

[1] Tom. vii. de Bapt. contra Donatist. lib. v. cap. 23. [t. ix. 156. "Apostoli nihil exinde præceperunt : sed consuetudo illa quæ opponebatur Cypriano ab eorum traditione exordium sumpsisse credenda est, sicut sunt multa quæ universa tenet Ecclesia, et ob hoc ab Apostolis præcepta bene creduntur, quanquam scripta non reperiantur."] T. C. l. i. p. 31. [18.] "If this judgment of St. Augustine be a good judgment and sound, then there be some things commanded of God which are not in the Scriptures; and therefore there is no sufficient doctrine contained in Scripture whereby we may be saved. For all the commandments of God and of the Apostles are needful for our salvation."
[2] Vide Ep. 118. [al. 54. t. ii. 124. A.]

that the Eucharist should be ministered after meat; or that the custom of church feasting should be renewed; or that all kind of standing provision for the ministry should be utterly taken away, and their estate made again dependent upon the voluntary devotion of men. In these things they easily perceive how unfit that were for the present, which was for the first age convenient enough. The faith, zeal, and godliness of former times is worthily had in honour; but doth this prove that the orders of the Church of Christ must be still the selfsame with theirs, that nothing may be which was not then, or that nothing which then was may lawfully since have ceased? They who recall the Church unto that which was at the first, must necessarily set bounds and limits unto their speeches. If any thing have been received repugnant unto that which was first delivered, the first things in this case must stand, the last give place unto them. But where difference is without repugnancy, that which hath been can be no prejudice to that which is.

[4.] Let the state of the people of God when they were in the house of bondage, and their manner of serving God in a strange land, be compared with that which Canaan and Jerusalem did afford, and who seeth not what huge difference there was between them? In Egypt it may be they were right glad to take some corner of a poor cottage, and there to serve God upon their knees, peradventure covered in dust and straw sometimes. Neither were they therefore the less accepted of God, but he was with them in all their afflictions, and at the length by working of their admirable deliverance did testify, that they served him not in vain. Notwithstanding in the very desert they are no sooner possest of some little thing of their own, but a tabernacle is required at their hands. Being planted in the land of Canaan, and having David to be their king, when the Lord had given him rest from all his enemies, it grieved his religious mind to consider the growth of his own estate and dignity, the affairs of religion continuing still in their former manner: "Behold now I dwell in an house of cedar-trees, and the ark of God remaineth still within curtains." [1] What he did purpose it was the pleasure of God that Solomon his son should perform, and perform it in manner suitable unto their present, not their ancient estate and condition. For which cause Solomon writeth unto the king of

[1] 2 Sam. vii. 2.

Tyrus, " The house which I build is great and wonderful, for great is our God above all gods."[1]   Whereby it clearly appeareth that the orders of the Church of God may be acceptable unto him, as well being framed suitable to the greatness and dignity of later, as when they keep the reverend simplicity of ancienter times.   Such dissimilitude therefore between us and the Apostles of Christ in the order of some outward things is no argument of default.

III. Yea, but we have framed ourselves to the customs of the church of Rome ; our orders and ceremonies are papistical.   It is espied that our church founders were not so careful as in this matter they should have been, but contented themselves with such discipline as they took from the church of Rome.[2]   Their error we ought to reform by abolishing all popish orders.   There must be no communion nor fellowship with Papists, *neither in doctrine, ceremonies, nor government.*   It is not enough that we are divided from the church of Rome by the single wall of doctrine, retaining as we do part of their ceremonies and almost their whole government ;[3] but government or ceremonies or whatsoever it be which is popish, away with it.   This is the thing they require in us, the utter relinquishment of all things popish.

Wherein to the end we may answer them according unto their plain direct meaning, and not take advantage of doubtful speech, whereby controversies grow always endless ; their main position being this, that " nothing should be placed in the Church but what God in his word hath commanded,"[4] they must of necessity hold all for popish which the church of Rome hath over and besides this.   By popish orders, ceremonies, and government they must therefore mean in every of these so much as the church of Rome hath embraced without commandment of God's word :

[1] 2 Chron. ii. 5.

[2] Eccles. Disc. fol. 12. [" Video architectos Ecclesiæ nostræ in ea restauranda soli doctrinæ intentos, de disciplina non laborasse, et talem fere qualem a Papistis acceperint retinere."] T. C. lib. i. p. 131. [102. Whitg. Def. 474.]

[3] T. C. i. 20. [al. 8, 9. ap. Def. 54.   " Judge whether they be more joined with the Papists which would have no communion with them, neither in ceremonies, nor doctrine, nor government ; or they which forsaking their doctrine retain part of their ceremonies and almost all their government : that is, they that separate themselves by three walls or by one."]

[4] T. C. i. 25. [al. 13. Def. 76. from Answ. 20.]

so that whatsoever such thing we have, if the church of Rome hath it also, it goeth under the name of those things that are popish, yea although it be lawful, although agreeable to the word of God. For so they plainly affirm, saying,[1] " Although the forms and ceremonies which they " (the church of Rome) " used were not unlawful, and that they contained nothing which is not agreeable to the word of God, yet notwithstanding neither the word of God, nor reason, nor the examples of the eldest churches both Jewish and Christian do permit us to use the same forms and ceremonies, being neither commanded of God, neither such as there may not as good as they, and rather better, be established." The question therefore is, whether we may follow the church of Rome in those orders, rites, and ceremonies, wherein we do not think them blameable, or else ought to devise others, and to have no conformity with them, no not so much as in these things. In this sense and construction therefore as they affirm, so we deny, that whatsoever is popish we ought to abrogate.

[2.] Their arguments to prove that generally all popish orders and ceremonies ought to be clean abolished, are in sum these : [2] " First, whereas we allow the judgment of St. Augustine, that touching those things of this kind which are not commanded or forbidden in the Scripture, we are to observe the custom of the people of God and decree of our forefathers ;[3] how can we retain the customs and constitutions of the papists in such things, who were neither the people of God nor our forefathers ? " Secondly,[4] " although the forms and ceremonies of the church of Rome were not unlawful, neither did contain any thing which is not agreeable to the word of God, yet neither the word of God, nor the examples of the eldest churches of God, nor reason, do permit us to use the same, *they being heretics and so near about us*, and their orders being neither commanded of God, nor yet such but that as good or rather better may be established." It is against the word of God to have conformity with the church of Rome in such things, as appeareth in that " the wisdom of God hath thought it a good way to keep his people from infection of idolatry and superstition, by severing them from idolaters in outward ceremonies, and therefore hath forbidden them to do things which are in

[1] T. C. lib. i. p. 131. [102.]

[3] [Ep. 36. 2. t. ii. 68.]

[2] T. C. lib. i. p. 30. [17.]

[4] T. C. lib. i. p. 131. [102.]

themselves very lawful to be done." And further, " whereas the Lord was careful to sever them by ceremonies from other nations, yet was he not so careful to sever them from any as from the Egyptians amongst whom they lived, and from those nations which were next neighbours unto them, because from them was the greatest fear of infection." So that following the course which the wisdom of God doth teach,[1] " it were more safe for us to conform our indifferent ceremonies to the Turks which are far off, than to the papists which are so near."

Touching the example of the eldest churches of God ; in one council it was decreed, " that [2] Christians should not deck their houses with bay leaves and green boughs, because the Pagans did use so to do ; and that they should not rest from their labours those days that the Pagans did ; that they should not keep the first day of every month as they did. [3] Another council decreed that Christians should

[1] T. C. lib. i. p. 132. [103. and Eccl. Disc. fol. 100. "A quibus nos tanto magis recedere et abhorrere debueramus, quanto gravius periculum nobis ab illis quam ab aliis hæreticis, quod inter eos versamur, immineat. Qua ratione etiam Dominus in Cananæos atrocius quam in reliquos idololatras sæviri voluit."]

[2] Tom. ii. [Ed. Surii.] Braca. 73. [Capitula Martini Episc. Bracar. A.D. 572. in Concil. t. v. 913. "Non liceat iniquas observationes agere Kalendarum, et otiis vacare gentilibus, neque lauro aut viriditate arborum cingere domos. Omnis hæc observatio paganismi est." This is not a decree of either of the councils of Braga, but one of a collection of oriental canons made by Martin archbishop of Braga (the reformer of the Gallican church from Arianism) and sent to the archbishop of Lugo, then the second see in the province, and to his provincial council. The oriental original of the seventy-third canon does not appear.]

[3] Con. Afric. cap. 27. ["Illud etiam petendum," (scil. ab imperatoribus) " ut quæ contra præcepta divina convivia multis in locis exercentur, quæ ab errore gentili attracta sunt, (ita ut nunc a Paganis Christiani ad hæc celebranda agantur, ex qua re temporibus Christianorum imperatorum persecutio altera fieri occulta videatur) vetari talia jubeant, et de civitatibus et de possessionibus imposita pœna prohiberi : maxime, cum etiam in natalibus beatissimorum martyrum per nonnullas civitates, et in ipsis locis sacris, talia committere non reformident. Quibus diebus etiam (quod pudoris est dicere) saltationes sceleratissimas per vicos atque plateas exercent, ut matronalis honor, et innumerabilium fœminarum pudor, devote venientium ad sacratissimum diem, injuriis lascivientibus appetatur ; ut etiam ipsius sanctæ religionis pœna fugiatur accessus." Concil. ii. 1649. The exact date of this canon seems to be uncertain : but it clearly refers not to Christians having feasts of their own as the Gentiles had, but to the danger they were in of being tempted to join with the Gentiles in *their* feasts, especially when happening on our sacred days. It is one of several canons, which

not celebrate feasts on the birthdays of the martyrs, because
it was the manner of the heathen." " ' O !' saith Tertullian,
'better is the religion of the heathen : for they use nc
solemnity of the Christians, neither the Lord's day,[1] neither
the Pentecost ; and if they knew them they would have
nothing to do with them : for they would be afraid lest they
should seem Christians ; but we are not afraid to be called
heathen.'"[2]   The same Tertullian would not have Christians to sit after they have prayed, because the idolaters did
so.[3]   Whereby it appeareth, that both of particular men
and of councils, in making or abolishing of ceremonies, heed
hath been taken that the Christians should not be like the
idolaters, no not in those things which of themselves are
most indifferent to be used or not used.

The same conformity is not less opposite unto reason ;
first inasmuch as "contraries must be cured by their contraries, and therefore popery being anti-christianity is not
healed, but by establishment of orders thereunto opposite.
The way to bring a drunken man to sobriety is to carry him
as far from excess of drink as may be.   To rectify a crooked
stick we bend it on the contrary side, as far as it was at the
first on that side from whence we draw it, and so it cometh
in the end to a middle between both, which is perfect
stra ghtness.[4]   Utter inconformity therefore with the church
of Rome in these things is the best and surest policy which
the Church can use.   While we use their ceremonies they

imply a kind of evil something similar to what Christians living in
India now experience.

The following is the summary of it given by Aristænus. Τὰ Ἑλ-
ληνικὰ συμπόσια πανέσθω, διὰ τὴν οἰκείαν ἀσχημοσύνην, καὶ τὸ πολλοὺς
ἀφέλκεσθαι Χριστιανῶν, καὶ ἐν ἡμέραις μνήμης μαρτύρων γίνεσθαι. Beve-
ridge, Synodicon. i. 598.]

[1] Lib. de Idololatria, [c. 14.   "O melior fides nationum in suam
sectam : quæ nullam solennitatem Christianorum sibi vindicat, non
Dominicum diem, non Pentecosten : etiam si nossent, nobiscum non
communicassent ; timerent enim, ne Christiani viderentur ; nos, ne
Ethnici pronunciemur, non veremur."]   He seemeth to mean the feast
of Easter-day, celebrated in the memory of our Saviour's resurrection,
and for that cause termed the Lord's day.

[2] [T. C. i. 103.]

[3] Lib. de Anima. [a mistake in Cartwright's reference, for "de
Oratione." c. 16.   (The error is noted by Whitgift, Def. 480.)
"Quum perinde faciant nationes, adoratis sigillaribus suis residendo,
vel propterea in nobis reprehendi meretur, quod apud idola celebratur."]

[4] [Abridged from T. C. i. 103.]

take occasion to blaspheme, saying, that our religion cannot stand by itself, unless it lean upon the staff of their ceremonies. They hereby conceive great hope of having the rest of their popery in the end, which hope causeth them to be more frozen in their wickedness. Neither is it without cause that they have this hope, considering that which Master Bucer noteth upon the eighteenth of St. Matthew,[1] that where these things have been left, popery hath returned; but on the other part in places which have been cleansed of these things, it hath not yet been seen that it hath had any entrance.[2] None make such clamours for these ceremonies, as the papists and those whom they suborn; a manifest token how much they triumph and joy in these things. They breed grief of mind in a number, that are godly-minded and have anti-christianity in such detestation, that their minds are martyred with the very sight of them in the Church.[3] Such godly brethren we ought not thus to grieve with unprofitable ceremonies, yea, ceremonies wherein there is not only no profit, but also danger of great hurt, that may grow to the Church by infection, which popish ceremonies are means to breed."[4]

This in effect is the sum and substance of that which they bring by way of opposition against those orders which we have common with the church of Rome; these are the reasons wherewith they would prove our ceremonies in that respect worthy of blame.

IV. Before we answer unto these things, we are to cut off that whereunto they from whom these objections proceed do oftentimes fly for defence and succour, when the force and strength of their arguments is elided. For the ceremonies in use amongst us being in no other respect retained, saving only for that to retain them is to our seeming good and profitable, yea, so profitable and so good, that if we had either simply taken them clean away, or else removed them so as to place in their stead others, we had done worse : the plain and direct away against us herein had been only to prove, that all such ceremonies as they require to be abolished are retained by us to the hurt of the Church, or

[1] [P. 144. ed. 1553. "His certe hodie debemus ut in multis locis, ubi diu prædicatum Evangelium fuit, adversa sint restituta omnia : quum id nusquam, ubi serio et pure prædicato Christo etiam ad ipsius verbum reformatæ ceremoniæ sunt, accidisse videamus."]

[2] T. C. lib. iii. p. 178.   [3] Ibid. p. 179.   [4] Ibid. p. 180.

with less benefit than the abolishment of them would bring. But forasmuch as they saw how hardly they should be able to perform this, they took a more compendious way, traducing the ceremonies of our church under the name of being popish. The cause why this way seemed better unto them was, for that the name of popery is more odious than very paganism amongst divers of the more simple sort, so as whatsoever they hear named popish, they presently conceive deep hatred against it, imagining there can be nothing contained in that name but needs it must be exceeding detestable. The ears of the people they have therefore filled with strong clamour: "The Church of England is fraught with popish ceremonies: they that favour the cause of reformation maintain nothing but the sincerity of the Gospel of Jesus Christ: all such as withstand them fight for the laws of his sworn enemy, uphold the filthy relics of Antichrist, and are defenders of that which is popish." These are the notes wherewith are drawn from the hearts of the multitude so many sighs; with these tunes their minds are exasperated against the lawful guides and governors of their souls; these are the voices that fill them with general discontentment, as though the bosom of that famous church wherein they live were more noisome than any dungeon. But when the authors of so scandalous incantations are examined, and called to account how can they justify such their dealings; when they are urged directly to answer, whether it be lawful for us to use any such ceremonies as the church of Rome useth, although the same be not commanded in the word of God; being driven to see that the use of some such ceremonies must of necessity be granted lawful, they go about to make us believe that they are just of the same opinion, and that they only think such ceremonies are not to be used when they are unprofitable, or "when as good or better may be established." [1] Which answer is both idle in regard of us, and also repugnant to themselves.

[2.] It is in regard of us very vain to make this answer, because they know that what ceremonies we retain common unto the church of Rome, we therefore retain them, for that

---

[1] T. C. iii. p. 171. "What an open untruth is it, that this is one of our principles, not to be lawful to use the same ceremonies which the papists did; when as I have both before declared the contrary, and even here have expressly added, that they are not to be used when as good or better may be established!"

we judge them to be profitable, and to be such that others instead of them would be worse. So that when they say that we ought to abrogate such Romish ceremonies as are unprofitable, or else might have other more profitable in their stead, they trifle and they beat the air about nothing which toucheth us ; unless they mean that we ought to abrogate all Romish ceremonies which in their judgment have either no use or less use than some other might have. But then must they shew some commission, whereby they are authorized to sit as judges, and we required to take their judgment for good in this case. Otherwise their sentences will not be greatly regarded, when they oppose their *methinketh* unto the orders of the church of England : as in the question about surplices one of them doth ;[1] "If we look to the colour, black methinketh is more decent ; if to the form, a garment down to the foot hath a great deal more comeliness in it." If they think that we ought to prove the ceremonies commodious which we have retained, they do in this point very greatly deceive themselves. For in all right and equity, that which the Church hath received and held so long for good, that which public approbation hath ratified, must carry the benefit of presumption with it to be accounted meet and convenient. They which have stood up as yesterday to challenge it of defect, must prove their challenge. If we being defendants do answer, that the ceremonies in question are godly, comely, decent, profitable for the Church ; their reply is childish and unorderly, to say, that we demand the thing in question,[2] and shew the poverty of our cause, the goodness whereof we are fain to beg that our adversaries would grant. For on our part this must be the answer, which orderly proceeding doth require. The burden of proving doth rest on them. In them it is frivolous to say we ought not to use bad ceremonies of the church of Rome, and presume all such bad as it pleaseth themselves to dislike, unless we can persuade them the contrary.

[3.] Besides, they are herein opposite also to themselves.

[1] Eccles. Discip. fol. 100. [in Cartwright's Transl. 134. "Si de colore agitur, mihi quidem magis decorus niger color videtur ; si autem de forma, talaris vestis honestior."]

[2] T. C. lib. iii. p. 176. "As for your often repeating that the ceremonies in question are godly, comely, and decent ; it is your old wont of demanding the thing in question, and an undoubted argument of your extreme poverty."

For what one thing is so common with them, as to use the custom of the church of Rome for an argument to prove, that such and such ceremonies cannot be good and profitable for us, inasmuch as that church useth them? Which usual kind of disputing sheweth, that they do not disallow only those Romish ceremonies which are unprofitable, but count all unprofitable which are Romish; that is to say, which have been devised by the church of Rome, or which are used in that church and not prescribed in the word of God. For this is the only limitation which they can use suitable unto their other positions. And therefore the cause which they yield, why they hold it lawful to retain in doctrine and in discipline some things as good, which yet are common to the church of Rome, is for that those good things are "perpetual commandments in whose place no other can come;" but ceremonies are changeable.[1] So that their judgment in truth is, that whatsoever by the word of God is not unchangeable in the church of Rome, that church's using is a cause why reformed churches ought to change it, and not to think it good or profitable. And lest we seem to father any thing upon them more than is properly their own, let them read even their own words, where they complain, "that we are thus constrained to be like unto the Papists in Any their ceremonies;" yea, they urge that this cause, although it were "alone, ought to move them to whom that belongeth to do them away, *forasmuch as they are their ceremonies;*" and that the Bishop of Salisbury doth justify this their complaint.[2] The clause is untrue which they add concerning the Bishop of Salisbury;[3] but the sentence doth

---

[1] T. C. iii. 174.

[2] "And that this complaint of ours is just in that we are thus constrained to be like unto the papists in any their ceremonies, and that this cause only ought to move them to whom that belongeth, to do them away, *forasmuch as they are their ceremonies;* the reader may further see in the Bishop of Salisbury, who brings divers proofs thereof." T. C. lib. iii. p. 177. [It may be worth observing that the Italics are Cartwright's own.]

[3] [Cartwright's margin refers to Apol. Part i. c. 2. div. 8. by mistake for div. 9. "They cry out . . . that we have rashly and presumptuously disannulled the old ceremonies which have been well allowed by our fathers and forefathers many hundred years past, both by good customs, and also in ages of more purity." On which Harding's remark is, "Concerning ceremonies: if ye shew us not the use of chrism in your churches; if the sign of the cross be not borne before you in processions, and otherwheres used; if holy water be abolished; if lights at the Gospel and Communion be not had; if peculiar vest-

shew that we do them no wrong in setting down the state of the question between us thus : Whether we ought to abolish out of the church of England all such orders, rites, and ceremonies as are established in the church of Rome, and are not prescribed in the word of God. For the affirmative whereof we are now to answer such proofs of theirs as have been before alleged.

V. Let the church of Rome be what it will, let them that are of it be the people of God and our fathers in the Christian faith, or let them be otherwise ; hold them for catholics or hold them for heretics ; it is not a thing either one way or other in this present question greatly material. Our conformity with them in such things as have been proposed is not proved as yet unlawful by all this. St. Augustine[1] hath said, yea and we have allowed his saying, "That the custom of the people of God and the decrees of our forefathers are to be kept, touching those things whereof the Scripture hath neither one way nor other given us any charge." What then ? Doth it here therefore follow, that they being neither the people of God nor our forefathers, are for that cause in nothing to be followed? This consequent were good if so be it were granted, that only the custom of the people of God and the decrees of our forefathers are in such case to be observed. But then should no other kind of latter laws in the Church be good ; which were a gross absurdity to think. St. Augustine's speech therefore doth

ments for Deacons, Priests, Bishops, be taken away ; and many such other the like : judge ye, whether ye have duly kept the old ceremonies of the Church." Jewel replies, "Verily, M. Harding, we hate not any of all these things. For we know they are the creatures of God. But you have so misused them, or rather so defiled and berayed them with your superstitions, and so have with the same mocked and deceived God's people, that we can no longer continue them without great conscience." This passage, it will be seen, refers to the ceremonies omitted, and not to those retained in the English church. Concerning the latter, although it is well known that he would not have disapproved of further concessions, (see his letters to Bullinger in Strype, Ann. i. i. 262. ii. 544.) yet it is equally certain that his views were not founded on the puritan principle of absolute unlawfulness in the use of things once abused. For in the very same year (1565-6) that he last wrote to Bullinger as above, he had refused his intimate friend, Humphrey, institution to a benefice in the diocese of Sarum, because Humphrey would not pledge himself to wear the habits. Strype, Park. i. 369, and Ann. i. ii. 133. Wordsworth, E. B. iv. 63. How far he differed with the Puritans on Church government may be seen by a paper of his in Whitg. Def. 423. and in Strype, Whitg. iii. 21. 1 App. No. x.]
[1] [See above, b. iii. c. xi. 13.]

import, that where we have no divine precept, if yet we have the custom of the people of God or a decree of our forefathers, this is a law and must be kept. Notwithstanding it is not denied, but that we lawfully may observe the positive constitutions of our own churches, although the same were but yesterday made by ourselves alone. Nor is there any thing in this to prove that the church of England might not by law receive orders, rites, or customs from the church of Rome, although they were neither the people of God nor yet our forefathers. How much less when we have received from them nothing, but that which they did themselves receive from such, as we cannot deny to have been the people of God, yea such, as either we must acknowledge for our own forefathers or else disdain the race of Christ?

VI. The rites and orders wherein we follow the church of Rome are of no other kind than such as the church of Geneva itself doth follow them in. We follow the church of Rome in more things; yet they in some things of the same nature about which our present controversy is: so that the difference is not in the kind, but in the number of rites only, wherein they and we do follow the church of Rome. The use of wafer-cakes, the custom of godfathers and godmothers in baptism, are things not commanded nor forbidden in Scripture, things which have been of old and are retained in the church of Rome even at this very hour. Is conformity with Rome in such things a blemish unto the church of England, and unto churches abroad an ornament? Let them, if not for the reverence they owe unto this church, in the bowels whereof they have received I trust that precious and blessed vigour, which shall quicken them to eternal life, yet at the leastwise for the singular affection which they do bear towards others, take heed how they strike, lest they wound whom they would not. For undoubtedly it cutteth deeper than they are aware of, when they plead that even such ceremonies of the church of Rome, as contain in them nothing which is not of itself agreeable to the word of God, ought nevertheless to be abolished; and that neither the word of God, nor reason, nor the examples of the eldest churches do permit the church of Rome to be therein followed.

[2.] Heretics they are, and they are our neighbours. By us and amongst us they lead their lives. But what then? therefore no ceremony of theirs lawful for us to use? We must yield and will that none are lawful, if God himself be a precedent against the use of any. But how appeareth it that God is so? Hereby they say it doth appear, in that[1] "God severed his people from the heathens, but especially from the Egyptians, and such nations as were nearest neighbours unto them,[2] by forbidding them to do those things which were in themselves very lawful to be done, yea, very profitable some, and incommodious to be forborne; such things it pleased God to forbid them, only because those heathens did them, with whom conformity in the same things might have bred infection. Thus in shaving, cutting,[3] apparel-wearing,[4] yea in sundry kinds of meats also, swine's flesh, conies, and such like,[5] they were forbidden to do so and so, because the Gentiles did so. And the end why God forbad them such things was to sever them for fear of infection by a great and an high wall from other nations, as St. Paul teacheth."[6] The cause of more careful separation from the nearest nations was the greatness of danger to be especially by them infected. Now papists are to us as those nations were unto Israel. Therefore if the wisdom of God be our guide, we cannot allow conformity with them, no not in any such indifferent ceremony.

[3.] Our direct answer hereunto is, that for any thing here alleged we may still doubt, whether the Lord in such indifferent ceremonies, as those whereof we dispute, did frame his people of set purpose unto any utter dissimilitude, either with Egyptians or with any other nation else. And if God did not forbid them all such indifferent ceremonies, then our conformity with the church of Rome in some such is not hitherto as yet disproved, although papists were unto us as those heathens were unto Israel. "After the doings of the land of Egypt, wherein you dwelt, ye shall not do, saith the Lord; and after the manner of the land of Canaan, whither I will bring you, shall ye not do, neither walk in their ordinances: do after my judgments, and keep my ordinances to walk therein: I am the Lord your God."[7] The speech is indefinite, "ye shall not be like them:" it is not general, "ye shall not be like them in any thing, or like to them in any thing indifferent, or like unto them in any indifferent ceremony of theirs." Seeing therefore it is not set down

---

[1] T. C. lib. i. p. 89, 131.   [2] Lev. xviii. 3.
[3] Lev. xix. 27.   [4] Levit. xix. 19; Deut. xxii. 11.
[5] Deut. xiv. 7; Lev. xi.   [6] Ephes. ii. 14.   [7] Levit. xviii. 3.

how far the bounds of his speech concerning dissimilitude should reach, how can any man assure us, that it
extendeth farther than to those things only, wherein the
nations there mentioned were idolatrous, or did against that
which the law of God commandeth? Nay, doth it not seem
a thing very probable, that God doth purposely add, " Do
after my judgments," as giving thereby to understand that
h s meaning in the former sentence was but to bar similitude
in such things, as were repugnant unto the ordinances, laws,
and statutes which he had given? Egyptians and Canaanites
are for example's sake named unto them, because the customs
of the one they had been, and of the other they should be
best acquainted with. But that wherein they might not be
like unto either of them, was such peradventure as had been
no whit less unlawful, although those nations had never
been. So that there is no necessity to think, that God for
fear of infection by reason of nearness forbad them to be
like unto the Canaanites or the Egyptians, in those things
which otherwise had been lawful enough.

For I would know what one thing was in those nations,
and is here forbidden, being indifferent in itself, yet forbidden only because they used it. In the laws of Israel we
find it written, " Ye shall not cut round the corners of
your heads, neither shalt thou tear the tufts of thy beard." [1]
These things were usual amongst those nations, and in
themselves they are indifferent. But are they indifferent
being used as signs of immoderate and hopeless lamentation
for the dead? In this sense it is that the law forbiddeth
them. For which cause the very next words following are,
" Ye shall not cut your flesh for the dead, nor make any
print of a mark upon you : I am the Lord." [2] The like in
Leviticus, where speech is of mourning for the dead ; " They
shall not make bald parts upon their head, nor shave off the
locks of their beard, nor make any cutting in their flesh." [3]
Again in Deuteronomy, " Ye are the children of the Lord
your God ; ye shall not cut yourselves, nor make you bald-
ness between your eyes for the dead." [4] What is this but
in effect the same which the Apostle doth more plainly
express, saying, "Sorrow not as they do who have no hope?" [5]
The very light of nature itself was able to see herein a fault ;
that which those nations did use, having been also in use

[1] Levit. xix. 27.   [2] Levit. xix. 28.   [3] Levit. xxi. 5.
[4] Deut. xiv. 1.   [5] 1 Thess. iv. 13.

with others, the ancient Roman laws do forbid.[1] That shaving therefore and cutting which the law doth mention was not a matter in itself indifferent, and forbidden only because it was in use amongst such idolaters as were neighbours to the people of God ; but to use it had been a crime, though no other people or nation under heaven should have done it saving only themselves.

As for those laws concerning attire : "There shall no garment of linen and woollen come upon thee ;"[2] as also those touching food and diet, wherein swine's flesh together with sundry other meats are forbidden ;[3] the use of these things had been indeed of itself harmless and indifferent : so that hereby it doth appear, how the law of God forbad in some special consideration such things as were lawful enough in themselves. But yet even here they likewise fail of that they intend. For it doth not appear that the consideration in regard whereof the law forbiddeth these things was because those nations did use them. Likely enough it is that the Canaanites used to feed as well on sheep's as on swine's flesh ; and therefore if the forbidding of the latter had no other reason than dissimilitude with that people, they which of their own heads allege this for reason can shew I think some reason more than we are able to find why the former was not also forbidden. Might there not be some other mystery in this prohibition than they think of? Yes, some other mystery there was in it by all likelihood. For what reason is there which should but induce, and therefore much less enforce us to think, that care of dissimilitude between the people of God and the heathen nations about them, was any more the cause of forbidding them to put on garments of sundry stuff, than of charging them withal not to sow their fields with meslin ;[4] or that this was any more the cause of forbidding them to eat swine's flesh, than of charging them withal not to eat the flesh of eagles, hawks, and the like ?[5]

[1] [Cic. Tusc. Quæst. ii. 23. "Ingemiscere nonnunquam viro concessum est, idque raro : ejulatus ne mulieri quidem : et hic nimirum est lessus, quem duodecim tabulæ in funeribus adhiberi vetuerunt."]

[2] Levit. xix. 19 ; Deut. xxii. 11.   [3] Deut. xiv. 7 ; Levit. xi.

[4] Levit. xix. 19. ["Meslin : mixt corn, as wheat and rye." John son, quoting Tusser :

> "If work for the Thresher ye mind for to have,
>   Of wheat and of meslin unthreshed go save."]

[5] Deut. xiv. ; Levit. xi.

Wherefore, although the church of Rome were to us, as to Israel the Egyptians and Canaanites were of old ; yet doth it not follow, that the wisdom of God without respect doth teach us to erect between us and them a partition-wall of difference,[1] in such things indifferent as have been hitherto disputed of.

VII. Neither is the example of the eldest churches a whit more available to this purpose. Notwithstanding some fault undoubtedly there is in the very resemblance of idolaters.[2] Were it not some kind of blemish to be like unto infidels and heathens, it would not so usually be objected ; men would not think it any advantage in the causes of religion to be able therewith justly to charge their adversaries as they do. Wherefore to the end that it may a little more plainly appear, what force this hath and how far the same extendeth, we are to note how all men are naturally desirous that they may seem neither to judge nor to do amiss ; because every error and offence is a stain to the beauty of nature, for which cause it blusheth thereat, but glorieth in the contrary. From thence it riseth, that they which disgrace or depress the credit of others do it either in both or in one of these. To have been in either directed by a weak and unperfect rule argueth imbecility and imperfection. Men being either led by reason or by imitation of other men's example, if their persons be odious whose example we choose to follow, as namely if we frame our opinions to that which condemned heretics think, or direct our actions according to that which is practised and done by them ; it lieth as an heavy prejudice against us, unless somewhat mightier than their bare example did move us, to think or do the same things with them. Christian men therefore having besides the common light of all men so great help of heavenly direction from above, together with the lamps of so bright examples as the Church of God doth yield, it cannot but worthily seem reproachful for us to leave both the one and the other, to become disciples unto the most hateful sort that live, to do as they do, only because we see their example before us and have a delight to follow it. Thus we may therefore safely

---

[1] Ephes. ii. 14.

[2] "The councils, although they did not observe themselves always in making of decrees this rule, yet have kept this consideration continually in making of their laws, that they would have Christians differ from others in their ceremonies." T. C. lib. i. p. 132.

conclude, that it is not evil simply to concur with the heathens either in opinion or in action; and that conformity with them is only then a disgrace, when either we follow them in that they think and do amiss, or follow them generally in that they do without other reason than only the liking we have to the pattern of their example; which liking doth intimate a more universal approbation of them than is allowable.

[2.] Faustus the Manichee therefore objecting against the Jews, that they forsook the idols of the Gentiles, but their temples and oblations and altars and priesthoods and all kinds of ministry of holy things they exercised even as the Gentiles did, yea more superstitiously a great deal; against the Catholic Christians likewise, that between them and the heathens there was in many things little difference; "From them," saith Faustus, "ye have learned to hold that one only God is the author of all; their sacrifices ye have turned into feasts of charity, their idols into martyrs whom ye honour with the like religious offices unto theirs; the ghosts of the dead ye appease with wine and delicates; the festival days of the nations ye celebrate together with them; and of their kind of life ye have verily changed nothing:"[1] St. Augustine's defence in behalf of both is, that touching matters of action, Jews and Catholic Christians were free from the Gentiles' faultiness, even in those things which were objected as tokens of their agreement with Gentiles;[2] and concerning their consent in opinion, they did not hold the same with Gentiles because Gentiles had so taught, but because heaven and earth had so witnessed the same to be truth, that neither the one sort could err in being fully persuaded thereof, nor the other but err in case they should not consent with them.[3]

---

[1] August. cont. Faust. Manich. lib. xx. cap. 4. [t. viii. 334. "Schisma aut nihil immutare debet ab eo unde factum est, aut non multum: ut puta vos, qui desciscentes a gentibus, monarchiæ opinionem primo vobiscum divulsistis, id est, ut omnia credatis ex Deo: sacrificia vero eorum vertistis in agapes, idola in martyres, quos votis similibus colitis: defunctorum umbras vino placatis et dapibus: solennes gentium dies cum ipsis celebratis, ut kalendas, et solstitia: de vita certe eorum mutastis nihil."]

[2] [Ibid. § 23. "Si usus quarundam rerum similis videtur nobis esse cum gentibus, sicut cibi et potus, tectorum, vestimentorum, &c. . . . longe tamen aliter his rebus utitur, qui ad alium finem usum earum refert; et aliter qui ex his Deo gratias agit, de quo prava et falsa non credit."]

[3] [Ibid. § 19. "Discat ergo Faustus, . . . monarchiæ opinionem

[3.] In things of their own nature indifferent, if either councils or particular men have at any time with sound judgment misliked conformity between the Church of God and infidels, the cause thereof hath been somewhat else than only affectation of dissimilitude. They saw it necessary so to do in respect of some special accident, which the Church being not always subject unto hath not still cause to do the like. For example, in the dangerous days of trial, wherein there was no way for the truth of Jesus Christ to triumph over infidelity but through the constancy of his saints, whom yet a natural desire to save themselves from the flame might peradventure cause to join with Pagans in external customs, too far using the same as a cloak to conceal themselves in, and a mist to darken the eyes of infidels withal : for remedy hereof those laws it might be were provided, which forbad that Christians should deck their houses with boughs as the Pagans did use to do,[1] or rest those festival days whereon the Pagans rested, or celebrate such feasts as were, though not heathenish, yet such as the simpler sort of heathens might be beguiled in so thinking them.

[4.] As for Tertullian's judgment concerning the rites and orders of the Church, no man having judgment can be ignorant how just exceptions may be taken against it.[2] His opinion touching the Catholic Church was as unindifferent as touching our church the opinion of them that favour this pretended reformation is. He judged all them who did not Montanize to be but carnally minded, he judged them still over abjectly to fawn upon the heathens, and to curry favour with infidels. Which as the catholic church did well provide that they might not do indeed, so Tertullian over often

non ex gentibus nos habere ; sed gentes non usque adeo ad falsos Deos esse delapsos, ut opinionem amitterent unius veri Dei, ex quo est omnis qualiscunque natura."]

[1] " Also it was decreed in another council that they should not deck their houses with bay-leaves and green boughs, because the Pagans did use so ; and that they should not rest from their labour those days that the Pagans did, that they should not keep the first day of every month as they did." T. C. l. i. p. 132 [103.]

[2] " Tertullian saith, O, saith he, better is the religion of the heathen ; for they use no solemnity of the Christians, neither the Lord's day, neither, &c. but we are not afraid to be called heathen." T. C. l. i. p. 132. [103.] " But having shewed this in general to be the policy of God first, and of his people afterward, to put as much difference as can be commodiously between the people of God and others which are not, I shall not, &c." T. C. l. i. p. 133.

through discontentment carpeth injuriously at them as though they did it, even when they were free from such meaning.

[5.] But if it were so, that either the judgment of these councils before alleged, or of Tertullian himself against the Christians, are in no such consideration to be understood as we have mentioned ; if it were so that men are condemned as well of the one as of the other, only for using the ceremonies of a religion *contrary* unto their own, and that *this cause* is such as ought to prevail no less with us than with them : shall it not follow that seeing there is still between our religion and Paganism the selfsame *contrariety*, therefore we are still no less rebukable, if we now deck our houses with boughs, or send new-year's gifts unto our friends, or feast on those days which the Gentiles then did, or sit after prayer as they were accustomed ? For so they infer upon the premises, that as great difference as commodiously may be there should be in all outward ceremonies between the people of God and them which are not his people. Again they teach as hath been declared, that there is not as great a difference as may be between them, except the one do avoid whatsoever rites and ceremonies uncommanded of God the other doth embrace. So that generally they teach that the very difference of spiritual condition itself between the servants of Christ and others requireth such difference in ceremonies between them, although the one be never so far disjoined in time or place from the other.

[6.] But in case the people of God and Belial do chance to be neighbours, then as the danger of infection is greater, so the same difference they say is thereby made more necessary.[1] In this respect as the Jews were severed from the heathen, so most especially from the heathen nearest them. And in the same respect we, which ought to differ howsoever from the church of Rome, are now they say by reason of our nearness more bound to differ from them in ceremonies than from Turks. A strange kind of speech unto Christian ears, and such as I hope they themselves do acknowledge unadvisedly uttered. " We are not so much to fear infection from Turks as from papists." What of that ? we must remember that by conforming rather ourselves in that respect to Turks, we should be spreaders of a worse infection into others than any we are likely to draw from papists by our conformity

[1] [Decl. of Discipl. 134.]

with them in ceremonies. If they did hate, as Turks do, the Christians; or as Canaanites did of old the Jewish religion even in gross; the circumstance of local nearness in them unto us might haply enforce in us a duty of greater separation from them than from those other mentioned. But forasmuch as papists are so much in Christ nearer unto us than Turks, is there any reasonable man, trow you, but will judge it meeter that our ceremonies of Christian religion should be popish than Turkish or heathenish? Especially considering that we were not brought to dwell amongst them, (as Israel in Canaan,) having not been of them. For even a very part of them we were. And when God did by his good Spirit put it into our hearts, first to reform ourselves, (whence grew out separation,) and then by all good means to seek also their reformation; had we not only cut off their corruptions but also estranged ourselves from them in things indifferent, who seeth not how greatly prejudicial this might have been to so good a cause, and what occasion it had given them to think (to their greater obduration in evil) that through a froward or wanton desire of innovation we did unconstrainedly those things for which conscience was pretended? Howsoever the case doth stand, as Judah had been rather to choose conformity in things indifferent with Israel when they were nearest opposites, than with the farthest removed Pagans; so we in the like case much rather with papists than with Turks. I might add further for more full and complete answer, so much concerning the large odds between the case of the eldest churches in regard of those heathens and ours in respect of the church of Rome, that very cavillation itself should be satisfied, and have no shift to fly unto.

VIII. But that no one thing may detain us over long, I return to their reasons against our conformity with that church. That extreme dissimilitude which they urge upon us, is now commended as our best and safest policy for establishment of sound religion. The ground of which politic position is that "evils must be cured by their contraries;" and therefore the cure of the Church infected with the poison of Antichristianity must be done by that which is thereunto as contrary as may be.[1] "A medled estate of the

[1] "Common reason also doth teach that contraries are cured by their contraries. Now Christianity and Antichristianity, the Gospel and Popery, be contraries; and therefore Antichristianity must be cured, not by itself, but by that which is (as much as may be) contrary unto it." T. C. l. i. p. 134. [103.]

orders of the Gospel and the ceremonies of popery is not the best way to banish popery." [1]

We are contrariwise of opinion, that he which will perfectly recover a sick and restore a diseased body unto health, must not endeavour so much to bring it to a state of simple contrariety, as of fit proportion in contrariety unto those evils which are to be cured. He that will take away extreme heat by setting the body in extremity of cold, shall undoubtedly remove the disease, but together with it the diseased too. The first thing therefore in skilful cures is the knowledge of the part affected ; the next is of the evil which doth affect it ; the last is not only of the kind but also of the measure of contrary things whereby to remove it.

[2.] They which measure religion by dislike of the church of Rome think every man so much the more sound, by how much he can make the corruptions thereof to seem more large. And therefore some there are, namely the Arians in reformed churches of Poland, which imagine the canker to have eaten so far into the very bones and marrow of the church of Rome, as if it had not so much as a sound belief, no not concerning God himself, but that the very belief of the Trinity were a part of antichristian corruption ; [2] and that the wonderful providence of God did bring to pass that the bishop of the see of Rome should be famous for his triple crown ; a sensible mark whereby the world might know him to be that mystical beast spoken of in the Revelation, to be that great and notorious Antichrist in no one respect so much as in this, that he maintaineth the doctrine of the Trinity. Wisdom therefore and skill is requisite to know, what parts are sound in that church, and what corrupted.

Neither is it to all men apparent which complain of unsound parts, with what kind of unsoundness every such part is possessed. They can say, that in doctrine, in discipline, in prayers, in sacraments, the church of Rome hath (as it hath indeed) very foul and gross corruptions ; the nature whereof notwithstanding because they have not for the most part exact skill and knowledge to discern, they think that amiss many times which is not ; and the salve of reformation they mightily call for, but where and what the sores are which need it, as they wot full little, so they think it not greatly material to search. Such men's contentment must be wrought by stratagem; the usual method of art is not for them.

[3.] But with those that profess more than ordinary and common knowledge of good from evil, with them that are able to put a difference between things naught and things indifferent in the church of Rome, we are yet at controversy about the manner of removing that which is naught: whether it may not be perfectly helped, unless that also which is indifferent be cut off with it, so far till no rite or ceremony remain which the church of Rome hath, being not found in the word of God.   If we think this too extreme, they reply, that to draw men from great excess, it is not amiss though we use them unto somewhat less than is competent;[1] and that a crooked stick is not straightened unless it be bent as far on the clean contrary side, that so it may settle itself at the length in a middle estate of evenness between both.   But how can these comparisons stand them in any stead ? When they urge us to extreme opposition against the church of Rome, do they mean we should be drawn unto it only for a time, and afterwards return to a mediocrity ? or was it the purpose of those reformed churches, which utterly abolished all popish ceremonies, to come in the end back again to the middle point of evenness and moderation ? Then have we conceived amiss of their meaning. For we have always thought their opinion to be, that utter inconformity with the church of Rome was not an extremity whereunto we should be drawn for a time, but the very mediocrity itself wherein they meant we should ever continue.   Now by these comparisons it seemeth clean contrary, that howsoever they have bent themselves at first to an extreme contrariety against the Romish church, yet therein they will continue no longer than only till such time as some more moderate course for establishment of the Church may be concluded.

[1] "If a man would bring a drunken man to sobriety, the best and nearest way is to carry him as far from his excess in drink as may be ; and if a man could not keep a mean, it were better to fault in pre-scribing less than he should drink, than to fault in giving him more than he ought. As we see, to bring a stick which is crooked to be straight, we do not only bow it so far until it come to be straight, but we bend it so far until we make it so crooked of the other side as it was before of the first side ; to this end, that at the last it may stand straight, and as it were in the midway between both the crooks." T. C. lib. i. p. 132. [103.]

[4.] Yea, albeit this were not at the first their intent, yet surely now there is great cause to lead them unto it. They have seen that experience of the former policy, which may cause the authors of it to hang down their heads. When Germany had stricken off that which appeared corrupt in the doctrine of the church of Rome, but seemed nevertheless in discipline still to retain therewith very great conformity; France by that rule of policy which hath been before mentioned, took away the popish orders which Germany did retain. But process of time hath brought more light into the world; whereby men perceiving that they of the religion in France have also retained some orders which were before in the church of Rome, and are not commanded in the word of God, there hath arisen a sect [1] in England, which following still the very selfsame rule of policy, seeketh to reform even the French reformation, and purge out from thence also dregs of popery. These have not taken as yet such root that they are able to establish any thing. But if they had, what would spring out of their stock, and how far the unquiet wit of man might be carried with rules of such policy, God doth know. The trial which we have lived to see, may somewhat teach us what posterity is to fear. But our Lord of his infinite mercy avert whatsoever evil our swervings on the one hand or on the other may threaten unto the state of his Church!

IX. That the church of Rome doth hereby take occasion to blaspheme, and to say, our religion is not able to stand of itself unless it lean upon the staff of their ceremonies,[2] is not a matter of so great moment, that it did need to be objected, or doth deserve to receive an answer. The name of blasphemy in this place, is like the shoe of Hercules on a child's foot.[3] If the church of Rome do use any such kind of silly exprobation, it is no such ugly thing to the ear, that we should think the honour and credit of our religion to receive thereby any great wound. They which hereof make so perilous a matter do seem to imagine, that we have erected of late a frame of some new religion, the furniture whereof we should not have borrowed from our

---

[1] [The Brownists, or Barrowists.]

[2] " By using of these ceremonies, the Papists take occasion to blaspheme, saying, that our religion cannot stand by itself, unless it lean upon the staff of their ceremonies." T. C. lib. iii. p. 178. [and i. 52.]

[3] [" Herculis cothurnos aptare infanti." See Quintilian VI. i. 3. and Erasm. Adag. Chil. iii. Cent. vi. Prov. 67.]

enemies, lest they relieving us might afterwards laugh and gibe at our poverty ; whereas in truth the ceremonies which we have taken from such as were before us, are not things that belong to this or that sect, but they are the ancient rites and customs of the Church of Christ, whereof ourselves being a part, we have the selfsame interest in them which our fathers before us had, from whom the same are descended unto us. Again in case we had been so much beholding privately unto them, doth the reputation of one church stand by saying unto another, " I need thee not ? " If some should be so vain and impotent as to mar a benefit with reproachful upbraiding, where at the least they suppose themselves to have bestowed some good turn ; yet surely a wise body's part it were not, to put out his fire, because his fond and foolish neighbour, from whom he borrowed perad- venture wherewith to kindle it, might haply cast him therewith in the teeth, saying, " Were it not for me thou wouldst freeze, and not be able to heat thyself."

[2.] As for that other argument derived from the secret affection of papists, with whom our conformity in certain ceremonies is said to put them in great hope, that their whole religion in time will have re-entrance, and therefore none are so clamorous amongst us for the observation of these ceremonies, as papists and such as papists suborn to speak for them, whereby it clearly appeareth how much they rejoice, how much they triumph in these things ; [1] our answer hereunto is still the same, that the benefit we have by such ceremonies overweigheth even this also. No man which is not exceeding partial can well deny, but that there is most just cause wherefore we should be offended greatly at the church of Rome. Notwithstanding at such times as we are to deliberate for ourselves, the freer our minds are from all distempered affections, the sounder and better is our judg- ment. When we are in a fretting mood at the church of Rome, and with that angry disposition enter into any cogitation of the orders and rites of our church ; taking particular survey of them, we are sure to have always one eye fixed upon the countenance of our enemies, and accord- ing to the blithe or heavy aspect thereof, our other eye

---

[1] " To prove the papists' triumph and joy in these things, I alleged further that there are none which make such clamours for these cere- monies, as the papists and those whom they suborn." T. C. lib. iii. p. 179.

sheweth some other suitable token either of dislike or approbation towards our own orders. For the rule of our judgment in such case being only that of Homer, "This is the thing which our enemies would have;"[1] what they seem contented with, even for that very cause we reject: and there is nothing but it pleaseth us much the better if we espy that it galleth them. Miserable were the state and condition of that church, the weighty affairs whereof should be ordered by those deliberations wherein such a humour as this were predominant. We have most heartily to thank God therefore, that they amongst us to whom the first consultations of causes of this kind fell, were men which aiming at another mark, namely the glory of God and the good of this his church, took that which they judged thereunto necessary, not rejecting any good or convenient thing only because the church of Rome might perhaps like it. If we have that which is meet and right, although they be glad, we are not to envy them this their solace; we do not think it a duty of ours to be in every such thing their tormentors.

[3.] And whereas it is said that popery for want of this utter extirpation hath in some places taken root and flourished again,[2] but hath not been able to re-establish itself in any place after provision made against it by utter evacuation of all Romish ceremonies: and therefore, as long as we hold any thing like unto them, we put them in some more hope than if all were taken away: as we deny not but this may be true, so being of two evils to choose the less, we hold it better that the friends and favourers of the church of Rome should be in some kind of hope to have a corrupt religion restored, than both we and they conceive just fear, lest under colour of rooting out popery, the most effectual means to bear up the state of religion be removed, and so a way made either for Paganism or for extreme barbarity to enter. If desire of weakening the hope of others should turn us

---

[1] Ἦ κεν γηθήσαι Πρίαμος. Il. A. [v. 255.]

[2] " Thus they conceiving hope of having the rest of their popery in the end, it causeth them to be more frozen in their wickedness, &c. For not the cause but the occasion also ought to be taken away, &c. Although let the reader judge, whether they have cause given to hope, that the tail of popery yet remaining, they shall the easilier hale in the whole body after: considering also that Master Bucer noteth, that where these things have been left, there popery hath returned; but on the other part, in places which have been cleansed of these dregs, it hath not been seen that it hath had any entrance." T. C. lib. iii. p. 179. [and i. 52.]

away from the course we have taken; how much more the care of preventing our own fear withhold us from that we are urged unto? Especially seeing that our own fear we know, but we are not so certain what hope the rites and orders of our church have bred in the hearts of others.

For it is no sufficient argument thereof to say, that in maintaining and urging these ceremonies none are so clamorous as papists and they whom papists suborn;[1] this speech being more hard to justify than the former, and so their proof more doubtful than the thing itself which they prove. He that were certain that this is true, must have marked who they be that speak for ceremonies; he must have noted who amongst them doth speak oftenest, or is most earnest; he must have been both acquainted thoroughly with the religion of such, and also privy what conferences or compacts are passed in secret between them and others; which kinds of notice are not wont to be vulgar and common. Yet they which allege this would have it taken as a thing that needeth no proof, a thing which all men know and see.

And if so be it were granted them as true, what gain they by it? Sundry of them that be popish are eager in maintenance of ceremonies. Is it so strange a matter to find a good thing furthered by ill men of a sinister intent and purpose, whose forwardness is not therefore a bridle to such as favour the same cause with a better and sincerer meaning? They that seek, as they say, the removing of all popish orders out of the Church, and reckon the state of Bishops in the number of those orders, do (I doubt not) presume that the cause which they prosecute is holy. Notwithstanding it is their own ingenuous acknowledgment, that even this very cause, which they term so often by an excellency, "The Lord's cause," is "*gratissima*, most acceptable, unto some which hope for prey and spoil by it, and that our age hath store of such, and that such are the very sectaries of Dionysius the famous atheist."[2] Now if there

---

[1] [T. C. i. 53. iii. 180.]

[2] Eccles. Disc. f. 94. [p. 127. as translated by T. C. "Hæc . . . oratio de episcoporum pompa et affluentia minuenda . . . gratissima nonnullis est, qui suam causam agi putant, et jampridem hæreditatem istam spe devorarint. . . . Habet enim ætas nostra multos ejusmodi milites, multos Dionysios, qui Deo togam auream neque ad æstatem neque ad hyemem commodam, sibi autem ad omnia utilissimam et commodissimam fore arbitrantur." Vide Cic. de Nat. Deor. iii. 34.]

upon we should upbraid them with irreligious, as they do us
with superstitious favourers ; if we should follow them in
their own kind of pleading, and say, that the most clamorous
for this pretended reformation are either atheists, or else
proctors suborned by atheists ; the answer which herein
they would make unto us, let them apply unto themselves,
and there an end.   For they must not forbid us to presume
our cause in defence of our church orders to be as good as
theirs against them, till the contrary be made manifest to the
world.

X. In the meanwhile sorry we are that any good and godly
mind should be grieved [1] with that which is done.   But to
remedy their grief lieth not so much in us as in themselves.
They do not wish to be made glad with the hurt of the
Church : and to remove all out of the Church whereat they
shew themselves to be sorrowful, would be, as we are persuaded, hurtful if not pernicious thereunto.   Till they be
able to persuade the contrary, they must and will I doubt
not find out some other good means to cheer up themselves.
Amongst which means the example of Geneva may serve for
one.   Have not they the old popish custom of using godfathers and godmothers in Baptism ? the old popish custom
of administering the blessed sacrament of the holy Eucharist
with wafer-cakes ?   These things the godly there can digest.
Wherefore should not the godly here learn to do the like both
in them and in the rest of the like nature ?   Some further mean
peradventure it might be to assuage their grief, if so be they
did consider the revenge they take on them which have been,
as they interpret it, the workers of their continuance in so
great grief so long.   For if the maintenance of ceremonies be
a corrosive to such as oppugn them, undoubtedly to such as
maintain them it can be no great pleasure, when they behold
how that which they reverence is oppugned.   And therefore
they that judge themselves martyrs when they are grieved,
should think withal what they are whom they grieve.[2]   For

---

[1] T. C. l. ii. p. 180. [and i. 53.]   " There be numbers which have
Antichristianity in such detestation, that they cannot without grief of
mind behold them."   And afterwards, " such godly brethren are not
easily to be grieved, which they seem to be when they are thus
martyred in their minds, for ceremonies which (to speak the best of
them) are unprofitable."

[2] [See a letter of Archdeacon Barfoot to Archbishop Whitgift in
Strype, Ann. iii. 1. 350. (1584.)   " Truly, my lord, the conformable
ministry is very much grieved hereat.   And divers said plainly, that if

we are still to put them in mind that the cause doth make no difference; for that it must be presumed as good at the least on our part as on theirs, till it be in the end decided who have stood for truth and who for error. So that till then the most effectual medicine and withal the most sound to ease their grief, must not be (in our opinion) the taking away of those things whereat they are grieved, but the altering of that persuasion which they have concerning the same.

[2.] For this we therefore both pray and labour; the more because we are also persuaded, that it is but conceit in them to think, that those Romish ceremonies whereof we have hitherto spoken, are like leprous clothes, infectious unto the Church, or like soft and gentle poisons,[1] the venom whereof being insensibly pernicious, worketh death, and yet is never felt working. Thus they say: but because they say it only, and the world hath not as yet had so great experience of their art in curing the diseases of the Church, that the bare authority of their word should persuade in a cause so weighty, they may not think much if it be required at their hands to shew, first, by what means so deadly infection can grow from similitude between us and the church of Rome in these things indifferent: secondly, for that it were infinite if the Church should provide against every such evil as may come to pass, it is not sufficient that they shew possibility of dangerous event, unless there appear some likelihood also of the same to follow in us, except we prevent it. Nor is this enough, unless it be moreover made plain, that there is no good and

they had thought this would have been the end, they would have joined with the other in their recusancy, rather than have offered themselves to such reproachful speeches, as were given out of them by some of that faction. For they told him, that there was a letter there in the country sent from Mr. Field of London, [a great Puritan,] to the ministers in those parts, recusants, exhorting them to stand stoutly to the cause; affirming the same not to be theirs, but the Lord's; boldly assuring, that such as had subscribed had made a *breach*, as he was informed Field termed it. And therefore rashly judging of them, that they never would do good hereafter, and slanderously terming them by the name of *branded menne*. He assured his grace, there was great grief conceived hereat." In a schedule of complaints from Suffolk Archdeaconry, 1586. "The communion was received by many sitting, and those that conformed to the Church called Time-servers." Whitg. i. 497.]

1 "Although the corruptions in them strike not straight to the heart, yet as gentle poisons they consume by little and little." T. C. lib. iii. p 171.

sufficient way of prevention, but by evacuating clean, and by emptying the Church of every such rite and ceremony, as is presently called in question. Till this be done, their good affection towards the safety of the Church is acceptable, but the way they prescribe us to preserve it by must rest in suspense.

[3.] And lest hereat they take occasion to turn upon us the speech of the prophet Jeremy used against Babylon, "Behold we have done our endeavour to cure the diseases of Babylon, but she through her wilfulness doth rest uncured;"[1] let them consider into what straits the Church might drive itself in being guided by this their counsel. Their axiom is, that the sound believing Church of Jesus Christ may not be like heretical churches in any of those indifferent things, which men make choice of, and do not take by prescript appointment of the word of God. In the word of God the use of bread is prescribed, as a thing without which the Eucharist may not be celebrated; but as for the kind of bread it is not denied to be a thing indifferent. Being indifferent of itself, we are by this axiom of theirs to avoid the use of unleavened bread in that sacrament, because such bread the church of Rome being heretical useth. But doth not the selfsame axiom bar us even from leavened bread also, which the church of the Grecians useth; the opinions whereof are in a number of things the same for which we condemn the church of Rome, and in some things erroneous where the church of Rome is acknowledged to be sound; as namely, in the article about proceeding of the Holy Ghost? And lest here they should say that because the Greek church is farther off, and the church of Rome nearer, we are in that respect rather to use that which the church of Rome useth not: let them imagine a reformed church in the city of Venice, where a Greek church and a popish both are. And when both these are equally near, let them consider what the third shall do. Without either leavened or unleavened bread, it can have no sacrament; the word of God doth tie it to neither; and their axiom doth exclude it from both. If this constrain them, as it must, to grant that their axiom is not to take any place save in those things only where the Church hath larger scope; it resteth that they search out some stronger reason than they have as yet alleged; otherwise they constrain not us to think that

[1] Jer. li. 9.

the Church is tied unto any such rule or axiom, no not then when she hath the widest field to walk in, and the greatest store of choice.

XI. Against such ceremonies generally as are the same in the church of England and of Rome, we see what hath been hitherto alleged. Albeit therefore we do not find the one church's having of such things to be sufficient cause why the other should not have them : nevertheless, in case it may be proved, that amongst the number of rites and orders common unto both, there are particulars, the use whereof is utterly unlawful in regard of some special bad and noisome quality ; there is no doubt but we ought to relinquish such rites and orders, what freedom soever we have to retain the other still. As therefore we have heard their general exception against all those things, which being not commanded in the word of God, were first received in the church of Rome, and from thence have been derived into ours ; so it followeth that now we proceed unto certain kinds of them, as being excepted against not only for that they are in the church of Rome, but are besides either Jewish, or abused unto idolatry, and so grown scandalous.

[2.] The church of Rome, they say, being ashamed of the simplicity of the gospel, did almost out of all religions take whatsoever had any fair and gorgeous show,[1] borrowing in that respect from the Jews sundry of their abolished ceremonies. Thus by foolish and ridiculous imitation, all their massing furniture almost they took from the Law, lest having an altar and a priest, they should want vestments for their stage ;[2] so that whatsoever we have in common with the church of Rome, if the same be of this kind we ought to remove it. "Constantine the emperor speaking of the keeping of the feast of Easter, saith, 'That it is an unworthy thing to have any thing common with that most spiteful company of the Jews.'[3]   And a little after he saith, 'That it is most absurd and against reason, that the Jews should vaunt and glory that the Christians could not keep

---

[1] Eccles. Disc. fol. 98. [in T. C.'s transl. p. 131, 2.] and T. C. lib. iii. p. 181.   "Many of these popish ceremonies faulty by reason of the pomp in them ; where they should be agreeable to the simplicity of the gospel of Christ crucified."   [2] [Eccl. Disc. ibid.]

[3] T. C. lib. i. p. 132. [103.] Euseb. de Vit. Const. lib. iii. c. 18. [Μηδὲν τοίνυν ἔστω ἡμῖν κοινὸν μετὰ τοῦ ἐχθίστου τῶν Ἰουδαίων ὄχλου. . . . ἐστὶ γὰρ ὡς ἀληθῶς ἀτοπώτατον, ἐκείνους αὐχεῖν ὡς ἄρα παρεκτὸς τῆς αὐτῶν διδασκαλίας ταῦτα φυλάττειν οὐκ εἴημεν ἱκανοί.]

those things without their doctrine.' And in another place it is said after this sort : ' It is convenient so to order the matter, that we have nothing common with that nation.'[1] The council of Laodicea, which was afterwards confirmed by the sixth general council,[2] decreed ' that the Christians should not take unleavened bread of the Jews, or communicate with their impiety.' "[3]

[3.] For the easier manifestation of truth in this point, two things there are which must be considered ; namely, the causes wherefore the Church should decline from Jewish ceremonies; and how far it ought so to do. One cause is that the Jews were the deadliest and spitefullest enemies of Christianity that were in the world, and in this respect their orders so far forth to be shunned, as we have already set down in handling the matter of heathenish ceremonies. For no enemies being so venomous against Christ as Jews, they were of all other most odious, and by that mean least to be used as fit church patterns for imitation. Another cause is the solemn abrogation of the Jews' ordinances ; which ordinances for us to resume, were to check our Lord himself which hath disannulled them. But how far this second cause doth extend, it is not on all sides fully agreed upon. And touching those things whereunto it reacheth not, although there be small cause wherefore the church should frame itself to the Jews' example in respect of their persons which are most hateful ; yet God himself having been the author of their laws, herein they are (notwithstanding the former consideration) still worthy to be honoured, and to be followed above others, as much as the state of things will bear.

[4.] Jewish ordinances had some things natural, and of the perpetuity of those things no man doubteth. That which was positive we likewise know to have been by the coming of Christ partly necessary not to be kept, and partly indifferent to be kept or not. Of the former kind circumcision and sacrifice were. For this point Stephen was accused, and the evidence which his accusers brought

---

[1] Socrat. lib. i. c. 9. [Τοῦτο οὕτως ἐπανορθοῦσθαι προσῆκεν, ὡς μηδὲν μετὰ τοῦ τῶν πατροκτόνων τε καὶ κυριοκτόνων ἐκείνων ἔθνους εἶναι κοινόν.]

[2] [Or rather by the council called Quinisextum. vid. Labb. Conc. vi. 1124, 1146.]

[3] Tom. i. Concil. Laod. Can. 38. [i. 1503. οὐ δεῖ παρὰ τῶν Ἰουδαίων ἄζυμα λαμβάνειν, ἢ κοινωνεῖν ταῖς ἀσεβείαις αὐτῶν.]

against him in judgment was, "This man ceaseth not to speak blasphemous words against this holy place and the Law, for we have heard him say that this Jesus of Nazareth shall destroy this place, and shall change the ordinances that Moses gave us."[1] True it is that this doctrine was then taught, which unbelievers condemning for blasphemy did therein commit that which they did condemn. The Apostles notwithstanding from whom Stephen had received it, did not so teach the abrogation, no not of those things which were necessarily to cease, but that even the Jews being Christian, might for a time continue in them. And therefore in Jerusalem the first Christian bishop not circumcised was Mark ; and he not bishop till the days of Adrian the emperor, after the overthrow of Jerusalem : there having been fifteen bishops before him which were all of the circumcision.[2]

The Christian Jews did think at the first not only themselves but the Christian Gentiles also bound, and that necessarily, to observe the whole Law. There went forth certain of the sect of Pharisees which did believe, and they coming unto Antioch, taught that it was necessary for the Gentiles to be circumcised, and to keep the law of Moses.[3] Whereupon there grew dissension, Paul and Barnabas disputing against them. The determination of the council held at Jerusalem concerning this matter was finally this : "Touching the Gentiles which believe, we have written and determined that they observe no such thing."[4] Their protestation by letters is, "Forasmuch as we have heard that certain which departed from us have troubled you with words, and cumbered your minds, saying, Ye must be circumcised and keep the Law ; know that we gave them no such commandment."[5] Paul therefore continued still teaching the Gentiles, not only that they were not bound to observe the laws of Moses, but that the observation of those laws, which were necessarily to be abrogated, was in them altogether unlawful. In which point his doctrine was misreported, as though he

---

[1] Acts vi. 13, 14.

[2] Vide Niceph. lib. iii. cap. 25. [Ἐπὶ δὲ τούτοις Ἰούδας πεντεκαιδέκατος· οὓς ἐξ ἐθνῶν μετὰ τὴν ἅλωσιν διαδέχεται Μάρκος· τοσοῦτοι μὲν ἀπὸ τῶν Ἀποστόλων ἐς τὸν εἰρημένον Ἰούδαν ἐπίσκοποι ἐκ περιτομῆς ἐν Ἱεροσολύμοις γεγόνασιν.] et Sulpit. Sever. p. 149. in edit. Plant. ["Tum Hierosolymæ non nisi ex circumcisione habebat Ecclesia Sacerdotem," p. 364. ed. Horn. 1665.]

[3] Acts xv.   [4] Acts xxi. 25.   [5] Acts xv. 24.

had every where preached this, not only concerning the Gentiles, but also touching the Jews. Wherefore coming unto James and the rest of the clergy at Jerusalem, they told him plainly of it, saying, "Thou seest, brother, how many thousand Jews there are which believe, and they are all zealous of the Law. Now they are informed of thee, that thou teachest all the Jews which are amongst the Gentiles to forsake Moses, and sayest that they ought not to circumcise their children, neither to live after the customs." [1] And hereupon they gave him counsel to make it apparent in the eyes of all men, that those flying reports were untrue, and that himself being a Jew kept the Law even as they did.

In some things therefore we see the Apostles did teach, that there ought not to be conformity between the Christian Jews and Gentiles. How many things this law of inconformity did comprehend, there is no need we should stand to examine. This general is true, that the Gentiles were not made conformable unto the Jews, in that which was necessarily to cease at the coming of Christ.

[5.] Touching things positive, which might either cease or continue as occasion should require, the Apostles tendering the zeal of the Jews, thought it necessary to bind even the Gentiles for a time to abstain as the Jews did, "from things offered unto idols, from blood, from strangled." [2] These decrees were every where delivered unto the Gentiles to be straitly observed and kept. [3] In the other matters, where the Gentiles were free, and the Jews in their own opinion still tied, the Apostles' doctrine unto the Jews was, "condemn not the Gentile;" unto the Gentile, "despise not the Jew." [4] The one sort they warned to take heed, that scrupulosity did not make them rigorous, in giving unadvised sentence against their brethren which were free; the other, that they did not become scandalous, by abusing their liberty and freedom to the offence of their weak brethren which were scrupulous. From hence therefore two conclusions there are which may evidently be drawn; the first, that whatsoever conformity of positive laws the Apostles did bring in between the churches of Jews and Gentiles, it was in those things only which might either cease or continue a shorter or longer time, as occasion did most

---

[1] Acts xxi. 20.   [2] Acts xv. 28, 29.
[3] Acts xvi. 4.   [4] Rom. xiv. 10.

require; the second, that they did not impose upon the churches of the Gentiles any part of the Jews' ordinances with bond of necessary and perpetual observation, (as we all both by doctrine and practice acknowledge,) but only in respect of the conveniency and fitness for the present state of the Church as then it stood. The words of the council's decree concerning the Gentiles are, "It seemed good to the Holy Ghost and to us, to lay upon you no more burden saving only those things of necessity, abstinence from idol-offerings, from strangled and blood, and from fornication."[1] So that in other things positive which the coming of Christ did not necessarily extinguish the Gentiles were left altogether free.

[6.] Neither ought it to seem unreasonable that the Gentiles should necessarily be bound and tied to Jewish ordinances, so far forth as that decree importeth. For to the Jew, who knew that their difference from other nations which were aliens and strangers from God, did especially consist in this, that God's people had positive ordinances given to them of God himself, it seemed marvellous hard, that the Christian Gentiles should be incorporated into the same commonwealth with God's own chosen people, and be subject to no part of his statutes, more than only the law of nature, which heathens count themselves bound unto. It was an opinion constantly received amongst the Jews, that God did deliver unto the sons of Noah seven precepts: namely, first, to live in some form of regiment under public laws; secondly, to serve and call upon the name of God; thirdly, to shun idolatry; fourthly, not to suffer effusion of blood; fifthly, to abhor all unclean knowledge in the flesh; sixthly, to commit no rapine; seventhly, and finally, not to eat of any living creature whereof the blood was not first let out.[2] If therefore the Gentiles would

---

[1] [Acts xv. 28.]

[2] Lib. qui Seder Olam inscribitur. [Or "The World's Order," being a summary of events and dates from the creation to the war of Bar Cochab, supposed to have been written about A.D. 130. Wolf. Bibl. Hebr. i. 491. ed. 1715. The passage cited is cap. 5. p. 16. ed. Meyer. Amstelæd. 1699. "From the Red sea they journeyed unto Marah. . . There were given unto Israel ten precepts;" [Exod. xv. 23, 25.] "seven of them, concerning which commandment had been given to the Sons of Noah."], 1. דינין [the judgments]: 2. ברכת השם [the malediction of the Name (of God)]: 3. עֶ[עבודת אלילים,]" (mor usually עבודת זרה "strange worship,") "the worship of idols

be exempt from the law of Moses, yet it might seem hard they should also cast off even those things positive which were observed before Moses, and which were not of the same kind with laws that were necessarily to cease. And peradventure hereupon the council saw it expedient to determine, that the Gentiles should, according unto the third, the seventh, and the fifth, of those precepts, abstain from things sacrificed unto idols, from strangled and blood, and from fornication. The rest the Gentiles did of their own accord observe, nature leading them thereto.

[7.] And did not nature also teach them to abstain from fornication? No doubt it did. Neither can we with reason think, that as the former two are positive, so likewise this, being meant as the Apostle doth otherwise usually understand it.[1] But very marriage within a number of degrees being not only by the law of Moses, but also by the law of the sons of Noah (for so they took it) an unlawful discovery of nakedness; this discovery of nakedness by unlawful marriages such as Moses in the law reckoneth up,[2] I think it for mine own part more probable to have been meant in the words of that canon, than fornication according unto the sense of the law of nature. Words must be taken according to the matter whereof they are uttered. The Apostles command to abstain from blood. Construe this meaning according to the law of nature, and it will seem that homicide only is forbidden. But construe it in reference to the law of the Jews about which the question was, and it shall easily appear to have a clean other sense, and in any man's judgment a truer, when we expound it of eating and not of shedding blood. So if we speak of fornication, he that knoweth no law but only the law of nature must needs make thereof a narrower construction, than he which measureth the same by a law, wherein sundry kinds even of conjugal copulation are prohibited

---

4. שפיכות דמים [the shedding of blood]: 5. גילוי עריות [the discovery of nakedness]: 6. הגזל [rapine]: 7. אבר מן החי [(partaking of) any member of a living creature.] Israel added unto these at that time the Sabbath, and (דינין) judgments," (on the difference between this and the first precept see Selden, De Jure Nat. et Gent. ap. Heb. vii. 5. p. 809.) "and the honouring of parents." The whole passage is quoted and illustrated by Selden, lib. i. c. 10. p. 123.]

[1] Heb. xiii. 4; 1 Cor. v. 11; Gal. v. 19.
[2] Lev. xviii.

as impure, unclean, unhonest. St. Paul himself doth term incestuous marriage fornication.[1] If any do rather think that the Christian Gentiles themselves, through the loose and corrupt custom of those times, took simple fornication for no sin, and were in that respect offensive unto believing Jews, which by the Law had been better taught; our proposing of another conjecture is unto theirs no prejudice.[2]

[8.] Some things therefore we see there were, wherein the Gentiles were forbidden to be like unto the Jews; some things wherein they were commanded not to be unlike. Again, some things also there were, wherein no law of God did let but that they might be either like or unlike, as occasion should require. And unto this purpose Leo saith,[3] "Apostolical ordinance (beloved,) knowing that our Lord Jesus Christ came not into this world to undo the law, hath in such sort distinguished the mysteries of the Old Testament, that certain of them it hath chosen out to benefit evangelical knowledge withal, and for that purpose appointed that those things which before were Jewish might now be Christian customs." The cause why the Apostles did thus conform the Christians as much as might be according to the pattern of the Jews, was to rein them in by this mean the more, and to make them cleave the better.

[9.] The Church of Christ hath had in no one thing so many and so contrary occasions of dealing as about Judaism : some having thought the whole Jewish Law wicked and damnable in itself; some not condemning it as the former sort absolutely, have notwithstanding judged it either sooner necessary to be abrogated, or further unlawful to be observed than truth can bear; some of scrupulous simplicity urging perpetual and universal observation of the Law of Moses necessary, as the Christian Jews at the first in the Apostles' times ; some as heretics, holding the same no less even after the contrary determination set down by

[1] 1 Cor. v. 1.
[2] [Selden in the work above cited (which is throughout an elaborate commentary on the seven Noachical precepts) approves this construction of the word πορνεία : though he does not think that the council of Jerusalem was referring to those precepts : lib. vii. c. 12, p. 845.]
[3] Leo in Jejun. Mens. Sept. Ser. 9. [vii. c. 1. "Apostolica institutio, dilectissimi, quæ Dom. Jesum Christum ad hoc venisse in hunc mundum noverat, ut legem non solveret sed impleret, ita Veteris Testamenti decreta distinxit, ut quædam ex eis sicut erant condita evangelicæ eruditioni profutura decerperet, et quæ dudum fuerant consuetudinis Judaicæ fierent observantiæ Christianæ."]

consent of the Church at Jerusalem; finally some being herein resolute through mere infidelity, and with open professed enmity against Christ, as unbelieving Jews.

To control slanderers of the Law and Prophets, such as Marcionites and Manichees were, the Church in her liturgies hath intermingled with readings out of the New Testament lessons taken out of the Law and Prophets; whereunto Tertullian alluding, saith of the Church of Christ,[1] "It intermingleth with evangelical and apostolical writings the Law and the Prophets; and from thence it drinketh in that faith, which with water it sealeth, clotheth with the Spirit, nourisheth with the Eucharist, with martyrdom setteth forward." They would have wondered in those times to hear, that any man being not a favourer of heresy should term this by way of disdain, "mangling of the Gospels and Epistles."[2]

[10.] They which honour the Law as an image of the wisdom of God himself, are notwithstanding to know that the same had an end in Christ. But what? Was the Law so abolished with Christ, that after his ascension the office of Priests became immediately wicked, and the very name hateful, as importing the exercise of an ungodly function?[3] No, as long as the glory of the Temple continued, and till the time of that final desolation was accomplished, the very Christian Jews did continue with their sacrifices and other parts of legal service. That very Law therefore which our Saviour was to abolish, did not *so soon* become unlawful to be observed as some imagine; nor was it afterwards unlawful *so far*, that the very name of Altar, of Priest, of Sacrifice itself, should be banished out of the world. For though God do now hate sacrifice, whether it be heathenish or Jewish, so that we cannot have the same things which

---

[1] Tertull. de Præscript. advers. Hæret. [c. 36. "Unum Deum novit Creatorem universitatis, et Christum Jesum ex Virgine Maria Filium Dei Creatoris, et carnis resurrectionem: legem et prophetas cum evangelicis et apostolicis literis miscet, et inde potat fidem: eam aqua signat, Sancto Spiritu vestit, eucharistia pascit, martyrio exhortatur."]

[2] T. C. lib. iii. p. 171. "What an abusing also is it to affirm the mangling of the Gospels and Epistles to have been brought into the Church by godly and learned men!"

[3] T. C. lib. i. p. 216. "Seeing that the office and function of priests was after our Saviour Christ's ascension naught and ungodly; the name whereby they were called, which did exercise that ungodly function, cannot be otherwise taken than in the evil part."

they had but with impiety; yet unless there be some greater let than the only evacuation of the Law of Moses, the names themselves may (I hope) be retained without sin, in respect of that proportion which things established by our Saviour have unto them which by him are abrogated. And so throughout all the writings of the ancient Fathers we see that the words which were do continue; the only difference is, that whereas before they had a literal, they now have a metaphorical use, and are as so many notes o remembrance unto us, that what they did signify in the letter is accomplished in the truth. And as no man can deprive the Church of this liberty, to use names whereunto the Law was accustomed, so neither are we generally forbidden the use of things which the Law hath; though it neither command us any particular rite, as it did the Jews a number, and the weightiest which it did command them are unto us in the Gospel prohibited.

[11.] Touching such as through simplicity of error did urge universal and perpetual observation of the Law of Moses at the first, we have spoken already. Against Jewish heretics and false apostles teaching afterwards the selfsame, St. Paul in every epistle commonly either disputeth or giveth warning. Jews that were zealous for the Law, but withal infidels in respect of Christianity, and to the name of Jesus Christ most spiteful enemies, did while they flourished no less persecute the Church than heathens. After their estate was overthrown, they were not that way so much to be feared. Howbeit, because they had their synagogues in every famous city almost throughout the world, and by that means great opportunity to withdraw from the Christian faith, which to do they spared no labour; this gave the church occasion to make sundry laws against them. As in the council of Laodicea,[1] "The festival presents which Jews or heretics use to send must not be received, nor holidays solemnized in their company." Again, "from the Jews men ought not to receive their unleavened, nor to communicate with their impieties." Which council was afterwards indeed confirmed by the sixth general council. But what was the true sense or meaning both of the one

---

[1] Conc. Laod. Can. 37, 38. ["Non oportet a Judæis vel hæreticis feriatica, quæ mittuntur accipere nec cum eis dies agere festos. Non oportet a Judæis azyma accipere, aut communicare impietatibus eorum." Conc. Reg. II. 116.] T. C. lib. i. p. 132. [103.]

and the other ? Were Christians here forbidden to communicate in unleavened bread because the Jews did so
being enemies of the Church ? [1] He which attentively shall
weigh the words will suspect, that they rather forbid communion with Jews, than imitation of them : much more, if
with these two decrees be compared a third in the council
of Constantinople, " Let no man either of the clergy or laity
eat the unleavened of the Jews, nor enter into any familiarity
with them, nor send for them in sickness, nor take physic at
their hands, nor as much as go into the bath with them. If
any do otherwise being a clergyman, let him be deposed ; if
being a lay person, let excommunication be his punishment."

[12.] If these canons were any argument, that they which
made them did utterly condemn similitude between the
Christians and Jews in things indifferent appertaining unto
religion, either because the Jews were enemies unto the
Church, or else for that their ceremonies were abrogated ;
these reasons had been as strong and effectual against their
keeping the feast of Easter on the same day the Jews kept
theirs, and not according to the custom of the West church.
For so they did from the first beginning till Constantine's
time. For in these two things the East and West churches
did interchangeably both confront the Jews and concur with
them : the West church using unleavened bread, as the Jews
in their passover did, but differing from them in the day
whereon they kept the feast of Easter ; contrariwise the
East church celebrating the feast of Easter on the same day
with the Jews, but not using the same kind of bread which
they did. Now if so be the East church in using leavened
bread had done ill,[3] either for that the Jews were enemies
to the Church, or because Jewish ceremonies were abrogated ;
how should we think but that Victor the bishop of Rome

[1] T. C. lib. iii. p. 176. [" What can be in itself more indifferent
than these two, forbidden the Christians for that they were used of the
enemies of the Church ! "]

[2] Conc. Constantinop. vi. cap. 11. [Μηδεὶς τῶν ἐν ἱερατικῷ τάγματι
ἢ λαϊκὸς τὰ παρὰ τῶν Ἰουδαίων ἄζυμα ἐσθιέτω, ἢ τοιούτοις προσοικειούσθω,
καὶ ἰατρείας παρ᾽ αὐτῶν λαμβανέτω, ἢ ἐν βαλανείῳ παντελῶς τούτοις συλ-
λουέσθω. Εἰ δέ τις τοῦτο πρᾶξαι ἐπιχειροίη, εἰ μὲν κληρικὸς εἴη, καθαι-
ρείσθω, εἰ δὲ λαϊκὸς, ἀφοριζέσθω. xvi. 618.]

[3] [So it stands in the original edition, p. 194. But it is most likely
an oversight, the sense requiring " not done ill," or " done well : "
which reading has been followed by all the editors except Mr. Hanbury.
The correction appears to have been Spenser's : at least it occurs in the
reprint of his edition, 1622.]

(whom all judicious men do in that behalf disallow) did well to be so vehement and fierce in drawing them to the like dissimilitude for the feast of Easter?[1]   Again, if the West churches had in either of those two respects affected dissimilitude with the Jews in the feast of Easter, what reason had they to draw the Eastern church herein unto them, which reason did not enforce them to frame themselves unto it in the ceremony of leavened bread?   Difference in rites should breed no controversy between one church and another; but if controversy be once bred, it must be ended.   The feast of Easter being therefore litigious in the days of Constantine, who honoured of all other churches most the church of Rome, which church was the mother from whose breasts he had drawn that food which gave him nourishment to eternal life; sith agreement was necessary, and yet impossible unless the one part were yielded unto; his desire was that of the two the Eastern church should rather yield.   And to this end he useth sundry persuasive speeches.

When Stephen the bishop of Rome going about to shew what the Catholic Church should do, had alleged what the heretics themselves did, namely, that they received such as came unto them, and offered not to baptize them anew; St. Cyprian being of a contrary mind to him about the matter at that time in question, which was, "Whether heretics converted ought to be rebaptized, yea or no?" answered the allegation of Pope Stephen with exceeding great stomach, saying, "To this degree of wretchedness the church of God and Spouse of Christ is now come, that her ways she frameth to the example of heretics; that to celebrate the Sacraments which heavenly instruction hath delivered, light itself doth borrow from darkness, and Christians do that which Antichrists do."[2]

Now albeit Constantine have done that to further a better cause, which Cyprian did to countenance a worse, namely the rebaptization of heretics, and have taken advantage at the odiousness of the Jews, as Cyprian of heretics, because the Eastern church kept their feast of Easter always the fourteenth day of the month, as the Jews did, what day of the

<hr />

[1] [Euseb. v. 24.]

[2] Cypr. ad Pomp. cont. Stephan. [Ep. 74. § 2. "Ad hoc enim malorum devoluta est Ecclesia Dei et sponsa Christi, ut hæreticorum exempla sectetur, ut ad celebranda sacramenta cœlestis disciplinæ lux de tenebris mutuetur, et id faciant Christiani, quod Antichristi faciunt."]

week soever it fell; or howsoever Constantine did take
occasion in the handling of that cause to say, " It is unworthy
to have any thing common with that spiteful nation of the
Jews :" [1] shall every motive argument used in such kind
of conferences be made a rule for others still to conclude
the like by, concerning all things of like nature, when as
probable inducements may lead them to the contrary? Let
both this and other allegations suitable unto it cease to bark
any longer idly against that truth, the course and passage
whereof it is not in them to hinder.

XII. But the weightiest exception, and of all the most
worthy to be respected, is against such kind of ceremonies,
as have been so grossly and shamefully abused in the church
of Rome, that where they remain they are scandalous, yea,
they cannot choose but be stumblingblocks, and grievous
causes of offence. Concerning this point therefore we are
first to note, what properly it is to be scandalous or offensive;
secondly, what kind of ceremonies are such; and thirdly,
when they are necessarily for remedy thereof to be taken
away, and when not.

[2.] The common conceit of the vulgar sort is, whensoever they see any thing which they mislike and are angry at,
to think that every such thing is scandalous, and that themselves in this case are the men concerning whom our Saviour
spake in so fearful manner, saying, "whosoever shall scandalize
or offend any one of these little ones which believe in me " [2]

---

[1] Socrat. Ecclesiast. Hist. lib. v. c. 22. "Plerique in Asia minore
antiquitus 14 die mensis, nulla ratione diei Sabbati habita, hoc festum
observarunt. Quod dum faciebant, cum aliis, qui aliam rationem in
eodem festo agendo sequebantur, usque eo nequaquam dissenserunt,
quoad Victor episcopus Romanus, supra modum iracundia inflammatus,
omnes in Asia qui erant τεσσαρεσκαιδεκατῖται appellati excommunica-
verit. Ob quod factum Irenæus episcopus Lugduni in Victorem per
epistolam graviter invectus est." Euseb. de Vita Constant. lib iii. cap.
18. "Quid præstabilius, quidve augustius esse poterat, quam ut hoc
festum, per quod spem immortalitatis nobis ostentatam habemus, uno
modo et ratione apud omnes integre sincereque observaretur? Ac
primum omnium indignum plane videbatur, ut ritum et consuetudinem
imitantes Judæorum (qui, quoniam suas ipsorum manus immani scelere
polluerunt, merito, ut scelestos decet, cæco animorum errore tenentur
irretiti) istud festum sanctissimum ageremus. In nostra enim situm est
potestate, ut, illorum more rejecto, veriore ac magis sincero instituto
(quod quidem usque a prima passionis die hactenus recoluimus) hujus
festi celebrationem ad posterorum seculorum memoriam propagemus.
Nihil igitur sit nobis cum Judæorum turba, omnium odiosa maxime.[5]"

[2] Matt. xviii. 6.

(that is, as they construe it, whosoever shall anger the
meanest and simplest artisan which carrieth a good mind,
by not removing out of the Church such rites and ceremonies
as displease him), "better he were drowned in the bottom of
the sea." But hard were the case of the Church of Christ, if
this were to scandalize. Men are scandalized when they
are moved, led, and provoked unto sin. At good things
evil men may take occasion to do evil ; and so Christ himself was a rock of offence in Israel,[1] they taking occasion at
his poor estate and at the ignominy of his cross, to think him
unworthy the name of that great and glorious Messias, whom
the Prophets describe in such ample and stately terms. But
that which we therefore term offensive because it inviteth men
to offend, and by a dumb kind of provocation encourageth,
moveth, or any way leadeth unto sin, must of necessity be
acknowledged actively scandalous.

Now some things are so even by their very essence and
nature, so that wheresoever they are found they are not
neither can be without this force of provocation unto evil ;
of which kind all examples of sin and wickedness are. Thus
David was scandalous in that bloody act whereby he caused
the enemies of God to be blasphemous :[2] thus the whole
state of Israel scandalous, when their public disorders
caused the name of God to be ill-spoken of amongst the
nations.[3] It is of this kind that Tertullian meaneth :
"Offence or scandal, if I be not deceived (saith he), is, when
the example not of a good but of an evil thing doth set men
forward unto sin. Good things can scandalize none save
only evil minds : " good things have no scandalizing nature
in them.

[3.] Yet that which is of its own nature either good or at
least not evil, may by some accident become scandalous at
certain times and in certain places and to certain men ; the
open use thereof nevertheless being otherwise without danger.
The very nature of some rites and ceremonies therefore is
scandalous, as it was in a number of those which the Manichees did use, and is in all such as the law of God doth
forbid. Some are offensive only through the agreement of

---

[1] 1 Pet. ii. 8.
[2] 2 Sam. xii. 14.
[3] Rom. ii. 24 ; Ezek. xxxvi. 20 ; Tertull. lib de Virgin. Veland. [c.
3. "Scandalum, nisi fallor, non bonæ rei sed malæ exemplum est,
ædificans ad delictum. Bonæ res neminem scandalizant, nisi malam
mentem."]

men to use them unto evil, and not else ; as the most of those things indifferent which the heathens did to the service of their false gods, which another, in heart condemning their idolatry, could not do with them in show and token of approbation without being guilty of scandal given. Ceremonies of this kind are either devised at the first unto evil, as Eunomian heretics in dishonour of the blessed Trinity brought in the laying on of water but once,[1] to cross the custom of the church which in baptism did it thrice ; or else having had a profitable use they are afterwards interpreted and wrested to the contrary, as those heretics which held the Trinity to be three distinct not persons but natures, abused the ceremony of three times laying on water in baptism unto the strengthening of their heresy.[2] The element of water is in baptism necessary ; once to lay it on or twice is indifferent. For which cause Gregory making mention thereof saith,[3] " To dive an infant either thrice or but once in baptism, can be no way a thing reprovable ; seeing that both in three times washing the Trinity of persons, and in one the Unity of the Godhead may be signified." So that of these two ceremonies neither being hurtful in itself, both may serve unto good purpose ; yet one was devised, and the other converted, unto evil.

[4.] Now whereas in the church of Rome certain ceremonies are said to have been shamefully abused unto evil, as the ceremony of crossing at baptism, of kneeling at the eucharist, of using wafer-cakes, and such like ; the question

[1] [Sozom. vi. 26. φασὶ δέ τινες, πρῶτον τοῦτον Εὐνόμιον τολμῆσα εἰσηγήσασθαι, ἐν μιᾷ καταδύσει χρῆναι ἐπιτελεῖν τὴν θείαν βάπτισιν, κα παραχαράξαι τὴν ἀπὸ τῶν Ἀποστόλων εἰσέτι νῦν ἐν πᾶσι φυλαττομένην παράδοσιν.]

[2] [Concil. Tolet. iv. Can. 6, t. v. p. 1706. " Propter vitandum schismatis scandalum, vel hæretici dogmatis usum, simplam teneamus baptismi mersionem ; ne videantur apud nos, qui tertio mergunt, hæreticorum approbare assertionem dum sequuntur et morem."]

[3] Epist. ad Leandrum Hisp. [lib. i. ep. 43. " De trina vero mersione baptismatis nil responderi verius potest quam ipsi sensistis : quia in una fide nihil officit ecclesiæ consuetudo diversa. Nos autem quod tertio mergimus, triduanæ sepulturæ sacramenta signamus, ut dum tertio infans ab aquis educitur, resurrectio triduani temporis exprimatur. Quod si quis forte etiam pro summæ Trinitatis veneratione æstimet fieri, neque ad hoc aliquid obsistit, baptizandum semel in aquis mergere : quia dum in tribus subsistentiis una substantia est, reprehensibile esse nullatenus potest, infantem in baptismate vel ter vel semel mergere : quando et in tribus mersionibus personarum Trinitas, et in una potest divinitatis singularitas designari." II. 532.]

is, whether for remedy of that evil wherein such ceremonies have been scandalous, and perhaps may be still unto some even amongst ourselves, whom the presence and sight of them may confirm in that former error whereto they served in times past, they are of necessity to be removed. Are these, or any other ceremonies we have common with the church of Rome, scandalous and wicked in their very nature ? This no man objecteth. Are any such as have been polluted from their very birth, and instituted even at the first unto that thing which is evil ? That which hath been ordained impiously at the first, may wear out that impiety in tract of time ; and then what doth let but that the use thereof may stand without offence? The names of our months and of our days we are not ignorant from whence they came, and with what dishonour unto God they are said to have been devised at the first.[1] What could be spoken against any thing more effectual to stir hatred, than that which sometime the ancient Fathers in this case speak ? Yet those very names are at this day in use throughout Christendom without hurt or scandal to any. Clear and manifest it is, that things devised by heretics, yea, devised of a very heretical purpose even against religion, and at their first devising worthy to have been withstood, may in time grow meet to be kept; as that custom, the inventors whereof were the Eunomian heretics. So that customs once established and confirmed by long use, being presently without harm, are not in regard of their corrupt original to be held scandalous.

[5.] But concerning those our ceremonies which they reckon for most popish, they are not able to avouch, that any of them was otherwise instituted than unto good, yea, so used at the first. It followeth then that they all are such, as having served to good purpose, were afterwards converted unto the contrary. And sith it is not so much as

---

[1] [Euseb. Emis.] Hom. xi. de Pasch. [p. 566. par. i. t. v. Biblioth. Patr. Colon.] " Idololatriæ consuetudo in tantum homines occæcaverat, ut Solis, Lunæ, Martis atque Mercurii, Jovis, Veneris, Saturni, et diversis elementorum ac dæmonum appellationibus dies vocitarent, et luci tenebrarum nomen imponerent." Beda de Ration. Temp. cap. 4. [6.] " Octavus dies idem primus est, ad quem reditur, indeque [l. eoque] rursus hebdomada inchoatur [l. semper orditur.] His nomina a planetis Gentilitas indidit, habere se credens a Sole spiritum, a Luna corpus a Marte sanguinem, a Mercurio ingenium et linguam, a Jove temperantiam, a Venere voluptatem. a Saturno tarditatem." Isid. Hisp. lib. v. Etymol. cap. 30. [p. 938, ed. Gothofred.] " Dies dicti a diis, quorum nomina Romani quibusdam sideribus sacraverunt."

objected against us, that we retain together with them the
evil wherewith they have been infected in the church of
Rome, I would demand who they are whom we scandalize,
by using harmless things unto that good end for which they
were first instituted. Amongst ourselves that agree in the
approbati n of this kind of good use, no man will say that
one of us is offensive and scandalous unto another. As for
the favourers of the church of Rome, they know how far
we herein differ and dissent from them ; which thing neither
we conceal, and they by their public writings also profess
daily how much it grieveth them ; so that of them there
will not many rise up against us, as witnesses unto the
indictment of scandal, whereby we might be condemned
and cast, as having strengthened them in that evil wherewith they pollute themselves in the use of the same ceremonies. And concerning such as withstand the church of
England herein, and hate it because it doth not sufficiently
seem to hate Rome ; they (I hope) are far enough from
being by this mean drawn to any kind of popish error.
The multitude therefore of them, unto whom we are
scandalous through the use of abused ceremonies, is not
so apparent, that it can justly be said in general of any one sort
of men or other, we cause them to offend. If it be so, that
now or then some few are espied, who, having been accustomed heretofore to the rites and ceremonies of the
church of Rome, are not so scoured of their former rust as to
forsake their ancient persuasion which they have had, howsoever they frame themselves to outward obedience of laws
and orders : because such may misconstrue the meaning of
our ceremonies, and so take them as though they were in
every sort the same they have been, shall this be thought a
reason sufficient whereon to conclude that some law must
necessarily be made to abolish all such ceremonies?

[6.] They answer, that there is no law of God which doth
bind us to retain them. And St. Paul's rule is, that in those
things from which without hurt we may lawfully abstain, we
should frame the usage of our liberty with regard to the
weakness and imbecility of our brethren. Wherefore unto
them which stood upon their own defence saying, " All
things are lawful unto me ;" he replieth, " but all things are
not expedient "[1] in regard of others. " All things are
clean, all meats are lawful ; but evil unto that man that eateth

[1] 1 Cor. vi. 12.

offensively. If for thy meat's sake thy brother be grieved, thou walkest no longer according to charity. Destroy not him with thy meat for whom Christ died. Dissolve not for food's sake the work of God.[1] We that are strong must bear the imbecility of the impotent, and not please ourselves."[2] It was a weakness in the Christian Jews, and a maim of judgment in them, that they thought the Gentiles polluted by the eating of those meats which themselves were afraid to touch for fear of transgressing the law of Moses ; yea, hereat their hearts did so much rise, that the Apostle had just cause to fear, lest they would rather forsake Christianity than endure any fellowship with such as made no conscience of that which was unto them abominable. And for this cause mention is made of destroying the weak by meats, and of dissolving the work of God,[3] which was his Church, a part of the living stones whereof were believing Jews. Now those weak brethren before-mentioned are said to be as the Jews were, and our ceremonies which have been abused in the church of Rome to be as the scandalous meats, from which the Gentiles are exhorted to abstain in the presence of Jews, for fear of averting them from Christian faith. Therefore, as charity did bind them to refrain from that for their brethren's sake, which otherwise was lawful enough for them ; so it bindeth us for our brethren's sake likewise to abolish such ceremonies, although we might lawfully else retain them.

[7.] But between these two cases there are great odds. For neither are our weak brethren as the Jews, nor the ceremonies which we use as the meats which the Gentiles used. The Jews were known to be generally weak in that respect ; whereas contrariwise the imbecility of ours is not common unto so many, that we can take any such certain notice of them. It is a chance if here and there some one be found ; and therefore seeing we may presume men commonly otherwise, there is no necessity that our practice should frame itself by that which the Apostle doth prescribe to the Gentiles.

Again, their use of meats was not like unto our of ceremonies that being a matter of private action in common life, where every man was free to order that which himself did ; but this a public constitution for the ordering of the

[1] Rom. xiv. 20 ; xv. 20.]   [2] [Rom. xv. 1.]
[3] Rom. xiv. ; xv. 1.

Church : and we are not to look that the Church should
change her public laws and ordinances, made according to
that which is judged ordinarily and commonly fittest for the
whole, although it chance that for some particular men the
same be found inconvenient ;[1] especially when there may
be other remedy also against the sores of particular inconveniences. In this case therefore where any private
harm doth grow, we are not to reject instruction, as being an
unmeet plaister to apply unto it ; neither can we say, that
he which appointeth teachers for physicians in this kind of
evil, is "As if a man would set one to watch a child all day
long lest he should hurt himself with a knife ; whereas by
taking away the knife from him, the danger is avoided, and
the service of the man better employed."[2] For a knife
may be taken away from a child, without depriving them of
the benefit thereof which have years and discretion to use it.
But the ceremonies which children do abuse if we remove
quite and clean, as it is by some required that we should,
then are they not taken from children only, but from others
also ; which is as though because children may perh ps hurt
themselves with knives, we should conclude, that therefore
the use of knives is to be taken quite and clean even from
men also.

[8.] Those particular ceremonies, which they pretend to
be so scandalous, we shall in the next Book have occasion
more thoroughly to sift, where other things also traduced in
the public duties of the Church whereunto each of these appertaineth, are together with these to be touched, and such
reasons to be examined as have at any time been brought
either against the one or the other. In the meanwhile
against the conveniency of curing such evils by instruction,
strange it is that they should object the multitude of other
necessary matters, wherein preachers may better bestow
their time, than in giving men warning not to abuse ceremonies :[3] a wonder it is, that they should object this, which

---

[1] Vide Harmenop. [Harmenopuli Promptuarium Juris.] lib. i. tit. 1.
sect. 28. [παραβαίνουσι γὰρ οἱ νομοθέται τὸ ἅπαξ ἢ τὸ δὶς γενόμενον. p.
20. ed. Gothofr.]

[2] T. C. lib. iii. p 178. [156.]

[3] T. C. lib. iii. p. 177. "It is not so convenient that the minister,
having so many necessary points to bestow his time in, should be driven
to spend it in giving warning of not abusing them, of which (although
they were used to the best) there is no profit." [See also i. 56, ap.
Whitg. Defence, 277. The words are, "A counsell not so convenient

have so many years together troubled the Church with quarrels concerning these things, and are even to this very hour so earnest in them, that if they write or speak publicly but five words, one of them is lightly about the dangerous estate of the church of England in respect of abused ceremonies. How much happier had it been for this whole Church, if they which have raised contention therein about the abuse of rites and ceremonies, had considered in due time that there is indeed store of matters fitter and better a great deal for teachers to spend time and labour in ! It is through their importunate and vehement asseverations, more than through any such experience which we have had of our own, that we are forced to think it possible for one or other now and then, at leastwise in the prime of the reformation of our church, to have stumbled at some kind of ceremony: wherein forasmuch as we are contented to take this upon their credit, and to think it may be ; sith also they further pretend the same to be so dangerous a snare to their souls that are at any time taken therein ; they must give our teachers leave for the saving of those souls (be they never so few) to intermingle sometime with other more necessary things admonition concerning these not unnecessary. Wherein they should in reason more easily yield this leave, considering that hereunto we shall not need to use the hundredth part of that time, which themselves think very needful to bestow in making most bitter invectives against ceremonies of the Church.

XIII. But to come to the last point of all ; the church of England is grievously charged with forgetfulness of her duty, which duty had been to frame herself unto the pattern of their example that went before her in the work of reformation. [1] For "as the churches of Christ ought to be most unlike the synagogue of Antichrist in their indifferent ceremonies ; so they ought to be most like one unto another, and for preservation of unity to have as much as possible may be all the same ceremonies. And therefore St. Paul, to establish this order in the church of Corinth,

that the ministers and pastors, which have so many necessary points to bestow their time on, and to inform the people of, should be driven to cut off their time appointed thereto, to teach them not to abuse these things, which if they use never so well, they can gain nothing."]

[1] T. C. lib. i. p. 133. [104.]

that they should make their gatherings for the poor upon
the first day of the sabbath, (which is our Sunday,) allegeth
this for a reason,[1] That he had so ordained in other
churches." Again, "As children of one father and servants
of one family, so all churches should not only have one diet
in that they have one word, but also wear as it were one
livery in using the same ceremonies." Thirdly, " This rule
did the great council of Nice follow,[2] when it ordained, that
where certain at the feast of Pentecost did pray kneeling,
they should pray standing : the reason whereof is added,
which is, that one custom ought to be kept throughout all
churches. It is true that the diversity of ceremonies ought
not to cause the churches to dissent one with another ; but
yet it maketh most to the avoiding of dissension, that there
be amongst them an unity not only in doctrine, but also in
ceremonies. And therefore our form of service is to be
amended, not only for that it cometh too near that of the
Papists, but also because it is so different from that of the
reformed churches."[3] Being asked[4] to what churches ours
should conform itself, and why other reformed churches
should not as well frame themselves to ours ; their answer
is, " that if there be any ceremonies which we have better
than others, they ought to frame themselves to us ; if they
have better than we, then we ought to frame ourselves to
them ; if the ceremonies be alike commodious, the later
churches should conform themselves to the first, as the
younger daughter to the elder. For as St. Paul in the
members, where all other things are equal, noteth it for a
mark of honour above the rest, that one is called before
another to the Gospel ;[5] so is it for the same cause amongst
the churches. And in this respect he pincheth the Corinths,[6]
that not being the first which received the Gospel, yet they
would have their several manners from other churches.
Moreover, where the ceremonies are alike commodious, the
fewer ought to conform themselves unto the more. Forasmuch therefore as all the churches " (so far as they know
which plead after this manner) " of our confession in

---

[1] 1 Cor. xvi. 1.
[2] Can. 20. The canon of that council which is here cited doth
provide against kneeling at prayer on Sundays, or for fifty days after
Easter on any day, and not at the feast of Pentecost only. [ii. 202, 226 ;
iv. 450.]
[3] T. C. lib. i. p. 182, 183.
[4] [By Whitgift, Def. 481.]
[5] Rom. xvi. 5, 7.
[6] 1 Cor. xiv. 36.

doctrine agree in the abrogation of divers things which we retain, our church ought either to shew that they have done evil, or else she is found to be in fault that doth not conform herself in that, which she cannot deny to be well abrogated." [1]

[2.] In this axiom, that preservation of peace and unity amongst Christian churches should be by all good means procured, we join most willingly and gladly with them. Neither deny we but that to the avoiding of dissension it availeth much that there be amongst them an unity as well in ceremonies as in doctrine. The only doubt is about the manner of their unity ; how far churches are bound to be uniform in their ceremonies, and what way they ought to take for that purpose.

[3.] Touching the one, the rule which they have set down is, that in ceremonies indifferent, all churches ought to be one of them unto another as like as *possibly* [2] they may be. Which *possibly* we cannot otherwise construe, than that it doth require them to be even as like as they may be without breaking any positive ordinance of God. For the ceremonies whereof we speak, being matter of positive law, they are indifferent, if God have neither himself commanded nor forbidden them, but left them unto the Church's discretion. So that if as great uniformity as required as is possible in these things ; seeing that the law of God forbiddeth not any one of them, it followeth that from the greatest unto the least they must be in every Christian church the same, except mere impossibility of so having it be the hinderance. To us this opinion seemeth over extreme and violent : we rather incline to think it a just and reasonable cause for any church, the state whereof is free and independent, if in these things it differ from other churches, only for that it doth not judge it so fit and expedient to be framed therein by the pattern of their example, as to be otherwise framed than they. That of Gregory unto Leander is a charitable speech and a peaceable ; [3] " In una fide nil officit ecclesiæ sanctæ consuetudo diversa : " " Where the faith of the holy Church is one, a difference in customs of the Church doth no harm." [4] That of St. Augustine to Casulanus is somewhat more particular. and toucheth what kind of ceremonies they are, wherein one church may vary from the example of another

---

[1] [T. C. iii. 183.]   [2] [T. C. i. 104.]
[3] Epist. lib. i. p. 41.   [4] Ep. 86. al. 36, c. 9.

without hurt : "Let the faith of the whole Church, how wide soever it have spread itself, be always one, although the unity of belief be famous for variety of certain ordinances, whereby that which is rightly believed suffereth no kind of let or impediment."[1] Calvin goeth further, "As concerning rites in particular, let the sentence of Augustine take place,[2] which leaveth it free unto all churches to receive each their own custom. Yea sometime it profiteth and is expedient that there be difference, lest men should think that religion is tied to outward ceremonies. Always provided that there be not any emulation, nor that churches delighted with novelty affect to have that which others have not."[3]

[4.] They which grant it true that the diversity of ceremonies in this kind ought not to cause dissension in churches, must either acknowledge that they grant in affect nothing by these words ; or if any thing be granted, there must as much be yielded unto, as we affirm against their former strict assertion. For if churches be urged by way of duty to take such ceremonies as they like not of, how can dissension be avoided ? Will they say that there ought to be no dissension, because such as be urged ought to like of that whereunto they are urged? If they say this, they say just nothing. For how should any church like to be urged of duty, by such as have no authority or power over it, unto those things which being indifferent it is not of duty bound unto them ? Is it their meaning, that there ought to be no dissension, because, that which churches are not bound unto, no man ought by way of duty to urge upon them ; and if any man do, he standeth in the sight of both God and men most justly blameable, as a needless disturber of the peace of God's Church, and an author of dissension ? In

---

[1] [" Sit ergo una fides universæ, quæ ubique dilatatur, Ecclesiæ . . . etiamsi ipsa fidei unitas quibusdam diversis observationibus celebratur, quibus nullo modo quod in fide verum est impeditur." t. ii. 77.]

[2] [Ep. 54. t. ii. 124.]

[3] Respon. ad. Med. " Responsio ad versipellem quendam Mediatorem, qui pacificandi specie rectum Evangelii cursum in Gallia abrumpere conatus est." " Quantum ad ritus particulares, vigeat sane Augustini sententia ; ut singulis ecclesiis liberum sit morem suum tenere ; immo interdum utile est, ne externis cærimoniis alligetur religio, aliquid esse varietatis : modo absit æmulatio, nec alii ab aliis novitate illecti diversum aliquid habere affectent." Tract. Theol. p. 414, Genev. 1597. The "versipellis Mediator" was Cassander, who in 1561 published a tract "De officio pii ac publicæ tranquillitatis vere amantis viri in hoc religionis dissidio."]

saying this, they both condemn their own practice, when they press the church of England with so strict a bond of duty in these things ; and they overthrow the ground of their practice, which is, that there ought to be in all kind of ceremonies uniformity, unless impossibility hinder it.

[5.] For proof whereof it is not enough to allege what St. Paul did about the matter of collections, or what noblemen do in the liveries of their servants, or what the council of Nice did for standing in time of prayer on certain days ; because though St. Paul did will them of the church of Corinth [1] every man to lay up somewhat by him upon the Sunday, and to reserve it in store, till himself did come thither to send it unto the church of Jerusalem for relief of the poor there ; signifying withal, that he had taken the like order with the churches of Galatia ; yet the reason which he yieldeth of this order taken both in the one place and the other, sheweth the least part of his meaning to have been that whereunto his words are writhed.   "Concerning collection for the saints, (he meaneth them of Jerusalem,) as I have given order to the church of Galatia, so likewise do ye," saith the Apostle ; "that is, in every first of the week let each of you lay aside by himself, and reserve according to that which God hath blessed him with, that when I come collections be not then to make ; and that when I am come, whom you shall choose, them I may forthwith send away by letters to carry your beneficence unto Jerusalem." [2]   Out of which words to conclude the duty of uniformity throughout all churches in all manner of indifferent ceremonies will be very hard, and therefore best to give it over.

[6.] But perhaps they are by so much the more loth to forsake this argument, for that it hath, though nothing else, yet the name of Scripture, to give it some kind of countenance more than the next of livery coats afforded them.[3] For neither is it any man's duty to clothe all his children or

---

[1] T. C. lib. i. p. 133. [104.]   "And therefore St. Paul, to establish this order in the church of Corinth, that they should make their gatherings for the poor upon the first day of the Sabbath, (which is our Sunday,) allegeth this for a reason, That he had so ordained in other churches."

[2] 1 Cor. xvi. 1.

[3] T. C. lib. i. p. 133. [104.]   "So that as children of one father, and servants of one master, he will have all the churches not only have one diet in that they have one word, but also wear as it were one livery in using the same ceremonies."

all his servants with one weed, nor theirs to clothe themselves so, if it were left to their own judgments, as these ceremonies are left of God to the judgment of the Church. And seeing churches are rather in this case like divers families than like divers servants of one family; because every church, the state whereof is independent upon any other, hath authority to appoint orders for itself in things indifferent: therefore of the two we may rather infer, that as one family is not abridged of liberty to be clothed in friar's-grey for that another doth wear claycolour, so neither are all churches bound to the selfsame indifferent ceremonies which it liketh sundry to use.

[7.] As for that canon in the council of Nice, let them but read it and weigh it well. The ancient use of the Church throughout all Christendom was for fifty days after Easter, (which fifty days were called Pentecost, though most commonly the last day of them which is Whitsunday be so called,) in like sort on all the Sundays throughout the whole year their manner was to stand at prayer; whereupon their meetings unto that purpose on those days had the name of Stations given them.[1] Of which custom Tertullian speaketh in this wise; "It is not with us thought fit either to fast on the Lord's day, or to pray kneeling. The same immunity from fasting and kneeling we keep all the time which is between the feasts of Easter and Pentecost."[2] This being therefore an order generally received in the Church; when some began to be singular and different from all others, and that in a ceremony which was then judged very convenient for the whole church even by the whole, those few excepted which brake out of the common pale: the council of Nice thought good to enclose them again with the rest, by a law made in this sort: "Because there are certain which will needs kneel at the time of prayer on the Lord's day, and in the fifty days after Easter; the holy synod judging it meet that a convenient custom be observed throughout all churches, hath decreed that standing we make our prayers to the Lord."[3] Whereby it plainly appeareth that in things

[1] De Cor. Milit c. 3. ["Die Dominico jejunium nefas dicimus, vel de geniculis adorare. Eadem immunitate a die paschæ in Pentecosten usque gaudemus."]

[2] T. C. lib. i. p. 133. [104.] "This rule did the great council of Nice follow, &c. Die Dominico et per omnem Pentecosten, nec de geniculis adorare, et jejunium solvere, &c. De Coro. Militis."

[3] ['Ἐπειδή τινές εἰσιν ἐν τῇ κυριακῇ γόνυ κλίνοντες, καὶ ἐν ταῖς τῆς

indifferent, what the whole Church doth think convenient
for the whole, the same if any part do wilfully violate, it
may be reformed and inrailed again by that general authority whereunto each particular is subject; and that the
spirit of singularity in a few ought to give place unto public
judgment : this doth clearly enough appear, but not that all
Christian churches are bound in every indifferent ceremony
to be uniform ; because where the whole hath not tied the
parts unto one and the same thing, they being therein left
each to their own choice, may either do as others do or else
otherwise, without any breach of duty at all.

[8.] Concerning those indifferent things, wherein it hath
been heretofore thought good that all Christian churches
should be uniform, the way which they now conceive to
bring this to pass was then never thought on. For till now
it hath been judged, that seeing the Law of God doth not
prescribe all particular ceremonies which the Church of
Christ may use ; and in so great variety of them as may be
found out, it is not possible that the law of nature and reason
should direct all churches unto the same things, each deliber-
ating by itself what is most convenient ; the way to establish
the same things indifferent throughout them all must needs
be the judgment of some judicial authority drawn into one
only sentence, which may be a rule for every particular to
follow. And because such authority over all churches is
too much to be granted unto any one mortal man, there yet
remaineth that which hath been always followed as the best,
the safest, the most sincere and reasonable way ; namely,
the verdict of the whole Church orderly taken, and set down
in the assembly of some general council. But to maintain
that all Christian churches ought for unity's sake to be
uniform in all ceremonies, and then to teach that the way of
bringing this to pass must be by mutual imitation, so that
where we have better ceremonies than others they shall be
bound to follow us, and we them where theirs are better ;
how should we think it agreeable and consonant unto
reason ? For sith in things of this nature there is such
variety of particular inducements, whereby one church may
be led to think that better which another church led by
other inducements judgeth to be worse : (for example, the

Πεντηκοστῆς ἡμέραις· ὑπὲρ τοῦ πάντα ἐν πάσῃ παροικίᾳ ὁμοίως παρα-
φυλάττεσθαι, ἑστῶτας ἔδοξε τῇ ἁγίᾳ συνόδῳ τὰς εὐχὰς ἀποδιδόναι τῷ
Θεῷ. Can. 20. apt. Routh, Script. Eccles. Opusc. 367.]

East church did think it better to keep Easter-day after the manner of the Jews, the West church better to do otherwise; the Greek church judgeth it worse to use unleavened bread in the Eucharist, the Latin church leavened; one church esteemeth it not so good to receive the Eucharist sitting as standing, another church not so good standing as sitting; there being on the one side probable motives as well as on the other) unless they add somewhat else to define more certainly what ceremonies shall stand for best, in such sort that all churches in the world shall know them to be the best, and so know them that there may not remain any question about this point, we are not a whit the nearer for that they have hitherto said.

[9.] They themselves, although resolved in their own judgments what ceremonies are best, yet foreseeing that such as they are addicted unto be not all so clearly and so incomparably best, but others there are or may be at leastwise, when all things are well considered, as good, knew not which way smoothly to rid their hands of this matter, without providing some more certain rule to be followed for establishment of uniformity in ceremonies, when there are divers kinds of equal goodness; and therefo e in this case they say, that the later churches and the fewer should conform themselves unto the elder and the more.[1] Hereupon they conclude, that forasmuch as all the reformed churches (so far as they know), which are of our confession in doctrine, have agreed already in the abrogation of divers things which we retain; our church ought either to shew that they have done evil, or else she is found to be in fault for not conforming herself to those churches, in that which she cannot deny to be in them well abrogated. For the authority of the first churches (and those they account to be the first in this cause which were first reformed,) they bring the comparison of younger daughters conforming themselves in attire to the example of their elder sisters; wherein there is just as much strength of reason as in the livery-coats beforementioned. St. Paul, they say, noteth it for a mark of special honour, that Epænetus was the first man in all Achaia which did embrace the Christian faith;[2] after the same sort he

---

[1] T. C. lib. iii. p. 183. "If the ceremonies be alike commodious, the latter churches should conform themselves to the first," &c. And again, "The fewer ought to conform themselves unto the more."

[2] Rom. xvi. 5.

toucheth it also as a special pre-eminence of Junia and Andronicus, that in Christianity they were his ancients;[1] the Corinthians he pinched with this demand, "Hath the word of God gone out from you, or hath it lighted on you alone?"[2]

But what of all this? If any man should think that alacrity and forwardness in good things doth add nothing unto men's commendation, the two former speeches of St. Paul might lead him to reform his judgment. In like sort, to take down the stomach of proud conceited men, that glory as though they were able to set all others to school, there can be nothing more fit than some such words as the Apostle's third sentence doth contain; wherein he teacheth the church of Corinth to know, that there was no such great odds between them and the rest of their brethren, that they should think themselves to be gold and the rest to be but copper. He therefore useth speech unto them to this effect: "Men instructed in the knowledge of Jesus Christ there both were before you, and are besides you in the world; ye neither are the fountain from which first, nor yet the river into which alone the word hath flowed." But although as Epænetus was the first man in all Achaia, so Corinth had been the first church in the whole world, that received Christ; the Apostle doth not shew that in any kind of things indifferent whatsoever this should have made their example a law unto all others. Indeed the example of sundry churches for approbation of one thing doth sway much; but yet still as having the force of an example only, and not of a law. They are effectual to move any church, unless some greater thing do hinder; but they bind none, no not though they be many, saving only when they are the major part of a general assembly, and then their voices being more in number must oversway their judgments who are fewer, because in such cases the greater half is the whole. But as they stand out single each of them by itself, their number can purchase them no such authority, that the rest of the churches being fewer should be therefore bound to follow them, and to relinquish as good ceremonies as theirs for theirs.

[10.] Whereas therefore it is concluded out of these so weak premises, that the retaining of divers things in the church of England, which other reformed churches have

[1] Rom. xvi. 7.   [2] 1 Cor. xiv. 36.

cast out, must needs argue that we do not well, unless we can shew that they have done ill;[1] what needed this wrest to draw out from us an accusation of foreign churches? It is not proved as yet that if they have done well our duty is to follow them, and to forsake our own course because it differeth from theirs, although indeed it be as well for us every way as theirs for them. And if the proofs alleged for confirmation hereof had been sound, yet seeing they lead no further than only to shew, that where we can have no better ceremonies theirs must be taken; as they cannot with modesty think themselves to have found out absolutely the best which the wit of men may devise, so liking their own somewhat better than other men's, even because they are their own, they must in equity allow us to be like unto them in this affection; which if they do, they ease us of that uncourteous burden, whereby we are charged either to condemn them or else to follow them. They grant we need not follow them, if our own ways already be better: and if our own be but equal, the law of common indulgence alloweth us to think them at the least half a thought the better because they are our own; which we may very well do, and never draw any indictment at all against theirs, but think commendably even of them also.

XIV. To leave reformed churches therefore and their actions for Him to judge of, in whose sight they are as they are; and our desire is that they may even in His sight be found such as we ought to endeavour by all means that our own may likewise be; somewhat we are enforced to speak by way of simple declaration concerning the proceedings of the church of England in these affairs, to the end that men whose minds are free from those partial constructions, whereby the only name of difference from some other churches is thought cause sufficient to condemn ours, may the better discern whether that we have done be reasonable, yea or no. The church of England being to alter her received laws concerning such orders, rites, and ceremonies, as had been in former times an hindrance unto piety and religious service of God, was to enter into consideration first, that the change of laws, especially concerning matter of religion, must be warily proceeded in. Laws, as all other

---

[1] T. C. lib. iii. p. 183. "Our church ought either to shew that they have done evil, or else she is found to be in fault that doth not conform herself in that which she cannot deny to be well abrogated."

things human, are many times full of imperfection; and
that which is supposed behoveful unto men, proveth oftentimes most pernicious. The wisdom which is learned by
tract of time, findeth the laws that have been in former ages
established, needful in later to be abrogated. Besides, that
which sometime is expedient doth not always so continue:
and the number of needless laws unabolished doth weaken
the force of them that are necessary. But true withal it is,
that alteration though it be from worse to better hath in it
inconveniences, and those weighty; unless it be in such
laws as have been made upon special occasions, which occasions ceasing, laws of that kind do abrogate themselves.
But when we abrogate a law as being ill made, the whole
cause for which it was made still remaining, do we not
herein revoke our very own deed, and upbraid ourselves
with folly, yea, all that were makers of it with oversight and
with error? Further, if it be a law which the custom and
continual practice of many ages or years hath confirmed in
the minds of men, to alter it must needs be troublesome
and scandalous. It amazeth them, it causeth them to stand
in doubt whether any thing be in itself by nature either good
or evil, and not all things rather such as men at this or that
time agree to account of them, when they behold even those
things disproved, disannulled, rejected, which use had made
in a manner natural. What have we to induce men unto
the willing obedience and observation of laws, but the weight
of so many men's judgment as have with deliberate advice
assented thereunto; the weight of that long experience,
which the world hath had thereof with consent and good
liking? So that to change any such law must needs with
the common sort impair and weaken the force of those
grounds, whereby all laws are made effectual.

[2.] Notwithstanding we do not deny alteration of laws
to be sometimes a thing necessary; as when they are
unnatural, or impious, or otherwise hurtful unto the public
community of men, and against that good for which human
societies were instituted. When the Apostles of our Lord
and Saviour were ordained to alter the laws of heathenish
religion received throughout the whole world, chosen I
grant they were (Paul excepted) the rest ignorant, poor,
simple, unschooled altogether and unlettered men; howbeit
extraordinarily endued with ghostly wisdom from above before they ever undertook this enterprise; yea their authority

confirmed by miracle, to the end it might plainly appear
that they were the Lord's ambassadors, unto whose sovereign
power for all flesh to stoop, for all the kingdoms of the
earth to yield themselves willingly conformable in whatsoever should be required, it was their duty. In this case
therefore their oppositions in maintenance of public superstition against apostolic endeavours, as that they might not
condemn the ways of their ancient predecessors, that they
must keep *religiones traditas*, the rites which from age to
age had descended, that the ceremonies of religion had
been ever accounted by so much holier as elder;[1] these
and the like allegations in this case were vain and frivolous.

Not to stay longer therefore in speech concerning this
point, we will conclude, that as the change of such laws as
have been specified is necessary, so the evidence that they
are such must be great. If we have neither voice from
heaven that so pronounceth of them; neither sentence of
men grounded upon such manifest and clear proof, that they
in whose hands it is to alter them may likewise infallibly
even in heart and conscience judge them so: upon necessity
to urge alteration is to trouble and disturb without
necessity. As for arbitrary alterations, when laws in themselves not simply bad or unmeet are changed for better and
more expedient; if the benefit of that which is newly better
devised be but small, sith the custom of easiness to alter
and change is so evil, no doubt but to bear a tolerable sore
is better than to venture on a dangerous remedy.

[3.] Which being generally thought upon as a matter that
touched nearly their whole enterprise, whereas change was
notwithstanding concluded necessary, in regard of the great
hurt which the Church did receive by a number of things
then in use, whereupon a great deal of that which had been
was now to be taken away and removed out of the Church;
yet sith there are divers ways of abrogating things established, they saw it best to cut off presently such things as
might in that sort be extinguished without danger, leaving
the rest to be abolished by disusage through tract of time.
And as this was done for the manner of abrogation: so

---

[1] [Min. Felix. c. 5. p. 50. ed. Gronov. "Venerabilius et melius,
antistitem veritatis majorum excipere disciplinam : religiones traditas
colere ; deos, quos a parentibus ante imbutus es timere quam nosse
familiarius, adorare ; nec de numinibus ferre sententiam, sed prioribus
credere." And see before, p. 110, not. 1.]

touching the stint or measure thereof, rites and ceremonies
and other external things of like nature being hurtful unto
the Church, either in respect of their quality or in regard
of their number; in the former there could be no doubt or
difficulty what should be done, their deliberation in the
latter was more hard.   And therefore inasmuch as they did
resolve to remove only such things of that kind as the Church
might best spare, retaining the residue; their whole counsel
is in this point utterly condemned, as having either proceeded
from the blindness of those times, or from negligence, or from
desire of honour and glory, or from an erroneous opinion
that such things might be tolerated for a while; or if it did
proceed (as they which would seem most favourable are
content to think it possible) from a purpose, [1] "partly the
easilier to draw papists unto the Gospel" (by keeping so
many orders still the same with theirs), "and partly to
redeem peace thereby, the breach whereof they might fear
would ensue upon more thorough alteration;" or howsoever
it came to pass, the thing they did is judged evil.   But such
is the lot of all that deal in public affairs whether of church
or commonwealth; that which men list to surmise of their
doings, be it good or ill, they must beforehand patiently
arm their minds to endure.   Wherefore to let go private
surmises, whereby the thing in itself is not made either
better or worse; if just and allowable reasons might lead
them to do as they did, then are these censures all frustrate.

[4.] Touching ceremonies harmless therefore in themselves, and hurtful only in respect of number: was it amiss
to decree, that those things which were least needful and
newliest come should be the first that were taken away, as
in the abrogating of a number of saints' days, and of other
the like customs, it appeareth they did; till afterwards the
Form of Common Prayer being perfected, Articles of sound
Religion and Discipline agreed upon, Catechisms framed
for the needful instruction of youth, churches purged of
things that indeed were burdensome to the people or to the
simple offensive and scandalous, all was brought at the
length unto that wherein now we stand?   Or was it amiss,
that having this way eased the Church as they thought of
superfluity, they went not on till they had plucked up even

---

[1] T. C. lib. ii. p. 29.   "It may well be, their purpose was by that
temper of popish ceremonies with the Gospel, partly the easilier to draw
the papists to the Gospel, &c., partly to redeem peace thereby."

those things also, which had taken a great deal stronger and deeper root; those things which to abrogate without constraint of manifest harm thereby arising, had been to alter unnecessarily (in their judgments) the ancient received custom of the whole Church, the universal practice of the people of God, and those very decrees of our fathers, which were not only set down by agreement of general councils, but had accordingly been put in ure and so continued in use till that very time present?

[5.] True it is, that neither councils nor customs, be they never so ancient and so general, can let the Church from taking away that thing which is hurtful to be retained. Where things have been instituted, which being convenient and good at the first, do afterwards in process of time wax otherwise; we make no doubt but they may be altered, yea, though councils or customs general have received them. And therefore it is but a needless kind of opposition which they make who thus dispute, "If in those things which are not expressed in the Scripture, that is to be observed of the Church, which is the custom of the people of God and decree of our forefathers; then how can these things at any time be varied, which heretofore have been once ordained in such sort?"[1] Whereto we say, that things so ordained are to be kept, howbeit not necessarily any longer, than till there grow some urgent cause to ordain the contrary. For there is not any positive law of men, whether it be general or particular; received by formal express consent, as in councils, or by secret approbation, as in customs it cometh to pass; but the same may be taken away if occasion serve. Even as we all know, that many things generally kept heretofore are now in like sort generally unkept and abolished every where.

[6.] Notwithstanding till such things be abolished, what exception can there be taken against the judgment of St. Augustine, who saith, "That of things harmless, whatsoever there is which the whole Church doth observe throughout the world, to argue for any man's immunity from observing the same, it were a point of most insolent madness?"[2] And surely odious it must needs have been for one Christian church to abolish that which all had received and held for the space of many ages, and that without any detriment unto religion so manifest and so great, as might in the eyes

---

[1] T. C. lib. iii. p. 30.   [2] Aug. Epist. 118. [al. 54. c. 5. t. ii. 126.]

of unpartial men appear sufficient to clear them from all blame of rash and inconsiderate proceeding, if in fervour of zeal they had removed such things. Whereas contrariwise, so reasonable moderation herein used hath freed us from being deservedly subject unto that bitter kind of obloquy, whereby as the church of Rome doth under the colour of love towards those things which be harmless, maintain extremely most hurtful corruptions ; so we peradventure might be upbraided, that under colour of hatred towards those things that are corrupt, we are on the other side as extreme even against most harmless ordinances. And as they are obstinate to retain that, which no man of any conscience is able well to defend ; so we might be reckoned fierce and violent to tear away that, which if our own mouths did condemn, our consciences would storm and repine thereat. The Romans having banished Tarquinius the Proud, and taken a solemn oath that they never would permit any man more to reign, could not herewith content themselves, or think that tyranny was thoroughly extinguished, till they had driven one of their consuls to depart the city, against whom they found not in the world what to object, saving only that his name was Tarquin, and that the commonwealth could not seem to have recovered perfect freedom, as long as a man of so dangerous a name was left remaining.[1]   For the church of England to have done the like in casting out of papal tyranny and superstition ; to have shewed greater willingness of accepting the very ceremonies of the Turk [2] Christ's professed enemy, than of the most indifferent things which the church of Rome approveth ; to have left not so much as the names which the church of Rome doth give unto things innocent ; to have ejected whatsoever that Church doth make account of, be it never so harmless in itself, and of never so ancient continuance, without any other crime to charge it with, than only that it hath been the hap thereof to be used by the church of Rome, and not to be commanded in the word of God : this kind of proceeding might haply have pleased some few men, who having begun such a course themselves must needs be glad to see their example followed

---

[1] [Liv. ii. 2.]

[2] T. C. lib. i. p. 131. "For indeed it were more safe for us to conform our indifferent ceremonies to the Turks which are far off, than to the papists which are so near."

by us.[1]   But the Almighty which giveth wisdom and inspireth with right understanding whomsoever it pleaseth
him, he foreseeing that which man's wit had never been
able to reach unto, namely, what tragedies the attempt of
so extreme alteration would raise in some parts of the
Christian world,[2] did for the endless good of his Church
(as we cannot choose but interpret it) use the bridle of his
provident restraining hand, to stay those eager affections in
some, and to settle their resolution upon a course more
calm and moderate : lest as in other most ample and heretofore most flourishing dominions it hath since fallen out,
so likewise if in ours it had come to pass, that the adverse
part being enraged, and betaking itself to such practices as
men are commonly wont to embrace, when they behold
things brought to desperate extremities, and no hope left to
see any other end, than only the utter oppression and clean
extinguishment of one side ; by this mean Christendom
flaming in all parts of greatest importance at once, they all
had wanted that comfort of mutual relief, whereby they are
now for the time sustained (and not the least by this our
church which they so much impeach) till mutual combus-
tions, bloodsheds, and wastes (because no other inducement
will serve) may enforce them through very faintness, after
the experience of so endless miseries, to enter on all sides
at the length into some such consultation, as may tend to
the best re-establishment of the whole Church of Jesus
Christ.   To the singular good whereof it cannot but serve
as a profitable direction to teach men what is most likely to
prove available, when they shall quietly consider the trial
that hath been thus long had of both kinds of reformation ;
as well this moderate kind which the church of England
hath taken, as that other more extreme and rigorous which
certain churches elsewhere have better liked.   In the meanwhile it may be, that suspense of judgment and exercise of
charity were safer and seemlier for Christian men, than the

---

[1] [Sarav. de divers.   Ministr. Evang. Grad. in Prolog.   "Ejectis
Tarquiniis Roma, Regis nomen postea non tulere Romani, quasi cum
nomine ejecta esset quam oderant tyrannis : qui tamen postea
plures tyrannidis formas perpessi sunt, quam si Regis nomen et
authoritatem retinuissent.   Non enim in regia potestate aut regis
nomine ulla inerat tyrannis, sed in Tarquinio.   Sic dico tyrannidem,
quæ Ecclesias Christi vastavit, non fuisse in primatu Episcoporum et
Archiepiscoporum, sed in iis qui primatu abusi sunt."]

[2] [France, Westphalia, Flanders, Scotland.]

hot pursuit of these controversies, wherein they that are most fervent to dispute be not always the most able to determine.   But who are on his side, and who against him, our Lord in his good time shall reveal.

[7.] And sith thus far we have proceeded in opening the things that have been done, let not the principal doers themselves be forgotten.   When the ruins of the house of God (that house which consisting of religious souls is most immediately the precious temple of the Holy Ghost) were become, not in his sight alone, but in the eyes of the whole world so exceeding great, that very superstition began even to feel itself too far grown : the first that with us made way to repair the decays thereof by beheading superstition, was King Henry the Eighth.   The son and successor of which famous king as we know was Edward the Saint : in whom (for so by the event we may gather) it pleased God righteous and just to let England see what a blessing sin and iniquity would not suffer it to enjoy.   Howbeit that which the wise man hath said concerning Enoch (whose days were though many in respect of ours, yet scarce as three to nine in comparison of theirs with whom he lived) the same to that admirable child most worthily may be applied, "Though he departed this world soon, yet fulfilled he much time." [1] But what ensued ?   That work which the one in such sort had begun, and the other so far proceeded in, was in short space so overthrown, as if almost it had never been : till such time as that God, whose property is to shew his mercies then greatest when they are nearest to be utterly despaired of, caused in the depth of discomfort and darkness a most glorious star [2] to arise, and on her head settled the crown, whom himself had kept as a lamb from the slaughter of those bloody times ; that the experience of his goodness in her own deliverance might cause her merciful disposition to take so much the more delight in saving others, whom the like necessity should press.   What in this behalf hath been done towards nations abroad, the parts of Christendom most afflicted can best testify.   That which especially concerneth ourselves, in the present matter we treat of, is the state of reformed religion, a thing at her coming to the crown even raised as it were by miracle from

[1] Sap. iv. 13.
[2] ["'That bright Occidental Star, Queen Elizabeth of most happy memory." Dedication to King James by the Translators of the Bible.]

the dead; a thing which we so little hoped to see, that even they which beheld it done, scarcely believed their own senses at the first beholding. Yet being then brought to pass, thus many years it hath continued, standing by no other worldly mean but that one only hand which erected it; that hand which as no kind of imminent danger could cause at the first to withhold itself, so neither have the practices so many so bloody following since been ever able to make weary. Nor can we say in this case so justly, that Aaron and Hur, the ecclesiastical and civil states, have sustained the hand which did lift itself to heaven for them,[1] as that heaven itself hath by this hand sustained them, no aid or help having thereunto been ministered for performance of the work of reformation, other than such kind of help or aid as the Angel in the Prophet Zachary speaketh of, saying, " Neither by an army nor strength, but by my Spirit, saith the Lord of Hosts."[2] Which grace and favour of divine assistance having not in one thing or two shewed itself, nor for some few days or years appeared, but in such sort so long continued, our manifold sins and transgressions striving to the contrary; what can we less thereupon conclude, than that God would at leastwise by tract of time teach the world, that the thing which he blesseth, defendeth, keepeth so strangely, cannot choose but be of him? Wherefore, if any refuse to believe us disputing for the verity of religion established, let them believe God himself thus miraculously working for it, and wish life even for ever and ever unto that glorious and sacred instrument whereby he worketh.

[1] [Exod. xvii. 12.] [2] Zach. iv. 6.

END OF VOL. I.

EVERYMAN'S LIBRARY was founded in 1906, and the series stands without rival today as the world's most comprehensive low-priced collection of books of classic measure. It was conceived as a library covering the whole field of English literature, including translations of the ancient classics and outstanding foreign works; a series to make widely available those great books which appeal to every kind of reader, and which in essence form the basis of western culture. The aim and scope of the series was crystallized in the title Everyman's Library, justified by world sales totalling (by 1960) some forty-four millions.

There were, of course, already in being in 1906 other popular series of reprints, but none on the scale proposed for Everyman. One hundred and fifty-five volumes were published in three batches in the Library's first year; they comprised a balanced selection from many branches of literature and set the standard on which the Library has been built up. By the outbreak of the First World War the Library was moving towards its 750th volume; and, in spite of the interruptions of two world wars, the aim of the founder-publisher, a library of a thousand volumes, was achieved by the jubilee in 1956, with Aristotle's *Metaphysics*, translated by John Warrington.

In March 1953 a fresh development of the Library began: new volumes and all new issues of established volumes in Everyman's Library were now made in a larger size. The larger volumes have new title-pages, bindings and wrappers, and the text pages have generous margins. Four hundred and twenty-two volumes in this improved format had been issued by 1960. In that year new pictorial wrappers appeared and they have provided the volumes with a surprisingly contemporary 'look'.

Editorially the Library is under constant survey; volumes are examined and brought up to date, with new introductions, annotations and additional matter; often a completely new translation or a newly edited text is substituted when transferring an old volume to the new format. New editions of Pepys's *Diary*, Caesar's *War Commentaries*, *The Anglo-Saxon Chronicle* and Professor T. M. Raysor's reorganization of Coleridge's *Shakespearean Criticism* are examples of this type of revision.

The new larger volumes are in keeping with the original 'home-library' plan but are also in a suitable size for the shelves of all institutional libraries, more so since many important works in Everyman's Library are unobtainable in any other edition. This development entails no break in the continuity of the Library; and fresh titles and verified editions are being constantly added.

A Classified Annotated Catalogue of the library is available free, the annotations giving the year of birth and death of the author, the date of first publication of the work and in many instances descriptive notes on the contents of the last revised Everyman's Library edition. Also available (as a volume in the Library, No. 889) is A. J. Hoppe's *The Reader's Guide to Everyman's Library*, revised and reissued in 1961. It gives in one alphabetical sequence references and cross-references of a comprehensive kind, including all authors and all works, even works included in anthologies, and a factual annotation of each work. Running to more than 400 pages, and referring to 1,260 authors, it is virtually a guide to all books of classic standing in the English language.